Western Conceptions of the Individual

Brian Morris

This is a comprehensive study of the varying conceptions of the human subject in the Western intellectual tradition. Although informed by an anthropological perspective, the work draws on material from all the major intellectual disciplines that have contributed to this tradition and offers biographical and theoretical vignettes of all the major Western scholars. By scrutinising the classical texts of the Western tradition Brian Morris succeeds in delineating the differing conceptions of the human individual which emerge from these writings, and gives a guide to the most important ideas in Western cultural traditions.

Brian Morris Reader in Anthropology, Goldsmiths' College, University of London

Western Conceptions of the Individual

Brian Morris

BERG

New York/Oxford

Distributed exclusively in the US and Canada by
St Martin's Press, New York

First published in 1991 by
Berg Publishers Limited
Editorial offices.
165 Taber Avenue, Providence, RI 02906, USA
150 Cowley Road, Oxford, OX4 1JJ, UK

British Library Cataloguing in Publication Data
Morris, Brian
    Western conceptions of the individual
    I. Title
    301.01

    ISBN 0–85496–698–6

Library of Congress Cataloging-in-Publication Data

Morris, Brian, 1936–
    Western conceptions of the
individual / Brian Morris.
        p.   cm.
    Includes bibliographical references and index.
    ISBN 0–85496–698–6 (cloth) : £37.00 ($59.95 U.S.)
    1. Anthropology—Philosophy.   2. Anthropology—Methodology.
    3. Ethnopsychology.   4. Individualism   5. Civilization, Western.
    I. Title.
    GN345.M67 1991   91–13878
    301'.01—dc20   CIP

Printed and bound in Great Britain by
Billing and Sons Ltd, Worcester

This study is dedicated to my friend and
colleague Olivia Harris who first suggested its
title and who knows that it is largely an exercise
in my own self-education

Contents

Contents

Acknowledgements

I should like to express my appreciation and thanks to all those friends and colleagues who have shown interest in my studies and who have encouraged me over the past decade: David Parkin, Maurice Bloch, Josep Llobera, Pat Caplan, Olivia Harris, Jacqui Morris, Jean LaFontaine, Laura Chase, Nici Nelson, Vicky Goddard, Ioan Lewis, James Woodburn, Simeren and Alfred Gell, Steve Nugent, Tim Ingold, Shelagh Weir and Madan Sarup.

To my daughter Dodo, and to Irene Goes, I am grateful for deciphering and typing up my scribbled manuscript.

Introduction

This study attempts to outline the varying conceptions of the human subject as indicated in the Western intellectual tradition. This tradition has an inherently androcentric bias, and one searches in vain among the textbooks on philosophy or in the standard histories of psychology and sociology for any mention of a woman scholar. In time perhaps this state of affairs will be rectified and a more balanced view of European thought will eventually emerge, but at the present juncture the key figures who are seen as representing this tradition are almost all men. Although the study is written from an anthropological perspective, it draws on material from all the major intellectual disciplines that make up this tradition – sociology, philosophy, psychology, Marxism, psychoanalysis, sociobiology, as well as anthropology. My aim has been to scrutinise the classic texts of this tradition – from about the time of Descartes – and to delineate the varying conceptions of the human individual that emerge from within these texts. The study is thus focused on specific scholars. I have throughout attempted, by means of biographical vignettes, to convey to the reader the kind of people these scholars were and something about their life circumstances. I dislike books that treat scholars as if they were a kind of cipher, and I think the huge (and deserved) popularity of Bertrand Russell's *History of Western Philosophy* stems less from its intellectual strengths and candour than from Russell's lively style and his treatment of the individual philosophers as real people – with foibles and fantasies. I attempt also to outline the social context and basic philosophical premises of the individual scholars before discussing at more length their conceptions of the human subject. Inevitably, I have had to curtail my discussion at times.

I have deliberately avoided dealing with ethical issues and political philosophy and, although offering a critique of the various theories, have not attempted to review the extensive critical literature on the many scholars whose work I review. The secondary literature, both expository and critical, on such theorists as Kant, Hegel, Freud and Marx, is quite staggering. At times I have simply foraged for ideas among a rich array of literature, but I have always taken pains to read the primary texts myself. Some of them – like Kant's *Critique of Pure Reason* and Heidegger's *Being and Time* – I found hard-going, but I trust that my discussion of them nevertheless has salience and value. As in my earlier study (1987), I have tried to adopt a standpoint of critical sympathy in approaching such classic works. I also regret that due to lack of space I have had to leave out of the study several important scholars – mention may be made of Rousseau, Jung, Fromm, Weber, Bergson, Whitehead and Laing – but there is a limit to what one can encompass within a single work.

Although its coverage is interdisciplinary, what the study outlines is a number of distinctive approaches to the human subject, which cut across disciplinary boundaries. Essentially, each of the chapters deals with a specific approach or orientation. Chapter 1 sets the intellectual scene and outlines the various philosophical traditions that developed during the Enlightenment period and attempted to situate the human subject within the mechanistic paradigm then emerging; the mechanical materialism of Hobbes, the rationalism of Descartes, Spinoza and Leibniz, and the empiricist doctrines of Locke and Hume. The chapter concludes with a discussion of Kant, whom I see as a major turning point in the development of Western philosophy. Subsequent chapters follow the developments of the different perspectives on the human subject, which we can trace from the turn of the nineteenth century.

Thus, chapter 2 deals with the 'psychology of the will', for an underlying theme of this chapter is the notion forwarded by several scholars that the will and instinctual strivings play a central role in human motivation. After outlining the perspectives of Schopenhauer and Nietzsche, the chapter focuses on the psychoanalytic theory of Sigmund Freud. The discussion centres on two key concepts of Freudian theory – libido, and unconscious – which are central to an understanding of the psychoanalytic conception of the person.

Chapter 3 is concerned to outline developments within the empiricist tradition, a tradition that tends to see the human subject as a reactive organism and to marginalise the importance of consciousness and subjective meanings. The chapter offers extended discussion on all the main varieties: evolutionary theory (Darwin), behaviourist psychology (Watson and Skinner), philosophical behaviourism (Wittgenstein and Royle) and sociobiology (Wilson).

Chapter 4 looks at the neo-Kantian tradition, especially as it was developed in the work of Dilthey, Wundt and Boas and in the writings of the cultural anthropologists. Among the latter I focus on the work of Kroeber, Benedict and Mead, who tended to see the human subject as a culture-bearing organism.

Chapter 5 presents on account of the Hegelian-Marxist tradition, which views the human subject as a fundamentally social being who is creatively and necessarily engaged in practical activities. I discuss in this chapter the founders of this philosophy of praxis – Hegel, Marx and Lukács. The chapter concludes with a discussion of two recent scholars – Sève and Vygotsky – who have attempted to establish a Marxist psychology.

Chapter 6 outlines the work of those scholars who have theorised within the sociological tradition established by the French positivist philosopher August Comte – Durkheim, Radcliffe-Brown and White. This tradition stresses the inherently social nature of the human person. In the final section I discuss the seminal writings of Dumont on holism and individualism.

Chapter 7 examines the work of the pragmatic philosophers – James, Dewey and George Herbert Mead – who were centrally concerned with the social dimensions of the human self. The chapter concludes with a discussion of symbolic interactionism and the work of Goffman.

Chapter 8 discusses the critical theory of the Frankfurt school, which followed a Hegelian-Marxist perspective, and I focus in particular on the writings of Horkheimer, Marcuse and Habermas.

Chapter 9 provides extended discussion of scholars whose work is situated in the phenomenological-existentialist tradition. After outlining the conceptions of the human subject evident in the work of the founders of this tradition – Kierkegaard, Husserl and Heidegger – the chapter deals with two existentialist scholars whose work has specifically focused on psychological issues – Sartre and Merleau-Ponty.

Chapter 10, which concludes the study, discusses structuralist and post-structuralist theories, including the various attempts that have been made to 'dissolve' or 'eradicate' the human subject from theoretical discourse. After an initial discussion on the origins of structuralism, in which I discuss the work of Lévi-Strauss, the chapter has sections on two important structuralist scholars, Piaget and Althusser, who share with Lévi-Strauss a commitment to scientific reason. The chapter concludes with a discussion of the recent work of the post-structuralists, Foucault and Derrida.

As the preceding conspectus indicates, the study focuses primarily on writers within the Western intellectual tradition who have adopted a standpoint of empirical naturalism. This seems to me to be the dominant tendency among intellectuals in Europe and America, although there are still many scholars – besides Kierke-gaard, Jung and Heidegger – who assume a religious standpoint in their conception of the human subject. It is as fallacious to identify European culture with materialist philosophy as it is to see Indian culture as fundamentally 'spiritual'. But the study does indicate that Western philosophy and the Western intellectual tradition more generally is by no means uniform or monolithic; there are in fact, as I outline, varying and contrasting conceptions of what constitutes the human subject, or at least how one must envisage the human subject if one is to gain a fuller understanding of the human condition.

-1-

Mechanistic Philosophy and the Human Subject

The revolution in scientific ideas that occurred in the seventeenth century has been described as perhaps 'the most important turning point in man's history' (Koestler 1959: 116). Whitehead, in his classic study *Science and the Modern World* (1926), likewise described the 'scientific outburst' of the seventeenth century as being equally radical and far-reaching, the 'century of genius', giving birth to a new conception of nature and to modern scientific materialism. Indeed, Whitehead felt that human knowledge of the natural world had hardly advanced since the time of the ancient Greeks, and remarked that in the year 1500 Europe knew less than Archimedes, who had died in the year 212 BC (1926: 16). The social and cultural changes wrought by this new mechanistic world-view were revolutionary. But although the mechanistic conception of the world, which is clearly expressed in the scientific writings of Copernicus, Kepler and Galileo, was related to broader socioeconomic changes, it is worth nothing that it was not until the end of the eighteenth century that industrial capitalism, based on this knowledge, began to develop.

This mechanistic conception of the world was shared by many seventeenth-century philosophers. Bacon, Descartes, Hobbes and Spinoza were the most important. But such philosophers essentially codified and expressed the new mechanistic cosmology, which emerged through the scientific studies of the aforementioned scholars – studies that were finally synthesised by Newton a century later. Copleston (1963: 22) has stressed that progress in astronomy and physics was attained more or less independently of philosophy. Thus it is important to note that the new paradigm was largely articulated through developments in physics and astronomy, and that psychology, as yet undeveloped as a science, was not part of the revolution.

In this chapter I explore those seventeenth- and eighteenth-century European philosophers who attempted to articulate the psychological and moral implications of the mechanistic world-view. In the first section I examine the classic writings of Descartes, whose rationalism and body/mind dualism has had such a profound influence on Western thought. The second section deals with the contrasting approach of Hobbes, who advocated a mechanistic materialism, which denied the autonomy of human consciousness and suggested a rigid determination that prefigured the views of many behavioural psychologists. In the following section I describe the rationalist philosophies of Spinoza and Leibniz, which although similar in their stress on conatus and self-activity, represent fundamentally contrasting viewpoints – Spinoza a quasi-materialist monism; Leibniz a pluralistic philosophy that demarcated the world into spiritual and physical realms. In section 1.4 I examine the theories of the two classic British empiricists, Locke and Hume, focusing on their differing conceptions of the self. In the final section I discuss Kant's alleged synthesis of the rationalist and empiricist traditions. Although this synthesis is not sustained, and Kant can, in many respects, be seen as offering a last-ditch defence of mechanistic science, I stress the complexity of Kant's philosophy and the intimations he makes of an alternative, dialectical world-view. I suggest that Kant represents a turning point within the Western intellectual traditions, suggesting insights that were later developed in varying theoretical directions. Throughout the chapter I attempt to articulate the differing conceptions of the human subject that emerge in the writings of these early philosophers, and their influence on later scholars within the human sciences.

1.1 Descartes

René Descartes has often been described as the founding father of modern philosophy. He was born in Touraine in north-west France and studied under the Jesuits at La Flèche, something he always valued in later life. When he was eighteen he left the college, resolved to learn from the 'book of the world', and so attached himself to a local Protestant army, that of the Prince of Nassau, even though he was a devout Catholic. Five years later, in 1619, while serving in Germany, Descartes had a kind of visionary experience, having spent the whole day shut up alone in a stove-heated room. Always something of a recluse, this vision crystallised his thoughts and convinced him that his mission in life was to seek truth by reason. He worked in relative obscurity for more than a decade after this experience, travelling widely throughout Europe. In 1629 he settled in Holland and there he remained until 1649, apart from short visits to France. Although a loyal Catholic all his life, Descartes feared the censure of the Church, and on hearing of the condemnation of Galileo, he withheld publication of his *Treatise on the Universe* (1633). But in 1637 he published his *Discourse on the Method of rightly conducting the Reason and Seeking for Truth in the Sciences*. It was the preface to a book on meteors and geometry. It is probably one of the most influential books on philosophy and is simply written in elegant French – not Latin – and is semi-autobiographical. In 1641 his equally well-known *Meditations on First Philosophy* was published in Paris, in Latin. It was to be translated into French in 1647 and included a set of objections by various authors together with Descartes' replies to them. These two texts, together with *The Passions of the Soul* (1649), which focuses on the relationship between the body and mind, provide us with a clear and very readable account of Descartes' philosophy.

Descartes' aim is through reason alone to find 'firm and solid foundation' for our knowledge of the world, and it is clear from the outset that Descartes sees mathematics, because of the 'certainty and self-evidence of its reasonings' (1637: 31), to be a model to follow. Only truths that are certain, clear and self-evident satisfy Descartes. Outlining four rules to follow, he suggests that in the search for truth one must not accept anything as true that is not self-evident, and that one should start with the most simple and clear ideas, and 'climb gradually' step by step towards more complex knowledge, following the 'chains of reasoning' which mathematicians use. For in the search for truth in the sciences only mathematicians, he writes, had been able to arrive at truths that were certain and self-evident. Thus the essential Cartesian method is to suggest that all scientific thought should follow the manner of mathematical reasoning, namely by deduction from axioms and by algebraic calculation.

This led Descartes to his famous 'method of doubt', to question all beliefs and claims to knowledge, and to reject all those that he had the slightest reason to doubt. 'We must doubt everything', was his maxim, and the crux of his method. Although thus appearing like Montaigne to be a sceptic, Descartes' aims were quite different, for his whole plan was 'the rejection of shifting ground and sand in order to find rock or clay' (1637: 50). Descartes, therefore, came to reject the writings of the scholastics, the common beliefs of his day, and even the validity of the senses as being sufficiently certain to form the foundations of knowledge. He extolled the value of travel: 'It is a good thing', he wrote, 'to know something of the customs and manners of various peoples in order to judge of our own more objectively and so not to think everything which is contrary to our ways is ridiculous and irrational' (1637: 30).

But customs varied and could not provide the basis of certain knowledge – any more than could poetry, theology, alchemy, astrology and the philosophy of his day. The latter, the scholastic philosophers, Descartes suggests, have an empiricist view of knowledge and 'never lift their minds above tangible things'. Their maxim, that there is nothing in the understanding that has not first been in the senses, is, he suggests, invalid, for ideas 'about God and the soul have never been' (1637: 57). Although Descartes did not wholly condemn the senses as Plato did, they did not, he felt, provide us with firm and certain knowledge – 'our senses sometimes play us false' (1637: 53). As Bronowski and Mazlish write: 'The books of scholars had shown Descartes that there is no certain truth on authority; the book of the world had shown him that there is none in custom – and now he had come to question even the validity of his senses (1960: 260).

What then would provide the foundation of true and certain knowledge? This is best answered by quoting the famous words of Descartes himself:

> While I decided thus to think that everything was false it followed necessarily that I who thought must be something; and observing that this truth: *I think, therefore I am*, was so certain and so evident that all the most extravagant suppositions of the sceptics were not capable of shaking it, I judged that I could accept it as the first principle of the philosophy I was seeking.

Seeing very clearly that in order to think one must exist, Descartes concluded that he

> was a substance, of which the whole essence or nature consists in thinking, and which in order to exist, needs no place and depends on no material thing; so that this *I*, that is to say, the mind . . . is entirely distinct from the body, and . . . that even if the body were not, it would not cease to be all that it is. (1637: 53–4)

From this basic first principle Descartes went on to deduce the existence of God, using the same kind of ontological argument first suggested by St Anselm in 1070, as well as the existence of the world and his own body, and the general accuracy of perception.

A number of points may be made regarding Descartes' general philosophy:

1. It is clear that one of Descartes' criticisms of the scholastic knowledge that derived from Aristotle was that it was primarily didactic and classificatory and did not lead to the generation of new knowledge. By contrast, he felt that the new scientific logic he advocated, based as it was on certain foundations, led us to direct our reason 'in order to discover those truths of which we are ignorant' (Copleston 1963: 82).

2. On concluding that the senses are intrinsically unreliable in discerning the reality of the physical world, Descartes came to reformulate the rationalist tradition, which stemmed from Plato, and to argue that knowledge is derived from rational reflection rather than from empirical observation. This led him to suggest that the essence of physical objects, their material substance, consists in extension (space), together with the various modes in and through which extension may change. He thus followed Galileo in distinguishing between the primary and secondary qualities of matter; the primary qualities were those of quantity, shape and motion and were presumed to be inherent in matter itself; the secondary qualities were those qualities such as colour, taste and feel of an object which impinge on a sensing organism. Descartes felt that the essential properties of matter (extension) could be ascertained by reason alone (Fancher 1979: 16).

3. Such rationalism led Descartes to postulate the existence of innate ideas of the soul. In fact, he speaks of all clear and distinct ideas as being innate. Such ideas as 'God', 'perfection', 'infinity' and the geometric axioms are also thought to be derived from thinking itself. Such ideas are not innate in the sense of being present in the child's mind from birth, but rather the mind produces them, as it were, out of its own potentialities on the occasion of some experience (Copleston 1963: 94). This kind of nativism was later developed by Kant.

4. Descartes came close to equating mathematics and natural science, for he suggests that the human mind produces the knowledge of nature by its own efforts in the same way as it does mathematics. This formulation leads to two problems. On the

one hand, there is the implied assimilation of a causal relation to that of logic – an equation that was essentially developed by Spinoza into a system of mechanistic monism. But as Hampshire writes, mathematical certainty 'by itself is insufficient for an empirical science; it lies in the purely logical interrelations of a theory and can carry in itself no predictive power or connection with the facts of experience' (1956: 67). On the other hand, if the truths of physics can be deduced *a priori*, where does experimental science fit into Descartes' metaphysics? Although Descartes does not refuse a role to experience and experiment in the natural sciences, Copleston stresses that he was far from being an empiricist, and was always pulled in the direction of 'pan-mathematicism'. He writes: 'The ideal of assimilating physics to mathematics remains always before his eyes and his general attitude is far removed from that of Francis Bacon' (1963: 93).

The contrast between the two men is a salient one. What Descartes lacked – a real commitment to experimental science – Bacon had. What Bacon lacked – any understanding of the potential of mathematics in advancing scientific understanding – Descartes had in profusion, though perhaps in extreme. But as Bronowski and Mazlish emphasise, science could only advance by a combination of the two methods: 'Bacon's notion that experiment will give results of itself is obviously ill founded. So equally is Descartes' notion that the universe can be constructed by thinking alone' (1960: 266; Kearns 1979: 31).

Besides seeing mathematical reasoning as the key to valid scientific knowledge, Descartes explicitly adopted the mechanistic conception of the world. The two conceptions are, in fact, intrinsically linked. As Descartes also had a rather scholastic propensity to present his ideas as a total world-picture, there is some justification in Bronowski and Mazlish's contention that Descartes was the first philosopher in modern times to present a comprehensive view of the world, which was fundamentally different from the Aristotelian-Christian one. This new cosmology, which saw the world as a machine rather than as a kind of organism, was both world-shaking and world-shaping (1960: 263; cf. Collingwood 1945; Merchant 1980: 203–4).

Given this mechanistic conception, there inevitably arises what Collingwood suggests is a problem, namely finding a placement for the 'homeless entity' – the human mind – within the metaphysical theory (1945: 103). Descartes' solution to this problem is well known, for he proposed a dualism of the body and mind, seen as two quite distinct substances, the one physical, the other entirely immaterial. This conception of the human person as composed of two distinct aspects, body and mind, is quite different from the Aristotelian notion of the soul, seen as the animating principle of the universe. For Aristotelian theory – that 'highbrow version of animism', as Koestler (1959: 113) significantly described it – distinguished three levels of the soul, with appropriate functions, reflecting varying degrees of complexity depending on the organism's place in the hierarchy of nature. At the lowest level there is vegetative soul, possessed by plants and subserving the functions of nutrition and reproduction. Higher organisms such as animals possess a sensitive soul, indicating an awareness of their surroundings, and the ability to experience pleasure and pain. Highest in the scale of souls is that possessed only by humans, the rational soul, which not only enables humans to reason but is seen as immortal. For Aristotle the human being was depicted as an essential unity, the soul standing to body as form to matter. Moreover, as the soul was regarded as the principle of biological, sensitive and rational life, it was not reducible to mind. But for Descartes soul and mind were equated and the mind seen as a thinking substance quite separate from the body. And as the extract quoted above indicates, Descartes did not see the body as belonging to the essence or nature of the human being. In the fifth part of the *Discourse on Method* he expressly writes that 'our soul is of a nature entirely independent of the body' (1637: 76), and had earlier expressed the view that what distinguishes humans from other animals is the possession of an immortal or rational soul. The implication is that, except for this soul or mind, a human being, or rather the body, is a machine. In an important sense Descartes conceived of the body as a machine, and thus its movements and actions were explicable in mechanical terms. Descartes was not the only person of his time to suggest a mechanistic view of the body, for William Harvey had demonstrated that the blood circulated through the body by analysing the mechanical properties of the heart as a pump (Francher 1979: 21).

Many writers have stressed the sharp dualism that Descartes made between the mind and body, the former having the property of thought and self-consciousness, while the latter is seen as part of a mechanistic universe. But as Copleston has suggested, there is within Descartes' writings two distinct lines of thought. On the one hand, Descartes emphasises a deep cleavage, a real distinction between mind and body, even conceiving of them as distinctive substances – hence a rigid dualism. On the other hand, he is reluctant to see the soul or mind as simply lodged in the body, 'like a pilot in his ship' (1637: 159). And he therefore devotes a good deal of discussion attempting to explore and explain the interaction between them. One short extract will suffice:

> Nature also teaches me by these feelings of pain, hunger, thirst, etc. that I am not only lodged in my body, like a pilot in his ship, but, besides, that I am joined to it very closely and indeed so compounded and intermingled with my body that I form as it were a single whole with it. (1637: 159)

Thus for Descartes the mind acquires information about the material world through the senses, and the desires and pains of the body are felt in consciousness, while in turn, the mind may direct the body. Aware from empirical observation that mutual interaction between the body and mind takes place, and that they must therefore constitute some kind of unity, Descartes in many contexts did not stress the dualism. Raymond Fancher expresses Descartes' 'interactive dualism' in the following words:

> Without a soul the human body would be an automaton responding to inner and outer stimulation according to the rules built into its mechanism. It would be without consciousness and completely under the control of its emotions and external stimuli. Conversely a soul without a body would have consciousness, but only of the innate ideas. It would lack the sensory impressions and ideas of substantial things that occupy human consciousness most of the time. Thus the body added richness to the contexts of the soul's consciousness while the soul added rationality and volition to the determinants of the body's behaviour. (1979: 31–2)

Thus in essence Descartes presents us not with a dualism but with a tripartite schema. There exists two distinct and separate substances; conscious substance or mind, which incorporates all cognition and volitional states, and material substance, the bodily mechanism referred to in terms of position, shape and motion. But then Descartes suggests we have experience 'which should not be referred to the mind alone nor yet to the body alone: they arise, as we shall see, from a close and intimate union of body and mind. To this class belong (1) appetites – hunger, thirst, etc.; (2) impulses or passions of the mind, which do not consist of mere consciousness – impulses towards anger, joy, sorrow, love, etc.; (3) all sensations – the sensations of pain, enjoyment, light and colours, sounds, odours, flavours, heat, hardness and other tactile qualities' (Anscombe and Geach 1954: 191).

Stressing that the body is 'really joined' to the soul or mind, Descartes went even further by locating their point of interaction. From his physiological studies he felt that the point of interaction was not the heart nor the whole brain even, but the small pineal gland in the brain. His reasons for thinking so is that the brain itself is 'double' – divided – while the soul is indivisible, a unified agency and therefore must be seated in a single organ. Although such ideas are highly speculative and unsatisfactory, they do indicate Descartes' dilemma, and the 'uneasy balance' between his stress on dualism and the implications of his analysis of the passions which suggests a complex interaction. His conception of the human subject is therefore an ambivalent one. On the one hand, he suggested that the person was a machine, and was thus open to being studied by the methods of the natural sciences. Not only the physical body was explicable in mechanistic terms, but also the many aspects of the body–mind interaction. Unlike Aristotle and the medieval faculty psychologists, Descartes implied that the faculties of memory and imagination, as well as passions and sensations, could be explained as bodily activities. Thus Descartes sought to account for as much of the mind as possible on materialist, mechanical terms within the sphere of natural science, only self-consciousness and volition falling outside the mechanistic paradigm. Hence Descartes gave a great impetus to the incorporation of mind within a mechanistic science (Leahey 1987: 95). On the other hand, Descartes seemed to suggest that what was most unique about humans, their self-conscious reflection and much of their cognitive attributes, was beyond the reach of mechanistic materialism, and could only be understood by introspection and rational reflection. Descartes is a truly paradoxical figure. Bronowski and Mazlish remark that 'it is ironic that the man who had an ecstatic experience revealing to him the nature of the universe should introduce into modern philosophy the dualism of mind and body which has plagued thought ever since' (1960: 265). He is difficult to fit into the well-known philosophical categories. A theist and a sincere Christian, his philosophy contained the seeds of materialistic atheism. As he denied the identity of mind with brain, and stressed a dualistic metaphysic, he is not a materialist. But his mechanistic view of the world, and of the human body and the psychology this implies, ultimately lends support to empiricism and behaviourism. As he does not accept that the body exists independently of the mind, he is not an idealist. But again, in his stress on reason as opposed to sense experience, in postulating innate ideas and in advocating absolute truth as opposed to relativism, he stands firmly within the rationalist tradition.

Although Descartes retained scholastic ideas – in explaining bodily functions in terms of 'humors' or 'animal spirits' and in utilising the concept of substance – his essential ideas are thoroughly modern, and many contemporary philosophical problems stem directly from him. As many writers have stressed, few scholars have left such an important intellectual legacy, and his influence has been profound. Copleston outlines the importance of Descartes in the development of Hegel's idealism, and in the foundation of the phenomenology of Husserl and Sartre, for all three writers stress 'subjectivity' as the Cartesian point of departure. He notes too the links between Descartes' mechanistic accounts of reality and the mechanistic materialism of the French Enlightenment philosophers like LaMettrie. But he argues that one should attempt to situate Descartes in an historical context, for Descartes was neither a mechanical materialist nor an idealist in any clear sense. Although Descartes grounded his philosophy on an existential proposition and subjectivity, he was neither an idealist nor a subjectivist, for he was concerned 'to establish an objective interpretation of reality which he did not regard as reducible to the activity of consciousness' (1963: 159).

Descartes' influence on psychology has been equally profound. Both Boring (1950) and Fancher (1979) stress that many of Descartes' fundamental conceptions still influence or even dominate psychology; the notion that the brain is pre-eminently the organ in mediating behaviour; the idea of the reflex as an elementary unit of behaviour (which became the cornerstone of behaviourism); the dualism of mind and body; the mechanistic approach; the doctrine of innate ideas, which was reformulated by Kant; the notion of emotions or passions as inner determinants of behaviour. All these ideas have influenced later students, and form the basis of the many different schools of psychology. (For further important studies of Descartes, see Kenny 1968; Reé 1974; B. Williams 1979; M. Wilson 1978.)

1.2 Mechanistic Materialism

In challenging religion and scholastic philosophy, both Bacon and Descartes, though paying lip-service to the idea of God, had in reality laid the foundations of modern materialism. Bacon had stressed the importance of experimental science and enunciated the principles of a materialist epistemology, while Descartes, along with Kepler and Galileo, had clearly established the mechanistic conception of nature. The 'natural philosophy' that Newton had expounded was to all intents and purposes materialist. And both Bacon and Descartes had emphatically rejected the Aristotelian doctrine of the final cause. A contemporary of these two philosophers, Thomas Hobbes (1588–1679), can rightly be cited as one of the founders of modern materialism. Although as a philosophical doctrine materialism is as old as philosophy itself, Hobbes, through his strident atheism and his espousal of mechanistic philosophy, firmly established materialism in European thought, making Britain the 'classic land' of the materialist mode of thought, as the neo-Kantian Friedrich Lange (1866) put it. (For historical perspectives on materialism, see M. N. Roy 1940; Chattopadhyaya 1959; Novack 1965.)

Thomas Hobbes described himself as a timid man, but by all accounts he was a man of strong personality, of powerful physique and he lived to the age of ninety-one. He was known for his wit and had a brilliant intellect. But he is almost universally despised as an atheist and materialist, and as a defender of absolutism. His study *Leviathan* ranks as one of the great books of political philosophy – a response to the far-reaching social and political changes of the seventeenth century, as well as a systematic application of the new mechanistic theory to social issues. Hobbes was born poor, the son of a dissolute clergyman. But he was rescued and supported by an uncle, who sent him to Oxford where he studied the classics and scholastic philosophy. He took a dislike both to scholasticism and to universities, and throughout his life he constantly criticised them. He became a tutor to the Cavendish family, who became his life-time patrons and gave him support. Hobbes became a friend of Francis Bacon, and although he shared Bacon's authoritarian politics and his dislike of Aristotelian philosophy, he had no great opinion of Bacon as a philosopher. In 1636 he visited Galileo in Italy and was deeply impressed by his theory of physics. He also met Descartes, who prompted him to think that geometry constituted an ideal model for systematic knowledge, but he was very critical of Descartes' *Meditations*. Throughout his criticisms of Descartes, Hobbes assumed a materialist position, suggesting that the mind is simply a body in motion. But Hobbes' interest in geometry did not develop until he had reached the age of forty. On one of his journeys to the continent, Hobbes happened to pick up a copy of Euclid's *Elements* while in Paris. He became so excited and impressed by Euclid's demonstrations that he fell in love with geometry and conceived the idea that all thought – and not just geometry – ought to be presented as an axiomatic system. Reason, therefore, is of the nature of reckoning and should start from clear definitions. From Galileo he also took the idea that motion, not rest, was the natural state of bodies. Everything was moving. Much of Hobbes' basic achievement was to turn Galileo's physics into a metaphysics, and to apply this mechanistic theory to humans and to social life. In Britain he popularised mechanistic philosophy by expressing it in a readable, non-mathematical language (Bronowski and Mazlish 1960: 230).

In 1640 Hobbes published his *Elements of Law* during the assembly of the Long Parliament – a text that argued for the need for an undivided authority, thus prefiguring the thesis of *Leviathan*. But when parliament impeached supporters of the monarchy like Land and Strafford, Hobbes was terrified and fled for his life. By the time the civil war started Hobbes was out of the country. Afterwards he confessed, or boasted, 'I was the first that fled.' In Paris he already had many friends, and was soon joined by other exiles supporting the Royalist cause. For a while he taught mathematics to the future Charles II. During the years of exile he spent his time writing his masterpiece *Leviathan*, which was published in 1651. Soon afterwards he returned to Britain, being granted permission to return by Cromwell, on the understanding that he abstained from political activity. After the Restoration Hobbes was received at Court, but because of his atheism was never fully in favour and was forbidden to publish his opinions. At the age of eighty-six he published a translation of Homer for want of something better to do. He died in 1679, a controversial figure to the end (Russell 1946: 568–79; Cranston 1972).

Carolyn Merchant expressed Hobbes' basic philosophy succinctly when she wrote: 'Hobbes, a throughgoing materialist, further mechanized the cosmos by denying any inherent force to matter, by reducing the human soul, will, brain and appetite to matter in mechanical motion, and by transforming the organic model of society into a mechanistic structure' (1980: 206).

A discussion of Hobbes' mechanical materialism can perhaps begin with his published objections to Descartes' *Meditations* (1641), although even in his *Little Treatise* (1630) he had developed a mechanical explanation of sensations, suggesting that they are simply particles of matter in motion. Hobbes makes a number of criticisms of Descartes' philosophy. First, he accuses Descartes of virtually equating the one who thinks with thinking itself, thus lapsing into scholasticism. It is like saying: 'I am walking, therefore

I am a walk.' Hobbes agrees that we are thinking beings, but it leads to obscurity to identity the human subject with thinking. He writes: 'I myself, who am conscious and distinct from my consciousness, and my consciousness is distinct, though not separated from me.' Thus, 'it may be that the thing that is conscious is the subject of mind, reason or intellect, and so it may be something corporeal.'

Descartes, he says, assumes the opposite, but never proves it. For Hobbes the 'conscious being' is something material or corporeal – 'for the subjects of all acts seem to be conceived only in terms of body or matter'.

Second, in questioning whether Descartes makes a clear distinction between imagination and a mental conception, Hobbes suggests that reasoning is nothing but a joining together and linking of names, and tells us nothing about the nature of things. Thus he concludes, 'reasoning will depend on names, names on imagination, and imagination perhaps (and this is my opinion) on the motions of bodily organs; and thus the mind will be nothing but motion in certain parts of an organic body.'

Finally, Hobbes questions Descartes' reliance on the notion that the idea of God is inherent in us. 'God's existence has not been demonstrated' by Descartes, he suggests, 'much less creation', and so Descartes' 'whole discussion falls to the ground' (Anscombe and Geach 1954: 128–43).

Hobbes' *Leviathan* is essentially divided into two parts; the first deals with human beings as individuals and forms the philosophical basis of part two, 'of commonwealth', which informs us how we can avoid the negative implications of the 'natural state' by forming communities under the central authority of a sovereign ruler. Throughout the study Hobbes adopts a mechanistic and materialistic approach, and views his conception of the state, 'an artificial man', in the same terms as he conceptualises the human subject – as a mechanism.

Critical of the 'vain' philosophy of Aristotle, which he thought full of jargon and absurdities and which attempted to explain the world in terms of abstract essences or forms, Hobbes suggests in contrast that the world is fundamentally corporeal and materialistic:

> The universe that is, the whole mass of all things that are, is corporeal, that is to say, body, and hath the dimensions of magnitude namely length, breadth, and depth; also every part of body is likewise body . . . consequently every part of the universe is body, and that which is not body is no part of the universe. (1651: 483)

This universe he sees as continually in motion, and following Galileo he writes: 'When a body is once in motion it moveth, unless something else hinder it, eternally' (1651: 23).

But if the whole world consists of bodies in motion, it follows that human beings too, being part of the world, can be conceived mechanistically, as a body, a machine in motion. In the introduction to *Leviathan* Hobbes wrote:

> For seeing life is but a motion of limbs, the beginning whereof is in some principal part within; why may we not say, that all automata (engines that move themselves by springs and wheels as doth a watch) have an artificial life? For what is the heart but a spring; and the nerves, but so many strings; and the joints, but so many wheels, giving motion to the whole body. (1651: 19)

Although Hobbes adopted the mechanistic paradigm and the axiomatic or geometric method of Galileo and Descartes, and was critical of Bacon's empirical method of science – and in this sense Hobbes was a rationalist – his basic concept and premises, as postulated in the early parts of *Leviathan*, are essentially empiricist. He begins by suggesting that all thoughts and representations are derived from the senses. 'The original of them all, is that which we call sense, for there is no conception in a man's mind, which hath not at first, totally, or by parts, been begotten upon the organs of sense' (1651: 21).

And the cause of sensation is the 'motions' of the external body or object, which 'presseth the organ proper to each sense'. He continues: 'Sense in all cases is nothing else but original fancy, caused by pressure that is by the motion of external things upon the eyes, ears and on the organs theron unto ordained' (1651: 22).

Hobbes is therefore suggesting that the qualities of experience do not inhere in the object itself, but in the experiencing person; what is without are motions and nothing more (R. I. Watson 1979: 25). Thus it is 'motions' in the objects that produce in us the sensation of the other qualities of colour, heat, and so on. This distinction between 'primary' and 'secondary' qualities was later elaborated by Locke.

Imagination – a term Hobbes uses for all mental images – he describes as 'decaying sense' – both essentially being derived from motions in the body. Imagination when asleep is dreaming; memory is to express the decaying sense and the memory of many things is experience. Hobbes discusses next the train of thought (imaginations), which he refers to as mental discourse, and he sees this as distinct from verbal discourse, which puts our thoughts into speech. He believed that there is 'nothing in the world universal but names for the things named are everyone of them individual and singular' (1651: 35).

Hobbes, as Russell (1946: 571) stresses, is an 'out and out nominalist'. As to reason, Hobbes sees this as nothing but 'reckoning', and truth consists of the right ordering of names. Following Descartes, Hobbes seems to suggest that all science follows a geometrical deductive system and all truths are analytic. But as Hampshire writes (1956: 48), such a system of truths could not in themselves give us an empirical science for no provision is made for empirical observations or for the prediction of future events.

But Hobbes' main interest is not in the theory of knowledge but in laying the foundations of his political theory. To do so he concedes of the human subject as a purely natural being – and society (the state) as an artifact. The human being, he thus suggests, is simply a natural machine and is driven by two powerful emotions; the desire for power and for self-preservation. All humans are essentially equal in their physical properties for even 'the weakest have strength, enough to kill the strongest' (1651: 98). As there is a 'restless desire' for power in all humans, Hobbes suggests that in a state of nature there is 'always war of everyone against everyone', and thus in his well-known phrase 'the life of man is solitary, poor, nasty, brutish and short' (1651: 100). This conception is opposite to that of Descartes, who thought that the passions 'are all good in their nature'. The natural human being for Hobbes is egotistic, competitive, aggressive, power-seeking, and civil society, the state, as he explained in part two of *Leviathan*, was the means whereby, through agreement, social order and civility were maintained. A mechanistic conception in humans and a fundamental opposition between the individual and society are the essential premises underlying Hobbes' important work.

Although Hobbes had attempted to provide philosophical foundations for the absolutist state, he not only offended the Parliamentarians – although he held that government was by the consent of the people – but he also upset the Royalists. For Hobbes presented a naturalistic theory of politics and simply poured scorn on the idea of the divine right of kings. In the final section of the book he was equally scathing of such Christian notions as the 'kingdom of God', 'spirits' and 'miracles'. Hobbes' theory of the human subject is merely a philosophical preamble for his theory of politics, which forms the substance of *Leviathan*. It is hardly surprising given the importance of the work that scholars have largely focused on his political philosophy (see Warrender 1957; MacPherson 1962).

But we may in summary fashion mention a number of important themes, which emerge in Hobbes' writings:

1. As a materialist and a sceptic, Hobbes, in attacking scholastic philosophy and their 'absurd speeches . . . without any significance at all', anticipated the methods of many later positivists and linguistic philosophers. As Hobbes put it: 'If a man should talk to me of a round quadrangle . . . or immaterial substance . . . or a free subject . . . I should not say he were an error but that his words were without meaning, that is to say absurd' (1651: 43).

2. Whereas Descartes believed that animals but not humans were entirely machines, Hobbes went a step further, claiming that spiritual substance (mind) is a meaningless idea. Humans are essentially self-moving and self-directing machines; only matter exists and the actions of people are fully determined. A voluntary act, according to Hobbes, 'preceedeth' from the will, and the will is essentially the last inclination or desire, and desires (appetites) are related to bodily motions. The whole analysis is mechanistic, deterministic and reductive.

3. Although Hobbes is often spoken of as a bourgeois philosopher, and he has been described as clearly and fully articulating the theory of possessive individualism (MacPherson 1962: 263–5), it is worth noting that in contrast to Locke there is little mention of the sanctity of property in the *Leviathan*. As Russell remarks (1946: 578), Hobbes seemed oblivious to the existence of class and class conflict.

4. In stressing that the human is corporeal, being endowed with instincts of self-preservation and with natural aggressive impulses – such instincts can even override the duty to the sovereign – Hobbes' theory has clearly been influential. The basic postulates of Nietzsche, Freud and Lorenz are essentially Hobbesian.

5. In his discussion of the 'train of imagination' or thought, Hobbes suggests that 'all fancies are motions within us, relics of those made in the sense as those motions that immediately succeeded one another, in the sense, continue also together after sense' (1651: 28). This idea forms the basis of associationist thinking, namely that we connect things in memory or in thought simply because they were connected in our original experience of them.

Although earlier writers had speculated along his lines, Hobbes was the first to present this doctrine in modern terms (Murphy and Kovach 1972: 28).

Having outlined the philosophical theories of both Descartes and Hobbes it can be seen that they had contrasting perspectives on the nature of the human subject, two contrasting ways of relating the human personality to the mechanistic universe. Descartes presents essentially a rationalist dualism, while Hobbes gives us the first consistent theory of monistic materialism. Descartes argues that humans can be defined and distinguished from animals by the possession of a spiritual soul (mind), that they are endowed with free choice and in having a soul humans partly transcend the system of mechanical causality. Descartes felt that all bodies are in the same sense machines, but by possessing a soul humans could not be reduced to a member wholly of the mechanical system. Apart from the mechanism, Descartes' theory was akin to that of Plato, who was (unlike Aristotle) a mind–body dualist. But as Copleston has suggested, and as we explained in the previous section, Descartes clearly had a problem, for a rigid stress on two contrasting sub-stances, mind and body, tends to undermine the obvious empirical unity of the human subject. In his theory of the passions, Descartes attempted to spell out the interaction and the way the body does act upon the mind.

On the other hand, Hobbes applied the fundamental ideas of Galileo's mechanics to all reality and thus interpreted mental phenomena as essentially material. He, therefore, as Bronowski and Mazlish stress (1960: 233), presents a view of causality that was rigidly deterministic and treated the mind as simply another body in motion. The mind is at best an epiphenomenon and human freedom virtually denied. Consciousness is interpreted as motion reducible to changes within the body system. Merchant is therefore misleading when she suggests that the machine metaphor was based on a dualism between body and soul, with the soul as an 'external operator' (1980: 156). The new mechanistic conception of Hobbes did not imply that the 'self' was 'master' of the passions and 'housed' in a machine-like body. Hobbes was a materialist monist. In fact, neither mind nor self is mentioned in the *Leviathan*. Humans for Hobbes are self-moving machines, which in their nature strive for the preservation of their own life and for power.

During the eighteenth century a number of philosophers adopted the mechanical materialist approach of Hobbes, especially in France. One of the most influential of these was the French physician and philosopher Julien Offray de la Mettrie (1709–51). In his well-known study *L'Homme Machine* (The Human Machine), published in 1748, La Mettrie praised Descartes for his materialism, suggesting that he was the first to conceive of animals as pure machines. Like Hobbes, la Mettrie took the further step: 'Let us boldly conclude that man is a machine,' he wrote. He went on to describe in detail how the state of the body necessarily affected the mind, for example, in the effects of drugs or disease. Rather than considering the 'soul' as an 'external operator', as Merchant (1980) suggests, this mechanist thought the soul an 'empty symbol'. Copleston (1963) suggests that he represented humans as a complicated machine and the theory of the spiritual soul as a fable. He felt that human mental processes no less than physical processes could be explained in terms of mechanistic and materialistic hypotheses. Many writers have indicated that la Mettrie was an important forerunner of the behaviourist doctrines of Watson and Skinner (Copleston 1963: 25; Leahey 1987: 125–6). Other French Enlightenment philosophers such as d'Holbach and Diderot adopted a mechanical materialistic standpoint along with atheism, conceiving of nature as a causal system, humans as essentially material beings and thought as a function of the brain. A later disciple of la Mettrie, the physician Cabanis, even went so far as to declare that the brain secretes thought as the liver secretes bile.

The mind–body problem was the inevitable outcome of the mechanistic paradigm and variations on both solutions – dualism and materialism – were explored by later scholars. But two philosophers are worth mentioning in the present context, for they represent contrasting responses to Descartes' metaphysic – Spinoza and Leibniz. Spinoza presented a pantheistic monism, which simply dissolved the mind–body problem; while Leibniz suggested a pluralistic approach, which left the dualism intact.

1.3 Spinoza and Leibniz

Baruch Spinoza (1632–77) – that most lovable and noblest of philosophers, as Russell described him (1946: 592) – was born in Amsterdam, of a family of Portuguese Jews. He lived for most of his life alone in various parts of Holland having been excommunicated from the Jewish community for his freethinking ideas. He never held an academic post, never sought the limelight, and made a living by polishing lenses. He died at the early age of forty-four of tuberculosis. His most famous work, *Ethics Demonstrated According to the Geometric Order*, was published posthumously in 1677.

In his basic premises Spinoza follows the mechanistic philosophy of Hobbes and Descartes. He accepts their materialistic and deterministic physics, suggesting that philosophy should inquire only into efficient and not into final courses. All things in the universe are determined, and there is no such thing as free will in the mental sphere, or chance in the physical world. He also accepts the geometric method, and *Ethics*, as its title suggests, follows the style of Euclid, beginning with definitions and axioms and following the deductive method. The essence of Spinoza's system is thus that everything could be demonstrated, and that following the geometric style not only gave clarity and rigour but was indispensable in the description of reality. It also leads to a certain detachment and impersonality. Thus Spinoza thought that the nature of the world and of human life could be logically deduced from self-evident axioms. But as with Descartes, this represents a serious flaw in his philosophy for it makes the untenable assumption that a causal relation is akin to the relation of logical implication and, as many have noted, scientific laws are to be discovered by observation not by reasoning alone (Russell 1946: 601; Copleston 1963: 217). But whereas Descartes begins his analysis with human subjectivity and thinking, and Hobbes, like the medieval scholastics such as Aquinas, with the objects of sense-experience, Spinoza begins his with God, or rather with what might be described as infinite divine substance, for Spinoza equates God with nature. It is quite misleading to see Spinoza as a religious thinker who conceived of God as a transcendental deity standing outside the world as its creator. Spinoza identifies God with nature and thus dissolves the distinction between the creator and creation, although he retained the distinction between *nature naturans* (nature creating) and *natura naturata* (nature as created). His early critics were quite justified in accusing Spinoza of being an atheist, for his theory did deny the existence of a personal spiritual being who transcends nature. But it is equally misleading to view Spinoza as a religious mystic like Plato or Aurobindo, for God was not equated with consciousness, or with a spiritual essence immanent in nature. There is only one substance, God or nature, and this divine substance is 'not only the effecting cause of the existence of things but also of their essence' (Spinoza, 1977: 21).

For Spinoza, then, God or nature is eternal, self-creating and self-created and is the cause of all things in the world. Only this divine substance is free, in the sense that it acts according to the necessary laws of its own nature — everything else is limited and determined. Spinoza's monism suggests that everything in the universe belongs to this single, intelligible, causal system (Hampshire 1951: 47–8). This system can be known and looked at from essentially two points of view; it can be conceived under the attribute of thought or under the attribute of matter (extension). But unlike Descartes, Spinoza does not conceive of these two attributes as two substances, or even two orders of reality. An uncompromising rationalist, Spinoza argues that there is only one order of nature (or God).

'The order and connection of ideas', he writes, 'is the same as the order and connection of things . . . thinking substance and extended substance are one and the same substance, which is now comprehended through this and now through that attribute' (1977: 41–2). And Spinoza continues:

'Whether we consider nature under the attribute of extension or under the attribute of thought . . . we shall find one and the same order and one and the same connection of causes' (1977: 42).

There seems to be neither dualism (as with Descartes) nor the reduction of thought to material bodies (as with Hobbes). If there is only one order of nature, it seems inadmissible to speak of the body and mind as two different orders – they are simply aspects of the one divine substance. The Cartesian problem of relating mind to body simply dissolves. What then, for Spinoza, is the exact relationship between the body and mind? Spinoza expresses this rather well:

> The mind and body are one and the same thing, which, now under the attribute of thought, now under the attribute of extension, is conceived. Whence it comes about that the order or concatenation of things is one . . . and consequently that the order of the actions and passions of our body are simultaneous in nature with the order of actions and passions of our mind. (1977: 86)

Copleston questions whether this is anything more than a 'verbal elimination' of the Cartesian problem (1963: 229), but clearly Spinoza is suggesting that there is an intimate and necessary connection between the mind and the body. This is confirmed when he suggests that the mind is the idea of the body and that it knows not itself save in so far as it perceives ideas of modifications of the body (1977: 58). It is equally confirmed when Spinoza denies that the mind (he never refers to the soul as such) is in any sense immortal: 'Our mind therefore can only be said to last, and its existence can be defined by a certain time, only in so far as it involves the actual existence of the body' (1977: 214).

Spinoza's whole account, while not explicitly suggesting a reductive materialism, is none the less infused with a naturalistic not a religious perspective. Scruton's suggestion (1981: 55) that Spinoza's theory is a 'thorough going pan-psychism' seems to me somewhat misleading, for Spinoza nowhere suggests the existence of a 'world soul', nor does he imply in his monism an animistic conception of the world. Pan-psychism is more properly reserved, as we shall see, to the philosophies of Leibniz and Schopenhauer – both idealists. It is difficult to pigeonhole Spinoza, but he was certainly not an idealist nor a theist, as many discussions of his writings imply. He has been described in that oft-quoted phrase, as 'a god-intoxicated man'; he would be better described as a 'nature-intoxicated' philosopher.

The problem remains that if the mind is determined for 'willing this or that by a cause', and thus cannot be the 'free cause of its actions' (1977: 74), as Spinoza's deterministic metaphysics suggests, how is human freedom and morality possible? For Spinoza's main interest in writing *Ethics* (as its title suggests) is not to present a causal theory of nature but is in salvation – in attaining a true peace of mind and freedom from the servitude of the passions (Copleston 1963: 268). He has the same aim as many mystics – salvation – but he is a thorough going rationalist, whose metaphysics is essentially opposed – opposite – to that of religious mysticism. In the final three sections of *Ethics* Spinoza thus presents us with his theory of the emotions, and with the role of the intellect in attaining this salvation.

All finite things in nature, Spinoza suggests, endeavour to persist in their own being, and, reviving a concept from Aristotle, Spinoza calls this conatus. This tendency of everything to preserve itself and to increase its power and activity Spinoza sees as identical with its essence. "The endeavour wherewith a thing endeavours to persist in its being is nothing else than the actual essence of that thing' (1977: 91). With humans this tendency, when it refers to both mind and body as a unity, is called 'appetite'. When a person becomes conscious of this it is called 'desire'. The move towards a conscious state of greater vitality or perfection Spinoza calls 'pleasure', while a transition to a lower state of perfection he calls 'pain'. In an important sense, as Hampshire writes, Spinoza's gives a naturalistic account of human emotion and conduct, for in his philosophy 'pleasure and pain always represent a change in psycho-physical state; they are the mental reflexion of the rise or fall in the power or activity of the organism' (1951: 127). Spinoza goes on to derive all emotion – love, hate, compassion, ambition, lust, anger – from the fundamental passions of desire, pleasure and pain. This analysis is very similar to that of Hobbes, although Spinoza by no means has a Hobbesian view of humans, but sees that natural passion in a more neutral sense. Morality derives in a naturalistic fashion from his theory of the emotions: 'By good I understand here all kind of pleasure and whatever may conduce to it, and more especially that which satisfies our fervent desires, what ever they may be; by bad all kinds of pain, and especially that which frustrates our desires' (1977: 111).

Given the causal origins of our emotions, moral praise and blame for the objects of our desires are quite out of place. There is no scope for moral judgements, as these imply that a person is free to determine his or her emotions. As Spinoza wrote, his doctrine 'teaches us not to despise, hate or ridicule anyone; to be angry with or envy no-one' (1977: 81). But Spinoza does make a distinction between passive emotions (passions) and active emotions. Active emotions are those of pleasure and desire, which are in a sense accompanied by adequate understanding of their causes. All actions that stem from the emotions, in so far as the mind is active, or understanding of the causes, Spinoza refers to as 'fortitude'; and he recognises two kinds – courage and nobility: 'I understand by courage the desire by which each endeavours to preserve what is his own according to the dictate of reason alone. But by nobility I understand the desire by which each endeavours according to the dictate of reason alone to help and join to himself in friendship all other men' (1977: 126).

For Spinoza, people think themselves free as they are conscious of their volitions and desires, and are ignorant of the causes by which they are disposed to will and desire. Superstition is thus ignorance of the causes of our emotions and actions. Freedom, Spinoza is suggesting, is not freedom from the causal system of nature, but rather the consciousness of the necessity that such a system implies. His moral philosophy, as Copleston (1963: 253–5) suggests, implies an analytic ethic, not an exhortatory one, and has striking similarities to that of the Stoics. For both stress the importance of knowledge and on understanding the place of individual things in the whole divine system of nature. But Spinoza's philosophy implied no ascetic ideal. He rather suggests, as did later Romantics and ecologists, that human wisdom consists of understanding the place of humans within the whole scheme of nature.

Spinoza's philosophy, like that of Hobbes, is in many respects highly egoistic, for he argues that the motives of self-seeking and self-preservation govern human behaviour. The basis of his political philosophy is thus the same as Hobbes', though he comes to very different conclusions. But this conception of wisdom is not that of a self-seeking egotist as normally understood. For Spinoza, wisdom consists not only of acting according to the laws of one's own nature but also according to the light of reason. 'Therefore to act according to virtue is nothing else in us than to act, to live, and preserve our being according to the guidance of reason, on the basis of seeking what is useful to oneself' (1977: 158). And this also implies, Spinoza suggests, that people 'desire nothing for themselves which they do not also desire for the rest of mankind, and therefore they are just, faithful and honourable' (1977: 155). As with the Stoics his philosophy leads logically to some doctrine of human solidarity (Copleston 1963: 254).

Copleston and others have remained unconvinced that Spinoza's deterministic theory could allow any room for real moral freedom. But in not allowing any mention of design or of final causes in the study of human life, and in adopting essentially a mechanistic, causal paradigm, Spinoza's ambitions and hopes for the human subject are necessarily curtailed. Absolute freedom, he senses, was a superstition. Hampshire has summed up his more limited vision when he wrote: 'In Spinoza it seemed that men can attain happiness and dignity only by identifying themselves, through their knowledge and understanding with the whole order of nature, and by submerging their individual interests in this understanding' (1951: 161).

Spinoza was a visionary, and his aim was salvation – but salvation was to be achieved through human reason, by understanding our place within the whole scheme of nature, and by directing all science in one direction – towards the attainment of human happiness and perfection. Spinoza never expressed the Promethean ethic of other mechanistic philosophers with their conception of 'dominion over nature'. This is why the Romantics of the early nineteenth century found his philosophy so appealing.

Many writers have noted the similarity between many of Spinoza's conceptions and those of Freud. There are evident parallels in Freud's concept of libido and Spinoza's conatus, in that both writers see emotional life as based essentially on a universal unconscious tendency to self-preservation, although Spinoza's conception lacks a sexual connotation. Both writers suggest that the epithets of praise and blame when applied to our particular desires are irrelevant and superstitious, and that we can free ourselves only by understanding the true causes of our desires and infirmities. Both writers insist – even if they do so in prophetic language – that the human subject should be studied scientifically, as organisms within nature. Above all, both were essentially concerned to point the way to human freedom and happiness through understanding and natural knowledge (Hampshire 1951: 141–4).

It would be difficult to find anyone who contrasted more, in both personality and philosophy, with Spinoza than did that other important rationalist philosopher, Gottfried Wilhelm Leibniz (1646–1716). Spinoza was an unworldly recluse, and he lived a simple, self-sufficient life. Leibniz in contrast was one of the most distinguished men of his time and he enjoyed the patronage of many eminent people. He was, Hampshire writes:

> accessible, organizing, power-loving, avaricious, was a courtier and politician, a man of encyclopaedic knowledge and many attainments; he was immersed in the public life of his time at every point, writing and publishing incessantly on a great variety of subjects in response to some immediate need or request. (1951: 233)

He was undoubtedly one of the greatest intellects of his generation and invented, independently of Newton, the idea of calculus. But while Spinoza, from his seclusion, was formulating a unitary view of the world and of the human subject's place within it, a monistic metaphysical system, Leibniz, a man of the world, was in contrast outlining a pluralistic philosophy. Their philosophies are in many respects directly contrasting in both aim and content.

Leibniz, like Spinoza and Descartes, was a rationalist philosopher who aimed to present, in mechanistic terms, an all-embracing philosophy of the universe. But whereas Descartes suggests two categories of substance, mind and body, and Spinoza a single substance, divine nature, and both rejected the theory of final causes, Leibniz postulated a pluralistic philosophy, believing in many substances. The universe as such, Leibniz suggests, consists of two 'natural kingdoms', the physical kingdom of nature in which bodies act according to efficient (causal) laws – this is the mechanistic world of matter – and the kingdom of minds, souls and lives, which act according to the laws of final causes – appetites and purposes. The world is made up of compound sustances or bodies, but the essential constituents of the world consist of simple substances or unities, the 'true atoms of nature' which Leibniz refers to as monads. These monads, or entelechies (another term he uses), are the 'elements' of things – but they are not, like Democritus suggests, material but immaterial. They represent the 'centre' of a compound substance (like an animal or human being) and are imperishable and indivisible. According to Leibniz: 'Each monad, together with a particular body, make a living substance. Thus there is not only life everywhere . . . but there are also infinite degrees of it in the monads' (Parkinson 1973: 196). Thus Leibniz combines a mechanistic philosophy – applicable to bodies – with a vitalistic theory that draws its inspiration from Aristotle's theory of final causes and the medieval conception of the 'great chain of being'. Lovejoy, in his classic study, suggests that the metaphysics of Leibniz is not so much a form of idealism but one of 'pan-psychism' (1936: 144). For Leibniz, then, the whole of nature is full of life, and a monad is essentially equivalent to the concept of soul. But the latter concept, for Leibniz, has biological and psychological connotations rather than a spiritual one, although he looked upon God, the supreme substance, as the creator of both kingdoms. Thus Leibniz describes a monad as having an internal principle of action, as being distinct and self-sufficient. They 'have no windows', as he put it (1936: 179), being in a state of continual change. Monads not only have internal actions (appetites) but also have perceptions, which Leibniz describes as the inner state of the monad representing the compound or the external world. Unlike the Cartesians, Leibniz felt that animals have souls with this characteristic, but that minds are souls raised to the level of reason. Such souls have apperception, which is consciousness or the reflective knowledge of the inner state of perception. Souls that enjoy apperceptions are called 'rational souls' or 'spirits'. Although all the universe is animate for Leibniz, in the sense that all things are ultimately composed of immaterial monads, he clearly senses that there are different levels of reality. He even suggests that for most of the time human beings act like animals – we behave merely like empiricists he remarks (1936: 183).

When it comes to the relationship between the body and mind, Leibniz suggests a harmony between the two kingdoms, which act according to different principles – that of efficient and final causes:

These principles provide one with a way of explaining naturally the union, or rather the conformity of the soul and the organic body. The soul follows its own laws, and the body its own likewise, and they accord by virtue of harmony pre-established among all substances, since they are all representations of one and the same universe. (1936: 193)

This theory of the mind-body relationship has come to be known as psycho-physical parallelism – a view also accepted by the Cartesian philosopher Malebranche, who concluded that there is correspondence but not interaction between the mind and body (Copleston 1963: 195).

Although Leibniz reintroduced Aristotle's theory of final causes into philosophy, and his idealist philosophy was described by Russell as 'esoteric', many modern conceptions were latent in his work. He was one of the first scholars to make a clear distinction between what he described as 'two kinds of truth; truths of reasoning and truths of fact. Truths of reasoning are necessary and their opposite is impossible: those of fact are contingent' (1936: 184). This distinction between necessary (analytic) and contingent truths – conflated by Spinoza, who tended to collapse causal and logical reasoning and held nothing to be contingent – has become a central tenet of modern philosophy. Equally of interest is that Leibniz's account of perception and apperception was later refined and developed by Wundt, who viewed his own psychology as a modern representative of the Leibnizian tradition (McRae 1976; Rieber 1980: 125; for further studies of Leibniz's philosophy, see Frankfurt 1972; Broad 1975; Rescher 1979).

1.4 The Empiricist Tradition

One of the cornerstones of the rationalist tradition of Descartes and Leibniz is that the mind – the soul – contains, as the latter writer puts it: 'originally the principles of various notions and doctrines, which external objects simply recall from time to time.' In other words, the mind is not entirely void, 'like a tablet where nothing has yet been written (*tabula rasa*)', as in the view of Aristotle; but rather contains innate ideas. Neither Descartes nor Leibniz denied the importance of sensory impressions, but they felt that the 'senses, although they are necessary for all our actual knowledge, are not sufficient to give us the whole of it, since the senses never give anything but instances, that is to say particular or individual truths'. Such was the opinion of Leibniz (Parkinson 1973: 150). The empiricist tradition is a reaffirmation of Aristotle's view, and rejects the idea that the mind contains conceptual principles or knowledge prior to and independent of sense experience. Although William of Ockham, Bacon and Hobbes were all important forerunners of British empiricism, it was John Locke's epoch-making study *An Essay Concerning Human Understanding* (1690) that perhaps laid the real foundations of the empiricist doctrine.

John Locke (1632–1704) was born in Somerset, the son of a Puritan who had fought on the side of Parliament during the civil war. Both his parents came from Puritan trading families, of minor gentry, not wealthy landowners. In 1652, supported by a friend of his father, he went to Oxford University, then still dominated by scholastic philosophy. Locke found the academic atmosphere uncongenial, and so he took up medicine, and in 1667 became the personal physician to Lord Ashley, later to become the first Earl of Shaftesbury, an important if not renowned Whig politician. Recognising Locke's talent, Ashley obtained for him a succession of official appointments. Thus Locke led a fairly comfortable life combining medicine with administration. Through Ashley's patronage Locke came to meet many important figures of the day, and became a friend of the chemist Boyle and Sydenham, whose medical researches he assisted. In 1683, after the fall and death of his patron, Locke felt himself threatened and fled to Holland. There he remained until the revolution of 1688. Until then Locke had published hardly anything of note, but while in Holland he had spent his time writing, and in 1690 his two most important philosophical works appeared: his *Essay*, which laid the foundations for classical empiricism and epistemology, and the *Two Treatises of Government*, published anonymously, which outlined the main tenets of philosophical and political liberalism. In the final decade of his life Locke became an immensely distinguished figure, working for the Board of Trade and conversing with Royal Society friends, such as Newton.

Maurice Cranston (1972) has suggested that Locke was something of a 'philistine'. Though versatile in his achievements as an economist, diplomat, physician and political scientist, he was not a great philosopher, even though he was a very important one. His philosophy appealed to practical men – scientists, industrialists, merchants, reformers (1972: 149–59). Bertrand Russell put it cogently when he said that no one had yet devised a philosophy that was both consistent and credible. Most of the great philosophers have been consistent in their ideas, but not credible to the ordinary public. Locke, he suggests, 'aimed at credibility, and achieved it at the expense of consistency' (1946: 637).

In the epistle to the reader that prefaces *An Essay Concerning Human Understanding*, Locke informs us as to the origins and the scope of his study. Apparently one evening in 1670, Locke was discussing with five or six of his friends various problems of morality and religion. Making little progress over the 'doubts which perplexed us', Locke proposed that what they needed to do first was to make an initial inquiry as to their intellectual abilities and to 'see what objects our understandings were, or were not, fitted to deal with' (1690: 56). This was the motivation for his study, to inquire into and critically assess the origins, nature and limits of human reason. His ideas took a long time maturing and he made several preliminary drafts of the *Essay*. He was fifty-seven years old when it was published. As to the scope of this philosophy, he was characteristically modest. Mentioning his admiration for the important scientific work of Newton, Huygenius, Boyle and Sydenham, Locke suggests that 'it is ambition enough to be employed as an under-labourer in clearing ground a little, and removing some of the rubbish that lies in the way to knowledge' (1690: 58).

It may be useful to summarise some of the main themes of Locke's essay.

The Rejection of Innate Ideas

In Book one of the study, Locke makes a sustained attack on the doctrine of innate ideas, the notion that human beings have innate knowledge of some truths, whether moral or speculative. He tries to indicate that the universal acceptance of some truth or principle does not make it innate, and that deductive reason or mathematical demonstrations are also not innately given. Some human beings, he suggests, go through their lives without ever being aware of deductive logic. As humans have widely differing views of moral principles and God, this can hardly suggest that such ideas are innately given. Scholars have often debated as to who is the target of his critique in Book one, but it is probable, as Russell indicates, that Locke is arguing against Plato, Descartes and the scholastics, and their varying conceptions of innate ideas or principles (1946: 633).

In suggesting that humans can acquire all the knowledge that they have simply by the 'use of their natural faculties', Locke vindicated the empirical road to knowledge suggested by Bacon and the experimental scientists, as against the rationalist and supernatural approaches. Thus knowledge was to be discovered by experience. But as many have observed, Locke's arguments in no way invalidate Leibniz's nativism, because, as we noted earlier, for Leibniz innate ideas were activated by sense-experience. In his important critique of Locke's theory – to which Locke never responded – Leibniz conceded that sensory experience is necessary if mind is to develop, but felt that such experience was insufficient for the acquisition of knowledge. Leibniz made the suggestion that the mind is not like a blank slate, but rather like a block of marble with veins already marked within it. Experience, like the sculptor, simply brings out the shape and inclinations of the mind. To the empiricist slogan 'there is nothing in the intellect which was not previously in the senses' (derived from Hobbes) Leibniz responded 'except the mind itself' (Parkinson 1973: 148–71; Cottingham 1984: 75–6).

The Mind as Tabula Rasa

Having denied that knowledge is derived from innate ideas, in Book two Locke presents his own positive theory, which suggests that the mind of the child at birth is like a blank tablet (*tabula rasa*). He himself uses the phrase 'white paper' and writes:

> Let us then suppose the mind to be, as we say, white paper, void of all characters, without any ideas; how comes it to be furnished? Whence has it all the materials of reason and knowledge? To this I answer, in one word, from experience. In that all our knowledge is found, and from that it ultimately derives itself. (1690: 89)

Ideas, Locke goes on to suggest, have two 'sources' or 'fountains'. They are either derived from our senses, which convey to the mind through sensations several distinctive perceptions of things – ideas such as yellow, white, heat, soft, hard, bitter, sweet – or they derive from the mind itself and its operations. The latter are the ideas of reflection, of introspection, such as perception, thinking, believing, willing, reasoning. These two sources, he writes, namely, 'external material things, as the objects of sensation, and the operations of our own minds within as the objects of reflection, are to me the only originals from whence all our ideas take their beginning' (1690: 91).

Crucial to Locke's quasi-mechanical conception of the mind is the distinction he makes between simple and complex ideas. Simple ideas, such as the taste of sugar, or the scent and whiteness of a lily, are rather like atoms, and can neither be created nor destroyed by us (1690: 99). In the reception of simple ideas, therefore, the mind is essentially passive, for the object of the senses 'obtrude their particular ideas upon us whether we will or no' (1690: 98). Complex ideas, on the other hand, are compounded out of simple ideas. But whereas the mind is 'wholly passive' in the reception of all its simple ideas, it is active in the framing of complex ideas. The ideas of relation, substance and abstraction, and the modes of space, number and duration, are all discussed by Locke as examples of complex ideas. Locke, following Galileo and Descartes, also makes a distinction between the primary and secondary qualities of material objects. Primary qualities are those that Locke felt to be 'inseparable' from the body – those of solidity, extension, figure and mobility – while secondary qualities were those produced 'by the operation of insensible particles on our senses' (1690: 112–13). Thus colours, smells, tastes and sounds are not in the objects themselves, but rather the latter have 'powers to produce various sensations in us' (1690: 114).

Locke's account of our knowledge of the physical world via the mediating of sensations and simple ideas has been criticised by many later philosophers, for Locke clearly believed that ideas correspond to things in the world. As Russell puts it: 'we experience the sensations, but not their causes. . . . The belief that sensations have causes, and still more the belief that they resemble their causes, is one which, if maintained, must be maintained on grounds wholly independent of experience' (1946: 636).

Isaiah Berlin (1956) puts the difficulties of Locke's position even more stridently, suggesting that although Locke starts from premises that seem close to those of common sense, he finally arrives at a 'paradoxical dualism' worse than that of Descartes. For his theory of representation traps human knowledge 'within the circle of the human mind' (1956: 107).

One of the main problems with Locke's analysis is that he uses the term *idea* – his crucial concept – in an extremely wide manner, thus leading to ambiguities. It seems to cover not only 'the object of the understanding when a man thinks', but the thinking itself, the perceiving of the object. Thus in one sense Locke views idea as a mental object, an intermediary between the knowing subject or mind and the external world. In this Locke has a representational theory of perception and knowledge. Aaron (1937: 102) suggests that Locke was by no means the originator of this theory, but that it was widely accepted among his contemporaries. (Aaron also indicates that the realist, who wishes to maintain that there are physical objects in the external world independent of the mind knowing them, would also find it difficult to avoid a theory of representation or some sort of perceptual dualism.) Locke, of course, never doubted the existence of the external material world, and his causal theory of perception presupposes it; but Aaron questions whether Locke has a rigid view of representation theory, namely that ideas are 'exact copies' of the originals. He questions too whether Locke can be interpreted as a 'sensationalist' – that we only know the external world in the act of sensation. Locke 'does seem to say that we know directly the existence of things in sensation and that we thus break out beyond ideas. In that case sense-experience is not merely having ideas, seeing colours, hearing sounds and the like. It is also a knowledge of the existence of physical objects' (Aaron 1937: 115).

Critique of the Metaphysics

In the third book of the *Essay* Locke deals with words and language, and his main aim appears to be to criticise the 'uncouth, affected or unintelligible terms' used by the scholastics who still followed Aristotelian doctrines, as well as by some Cartesians. In a sense the book aims to clear away the 'rubbish' he refers to in the epistle to the reader, and his main target is the 'schools' of traditional philosophy. The text is polemical and its focus seems to be a concept of essence, which in Aristotelian philosophy was linked to an *a priori* classificatory system. For Locke the only viable notion of essence in the 'real constitution of anything which is the foundation of all those properties that are combined in, and are constantly found to co-exist with, the nominal essence' (1690: 286). Thus, like Hobbes, Locke takes up an extreme nominalist position. All that exists in reality are particular things, and the general ideas that we use – metal, horse, man – are given names and then applied to particular things. Words for Locke are simply conventional signs which we agree upon for the purposes of intercourse, and most of 'those obscure and unintelligible discourses and disputes' of scholastic philosophy are purely verbal. 'The greatest part of the questions and controversies that perplex mankind', he wrote, 'depend on the doubtful and uncertain use of words' (61). The 'schoolmen' he concluded, speak a lot of 'gibberish' (Aaron 1937: 193–219; Hawton 1956: 55–6).

The Extent of Human Knowledge

In the fourth and final book of the *Essay* Locke explicitly sets forth his ideas on the nature of knowledge. We have, he suggests, three kinds of knowledge of real existence: 'we have the knowledge of our own existence by *intuition*; of the existence of God by *demonstration*; and that of other things by *sensation*' (1690: 378). Although it is evident that with respect to our own existence Locke departs from a strictly empiricist position, the main thrust of his approach is to suggest that there are strict limits to human knowledge. We can never have certain knowledge of general truths about the world.

Locke is rightly regarded as one of the founding inspirations of psychology, and his writings and approach to psychological problems proved to be extremely influential in the subsequent two centuries. Although his classic study is concerned with what we know rather than in the processes of knowing, the book raises many important issues. Three are worth mentioning.

Although Locke is often interpreted as viewing the mind as a purely 'passive' medium, it is clear that for Locke mind has a double meaning. On the one hand, it is the place or locality of ideas, a 'white paper' on which experience inscribes. But on the other hand, mind is the knowing, the experiencing and the willing agent. In the first sense the mind contains ideas; in the second sense it perceives them (Aaron 1937: 106). But following the conventions of his day that mind is a substance, Locke also felt uneasy about the Cartesian dualism of material body and immaterial mind. If thinking was the essence of mind, then there should be no break in thought. This Locke felt was not supported by the evidence, and so although thinking was one of the operations of mind it was not its essence (93–4). Such a rigid dualism also violated Locke's feeling that the human personality was an essential unity of body and mind. But Locke was equally hesitant to adopt a materialist approach and thus like Hobbes to look upon the mind as an abstraction, a way of talking about the 'thinking-body'. For Locke the world could not be explained in terms of either matter alone, or mind alone. No reduction of one to the other was possible: 'it is impossible to conceive that ever bare incogitative matter should produce a thinking intelligent being, as that nothing should of itself produce matter' (1690: 382). Locke also spoke of two powers or 'faculties' of the mind, those of 'perception or thinking, and volition or willing' (1690: 107). He also speaks of two other simple ideas, which are conveyed to the mind by sensation and reflection – the capacity to feel pleasure and pain. But he did not see the two faculties of understanding and volition as standing for 'some real beings in the soul', as being distinct 'agents' in our minds (1690: 165). He cannot, therefore, be held responsible for the later development of 'faculty theory'.

A second important theme in Locke is his discussion of personal identity. Although he makes a distinction between three levels of human identity or existence – as a living body, as a person and as an immaterial substance – it is clear that Locke views the human subject as a psychosomatic unity. But he sees this subject as having two types of identity, as an organism (man) and as a person, both expressed and experienced as a continuity in time. As an organism humans have identity through participation in the same continued life, a 'succession vitally united to the same organized body' (1690: 210). But we also know that we have 'in us something that thinks', and thus the person can be conceived as a 'thinking intelligent being that has reason and reflection, and can consider itself as itself, the same thinking thing, in different times and places, which it does only by that consciousness which is inseparable from thinking'. He continues: 'When we see, hear, smell, taste, feel, meditate, or will anything, we know that we do so. Thus it is always as to our present sensations and perceptions; and by this everyone is to himself that which he calls self' (1690: 211). Personal identity is therefore linked by Locke to consciousness, the 'same consciousness' through time. 'Consciousness alone makes self' (1690: 218), he concludes. Locke, therefore, suggests that there is a consciousness of a permanent self, and that the human person is more than a series of perceptions – a viewpoint that, as we shall see, is radically different from that of Hume.

A final important aspect of Locke's study, which was to have an influence on the development of psychology, was his theory of the association of ideas. This theory is not central to his *Essay*. The chapter on the association of ideas did not appear until the fourth edition of his work, and only takes up a few pages. The theory in fact goes back to Aristotle and, as we have noted, was suggested by Hobbes. But in giving a clear analysis of the origin and organisation of our own ideas, Locke made possible and explicit the possibilities for a theory of association. For he argued that while some of our ideas have a natural correspondence and connection with one another, chance or custom also give rise to the connection of ideas. Ideas, he wrote, 'that in themselves are not at all of kin come to be so united in some men's minds that it is very hard to separate them; they always keep in company' (1690: 251).

We have noted above that Locke had in a sense two theories of perception and knowledge. In the one, the representation theory, ideas are conceived as mental objects, as furniture in the mind, and our knowledge is limited to them. In the other, the 'direct realist' conception of perception, ideas are conceptualised in terms of a kind of mental act, that act of perception in which the mind interacts with the material world. This allows for two interpretations of Locke's theory of ideas, and Leahey (1987) writes that both conceptions were developed in the late nineteenth century by academic psychologists. In the introspection psychology of Titchener (1921), sensations were believed to be irreducible atomic constituents of consciousness – the elementary content of the mind. On the other hand, Brentano (1973) developed the realist implications of Locke's work, in his psychology of act, in which any mental event is construed as a mental act referring to something in the outside world. This account follows that of Thomas Reid, the Scottish 'common sense' philosopher (1987: 98).

Although Locke was not a materialist, and never doubted the truths of theism and Christianity, his theories were conceived by many as dangerous to both religion and morality. His suggestions seemed akin to those of Hobbes, and to deny the immortality of the soul. Certainly, as Will Durant (1952: 256) wrote, since only material things can affect our sense, we know nothing but matter, and must accept a materialistic philosophy. Such are the implications of Locke's theory of knowledge. (For further studies of Locke's empiricism, see Yolton 1956, 1970: Woolhouse 1971.)

The significance of George Berkeley (1684–1753) is that he took one interpretation of Locke's theory of ideas and thus used empiricist doctrine not only to reinstate God's function in the universe – which he felt had been undermined by mechanistic philosophy – but to deny the existence of matter itself. If, as Locke seemed to imply, all our knowledge of the world is simply our sensations of it, and the ideas derived from these sensations, then all we can know are thoughts, feelings and sensations. To introduce consistency and continuity to our experience Berkeley introduced the omniscient perceiver – God. Berkeley thus combined a thoroughgoing empiricism with regard to the material world – sensationalism – with the belief in a spiritual reality.

If Berkeley, the idealist, could, using Locke's empiricism, undermine the reality of the material world, then Hume the sceptic took empiricism to its logical conclusion and undermined the two remaining verities of eighteenth-century thought. For he was not content only to undermine orthodox theism by dissipating the concept of mind (soul), but he also cast doubt on the central concept of mechanistic science – that of causality. He thus took the final step, as Barrett puts it, in the dialectical drama of British empiricism: 'As Berkeley reduced Locke's material substance to a conglomerate of sense perceptions, so Hume seeks to reduce Berkeley's mind to a heap of sense impressions' (1986: 43). In a certain sense, as Russell remarked, Hume took empiricism to a 'dead end' (1946: 685), and we are left with neither mind nor matter, but simply with sense impressions.

David Hume (1711–76), who is widely regarded as the greatest and most influential of British philosophers, was born in Edinburgh, the son of a minor laird. His father died when he was an infant, and his mother, an ardent Calvinist, managed the family estate. After a desultory attempt to study law, and a period of work as a clerk in a merchant firm in Bristol, Hume went through an intellectual crisis. He had an 'insurmountable aversion' to anything but the study of philosophy and in 1734 left for France. He spent three years at Rheims and La Flèche (where Descartes had studied) and, living off his small private income, he wrote the greater part of his important philosophical text, *A Treatise of Human Nature*, and finished it when he was barely twenty-six years old. He returned to London and eventually published the book (1739–40). Never was a literary attempt, he later recalled, more unfortunate, for 'it fell dead born from the press'. This was not altogether true. Undiscouraged, he published two volumes of essays shortly afterwards, *Essays, Moral and Political* (1741–2). Unable to secure a university post, he took a job as a tutor with an eccentric nobleman. The salary was low, but it offered Hume ample leisure to study, and in 1748 he published some further essays and his *An Inquiry concerning Human Understanding*. The latter work is a shortened version of the *Treatise*, from which it differs more in emphasis than in argument. In 1752 he returned to Edinburgh and began publishing his famous *History of England*. It was considered by his contemporaries to be an outstanding work, and although well written and researched, it exposed his Tory inclinations. He did not consider history, Russell chided, worthy of philosophic detachment (1946: 686). In 1764 he visited Paris and enjoyed much social acclaim, becoming friendly with the French Encyclopédistes, Diderot, d'Alembert and d'Holbach. He returned to Edinburgh in 1766 and remained there for the remainder of his life. He died as he had lived, an atheist, loved by many friends. He was, as he described himself in his own 'funeral oration', a man of a mild disposition, of cheerful humour, who practised moderation in all his passions. (For Hume's biography, see Hume 1955: 3–11: Mossner 1954.)

The classic text *A Treatise of Human Nature* is subtitled as *An attempt to introduce experimental reasoning into moral subjects* – moral philosophy being what we today would describe as the human or social sciences. In his introduction to the work, Hume makes it clear that he sees 'the science of man' as the only foundation for the other sciences – logic, mathematics, natural philosophy (science) and natural religion being those mentioned. All these, he suggests, are in some measure dependent on the science of man, for their connection with human nature is close and intimate. Hume set out to explore 'the principles of human nature'; to explore, like Locke, the nature and limits of human knowledge as this was based on experience. He shared also Locke's belief that the experimental methods of reasoning, which had been so successful in Newtonian physics, could be applied to the moral sciences. Because he felt that all science was based on human thought – 'the cognizance of man' – psychology not metaphysics was in essence to be the new foundation for all the sciences. The principles of human nature, Hume affirmed, could provide the only security for a complete system of sciences. Isaiah Berlin (1956: 163–4) suggests that Hume's empirical 'science of man' is the true beginning of modern philosophy, and that his theory of knowledge, conducted mainly in the field of introspective psychology, is indeed hardly distinguishable from his philosophy.

Like Locke, Hume begins his *Inquiry* by examining the contents of the human mind. All its 'perceptions', he suggests, can be divided into two distinct kinds, impressions and ideas, distinguished by their different degrees of force and vivacity. By impressions he means all sensations, passions and emotions as they make their first appearance in the soul (mind). Ideas are the 'faint images' of these impressions in thinking and reasoning as well as the images of memory and imagination. Every simple idea we have, Hume suggests, are derived from impressions, and exactly represent them. Thus impressions are prior to their corresponding ideas, and are of two kinds; those of sensation and those of reflection. An idea he describes as a 'copy' taken by the mind which remains after the impression. Complex ideas are built up out of simple ideas and in turn are divided into three kinds – relations (such as those of time and space), modes and substance. The latter two, he writes, 'are nothing but a collection of simple ideas that are united by the imagination, and have a particular name assigned them' (1955: 16). There is thus no idea of substance, Hume simply accepting Berkeley's view that what we ordinarily call a physical object is no more than a collection and succession of sense impressions. Unlike Locke, Hume often refers to impressions as 'innate', but it is clear, as Ayer suggests (1980: 26), that what is inherent in human nature are certain passions such as sexual love and self-preservation.

As all complex ideas are made up of simple ideas and the latter are simply copies of previously experienced and more vital impressions, it is evident that Hume's empiricism is a descriptive psychology, which is best described as 'atomistic sensationalism' (Berlin 1956: 166).

In connecting or associating simple ideas the faculty of imagination acts as a 'gentle force'. Hume suggests, and it does so through three principles of association – resemblance, contiguity in time and space, and cause and effect. These principles are the only bonds that 'unite our thoughts together, and beset that regular train of reflection or discourse which . . . takes place among all mankind' (1955: 64). He seems to have looked upon himself as the originator of the principle of association of ideas, although, as we noted, both Locke and Hobbes made similar suggestions. Berlin (1956: 173) suggests that Hume may have derived the doctrine from his contemporary, David Hartley. These principles of association – 'the cement of the universe' – in which ideas are connected by a 'kind of attraction' (1956: 12), are clearly consonant with the mechanistic conception of the natural world, and indeed Hume writes that all our reasoning about facts or existence is based on the idea of cause and effect (1955: 87).

Hume makes a clear distinction, following Leibniz, between two kinds of truths or understanding – demonstrative reasoning and moral or probable reasoning:

> All the objects of human reason or inquiry may naturally be divided into two kinds, to wit, 'relations of ideas' and 'matters of fact'. Of the first kind are the sciences of geometry, algebra and arithmetic, and in short, every affirmation which is either intuitively or demonstratively certain . . . matters of fact (on the other hand) are not ascertained in the same manner, nor in our evidence of their truth . . . of a like manner. (1955: 40)

Relations of ideas are thus purely conceptual and give us no information about the world, while matters of fact, he writes, 'seem to be founded on the relation of cause and effect. By means of that relation alone we can go beyond the evidence of our own memory and senses' (1955: 41). Using these two forms of truth as the only criteria of meaning, Hume, like Locke before him, goes on to make a critique of 'divinity and school metaphysics'. He thus concludes his *Inquiry* with those oft-quoted words: 'Let us ask: Does it contain any abstract reasoning concerning quantity or number? No. Does it contain any experimental reasoning concerning matters of fact and existence? No. Commit it then to the flames for it can contain nothing but sophistry and illusion' (1955: 173). This aphorism became a clarion call and a guiding principle for the later logical positivists.

Besides questioning the reality of God, Hume's scepticism was, as earlier noted, directed towards three fundamental conceptions which underpinned science and common sense – the existence of a material world independent of ourselves; the matters of fact, the truths based on causal reasoning; and the existence and continuance of a permanent self. Book one of his *Treatise* is largely taken over to a discussion of these three issues. As to the existence of a material world independent of our perceptions of it, Hume argued that this could not be known or demonstrated. Although Locke had maintained a materialistic perspective throughout his writings, by making a distinction between objectively existing primary qualities and purely subjective secondary ones Locke had paved the way for phenomenalism. Thus Berkeley came to criticise and collapse this distinction, recognising only the reality of perceptions. Hume agrees with Berkeley, arguing that the mind knows nothing but perceptions, and that though we may experience the external world by 'natural instinct', its existence is not confirmed by reason (1955: 163): 'Let us chase our imagination to the heavens, or to the utmost limits of the universe: we never really advance a step beyond ourselves, nor can we conceive of any kind of existence, but the perceptions which have appeared in that narrow compass' (*T*: 67–8).

We cannot, Hume suggests, infer the existence of objects from our perceptions, and he concludes that the cause of our impressions must remain 'inexplicable' to human reason.

He follows this radical separation of the material world from our perceptions of it with his celebrated discussion of causality. Applying his sceptical doubt to causal reasoning, on which 'matters of fact' are based, Hume suggests that our sense impressions do not provide us with any evidence that there is a necessary connection between events in the world, such that we could infer to causal link. Although all our conduct in life, as well as our belief in history and mechanistic science, is founded on causal inference, such an inference, Hume maintains, is invalid. He writes that we can never

> discover anything but one event following another without being able to comprehend any force or power by which the cause operates, or any connection between it and the supposed effect. The same difficulty occurs in contemplating the operations of mind on body . . . all events seem entirely loose and separable. One event follows another, but we never can observe any tie between them. They seem conjoined, but never connected. (Hume 1955: 84–5)

Thus Hume reduced causality to contiguity and suggests that it is derived from that 'great guide of human life' – habit or custom. It is custom, he writes, which leads us to expect, in the future, a similar train of events to those that have appeared in the past. He is equally sceptical of arguments by induction. Hume pursued the question of causality at great length, and his text has given rise to much subsequent debate as to the nature of causality and induction, although it is worth noting, as Ayer remarked, that the popular notion of causality never did imply a logical or necessary connection between events (1980: 59).

The implication of the first two aspects of Hume's scepticism is that for Hume human consciousness is 'essentially bodiless' and that the mind sits precariously, external to the body, receiving from it the discrete data of impressions. 'It is never a mind embedded in its body' (Barrett 1986: 46). But as is well known, Hume goes even further, and beyond Berkeley, in suggesting that we have no grounds for believing in a permanent self, apart from a succession of our inner perceptions. It is perhaps best to outline Hume's conception of the self in his own words. He writes in his abstract of the *Treatise*:

[The author] asserts that the soul, as far as we can conceive it, is nothing but a system or train of different perceptions – those of heat and cold, love and anger, thought and sensations – all united together but without any perfect simplicity or identity. Descartes maintained that thought was the essence of the mind – not this thought or that thought, but thought in general. This seems to be absolutely unintelligible, since everything that exists is particular; and therefore it must be our several particular perceptions that compose the mind. I say compose the mind, not belong to it. The mind is not a substance in which the perceptions inhere. (1955: 194)

In the *Treatise* itself, Hume writes:

The mind is a kind of theatre, where several perceptions successively make their appearance, pass; re-pass; glide away, and mingle in an infinite variety of pastures and situations. There is properly no simplicity in it at one time, nor identity in different . . . The comparison of the theatre must not mislead us. They are the successive perceptions only that constitute the mind. (1739–40: 253)

Hume's scepticism with regard to the self is said to have caused as much scandal among philosophers as his undermining of causation and inductive generalisations (Berlin 1956: 216). And certainly his writings seem to deny any immortality of the soul, which is a fundamental tenet of religious conceptions of the world. Hume himself did not believe in immortality and doubted whether it could be proved either by metaphysical or moral arguments (Copleston 1959: 304).

But it is important to note that Hume made a distinction between two forms of personal identity – in relation to thought and imagination (where identity is conceived as a 'fictitious one' – a succession of perceptions) and 'as it regards our passions or the concern we take in ourselves' (1739–40: 253). For Hume viewed the human subject not only as a rational being, but also as an active and social being. Although the implications of Hume's scepticism is to suggest that only sense-impressions are real, and that nothing exists except 'the solitary individual and then only at the present moment' (Novack 1969: 69), his scepticism only seems to apply in a limited way to rational knowledge. His denial of material existence apart from our sensations of it; his reduction of causality and inductive generalisation to custom: and his denial of an integrated self – all imply merely a limitation of rational knowledge not their invalidity in a practical sense. Causal reasoning based on a belief in an external world and on an integrated self is, he seems to suggest, essential to the subsistence of all human creatures. And rather than viewing the human subject as 'isolated', Hume contends that the 'mutual dependence' of humans is so great in all societies that scarcely any human action is performed without reference to others (1955: 98).

Hume uses the term 'passion' to cover all emotions, feelings and effects, and regards them, along with other sensations, as impressions. He distinguishes between calm passions such as a sense of beauty and violent passions such as love and hatred, grief and joy, pride and humility. He also divides passions into direct and indirect kinds. The former arise from 'a natural impulse or instinct' and include, besides the violent passions noted above, also those that arise from the experience of pleasure or pain – desire, aversion, fear, despair and security are mentioned by Hume (*T*: 276–7). Like many writers of his day, Hume saw a 'struggle' or 'contrast' taking place between reason and the passions, but he differed from most of these philosophers, he writes, in viewing reason as subservient to the passions. Reason, he argues, can never be the motive for any action of the will, and is secondary to the passions in its direction.

And in another oft-quoted passage Hume writes: 'Reason is, and ought only to be the slave of the passions, and can never pretend to any other office than to serve and obey them' (*T*: 415). Passion is an impulse, an 'original existence' and cannot be contradictory to truth or reason. For Hume even morality is a matter of feeling (passion), and he clearly articulated an 'emotive theory' of ethics.

Hume's stress on the 'natural instincts' and on the 'passions' is a corrective to his scepticism, and leads him to suggest that there is great uniformity among the actions of humans, and that 'human nature', in terms of its principles and operations, is the same everywhere. With regard to the passions he writes, 'mankind are so much the same, in all times and places' and their actions and enterprises are largely motivated by ambition, avarice, self-love, vanity, friendship, generosity and public spirit (1955: 93). Thus Hume came to view the passions, rather than reason, as the essential part of 'human nature'; as the critical dimension of the human subject.

Although Hume's philosophical works were little read, his scepticism and his 'psychological atomism' had a profound effect on European philosophy, particularly in arousing Kant from his 'dogmatic slumbers'. (For useful studies of Hume's philosophy, see N. K. Smith 1941; Passmore 1952: Aver 1980.)

1.5 The Kantian Synthesis

The empiricist tradition from Bacon to Hume was, as George Novack and others have written, a powerful stimulus to the progress of European thought. It switched the main function of philosophy away from providing theoretical arguments for religious dogmas and towards serving the practical needs of humankind. 'It challenged medieval ideas, shattered scholasticism, dislodged many props of feudal theology, and undercut established modes of idealism' (Novack 1969: 16). But empiricism was not in itself a worldview or ontology; it was essentially a theory of knowledge – an epistemology that took for granted, and gave support to the mechanistic conception of nature. The empiricists, as well as the rationalists like Descartes, sought both to provide a theory of knowledge that was in line with mechanistic philosophy, and to extend the methods of the natural scientists like Galileo and Newton to the problems of social life and to the understanding of the human subject. In the writings of Locke, mechanistic science, bourgeois political economy and empiricist philosophy form an essential unity and express a similar underlying pattern. With respect to nature a 'one-sided atomism', with respect to social life, a 'metaphysics of individualism' with respect to the human mind a focus on discrete and self-sufficient 'ideas'. All conceptions are consonant with the conditions of mercantile capitalism, which was then beginning to emerge in Western Europe (Novack 1969: 52–7). In an important sense Immanuel Kant (1724–1804) provides a last-ditch defence of mechanistic philosophy, although, as we shall note, mechanistic theory still permeates contemporary thought and, as Lucien Goldman suggests, Kant can be seen not simply as a representative of the German bourgeoisie, but as someone who 'laid the foundations for an entirely new conception of the world' (1971: 224).

An important influence on Kant and the development of German philosophy was Christian Wolff (1679–1754). A follower of Leibniz, Wolff was a thoroughgoing rationalist and held that rational thought was a means of obtaining truth about the world that was vastly superior to that of empirical methods. Although not an original thinker, and accused by Kant of dogmatism, Wolff was a systematic one, and developed the thought of Leibniz into an elaborate metaphysical system. His metaphysics consisted of four divisions; ontology, dealing with being as such; rational theology, which took as its subject matter the existence and attributes of god; cosmology, which treats the cosmic system; and rational psychology, concerning the soul. It is this last division that concerns us here, for in his study *Rational Psychology*, published in 1734, Wolff laid the foundations of what came to be known as faculty psychology. The idea that the mind has a number of separate powers or faculties, such as intellect, memory, will, understanding, was implicit in ancient and scholastic philosophy. And although Reid had divided the mind into separate components, each of which is assigned a specific role in mental life and knowledge, Wolff is considered to be the first real proponent of faculty psychology.

In Wolff's metaphysical philosophy, the soul is a simple substance, whose existence is proved by consciousness – consciousness of the external world as well as self-consciousness. The soul possesses active powers, of which two are fundamental: knowing and desiring. The relationship between the body and mind is, for Wolff, as with Leibniz, one of pre-established harmony. But though Wolff suggested that there are distinct faculties of the mind or soul, and the soul enters into each activity, he none the less saw the soul as having an essential unity, and is never a mere sum of its constituent parts. This became a central tenet of later German philosophy, and was expressed in Kant's theory of apperception. It meant, as Murphy and Kovach write (1972: 37), that faculty psychology and associationism stood at 'opposite poles' in their conceptions of the human mind. Although faculty psychology has often been regarded as an historical curiosity, it has recently been revived in discussions of the modularity of the mind (Fodor 1983; for further discussions of Wolff's philosophy, see Copleston 1960: 126–135).

We turn now to the writings of Immanuel Kant, whom many have seen as the greatest of modern philosophers and as the philosopher who laid the methodological foundations of cognitive psychology. My own feelings tend to accord with those of Bertrand Russell – that Kant, while no doubt an important figure, has been somewhat overrated. This no doubt stems from the fact that, unlike Hume, Locke and Leibniz, Kant was an academic philosopher and by his own admission wrote in a prose that was dry, obscure, long-winded and opposed to all ordinary notions (1783: 9). Academics have an insatiable attraction, it seems, to scholars who write obscurely – witness the profuse secondary literature on Derrida and Lacan – and this is no doubt a factor that draws university scholars to the writings of Kant. In fact, the volume of literature on Kant's philosophy is quite staggering.

The only dramatic quality of Kant's life, Copleston suggests, is the contrast between the greatness of his intellectual influence and his quiet and comparatively uneventful life. Born in Königsberg in East Prussia (now part of the Soviet Union) in 1724, the son of a saddler, Kant spent all his life in or near the town. His family belonged to the Pietists, a Protestant sect somewhat like the Quakers, and Kant retained throughout his life a deep ethical orientation and lack of dogmatism in religious matters. His study *Perpetual Peace* (1795), published in his old age and revealing an unusual vigour and freshness, expresses liberal politics and condemns all war as contrary to reason. Unlike Leibniz, he never travelled widely and as he led a life of methodical regularity and punctuality he has, unlike Nietzsche, never been the subject of psychological analysis. The poet Heinrich Heine wrote that it was hard to write anything about Kant's uneventful life – although he lived through the Seven Years War and the French Revolution – 'inasmuch as he had neither life nor history for he lived a mechanically ordered and abstract bachelor life in a quiet retired street in Königsberg'. Neighbours were reputed to set their clocks by him, so regularly did he take his afternoon walk.

But though perhaps a recluse, this picture of him is something of a caricature. He was of diminutive size (he was scarcely five feet tall), and he did lead a quiet and well-regulated life; but he integrated himself into the local community and Herder has noted his lively personality and youthfulness, even in old age, and described his lectures as 'most entertaining talks', full of wit and humour. After working as a tutor for a number of years, Kant became a lecturer at the University of Königsberg in 1755. He lectured on a variety of topics, and took a great interest in physical geography and science. In 1770 he was appointed professor of logic and metaphysics at the same university. At that time Kant was still steeped in the rationalism of Christian Wolff, and only slowly did he develop his own thoughts. He was in fact something of a late developer. For the next decade Kant did not publish anything. Then in 1781, at the age of fifty-seven, he published his classic work, *Critique of Pure Reason*. Other important works followed in quick succession; a short introduction to the *Critique* – *Prolegomena to any Future Metaphysics* (1785); *Critique of Practical Reason* (1788) and *Critique of Judgement* (1790). This simple, frail, little man, as Will Durant describes him (1952: 264), lived to the age of eighty. (For biographies of Kant, see Copleston 1960: 209–41; Paulsen 1963; Cassirer 1981.)

Kant's *magnum opus*, *Critique of Pure Reason*, which took him more than a decade to write, is written in a formidable style, highly abstract, intrinsically difficult and exceedingly obscure, for it is replete with his own technical terms. As earlier noted, the amount of expository and critical writing on Kant is prodigious, especially on this text, but as Joad remarked (1936: 360), little of this vast corpus has succeeded in reducing Kant's views to a clear and simple statement (cf. Körner 1955; Strawson 1966).

Kant's aims in writing the *Critique* are clearly stated in the Preface to the first edition to the study; it is 'but a critical inquiry into the faculty of reason, with reference to the cognitions to which it strives to attain without the aid of experience; in other words, the solution of the question regarding the possibility or impossibility of metaphysics, and the determination of the origin, as well as of the extent and limits of this science' (1781: 3). Kant's concerns seem to be philosophical, and many have interpreted his study and work as essentially an attempt to mediate between the rival philosophical schools of rationalism and empiricism. He is credited with having proposed a 'Kantian synthesis'. As we have earlier discussed, the rationalists – Descartes, Spinoza and Leibniz – basically saw themselves as scientists whose function it was to clarify and then apply the same methods that had proved so successful in the development of mathematics and mechanistic science to the larger problems of existence. They never doubted that human reason was able to discern, through reason alone, the essential structure of the world. For these scholars 'the human mind thinks "cause-wise" precisely because the mind itself is, in effect, a mirror that reflects without distortion the indwelling structure of the external world. Reason knows such principles to be true "self-evidently" because it "sees" through an act of intellectual intuition, that they are neccessarily true of the nature of things' (Aiken 1956: 31). The empiricists denied that this was so, arguing that all human knowledge is based on sense-impressions and experience. Kant was interested in this philosophical debate and in a sense provided a solution to the issue. As he wrote in the introduction to the *Critique*:

> though all our knowledge begins with experience, it by no means follows that all arises out of experience. For on the contrary, it is quite possible that our empirical knowledge is a compound of that which we receive through impressions and that which the faculty of cognition supplies from itself . . . knowledge of this kind is called a priori, in contradiction to empirical knowledge, which has its sources a posteriori, that is, in experience. (1781: 25)

A large part of the *Critique* is devoted to exploring the nature of this kind of knowledge – *a priori* synthetic judgements as he calls them. But Kant is concerned not simply with a philosophical debate as to the nature of knowledge and its sources, but with much more fundamental issues, with the intellectual problems that deeply troubled him. These were threefold.

First, there was the question as to the validity of mechanistic science. No philosopher, as G. Warnock (1964) rightly argues, has accepted more wholeheartedly than Kant the essential truth and importance of the scientific world-view, as this had been propounded by mechanistic philosophers such as Galileo and Newton. Kant himself had a deep interest in natural science, and his early publications had been in geophysics and astronomy. The problem was that Hume's critique of the concept of causality had completely undermined the central concept of mechanistic science. This is why his reading of Hume had affected him so profoundly and interrupted what Kant called 'my dogmatic slumber', for until then Kant had happily accepted the validity and premises of both mechanistic science (Newton) and rationalist philosophy (as expounded by Wolff). Kant had to find some philosophical justification for the principle of causality, as a necessary principle, to make science possible.

Secondly, Kant was troubled that Hume's scepticism and attack on metaphysics made philosophical reasoning unnecessary and redundant. As we have seen, Hume made a distinction between two forms of knowledge, the contingent findings of empirical science, and the formal exercises in calculation as characterised in mathematics or logic. All else, as far as Hume was concerned, was 'sophistry and illusion'. If one accepted this dichotomy, as Kant appeared to do, then there was a problem. What role was there for philosophy or human reason? Was metaphysics possible? Kant asked.

Thirdly, if one accepted the findings of mechanistic science, as Kant did, this implied that the human subject was causally determined. But for Kant this also implied a fundamental incompatibility between accepting a universal causal determinism and the supposition that humans are free and responsible moral agents. Given a mechanistic universe, where did our beliefs in God, immortality, human freedom and morality fit in? This was another intellectual problem to be solved, far wider in its scope than the philosophical debate between the two schools of philosophy. The conflict that Kant wished to resolve was between 'on the one side, not Hume, but Newton, and on the other side, not Leibniz but the essentials of morality and religion. This was not a domestic quarrel within the field of philosophy. It was an issue involving the deepest interests of every man' (G. Warnock 1964: 297).

In the introduction to the *Critique*, Kant outlines his classification of judgements which form the basis of his critical or transcendental philosophy. He makes two distinctions. The first is between *a priori* and *a posteriori* judgements. An *a priori* judgement is one that can be known without reference to experience, while *a posteriori* judgements can only be known by reference to empirical facts. It is the distinction between necessary and contingent truths. But Kant also makes a distinction between analytic and synthetic judgements. The first related to judgements where the predicate is contained in the subject (such as a bachelor is unmarried), while synthetic judgements give us substantive information about the world. All propositions that we know through experience are synthetic and all analytic judgements are *a priori*. But Kant contends and argues that there is a third class of judgements, *a priori* synthetic judgements, and the main problem for pure reason is to determine how such judgements are possible. The solution to this problem also entails an answer to another question: how is mathematics and mechanistic science possible? The answer to these two questions constitutes the main themes of the first part of *Critique of Pure Reason*.

Like Hegel, Kant's thought often expresses itself in the form of triads. And the *Critique* essentially has a triadic pattern, dealing respectively with three human faculties – sensibility, understanding and reason. The three sections of the book – transcendental aesthetic, transcendental analytic and transcendental dialectic – deal with each of these faculties, and correspond to his discussion, respectively, of mathematics, natural science and metaphysics, the latter section dealing with the limits of reason and its practical application. We may discuss each of these sections in turn.

Transcendental Aesthetic

The process by which the raw material of sensations are transformed into products of thought consists, Kant suggests, of two stages. Using the term aesthetic in the original sense as connoting sensation or feeling, the first stage is the co-ordination of sensations by applying to them the forms of perception – time and space – which Kant calls forms of intuition. In the second stage perceptions are co-ordinated by applying to them the forms of understanding – the 'categories' of thought – fully dealt with under the section on transcendental analytic:

> By means of sensibility objects are given to us, and it alone furnishes us with intuitions; by the understanding they are thought, and from it arise conceptions. But all thought must directly or indirectly relate ultimately to intuitions; consequently to sensibility, because in no other way can an object be given to us. (1781: 41)

The undetermined object of an empirical intuition Kant calls phenomenon, and that which affects the phenomenon he calls its forms. Thus time and space for Kant are not simply given features of the world, they are only 'mere forms of sensibility', which must precede all empirical intuitions, that is, our perception of actual objects. As he puts it, time and space are not qualities 'of things in themselves, but a form of our sensuous faculty of representation' (1783: 31–5). Both mathematics and geometry, Kant contends, are based on these forms of intuitions, as is our ordinary experience of the world, and thus are *a priori* synthetic judgements. Kant therefore disputes Hume's suggestion that mathematics and geometry are analytical truths. Kant denied that his approach is a form of idealism. It never came into my head, he says, to doubt the reality of the material world. But he does suggest that while the objects of our senses, existing outside us, are given: 'we know nothing of what they may be in themselves, knowing only their appearances' (1783: 36).

Transcendental Analytic

Kant divides transcendental logic into two divisions, analytic and dialectic, which correspond to his distinction between understanding and reason. Spatial and temporal concepts, as forms of intuition, are those modes of cognition that are 'applied', as it were, during the act of perception to the material world. They are *a priori* synthetic judgements which are associated with our 'sensibility'. In the section in the *Critique* on transcendental analytic logic Kant explores those *a priori* synthetic judgements that are concerned not with sensibility but with understanding. Developing Aristotle's notion of categories, and sensing that some kind of order is a fundamental condition for the 'possibility of experience', Kant proposed that there are forms or categories of understanding that are both *a priori* and synthetic. Making a distinction between judgements of perception and judgements of experience, Kant suggests that while the latter are empirical (in the sense that they are grounded in immediate sense perception) they involve more than sensuous intuition for concepts of understanding have been 'super-added' (1783: 245). Thus these *a priori* synthetic concepts have a transcendental aspect. Kant therefore is not suggesting that the mind itself is the only reality, as implied in the 'mystical and visionary idealism' of Berkeley; nor is he suggesting that the mind creates its world from sense impressions as the empiricists suggested; nor again, as noted, does he doubt that there is a material world existing independently and outside the mind. But rather, Kant holds that the 'concepts of understanding' inherent in the mind, acting upon sense data, form our experience of the world – as it appears to us: 'all intuition possible to us is sensuous; consequently our thoughts of an object by means of a pure conception of the understanding, can become cognition for us only in so far as this conception is applied to the objects of the sense' (1781: 102).

Sensory impressions are therefore necessary to give the content of experience. As he expressed in a now famous quote: 'thoughts without content are empty; intuitions without concepts are blind.' The world then, for Kant, has order, not of itself (for that is not known), but because the mind itself is an ordering mechanism:

'The understanding does not derive its laws from, but prescribes them to, nature' (1783: 67).

Kant outlined the categories of understanding in schematic form as follows:

Quantity	unity, plurality, totality
Quality	reality, negation, limitation
Relation	substance, causality, reciprocity
Modality	possibility, existence, necessity
(1781: 79)	

The business of the senses, Kant writes, is to intuit; that of the understanding is to think, and thinking is the uniting of representations in one consciousness. The term apperception is given to this act of synthetic unity; it is a virtual synonym of consciousness. All empirical knowledge then, for Kant, implies categories or forms of understanding that are *a priori* and synthetic. And they form the fundamental principles not only of the physical sciences but of human experience itself. 'The claims of the scientific outlook have never been pitched higher than this. No one has ever nailed his colours so firmly to Newton's mast' (G. Warnock 1964: 304). Thus as the forms of intuition, time and space, are linked by Kant to both perception and to mathematics and geometry, so the categories of understanding – causality, substance – are linked both to ordinary empirical knowledge and to the foundations of mechanistic science. And both the forms of intuition and the principles of understanding involve *a priori* synthetic judgements.

Transcendental Dialectic

The outcome of Kant's *Critique of Pure Reason* is essentially a negative one. For he argues that the forms of intuition and the categories of understanding have no proper application beyond what is given in sense experience. For the possibility of *a priori* synthetic principles such as causality or the notion of substance, we must, Kant felt, pay the price of restricting their application to the world of experience. Any attempt to apply these concepts of understanding beyond experience leads to inconsistencies and errors. Thus the speculative use of reason in metaphysics leads to arguments that are either contradictory or meaningless. In this sense he comes close to Hume's conclusions about metaphysics. Arguments relating to the existence of God or the nature of the cosmos or the immortality of the soul inevitably lead to 'anti-nomies'. In a famous section (1793: 342–73), Kant presents arguments that demolish all the classic intellectual proofs of the existence of God – he smashed them to pieces, Hawton suggests (1956: 92), and outside the Catholic Church no reputable philosopher has dared to revive them. With regard to the soul as a substance that was immaterial and immortal – the position of rational psychology – Kant argues that these beliefs have no empirical or rational foundation. The immortality of the soul cannot be proved, as clearly there is no thought without a subject and no substantial evidence within experience, to support this belief:

> If from the concept of the soul as a substance we would infer its permanence, this can hold good as regards possible experience only, not of the soul as a thing in itself and beyond all possible experience. Life is the subjective condition of all our possible experience; consequently we can only infer the permanence of the soul in life. (1783: 83)

Kant, furthermore, argues that our empirical knowledge of the world and ourselves pertains to the level of 'phenomena', which are the objects of experience, not to 'things-in-themselves' (noumena), which Kant regards as unknowable.

But the empirical use to which pure reason limits understanding and knowledge does not 'satisfy the proper calling of reason' (1783: 76). For Kant felt that reason not only had a practical use, but was intrinsically always trying, as it were, to go beyond the limits of experience. Kant seems to use the term 'dialectic' not only as a critique of the pretensions of metaphysics, but also as that dimension of reason that strives to go beyond understanding. He seems, as Warnock (1964: 305) suggests, to sense that human beings have a persistent desire to construct a picture of the world, and their own place in it, that would be rationally satisfying. Yet our actual knowledge of the world must always be incomplete, and our explanations never more than conditional; there always seems to be a disjunctive between what is known and what could rationally satisfy our demands. The ambitious attempts of reason to penetrate beyond the limits of experience often end, Kant writes, in disappointment, and lead us to the errors of speculative metaphysics which pure reason has to check, but nevertheless the human mind has an 'extinguishable desire' to 'find a firm footing in some region beyond the limits of the world of experience' (1781: 452). For Kant this was the realm of practical reason. Thus Kant came to construct a dualistic metaphysic in which the three 'ideas of reason' – the existence of God, moral freedom and the immortality of the soul – have a crucial role. Although reason itself cannot prove their reality, these ideas have a practical use, that is, a moral function. The right use of reason beyond the limits of experience should be, Kant felt, directed towards moral ends. I must, Kant wrote, abolish knowledge, to make room for belief – in God, freedom and immortality (1781: 18).

Kant's moral theory is based on rationalist premises and is almost completely opposite to that of Hume. Kant argued for a universal moral ethic based on *a priori* principles, and two of the 'categorial imperatives' he postulated are well known – to treat humans, including oneself, as an end in themselves, and to act on the maxim that whatever you do would have universal validity.

Kant's conception of the human subject is complex and difficult to extract from his dualistic metaphysic. Employing the concepts of faculty psychology Kant divides human psychological faculties into three main categories: the senses, the understanding and the will. The first two are dealt with in the first two sections of the *Critique*. Neither of them give us direct knowledge of the material world, but together they give us knowledge of the world of phenomena. Importantly, for Kant, the mind is neither the passive container of ideas derived from sense impressions, as the empiricists suggest, nor is it endowed with innate ideas which give us knowledge of reality without reference to experience. For Kant, the mind is active, and its forms of intuition and the categories of understanding, inherent in the mind itself, 'create' the phenomenal world as we experience it. They do not fashion it out of nothing, but nevertheless our knowledge of the world is limited to experience. But when we come to the will, which Kant sees as intrinsically free and rational, we have a kind of knowledge that is neither sensuous not intellectual. Kant seems to suggest that the will, as a moral agent, is a kind of free activity that is independent of the law of cause and effect, which dominates the world of phenomena. When the human subject is considered from the point of view of the empirical sciences, he or she is subject to the law of cause and effect. They are, therefore, completely determined. Even the will expressed in the phenomenal sphere is necessarily obedient to the law of nature. Man, he wrote, 'as one of the phenomena of the sensuous world' is subject to natural causes, 'the causality of which must be regulated by empirical laws. As such, he must possess an empirical character, like all other natural phenomena' (1781: 323). Man is a phenomenon he writes; but he then goes on to suggest that reason itself is is not a phenomenon, and therefore not subject to sensuous conditions (1781: 326) – the term noumenon applying to such things. Thus Kant came to make a distinction between the phenomenal or 'empirical self', which is passive and subject to natural laws, and the transcendental or 'noumenal' self, which is the subject of moral agency and the rational will. By postulating this distinction, Kant appears to think that he has resolved the dilemma between the advocacy of causal necessity underlying the premises of mechanistic science and the notion of human moral freedom, which is at the basis of religion and morality. But the problems of this distinction are twofold. One is that the noumenal realm, the world of the 'thing-in-itself', is, Kant argues, unknowable. So human freedom and morality can hardly belong to this realm. The other is the difficulty of fitting his philosophy of mind into this dichotomy. The intrinsic properties of mind, expressed in the forms of intuition and the concepts of understanding – the 'thinking self', as Kitcher (1984) describes it – does not seem to fit happily into the phenomenal – noumenal distinction. And by suggesting that the self, as a rational, moral agent, is not phenomenal (otherwise it would be subject to natural causality), Kant gets himself caught up in intractable contradictions. What he ought to have done to avoid these dilemmas, Kitcher (1984: 138) suggests, is to assent that the real self – the thinker – is a real, albeit phenomenal, self. There are also contradictions in Kant's general theory, as both Joad (1936: 395) and Russell (1946: 735) long ago pointed out. Kant presents us with three entities; the knowing mind, the phenomenal world and the noumenal 'things-in-themselves', which are the cause of our sensations. If the mind only knows phenomena, how can we know that the noumenal world exists and is the cause of phenomena?

Many writers have expressed dissatisfaction with Kant's attempt to resolve the antimony between free will and moral freedom on the one hand and universal causal determinism on the other, as implied by mechanistic science. His bifurcation of reality into phenomenal and noumenal realms, and the corresponding distinction between 'two selves' – the empirical and real (moral) self – in essence simply replicates the antimony rather than resolving it. Moral experience is intrinsically related to other forms of experience, and as Hegel was to stress, his concept of human freedom is essentially abstract. Although he looked upon himself as a kind of Copernicus who had created a new science, he did nothing of the sort, for he remained essentially a religious thinker, and the concepts of God, the soul and immortality were retained in the sphere of practical reason. The dichotomies of freedom and necessity, consciousness and mechanism, subject and object, and morality and science became entrenched in Kantian thought rather than resolved. (For further discussions of Kant, with particular reference to his moral theory, see H. E. Jones 1971; Ameriks 1982; Wood 1984.)

Kant's influence on philosophy has been enormous; his influence on the psychological sciences has also been important, although some writers have questioned whether he departed in any essential way from Hume and Reid. (Leahey 1987: 118). My own feeling is that he did. In general terms Kant gave impetus to three trends in psychology; one was to present, in essence, a critique of associationist psychology, and to suggest that the act of perception involves an act of unity or synthesis that is intrinsic to the mind, not simply of habit. Secondly, he gave impetus to faculty psychology, and later writers utilised and explored the three great subdivisions of mental activity he postulated – feeling, knowing and willing. But many have felt that the rigid separation of willing from the other two faculties to be limiting and retrogressive. Finally, Kant stressed that knowledge of the external world involves the creative 'contribution' of the mind itself and thus that there is no perfect one-to-one relationship between objects in the external world and our sensations of those objects in the inner world of consciousness (Fancher 1979: 89–90).

Locke, Descartes and Kant all conceive of the mind as simply a 'mirror of nature' (Rorty 1980). But it's a strange mirror that determines the world as it appears to us, and is unable to reflect the world as it really is – as noumena; for this was Kant's conception of the mind (cf. Barrett 1986: 72).

But in his critique of rational psychology, and in stressing that the self or soul cannot be known as a thinking subject – for in its transcendental aspect it has only a noumenal status – Kant would appear to deny the possibility of a science of consciousness. In terms of the empirical subject, however, Kant advocated the study (*logos*) of humans (*anthropos*) – anthropology. In a series of lectures published as *Anthropology from a Pragmatic Point of View* (1798), Kant discussed the relationship of body and mind, and knowledge of our minds that can be gained through introspection. In this respect he had an important influence on Wundt, though Kant's emphasis on introspection and his radical dualism have been seen as negative influences on contemporary psychology (Wolman 1968; Leahey 1987: 119–21).

Holding with such tenacity to both the mechanistic conception of nature and the essential belief in human freedom and moral agency, Kant got himself into difficulties – resolved only by a radical dualism between empirical science and moral freedom. But Kant's work had a radical impact in two senses. First, he was aware that certain kinds of natural phenomena – biological organisms – did not fit the mechanistic paradigm, and in a famous passage in his *Anthropology* he even suggests the possible animal origin of the human species (Durant 1952: 263; G. Warnock 1964: 316). Secondly, as Lucien Goldman has argued (1971), Kant was the originator, or at least the initiator, of a new world-view, which was distinct both from the individualist and atomistic doctrines of the Enlightenment thinkers (including both rationalists and empiricists – Descartes, Leibniz, Locke, Hume) and the collectivist doctrines of the mystical philosophies of feeling and intuition expressed by writers like Schelling and Bergson. In the first philosophical attitude confirmed by both the positivists and the neo-Kantians, the concepts of 'atom', 'monad' and 'sensation' have primacy; while in the second, the categories of 'feeling', 'intuition', 'life-principle' are central ideas. The first approach sees the human subject as autonomous or isolated from the collectivity or cosmos, the second tends to renounce all autonomy and 'lose' the human subject in God, the state or nation. In the latter attitude the part exists only as a necessary means to the existence of the whole. The world-view, which Goldman feels Kant initiated, suggested a reciprocal relation between the autonomy of the human person and the reality of the whole – the human community and the cosmos. The stress is on totality, not as something given and existent, but as a goal to be obtained through human activity. This approach, Goldman argues, is implicit in Kant's writings on the dialectic, and is developed in the works of Hegel, Marx and Lukács.

Kant does not represent a Copernican revolution in philosophy, but he does, as Barrett (1986: 54) suggests, constitute a 'turning point'. Adopting his schema we can suggest the following 'gathering and dispersion' in intellectual trends. Such trends will be explored in subsequent chapters.

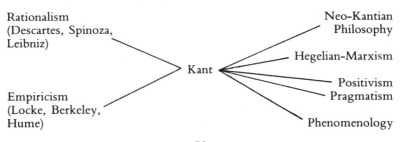

Rationalism
(Descartes, Spinoza,
Leibniz)

Empiricism
(Locke, Berkeley,
Hume)

Kant

Neo-Kantian
Philosophy

Hegelian-Marxism

Positivism
Pragmatism

Phenomenology

The Psychology of the Will

Kant was a revolutionary thinker with a comprehensive vision, and with regard to his influence, Durant (1952: 291) has suggested that the entire philosophical thought of the nineteenth century revolved around his speculations. This may be something of an exaggeration, but certainly the German idealist philosophers saw themselves as the spiritual heirs of Kant. Kant, as we have noted, was a dualist thinker like Descartes, but whereas Descartes made a distinction between consciousness and mechanism, Kant drew a distinction between the world of appearances and the 'things-in-themselves'. That is to say, we have the phenomenal world, the world of mechanistic science and causal laws on the one hand, and, on the other, the super-sensuous world of God and moral agency. As Copleston wrote, Kant left us with 'a bifurcated reality'. The noumenal world could not be known or reached by theoretical reason. But Kant argued that this world, 'the thing-in-itself', could be reached by practical reason, as this was expressed by the moral will of a rational free agent. Thus Kant follows Rousseau in stressing the primacy of the will over theoretical reason.

Kant's critique of reason and his exaltation of feeling and will undoubtedly prepared the way for the voluntarism of Schopenhauer and Nietzsche, whose philosophies are the subject of the present chapter. But, as I stress, these later writers interpreted the 'will' in ways that are quite different from those of Kant, for whom the will was rational and expressed in universal moral imperatives. But there is a real sense in which Kant's practical reason was developed by Schopenhauer and Nietzsche, and turned from a moral into a biological category. The first two sections of this chapter deal respectively with the theories of the subject that emerge from the writings of Schopenhauer and Nietzsche. In the following two sections I outline the life-work and the psycho-analytical theory of Freud, whose basic philosophy stands firmly in the tradition of these two earlier scholars.

2.1 Schopenhauer

Schopenhauer's philosophy also begins with Kant; indeed, Schopenhauer thought that he alone had truly understood Kant, and that Kant's other successors like Hegel were imposters or charlatans. But he emphasised aspects of the *Critique* quite differently from those stressed by Hegel and Fichte. They essentially eliminated the 'thing–in–itself' and made metaphysical idealism possible; Schopenhauer retained the 'thing–in–itself', but identified it with the will, as a vital force, a blind and unconscious striving, which is inherent in the world. Yet whereas Fichte, like Kant, had seen the will as rational and moral, Schopenhauer views it as non-rational and a moral. Indeed, he personifies it to the extent that it is almost seen as an evil force within the universe. He contrasts even more with Hegel. Hegel remained true to the rationalist spirit in Kant, and sought to advance the scope of critical reason. He thus came to see the ultimate reality as a rational process, the self-thinking thought actualising itself as concrete spirit. The real and the rational are thus equated. By contrast, Schopenhauer sees reality as irrational, the world being a manifestation of a blind impulse or energy – the will (Copleston 1963: 287).

Arthur Schopenhauer (1788–1860) was born in Danzig (Gdansk), the son of a wealthy merchant of Dutch descent. His father was a man noted for his ability and culture, and he sent Schopenhauer to England and France to prepare him for a business career. In 1805 his father was found lying dead in a canal, apparently having committed suicide. Having no relish at all for business, his mother allowed Schopenhauer to continue his studies. In 1809 he entered Göttingen University to study medicine and science, but in his second year changed to philosophy. His tutor advised him to confine his reading to Plato and Kant, and this is what he essentially did. After his father's death his relations with his mother deteriorated. She was a talented woman, a popular novelist in her day, and after her husband's death had moved to Weimar. She had an easy-going temperament and ran a salon at which Goethe and other notables appeared from time to time. In 1814 Schopenhauer quarrelled violently with her. He left Weimar with much bitterness, and though she lived for another twenty-four years they never saw each other again. The extreme misogyny that Schopenhauer expressed throughout his life is no doubt related to this episode. From 1814 to 1818 Schopenhauer lived in Dresden and there he wrote his *magnum opus*, *The World as Will and Idea*. It was published in 1819 but was a flop; nobody bought it and nobody read it, although Schopenhauer had the consolation that some philosophers like Herbart took notice of it. Some sixteen years after its publication Schopenhauer was informed that the greater part of the edition had been sold as wastepaper. Schopenhauer was only twenty-eight when the book was published. In 1844 he issued an expanded second edition, but his philosophical views remained essentially unchanged. Hollingdale (1970) has remarked that Schopenhauer had an 'immovable mind'. In 1820 Schopenhauer went to Berlin, and though having no university appointment, started lecturing there. He deliberately chose to lecture at the same hour as Hegel – then at the height of his fame. Needless to say, nobody attended Schopenhauer's lectures. He gave up lecturing and never ceased to pour scorn on academic philosophers. He described Hegel as a 'stupid and clumsy charlatan' and Fichte as an opportunist who had caricatured Kant, and thereby wrapped the German people in a 'philosophic fog'. After some wandering Schopenhauer finally settled in Frankfurt in 1833, living modestly on a small income derived from an interest in his father's firm. For the last twenty-seven years of his life he lived alone in a boarding house, his only companion a dog, and like Kant followed an identical routine. As Durant put it: 'He had no mother, no wife, no child, no family, no country' (1952: 304) – and few friends either it seems. In his study he had a bust of Kant and a bronze Buddha, for he always had a deep interest in oriental religions, particularly the Upanishads. But in his personal life Schopenhauer was no ascetic; he dined well and had numerous, but always casual love affairs. By all accounts Schopenhauer was not an amiable or admirable character. He was selfish, quarrelsome, vain, unusually avaricious, anti-democratic, paranoid and hostile towards women. But he was free of the nationalism that characterised his contemporaries, had a secular outlook, a deep and genuine love of philosophical truth, and like Nietzsche, in his best moments gives us profound insights into the human condition. He understood more vividly than anyone, Hollingdale writes, 'the suffering involved in life, and the need felt by all created things for love and sympathy' (1970: 34).

After the publication of his essays *Parerga and Paralipomena* in 1851, Schopenhauer came by degrees to receive the acclaim and the fame he had always yearned for. And in the last decade of his life he became famous and something of a cult figure. He died alone in 1860 aged seventy-two. (For accounts of Schopenhauer's life and work, see Copleston 1946; Durant 1952; 300–50; Hollingdale 1965.)

Schopenhauer's basic premises are derived from Kant's epistemology, and he begins the study *The World as Will and Idea* with the famous words 'The world is my idea'. Following Kant's distinction between the phenomenal world, the world as it is experienced and rationally understood, and the noumenal world, or the world as it is 'in itself', Schopenhauer argues that the world is rationally known only in so far is it is capable of being sensed and rationally interpreted. According to Schopenhauer, then, our ideas provide no access to a world beyond our sense impressions. And simplifying Kant, he looks upon the universal forms of all objects, space, time and causality as lying *a priori* in our consciousness. Making a distinction between ideas of perception and abstract ideas or concepts, which are the unique possession of humans, Schopenhauer goes on to suggest that 'the whole world of objects is and remains idea, and therefore wholly and for ever determined by the subject; that is to say, it has transcendental ideality' (Edman 1928: 17). Although linking Kant's phenomenal realm with the Hindu concept of Mâya, Schopenhauer denied that this realm is an illusion or mere appearance; it is the world or representation of ideas that is known to us – the only world that we know. Although Schopenhauer's philosophy has been described as 'voluntaristic idealism', he himself argues that he is advocating neither materialism nor idealism. The old antithesis between mind and matter, he writes, is fundamentally false. All systems of materialism that start with the object and derive the mind from material substance – he mentions Democritus, Bruno, Spinoza and the French mechanistic materialists – are, Schopenhauer contends, 'absurd', for 'the world is entirely idea, and as such demands the knowing subject as the supporter of its existence' (1819: 27). But he is equally critical of the metaphysical idealists like Fichte who begin with the subject and try to derive the object from it. This is just the converse of materialism, and indicates that Fichte, for all his eloquent polemics, had not understood Kant, for 'no subject is thinkable without an object'. Both materialism and idealism, Schopenhauer suggests, are misconceptions: 'We start neither from the object nor from the subject, but from the idea, as the first fact of consciousness' (1819: 31). Thus for Schopenhauer the 'world as idea' or representation (*Vorstellung*) comprises both the subject and the material world.

In his discussion of concepts, Schopenhauer makes a distinction between concrete and abstract ideas, and suggests that knowledge, remaining always subordinate to the service of the will, has as its primary function a practical value, as an instrument of physical needs.

Like Kant, Schopenhauer has a dualistic concept of the human subject. A person has a phenomenal aspect, a body and mind that is known within a spatial, temporal and causal context. But the human subject can also have a noumenal aspect; for Schopenhauer this is will, which he equates with the Kantian 'thing-in-itself', and with the Platonic realm of ideas: 'The will, as the thing-in-itself, is the common stuff of all beings; consequently we possess it in common with each and every man, indeed with the animals, and even further on down' (1970: 1).

With regard to the human body he writes that it:

> is given in two entirely different ways to the subject of knowledge, who becomes an individual only through his identity with it. It is given as an idea in intelligent perception. And it is also given in quite a different way as that which is immediately known to every one, and is signified by the word will. . . . The action of the body is nothing but the act of the will objectified . . . I shall call the body the objectivity of will. (Edman 1928: 64)

Every emotion, therefore, Schopenhauer comes to see as 'agitations' of the will – hatred, joy, fear, anger. The idea is to phenomenal existence as the will is to the noumenal realm, and the latter provides Schopenhauer with the key, or fundamental category, to make sense of the nature of the world. For he sees the will as manifested in a wide range of empirical phenomena; the force that germinates and vegetates plant life, the force through which crystals are formed, the instinctive activities of spiders, birds, ants and other forms of animal life, the gravitational forces in nature, as well as human emotions and volition. Schopenhauer describes the will as being without knowledge, as 'the essence of the world', as a 'blind incessant impulse' or force of nature that appears in all unorganised vegetable nature, including our own, as the 'vital force' within the world. His dualism comes through strongly when he suggests that the world in which we live and have our being is in its whole nature through and through both will and idea. But importantly, will has primacy; for it is seen as the 'motive power' of the intellect. This aphorism will perhaps convey the relationship between the will and knowledge as Schopenhauer conceives it:

> Life is known to be a process of combustion; intellect is the light produced by this process. . . .
> The intellect is fundamentally a hard-working factory-hand whom his demanding master, the will, keeps busy from morn till night. (1970: 121, 127).

A number of interesting points emerge from Schopenhauer's discussion of will as the vital force within the world.

First, it is clear that Schopenhauer sees the will as fundamentally expressing itself in 'the affirmation of the will to live' and in the sexual impulse. He speaks of the genitals as being entirely subject to the will, and the 'kernel' of the will to live to be in sexual passions and procreation. In the final section of his study, appropriately called 'The Metaphysics of the Love of the Sexes', he suggests that the prime function of the sexual instincts and passions is focused essentially on the procreation of the species. Our true nature, he writes, 'lies more in the species, than in the individual' (Edman 1928: 374). Although his writings on women are marred by his extreme misogyny, it is of interest, given the primacy that he gives to the organism and the will, that he sees the male sex as being associated with will, and the female with intellect (1970: 73).

Secondly, as Schopenhauer's concept of the will clearly foreshadows Freud's concept of the id, even with respect to its sexual connotations, so it also anticipates Freud's theory of the unconscious. Schopenhauer continually writes of the will as an 'unconscious' striving or impulse, as well as writing that 'half our thinking takes place unconsciously' (1970: 123).

Thirdly, Schopenhauer also anticipates some of the central ideas of the French philosopher Henri Bergson, both with respect to the practical function of intelligence and with respect to the important role that intuition and the concept of *élan vital* (life force) plays in Bergson's philosophy (Copleston 1963: 271).

Finally, there is the important issue as to the evident contradiction in Schopenhauer's argument. His study is full of vivid illustrations outlining the empirical manifestations of the 'will to live' or the 'vital force' (will), yet he argues, like Kant, that the thing-in-itself (will) is unknowable.

If the essence of the world is will, and will is portrayed as a blind urge, as a universal striving without aim or purpose, it is hardly surprising that Schopenhauer comes to describe the world and the human condition in highly pessimistic terms. As in Vedanta and Buddhist texts, Schopenhauer thought that human life was intrinsically meaningless and full of suffering and affliction. Happiness is always transitory, and the gratification of our desires can never give us lasting satisfaction. 'So long as we are the subject of willing, we can never have lasting happiness or peace.' Life itself, Schopenhauer describes as a sea full of rocks and whirlpools, which even if a person succeeds in negotiating with effort and skill, only leads him or her 'nearer at every step to the greatest, the total, inevitable, and irremediable shipwreck, death' (Edman 1928: 253). The majority of humans, he felt, were egoistic, unjust, inconsiderate, deceitful and sometimes even malicious. His views on human nature and the neccessity of the state followed those of Hobbes. Humans compare with tigers and hyenas in their cruelty, he wrote, and go one worse, they often deliberately inflict pain on others. In his *Essays* he drew attention to the injustices of industrial exploitation, to wars and slavery, to cruelties inflicted on animals and humans alike, and concluded that not only was existence wretched, but 'that human life must be some kind of mistake' (1970: 53). But though like the Buddha Schopenhauer stressed the 'suffering of the world', he also felt that the chief source of human ills were those inflicted by humans themselves. Schopenhauer's pessimism is thus metaphysical and social – though he showed little sympathy for the 1848 revolutions.

It is hardly surprising that Schopenhauer poured scorn on those rationalist thinkers like Leibniz and Hegel, who, while acknowledging the suffering in the world, tended to situate it in the context of a wider rationality.

Schopenhauer discussed two avenues of escape or salvation from the suffering engendered by the will, and the inescapable conditions of human existence. One was by 'aesthetic contemplation', through art and music and delight in perceptive knowledge – 'an oasis in the desert' as Copleston described it (1963: 277). The other was through the development of compassion, which along with egotism and malice, Schopenhauer considered one of the primary human motives, and through ascetic practices – chastity, poverty and self-mortification. This was the path of salvation advocated in the teachings of the Buddha, which Schopenhauer extolled. Needless to say, Schopenhauer never attempted this second path (Copleston 1963: 277–85; R. Taylor 1964: 382).

Schopenhauer, though hardly mentioned in texts on the history of psychology, nevertheless had an important influence on later scholars, although this is often unacknowledged. The central emphasis he put on the will and on instinctual striving was taken up later, not only by Nietzsche, but by Freud, Wundt, Bergson, James and Dewey. His writings also stimulated in Germany an interest in oriental thought and religion. Although he was not explicitly anti-rationalist, by stressing that the intellect is subservient to the will and is 'entirely practical in its tendencies', Schopenhauer is essentially seen as belonging among the Romantics and as sustaining a counter-metaphysics that was opposed to the 'ontological intellectualism' of the main Western philosophical tradition. The thesis of instrumental reason in the service of life is evident in the writings of Freud, Nietzsche and Heidegger and in Horkheimer's critique of instrumental reason (Schnädelbach 1984: 143–4). Horkheimer reiterates the importance of Schopenhauer – a 'modern' thinker driven by a passion for the truth – with respect to Freudian theory. He writes: 'Schopenhauer's theory of consciousness as a small part of the psyche, by which it is used as a tool . . . anticipates the basic principle of modern psychoanalysis' (1974: 74).

An important figure in translating Schopenhauer's will into the idea of the unconscious was Eduard von Hartmann (1842–1906). His well-known work *The Philosophy of the Unconscious* (1869) was an attempt to synthesise the philosophies of Schopenhauer, Hegel and Schelling, and argued that the unconscious, as the ultimate reality had the attributes of both will and idea (reason).

We turn now to the writer who regarded himself as the successor to Schopenhauer, Friedrich Wilhelm Nietzsche (1844–1900); indeed, Nietzsche described Schopenhauer as 'my great teacher' (1956: 153).

2.2 Nietzsche and the Will to Power

Friedrich Nietzsche has been described as one of the great visionaries and myth-makers of our time. His writings had a prophetic quality, yet in essence he is both a tragic and a paradoxical figure. He described himself as the 'first immoralist', and his nihilistic way of thinking has presented us with some of the most devastating critiques of contemporary thought and culture – in all its aspects. Yet he is, first and foremost, a moralist, who suggested an ethic – the will to power – that was the 'transvaluation of all values'. He was vehemently anti-Christian, yet he remained throughout his life a kind of preacher, suggesting the possibility of salvation and postulating the quasi-religious doctrine of eternal recurrence. Nietzsche also offered some important critiques of the pretensions of science and rationalist metaphysics, but at heart he was a rationalist and a materialist. Aiken (1956: 207) suggests that he had a nostalgia for the Enlightenment, though knowing its ideals could no longer be his. He was indeed a critical thinker who attempted to remain true to the rationalist tradition. As Walter Kaufmann put it:

He tried to strengthen the heritage of the Enlightenment with a more profound understanding of the irrational – something Hegel had attempted three-quarters of a century earlier, but metaphysically and rather esoterically. Nietzsche was determined to be empirical, and he approached his subject – as it surely should be – with psychology. (1971: 16)

Psychological insights and a profound historical consciousness indeed permeate all Nietzsche's writings, and it is this that makes him such an important figure in modern thought, in spite of his reactionary politics. His contradictory personality was perhaps best described by Bertrand Russell when he labelled Nietzsche an 'aristocratic anarchist' (1946: 789).

Many writers have linked Nietzsche with Marx and Freud as one of the three key thinkers who have influenced twentieth-century thought. All three were German speakers and lovers of classical Greek thought. All were passionate thinkers who deeply sensed the need for radical change, and in various ways were profoundly critical of the temper and culture of their own age. All three had a profound distrust of moral discourse and everyday consciousness, and they collectively represent what Ricoeur has called the 'school of suspicion', united in a 'common opposition to the phenomenology of the sacred' (1970: 32). Indeed, all three scholars were professed atheists and looked upon belief in God as an historically determined symptom of human weakness and subordination. Finally, all three directed their thought towards a single leading idea – for Marx praxis; for Freud sexual motivation; for Nietzsche, the will to power (Stern 1978: 13–17).

Nietzsche was born at Röcken in Germany in 1844, the heir to a long line of Lutheran pastors. He was named Friedrich Wilhelm, after the king. (Later Nietzsche tended to repudiate his German origins.) His father died of a mental disorder when Nietzsche was aged four, and he was brought up in an all-female household, consisting of his mother, grandmother, sister and two aunts. After studying classical philosophy at the universities of Bonn and Leipzig and undertaking military service, in 1869 Nietzsche obtained a post at Basle as a professor extraordinary. He was only twenty-five years old at the time, but had apparently made a great impression on one of his professors, Friedrich Ritschl, a distinguished philologist. Taking Swiss citizenship, while at Basle, he formed friendships with the historian Jacob Burckhardt and Richard Wagner. During the Franco-Prussian War (1870–1) he wrote his first important book *The Birth of Tragedy from the Spirit of Music* (1872), drawing a contrast between Greek culture before and after Socrates, and noting the similarity between contemporary German culture and the 'Hellenic disintegration'. The book ends with a polemic in favour of Wagnerian music. Between 1873 and 1876 Nietzsche published four essays, which were collectively printed as *Thoughts out of Season* (1876). The study included important essays on Schopenhauer and Wagner. By this time, however, Nietzsche and Wagner had already drifted apart. In 1878 Nietzsche published his first aphoristic work *Human-all-too-Human* – he adopted the aphoristic style apparently on account of his deteriorating eyesight. In fact, over the decade his health deteriorated further and Nietzsche suffered from several ailments – migraine, stomach troubles, insomnia, as well as worsening eyesight. In 1879 he resigned his professorship at Basle on the grounds of ill health, and for the next decade, living on a small pension, he became something of an 'eternal fugitive', as he described himself. He wandered around Europe, living an increasingly solitary and lonely life, looking for some place or climate that might ease or stay his steadily deteriorating health. While in Messina, Sicily, in 1882, he met a young Russian woman, Lou Salomé, with whom Nietzsche became emotionally involved, but she never returned his feelings, and turned down his proposal of marriage. Nietzsche even asked his friend Paul Rée to propose to her on his behalf. Nietzsche was thirty-eight when he parted from Lou and he never saw her again, nor did he have any other emotional involvement. It was during this painful ten-year period that Nietzsche, filled with a sense of urgency and mission, wrote his major works: *The Gay Science* (1882), *Thus Spoke Zarathustra* (1883–5), *Beyond Good and Evil* (1886), *The Genealogy of Morals* (1887) and *The Twilight of the Idols* (1889).

Hollingdale (1965) has suggested that it was only his sense of mission that kept Nietzsche alive during the latter part of the decade. But in 1889 Nietzsche's solitary wanderings came to an end, and dramatically. He left his lodgings one morning and seeing a cabman beating his horse in the public square of Turin, he ran across and flung his arms around the horse's neck. He thereupon collapsed of apoplexy. He was taken, at first, to an asylum, but his mother later claimed him. He never regained his sanity, and remained in a childlike state for the rest of his life, cared for by his mother, and then, after 1895, by his sister Elizabeth. Nietzsche died in Weimar eleven years after his collapse, aged fifty-six. The evidence suggests that his illness and insanity may have been due to a syphilitic infection contracted when he was a young man. (For biographies of Nietzsche, see Kaufman 1950; Hollingdale 1965; Lavrin 1971.)

Compared with writers like Kant and Hegel, Nietzsche's writings are easy to understand; they are informative, aphoristic, lively, provocative, enigmatic, full of arresting metaphysics and profound psychological insights. But his thoughts are disordered and unsystematic; he's like a 'self-taught eccentric' or an 'intellectual Bohemian'. This makes it difficult to discern the main threads of his philosophy, or the important psychological themes that emerge from his writings, for these are scattered almost randomly in his studies. He was undoubtedly an important moral and social critic, but he was also a philosopher, and as Lavrin (1971) remarked, one of the great psychologists of the last century. And it is with respect to these last two roles that we shall largely be concerned with here, though we can hardly ignore his importance as a social critic. To do this we can be guided by Arthur Danto's (1964) important study of Nietzsche as a philosopher.

Nietzsche had read Schopenhauer when he was a student at Leipzig, and Schopenhauer's study *World as Will and Idea* was a powerful stimulus for him. He described Schopenhauer as 'my great teacher' and as being a 'European event', like Goethe and Hegel. The 'root metaphor' of Nietzsche's philosophy, the will to power, is indeed a modification, via Darwin, of Schopenhauer's 'will to live'. Whereas for Kant the will had only ethical significance, Nietzsche follows Schopenhauer in seeing the will as having a metaphysical function, as well as an ethical one. The will to power is indeed Nietzsche's key concept. 'The World', he declared, 'is the will to power – and nothing else! And you yourselves are this will to power – and nothing else!' But Nietzsche rebelled against Schopenhauer's ethic of renunciation and his 'nihilistic total devaluation of life' which made him the heir to Christian moralism with its anti-sensual metaphysics. We must, he wrote, 'first of all deny Schopenhauer'. Thus unlike Schopenhauer Nietzsche's thought is always towards the affirmation of life rather than towards its negation (Nietzsche 1968: 79–89; Copleston 1963: 396–407). Equating Schopenhauer's philosophy with Christianity and the ascetic ideal – of poverty, humility, chastity and self-denial – Nietzsche declared himself an 'anti-nihilist'. For Nietzsche, nihilism was associated with this ascetic ideal, with 'all the unnatural inclinations – the longing for what is unworldly, opposed to the senses, to instinct, to nature, to the animal in us, all the anti-biological and earth-columniating ideals' (1956: 229). The will to extinction, the anti-sensual resentments and attitudes, the denial of the self and of the natural instincts – all this for Nietzsche was nihilism. Classical philosophy itself accepted this 'spirit of asceticism'. What great philosopher has ever been married, he asked. Heraclitus, Plato, Descartes, Spinoza, Leibniz, Kant, Schopenhauer – not one of them ever married, and it is difficult to imagine them being so (1956: 242). But although in his critique of the ascetic ideal Nietzsche was himself 'anti-nihilist', his own philosophy was essentially a nihilistic one. For he agreed with Schopenhauer that the world and human life had no purpose or meaning. Retaining Schopenhauer's metaphysical interpretation of the 'thing-in-itself' as an impersonal will, an absolute reality underlying the world and all thought, Nietzsche came to the conclusion that the world had no purpose or value. As he expressed it in his unpublished notes:

> The feeling of valuelessness is attained when one apprehends that the general character of existence must not be interpreted with the concept of 'purpose', or 'oneness', or of 'truth'. . . . The world fails to have in the plentitude of happening any overarching unity'. (Danto 1965: 32)

Unlike the Russian nihilists of the same period, Nietzsche took his critique even further and repudiated the objectivity of scientific materialism. Nietzsche was, as Hollingdale suggests, a 'thoroughgoing materialist' (1968: 192), but he looked upon materialism, as with all scientific theories, only as a form of 'interpretation' not truth itself. Science, for Nietzsche, was not a repository of truths or a method of discovering them, but essentially a set of 'fictions', a perspective on the world that had a practical significance. It was an instance – like religion, morality, and philosophy, as well as with the common-sense realism that was embodied in language – of the 'will to power', a manifestation of the impulse to impose form and structure on an essentially chaotic reality. All knowledge, as Nietzsche puts it, 'works as an instrument of power'. Copleston expresses Nietzsche's approach cogently when he writes:

> We desire to schematize, to impose order and form on the multiplicity of impressions and sensations to the extent required by our practical needs. Reality is becoming; it is we who turn it into Being, imposing stable patterns on the flux of Becoming. And this activity is an expression of the will to power. (1963: 408)

The fact that the world itself is devoid of form or meaning Nietzsche accepts and affirms; and thus a philosophy of metaphysical nihilism forms the basis not for an attitude of pessimism or ascetic denial (as with Schopenhauer) but of life affirmation, of an exuberant stress on the instincts of life and the will to power. His respect for Heraclitus was precisely that this Greek philosopher stressed the evidence of the senses, of plurality and change.

In his study *Beyond Good and Evil* Nietzsche poses the question: what really prompts us to want always to know 'the truth'? What is the value of this search for truth? And in answering this question in three sections 'on the prejudices of philosophers' and in his other writings, Nietzsche comes to suggest that there is no objective truth, and that all knowledge is a form of interpretation based on human vital needs and the will to power. Thus the general view – known as the 'correspondence theory of truth' – that there is an objective structure or order in the world, and that a theory is true or false to the degree that it reflects or mirrors this structure, is rejected by Nietzsche. Truth, he writes, 'is that sort of error without which a particular type of living being could not live. The value for life is ultimately decisive'. Thus we have to recognise, he suggests, that untruths are 'a condition of life', and that some of our falsest judgements are the most indispensable to us (1972: 17). 'All seeing', he writes elsewhere, 'is essentially perspective and so is all knowing' (1956: 255).

Nietzsche, therefore, comes to develop both an instrumental or pragmatic theory of truth, and a 'perspectivist' conception of knowledge. He also, in the spirit somewhat of the later logical positivists, offers a critique of metaphysical philosophy, although accepting that both reason and science are in themselves nothing but 'useful fictions':

> We possess scientific knowledge today to precisely the extent that we have decided to accept the evidence of the senses – to the extent that we have learned to sharpen and arm them and to think them through to their conclusions. The rest is abortion, and not-yet-science, which is to say metaphysics, theology, psychology, epistemology. (1968: 36)

Nietzsche is particularly critical of writers like Plato and Kant, who make a distinction between the phenomenal world and the real world of ideas or noumena. This implies, he felt, a devaluation of the senses as well as a lack of historical consciousness. In their radical hostility towards sensuality, metaphysical philosophers are often worse, he suggests, than the Christian ascetics. Although Nietzsche's critiques of metaphysics are in the spirit of the later positivism – his theory of knowledge, unlike the positivists, is not

an empiricist one: 'Against positivism, which halts at the phenomena – "There are only facts" – I would say: No, facts are precisely
what there are not, only interpretations.'

He suggests, therefore, that the idea of 'cause' and 'effect' are not
material things, as mechanistic science sometimes suggests, but are
only concepts, they are 'conceptual fictions' that serve mutual
understanding, not explanation (1972: 33). Logic too is only an
instrument of knowledge that serves practical purposes.

With respect to metaphysical philosophy, Nietzsche makes two
important points; one is that much of this knowledge is useless for
practical life, 'more useless even than knowledge of the chemical
composition of water must be to the sailor in danger of shipwreck'
(1986: 16). The other is that many philosophical concepts and ideas
that are postulated as being the basis for the form of phenomenal
reality are in fact derived from commonsense understanding as this
is embodied in language. The so-called categories of understanding, for example, which Kant felt could not be derived directly
from experience, are in fact built into the structure of our language.
As Danto (1964) writes, it is Nietzsche's contention that metaphysical philosophers have mistaken certain general features of
their language, the subject–attribute distinction for example, for
generic traits of existence, and have gone on to base their rejection
of commonsense understanding on exactly the presuppositions of
commonsense (1964: 388). But the practical realism built into our
language is nevertheless only a 'perspective', necessary though it is
for the conditions of life. It is not in Nietzsche's sense true. As he
wrote:

> We have arranged a world for ourselves in which we might live, with
> the accepting of bodies, lines, surfaces, causes and effects, motion and
> rest, form and content. Without these articles of faith, no one now
> would be able to live! But this hardly constitutes a proof. Life is no
> argument. Among the conditions of life, error might be one.

There is thus a primordial realism inherent in our language
categories and grammar that serves a practical function, and enables
us to cope with the exigencies of life. But, Nietzsche argued, there
is a philosophical mythology concealed in a language, and words
and concepts are apt to mislead us into thinking that the things in
the material world are simpler than they really are (1986: 306).
Nietzsche thus offers a critique of common sense as well as defend-
ing it in his criticisms of 'life denying' metaphysical philosophy

(Danto 1964: 386–9). It is important to note that Nietzsche's theory of knowledge is essentially materialist; he is neither an idealist nor a phenomenalist, and he tends to see science as essentially a refinement of commonsense realism.

Although Nietzsche stressed the practical importance of ordinary language, his approach to language differs markedly from that of later linguistic philosophers, who tend to have an almost sacrosanct attitude towards it. Whereas Wittgenstein tended to see deviations from ordinary language use as leading to 'non-problems' in philosophy, Nietzsche was critical of ordinary language. Although the grammatical structure of language had been innocently accepted by metaphysical philosophers as reflecting the structure of reality, Nietzsche also felt that language tended to condition and depersonalise us.

It will be evident from what we have already written about Nietzsche's general philosophy that his conception of the human subject is complex. Posing the question as to what gives a human being his or her qualities, Nietzsche writes: 'Not god, not society, not his parents, or ancestors, not he himself. No one is accountable for existing at all.' Humans are not the result of any special design, will or purpose, but rather they have a certain fatality that 'cannot be disentangled from all that which has been and will be' (1968: 54). *Amor fati*, loving one's fate, is one of Nietzsche's essential premises. Thus although Nietzsche had been seen as one of the founders of existentialism, his stress is not on the uniqueness of the individual, or even on egoism, but rather he regards every individual as representing either the ascending or descending line of life as an evolutionary process. He writes later in the same study, *Twilight of the Gods*: 'the individual, the "single man", as people and philosophers have hitherto understood him, is an error; he does not constitute a separate entity, an atom, a "link in the chain" – he constitutes the entire single live "man" up to and including himself.' In a sense, for Nietzsche, the person is a 'species-being'. If he represents the descending development – decay, degeneration – then he has little value, while if he represents the ascending line of life then his value is extraordinary (1968: 85–6). Although psychology is fundamental to Nietzsche's approach, both his ethics and metaphysics are evolutionary and biological. Not only is the focus on the individual misleading, but Nietzsche takes a fundamentally anti-Cartesian stance in questioning the self as a permanent substance, and abolishing the body/mind dualism. Questioning the validity of materialistic atomism. Nietzsche also 'declares war' on what he calls 'soul atomism' – the belief in something indestructible, eternal, as a monad, the soul of Christianity. This belief Nietzsche felt to be unjustified, and ought to be jettisoned from science (1972: 25). But even modern philosophers like Descartes continue to be misled by certain structural features of language and the general disposition we have to regard whatever happens as the action of some agent. Reason, Nietzsche suggests, a reason that is derived from the rudimentary form of psychology inherent in language, 'believes generally that wills are causes. It believes in the ego as a being, a substance, and projects this belief in ego-substance onto all things' (1968: 38). But the notion of an ego or self, as a permanent substance, is, for Nietzsche, an inferred entity, a creation of the human intellect for practical purposes. It is a useful fiction, a necessary one, but devoid of 'objectivity'. The distinction between subject or agency and activity Nietzsche felt to be a 'popular superstition' for 'no such agent exists, there is no "being" behind the doing, acting, becoming; the doer has simply been added to the deed by the imagination – the doing is everything' (1956: 178–9). As Copleston (1963) suggests, this idea has its problems; one is prompted to ask, who is doing the imagining? But Nietzsche makes the same point when he writes: 'A thought comes when "it" will, not when "I" will.'

One of the most original themes in Nietzsche's philosophy is his analysis of consciousness, for though critical of Descartes, and stressing the unacknowledged presuppositions that lay behind the notion 'I think', Nietzsche was intrigued over the phenomenon of introspection. Nietzsche was puzzled not over the fact that one had thoughts, but rather because we seemed to be *aware* of them. It was possible to make a distinction between consciousness and self-consciousness. The question was: what purpose did self-awareness have? As he wrote in *The Gay Science*: 'Consciousness first becomes a problem for us when we begin to appreciate the degree to which it is dispensable.' For the fact is that 'we could think, feel, will, remember; we could likewise "act" in every sense of the word; and yet none of this would need to "come into consciousness" (to put it metaphorically)' (354; Danto 1965: 117).

Much of what we do takes place without us being conscious of it, including many of our vital functions. The whole of life, in fact, Nietzsche suggests, might be possible 'without its seeing itself, so to speak, in a mirror'. The question, therefore, is what extra function does consciousness serve. Nietzsche's answer to this, as Danto writes, is to sense that consciousness is an extraordinary development, and has little to do with the individual *per se* – who could quite easily function in some instinctual or automatic fashion.

Offering what he termed 'an extravagant hypothesis', Nietzsche argued that it was a fundamental mistake to think of consciousness as an individual attribute, but rather it is to be understood 'as a tool, in the collective life'. Consciousness is a means of communication, which develops through social interaction and with respect to specific social interests. Thus Nietzsche writes that 'consciousness is only a connecting network between man and man' which develops 'only in proportion to its utility'. Self-awareness and reflection, which philosophers have seen as essentially a private matter, is social in its essence and origins. It is only as a social animal that humans became conscious of themselves, and the development of language and consciousness are inextricably linked. But thinking in itself need not be conscious: 'Man, like every living creature, thinks continuously without knowing that he does; the thinking which becomes conscious is the smallest part, according to us the most superficial and the worst.' And he continues, 'my motion is that consciousness does not belong to the individual existence of men, but to what is the community' (1956: 354; Danto 1965: 117–21).

Nietzsche's essential argument is a pragmatic one, that our consciousness has its origins in sociality and in our relationship with the outer world, and is related to the conditions of human life and our instinctive activities. Self-consciousness and individuality are thus bound up with collective life and are a late development. His theory is therefore quite different from the speculative theories of Hobbes and Locke, for whom the individual is a primordial reality, and social relations to some extent 'artificial' (Danto 1965: 141).

The Cartesian dualism of body and mind, the 'ghost in the machine' as Gilbert Ryle (1949) was later to express it, disappears with Nietzsche, for his conception of the human person is a unified one, in the sense that cognition and action are not separate functions but were both aspects of the operation of the will (M. Warnock 1970: 15). Likewise, Nietzsche sees no necessary conflict between the reason and the passions, and the suggestion that he is an anti-rationalist is far from the truth. He is in fact only critical of reason when reason is opposed to the senses and life, as with Plato. But he is equally critical of the unbridled passions, even though he continually acknowledges the primacy of human emotions and impulses. In his early study *The Birth of Tragedy*, Nietzsche draws a distinction between two creative tendencies in Greek culture, represented by the deities Apollo and Dionysus. The Dionysian tendency represents 'mystical jubilation' and is identified with the stream of life, with music and intoxication, and with the Bacchic rites, which tend to break down 'the spell of individuation'. Through the Dionysian rites the individual experiences 'primordial unity' with nature itself; it 'opens a path to the material womb of being' (1956: 97). Apollo, on the other hand, is the symbol of light, of dream experiences and of art and sculpture; the deity represents restraint and individuation. The duality and 'fierce opposition' between these two aesthetic tendencies is reflected in other oppositions: male and female; form and ecstacy; reason and passion. But although Nietzsche throughout his writings applauds and advocates the Dionysian spirit, the genius of Greek culture, he suggests, was in an integration of the Dionysian and Apollonian elements. The ideal for Nietzsche, therefore, is not unlicensed passion, but Hellenised Dionysianism, passion guided by reason, and restraint. The aim was 'to convert passions into joys'.

It is beyond the scope of the present study to discuss fully Nietzsche's theory of morals, but a short discussion may be appropriate as his writings on moral issues are full of interesting psychological insights.

Nietzsche's moral philosophy, clearly expounded in *The Genealogy of Morals*, published two years before he went insane (1887), rejects both the utilitarian theory of Spencer – the notion that good is what is useful and promotes pleasure – and the ethical theory of Kant. The latter theory suggests that ethical values are fixed and stable, and can be ascertained by pure reason or intuition. Nietzsche suggests that morals are relative, but if looked at historically – something that philosophers rarely do, he chides – then they can be seen to consist of two main types. On the one hand, there is the morality of the ruling aristocracy or warriors, the nobility. The morality of this class is one of self-glorification, growing out of triumphant self-affirmation. The virtues of the nobility, whether Roman, Arabian, German or Japanese, stress power, heroism, honour, pride and individual autonomy. The distinction it makes is between good and bad, the latter signifying what is contrary to its own values. Within the aristocratic class there is no sense of guilt for the will-to-power, the aggressive instincts are freely discharged. On the other hand, there is the morality of the people of the dominated class, the plebeians or slaves – the ethics of the 'herd', as Nietzsche describes them. These people suffer and are subjected to violence. The virtues they come to stress, therefore, are those functional and beneficial to a subjected people – the qualities of kindness, humility, sympathy, love; the Christian virtues in fact. The distinction made by the slave morality is not between good and bad but between good and evil, and being unable to express their resentments openly, the slaves develop a sense of bad conscience or guilt. When a nobleman feels resentment, Nietzsche writes, 'it is absorbed in his instantaneous reaction and therefore does not poison him' (1956: 173). But with the plebeians, their resentments and instincts are not able to find expression, and they become turned upon themselves. It is almost a form of sickness. And yet this 'bad conscience, the desire for self-mortification, is the wellspring of all altruistic values' (1956: 221). It also leads to an inner sense of self:

All instincts that are not allowed free play are turned inward. This is what I call man's interiorization; it alone provides the soil for the growth of what is later called man's soul. Man's interior world, originally meagre and tenuous, was expanding in every dimension, in proportion as the outward discharge of his feelings was curtailed.' (1956: 217–18)

This slave morality finds its expression in Christianity and the ascetic ideal; indeed, he describes the ascetic priest as the 'virtuoso of guilt' (1956: 177). Nietzsche is extremely critical of the slave morality, seeing it as an 'anti-natural' morality, that is against the instincts of life. It constitutes a 'formula for decadence', and Nietzsche felt it permeated European culture, for not only Christianity, but idealist philosophers, anarchists and democratic and socialist movements all expressed this ethic. Indeed, Nietzsche looked upon socialism as simply a derivative of Christianity. Rather than offering redemption, all these decadent tendencies were a 'deep-seated malady', representing the 'descending line of life'.

Throughout the work Nietzsche expresses his sympathies for the warrior ethic, and it is in relation to this context, to what he felt was a climate of decadence, that Nietzsche preferred his own ethic to counter the malaise. This he described as a 'naturalism in morality', a morality dominated by an instinct for life, by the will-to-power. It expressed a 'revaluation of all values' and the symbolism of the Dionysian. Nietzsche graphically portrayed this new ethic with the idea of a 'higher type of man', an anti-Christ or superman (*Übermensch*). His classic prose-poem *Thus Spoke Zarathustra* vividly and beautifully expresses Nietzsche's reactionary vision. It expresses both his elitism and his feeling that humankind might be able to attain higher forms of excellence: 'Man is something which must be surpassed.' Copleston (1963: 414) suggests that the superman is all that the ailing, lonely, tormented and neglected Nietzsche would like to have been. The book also carries the idea of the eternal recurrence, the notion – an ancient one – that the same cycle of life is endlessly relived.

The superman in a sense personifies Nietzsche's concept of the will-to-power, which is Nietzsche's central, organising concept. This is not a mentalistic concept, nor is it to be identified simply with human volition. It is defined by Nietzsche as 'all effective energy' and is in essence the inner reality of the universe which manifests itself particularly in living organisms. Discerning manifestations of the will-to-power in human physical processes, Nietzsche extended this idea to organic life in general. And he saw this will-to-power as precisely power over others, and over aspects of the world:

> Life itself is essentially appropriation, injuring, overpowering the alien and the weak. It is oppression, hardness, imposing one's form. . . . Life just is will-to-power . . . it belongs in essence to living things, as a basic organic function. It is a consequence of the will-to-power which is but the will to life.

The search for truth and the struggle for existence are both, for Nietzsche, expressions of this will-to-power. Spinoza's conatus, the tendency of each person or thing to retain its integrity, he sees as a consequence of this struggle for power. Although Nietzsche's ideas clearly reflect Darwinian tendencies, Nietzsche was critical of Darwinian theory; he felt that Darwin overrated external circumstances and that the vital factor was not the struggle for existence, but rather for richness, for profusion. Where there is struggle, he suggests, it is a struggle for power and the essential process is 'precisely the tremendous power to shape and create forms from within, a power which uses and exploits the environment'. Nietzsche abandoned the mechanistic conception of the world, but he retained the Promethean ethic of some Enlightenment philosophers, seeing human relations with the world as essentially one of power and control (Copleston 1963: 407–11; Danto 1964: 396).

Although Nietzsche has had a tremendous influence on Western thought, he has had a bad press. In particular, in his praise of the warrior ethic and in his attack on socialism and democratic ideals, he has been seen as a forerunner of irrationalist ideologies of power, which found their apotheosis in fascism. But many aspects of Nietzsche's philosophy are incompatible with fascism; he was critical of German nationalism, he was not anti-Semitic and, although he espoused the values of an aristocratic elite in *Thus Spoke Zarathustra* (that 'extended hymn to solitude and individuality', as Hollingdale called it (1961: 27)), he launched an eloquent critique of that 'new idol', the state, describing it as 'the coldest of all cold monsters'. The state, he suggests, is contrary to life and human freedom (75–7). And his ideal of the superman seems to be less of a warrior than a creative artist or religious prophet. He seems throughout his writings to have Goethe in mind (Aiken 1956: 202–3; Hollingdale 1961: 29).

Nietzsche has had an important influence in many areas of study. His pragmatic theory of truth anticipates those of James and Dewey; his ideas on the social context and objectivity of human knowledge have been taken up by writers like Mannheim, Kuhn and Foucault; and his radical atheism and his highly individualistic philosophy has led many writers to see Nietzsche as one of the key founders – along with Kierkegaard – of existentialism (Blackham 1952: 23–42; Barrett 1958: 158–83; M. Warnock 1970: 13–22). But perhaps his most crucial influence has been in the development of psychology, particularly on the psychological theories of Adler and Freud, to whom we may now turn. For like Nietzsche, Freud felt that the essence of human nature consists of instinctual impulses that have a pan-human significance.

2.3 Freud – His Life and Work

Sigmund Freud (1856–1939) is a difficult figure to approach in an unprejudiced manner. On the one hand, he has been described as an 'inscrutable genius' who, along with scholars of the stature of Newton, Darwin and Einstein, has revolutionised human thought; on the other, he has been labelled 'the greatest con man in the history of medicine'. But whatever the final verdict, no one can question the fact that Freud has had a profound influence on Western thought. Even E. M. Thornton, who in her 'alternative biography' of Freud relates his revolutionary new theories to cocaine addiction, has to admit that 'probably no single individual has had a more profound effect on twentieth-century thought than Sigmund Freud', and that his theories have left their imprint on almost every facet of human existence (1983: 9). Freud, a prophet without a real message, tended to see himself as a world-historical figure. In his *Introductory Lectures on Psychoanalysis* (1915–17), Freud wrote that in the course of time humanity has had to suffer 'two great outrages upon its naive self-love'. The first outrage was a

cosmological one, and associated with the mechanistic philosophers of the seventeenth century. This made us realise that our
earth was not the centre of the universe, but only a tiny speck in a
vast world-system. The second was when biological research initiated by Wallace and Darwin made us realise that we were not
especially created in God's image, but were descended from the
animal world, and had an 'ineradicable animal nature' within us.
The third and most bitter blow to human 'craving for grandiosity'
was, Freud suggested, coming 'from present-day psychological
research which is endeavouring to prove to the "ego" of each one
of us that he is not even master in his own house' (1953: 296).

Frank Sulloway (1979), in his important biography of Freud – a
study that is both critical and sympathetic (an unusual combination
in the writings on Freud) – makes the significant point that while
Freud did indeed deliver this third blow to humans' narcissistic
pride, his achievement was in essence a direct extension of the
second, Darwinian revolution. The revolutionary doctrines of both
Darwin and Freud did indeed, he suggests, bring about 'a kindred
metaphysical shift in Western intellectual thought', but Freud drew
both inspiration and his central ideas from Darwin's evolutionary
theory – his historical approach, and his stress upon the dynamic,
the instinctual and above all, the non-rational in human behaviour
(1979: 276).

Writings on Freud since the publication of Ernest Jones' official
biography of Freud (1953–7) have tended to focus on three essential
themes: a critique of Freud from the standpoint of a positivistic
conception of science; a debunking of the 'great myth' of Freud as a
hero; and the attempt to suggest that psychoanalysis is simply a
hermeneutic science.

The positivistic critique of Freud and psychoanalysis has been
most forceably presented by the behaviourist psychologist Hans
Eysenck (1985), who sees Freudian theory as a 'pseudo-scientific
doctrine', which has done irreparable harm to both psychology and
psychiatry. Freud has, he thinks, set back the study of these
disciplines by something like fifty years or more, and he concludes
that the Freudian legacy must be regarded as a failure. It is an
'historical curiosity' that is best forgotten. With regard to Freudian
theory he writes:

We are left with nothing but imaginary interpretation of pseudo-events,
therapeutic failures, illogical and inconsistent theories, unacknowledged
borrowings from predecessors, erroneous 'insights' of no proven value,

and a dictatorial and intolerant group of followers insistent not on truth but on propaganda. (1985: 201–2)

Thus Eysenck suggests that Freud's place in history is not with Copernicus and Darwin, but with fairy tale writers like Hans Christian Anderson. What is valid in Eysenck's critique is lost in his strident polemics, which seem to have an underlying purpose of advocating and promoting behavioural therapy. Ignoring Freud's own insistence on the limitations of psychotherapy, Eysenck applies standards of empirical validation to psychoanalysis which inevitably highlight its limitations and inadequacies. Had he applied the same rigorous standards and the same critical acumen to other forms of therapy and psychiatric treatment, or even to biomedicine itself, he may well have come to the conclusion that biomedical therapy is not only limited in its effects but in many ways a threat to health. Eysenck is still entrenched in the positivistic conception of natural science, which stems from Bacon and the mechanistic philosophers of the seventeenth century, and thus has a narrow conception of psychology, which excludes human subjectivity and human consciousness. He is equally stuck with a neo-Kantian dualism and the distinction between a natural science based on a mechanistic conception of the world and hermeneutic understanding, unaware that the world-view presented by Darwin has made this dichotomy, and the 'eternal struggle' (1985: 194) between these two approaches, a redundant one. Additionally, whatever seems to be of value in Freud's writings Eysenck tends to dismiss or ignore, largely on the grounds that it was not original to Freud. All important scholars are unoriginal in the sense that many of their concepts and ideas are derived from earlier scholars; what makes them important is that they present us with a new creative synthesis of these ideas and thus take us to a new level of understanding. Freud was not unaware that many of his key ideas had been anticipated by earlier writers; he simply had a psychological need to stress his own 'originality'. (For further discussions of the 'scientific' status of psychoanalysis, see Ellenberger 1970; Cioffi 1970; Gruenbaum 1984.)

A second important theme in recent studies of Freud is to suggest that both Freud and his earlier biographers tended to see his life-work as a kind of heroic journey. Freud saw himself, and is so portrayed by his colleague and biographer Ernest Jones, as a scientific hero, and yet this portrait deviates substantially from the actual historical features that characterise this 'myth of the hero' in psychoanalytic history, and which have been emphasised by both Ellenberger and Sulloway. The first is the stress that is put on Freud's intellectual isolation during the formative years of discovery – the decade after 1895 – and that tends to exaggerate the hostile reception given to his theories: 'I had no followers. I was completely isolated. In Vienna I was shunned; abroad no notice was taken of me. My *Interpretation of Dreams* published in 1900, was scarcely reviewed in technical journals,' Freud wrote in his autobiographical study published in 1925 (1986: 231). But the actual record shows that Freud's writings were widely reviewed and that the reception to his theories, even to his sexual theories, were by no means hostile (Ellenberger 1970: 547; Sulloway 1979: 446–67).

The second feature of the hero legend depicts Freud's 'absolute originality' as a scientist, and suggests that Freud was unconcerned about the issue of scientific priority. But as many scholars have suggested, Freud was not only highly conscious of the issue of priority – and to be fair, he always acknowledged the priority of others where it was due – but that many of his key ideas – specifically the importance of childhood sexuality and the unconscious mind – were by no means original to Freud. Of particular interest is Freud's relationship and attitude towards Schopenhauer and Nietzsche, whose basic premises clearly anticipate those of Freud. As Sulloway writes:

> Like Freud, both philosophers described the unconscious and irrational sources of human behaviour and stressed the self-deluding character of the intellect. But whereas Schopenhauer and Freud considered sexuality as the most important instinct, Nietzsche emphasized the aggressive and self-destructive drives of man. Nietzsche, however, preceded Freud in the use of the terms sublimation and id (*das es*) as well as in the idea that civilization is founded upon a renunciation of instinct. (1979: 467; cf. Gellner 1985: 20–6)

In his autobiography Freud mentions both Schopenhauer and Nietzsche. He acknowledges that in emphasising the dominance of the emotions and the supreme importance of sexuality, Schopenhauer's philosophy coincides with psychoanalysis, but Freud suggests that he did not read the philosopher until late in life. As to Nietzsche, Freud indicates that he avoided Nietzsche on purpose so as not to be hampered in working out his own ideas. Freud was thus clearly aware of the content of Nietzsche's work – otherwise why deny himself the pleasure of reading the works of Nietzsche

(1986: 73)? Within the circles in which Freud moved, the writings of Schopenhauer and Nietzsche were widely discussed, and Nietzsche's friend Lou Salomé, who came to Vienna in 1912 to join Freud's circle, later became a close confidant of Freud (Lavrin 1971: 60; Roazen 1976: 320–1). The concept of the unconscious mind, in fact, has a long history, a history that has been detailed by both Whyte (1960) and Ellenberger (1970). Freud never denied this. Freud did not 'discover' the unconscious; what he stressed was that the acceptance of unconscious mental processes represents a decisive step in science (1953: 26).

A third theme is the growing tendency to see Freud's contributions as being outside the scope of scientific understanding – to suggest that Freud can be understood only in terms of hermeneutics. Eysenck rightly argues that Freud would have rejected this interpretation of his work, that he always looked upon his psychoanalytical studies as falling within the scientific *Weltanschauung*. What Eysenck fails to realise is that Freud not only rejected hermeneutics in its narrow sense, but was also critical of the limitations of behaviourist and physiological psychology. But having rejected Freud's claims as a scientist, Eysenck also pours scorn on any insights to be derived from Freud's work. Eysenck, in a very jaundiced fashion, is unable, it seems, to see any value at all in Freud's writings: 'There is no reason to assume that Freud's "insights" into his own suffering are in any way relevant to the behaviour of other human beings, just as there is no reason to assume that his "insights" are in fact accurate' (1985: 196).

Such a view informs us not about Freud, but about Eysenck's own commitment to scientism rather than to science. Reading Freud is open and refreshing by comparison. But given this kind of criticism from positivists, many defenders of Freud have tended to stress that Freud's psychoanalytic theory is essentially a form of hermeneutics, a form of interpretative understanding concerned with everyday life (Habermas 1972; Stevens 1983). But the writer who has expressed this viewpoint most cogently is Bruno Bettelheim.

Bettelheim's study *Freud and Man's Soul* (1983) is largely concerned with indicating that the English translation of Freud's work have tended to obliterate Freud's essential humanism and to present us with writings that are abstract, depersonalised, highly theoretical and mechanised. All the translators have tended to replace words in ordinary use with medical terms and learned borrowings from Greek and Latin. Thus the German terms *Ich* and *es*, are not translated as 'I' and 'it', which is how Freud used them, but as 'ego' and 'id' – thus making them cold technical terms which arouse no personal associations. Similarly, words like parapraxis and cathexis are coined by the translators – even though Freud himself always shunned arcane technical terms. The reasons for these mistranslations seems to Bettelheim clear; it was to translate an introspective psychology into a behavioural one, which observes from the outside. It reflected the American tendency to view psychoanalysis as a medical speciality, as a handmaid of psychiatry, or as a behavioural psychology concerned with 'adjustment'. This was quite contrary to Freud's intentions. For not only was Freud not really enthusiastic about psychoanalysis as a therapy, but in his famous essay *The Question of Lay Analysis* (1926), published when he was seventy, Freud strongly argued against the idea that psychoanalysis was a medical speciality or should be purely the concern of the medical profession. But rather, it was important, he suggests, in that it gave us insights into understanding the human condition. Psychoanalysis, he wrote, 'is a part of psychology. It is not medical psychology in the traditional sense, nor the psychology of pathological processes. It is psychology proper; certainly not all of psychology, but its substratum' (1986: 356–7; Bettelheim 1983: 33). And elsewhere Freud writes that psychoanalysis had never claimed to be a complete theory of psychology but should be 'applied to supplement and correct the knowledge acquired by other means' (1986: 110). Freud described his kind of psychology as 'depth psychology' or 'the psychology of the unconscious' (1986: 306). Thus Bettelheim comes to suggest that the distinction drawn by German neo-Kantian philosophy between hermeneutic-spiritual knowledge and positivistic-pragmatic knowledge is apposite for understanding Freud. For whereas the English translators tended, following the Anglo-Saxon psychological tradition, to interpret Freud in terms of the positivistic tradition, in essence, Bettelheim contends, Freud must be seen as working within the framework of the *Geisteswissenschaft* (science of the spirit), applying the methods appropriate to an idiographic science. Psychoanalysis, he writes, 'is plainly an idiographic science, utilizing unique historical occurrences to provide a view of man's development and behaviour' (1983: 41–3).

Freud stood at the watershed in the development of social theory. As a student at the Brück Institute of Physiology in Vienna, Freud took as his idol the German scientist Hermann Helmholtz (1821–94), whose school of medicine advocated experimental methods and was hostile to any form of vitalism within biology. Within this perspective all mental diseases were seen as due to organic disorders. Given this background it is hardly surprising that Freud inherited a positivistic conception of science. He aimed, as Rycroft notes (1985: 43), to establish a 'scientific psychology' by applying the same principles of causality that were in his time considered valid in physics and chemistry. Freud thus accepted the principle of 'psychic determinism' and, as Hughes suggested (1958: 134–5), even to the end of his life Freud tended to use a mechanistic vocabulary drawn from nineteenth-century physics. But in essence Freud's guiding thoughts were biological rather than mechanistic, and Sulloway has rightly argued that his 'fundamental conceptions were biological by inspiration as well as by implication'. Freud, he suggests, offers us not a 'pure psychology' but a psychobiological perspective which places him squarely in the intellectual lineage of Darwin and other evolutionary thinkers (1979: 5).

Lomas has implied that Freud was unable to 'emancipate himself from the physical frame of reference' (1966: 152). But as I have suggested elsewhere (1987: 152), what is significant about Freud is that he shifted his theoretical perspective and avoided any kind of simple biological reductionism, without losing sight of the fact that the human being is a psychobiological entity, or abandoning causal analysis. As Engels had compared Marx with Darwin as the founder of historical science, so Freud's own biographer, Ernest Jones, was right to bestow upon Freud the title of 'Darwin of the Mind', for both Marx and Freud saw the human species as rooted in society and nature. But the theoretical shift that Freud made is important.

Psychoanalysis as it developed did not therefore remain entrenched in a mechanistic framework. Beginning as a study by Freud of neurosis, and as a theory that aimed to explain its origin and development, psychoanalytic thought shifted the focus away from 'organicism' and the general nineteenth-century notion that mental illnesses were physical in origin. For around 1900 Freud invoked in his studies a totally new principle of explanation, which ran counter to the tenor of thought prevalent at that period. Expressed simply, Freud argued that neurotic symptoms have a meaning and, as Home wrote, this opened up a new way of understanding functional illness: 'In discovering that the symptom had meaning and basing his treatment on this hypothesis, Freud took the psychoanalytic study of neurosis out of the world of science into the world of humanities, because a meaning is not the product of causes but the creation of a subject' (Home 1966: 42).

Accepting that there is a radical difference in logic and method between the humanities and science, Home thus felt that Freud had made a radical break with past interpretations of neurosis. He had abandoned the earlier attempts at physiological reductionism for a psychological mode of understanding based on the interpretation of meaning. My feeling is that this disjuncture is false; for as with Marx, what Freud essentially tried to do was to create a humanistic science. In doing so he employed, as many have noted (Bocock 1976: 23–9), two methodological approaches. In attempting to understand human life Freud, therefore, adopted both a natural scientific position, with its causal analyses and a rather mechanistic model of energy flows, and an interpretative account based on meaning. In essence he did not confuse, but rather fused the two approaches. As Ricoeur put it, Freud's theory reflects a 'mixed discourse' (1970: 363). But it is important to realise that the mode of interpretative understanding that Freud advocated is quite different from the kind of hermeneutics that stems from German idealism. To say that 'Freud's psychology belongs to the kind which seeks to understand human behaviour rather than to explain it on a scientific basis; that is it is *Verstehende* psychology' (Bocock 1976: 21), is to accept the kind of dichotomy which Freud (and Marx) were attempting to go beyond. Freud did not simply propound a theory of meaning in the understanding of neurosis (or culture) but linked that understanding to a biological reality. In Ricoeur's terms, he did not aim at the 'restoration of cultural meanings' nor link such meanings to a 'sacred' reality, (as with phenomenological analyses), but rather belonged to the 'school of suspicion' which advocated a 'science of meaning'. This latter approach viewed interpretation as a 'process of demystification' (Ricoeur 1970): 32–6). As Rycroft rightly indicated (1985: 49), to accept psychoanalysis simply as a theory of meaning is incomplete and misleading without realising that it is also a 'biological theory of meaning'.

In attempting to bridge the gulf between the sciences and the humanities or, to put it another way, in attempting to go beyond the positivistic conception of science – that is, to broaden its scope – Freud never lost his commitment to the scientific *Weltanschauung* (world view). Although in his personal life he seems to have surrounded himself with uncritical disciples and a sect-like organisation (Fromm 1970: 17–24), his writings convey an open-mindedness and a strong commitment to science, defining the latter as radical enquiry into human life based on empirical knowledge. As he put it: the aim is not 'at producing conviction – my aim is to stimulate enquiry and to destroy prejudices' (1953: 256). But inevitably, he has been subject to criticisms from both sides of the intellectual divide. Those who, in the positivist tradition, have narrowly interpreted all science on the model of the physical sciences – as involving causal theory and experimental methods – have naturally pronounced psychoanalysis to be unscientific and 'mentalist' (Skinner 1954; Eysenck 1953, 1985). On the other hand, existential psychologists like Sartre (1943: 50–4) have denounced Freudian theory as deterministic, and as presenting a dehumanisation of the human personality. C. Wilson (1981: 62) has gone even further and described Freud's theory as a 'philosophy of helplessness' – a perspective that seems to me to run counter to the whole tenor of Freud's thought. For though, like Schopenhauer, he presents us with a pessimistic vision, Freud never advocates despair or mysticism.

Sigmund Freud was born of Jewish parents in Freiberg, Moravia, a small town then part of the Austro-Hungarian Empire, now in Czechoslovakia. When he was four years old, his family moved to Vienna, and here Freud lived for most of his long life. At school Freud proved to be outstanding at languages. Although he was interested mainly in literature and philosophy, he decided to study medicine, and entered the University of Vienna in 1873 when he was seventeen years old. He admitted in his autobiography that he never had any particular predilection for the career of a doctor, and apart from psychiatry took little interest in the various branches of medicine. He was thus negligent in his studies and did not graduate until 1881, eight years later. But from 1876 he worked for six years as a research assistant in the physiology laboratory of Ernst Brücke – physiology then being a newly emerging science. He had the highest regard for Brücke, and wrote several papers on the histology of the nervous system. Having met his future wife Martha Bernays in 1882, and being in financial difficulties, Freud took his tutor's advice and became a junior physician at the General Hospital in Vienna. But continuing his interest in neuropathology, in 1885 Freud went to Paris on a scholarship, to study under Charcot at Salpêtrieve, the famous mental hospital. Charcot was an authority on nervous disorders, and experimented in the use of hypnosis for the treatment of hysteria – the 'daughter's disease' – an ailment that particularly affected young middle-class women. Hysteria took the form of various physical symptoms like paralysis, or of phobias, there being no obvious organic disease or damage to account for the nervous disorder. By careful observation and the use of hypnosis, Charcot was able to prove that hysterical symptoms, while produced by emotions rather than by physical injury, were genuine, and not under the conscious control of the patient. At the time, hysteria was regarded as either pure imagination or malingering, or else a peculiar disorder of the womb (*hysteria* being Greek for womb) and thus only affecting women. It was treated either by electrotherapy, by 'extirpation of the clitoris', or by the administering of valerian root, which is a powerful sedative (E. Jones 1964: 204). Charcot also indicated to Freud the frequent occurrence of hysteria in men, and it was not therefore simply related to the female reproductive system. Although there was evidently no direct relationship between hypnosis and hysteria, Freud was clearly sympathetic to Charcot's emphasis on possible psychological causes of this 'strange disorder'. Thus, as Thornton (1983) suggests, Freud came away from Salpêtrieve a strong believer in the psychogenic origin of hysteria. Believing both hypnosis and hysteria to be caused by 'temporal lobe epilepsy', Thornton naturally thought this to be a retrogressive step on the part of Freud (Thornton 1983: 53–122; Showalter 1985: 147–8).

During this period (1884–7), Freud also made some early experiments on the potential therapeutic uses of cocaine, and as he wrote in a letter to his fiancée, he sang the praises of this 'magical substance'. One of his friends, Carl Koller, established the use of cocaine as a local anaesthetic, thus denying Freud the 'fame' he so eagerly sought after.

On his return to Vienna, Freud became friendly with a medical colleague, Joseph Breuer, who was fourteen years his senior and who had for several years been using hypnosis in the treatment of hysteria. Breuer was a lovable man, of striking intelligence and wide knowledge, and even after their later estrangement Freud continued to speak highly of him. Talking with Breuer, Freud wrote, is 'like sitting in the sun', for he radiated light and warmth. Breuer related to Freud the case history of one of his patients, a young woman of unusual education and gifts who had fallen ill while nursing her father. She suffered from various forms of paralysis and mental confusion. Quite by chance and primarily on the instigation of the young woman herself, Breuer discovered that her symptoms disappeared after she had verbalised, under hypnosis, her emotional feelings and past experiences. This process Breuer called 'catharsis'. Thus was the origin of the 'talking cure' as the woman herself described it, which proved to be a new treatment of hysteria. The patient, Bertha Pappenheim, was treated by Breuer for hysteria from 1880 to 1882 and, under the pseudonym of 'Anna O.', she figured as the first case-history in Breuer and Freud's important work *Studies on Hysteria* (1895), published thirteen years later. 'Anna O.', in fact, was the inventor of the 'talking cure' of psychoanalysis, for as Showalter writes (1985: 155) she was Breuer's partner in a remarkable, shared and egalitarian therapeutic exchange. The case of 'Anna O.' has since become a topic of much research. Breuer's treatment it is argued, did not, in fact, effect a cure, as the young Bertha Pappenheim was suffering from tuberculosis and later spent some time in a sanatorium. But eventually she recovered and in later life she became a social worker, founded a League of Jewish Women (1904) and was an important pioneer in the woman's movement (Edinger 1968; Sulloway 1979: 54–9; Thornton 1983: 123–50).

Freud took over Breuer's cathartic method of treating hysteria but eventually gave up trying to hypnotise patients. He found he could not hypnotise every patient nor put individual patients into as deep a state of hypnosis as he would have wished (1986: 200). So Freud began to develop an alternative therapeutic technique, and simply allowed his own patients to 'talk out' their problems and difficulties by free association, and by relating their dreams. The book he wrote with Breuer, *Studies on Hysteria*, marked the beginning of psychoanalysis both as a therapeutic method and as a theory of human personality and culture. The book was an important landmark, for it lay the foundations of a culturally aware therapy that took women's words and women's lives seriously and allowed women a say in the management of hysterical symptoms (Showalter 1985: 158).

The following year, after the death of his father, an event that greatly disturbed Freud ('I feel quite uprooted,' he had written to his friend Wilhelm Fliess) Freud began 'his most heroic feat – the psychoanalysis of his own unconscious' (E. Jones 1964: 276). Realising the importance of dreams as a source of data in the understanding of neurosis, in uncovering the hidden motives and conflicts within the individual, Freud focused his own self-analysis on the recording and interpretation of his own dreams. The outcome was the writings of his classic study *The Interpretation of Dreams* (1900), which many have regarded as his best work.

During the last decade of the nineteenth century, roughly from 1892 to 1900, a remarkable transformation took place in Freud's personality. At the beginning of the decade Freud was a respectable member of the bourgeoisie, happily married with six children, and with a lucrative private medical practice, Freud specialising in the treatment of nervous diseases. Then by degrees Freud began to form an intense admiration and devotion towards an eccentric Berlin physician Wilhelm Fliess, as well as to develop severe neurotic and physical ailments. His biographer Ernest Jones tells us that during this decade Freud suffered from very considerable psychoneurosis, from anxiety, from alternating moods of elation and self-confidence and severe depression and doubt. Freud also suffered from migraine, nasal infection and unexplained symptoms of cardiac irregularity. His sexual vitality also declined. Jones discusses Freud's heavy smoking, but is unable to explain Freud's ailments and his constant struggles against spells of depression and anxiety (E. Jones 1964: 263–9). It was during this period that Freud formulated and developed all the key concepts of psychoanalysis, but particularly his theory of the sexual origins of neuroses, and the concept of the Oedipal complex. Thornton, in her important study of Freud, which is marred only by her own excessive adherence to biological explanation of mental disorders, provides much evidence to suggest that during this period Freud became addicted to cocaine. This drug was widely used at the time, and was taken by Freud as a remedy for his nasal swellings and severe migraines. However, Thornton suggests that not only are Freud's various ailments explicable in terms of the effects of cocaine, but also his 'messianic obsession with sexuality'. She ponders on how 'this mélange of ignorance, obsolete medicine and the products of a drugged brain' – psychoanalysis – ever became accepted as a revolutionary new science (1983: 13–14).

In attempting to understand neurosis and dreams, and in his own self-analysis, Freud came to the conclusion that many of the unconscious wishes revealed in analysis had their locus in past experiences or fantasies of a sexual nature. As Freud wrote: he learned from his increasing experience as a doctor that the phenomena of neurosis – whether hysteria or neurasthenia – were inevitably associated with actions of a sexual nature 'whether it was a current sexual conflict or the effect of earlier sexual experiences' (1986: 207). Traumatic experiences from early sexual life thus were 'at the root of the formation' of every neurotic symptom (140). In earlier writings he stressed that neuroses were the result of a sexual assault or seduction in infancy. But later he came to reflect that these sexual traumas were often fictitious and that the patients 'create such scenes in fantasy and this psychical reality requires to be taken into account alongside practical reality' (1986: 75). Although Masson, in his study *The Assault on Truth* (1984), is strongly critical of Freud for having abandoned the 'seduction theory' and for 'suppressing' the reality of severe sexual traumas inflicted on immature girls, in stressing the importance of fantasy Freud never in fact denied the reality of sexual abuse. As he expressed it in one of his lectures given twenty years after his paper on *The Aetiology of Hysteria* (1896): 'Do not suppose however, that sexual misuse of children by the nearest male relatives is entirely derived from the world of phantasy; most analysts will have treated cases in which such occurrences actually took place and could be established beyond doubt' (1953: 379).

In 1904 Freud published *The Psychopathology of Everyday Life*, applying his theory of unconscious motivation to such normal everyday phenomena as 'slips' of the tongue and the inability to recall names. He argued that such phenomena are not accidental, nor are they related to physiological factors, but rather they have a meaning and can be interpreted with reference to repressed or restrained impulses. Two years later an important event in the history of psychoanalysis occurred, for he made contact with Eugen Bleuler and his assistant Carl Jung, psychiatrists at the renowned Burghölzli mental hospital in Zurich. Both men had taken an interest in Freud's psychoanalytic theories. In 1908 the first international meeting of psychoanalysts was held in Salzburg, and the following year Freud, with Jung, was invited by the well-known child psychologist, G. Stanley Hall, to give a series of lectures at Clark University in Worcester, Massachusetts. That event signified the end of Freud's feeling of 'isolation' and established him as a psychologist with an international reputation. The psychoanalytic movement grew in membership and beyond the small clique of Jewish intellectuals with whom Freud was initially associated in Vienna. The period 1911–13 saw 'two secessionist movements' spring up from within the psychoanalytic tradition, movements associated with the names of Alfred Adler and Carl Jung. Their differences with Freud were both intellectual and personal, and both scholars came to focus their differences on a rejection of Freud's stress on the importance of sexuality in human life. Adler came to establish his own 'Individual Psychology' with its stress on the ego and on the Nietzschean 'will to power', while Jung spiritualised the libido and established his own school of 'Analytic Psychology'. Freud gave his own account of these two 'opposition movements' in his history of the Psychoanalytic Movement (1914, 1986: 108–28; for further accounts of the two movements, see J. A. C. Brown 1961; Roazen 1976).

Freud never conceived of psychoanalysis as simply a form of therapy, and even as a therapy he clearly felt that it had a limited application and was of little use in treating war neuroses and severe psychotic illnesses. But rather Freud, as Bettleheim stressed, saw psychoanalysis as a 'depth psychology' which would throw important light on all aspects of human existence, not only dreams or the psychology of jokes or errors, but of religion and other aspects of social life. It deserves a 'better fate', Freud suggests, than merely being seen as one form of therapy available to the psychiatric profession. Psychoanalysis, he writes, 'as a "depth psychology", a theory of the mental unconscious, can become indispensable to all the sciences which are concerned with the evolution of human civilisation and its major institutions such as art, religion, and the social order' (1986: 351). In his later years he wrote some important studies on religion and human culture – *Totem and Taboo* (1912–13), *The Future of an Illusion* (1927) and *Civilisation and its Discontents* (1930). As I have discussed these writings fully in an earlier study, little needs to be added here; the reader is referred to this discussion (1987: 155–63).

In his last years Freud suffered from cancer and underwent a series of operations. When the Nazis seized power in Germany his books were publicly burned, and in 1938 when Hitler invaded Austria, Freud was forced to leave the country. He settled in London with his daughter Anna, where he died the following year, shortly after the declaration of war. (Useful biographies of Freud are E. Jones 1964; Robert 1966; Roazen 1976; R. W. Clark 1980.)

2.4 Libido and the Unconscious

Freud's 'depth psychology' and his understanding of the human mind focused on two interrelated concepts – the unconscious and the libido. Around these two ideas an intricate and complex structure of related concepts were suggested, defined and even modified by Freud as his ideas and theories developed over the years. Always self-critical and never hesitating to revise his concepts and theories, and, like Marx, essentially a dialectical thinker, Freud is a difficult theorist to understand fully, although his prose is lucid and engaging. Psychoanalytic theory is therefore difficult to summarise, and is subject to diverse and conflicting interpretations. But one can only agree with Comfort that the best summary of Freud's work are his own lectures; for no subsequent exposition of his ideas are 'livelier or more intelligible' (1964: 35).

Freud's psychology was quite different from that of Wundt. Although Wundt, like Freud, was concerned to establish psychology as a discipline independent from physiology, Wundt (in common with contemporary psychologists and anthropologists) put an essential focus on consciousness. He was interested in those psychological functions – sensation, perception, learning, thinking, memory – which for Freud were basically ego functions, related to the individual's adaption to reality. But for Freud this was not the primary process, for in contrast he put the emphasis not on consciousness but on unconsciousness, on affectivity, on sexuality and on the role of fantasy. A fundamental postulate for Freud, then, was that mental processes are essentially unconscious. The mind or psyche could not, he felt, be equated with consciousness. Moreover, he did not perceive the unconscious as a descriptive notion, depicting simply those ideas or motivations of which we are unaware, but rather as a dynamic conception, consisting of those impulses and instinctive strivings which supply the motive power for psychological experience. He admitted that the unconscious mind was not a new idea; it was evident from studies of hypnosis, and such philosophers as James and Schopenhauer had also employed the term, but Freud aimed to give the concept a new significance.

In ordinary experience and knowledge, Freud suggests, we normally recognise a mental agency that mediates, as it were, between sensory stimuli and perception of our bodily needs on the one hand, and our motor activities on the other. We call this agency *Ich* (I or me). But this, Freud felt, did not exhaust the description of our mental apparatus – the 'structure of our soul' or psyche, as Freud described it. There is another mental region, unconscious, dynamic, obscure; this Freud referred to as the *es* (it), following Nietzsche. You may complain that I have chosen to use simple pronouns to describe these two regions of the mind, instead of giving them 'orotund Greek words', Freud writes (1986: 295), but there is a need, he responds, to keep contact with the popular mode of thinking. So ironically translators of his work have tended to mistranslate Freud and have used the misleading Greek concepts the ego and the id. These terms have become so widely used in discussion of Freud's ideas that at this late date it is difficult to avoid them. The relation between the ego and the id was Freud's immediate concern, and this relation could only be conveyed, he suggests, by the use of analogies. He thus speaks of the ego as an external cortical layer of the id, a frontage or protective layer that lies between reality and the id; or the relation of the ego to the id is like a man on horseback, who has to hold in check the superior strength of the horse – with the difference that the man's strength is derived from the horse (1937: 215); or with a vehicle, the driving force being derived from the id, while the ego does the steering (1986: 301).

With the human subject the forces or impulses which drive the mental apparatus into activity are, Freud stresses, derived from somatic needs. He quotes the poet Schiller in saying that hunger and sex are what moves the world, and refers to these primary impulses as drives. Freud uses the German term *Trieb*, which is more commonly translated as impulse or drive, not as instinct (*Instinkt*), a term he only employs when referring to the inborn instincts of animals (J. A. C. Brown 1961: 10; Bettelheim 1983: 104). The ego is associated with consciousness, and with synthesis, and with the self-preservation of the organism. During the early years of life the ego is weak, and little differentiated from the id.

Thus Freud comes to recognise two 'instincts'; those for self-preservation, the ego instincts, and the sexual instinct, the dynamic manifestation of which in mental life Freud calls libido. The libido or sexual energy Freud conceptualised rather broadly and 'included under it all the urges, which, like the genital impulses, are physically conditioned, attached to certain erogenous zones of the body, and seek for pleasurable tension release' (Fromm 1970: 151). The urge to discharge or reduce instinctual tensions derived from the libido, thus giving pleasure to the organism, Freud called the pleasure principle. In a very young child these instinctual drives act automatically. If, however, normal reflex action is not sufficient to discharge tension and frustration built up in the human organism, then, Freud believed, the child will form an image of an object in order to reduce the tensions. This imagery is pure wishful thinking, but such wish-fulfilment, he felt, persisted throughout life and was evident in adult dreams. Freud termed these unconscious substitute satisfactions (exemplified later in neurotic symptoms as well as dreams and fantasies) the primary processes. But adjustment to the social and physical environment also demands that the ego, the largely conscious aspect of the personality, mediates on behalf of the organism. Thus when reflex action and fantasy have both failed, or become inoperative, the ego is said to obey the 'reality principle', and to operate by means of the secondary processes – the thinking and problem-solving that guide the personality. And thus, as Schellenberg puts it, 'the stage is set for the inevitable conflict, essentially unconscious, between pleasure and reality. The forms taken by this conflict are the primary basis of the personality patterns and neurotic symptoms given central attention by psychoanalysis' (1978: 24).

In his later writings, Freud (1920) modified his ideas on the unconscious drives, and subsumed the two earlier instincts, libido and ego, under the concept of Eros, the life-maintaining drive, which was set against the death instinct, Thanatos, the latter operating according to the Nirvana principle, the notion that all living processes tend to return to the inertia of the inorganic world.

Freud (1923) also introduced a structural theory of the personality with the tripartite division of id, ego and super ego; the latter being a differentiation of the ego reflecting an individual conscience or ego ideal: 'It is the internal representative of the traditional values and ideals of society as interpreted to the child by his parents' (Hall and Lindzey 1957: 35). Thus Freud's conception of the human personality incorporates a biological (id), psychological (ego) and social (super ego) dimension. Together they constitute the 'structure of the soul (*Seele*)'.

Also important in psychoanalytical thought are the various kinds of ego defence mechanisms, which Freud suggested in his writings. Serving to protect the ego from pain and anxiety, the most important of these were: repression (keeping painful experiences from becoming conscious), sublimation (directing an unacceptable impulse towards a socially acceptable goal), regression (the return to an earlier stage of libidinal satisfaction) and projection (attributing the source of the anxiety to some external person or object). His daughter Anna developed these ideas after Freud's death in an influential book (A. Freud 1936).

Neurosis for Freud was essentially the outcome of a conflict between the ego and the id, when the weak ego was unable to handle instinctual impulses of a sexual nature. It – the ego – therefore repressed those sexual impulses that seemed incompatible with its integrity or with its ethical standards. The impulses, not finding expression in consciousness, become converted, for the 'damned-upon libido' expresses itself in neurotic symptoms. Consequently, the symptoms are in the nature of a compromise between repressed sexual impulses and the ego instincts. Psychoanalytic therapy is essentially an attempt to make these repressed impulses conscious (1986: 144). Freud recognised that the same psychological mechanism may have a varied and complex aetiology, that organic factors are important in many nervous diseases, and that actual neuroses are beyond the scope of psychotherapy. In his later discussions of narcissism he explored the situation where the subject's libido becomes focused on his or her own ego rather than on other people – self-preservation leads to the withdrawal of the libido from objects, thus giving rise to such disorders as melancholia, paranoia and schizophrenia, which Freud suggests are beyond analytic therapy (1986: 147).

Central to Freud's libido theory was his notion of infantile sexuality, and his theory of libidinal development. For Freud (1905) sex did not suddenly spring forth at puberty; children from their earliest years were sexual. And he suggested that at different ages a child's sexual pleasures are linked to specific erogenous zones of the body. In the initial oral phase, the child's mouth is the primary organ of pleasure, sucking and biting being two important modes of oral activity. This phase is succeeded by the anal phase, when the child will begin to experience pleasure in the anal zone with its two modes of functioning, the retention and expulsion of the faeces. As there are often tensions built up during this phase, with regard to the method of toilet training used by the mother, it was thought that certain character traits of the adult personality have their roots in these early periods of development. Around the age of four the phallic phase begins, and the child's interest becomes focused, according to Freud, not on the genitals as such, but on the penis. Autoerotic pleasures and various phantasies focused on such activity set the stage for the familiar Oedipus complex, so-called from the Greek legend (by Sophocles) about King Oedipus who, unwittingly (and deliberately trying to avoid the fate prophesised by an oracle), killed his father and married his mother, and thereby brought the plague to Thebes. Hall and Lindzey define it cogently:

> The Oedipus complex consists of a sexual cathexis for the parent of the opposite sex and a hostile cathexis for the parent of the same sex. The boy wants to possess his mother and remove his father, the girl wants to possess her father and displace her mother. These feelings express themselves in the child's fantasies during masturbation and in the alternation of loving and rebellious action towards his parents. The behaviour of the three to five year old child is marked to a large extent by the operation of the Oedipus complex, and although it is modified and suffers repression after the age of five, it remains a vital force in the personality throughout life. Attitudes toward the opposite sex and toward people in authority, for instance, are largely conditioned by the Oedipus complex. (1957: 53)

And, it may be added, its resolution is of great importance in the psychoanalytic explanation of neurosis.

According to Freud, during the Oedipus period, a boy becomes afraid that his father will castrate him and this castration anxiety induces the repression of his sexual desire, while the girl is supposed to develop penis envy and, after becoming attached to her father, eventually has to renounce the 'wish to be a man'. There follows, a period of sexual latency, lasting until the child is about twelve years of age, when the genital stage is reached. From the onset of puberty, Freud suggests, the great task of the individual is 'freeing himself from the parents' (1953: 345).

That the early years of life are crucial for the development of the personality, as well as for the understanding of neurosis, has generally been accepted by later psychologists and psycho-therapists. Indeed child-rearing practices become a central focus, as we shall see, in the studies of the 'culture and personality' theorists. But no aspect of Freud's theory has been subject to more strident criticisms than his theory of human sexuality. Feminists in particular (Figes 1970; Millett 1971: 179–203) have seen Freudian theory as an ideological system, a form of brainwashing that has served to uphold patriarchial attitudes and sexual inequalities. The concept of penis envy, and the notion that vaginal orgasm has priority over clitoral stimulation, has, in particular, come in for a good deal of criticism. Although some feminists have defended Freud's integrity (e.g. Mitchell 1974), there is I think substance in these criticisms, for Freud implicitly accepted the prejudices of his class and period. As Fromm (1970) remarked, he followed the Victorian idea that a woman's desires in maturity 'were almost entirely directed to the bearing and upbringing of children – and to serve the man'. Freud gave clear expression to this when he wrote 'the libido is masculine' (Fromm 1970: 58). But two points are worth making in this context.

The first is that Freud, although something of a puritan in his personal life, generally expressed liberal attitudes in sexual matters, and stressed the need for women to have more freedom to express and explore their sexuality. Although he can hardly be credited with having inaugurated the 'sexual revolution' – this, as Fromm suggests, is probably related to changing patterns of consumption in industrial capitalism and thus has negative implications – Freud was generally progressive in his attitudes, as his views on homo-sexuality reveal (Mitchell 1974: 11; Freud 1930: 51–3).

Secondly, there is an important point stressed by many feminist scholars, namely that Freud assumed that every person is inherently bisexual. Thus Freud advanced a non-essentialist (non-biological) theory of sexuality. The child is seen as 'polymorphously perverse' in seeking all forms of sensual gratification, and Freud insisted that the sexual behaviour of young children of both sexes is indis-tinguishable. Gender identity is something that is socially con-structed not biologically given, and this inevitably complicates the Oedipus complex, for a person's feelings for both parents are essentially ambivalent (Coward 1983: 192).

In his later writings, particularly in his essay *Civilisation and its Discontents* (1930) (a more appropriate translation of which would have been 'The Uneasiness Inherent in Culture' (Bettelheim 1983: 99)), Freud's basic concern was in the promotion of human happiness and well-being. He assumes that there are 'two great powers' reflected in the human condition; that the communal life of mankind is based on a twofold foundation, 'the compulsion to work, which was created by external necessity, and the power of love' (1930: 48). Thus Freud starts from materialist premises, and in his writings implics that patriarchy is at the centre of human life. Engels had also written of history, the production and reproduction of immediate life, as being of a 'two-fold character'. On the one hand, there was the production of the means of subsistence, food and shelter, and on the other, the reproduction of human beings (Marx and Engels 1968: 449). But the crucial difference is that Freud played down the significance of human labour, and like many conservative thinkers, viewed work as a painful necessity, seemingly unrelated to pleasure and creativity. On the other hand, unlike Engels, sex was not tied to procreation. Rather, Freud thought of sexual love, as we have seen, as a kind of energy that was intrinsically linked to the pleasure principle, but which, through deflection, could be put to the service and development of culture. For Freud culture was thus not the product of human praxis as with Marx, but of the renunciation of the libido, of the sublimation of sexual energy. There was, therefore, a fundamental antithesis between culture and sexuality.

Accepting that we are a part of nature and have limited capacity to control our lives, Freud agrees with Schopenhauer that most of our sufferings and unhappiness – war, intercommunal conflict, neurosis – come not from nature but from social relationships. The contention holds, he writes, 'that what we call culture is largely responsible for our misery' (1930: 33). Stressing that the motive force behind human activites is utility (necessary work) and the striving for pleasure, Freud deeply sensed that Eros (sexual life) was the 'prototype of all happiness' and that human beings left to themselves would 'seek the satisfaction of happiness, along the path of sexual relations'. We can imagine, he writes, an ideal cultural community, consisting of loving couples who 'libidinally satisfied in themselves, are connected with one another through the bonds of common work and common interests' (1930: 55). But this kind of community (which resembles what Reich clearly envisaged as a social possibility), Freud suggests, has never existed: the reality is quite different. Love appears to be opposed to civilisation, while civilisation 'threatens love with substantial restrictions'. This antithesis between culture and sexuality has significant consequences.

A dichotomy emerges between the family and sexual life focused on women, and civilisation, which has become increasingly the concern of men. 'Thus the woman finds herself forced into the background by the claims of civilisation.' Freud clearly gave the impression that he did not approve of this state of affairs. Linked with this, sexuality was not only restricted to heterosexual genital love, but such relationships were geared to procreation – to legitimacy and monogamy. Present-day society, he writes, make it plain 'that it does not like sexuality as a source of pleasure in its own right' (1930: 52). And Freud concludes by suggesting that 'the sexual life of civilised man is . . . severely impaired . . . one is probably justified in assuming that its importance as a source of feelings of happiness, and therefore in the fulfilment of our aim in life, has sensibly diminished . . . the life of present day civilised people leaves no room for the simple natural love of two human beings' (1930: 52).

All this amounts to a radical critique of Western culture. Human beings instinctively seek pleasure through sexual love, and this is fundamental to their well-being; but culture represses these natural feelings to the detriment of the individual. Neuroses are the outcome of the ensuing frustrations and Freud even poses the question that specific cultures, or even the whole of mankind, may have become neurotic (1930: 91). Thus a further question may be posed, and Freud himself raises it: namely, whether a 're-ordering of human relations' is possible 'by renouncing coercion and the suppression of the instincts' (1928: 3). But Freud did not think such a communal life was possible, and he offers some critical observations on socialist theory. The abolition of private property and economic inequalities (which Freud is clearly unhappy about) would not make any difference. Private property, he felt, was one of the instruments of aggression, not the cause of it. Every civilisation, he felt, 'must be built upon coercion and renunciation of instinct' (1928: 3), essentially because of the original nature of mankind, and here Freud took a very Hobbesian view, suggesting that human beings by nature were not 'gentle creatures who want to be loved' (1930: 58), but on the contrary, destructive, aggressive, anti-social and anti-cultural. As with other bourgeois thinkers, Freud saw the individual as an isolated, self-sufficient entity, in opposition to culture (cf. Fromm 1970: 47). Evidence of this aggressiveness Freud considered to be apparent in the historical record and the atrocities and horrors committed in the acts of genocide and war (1930: 59). It was in relation to such thoughts that Freud came to revise his instinct theory and to posit aggression as an original, self-subsisting, instinctual disposition in mankind. This aggressive instinct, 'the hostility of each against all and of all against each' (1920: 69) (echoing Hobbes' famous phrase), makes 'civilisation' necessarily coercive and demanding of instinctual renunciation. And thus detrimental to individual happiness. Hence the discontents. The history of mankind becomes, therefore, a continuing struggle between Eros and Thanatos, between the instinct of life and the instinct of destruction, and with the possibility that humans could, Freud notes, and with no difficulty, exterminate 'one another to the last man' (1930: 92) the future can only be uncertain. It is an extremely pessimistic vision.

Marcuse presented the essence of Freud's social theory when he wrote: 'The concept of man that emerges from Freudian theory is the most irrefutable indictment of Western civilisation – and at the same time the most unshakeable defence of this civilisation' (1969: 29). (For an illuminating discussion of the Hobbesian perspective of Freud and his political philosophy, see Rieff 1959: 220–56.)

The achievement of Freud's psychoanalytic theory, Mark Poster writes, 'is to unmask the illusion of individualism, of the self-contained, autonomous nature of personal experience and motivation. As an isolated unit, the individual is unintelligible' (1978: 2). Freud did this by situating the individual within a family context. The family for Freud is 'the secret of the individual'. Unfortunately, given his ardent psycho-Larmarckian tendencies, Freud's social theory took the form of phylogenetic explanations (as in *Totem and Taboo*), and he was thus unable to set his theorising in the wider context of historical and social theory. The human subject for Freud is not a 'closed system' (cf. Greenberg and Mitchell 1983), for not only is the structure of the mind formed within the family nexus, but the Oedipal complex itself is, in a sense, inherent within us. But what Freud fails to do is to situate this nexus within an historical setting, or within a wider social structure. Freud's historical consciousness is focused on the individual not on human culture, and thus he never articulates a truly social psychology. This concern for the individual, as opposed to culture, Rieff attributes to the *Zeitgeist* Freud inherited – one 'thoroughly saturated with Schopenhauer and Nietzsche' (1959: 254). It gave Freud an elitist tendency, and in his essay *Group Psychology and the Analysis of the Ego* (1921), Freud seems to follow the profoundly anti-democratic theorist Gustave Le Bon, author of *The Crowd* (1920), in seeing all group actions, particularly revolutionary action, as being essentially irrational and as giving rise to illusions and destructive instincts (1937: 137; Rieff 1959: 229–30; Poster 1978: 31).

In an important sense, then, Freud tends to take the Western bourgeois family as a universal and necessary institution, and his theory of the psyche had meaning and relevance only if it is read, as Poster suggests, with this perspective in mind. By insisting on the importance of unconscious motivations, Freud, like Nietzsche, undermined any blind trust in consciousness or rational thought. Some writers have implied that Freud, in consequence, was an anti-rationalist. But in spite of his pessimism and his stress on the unconscious, Freud never lost his faith in rational thought, and one can do no better than to conclude this section with an extract from his writings.

We may insist as often as we like that man's intellect is powerless in comparison with his instinctual life, and we may be right in this. Nevertheless, there is something peculiar about this weakness. The voice of the intellect is a soft one, but it does not rest until it has gained a hearing. Finally, after a countless succession of rebuffs, it succeeds. This is one of the few points on which one may be optimistic about the future of mankind. (1928: 49)

Freud always saw himself in the tradition of the Enlightenment thinkers, as a humanistic scientist setting forth to dispel outworn superstitions and to discredit humanity's 'naive self-love'. Bettelheim confirms Freud's essential humanism. In Freud's view, he suggests: 'A good life denies neither its real and often painful difficulties nor the dark aspects of our psyche; rather it is a life in which our hardships are not permitted to engulf us in despair and our dark impulses are not allowed to draw us into their chaotic and often destructive orbit' (1983: 110). (For further important studies of Freud, see Rieff 1959; Wollheim and Hopkins 1982; Erdelyi 1985.)

-3-

The Varieties of Empiricism

In the first two chapters I have, in essence, outlined three lines of philosophical inquiry, three conceptions, as it were, of the human subject.

The first was the rationalist approach, which received its philosophical culmination in the writings of Immanuel Kant, who, as Flügel remarked, still casts a 'gigantic shadow over the whole of philosophy' (1964: 13). Kant insisted on the unity of perception, and on the notion of the self as an active agent which organises experience with the help of the inherent categories of time, space and causality. He stressed too the importance of three major mental faculties, knowing (cognition), feeling (affection) and willing (conation). Although Kant is often seen as a precursor of the functionalist and Gestalt schools of psychology, his influence on psychology was in fact limited, particularly as Kant conceived of the will primarily in ethical terms. And his faculty theory is seen as eventually developing into a sterile cul-de-sac in the first physiological theory of psychology, the phrenology of Franz Joseph Gall (1758–1828). Although it has to be said that the phrenological spirit is still alive in the writings on the modularity thesis of the mind, and on 'modes' of consciousness (Ornstein 1972; Fodor 1983; for brief discussions of phrenology see Flügel 1964: 31–8; Fancher 1979: 44–59; Leahey 1987: 156–8).

The second line of inquiry was discussed in chapter 2, namely the development of Kant's theory of the will into a dynamic psychology. Whereas Kant saw the will as essentially ethical, rational and 'mental', the theories of Schopenhauer, Nietzsche and Freud developed this line of thought along a quite different track, conceiving the will as something impersonal, instinctive, non-rational and dynamic. By a strange turn of fate, Kant's categorical imperative became a biological impulse.

The third conception of the human subject was that advanced by the empiricist philosophers – Hobbes, Locke and Hume – who essentially viewed the mind as a passive mechanism, which through the 'laws of association' responded in a complicated but causally related way to the influence of the environment. Developments in this empiricist tradition are the subject of the present chapter, a tradition that was given a new lease of life in the early years of the nineteenth century with the development of utilitarianism and an empiricist psychology that put a focal emphasis on the association of ideas. The main scholars in this tradition were Bentham, James and John Stuart Mill and Alexander Bain. It is beyond the scope of the present study to cover all the various developments in the empiricist tradition – Spencer's synthetic philosophy, Haeckel's monistic materialism, Galton's psychology, and the logical positivism of Mach, Carnap and A. J. Ayer all being noteworthy. I shall instead focus on four selected themes, all of which in essence derive from Darwin's evolutionary theory.

In the first section I outline Darwinian theory, focusing on the theory of the human subject that emerges in Darwin's later writings. In the following two sections I discuss the behaviourist tradition in psychology, a tradition that tends to see the human subject as a reactive organism and to play down the importance of consciousness and subjective meanings. In these sections I focus respectively on the work of J. B. Watson and B. F. Skinner. In section 3.4 I turn to the empiricist philosophies of Wittgenstein and Ryle, and explore the behaviourist tendencies in their work. The final section is devoted to an outline and critique of the newly-emerged subdiscipline sociobiology, and in this I focus on the writings of E. O. Wilson.

3.1 Darwin and Evolution

Associationist psychology, the phenomenalism of John Stuart Mill and the utilitarian theory of ethics all had their roots, as Copleston suggests, in the eighteenth century. But around the middle of the nineteenth century a new doctrine began to emerge, one that was closely associated with empiricist philosophy, and which was to alter radically the ethos and temper of Western culture and science; this was the theory of evolution. The idea of evolution has a long history. As an idea it goes back at least to Lucretius, while in the eighteenth century Buffon and Lamarck had developed theories in biology that indicated that natural species were not immutable. But the two scholars whose names are indubitably linked with the theory of evolution were both English – Charles Darwin (1809–82) and Herbert Spencer (1820–1903).

Darwin was born in Shrewsbury, the grandson of the eighteenth-century biologist and radical Erasmus Darwin. Quite undistinguished at school, preferring outdoor pursuits like rat-catching to study, he went on to study medicine at Edinburgh University. Finding this uncongenial, Darwin transferred to Cambridge to train for the priesthood. But again he neglected his basic studies, being mainly interested in biology and geology. Fortunately, Darwin was befriended by a Professor of Botany, John Henslow, who encouraged him to join an expedition around the world under the command of Captain Fitzroy of *HMS Beagle*. Darwin's father was none too happy about this, fearing that it would jeopardise Darwin's future career as a clergyman. Ultimately it did, though Darwin never renounced his intention to enter the Church; it merely lapsed with time. Darwin was twenty-three years old when he joined the expedition as its chief naturalist, and the voyage of the *Beagle* was to last five years (1831–6). The voyage he recorded in his autobiography was 'the most important event' in his life, and one that determined his whole career. The voyage took Darwin to South America and the Galapagos Islands, and Antony Flew records that the voyage was a story of travel, observation, speculation and adventure (1984: 6; Moorehead 1969). In 1839 Darwin married his cousin Emma Wedgwood and in that same year was elected as a Fellow of the Royal Society and wrote his 'Journal of Researches', better known under the title *The Voyage of the Beagle*. A year earlier Darwin had read Thomas Malthus's *Essay on the Principle of Population* (1795) and this had a crucial impact on his thought. As he wrote in his autobiography:

> Being well prepared to appreciate the struggle for existence which everywhere goes on from long-continued observation of the habits of animals and plants, it at once struck me (on reading Malthus) that under these circumstances favourable variations would tend to be preserved and unfavourable ones to be destroyed. The result of this would be the formation of new species. Here then I had at last got a theory by which to work. (quoted in Toulmin and Goodfield 1965: 248)

Thus, soon after returning to England, and while still only thirty, Darwin had already formulated the basic ideas of his theory of evolution. In 1842 he moved with his family to Down in Kent, and there he remained as a kind of scholarly recluse for the remainder of his life. He suffered much from headaches and chronic exhaustion, possibly due to a trypanosome infection (a parasitic infection of the blood). In 1844 he drafted what he called 'a sketch of my species theory' and for almost two decades worked steadily, concentrating on geological problems. He published two detailed and important studies, *The Structure and Distribution of Coral Reefs* (1842) and *A Monograph of the Fossil Lepadidae* (1851), the latter work, on fossil barnacles, indicating that the fossil record showed a sequence of evolutionary changes. In 1856 he began work on what was to be a treatise on the 'species problem' but then, two years later, Darwin received a paper written by Alfred Wallace, who was a young botanist living in the Moluccas, and who had also been stimulated by reading Malthus. Wallace's paper essentially outlined Darwin's theory of natural selection. It came, Darwin wrote, like a 'bolt from the blue' and he was shattered. Darwin consulted his friends Charles Lyell the geologist and the botanist J. D. Hooker as to what he should do. They suggested that a joint paper should be presented to the next meeting of the Linnaean Society in London. This was done, neither Darwin or Wallace being present. The paper passed virtually unnoticed. In the following year, 1859, Darwin, having quickly written up the material he had been gathering over two decades, published his work *On the Origin of Species by Means of Natural Selection* (its sub-title reads *The Preservation of Favoured Races in the Struggle for Life.*) The first edition sold out on the day of publication. It was soon reprinted and translated into many languages, and has since become a classic. Its importance as a scientific work cannot be overestimated, and like Newton's *Principia* it has revolutionised human thought, even though its basic tenets were not in fact original. The general theory of evolution and the mutability of species was already widely accepted, and had been expressed not only by Lamarck, but in the writings of Spencer and in Lyell's *Principles of Geology* (1830–3). What made Darwin's work so significant is that it both presented a wealth of detail relating to many years of experience in geology, botany and zoology, and provided a viable mechanism to explain biological evolution. As Wilma George writes: 'It was to the biological sciences what the Copernican revolution was to the cosmological sciences: a working hypothesis stimulating experiment and observation, a hypothesis whose repercussions were felt throughout society because the world would never look the same again' (1982: 17).

In the remaining years of his life, Darwin wrote several more important texts, though his interests shifted away from geology and more towards botany. With respect to the present study, of particular relevance are *The Descent of Man* (1871) and *The Expression of the Emotions in Man and Animals* (1872). In 1881, the year before his death, Darwin published a book on a topic that had fascinated him for over some forty years, one of his 'hobby horses'. The book is titled *The Formation of Vegetable Mould through the Action of Worms, with Observations on their Habits*. It typifies Darwin's unique strength: the careful observation of an amateur naturalist. 'The picture of the natural world we all take for granted today', write Toulmin and Goodfield, 'has one remarkable feature, which cannot be ignored in any study of the ancestry of science: it is a historical picture' (1965: 17).

Thus, as Hegel was to do in the realm of philosophy, Darwin put forward a view of reality that conceived the world not as a mechanism but as a kind of historical process. Mary Midgley has described Darwin's theory of evolution as 'the creation myth of our age', a kind of cosmic mythology that gives meaning and structure to the modern scientific world-view (1985: 30). Tim Ingold (1986: 1–28), in an important study, has also stressed the historical nature of Darwin's theory, a non-teleological theory based on natural selection, and its distinction from the evolutionary theories of Lamarck, Spencer and Tylor.

Darwin's theory can perhaps best be expressed in his own words:

As many more individuals of each species are born than can possibly survive: and as, consequently, there is a frequently recurring struggle for existence, it follows that any being, if it vary however slightly, in any manner profitable to itself, under the complex and sometimes varying conditions of life, will have a better chance of surviving, and thus be *naturally selected*. (1859: 68)

He goes on explicitly to state that 'this is the doctrine of Malthus applied with manifold force to the whole animal and vegetable kingdom' (117). The theory thus has three aspects: variation – that members of a species vary among themselves and those that survive are adapted to their surroundings; the struggle for existence – consequent on the fact that animals and plants produce more offspring than can possibly survive; and natural selection – those organisms that survive have traits conducive to survival. Darwin developed his hypothesis by analogy with the artificial breeding of domestic animals by humans. Through this process animal and plant species develop. It is important to note that although the theory is termed evolution through natural selection, no selective agent or process is evident, it is rather a process of 'natural preservation' (Flew 1984: 25). As Ingold and others have stressed, there is no plan or progress in Darwin's conception of evolution, for it suggests a phylogenetic rather than an orthogenetic process, a process of ever-increasing diversity. It is a 'history without progress' and denies that there is any divine creation or divine purpose in the universe. It also had the disturbing implication that humans were not unique, but were 'descended' from animal life. It is hardly surprising that his book aroused widespread controversy and was hotly disputed by Christian theologians.

In the *Origin of Species* Darwin has little to say on the human species, except to hint that sexual selection may perhaps be important in human evolution, and to recognise that his study may throw some light 'on the origin of man and his history'. In *The Descent of Man* he specifically turned his attention to the human subject even though almost half the book deals with sexual selection among animals. As George put it: 'Darwin filled his pages with colour and song – from the song of the linnet to the feathers of the Argus pheasant' (1982: 70). It is also important to note that prior to the publication of *The Descent of Man*, several of his friends had published works offering an evolutionary perspective on the human species – Huxley's *Man's Place in Nature* and Lyell's *The Antiquity of Man* were both published in 1863, and in the following year Wallace wrote an article in the *Anthropological Review* suggesting that natural selection could account for the evolution of humans. But what is remarkable about Darwin's book on the 'descent of man' is that it eschews the theory of natural selection, and the theory of the book and its argument are, as many writers have suggested, essentially Lamarckian. It represents, as Ingold writes, an 'about turn' in his approach, 'from a relativistic view of nature to a firm belief in man's rise towards moral and intellectual enlightenment' (1986: 48).

In *The Descent of Man* Darwin argued that humans were descended from ape-like ancestors and came to the conclusion that

the difference in mind between man and the higher animals, great as it is, is certainly one of degree and not of kind. We have seen that the senses and intuitions, the various emotions and faculties such as love, memory, attention, curiosity, imitation, reason etc., of which man boasts may be found in an incipient, or even sometimes in a well-developed condition in lower animals.

What he felt had led humans to become 'the most dominant animal' on earth was the superiority of human intellectual faculties, particularly the habitual use of articulate language, their social habits which expressed themselves in instinctive love and sympathy for other humans, and the corporeal structure of humans. In the remote epoch before the human species became fully human, we would, he writes 'have been guided more by instinct and less by reason than are the lowest savages at the present time' (Alland 1985: 143).

Although Darwin concluded that 'man is derived from some lower animal form' and argued that the several races of mankind have a 'specific unity', that is, belong to a single species, he nevertheless tended, like his contemporaries Spencer and Tylor, to see pre-literate societies as lower stages in social evolution. Accepting that there was a close relationship between brain size and the development of intellectual faculties, Darwin even suggested that this was 'supported by the comparison of skulls of savage and civilised races' but then had to admit that the skull of the Neanderthal man (discovered near Düsseldorf in 1857) was well developed and capacious. Darwin had difficulty in applying natural selection theory to the human species, for it was evident that many of the more important aspects of 'civilised nations' – the sympathy and aid given to the sick and helpless, which he thought expressed the social instincts – seemed to counter the natural 'process of elimination'. But he nevertheless thought that the 'wonderful' progress of the United States was due to natural selection.

However, to explain the racial differences of mankind, Darwin adopted a very different strategy, one that he had briefly discussed in the *Origin of Species*, namely sexual selection. Aware that there was no evident correlation between races and environmental conditions – the disjuncture between environment and the kinds of species found in the Americas and the Old World had earlier prompted his thoughts on evolution – Darwin came to postulate that the major influence on the evolution of humans was sexual selection, not natural selection:

> The strongest and most vigorous men – those who could best defend and hunt for their families, who were provided with the best weapons and possessed the most property – would succeed in rearing a greater average number of offspring than the weaker and poorer members of the same tribe. (Alland 1985: 198)

Such variable human racial traits as skin colour, the texture and colour of hair, and facial features are all seen by Darwin as the result of sexual selection. Linked with this theory was Darwin's stress on the innate differences between men and women. Women, because of their maternal instincts, are seen as tender, unselfish, intuitive, and such inherent characteristics, Darwin suggests, are similar to those of the 'lower races'. Men in contrast are more competitive and more courageous and energetic than women, and have a more inventive genius. They have an intellectual pre-eminence over women, which is innate. His misogyny is not as pronounced as Schopenhauer's and Nietzsche's, but on the subject of women, Alexander Alland Jr (1985: 24) suggests, Darwin is at his worst and a crude biological determinist.

In his introduction to a collection of Darwin's writings on 'human nature', Alland stresses that Darwin shared the prejudices of his age and class, and was writing before the emergence of anthropology as a distinct discipline. Nevertheless, Darwin was a keen observer of the human species and made some shrewd judgements about race and human intelligence. These judgements were, for the most part, ahead of their time. Darwin's attitude and theories, he suggests, were largely tempered by three factors – the exigencies of his own theory of natural selection, his reading of the available literature by his scientific contemporaries, and his own first-hand observations of pre-literate people, particularly those made on the voyage of the Beagle. Alland rightly suggests that while Darwin was an excellent observer, capable of accurate description and analysis – and thus often saw people as they were rather than accepted stereotypes – he tended to be gullible in his uncritical acceptance of the data and theories of his contemporaries. Not surprisingly, Darwin's views on the human subject are often inconsistent and contradictory. Following a distinctly Lamarckian orientation – he speaks of the short-sightedness of watchmakers as being inherited – and accepting a modified form of social Darwinism, Darwin looked upon pre-literate cultures as representing an early stage of the social evolution of the human species. Throughout the study he uses contemporary pre-literate peoples as examples of biologically intermediate forms of the human species. Thus although Darwin held enlightened liberal views on slavery and deplored the maltreatment of Indians and slaves, his writings often carry a decidedly racist tone, and towards the Fuegian hunter-gatherers he expresses little but contempt. He could not understand their egalitarian society, their lack of property and fixed abode, and their nomadic, foraging economy. As with the more enlightened men of his period, Darwin never seems to have doubted the innate superiority of his own culture.

With respect to his views on the human subject, Darwin's

writings suggest several important themes which are of interest.

First, in comparing the different races of humankind – the differences between, for example, the Maoris, Tahitians and the Fuegians – Darwin seems to be insisting on a distinction between race and culture. As Gruber suggests: 'Darwin consistently took these differences to be the products of history, culture, education and habitat rather than a reflection of a fixed inheritance of psychological traits' (1974: 184). Darwin in fact seems to be suggesting several different ideas at once – that humankind has a species-unity and that the mental faculties of all races are similar; that racial differences are due to the evolution of culture, those more 'civilised' having property, agriculture and chiefs; that there is an essential continuity between humans and animals and the difference is only one of degree; and finally, that all humans have evolved from a single progenitor and that the racial differences now evident are due to sexual selection.

Secondly, in suggesting an evolutionary perspective with regard to psychology, this did not imply a disregard for consciousness – quite the opposite. For Darwin was concerned to show that animals, particularly the higher mammals, have the rudiments of consciousness. The evolution of consciousness was an important theme in Darwin's writings. As Gruber has cogently put it: 'Darwin had studied animal behaviour largely to elucidate the origins of human mental processes and was completely unabashed in his search for primordial signs of higher mental processes in lower animals and in his use of a vocabulary based both on human introspection and on behaviour description' (1974: 235).

The reductionist tendencies of Lloyd Morgan, J. B. Watson and Skinner, who in their behaviourist approach expunged all reference to inner experience from scientific psychology, represent, Gruber suggests, a complete distortion of Darwin's achievement: 'Rather than considering mental processes as part of natural science, the behaviourists have lost sight of Darwin's evolutionary aim and eliminated mind from psychology' (ibid.: 235). He implies that both psychoanalysis and Gestalt psychology are much closer to the Darwinian perspective.

Thirdly, to support both the idea of the specific unity of humankind and the notion that humans are 'derived' from some lower animal form, Darwin made a detailed study of The Expression of the Emotions in Man and Animals. It was one of the very first cross-cultural studies, and Darwin sent out a questionnaire to missionaries and government officials across the world inquiring about emotional expressions. He also made inquiries about the mentally insane. Though much of the material was anecdotal, Darwin's study was strictly empirical, and he concluded that emotional expressions 'exhibited by man are the same throughout the world'. The study became a classic in psychology and in many ways initiated the nature versus nurture (culture) debate with respect to bodily expression (see Polhemus 1978: 30–112).

Finally, Darwin expressed a thoroughgoing materialism, suggesting that all mental activity was intrinsically connected with the functioning of the brain. His approach, Gruber writes, helped to lay the foundations for the modern view of the brain as the organ in which mental functions are centred. Darwin's views, in fact, were similar to those of his friend and disciple Thomas Henry Huxley (1825–95), who held that 'consciousness is a function of the brain'. Huxley suggested that consciousness was a kind of 'epiphenomenon' which had emerged when matter had developed a special form of organisation. It had no energy of its own (Passmore 1957: 39; Copleston 1966: 106; Gruber 1974: 218).

Darwin's influence on the development of psychology and the social sciences has been profound. Darwin presented an entirely new approach to the human subject, although his psychology is only part of a materialistic evolutionary biology. In their materialism and in their historical outlook there is an essential affinity between Marx, Freud and Darwin, which Flew, given his negative feelings towards both the later writers, tends to ignore (1984: 92–113). Another empiricist, Gellner (1985), is equally myopic in ignoring Darwinian tendencies in the psychoanalytic movement. Comparative psychology and the study of animal behaviour – both as an independent discipline and as an aspect of psychology – owe their inspiration to Darwin, and in stressing the importance of 'adaptation' Darwin encouraged the development of functional psychology in opposition to the structural psychology that stemmed from the associationist tradition. Darwin's approach to the human subject is genetic and developmental, and with his *A Biographical Sketch of an Infant* (published in 1877 but describing the development of his first children and written thirty-seven years earlier), Darwin can with some justification be considered the first child psychologist.

3.7 Behaviourism

Around the end of the nineteenth century academic psychology seems to have focused on three separate theoretical tendencies. The first is the introspective psychology associated with Wilhelm Wundt and his disciple Edward Titchener (1867–1927), an approach that put a central focus on the 'contents' of human consciousness, and advocated introspection as its principal experimental method. It is often referred to by early writers as 'structuralism' or 'existentialism' (Woodworth 1931) – although this approach to psychology has little in common with the recent movements that go under the same names. Wundt has often been viewed, particularly by his early followers Titchener and Boring, as following in the empiricist tradition of Locke and J. S. Mill, but recent scholarship has shown that this is a serious misunderstanding of Wundt's conception of psychology. In his voluntarism and in his stress on the synthetic activity of the mind, Wundt stood not in the empiricist camp, but in the tradition of Leibniz and Kant. Consequently, we shall discuss Wundt in the following chapter, along with the neo-Kantians.

The second tendency is particularly associated with the writings of Dewey and William James. Through the influence of Darwin and Spencer, a form of empiricist psychology developed towards the end of the century which, while still keeping a focus on human consciousness, conceived of the mind in functional terms. Pragmatic philosophy and functional psychology, which are intimately linked, represent this tendency. This tendency too, will be dealt with in a later chapter.

Finally, the influence of Spencer's psychology of adaptation, as well as of Comte's positivism, was instrumental in the early decades of the century in providing the impetus for the development of behaviourism. Both the signal call and the manifesto of this new psychological approach was provided by John B. Watson (1878–1958), who in 1913 published his classic paper 'Psychology as the Behaviourist Views it'. Although Watson is often seen as the founder of this new movement in psychology, which became the dominant tendency in American psychology during the interwar years, behaviourism in essence crystallised three important developments within psychology. It may be useful to mention these briefly before discussing Watson's own brand of psychology.

The first development took the form of a protest – a protest against the limitations of the classical method of introspection and against the notion that psychology was the study of consciousness. Although the development of the biological sciences during the nineteenth century involved something of a struggle between the physicalist and developmental conceptions of science, the general tendency was towards a more materialistic outlook on the world, as the writings of Spencer and Haeckel indicated: 'Helmholtz's disgust with the "philosophy of nature" was typical of the general nineteenth-century movement of the exact sciences away from dualisms of every type, and in support of a conception of life which placed it squarely within the orbit of ordinary natural – that is, physical – law, and of mind within the scope of the law of life' (Murphy and Kovach 1972: 237–8). The promise of the mechanical materialism of La Mettrie and Hobbes, of a 'psychology without a soul', seemed a distinct possibility.

The second development within psychology which is of importance is that of animal psychology – and as the method of introspection could not be applied to animals, behavioural observations became the dominant research technique. It also involved the development of elaborate experimental strategies – the maze, the puzzle box – in order to study the processes of animal learning. Two American scholars were of importance in these new experimental researches into animal psychology, Edward L. Thorndike (1874–1949) and Robert Yerkes (1876–1956). But what is of interest about these students of animal psychology is the shift of emphasis that they initiated, a shift away from Darwinian psychology. For one, the locus of the research was shifted away from natural history, from the observations of animals in their natural habitats towards the observation of animals in controlled laboratory conditions. Secondly, whereas biologists like Haeckel had been concerned to emphasise the unity between animals and humans by stressing the social and conscious aspects of animal life, these new researchers began to explore the possibility of a more purely mechanical explanation of animal behaviour. Thorndike called his own theory 'connexionism', but unlike the early empiricists the associations were not mental but behavioural, a 'bond between the situation and the impulse'. Animals, he argued, did not reason, but learned solely by trial and error, reward and punishment. Thus the elimination of consciousness and reasoning from the psychology of humans simply followed on from its elimination from the study of 'animal psychology'.

The third important development, and one of crucial significance in the development of behaviourism, is associated with the researches of two pioneer Russian physiologists, Ivan P. Pavlov (1849–1936) and Vladimir M. Bechterev (1857–1927). Pavlov was a specialist in the physiology of digestion, research on which won him the Nobel Prize in 1904. As is well known, Pavlov discovered that the dogs used in his experiments would salivate not only when given food but also when presented with a stimulus – like the sight of the keeper or the ringing of a bell – that was associated with food. This led Pavlov to develop the concept of the 'conditioned reflex' and to adapt an approach to the study of animals that was uncompromisingly materialistic and objective. He rejected any appeal to an active, inner agency or mind, favouring the detailed analysis of environmental conditions. Apparently, he formally banned all psychological terminology from his laboratory, threatening to fire anyone who used subjective terms, and to the end of his life maintained that he was not a psychologist, but a physiologist studying the brain. His analysis of thought processes was entirely atomistic and reflexive. 'The entire mechanism of thinking', he wrote, 'consists in the elaboration of elementary associations and in the subsequent formation of chains of associations.' Like Thorndike, Pavlov followed the associationist tradition of the empiricists, but replaced the association of ideas with a reflexology that studied the relationship between a stimulus and a response. The conditioned reflex was gradually to become one of the principal methods and working concepts of behaviourism (Flügel 1964: 217–19; Fancher 1979: 295–308; Leahey, 1987: 284–5).

The great populariser of reflexology in Russia was Pavlov's rival, Vladimir Bechterev. It was Bechterev who first coined the term. A specialist in brain physiology and on nervous and mental disorders, Bechterev's studies, like Pavlov's, led him to the conception of what he called 'associated reflexes'. His book *Objective Psychology* (1907) is regarded by Flügel as the first systematic exposition of behaviourism (1964: 217).

All these three tendencies – the rejection of introspective psychology, the developments in animal studies and reflexology – found their expression in Watson's theory of behaviourism, which was announced to the world with a certain flamboyance in 1913 in an article in the *Psychological Review*, and in the following year developed in his book *Behaviour: An introduction to comparative psychology*.

John B. Watson was born in South Carolina and reared in a highly religious fundamentalist household. He studied at Chicago under Angel and Dewey (he admitted in his autobiography that he never understood what Dewey was talking about). Working as a laboratory assistant, Watson wrote his doctorate thesis on the *The Psychical Development of the White Rat* (1903), and then went on to obtain a professorship in psychology at Johns Hopkin University at the early age of thirty-one. His academic career ended suddenly in 1920, when Watson, then a married man, became emotionally involved with one of his graduate students, Rosalie Rayner, whom he later married. The affair cost Watson his job, and for the remainder of his life Watson worked in advertising, though continuing to write popular accounts of psychology. (For details of Watson's life, see Fancher 1979: 314–22; D. Cohen 1979.)

Watson's programmatic statement was largely concerned with the question of what kind of science psychology ought to be, and in the opening paragraph of his article his essential message is made clear:

> Psychology as the behaviourist views it is a purely objective natural science. Its theoretical goal is the prediction and control of behaviour. Introspection forms no essential part of its methods, nor is the scientific value for its data dependent upon the readiness with which they lend themselves to interpretation in terms of consciousness. The behaviourist in his efforts to get a unitary scheme of animal response, recognizes no dividing line between man and brute. (1913: 158)

Several important points emerge from this statement.

First, Watson rejected the method of introspection in psychology, arguing that behavioural – observable – data should be used as data. He felt that all psychological functions could be described in terms of responses, since it is these that are involved in the organism's (including humans') adaptation to the environment.

Secondly, and arising from this, Watson disagreed with both the structuralists (Wundt and Titchener) and the functionalists (James) in conceiving of psychology not as the science of consciousness or, as James put it, 'the science of mental life', but as the 'science of behaviour'. The whole idea of consciousness for Watson seemed to involve a dualism of body and mind, and as an avowed mechanical materialist in the tradition of Hobbes, he completely rejected the entire concept of mind or consciousness as a remnant of an earlier religious way of thinking. Wundt and James are put on par with Voodoo doctors and magicians (1924: 2–5).

Thirdly, Watson wished to eliminate the traditional distinction many psychologists had drawn between human beings and animals. But as with the animal psychologists, Watson thought that consciousness was an irrelevant issue in this context; thus he came to see the human subject as essentially an organism, like the rats, pigeons and apes, which also became important aspects of study, responding in terms of physiological or environmental conditions. The term 'objects' is perhaps inappropriate here, for in no sense were humans seen as conscious subjects.

Finally, Watson saw behaviourism not only as a natural science, but also as a practical one: 'Whereas traditional psychologies sought to describe and explain conscious states, Watson's goals were to predict and control overt behaviour' (Fancher 1979: 319). Not surprisingly, Watson came to praise and advocate all forms of applied psychology – psychopathology, educational psychology, mental testing and legal and advertising psychology. In fact, in his later books (1919, 1924) Watson attempted to show not only the practical significance of behaviourism, but how such subjects as language, thought, personality, emotional disorders and child development could all be understood from a behaviourist perspective.

The starting point of Watson's psychology is the suggestion that organisms – humans and animals alike – adapt and adjust themselves to environmental conditions. The focus of the behaviourist psychologist is therefore on behaviour, 'what the organism does or says'. Thinking, for Watson, was largely 'subvocal talking'. Following Pavlov, Watson felt that behaviour can be described and explained in terms of stimulus and response. A stimulus is any physiological change within the organism or any impinging object in the environment; while a response is 'anything the animal (or human) does', anything, that is, from jumping at a sound to writing a book (1924: 6). Both instincts and habits are seen by Watson to arise from reflexes, instincts being inherited sequences while habits are acquired by experience.

Watson also applied Pavlov's theory of 'conditioned reflexes' to the human emotions, and with his wife and colleague also conducted experiments with young children, including a notorious experiment with an eleven-month-old child named Albert. Watson suggested that there were only three innate human emotions, those of fear, rage and love. Fear is invoked by two primary stimuli, hearing a loud and unexpected noise, and the experience of a sudden loss of support; rage is invoked when physical movements by the child are hindered in some way; finally love is invoked by stroking, caressing or gently rocking. Watson felt that all other human emotions were nothing more than conditioned responses based upon these three primary unconditioned emotional reflexes. By associating the presence of a white rat, towards which the young Albert had initially expressed no fear, with a loud and sudden noise, Watson deliberately conditioned the child to fear the animal. Similar conditioned fear responses were produced with other furry animals. These experiments had a propaganda purpose, though one may question the research ethics (Fancher 1979: 326–32).

Although behaviourism made little headway in Europe, this style of psychology appears to have been enthusiastically received in America. A reviewer in the *New York Times* of Watson's *Behaviourism* (1924) described it as marking 'a new epoch in the intellectual history of man'. Another reviewer described it as 'the most important book ever written' (Woodworth 1931: 97). There is a sense in which Watson's writings became a 'myth of origin' for behaviourism, for Watson expressed little that was new; he simply advocated the new style of psychology with a strident voice (Leahey 1987: 306). But it is certain that Watson's popular writings had an enormous influence during the inter-war years – he wrote perhaps the first popular guide to child care. Equally evident is that the inter-war years saw behaviourism emerge as the dominant approach in American psychology, although it was not without its critics. Many considered it as a 'religion to take the place of religion'. But what was significant about Watson's behaviourism is that it represented a radical form of environmentalism in stark contrast to the views expressed by Galton in his *Hereditary Genius*. There is no such thing, he wrote, 'as an inheritance of capacity, talent, temperament, mental constitution and characteristics'. Apart from the three innate emotions, there are also no such things as instincts. What psychologists have called instincts are largely the result, Watson argued, of learned behaviour (1924: 94).

It is beyond the scope of the present study to discuss fully the many developments in behaviourist psychology, though two writers are worth mentioning. One is Edward Tolman (1886–1959) who, while continuing to reject the notion of mind and consciousness, introduced some flexibility with his stress on purposive behaviour and by introducing the notion of a 'cognitive map' which structures an animal's response to the environment. It has been suggested that he is the founding father of cognitive psychology (Murphy and Kovach 1972: 317–19). The other is Clark L. Hull (1884–1952), whose mechanistic behaviourism stressed the importance of intervening variables, such as drives or habits, that mediate between the stimulus and the response. (For useful discussions of behaviourism, see MacKenzie 1977; O'Donnell 1985; Leahey 1987: 301–25.)

3 3 Skinner and Operant Conditioning

Although behaviourism reached its heyday in American in the years before the Second World War, its influence continued in spite of important critiques by phenomenologists and humanistic psychologists (cf. Wann 1964). Through the writings of George C. Homans (1961) and Clyde Kluckhohn, behaviourism also had an important influence on sociology and anthropology. Both in his *Navaho Witchcraft* (1944) and in his classic paper on culture and behaviour (1954), Kluckhohn attempted to unite the perspectives of cultural anthropology, psychoanalysis and behaviourism. In his programmatic statement Kluckhohn argued against single-factor explanations – whether in terms of biological inheritance, environment or culture. Except for reflexes or behaviour under extreme physiological stress, human beings, Kluckhohn suggested, do not behave simply as organisms, nor are they, as some cultural anthropologists implied, purely a microcosm or a receptacle of cultural patterns. But given his behaviouristic tendencies, Kluckhohn saw the individual subject as only an 'emergent entity' and a 'locus' of behaviour within an abstract triad consisting of biological, cultural and environmental factors.

But in the period after the Second World War, behaviourism was given a new lease of life in the writings of Burrhus Frederick Skinner, an enigmatic figure whose radical behaviourism, if accepted, is said to constitute 'a momentous understanding of the human self' (Leahey 1987: 379). He has indeed been compared with Darwin, and his theory of operant conditioning, it has been suggested, presents us with a 'Copernican revolution' in our way of thinking (Wheeler 1973: 5) – although it is often forgotten that monistic materialism, a theory implying an all-embracing determinism, had been suggested by many earlier scholars, as different as Hobbes, Spinoza and Haeckel. Skinner was by no means the first person to deny humans 'free will'.

Skinner was born in Pennsylvania in 1904 and at college studied primarily philosophy and English literature. He had early hopes of becoming a professional writer, but gave this idea up and returned to university, becoming a graduate student in psychology at Harvard. After working at Minnesota and Indiana for some twenty years, he returned to Harvard in 1948, as professor of psychology, and has remained there ever since, building up a reputation as one of the most important psychologists of the present century. His interest in behaviourism was apparently stimulated by reading one of Bertrand Russell's books on philosophy, which included a critique of Watson's behaviourism.

It may be useful to summarise some of the basic tenets of Skinner's form of behaviourism.

First, Skinner adopted the kind of scientific attitude advocated by the logical positivists and by the philosopher P. W. Bridgman (1927) in his theory of 'operationalism', which suggested that all scientific concepts are definable in terms of the set of operations and experiments by which they are apprehended. Skinner's first paper on psychology was in fact the application of Mach's radical positivism to the concept of the reflex. The essence of this positivistic attitude was to stress the importance of physically observable phenomena, and the criteria of public verification of theories:

> Rudolf Carnap and the Vienna Circle of positivists originally propagated strongly the thesis of 'physicalism', according to which all theory (if clarity and freedom from metaphysical 'obscurantism' were to be gained) had ultimately to rest in physical observables. This thesis is the complete theoretical equivalent, in the physical sciences, of behaviourism. (Wilkinson 1973: 154; cf. Malcolm 1964).

This positivist programme Skinner consciously adopted, stressing the importance of variables that are observable, and suggesting an analysis based on verifiable causal explanations (1953: 3–42).

Secondly, and stemming from this, Skinner rejected all psychological explanations that made reference to what he termed 'psychic inner causes'. He was particularly critical of psychoanalysis and Cartesian dualism, both of which implied that the human mind was both 'free' and a causal agent. Skinner did not doubt the reality of inner thoughts, perceptions and feelings, rather he refused to accept that these had any explanatory significance in the understanding of human behaviour. Skinner thus follows Watson in adopting a position of radical behaviourism. Skinner applauds Freud's deterministic theory in linking human behaviour to unconscious causes, but felt that there was no need at all to posit a mental apparatus – id, ego and super ego – as an intervening link between environmental and behavioural events, between the trauma and the hysterical condition. The Cartesian conception of the 'rational soul', or mind, Skinner suggests are 'explanatory fictions', which have no function in psychological science. Descartes' problem of relating human consciousness to a mechanistic universe is completely collapsed, for the human subject is conceptualised by Skinner, as with Hobbes, as a machine-like organism, which can thus be appropriately studied by a 'science of behaviour' Since Descartes' time 'machines have become more life-like and living organisms have been found to be more like machines' (Skinner 1953: 46). For Skinner therefore the human subject or self is simply a 'mode of action', a 'functionally unified system of responses' (1953: 285).

Thirdly, adopting a materialist philosophical position, Skinner resists the temptation to reduce or identify psychology with neuro-physiology. Skinner appears to advocate a functionalist approach, and to conceive of psychology – as the 'science of behaviour' – as methodologically autonomous from the physical and biological sciences. Skinner thus conceives of psychological explanations neither in terms of inner mental states, nor in terms of neuro-physiology, but rather in terms of environmental conditions. As he writes: 'The objection to inner states is not that they do not exist, but that they are not relevant in a functional analysis. We cannot account for the behaviour of any system while staying wholly inside it: eventually we must turn to forces operating upon the organism from without' (1953: 35).

Behaviour, for Skinner, is the 'function' of independent causal variables that are environmental. Like Watson, Skinner is thus an extreme environmentalist (Flanagan 1984: 85–93; Churchland 1984: 36–8).

Although Skinner has been described as operating in terms of a strict stimulus–response model (R. Thompson 1968: 233), this is not strictly true, for Skinner's theory of operant conditioning is both distinct from, and a development of, the classical conditioning theories of Pavlov and Watson. In his first book *The Behaviour of Organisms* (1938), which was largely based on his laboratory experi-ments with rats and pigeons, Skinner made a distinction between two fundamentally different forms of behavioural response. The first he referred to as respondent conditioning, response behaviour being seen as a function of antecedent stimulus events. This corre-sponds to Pavlov's conditioned reflex. Secondly, Skinner spoke of operant conditioning, behaviours (responses) that are in a sense mediated by the central nervous system. While 'stimulus–response leads us to concentrate on prior conditions; operant conditioning leads us to concentrate on what happens after behaviour occurs' (Wheeler 1973: 9). Crucial to this second perspective are those environmental contingencies, such as approval or disapproval, within which the behaviour takes place, and which may condition future responses. Skinner suggests that behaviour will tend to be reinforced when the stimulus has the likely effect of increasing the probability that a response will recur in the future. Any increase in the rate of reinforced behaviour is called operant conditioning, and the stimulus a 'positive reinforcer'. Negative reinforcement, like punishment, has a quite different effect. Skinner thus denied that he was a stimulus–response psychologist; he also felt that he had overcome the problems of the classical conditioning paradigm – namely, how to account for novelty and purpose, both of which are denied in the mechanical model of antecedent causes (Flanagan 1984: 104–12).

Skinner felt that he had formulated a general theory of psychology with his concept of operant conditioning, and he applied these ideas to the acquisition of language in his controversial *Verbal Behaviour* (1957). Arguing that thought itself is simply behaviour, Skinner attempted to show in the study that language could be explained entirely in terms of schedules of reinforcement. The analysis provoked a strident critique from the young Noam Chomsky (1959), who not only criticised Skinner's work, but empiricist ideas in psychology, philosophy and linguistics more generally. Since then Skinner has continued to be a controversial figure, and has been increasingly concerned with the practical applications and philosophical implications of his operant conditioning theory. He was instrumental in the advocacy of teaching machines and programmed learning, and 'behaviour therapy' (a term first coined by Skinner) was developed by many of his followers in the treatment of psychotics and in psychotherapy.

But as with Bentham and other writers in the empiricist tradition, Skinner is more than an academic psychologist; he is a strong advocate of social reform based on his operant conditioning theories. In his best-selling novel *Walden Two* (1948), Skinner had already outlined a social utopia based on behaviourist principles, and more than two decades later he produced a sustained and readable outline of his answer to the problems of the contemporary world – the threat of a nuclear holocaust, world famine, poverty, pollution of the environment, overcrowding of the planet. What is needed, he suggests, is to make radical changes in people's behaviour, and this can be done by a 'technology of behaviour', by instituting a behavioural technology based on his theory of operant conditioning. We can, he writes, 'follow the path taken by physics and biology by turning directly to the relation between behaviour and the environment and neglecting supposed mediating states of mind' (1971: 20). We need to reject the notion of an 'autonomous man', which pervades our current understanding of human life, for such 'mentalistic explanations' are of little help in explaining human behaviour; we must, he argues, go 'beyond freedom and dignity', as the title of the book suggests. Accepting the postulate that all human behaviour is determined by environmental conditions, there is in essence no human 'freedom', and human dignity – the assigning of credit or blame to a human agent responsible for his or her actions – is largely false and irrelevant. A scientific analysis shifts the credit as well as the blame to the environment, Skinner writes (1971: 27). He thus argues that a technology based on the natural sciences alone cannot solve current problems, but only the development of a science and a technology based on behaviour; on studying the interaction between the human organism and the environment and the effects of operant conditioning.

Skinner's study has provoked a good deal of hostile criticism, and the philosopher Max Black has described it as a 'mélange of amateurish metaphysics, self-advertising "technology", and illiberal social policy' – a document that offers us little in our attempts to improve the human condition' (1973: 134). Others have seen it as a crypto-fascist text, and as suggesting the approval of a happy yet highly controlled totalitarian society. But it is well to keep in mind Skinner's radical criticisms of punitive systems of social control, and the fact that his ideals seem to be those of the Enlightenment thinkers – a society that is essentially egalitarian, where governmental power is limited and democratic decision-making procedures upheld, to enable people rationally and creatively to choose their patterns of life (Flanagan 1984: 112). What is at issue, therefore, is his overall behaviourist doctrine and its social implications. Important criticisms of Skinner's theory focus on five issues.

First is the observation that Skinner uses an essentially 'mentalistic' language, which is embedded in ordinary discourse, in order to convey his own ideas. For example, he speaks of individuals being 'induced' by their culture to act in ways conducive to its survival (1971: 177) – a form of words that is inadmissible according to his own behaviourist thesis (Toynbee 1973: 117).

Secondly, Skinner uses concepts in an extremely wide sense, such that they sometimes lose their proper meaning. As the environment is seen by Skinner as 'controlling' us, every force or influence upon us – whether love or a pat on the back – is seen as a form of control. Chomsky also indicated that many of Skinner's key concepts, which have sense and meaning in the laboratory setting – concepts like stimulus and reinforcement – become hopelessly vague when applied in a general manner (Chomsky 1959: Black 1973).

Thirdly, Skinner's approach is narrowly focused on the psychology of organisms – individual organisms – and he sees nothing else. He analyses social institutions in the chapter on 'Social Behavior' in *Science and Human Behaviour* (1953: 297–312), and in his later study (1971), but although he is critical of notions like 'group mind' and 'national character', he tends to view the social essentially in terms of dyadic relationships. Structural forces such as capitalism, and ideational forces such as the Protestant ethic, he singularly ignores. Social problems are therefore seen as individual problems, and human institutions are seen in terms of the behaviour of individuals (Wheeler 1973: 12–14; Schellenberg 1978: 100).

Fourthly, although it may perhaps be important to maintain a distinction between the psychological and neurological approaches to the human subject, these domains are not rigidly demarcated and there is much overlap and interaction between them, as even Descartes was aware. To discount completely genetic-neurological explanations of human behaviour is therefore a limited perspective, and Karl Pribram (1973: 112) has argued that cultures (environments) cannot, in and of themselves, completely specify behaviour. Pribram, in fact, suggests four levels of 'language' or understanding – cultural, mental, behavioural and biological (brain) (ibid.: 109), all of which are relevant in understanding the human person.

Finally, and linked with this, the suggestion that human behaviour is completely determined either by our genetic endowment or by the environmental (social) setting is misleading, for although much of our behaviour is conditioned, certain aspects of our conduct is self-determined. Toynbee (1973) suggests that this self-determining aspect, the striving of every living organism for life and independence, is virtually a synonym for life itself. And he argues that Skinner's analysis presupposes this kind of determination, for passages in the book assume that some participants in a human society design cultural practices, create cultural environments and control the behaviour of other human beings. If humans are wholly determined by their environment, how is it possible for a human being to have a policy? Toynbee asks (1973: 115–16). The problem that Skinner sets himself: 'Who is to construct the controlling environment and to what end?' (1971: 27) – the issue of value – Skinner never adequately answers, and it is difficult to see how he could do this given his postulate of a 'complete determinism' of human behaviour. In responding to his critics, Skinner simply asks us to consider 'the possibility that human behaviour is always controlled', and to 'look instead to the culture' – refusing even to specify values let alone 'who' is to do the controlling. But what comes out of his analysis is a concern for survival – for the individual and the culture – and a plea to design a culture where no person or group can emerge with despotic powers. It is paradoxical that a scholar who values human freedom and democratic principles should conceive of the human subject as essentially machine-like and unfree.

3.4 Wittgenstein and Philosophical Behaviourism

Ludwig Wittgenstein (1889–1951) has been described as a genius and as the greatest philosopher of the twentieth century, although he was significantly ignored in the early popular accounts of philosophy by Joad and Durant. But while undoubtedly an important scholar, he has, I think, been somewhat overrated, and his writings have invoked what can best be described as a cult of adulation. Many studies of Wittgenstein are little more than philosophical eulogies, and contain not a single note of real criticism (e.g. Pears 1971).

Wittgenstein was born in Vienna and was of Jewish descent, although baptised a Catholic. His father was a wealthy industrialist. On the death of his father in 1912, Wittgenstein became a very rich man, but seemingly influenced by Tolstoy's philosophy, he gave all his wealth away to his immediate family. For most of his life he lived a frugal existence and avoided publicity. In 1908 Wittgenstein came to Britain, and became a research student at Manchester University, being especially interested in aeronautics and mathematics. Deciding to give up his studies in engineering, he went to visit Frege at Jena, who advised Wittgenstein to go to Cambridge and study philosophy under Russell. Wittgenstein spent almost two years at Cambridge (1912–13), and greatly impressed his tutors, Russell and Moore, who treated him as their intellectual equal. Serving in the Austrian army during the First World War, Wittgenstein spent much of his time writing philosophical reflections in a notebook which he carried around in his rucksack. On leave in Vienna in 1918 he assembled a selection of these notes into a small treatise, which, largely through the efforts of Bertrand Russell, was published in 1921. Entitled *Tractatus Logico-Philosophicus*, it is considered by many to be one of the most important philosophical texts of the present century. Considering, somewhat arrogantly, that he had solved all the problems of philosophy, Wittgenstein retired from academic life. The *Tractatus* was the only book that Wittgenstein published during this lifetime. From 1920 to 1926 Wittgenstein taught in various village schools in Austria but eventually had to resign due to parents' complaints that he was ill-treating their children. As Norman Malcolm (1984), in his sympathetic memoir of Wittgenstein, admits that students at Cambridge 'feared' him, it's hardly to be wondered that children found his manner threatening. In 1929 Wittgenstein returned to Cambridge, and there he continued to teach philosophy until 1947. His *Philosophical Investigations* (1953) and other works, based on his notebooks, were published posthumously. By all accounts Wittgenstein was a strange, eccentric figure. He had a fear of going insane – of his four brothers three had committed suicide – he was elitist and arrogant, and seems to have had little but contempt for ordinary people; he suffered from paranoia, and had an obsessive fear that his ideas were being plagiarised, although he himself never seemed to acknowledge his own intellectual debts; he was domineering and suggested to Malcolm that it was unlikely that anybody in his class should think of something of which he had not already thought. Nevertheless, he seems to have surrounded himself with admiring students, although he admitted that his influence on others was perhaps a stifling and negative one. (For further biographical details, see Bartley 1973; Malcolm 1984; Ayer 1985: 1–16.)

Wittgenstein has the unusual merit of having produced not one, but two different philosophies which are in many respects in opposition to each other. The *Tractatus* (1921) offers a philosophy in the tradition of logical positivism, while *Philosophical Investigations* presents a development of Moore's conception of philosophy as one involving the analysis of ordinary language. There are, naturally, links between the 'early' and 'later' Wittgenstein, for he was throughout fundamentally concerned with the philosophy of language, but the contrast between the two philosophies is nevertheless a fundamental one. We may consider them separately here.

In the *Tractatus* Wittgenstein is largely concerned with language as a means of representation, as a way of conveying how things are in the world. Accepting that tautologies – the propositions of logic and pure mathematics – provide us with no information about the world, Wittgenstein suggested that underlying ordinary language, there is a structure of elementary propositions. These elementary or factual propositions are seen as logically independent of one another, and tend to be identified by Wittgenstein with the propositions of the natural sciences (Copleston 1966: 496). Such propositions are seen by Wittgenstein as 'mirroring' or as a 'picture' of the world, seen as a totality of 'atomic facts' or 'states of affairs'. Wittgenstein thus offers a 'picture theory' of meaning.

As with other logical positivists, what lies beyond factual propositions is considered by Wittgenstein to be metaphysical, and thus nonsense. Pears (1971) links Wittgenstein's project with that of Kant, but whereas Kant is concerned with epistemology and the limits of reason (scientific knowledge), Wittgenstein is concerned with the limits of language, or rather factual discourse about the world. But Wittgenstein differs from other logical positivists on two counts. First, he is extremely vague ('mysterious') about both what constitutes the elementary propositions (he gives no examples), and exactly what the 'facts' of the world consist of – whether material particulars or sense data. Secondly, while positivists are generally hostile to religion and metaphysics, Wittgenstein is more circumspect, and while stressing that religion, morality and aesthetics lie outside factual discourse, Pears has suggested that he was not rejecting them, but 'trying to preserve them' – from, one presumes, criticism and empirical explanation. On these grounds Pears suggests that Wittgenstein is neither an empiricist nor a positivist (1971: 55–82). The problem is that Wittgenstein's writings are obscure and elliptic, even mystical – and deliberately so; it is therefore often difficult to grasp his meaning. This is particularly so towards the end of the *Tractatus*, when he writes on the question of solipsism and the human subject:

> The limits of my language mean the limits of my world . . .
> We cannot think what we cannot think; so what we cannot think we cannot say either.
> This remark provides the key to the problem, how much truth there is in solipsism.
> For what the solipsist means is quite correct; only it cannot be said, but makes itself manifest.
> The world is my world . . .
> I am my world (the microcosm).
> There is no such thing as the subject that thinks or entertains ideas.
> The subject does not belong to the world, rather, it is a limit of the world.
> Where in the world is a metaphysical subject to be found . . .
> The philosophical self is not the human being, not the human body, or the human soul, with which psychology deals, but rather the metaphysical subject, the limit of the world not a part of it. (1921: 5.6–5.641)

It is hardly surprising that many people have found these passages difficult to understand. Many of the statements are simply not true, even if they are expressed in oracular fashion. To suggest that 'there is no such thing as the subject that thinks' is literally false, unless it is intended to deny the uniqueness of the subject. Similarly, to claim that 'the world is my world' is obviously false, for the world exists prior and independently of Wittgenstein. Perhaps the best that can be said of Wittgenstein's thought in *Tractatus* is that it contains 'important nonsense'. Ayer and others have noted

Wittgenstein's debt to Schopenhauer in his notion of the metaphysical self, the transcendental ego. In his later writings Wittgenstein continually returned to the issue of solipsism, the idea that I am the sole existence (Ayer 1985: 27–33).

In his later writings, although still concerned with the scope and limits of language, Wittgenstein presents us with a radically different philosophy from that expressed in the *Tractatus*. And in many ways his later ideas about language are incompatible with logical positivism. He abandons the idea that there is an underlying structure of language which 'mirrors' an objective reality which is its foundation, and suggests instead that the meaning of language is to be found in its use or function. Language comes to be seen in *Philosophical Investigations* as essentially a social instrument used for a variety of purposes and in a variety of different social contexts. To explain his ideas about meaning he often uses the analogy of 'games', suggesting that if we want to understand what a 'game' is, we have to look at this phenomenon in a variety of different contexts, for no single criterion signifies its meaning. There is no one feature or set of features that is common to all games, but rather 'we see a complicated network of similarities overlapping and criss-crossing'. Wittgenstein refers to these similarities as 'family resemblances', concluding that games form a family. In his later writings, therefore, the 'picture' analogy of language and meaning is replaced by one based on 'tool' and 'game' analogies. A number of important points emerge from this new conception of language.

First, Wittgenstein sees the function of philosophy differently. Whereas in *Tractatus* Wittgenstein saw philosophy as having an essentially negative function, in delineating the limits of factual discourse, now it has a more positive function. In *Tractatus* Wittgenstein essentially took the language of science as the model for factual discourse, all other non-tautological propositions being deemed metaphysical and nonsensical. Wittgenstein was well aware of the dilemma in this position, for the Achilles' heel of logical positivism is that its own central principle of verifiability was neither a tautology nor itself amenable to empirical verification:

> The right method of philosophy would be this. To say nothing except what can be said, i.e. that the propositions of natural science, i.e. something that has nothing to do with philosophy. . . . My propositions are elucidatory; he who understands me finally recognizes them as senseless when he has climbed through them, on them, over them (He must so to speak throw away the ladder, after he has climbed upon it). Whereof one cannot speak, thereof one must be silent. (1921: 6.53 7)

Having tripped themselves up on their own boot laces, the logical positivists did themselves out of a job; their only function as philosophers was to be underlabourers to science, to provide the logic of science, as Ayer put it. But in his later philosophy the scope of this discipline was greatly expanded. It would become the descriptive understanding of language, or, as Pears puts it, 'a sort of anthropological study of conceptual systems' (1971: 104).

Secondly, seeing philosophy now as a kind of 'philosophical anthropology', Wittgenstein, in his later writings, was adamant that this mode of interpretation should be non-theoretical. 'We may not', he wrote, 'advance any kind of theory. There must not be anything hypothetical in our considerations. We must do away with all explanations and description alone must take its place. And this description gets its power of illumination – i.e. its purpose – from the philosophical problems. These are, of course, not empirical problems; they are solved, rather, by looking into the workings of our language' (1953: 1.109).

Philosophy thus becomes centrally focused on language and its usage; negatively, it elucidates the misuses of language which are thought to give rise to the philosophical problems that have puzzled philosophers over the centuries: positively, it has the function of describing the actual use of language. As with Moore, Wittgenstein's later philosophy presupposes that ordinary language is all right as it is, and unproblematic. Later British linguistic philosophers have tended to follow Wittgenstein's positive programme of describing the actual use of language (Copleston 1966: 502–3). Wittgenstein's own style of philosophy would, however, tend to suggest that the function of philosophy is more a kind of therapy than a descriptive anthropology concerned with delineating 'conceptual systems' and their corresponding 'forms of life'.

Thirdly, although many writers have been concerned to emphasise, as Wittgenstein did himself, the originality of his theories, neither the correspondence theory of truth (meaning – objectivism) nor the pragmatic theory implicit in his later writings is in fact particularly original. His pragmatism and his 'anthropocentrism' (as Pears describes it) has affinities with Dewey and the pragmatists (M. White 1955: 228); many of Nietzsche's ideas seem to anticipate those of Wittgenstein; while both Mach and Dilthey long ago stressed the two contrasting approaches to human life, both of which Wittgenstein seemed to espouse at different times in his life – namely logical positivism and hermeneutic understanding.

Throughout the later part of his life, Wittgenstein was particularly concerned with investigating our use of psychological concepts, and his interest largely focused on the issue as to whether the language we use to describe our sensations can in any sense be a private one. A private language, in the sense discussed by Wittgenstein, is a language whose words 'refer to what can only be known to the person speaking; to his immediate private sensations' (1953: 1.243). Apart from Wittgenstein himself, I find it difficult to find any philosopher who is committed to such a thesis. Anthony Kenny (1973) suggests that Wittgenstein is arguing against his own earlier views expressed in the *Tractatus* and against an earlier tradition of Western philosophy exemplified in the writings of Hume and Descartes. There was no school of thought in his own day, Kenny suggests, committed to a defence of 'private language'. It is doubtful if the mirror theory of meaning implies such a thesis, and although there is a long tradition of philosophy that implied a dualism between the conscious subject and an external reality – a tradition that both Kant and Hegel tried to transcend – such a subjectivist epistemology did not entail either Descartes or Hume embracing a theory of 'private language'. The first person approach, the traditional epistemological approach, which envisages the world from the standpoint of individual subject, and inquires as to how the world comes to be known – this approach does not imply solipsism. Only if sensations are mind-dependent – something that Descartes did not hold – does the issue of solipsism (private language) become a problem. And it was clearly a problem for Wittgenstein.

Wittgenstein argues that although sensations and our own inner mental states have a certain immediacy, and through introspection seem to have a privileged status in being concretely known to us, a private language about such states is impossible. He suggests that to conceive of the phenomena of mind and of sensations as if they were simply private inner states is misleading, for it prevents us, as Malcolm writes, 'from observing the situations and activities, the contexts, to which words like "remember", "mean", "think" etc. belong and which give them all the significance they have' (1977: 142). Our thoughts and our sensations only have meaning in terms of a public language which we share with others. But Wittgenstein does not deny that we have inner experiences, such as those of pain, thoughts, or feelings in the body, but these cannot be understood solely in terms of inner mental states. Similarly, Wittgenstein does not suggest that a person's feelings and sensations can be understood simply as manifestations of behavioural or physical events. A person's inner experiences are not explicable only in terms of physiological states or as dispositions to overt behaviour, as the writings of Carnap and, as we shall see, Ryle, seem to imply (Malcolm 1977: 143; Ayer 1982: 150). In a sense, as Kenny writes, Wittgenstein attempts to avoid the pitfalls of both behaviourism and a rigid Cartesian dualism:

> Wittgenstein rejected both dualism and behaviourism. He agreed with dualists that particular mental events could occur without accompanying bodily behaviour; he agreed with behaviourists that the possibility of describing mental events at all depends on their having, in general, an expression in behaviour. In his view, to ascribe a mental event or state to someone is not to ascribe to him any kind of bodily behaviour; but such ascription can only sensibly be made to beings which have at least the capability of behaviour of the appropriate kind. (1973: 17)

Wittgenstein felt that philosophy should not try to explain the phenomena of mind, but should only describe language usage, and thus the ways in which we use mental terms. But of course, ordinary language has always implied both a first and a third person point of view. Equally important is the fact that long before Wittgenstein philosophers had been critical of Cartesian dualism, without in the process advocating either behaviourism or a reductive materialism. (For useful studies of Wittgenstein, see Pears 1971; Kenny 1973; Ayer 1985.)

The writer from within the school of linguistic philosophy who may be usefully discussed in the present context is Gilbert Ryle (1900–76), for his classic study *The Concept of Mind* (1949) is directly concerned with the issues that Wittgenstein raised. Interestingly, Wittgenstein is not mentioned in the text. Ryle spent his whole life, apart from war service and lecturing abroad, as a philosophy scholar at Oxford University. Ryle's study is a sustained and critical polemic against the Cartesian conception of mind, which he saw as a kind of malady which still affected contemporary thought. He admits to a 'deliberate abusiveness' in addressing what he described as the myth of dogma of 'the ghost in the machine'. This myth represents, he suggests, a 'category mistake', namely it represents the facts of mental life as if they belonged to one logical type or category when they actually belong to another (1949: 17). The notion that there are two kinds of processes – one mental, the other physical; the idea that introspection gives us immediate and direct access to present states and operations of the mind; the notion that the workings of the mind are essentially private; and finally, the idea that a person's thinking and feelings are mysteriously ensconced as a kind of ghost in a machine – all these are elements of a myth that Ryle intends to explode. He does not deny of course that mental processes occur, but he does question whether such processes can be understood as if they were the function of a ghostly entity called mind.

His response can perhaps best be expressed in his own words, for they indicate clearly the behaviouristic tendencies inherent in his outlook. In opposition to the dogma of the 'ghost in the machine', he writes:

> I am arguing that in describing the workings of a person's mind we are not describing a second set of shadowy operations. We are describing certain phases of his own career; namely we are describing the ways in which parts of his conduct are managed . . . overt intelligent performances are not clues to the workings of minds; they are those workings. (1949: 49–57)

He goes on to argue that the concept of will or volition is a redundant one, and that such emotions as moods and motives are not different in kind from gestures and other modes of communication. He argues too that mechanism has become something of a 'bogey', but suggests that deterministic theories do not entail a rigid determinism any more than the grammar of language or the rules of a game curtail our personal autonomy. Although Ryle does not develop a consistent philosophical theory – given his polemical intent – he indicates his opposition to phenomenalism (accepted by both Mach and Ayer) and to mechanistic materialism (Hobbes), and accepts a behaviouristic interpretation of his study. Many writers have looked upon *The Concept of Mind* as exemplifying a philosophical behaviourist approach, but it is doubtful, as Ayer suggests, whether Ryle aimed at a strong thesis which suggests that all our talk about mind is referrable to behavioural modes. His thesis rather allows for the existence of inner processes but minimises their importance. In this sense there are close affinities between the approaches of Wittgenstein and Ryle. But although Ayer applauds their work, he suggests that their behavioural approach leaves a great deal of mental activity unaccounted for: 'It includes a considerable part of the exercise of the memory and the imagination and it includes every form of sentience. Most importantly, it has not been shown that perceiving can be analysed in behavioural terms' (Ayer 1982: 168).

But given the fact that both Wittgenstein and Ryle are concerned only with describing the meanings involved in ordinary language usage, such questions as these, demanding empirical examination and explanations are beyond their purview. It is of interest that while psychological behaviourists like Watson and Skinner advocated behaviourism because of its scientific and explanatory possibilities, Wittgenstein follows these tendencies while exploring ordinary language, and holds to a non-theoretical standpoint.

Pears applauds Wittgenstein's conception of philosophy for the fact that it 'brought philosophy down to earth without turning it into a science' (1971: 112). Ironically, a whole host of critics of linguistic philosophy have been concerned not with its 'earthly' qualities, but with its unearthly tendencies, and the fact that the analysis of ordinary language has degenerated into a scholastic and ivory tower occupation. Bertrand Russell described linguistic philosophy as a 'curious kind of arid mysticism' which might at best be of some help to lexicographers, and at worst an idle tea-table amusement (1959: 217). Ernest Gellner (1959: 26), in an important critique, bewails its influence, though accepting that its contributions to the philosophy of mind is of genuine interest, even though Wittgenstein did not succeed, as claimed, in solving the important problem of body–mind interaction. (For further criticisms of linguistic philosophy, see Cornforth 1965: Novack 1969: 107–12, Barrett 1986: 152–4.)

3.5 Sociobiology

The general implication of both psychological behaviourism and linguistic philosophy was to eradicate or play down the importance of mind, or of human agency, and to put an emphasis on function or utility. Barrett (1986) has stressed the persistent and consistent behaviourism of Wittgenstein's later philosophy, and notes how ironic this is; for ordinary language abounds with introspective and subjective references and is centrally concerned with the human world of action, purpose and need. It makes no sharp division between the inner and outer aspects of human life, between its introspective and behavioural dimensions. Writing on the issue of the 'disappearing self', Barrett concludes that Wittgenstein seems to share this 'fear' of the mind, which haunts so many other contemporary philosophers (1986: 152–4). This denial of the mind and of subjective agency is equally evident in the latest explication of positivism and Darwinian evolutionary theory – sociobiology – and we can conclude this chapter by briefly examining some of its central tenets.

Sociobiology suddenly burst upon the intellectual scene in the spring of 1975, amid a fanfare of publicity. It marked the publication of *Sociobiology: The new synthesis* by the Harvard biologist Edward O. Wilson, a scholar who, until then, was hardly known outside the narrow halls of academia, although four years earlier he had published an important study on *The Insect Societies*. *Sociobiology* is a massive tome of nearly 700 pages, and aims to provide a comprehensive synthesis of existing knowledge on the social behaviour of animals. Although well illustrated and in coffee-table format, its subject matter was hardly of the kind to appeal to the ordinary person in the street, but anticipating that the book would be a controversial one, its publisher gave it maximum publicity. The book did indeed become the subject of controversy, and the author suddenly found himself a celebrity. What caused the furore was that Wilson applied his theories – sociobiology, as a branch of evolutionary biology, he defined as 'the systematic study of the biological basis of all social behaviour' – not only to animal life, from the lower invertebrates to primates, but also to humans. And in the study, particularly in the final chapter entitled 'Man: From Sociobiology to Sociology', he argued that biological principles can be applied to the social sciences and offers a biological explanation for such human cultural manifestations as religion, warfare, ethics, competition, entrepreneurship, altruism, tribalism and genocide. Although this study was reviewed favourably in some journals, the book aroused what Flew describes as 'an explosive outburst of fury and execration' (1984: 113), for it was angrily attacked by geneticists and anthropologists on both intellectual and ideological grounds. Much of this criticism, as we shall see, has substance, but some was personal and unfair, for Wilson's ideas on biological determinism were linked not only to reactionary ideas in general but to those of the most extreme form, to the gas chambers in Nazi Germany. Wilson was clearly unprepared for the bitterness of the attack, especially as many of his critics were colleagues. But Wilson's study also generated a good deal of intellectual excitement, and over the last decade sociobiology has become something of a subdiscipline, and has now many adherents in psychology and anthropology as well as the social sciences more generally (Barash 1977; Alexander 1979; Freedman 1979). It is not my intention to review the extensive literature on sociobiology here; I shall instead focus on the writings of Wilson, particularly on two texts – *On Human Nature* (1978), which is specifically on human sociobiology, and *Promethean Fire*, co-authored with the physicist Charles J. Lumsden. The latter is a reflection on the origin of mind, presenting in a more readable form, and free from sophisticated-looking mathematical equations, the ideas earlier expressed in *Genes, Mind and Culture* (1981). I shall conclude the section by reviewing some of the key criticisms levelled at sociobiology, the latest of a long line of biological theories of culture. In fact, in the previous decade a whole series of books had been published which have been aptly called 'pop-ethology', all of which suggested a reductionist, biological explanation of human existence and culture – Ardrey's *The Territorial Imperative* (1966), Lorenz's *On Aggression* (1966), Morris's *The Naked Ape* (1967) and Tiger and Fox's *The Imperial Animal* (1970). All these works propagate the myth of 'man the mighty hunter' and support the view of humans as innately aggressive, territorial, entrepreneurial and male-dominated. They essentially present a Hobbesian view of the human species (S. Rose et al. 1984; see my review of Ardrey 1979).

Wilson's sociobiology is motivated by a desire to study human nature as part of the natural sciences, and to integrate these sciences with the social sciences and humanities. But this intended integration is not in the form of a marriage, but as Edmund Leach (1981) graphically expressed it more in the nature of rape: a 'jargon-loaded take-over bid', a reductionist analysis that Wilson misleadingly assumes to be the traditional method of scientific analysis. Thus Wilson does not suggest or offer a needed integration of biology and the social sciences, but rather the uncompromising application of evolutionary biology to all aspects of human existence. Biology, he writes, 'is the key to human nature' (1978: 13).

Wilson's theory, his essential argument, is contained in the following extract:

> The heart of the genetic hypothesis is the proposition, derived in a straight line from neo-Darwinian evolutionary theory, that the traits of human nature were adaptive during the time that the human species evolved and that genes consequently spread through the population that predisposed their carriers to develop those traits. Adaptiveness means simply that if an individual displayed the traits he stood a greater chance of having his genes represented in the next generation than if he did not display these traits. The differential advantage among individuals in this strictest sense is called genetic fitness. (1978: 32)

Such a postulate seems to imply a close relationship or 'fit' between genotype and phenotype, and to introduce a teleological element into the evolutionary process; individuals consciously or unconsciously seeking to propagate their genes or to ensure that their genes are transmitted to a future generation. Dawkins introduced the notion of the 'selfish gene', the human person being seen as simply the receptacle whereby genes are preserved unaltered. 'We are survival machines', he wrote, 'robot vehicles blindly programmed to preserve the selfish molecules known as genes' (1976: 4–7). Wilson is less graphic and mystifying than this, but his argument is basically the same, and has an essential circularity, gene, organism, mind and culture being almost functionally equivalent. Thus the possession of certain genes predisposes the individual to think and act in a certain way, such traits or social responses convey superior fitness for the individual (as these traits proved their adaptive worth in the by-gone days of hunter-gathering), and thus the genes themselves will gain an increase in the next generation (1976: 33). Variations would seem to arise from genetic mutation; the individual organism ceases to be the agent on which the forces of natural selection operate and a 'substantial fraction', as Wilson puts it, of human behavioural variation is based on genetic differences among individuals. In essence, then, Wilson proposes a theory of 'genetic determinism', suggesting that human social behaviour is genetically determined. He disclaims, however, that this theory implies a rigid determinism, 'a single channel, running from a given set of genes to the corresponding single predestined pattern of behaviour' (1976: 55). And arguing against the kind of cultural determinism which he sees as inherent in much Marxism and social science, he writes: 'Each person is moulded by an interaction of his environment, especially his cultural environment, with the genes that affect social behaviour' (1976: 18). Elsewhere, in similar vein, he writes: 'The evidence is strong that almost all differences between human societies are based on learning and social conditioning rather than on heredity,' but he adds the proviso: 'yet perhaps not quite all' (1976: 48).

Wilson also concedes that virtually all the social changes that have occurred over the last several thousand years have been due to 'cultural rather than genetic evolution', and he suggests that cultural evolution, unlike biological evolution, is 'Lamarckian and very fast'. But what interests Wilson is the extent to which the hereditary qualities of hunter-gatherer existence have influenced the course of subsequent cultural evolution. On cultural change he writes: 'The directions this change can take and its final products are constrained by the genetically influenced behavioural predispositions that constituted the earlier, simpler adaptations of preliterate human beings' (1976: 9). He therefore speaks of contemporary social behaviour as 'hypertrophic outgrowths of the simpler features of human nature joined together into an irregular mosaic' (1976: 95) (hypertrophy being the extreme growth of a pre-existing structure, like the tusk of an elephant). History, therefore, for Wilson is guided by the biological evolution that preceded it and the culture of each society 'travels along one or the other of a set of evolutionary trajectories whose full array is constrained by the genetic rules of human nature' (1976: 207). His whole approach is summed up in that oft-quoted phrase: 'The genes hold culture on a leash' (1976: 167).

To substantiate his theory Wilson draws on the literature, particularly from anthropology, to indicate how social phenomena can best be understood by relating them to genetic factors. His examples and strategies are somewhat *ad hoc*. Here are some samples:

- although we all have the capacity to become schizophrenic, some people have distinctive genes predisposing them to this condition.
- psychologists have shown that there are universal expressions of emotion.
- Chomsky and other linguists have indicated that there is a 'deep grammar' facilitating the rapid acquisition of language by all humans.
- the inefficiency, brutality and inhumanity of slavery as a human institution, and the fact these institutions 'fail', suggest that they are contrary to human nature.
- the fact that warfare has been endemic to all societies throughout history indicates that human beings are innately aggressive – we do not have an instinct but a 'marked hereditary disposition' (1976: 100). Like the earlier ethologists, he suggests that human beings are ecologically akin to lions, wolves and hyenas.
- altruism (which would appear to be contrary to classical Darwinian theory, especially if it involves self-sacrifice) is ultimately self-serving, for it may lead to the continuance of the individuals' genetic capital if those supported are close kin. (Under the theory of kin selection this topic has generated a wealth of literature, which tends to be bedevilled with contradictions and anthropological naivety. See Sahlins 1976: 17–67 for an important critique.)
- incest taboos are universal because sexual relations with close kin entail loss of genetic fitness.
- Hypergamy, polygamy and infanticide can be explained in terms of an inherited disposition to maximise the number of offspring

in competition with other members of the society. Even religion, tribalism and racism make sense seen in the context that they confer genetic or biological advantage on their adherents. Racism, he seems to suggest, is just like the springtime singing of male birds (1976: 70).

Although when discussing chimpanzees Wilson stresses that these animals have a consciousness of self and the ability to communicate ideas (1976: 27), when discussing the human species in *On Human Nature* he is strangely silent on this subject. Other than suggesting that the mind can be explained as 'an epiphenomenon of the neuronal machinery of the brain' (1978: 197), and that the self is a 'leading actor in this neural drama' (of memory and fantasy) Wilson has nothing to say on what is unique about the human subject – our language, our symbolic propensities and our developed sense of consciousness. Wilson's later writings had the specific aim of attempting to rectify the limitations of the earlier studies, namely to provide an adequate theory of the mind.

Promethean Fire, co-authored with Lumsden, is sub-titled *Reflections on the origin of mind*. The authors argue against the notion that culture (or mind) is separate and independent of the physiology of the brain, like 'a layer on top of the biological mechanism capable of being explained only by means of unique procedures and laws', and suggest instead that the evolution of mind is due to a mechanism they call 'gene-culture co-evolution', which is both explicable in terms of physical laws and unique to the human species. This mechanism connotes an 'interaction in which culture is generated and shaped by biological imperatives while biological traits are simultaneously altered by genetic evolution in response to cultural innovation' (1983: 19). They thus see a 'tight linkage' between genetic evolution and cultural history. They also postulate what they term epigenetic rules. These are in the nature of universal constraints: certain cognitive mechanisms, universal expressions of emotion, phobic reactions, the tendency to avoid sex with close kin, patterns of mother–infant bonding are among those discussed. Such epigenetic rules, they suggest, cause individuals to adopt cultural choices that enable them to survive and reproduce more successfully. Over many generations these rules and the genes prescribing them will tend to increase in the population. Hence they suggest that culture affects genetic evolution. To facilitate analysis they suggest we should consider culture atomistically, as consisting of specific elements or basic units, which they refer to as culturgens – discrete entities, which they clearly associate with specific genes. The preference for incest and outbreeding they see as two such culturgens. They assume that human culture can be broken down into clusters of traits – an idea that anthropologists long ago abandoned (Leach 1981: 267).

Throughout the study Lumsden and Wilson focus on the relation between gene and culture (the mind, human subjectivity and practical concerns are of secondary interest) and assume a 'complicated sequence' or 'circuit': a long 'chain of causation' stretching from genes to culture. As they put it, a proper understanding of mind and culture involves an understanding of gene-culture co-evolution, 'the great circuit of causation that runs from the genes to brain architecture and the epigenetic rules of mental development, then to the formation of culture, and finally back to the evolution of the genes through the operation of natural selection and other agents of evolution' (1981: 170). Hereditary and environmental factors, they conclude, cannot be separated. They admit that new forms of behaviour, the 'mutations' of culture, as they describe them, are invented by the mind, but which forms occur, they insist, 'is very much influenced by the genes'. They contrast their own approach with the view of human evolution that sees culture as a new emergent force which has replaced genetic evolution (1981: 153). Although appearing to stress the importance of culture and the human mind, consciousness has little function, and the whole analysis emphasises a genetic determinism; genes determine the configuration of brain cells, these determine the epigenetic rules, and the latter, having been of survival value in prehistory, 'shape' or 'affect' which cultural innovations will be invented and adopted.

A number of criticisms have been made of Wilson's attempt to apply sociobiological principles to the human subject.

First, many anthropologists have been critical of Wilson's presentation of empirical data which is selective and which tends to universalise what are essentially the values and attributes of a particular kind of society – one with a capitalist market economy. Wilson's depiction of hunter-gatherers as aggressive carnivores hardly matches the empirical evidence, and although he notes that not all societies are engaged in genocidal warfare and that meat only forms a minor proportion of the food intake of hunter-gatherers, he follows the early ethologists in seeing hunting and aggressive conflict as ubiquitous. Equally evident is Wilson's tendency to describe other cultures in terms that derive from his own culture: indeed, his whole discourse is permeated with the values and ideas, which MacPherson (1962) described as possessive individualism.

Human beings are seen, universally, as being territorial and xeno-phobic, as being self-aggrandising and selfish creatures, who are essentially concerned with the maximisation of their own repro-ductive fitness. Even the genes they possess are described as capital, and all co-operative aspects of human life are viewed as really a form of selfishness (Rose et al. 1984: 245). As with Hobbes, Wilson seems to equate the state of human nature with the ideology of capitalism. Sahlins has written perceptively on the reciprocal influ-ences between bourgeois political economy and biological theory, and how the Hobbesian vision of humans in the natural state is almost the 'origin myth' of Western capitalism. Darwin, as Engels and others noted, applied the ideas of the classical economists like Malthus to biology, and in turn, social Darwinists like William Sumner transferred Darwin's teaching back to their original source – society. Wilson is engaged in a similar endeavour, though he moves back and forth between the biological and cultural domains, often using social concepts, such as caste or slavery, quite inappro-priately in discussing insect life. Sahlins concludes that sociobiology is a form of scientific totemism, which represents 'the modern en-compassment of the sciences, both of culture and of life, by the dominant ideology of possessive individualism' (1976: 93–107). Other anthropologists have been critical of Wilson's 'astonishing ignorance' of non-Western cultures (Leach 1981; Ingold 1986: 68).

Secondly, many writers have been critical of the genetic deter-minism implicit and stressed by Wilson's brand of sociobiology. As one critic suggests: 'The trouble with the simple deterministic model of gene control is that the manifest traits of an organism, its phenotype, are not in general determined by the genes in isolation but are a consequence of the interaction of genes and environment in development' (Rose et al. 1984: 252).

If this is the case with the phenotype (organism), human behav-iour and culture as phenotypical attributes would seem even less determined. There is also the erroneous suggestion that the gene rather than the individual organism is the unit of natural selection – as it is in classical Darwinian theory. Although there has been a long debate in biology as to whether the group or the individual is the unit of selection, the general consensus is that selection operates on the phenotype – on the organism and its behavioural responses. Genes are not selected, they are only replicated, as even Dawkins (1982) seems to suggest. But even the term selection is an inap-propriate one here, for as Flew notes, there is no agent as such doing the selecting (1984: 119; see Gould 1980: 72–8 for a good discussion of these issues). There is the question, however, of whether sociobiologists are suggesting that only the universal features of human nature – the epigenetic rules – are determined by our genes, and thus whether these rules only constrain culture. If this is the case they have yet to specify how the constraints operate, or whether specific culturgens have in fact associated genes. Although jesting, Flanagan makes an important point when he writes: 'it would be odd to think that there was some specific gene or set of genes that underwrote car-driving and that therefore was decreasing in frequency because 50,000 Americans with the gene(s) died in automobile accidents every year' (1984: 269). If the genes of epigenetic rules are seemingly only constraints like gravity (to which human beings must also adapt), then they explain nothing. Wilson continually disclaims that all culture can be explained by genetic factors – as the quotations cited earlier denote – and he is quoted as suggesting that perhaps only 10 per cent of social life can be laid to biology. But as Sahlins has argued (1976: 65), this kind of factorial specification is meaningless, for all the organic and inorganic constraints on human life are in some sense always 100 per cent involved. The constitution of the human subject is in some ways like the baking of a cake – and this is just an analogy. To make a cake four elements are involved – the ingredients (genes), the oven (environment), the recipe (culture) and the cook (the human agent). It is quite misleading to attempt to express these elements as percentages in the process of baking a cake. Ten per cent determined by the ingredients?

Finally, although Sahlins' critique is offered from the standpoint of the Boasian tradition, which, as we shall explore in the next chapter, is a limiting cultural determinist perspective, other anthropologists, while accepting the importance of biology in understanding the human subject, have found Wilson's approach too limiting. William Durham (1979), for example, argues that Wilson, though claiming to offer a 'new synthesis', in fact presents a one-sided account and focuses entirely on the genetic-inheritance mechanism, thus ignoring the importance of the cultural mechanism as a mode of human adaptation. Durham postulates that human beings have two principal inheritance mechanisms, and that the cultural mechanism – cultural patterns and behavioural attributes that serve to enhance human adaptation and survival, and are acquired through learning – is no less important than the biological one. The human capacity for culture allows human beings to modify aspects of phenotype without any concomitant genotypic changes, he suggests, and an adequate co-evolutionary theory must embrace both mechanisms. The process of 'cultural selection' functionally complements that of natural selection. The problem with this theory, as with Wilson's, is that it takes what Flanagan has called a 'vertical' approach to human behaviour, and implies that whatever cultural manifestations are in evidence have functional value for human survival. With Wilson you have the suggestion, earlier made by Marvin Harris, that the religiously sanctioned cannibalism of the Aztecs was an adaptive strategy, a cultural response to a genetically programmed need for protein (1978: 94; Harris 1977: 110–25; but cf. Arens 1979). Any attempt to argue that every aspect of human culture is specifically adaptive, whether cannibalism or xenophobia, is essentially to justify things as they are. Many have seen Wilson's analyses as thus legitimating the status quo. The 'vertical' nature of Wilson's approach – the chain of causation from genes to culture – is limiting, for it ignores what Flanagan calls the 'horizontal' dimension of human life, the cultural patterns and behaviour that are embedded in complex social and historical contexts. Equally, the stress on gene–culture co-evolution mediated only by epigenetic universal rules inevitably tends to underestimate the transformational power of the mind, and its ability to mediate between higher and lower levels of organisation (Flanagan 1984: 262–6). Thus a response to Wilson's genetic determinism with its reductive tendency should not be an equally one-sided cultural determinism (as Sahlins appears to suggest) and a complete denial of biology, but rather an integrated understanding of the relationship between the biological and the social. 'Humanity cannot be cut adrift from its own biology, but neither is it enchained by it' (Rose et al. 1984: 10).

Like Skinner's, Wilson's writings often have a prophetic quality and offer a technocratic solution to human problems. And though they express very contrasting viewpoints – one an extreme environmentalism, the other a form of biological determinism – both Skinner and Wilson have much in common in their positivistic approach and in excluding or playing down what is perhaps fundamental about the human species – human consciousness and the structures of meaning that constitute human culture. As Lucien Goldman wrote in referring to the anti-positivist tradition that stemmed from Hegel and Marx, and that attempted to go beyond the dualistic metaphysics of the earlier 'philosophers of individualism' – and this long before Wittgenstein:

Man is not opposite the world which he tries to understand and upon which he acts, but within this world which he is a part of, and there is no radical break between the meaning he is trying to find or introduce into the universe and that which he is trying to find or introduce into his own existence. This meaning common to both individual and collective human life, common as much to humanity as, ultimately, to the universe, is called history. (1977: 6)

Given their shared natural scientific standpoint, what is lacking in both Wilson and Skinner is any real sense of human history and human agency. (For further interesting studies of sociobiology, see Ruse 1979; Chagnon and Irons 1979; Bock 1980.)

−4−

Culture and Psychology: Neo-Kantian Perspectives

In this chapter I explore writers who can be seen as standing within the neo-Kantian tradition, which emerged towards the end of the nineteenth century. This tradition followed the dualistic metaphysics inherent in the writings of Leibniz and Kant, and drew a clear line of demarcation between the natural and the social sciences. The person thus came to be seen as essentially a 'culture-bearing organism'. In the first section I introduce the neo-Kantian school, and outline the influential theories of Wilhelm Dilthey and his advocacy of an 'interpretative' or humanistic science. In the next two sections I describe the work of two figures who played a fundamental role in the founding of the academic disciplines of psychology and anthropology – Wundt and Boas – and I stress their affinity with the neo-Kantian perspective. After examining the writings of Kroeber, whose vision of the human sciences was much more dualistic than Boas's, I outline in the final two sections the theories of two other important students of Boas – Benedict and Margaret Mead. I focus on their earlier, more seminal work and the conceptions of the human subject which emerge from their writings.

4.1 Dilthey and the neo-Kantian School

Towards the end of the nineteenth century there arose in Germany a philosophical movement whose basic message was a 'return to Kant', a movement that drew its inspiration from his spirit, method and writings. Three tendencies prompted this 'back to Kant' movement. One was a growing dissatisfaction with the idealist metaphysical philosophy associated with Hegel and Schelling, which seemed to go well beyond the limits of critical reason (science) that Kant had specified as possible. A second tendency which also caused concern was the positivist programme articulated by Comte, J. S. Mill and Mach, which suggested that the theories and methods of the natural sciences could be applied to what Hume had called the 'moral sciences' – to all aspects of human life. Nurtured in the German idealist and historicist tradition, these suggestions stirred deep misgivings in the hearts of German academic philosophers. Finally, there was a concern – a move – within this tradition to provide a philosophical foundation for the newly emerging empirical sciences of sociology and psychology, and for the important developments in historical scholarship associated with Leopold von Ranke and Theodor Mommsen. The neo-Kantian school became a dominant influence in Germany in the period between 1870 and 1920, and most academic philosophers were influenced by, or were representatives of, the movement. Although all shared a common aim, to avoid 'the extravagance of metaphysics without falling into the dogmatism of the materialists' (Copleston 1963: 361), it was by no means a unified movement, and different schools emerged within neo-Kantianism, emphasising different aspects of Kant's work. The Marburg school, associated with Hermann Cohen, was mainly concerned with the philosophy of science, while the Baden or 'south-west German' school of neo-Kantian philosophy focused on the philosophy of values and on the epistemology of the cultural sciences. The two important philosophers of this school were Wilhelm Windelband (1848–1915) and Heinrich Rickert (1863–1936). Many other scholars were associated with the neo-Kantian movement, including Freidrich A. Lange, Hermann von Helmholtz, Wilhelm Dilthey, Gustav Fechner, Ernst Cassirer and the sociologist Georg Simmel, and it had an important influence on Max Weber (B. Morris 1987: 57–8).

The basic tenet of neo-Kantian thought was to suggest a radical cleavage between the phenomenal and the spiritual realms, between the world of the natural sciences (nature) and the world of human activity (history). Thus the neo-Kantians firmly rejected materialism in favour of Cartesian dualism, or rather, in terms of the distinction made by Leibniz between the physical 'kingdom' of nature, where causal law reigns, and the 'kingdom' of substances, where purpose and consciousness inhere. The philosophical psychologist Hermann Lotze (1817–81), who was much influenced by Leibniz, made in his study *Microcosm* (1856) a radical distinction between Nature as the realm of necessity and History as the realm of freedom, and thus saw the human subject as having a dual nature (Collingwood 1946: 156; Copleston 1963: 376–81). But the writer who most clearly expressed the difference between history and science was Windelband, who in 1894 delivered a famous address at the University of Strassburg on 'History and Natural Science'. Windelband argued that the distinction between the natural (*Naturwissenschaft*) and the historical sciences (*Geisteswissenschaften*) is based not on ontology or subject matter, but rather on different forms or modes of knowledge. He suggested that whereas the natural sciences are concerned with the formulation of general laws, and are thus nomothetic, history is an idiographic science and is concerned with the singular and the unique. He claimed that these two approaches are independent and distinct, and that the event and a law are incommensurable entities. Windelband's student Rickert, who was a colleague and friend of Max Weber, explored this distinction further in his *The Limits of Concept Formation in Natural Science*, first published in 1902 (1986). Like Windelband, Rickert insists that what is at issue is the logic of the sciences rather than the 'material' or object of investigation, and is concerned to outline a science of history that is independent of both positivism (which would reduce the psychic to the physical) and neo-Hegelian idealism. Rickert is thus concerned to show that history is a substantive form of scientific knowledge (Schopenhauer had denied that it was), and to demarcate the limits of natural science.

Although there is some debate as to what degree Wilhelm Dilthey can be described as a neo-Kantian philosopher, he was certainly associated with the neo-Kantian school and showed a keen interest in developing many of Kant's insights. He was also one of the most important and influential philosophers of his day, and has been sadly neglected by most historians of psychology and philosophy. If Wittgenstein can be said to be overrated as a seminal philosopher, then Dilthey, who anticipated many of the ideas of the later Wittgenstein, has, I think, been rather underrated. He was, as Collingwood writes, a 'lonely and neglected genius' (1946: 171), someone whose recognition has been long overdue.

A complex and versatile scholar, an historian of ideas as well as a philosopher, Dilthey wrote on a wide range of subjects – poetry, religion, history, a biography of Schleiermacher, hermeneutics, educational reform, as well as on the philosophy of the social sciences. His own intellectual concerns were diverse and eclectic, although he attempted to combine them into a coherent synthesis. Stuart Hughes writes of his concerns:

These were a curious and rather unstable combination of Kantian memories, strict historical training, a nostalgia for the spiritual world of the Enlightenment, a respect for the aims of positivist investigation, and, still hovering in the background, the misty pantheism of Romantic theology. A gentle and conciliatory spirit, Dilthey was to strive mightily to bring his diverse orientations into some sort of synthesis and to leave behind him a major work of philosophical integration. (1958: 193)

In a sense Dilthey tries to evaluate and combine many diverse currents of thought; the hermeneutic approach suggested by Schleiermacher; Goethe's and the Romantics' emphasis on receptivity, intuition and individuality; Hegel's conception of reality as a process of historical change; Kant's critical philosophy; and the emphasis that Nietzsche, Ruskin and Tolstoy put on the philosophy of life. Spinoza, too, was an important influence on Dilthey.

Dilthey was born in a small Rhineland village, and in 1852 enrolled at Heidelberg University, intent on studying theology. But finding theology too narrow, he became interested in history and philosophy and attended the lectures of Mommsen, and of Ranke on universal history. Deciding on an academic career, in 1864 Dilthey completed his doctoral studies, a thesis on Schleiermacher's ethics, and became a university professor, first at Basle, then in 1882 the chair at Berlin, once occupied by Hegel. Dilthey's life, as Rickman notes, 'was that of a respectable and successful academic and there is nothing spectacular about it except this single-minded devotion to scholarship' (1976: 2).

Dilthey's central concern was to lay the philosophical foundations of the human sciences (*Geisteswissenschaften*; the science of spirit or mind), to gain an understanding of what he described as social-historical reality. In 1883, eleven years before Windelband, Dilthey published his *Introduction to the Human Sciences*, his only substantial book on the subject, although for the rest of his life he continued to publish important and interesting reviews and critical essays, which threw light on his understanding of human culture. He had plans for writing a great 'Critique of Historical Reason', on the lines of Kant's classical study, but his project was never completed. In attempting to provide the philosophical foundations for the human sciences, Dilthey was concerned that while over the centuries the study of history and society had gradually been able to emancipate itself from metaphysical philosophy, the appearance of positivist science in the nineteenth century seemed to entail a new kind of slavery. The growing power of science, he wrote, has 'led to a new bondage which is no less oppressive than the old' (Rickman 1976: 159). Thus it was Dilthey's intent to combat positivism, while attempting to avoid a return to metaphysical idealism. Comte, J. S. Mill and other empiricists had seemed to 'truncate historical reality' in order to assimilate it to the concepts and methods of natural science. He sympathised with the attempts of Comte and Mill to make the human sciences into rigorous, empirical and scientific disciplines, but profoundly opposed positivism on a number of points. First, he questions the epistemological realism inherent in the empirist approach, indeed in traditional epistemology, from Descartes to Kant, which sees the human subject as essentially a cognitive being standing against and separate from the world. The epistemology of Kant and the empiricists had up to now, Dilthey writes, 'explained experience and cognition merely from the facts of apprehension. No real blood flows in the veins of the knowing subject constructed by Locke, Hume and Kant; it is only the diluted juice of reason, a mere process of thought.' Our knowledge of ourselves, of the external world and of human culture can only be explained, Dilthey continues, 'in terms of the whole of human nature in which willing, feeling, and thinking are only different aspects of the real process of life. The questions we all ask of philosophy cannot be answered by rigid a priori conditions of knowledge but only by a history which starts from the totality of our nature and sketches its development' (ibid., 162). Thus for Dilthey, experience is not, as for the positivists, the imprint of the external world on a passive mind. He rejected the doctrine of phenomenalism, and the narrowing of experience to the perception of sense data – and thus the assumption of epistemological realists that experience and thought is a mirror-image of objective reality (Rickman 1976: 21). Dilthey writes: 'To the perceiving mind the external world remains only a phenomenon but to the whole human being who wills, feels and imagines, this external reality is something independent and immediately given and certain as his own self – it is part of life, not a mere idea' (162). We must, he concluded, put the epistemological foundation of the human sciences on a much broader basis than that suggested by the empiricists.

Secondly, Dilthey is critical of the behaviourist implications of positivism. Comte has claimed in his positive philosophy that all human mental attributes could be properly and exhaustively studied by biology and sociology, and thus refused to give a legitimate place to psychology as a science – a viewpoint which, as we shall see, was also adopted by later anthropologists like Durkheim and

Leslie White. Dilthey considered that to limit the human sciences to the study of behaviour, to external observation alone, was narrow and misleading. Any empiricism, he wrote 'which forgoes an explanation of what happens in the mind in terms of the understood connections of mental life is necessarily sterile' (Rickman 1976: 89; Makkreel 1975: 37).

To understand such subjects as jurisprudence, religion and political science requires, he suggests, psychological insights and psychological analysis:

> The systems of culture, commerce, law, religion, art and scholarship and the outer organisation of society in family, community, church and state, originated from the living context of the human mind, and, ultimately, can only be understood through it. Mental facts form their most important constituents so they cannot be grasped without psychological analysis. (1976: 90)

Schnädelbach (1984: 54) understands Dilthey's approach as suggesting that he is offering a psychologistic variant of the Kantian programme, a grounding of historical knowledge by means of an analysis of the facts of consciousness. This is to suggest that Dilthey is proposing a form of psychologism. This is the complete opposite of what Dilthey is in fact proposing. Rather than grounding history in psychology, Dilthey is suggesting not only that the psyche can only be understood in a socio-historical context, but also that social phenomena are intrinsically mental and cannot be studied from a purely behavioural perspective. Dilthey is equally against the limitations of a purely introspective approach, as well as the analytic approach of the empiricists, which thought of the mind as consisting of basic elements linked by laws of association. But Dilthey's stress on the psychological dimension of social phenomena did not, as Rickman stresses, imply that Dilthey was a methodological individualist. Although the entities that make up the cultural and intellectual heritage of mankind – religion, language, codes of law, political ideologies – are the collective products of human minds, 'they can and sometimes have to be studied without reference to individual authors' (1976: 7).

We do not, Dilthey felt, do justice to the great thinkers of the eighteenth century simply by transferring the methods of natural science to the domain of human culture and history. To be true disciples of the Enlightenment thinkers we must adjust our knowledge to the nature of the subject matter. Thus, like other neo-

Kantian philosophers, Dilthey came to make a distinction between the historical and the cultural sciences on the one hand, and the natural sciences on the other. As he wrote:

> The human studies differ from the sciences because the latter deal with facts which present themselves to consciousness, as external and separate phenomena, while the former deal with the living connections of reality experienced in the mind. It follows that the sciences arrive at connections within nature through inferences by means of a combination of hypotheses, while the human sciences are based on directly given mental connections. We explain nature but we understand mental life. (1976: 89)

Unlike the neo-Kantians Windelband and Rickert, Dilthey did not see a sharp and rigid distinction between these two forms of science, and in the long controversy between these two writers Dilthey was to insist that both ideographic and nomothetic interests were legitimate within the human sciences (Harris 1969: 270). The distinction could be articulated at different levels, in terms of the research field, in terms of experience, or in terms of the attitude of the investigator. Dilthey used the term *Geisteswissenschaften* rather broadly to cover not only the disciplines that deal with the human mind or spirit (*Geist*) but psychology and the social sciences generally – history, jurisprudence, political science, sociology, linguistics, literary criticism, religious studies and economics. To translate *Geisteswissenschaften* as simply the 'science of mind' or 'mental sciences' is misleading.

Knowledge of history and of culture, of what Dilthey referred to as the 'objectifications' of the human mind, could be derived, he argued, through some form of internal process – through lived experience and through understanding. A necessary condition for the understanding of social phenomena Dilthey felt to be what he described as 'lived experience' (*Erlebnisse*), a person's conscious involvement with the immediate social milieu. But this in itself did not constitute knowledge; what was also required was understanding (*Verstehen*) – not the understanding of the human mind in terms of its interiority or inner states, but understanding of the external objectification of the human mind – such cultural manifestations as art, state, religion, economy, world-views. This involved understanding the meaning and purposes of human activity and culture. The understanding of a complex cultural phenomenon Dilthey referred to as 'interpretation' and its methodology 'hermeneutics'.

His approach is summed up thus: 'Knowledge of the mind-constructed world originates from the interaction between experience, understanding of other people, the historical comprehension of communities as the subject of historical activity and insight into objective mind' (1976: 211).

Although, following Hegel, Dilthey used the term objective mind to refer to human culture, he distinguished his own approach from that of Hegel. We cannot understand the objective mind by relating it, as Hegel does, to a universal reason, which is itself an expression of the nature of the world spirit, but rather, Dilthey suggests, must start with its historical reality; we must go back to the structural connections of persons, and, by extension, of communities. We must replace Hegel's universal reason with life in its totality, and then a new understanding of objective mind becomes possible – we see it as cultural manifestations such as language, customs, family, state, society and styles of life (1976: 194–5). Dilthey was equally critical of the tendency of German idealist philosophers to reify the national spirit. Dilthey argues that such entities as the 'collective mind' or the 'nation' have no real, independent existence; that nations are only 'relatively independent centres of culture', and that real movers of history are individuals subject to psychological elucidation (Makkreel 1975: 57). It is also worth noting that in writing of the objective mind, Dilthey makes a distinction between systems of culture (law, economy, religion, art) and the outer organisation of society – a distinction of importance to later anthropologists.

Consonant with his approach towards human culture, Dilthey advocates a descriptive psychology that complements that of experimental psychology. He stresses that the human mind is a unified whole and argues against the associationist doctrines of the empiricists. Mental life, he writes, 'does not arise from parts growing together; it is not compounded of elementary units; it does not result from interacting particles of sensation or feeling; it is always an encompassing unity' (1976: 95). But the human mind cannot be understood apart from the human subject, or separate from the socio-historical context. To illustrate Dilthey's views on the human subject it is perhaps useful to quote extracts from his own writings for they indicate the close links that Dilthey saw between history and psychology, and his attempts to situate the subject in a natural, social and historical context:

Language, myth, religious tradition, custom, law and outer organisations are products of the collective mind in which human consciousness, to use Hegel's phrase, has become objectified and so open to
analysis. Man does not discover what he is through speculation about
himself or through psychological experiments but through history. . . .

The psycho-physical unit, man, knows even himself through the
same mutual relationship of expression and understanding; he becomes
aware of himself in the present; he recognizes himself in memory as
something that once was; but, then he tries to hold fast and grasp his
states of mind by turning his attention upon himself, the narrow limits
of such an introspective method of self knowledge show themselves;
only his actions and creations and the effect they have on others teach
man about himself. . . .

The germinal cell of the historical world is the experience in which the
subject discovers himself in a dynamic relationship with his environment. The environment acts on the subject and is acted upon by him. It
is composed of the physical and cultural surroundings. In every part of
the historical world there exists, therefore, the same dynamic connection
between a sequence of mental events and an environment. This is why
the influence both nature and his cultural environment have on man
must be ascertained and evaluated. (1976: 93, 176, 203)

In his criticisms of Hegel's universal reason, Dilthey suggests
that we must begin with 'the reality of life', and Dilthey indeed
described his own approach as a 'philosophy of life', an approach he
felt was akin to that of Tolstoy and Nietzsche. But for Dilthey, life
(*Leben*) is not used in a purely biological sense, but refers essentially
to the socio-historical reality – the 'human world' – which in itself
is conditioned by the natural world. Life for Dilthey is thus both
the starting point of the human sciences and the abiding context for
the human subject. As Copleston writes, Dilthey 'regards the study
of life, of history as a whole, as a constant approximation to an
objective and complete self-knowledge by man. Man is fundamentally an historical being, and he comes to know himself in
history' (1963: 372). This was Hegel's view, but he expressed it
metaphysically. There is the implication, of course, that Dilthey's
philosophy implies a cultural relativism, but Dilthey pleads for the
development of an historical consciousness which is no longer
abstract and metaphysical, and which could form a 'basis for the
unity of mankind in universally valid thought'. He did indeed
argue that as all human beings share the same external world,
which is experienced by a common mental structure, then similar
patterns and ideals of life are developed everywhere. Hegel's

postulate of a universal reason and Schopenhauer's concept of will express in metaphysical abstractions, the fact of human kinship (97). Stuart Hughes (1958: 199) stressed that Dilthey continually struggled to escape from the sceptical and relativist implications of his own thought.

Long, before Wittgenstein, Dilthey was advocating the need for a philosophical anthropology, and one, moreover, based on a much broader basis than that envisaged by linguistic philosophy. For Dilthey's final aim, as Rickman suggests, 'was to co-ordinate and integrate all the disciplines concerned with the various aspects of human life, ranging from man's physiology to his intellectual and cultural products; from the working of individual minds to the functioning of social systems' (1976: 24).

He called this perspective anthropological, and it was one that was intrinsically both historical and psychological.

Dilthey has had an enormous, even if often unacknowledged influence on all the human sciences. Harris (1969: 268–9) noted his influence on Boas and cultural anthropology; Bleicher (1982: 61–2), describing Dilthey as an eminent sociological theorist, suggests that he anticipated, or shaped, much current sociology; many have noted his influence on Max Weber, and Rickman (1976: 1) has observed that the most important German philosophers, particularly the founders of phenomenology and existentialism – Husserl, Heidegger and Jaspers – have been influenced by him. Unfortunately, Dilthey tends to be seen only as a precursor of later theorists and the originality of his views are consequently undervalued. But he was without doubt a 'pathfinder' to the thought of the present century – hermeneutics, cultural anthropology, phenomenology, existentialism, interpretative sociology all bear the impress of his thought. (For further studies of Dilthey, see Hodges 1952; Rickman 1961; Makkreel 1975.)

4.2 Wundt and the Leibnizian Tradition

In the last two chapters we have continued to explore the two contrasting approaches to the human subject which stem from the rationalist and empiricist philosophical traditions. Several writers have suggested that current schools of psychology orient themselves towards one or other of these two polar conceptions, which have been described as the Leibnizian and Lockean traditions (Peters 1953; Allport 1955). The Lockean tradition assumes that the human subject is a *tabula rasa* at birth, and that all knowledge is based on sense impressions. It combines empiricism and an emphasis on sensations with an atomistic approach, leading to the analysis of conscious experience into elements or simple ideas that form the basic building-blocks, as it were, of the mind. Such 'ideas' are seen as basic and fundamental, and prior to the complex ideas that are built up by laws of association. The Lockean tradition sees the human mind as a rather private and personal entity, and knowledge as based essentially on external observations. Besides Locke, Hume, Hartley and J. S. Mill, Bain and Spencer are in this tradition. It was closely allied to positivism – the belief that the methods and concepts of the natural sciences can be applied to all aspects of human life, as well as to evolutionary theory. Behaviourism, Skinner's operant conditioning, and sociobiology belong to this tradition, and the human mind is either bypassed or regarded as of little or no importance. Stressing the positivistic spirit of the Lockean tradition, Allport summed up this psychological approach as having a preference 'for externals rather than internals, for elements rather than patterns, for geneticism, and for a passive or reactive organism rather than for one that is spontaneous and active' (1955: 7–12; G. Miller 1964: 25–9). It is worth noting that this tradition was embraced particularly by Anglo-American psychologists.

The Leibnizian tradition, by contrast, conceptualises the human subject not as a locus of acts, but as the source of activity, and sees the human mind, as with Kant, as an active entity, with inherent categories of thought. Spinoza's concept of conatus, the striving towards self-preservation and self-affirmation, was part of this tradition, and as we have seen in chapter 2, Fichte, Schopenhauer, Nietzsche and Freud all developed Kant's practical reason into a psychology of the will. Besides Kant and Spinoza, Hegel, Schelling, Herbart, Brentano and the Gestalt psychologists are all considered to belong to the Leibnizian tradition.

What is of interest about Wilhelm Wundt (1832–1920) is that until recent scholarship, he was considered by all historians of psychology to stand firmly within the Lockean empiricist tradition. He was considered to be the German version of John Stuart Mill, and to have adopted the atomistic approach of the British psychological empiricists. He is portrayed by Edwin Boring (1950) as having a narrow vision of psychology based on introspection, as denying that human consciousness is an active agency, and as borrowing his ideas from Mill and the British associationist psychologists. During the 1980s, however, scholars indicated that the views expressed by his disciple Edward Titchener (1921) and

Boring have completely misrepresented and misinterpreted Wundt's psychological theories, and that such views have become a hindrance to a proper understanding of Wundt. Rather than adopting the British empiricist tradition of J. S. Mill and Bain, contemporary scholars have stressed that Wundt viewed his psychology as the modern representative of the Leibnizian tradition. Among the influences on Wundt, Blumenthal suggests, were:

> Leibniz's notions of volition, levels of consciousness, and holistic orientations; Spinoza's assertion that volition, or desiring and striving, is the supreme human faculty; Wolff's analyses of the distinctions between empiricists and rationalist psychology; Kant's notion of volitional apperception; Hegel's use of developmental laws; Schelling's and Teten's writings on emotion and volition; and finally Fichte and Schopenhauer's as more direct sources of Wundt's voluntarism. (1980: 125–6)

Wundt therefore stood firmly in the German rationalist tradition.

Although Wundt has been rightly acclaimed as one of the true founders of psychology (along with Fechner, Bain and William James), his anthropological studies have largely passed unnoticed. Several texts on the history of social theory give him no mention (e.g. Harris 1969); one of the essays in Bottomore and Nisbet's *A History of Sociological Analysis* (1979: 194) described Wundt as 'one of the great figures of modern social science', yet he is hardly mentioned in the text. Very little of his work was translated into English, and that which was translated was selective – mainly his popular introductory texts in psychology (Danziger 1980: 74). Like Dilthey, Wundt may be due for a re-appreciation.

Wundt was born in a suburb of Mannhein in south west Germany, the son of a Lutheran pastor. As a young boy he seems to have had few friends, and was a rather lonely child given to fantasy and daydreaming. His only companion was a somewhat older, mentally retarded boy who could barely speak. When he was about eight, Wundt's education was entrusted to his father's young assistant, and Wundt later went to live with him. By all accounts, Wundt was always a serious, indefatigable scholar from the day he was born. Deciding to become a physician, he enrolled at the University of Heidelberg, and in his first years he studied anatomy, physiology, physics and chemistry as well as medicine. Although Wundt qualified as a medical doctor he soon realised that his calling lay elsewhere, and he consequently spent a few months in 1856 studying with the great experimental physiologist Johannes Müller at his institute in Berlin. In 1858 Wundt became research assistant to Hermann Helmholtz, perhaps one of the greatest scientists of the nineteenth century, and a scientific 'idol' also of Freud. It was Helmholtz who stated the law of the conservation of energy. Wundt spent thirteen years at Heidelberg with Helmholtz, undertaking researches into physiology, mainly conducting and demonstrating experiments into nerve impulses and the physiology of the senses. Helmholtz was a reticent man, and although Wundt and Helmholtz (who was eleven years his senior) seemed to have respected each other and their relations were cordial, there was no intimacy or collaboration between them. While working at Heidelberg Wundt gradually lost interest in pure physiology and began to formulate his ideas on a new discipline, that of psychology. In 1862 he published an important study, *Contributions to the Theory of Sensory Perception* (the *Beiträge*), consisting of six articles on the psychology of sense perception. What is important now about the study is that Wundt, then thirty years of age, outlined in the introduction the three projects that were to constitute his life-work, which, with an unmatched thoroughness, he eventually carried through. These were: to create a science of consciousness – psychology – based on experimental methods; to create a psychology based on *Geschichte*, the natural history of humankind, an historical, comparative and ethnographic analysis; and, to develop a truly scientific metaphysics, a philosophy that would integrate and interrelate all the sciences. At different periods of his life Wundt worked consistently on each of these projects, and completed them to his satisfaction, although aware that knowledge is an ongoing enterprise. But it is important to note that all three projects were always in his mind. It is worth noting, for instance, that Wundt was giving a lecture course on 'the natural history of man' (history and cultural anthropology) as early as 1859, even before his first course on 'physiological psychology' (1867) (Diamond 1980: 39).

In 1871 Helmholtz left Heidelberg to become a professor of physics in Berlin, and four years later Wundt moved to Leipzig as professor of philosophy. He remained there until his retirement in 1917, forty-two years later, by which time he had become something of an institution (Fancher 1979: 135).

Once established at Leipzig, Wundt set about the first of his projects, making his proposed experimental psychology into a concrete reality. In 1874 he published the first edition of his *Principles of Physiological Psychology*, based on his lectures at Heidelberg, which many have considered to be the most important book in the history of modern psychology (Boring 1950: 322). It was the symbol of Wundt's metamorphosis from physiologist to psychologist, and attempted to mark out, as Wundt put it, 'a new domain of science'. The book went through six editions between 1873 and 1911, and though Wundt developed and changed many of his ideas and greatly expanded the text, its structure remained essentially the same. It firmly established psychology as a laboratory science with its own problems and experimental methods. In 1879 Wundt established his own laboratory – the first formal psychological laboratory in the world – and two years later founded a journal in experimental psychology, *Philosophische Studien*. Experimental research in Wundt's laboratory was in essence a development of the important studies in physiology pioneered by such researchers as Helmholtz, Müller and Gustav Fechner. What Wundt essentially argued was that conscious states could be studied scientifically through the systematic manipulation of antecedent variables, and analysed by carefully controlled techniques of introspection. But as Fancher and others have stressed, this self-observation or introspection was not the simple sort of self-analysis or inner pondering usually associated with the term, but rather a rigorous and highly controlled technique for separating and examining conscious experience in terms of its most basic elements (1979: 139).

After establishing his psychological laboratory, Wundt spent the following decade largely in the writing of his philosophical studies – *Logic* (1880–3), *Ethics* (1886) and *System of Philosophy* (1889). The three books amount to some 2,500 pages and by no means exhaust his activities during that period. It indicates what a prodigious scholar he was: it has been estimated that during his lifetime he wrote over 500 articles and books, and that reading fifty pages a day, it would take a person almost three years to get through Wundt's works (Fancher 1979: 130). Summing up his philosophy, motivated by the aim to integrate all the natural sciences, Copleston suggests that Wundt conceived of reality as 'the totality of individual agents or active centres which are to be regarded as volitional unities of different grades. These volitional unities form a developing series which tends towards the emergence of a total spirit (*Gesamtgeist*). In more concrete terms, there is a movement towards the complete spiritual unification of man or humanity' (1963: 383). Wundt therefore produced a variant of rational idealism in the tradition of Leibniz and Hegel.

Given the stress on volition, which links Wundt with Schopenhauer, Nietzsche and Freud, it is hardly surprising that Wundt described his own form of psychology as 'voluntarism'. Psychology, as he defined it, was concerned with the study of consciousness, and the latter he felt could be analysed into elementary sensations and feelings. This is the only thing he has in common with the empiricist psychologists like J. S. Mill and Bain, but it is important to realise that he looks upon these elements not as inert static units but as processes. Moreover, he looked upon categories like sensation, feeling and volition as essentially theoretical constructs, 'whose referents exist not as separate entities but only as components in a complex process that follows a course of development marked by changing interrelationships among the components' (Danziger 1980: 97). Wundt did not see psychology as dealing with inner conscious experience; for the distinction between inner and outer experience is invalid. Feeling is inner in that it is consciously subjective, and perception is outer in that it refers to the external world; but psychology for Wundt deals with both. Nor did Wundt see consciousness as separate from our whole physical and mental being, it is only the 'mental side of this being' (1912: 6). But importantly, Wundt rejects the atomistic approach of the empiricists and the theory that mental processes involve the association of ideas. This approach, he suggests, involves the 'false materialisation of ideas' and assumes that an 'idea' is an unchanging entity like the object it represents. But any mental idea, Wundt argues, is no more than a constant thing than is a feeling or emotion or volitional process. There exists only changing and transient conscious processes. Moreover, just as ideas are not permanent objects, neither are they processes that take place independently of feelings and emotions, for these influence what he described as apperception (1912: 121–2). The concept of apperception, which Wundt derived from Leibniz and Herbart, refers to the constructive activity of the mind, to the active process of selecting and structuring internal experience, particularly relating to the focus of attention within the field of conscious experience. While apprehension is simply the entrance of some content into consciousness apperception is the active grasping of this by attention (1912: 35). Wundt thus makes a distinction between the periphery of consciousness which is perceived, and the focalised aspect of consciousness which is apperceived. But Wundt saw apperception as an active principle, as essentially a manifestation of volition, a principle that gave structure and direction to both experience and movement (Danziger 1980: 104). Volition or will, however, for Wundt is not simply an intellectual process as Kant and other philosophers had implied, but always involves affective processes, feelings and emotions. As mental processes, apperception and volition are interlinked and both involve cognition and feeling. Both are active processes.

Wundt also described feelings in terms of three pairs of contrasts, relating to pleasure and pain, strain and relaxation, excitement and calm. With respect to the self or ego, Wundt described this as 'neither an idea nor a specific feeling, but it consists of those elementary volitional processes of apperception which accompany the process of consciousness' (1912: 68). The ego, always present but always changing, forms the lasting substratum of our self-consciousness. The self for Wundt is neither a special substance nor can it be reduced, as with Hume, to a discrete series of sense perceptions.

It is important to stress that although Wundt looked upon psychology as a science, and spoke of the 'laws of psychical life', he made a distinction between physical and psychological laws, and opposed the reduction of all sciences to physics. He was consistently anti-positivist. He was critical of writers like Dilthey who advocated a purely descriptive psychology and who considered laws, in the sense of universally valid rules, to be restricted to the natural sciences. Psychical laws, universal regularities, pertain also to the processes of consciousness, Wundt felt. But he was also critical of a materialist psychology that reduced consciousness to physical laws (1912: 154–7). As he expressed it in his *Outlines of Psychology*:

> Materialism does away with psychology entirely and puts in its place an imaginary brain physiology of the future, or when it tries to give positive theories falls into doubtful and unreliable hypotheses of cerebral physiology. In thus giving up psychology in any proper sense, this doctrine gives up entirely the attempt to furnish any practical basis for the mental sciences. (1907, in Rieber 1980: 184)

Mind, for Wundt, was not a substance, but an actuality, and he conceived of the relationship between the body and mind as involving the 'principle of psycho-physical parallelism' (1980: 187). But he was against the Cartesian dualism that saw the body and mind as substances, and though rejecting materialism, which he referred to as a monistic view, he never doubted the objectivity of the natural world, or the fact that psychical phenomena, such as sensations and feelings, are intrinsically bound up with physical processes. In essence he argued that the mental and the physical belong to connected but separate realms, each with its own laws of causality. His thoughts seem similar to Spinoza; there is only one reality, but it can be examined from two points of view. Popper and Eccles would appear to espouse a similar, interactionist, view of mind/body dualism (Popper and Eccles 1977; Eccles and Robinson 1985).

The human subject, then, as conceived by Wundt, is essentially a 'psycho-physical' being, as we in reality experience ourselves. It is thus inadequate to conceive of the human subject from a purely physical or a psychical point of view, Wundt contends, and to understand the life of the human subject, 'the psycho-physical being given to us in its unity', we must combine the natural sciences and psychology for their approaches essentially 'supplement' each other (1912: 183–4). Physiology and psychology are simply different standpoints – they both have the psycho-physical unity, the human being as their subject matter. Wundt makes the important point that science (as with art) involves both imagination (concrete thought) and understanding (knowledge).

I have so far discussed only two of Wundt's projects – philosophy and experimental psychology. We can turn now to his third project – that of establishing a cultural psychology, *Völkerpsychologie*. Wundt viewed psychology as occupying an intermediate position between the natural sciences, like physics, chemistry and biology, and the mental, or social sciences as we would now describe them – history, jurisprudence, political science and the philosophies of art and religion. Wundt thus divided his psychology into two parts – experimental and cultural, the natural history of the mind, as he writes. Simple mental functions – sensation, perception, memory, simple feelings – could be studied through experimental methods with individuals, but our higher mental processes could only be understood by reference to history and ethnology· 'Psychology must not only strive to become a useful basis for the other mental sciences, but it must also turn again and again to the historical sciences, in order to obtain an understanding for the more highly developed mental processes' (1912: 194).

Wundt therefore, like Dilthey, firmly situated himself in the German historical tradition that stemmed from Herder and Hegel, and firmly believed that only by understanding the products of the human mind – Dilthey's objective spirit – could we understand the higher processes of human thought. To understand the development of the human mind we must have recourse to human culture and history. This aspect of Wundt's psychology has been singularly ignored by British and American academic psychology, which has followed the empiricist tradition and concerned itself solely with the psychology of isolated, ahistorical individuals. American social psychology has also followed this tradition (Danziger 1980: 82).

By *Völkerpsychologie* (best translated as ethnic or cultural psychology) Wundt understood the psychological study of the products of collective life, particularly religion, language, myth and custom. Although his writings on the subject had begun as early as 1860, it was not until 1900 that he began work on his monumental study *Elements of Folk Psychology*, which he published in ten volumes (1900–20). Marvin Harris (1969) has written that few of the great anthropologists of the nineteenth century escaped the effects of the pervasive racial deterministic outlook of the period – Spencer, Tylor and Morgan, all cultural evolutionists, are the important figures here. But there was nevertheless a growing feeling towards the end of the century that there was an essential 'psychic unity' common to all humankind. The writings of Adolph Bastian strongly expressed this doctrine of psychic unity, for he rejected both racial and geographical determinism and used the concept to account for the apparent similarities to be found in varied cultural traditions. Wundt followed this ethnological tradition in two senses.

First, he adopted an evolutionary perspective, inferring from the ethnographic record several stages of cultural evolution – a 'totemic age' giving rise to an 'age of heroes and gods', which in turn led to the 'age of humanity'. But although many human cultures throughout the world were still at the 'totemic' stage of evolution, this 'did not at all imply that within the narrow sphere that constitutes his world, the intelligence of primitive man is inferior to that of cultural man', and, Wundt continued, 'the intellectual endowment of primitive man is in itself approximately equal to that of civilised man, primitive man merely exercises his ability in a more restricted field' (1916: 112–13).

Secondly, Wundt senses that individual psychology could only be meaningful if it took into account cultural facts. But though Wundt wrote of the folk spirit or soul (*Volksgeist*), he did not overemphasise the social, nor, like many of his contemporaries, conceive of the folk-spirit as a quasi-religious entity that transcended human collective life. Equally, he was well aware that culture could not be interpreted simply in terms of individual psychology. As he wrote, folk psychology relates

to those mental products which are created by a community of human life and are therefore inexplicable in terms merely of individual consciousness, since they presuppose the reciprocal action of many . . .

thus, then, in the analysis of the higher mental processes, folk psychology is an indispensable supplement to the psychology of individual consciousness. (1916: 3)

Wundt had an encyclopaedic mind, and an almost unrivalled ability to bring together a vast amount of empirical material and present it as a systematic structure. He was driven by a deep sense of pride that arose from early feelings of loneliness and inferiority, and he had a passion for orderliness. Even his death, Boring records, seems to have accorded with his systematic habits. Having completed his *Völkerpsychologie* and the revisions of his early psychological texts and written his autobiography in 1920, he died shortly thereafter. He was eighty-eight years old (1950: 327).

Although acclaimed as the founder of experimental psychology, Wundt is a much neglected figure, particularly in anthropology. But his influence was enormous, and many of his students at Leipzig later became important scholars in their own right – Titchener, Kraepelin, Stanley Hall, Cattell, Angell and Külpe. He has had an important influence on Durkheim, Boas and Malinowski, and this influence, Bock suggests (1980: 26), is probably far greater than is generally recognised. His importance was earlier noted by Irving Hallowell (1976), who wrote that Wundt made an 'heroic effort' to relate cultural data to psychology, at a time when the major emphasis in this discipline was individualistic, physiological and biological. Wundt's insistence that cultural and historical data are essential material for the psychologist was, Hallowell remarked, of critical historical importance (1976: 186–9), for Wundt clearly envisaged problems that centred on the complex interrelationships between individual and cultural forms – problems that have only recently been reaffirmed by researchers – particularly those concerned with culture and cognition (e.g. Berry and Dasen 1974). Wundt, having been misunderstood or ignored for so long, is now being seen by many scholars as a genuine innovator whose ideas anticipated those of many contemporary psychologists and psycholinguistics like Chomsky (Fancher 1979: 146–9; Leahey 1987: 188).

It is of interest that of the two schools of psychology that emerged during the early decades of the present century, one, the structuralist school associated with Edward Titchener (1897), was virtually identified with Wundt's psychology, Titchener being described as a disciple of Wundt; while the other, the Gestalt school, was seen as emerging later (along with behaviourism) as a 'revolt' or rejection of the 'brick and mortar psychology' of Wundt. This is the opinion of the dynamic behaviourist Robert Woodworth (1931: 100–1). Nothing could be further from the truth, for the reality is the opposite. The psychological systems of Wundt and Titchener are quite distinct, for Titchener's structuralist theory followed the tradition of British empiricist psychology, and though he claimed to be a follower of Wundt, in his hands Wundt's basic ideas of volition, apperception, cultural psychology, were either muted or fundamentally changed. There is an 'enormous cultural and intellectual gulf' separating Wundt's voluntarism and Titchener's structuralism (Danziger 1980: 84; Blumenthal 1980: 128).

4.3 Cultural Anthropology

In many ways Franz Boas (1858–1942) played the same role in founding cultural anthropology that Wundt played in founding experimental psychology as an academic discipline – he literally presided over, though in a creative manner, the establishment of anthropology as an university-based discipline. His accomplishments as a teacher, administrator and scholar are, like Wundt's, unique and breath taking to consider. Yet though a central figure in anthropology, Boas has tended to be ignored by British anthropologists, who have followed Durkheim in seeing anthropology as the study of society rather than the science of humankind. Ingold (1986) has recently made a renewed plea from within this tradition for a Boasian approach, which unites the biological and cultural dimensions of human life.

Boas was born in Minden in Germany, and came from a liberal, freethinking background. His university studies were in physics and mathematics and his doctoral dissertation was in physics, on the colour of seawater. But being a keen nature lover and botanist, he developed an interest in geography and, in 1883, at the age of twenty-five, he went to Baffinland to undertake research in physical and human geography. Living with the Inuit, his fieldwork experience had a profound effect on Boas and it is often spoken of as a kind of 'conversion experience', for it radically changed his theoretical disposition. Boas came to realise the inadequacy of trying to interpret cultures in terms of environmental factors, although he had initially, under the influence of Ratzel, accepted the main tenets of 'geographical determinism'. In postulating the relative autonomy of culture, Boas thus not only became an anthropologist, but in a real sense laid the foundations of modern anthropology, several decades before Malinowski. After further fieldwork studies among the north-west coast Indians, Boas eventually became, through his writings and his contribution to the development of anthropology as an academic discipline, one of the most influential figures in the history of social science. He was, as Goldenweiser remarked (1941: 153), anthropology's 'culture hero'. And as many American anthropologists were trained by Boas – Kroeber, Lowie, Sapir, Radin, Mead, Benedict – it is possible, as Kardiner and Preble note (1961: 133), to link Boas with almost every major theoretical and methodological doctrine in American anthropology. Of particular importance were his links to the culture and personality school, which we shall discuss below.

The kind of anthropology Boas advocated has been described by Harris (1969: 25–289) – and I think justly – as 'historical particularism'. Boas had a strong empiricist background and was of a critical and sceptical disposition, and he was also influenced by the German historical school, which is associated with Dilthey. As we have seen, this tradition clearly differentiated between the natural and the human sciences, the one concerned with explanation, the other with understanding. Boas repudiated the mechanistic approach to cultural life, and clearly stood in the humanistic tradition. He is reputed to have read Kant on his trips to Baffinland, during the long, cold evenings. But although Boas stressed the need for careful descriptive studies, of understanding culture from 'within', and emphasised the importance of critical objectivity (which, as Kroeber (1935: 540) remarked, he derived from his scientific background), Boas never advocated pure description or ideographic studies. Like Dilthey, he had a strong sense that culture was essentially of an historical nature and that the aim of the social sciences should be the formulation of generalised and cultural regularities. But as Lévi-Strauss remarked, he imposed on anthropological studies conditions of validity 'so exacting and impossible to meet that they would have withered scientific development in any field' (1963: 281). As Harris noted, Boas had an empiricist, somewhat Baconian conception of science. Thus, rather than seeing a dialectic relationship between fact and theory, Boas saw knowledge as essentially involving the collection of reliable facts from which inductive generalisations could later be drawn. The larger the corpus of sound ethnographic data the better the foundation for their formulation. But as Harris cogently remarked: 'Science consists of more than responsibility to the data; the data must be made responsible to theory. Neither one without the other suffices. It is impossible to be faithful to the facts and at the same time indifferent to theory' (1969: 285).

The essence of the Boasian approach is summed up here:

> When we have cleared up the history of a single culture and understand the effects of environment on the psychological condition that are reflected in it we have made a step forward, as we can then investigate in how far the same causes or other causes were at work in the development of other cultures. Thus by comparing histories of growth general laws may be found. (Boas 1940: 279)

In 1911 Boas published his classic study *The Mind of Primitive Man*. It was a summation of his earlier studies and it represents a seminal contribution to social thought. The book contains three essential theses.

First, it is critical of early evolutionary theories. Kardiner and Preble (1961) suggest, not without some exaggeration, that Boas 'dealt a blow to evolutionary theory and the comparative method from which American anthropology has never recovered'. Through the writings of Steward (1960) and White there had been a reaffirmation and reappraisal of evolutionary theory. The important point, however, is that Boas never repudiated cultural evolution; what he criticised were the speculative theories of the late nineteenth century, particularly those that implied that all cultures pass through a necessary pre-determined process of change. As he wrote:

> The development of ethnology is largely due to the general recognition of the principle of biological evolution. It is a common feature of all forms of evolutionary theory that every living being is considered as a result of an historical development. This point of view introduced an historical perspective into the natural sciences and has revolutionised their methods. (1940: 633)

Thus, as Lesser (1981: 22–5) stressed, Boas accepted biological evolution and affirmed the principle of cultural evolution, but this was seen in historical terms, not orthogenetic. It was speculative theories of evolution that Boas rejected.

Secondly, in stressing the relative autonomy of social phenomena, and the cultural diversity that ethnographical studies had indicated, Boas argued that race (physical type), language and culture were independent concepts. He cogently demonstrated that not only was there little evidence to support environmental determinism, but racial deterministic theories of culture were also untenable.

Finally, though his writings implied a 'cultural relativist' stance (which was later taken up by his students, Herskovits in particular), a central theme of this study is to show that human beings the world over share fundamentally the same mental processes. Boas begins by stressing a viewpoint, one more balanced than most anthropologists, that human beings differ from animals along three crucial dimensions – the possession of language, the use of tools and the power of rational thinking – indeed he considers the cognitive functions of reason, the ability to form conclusions from premises and the desire to seek for causal relation, as basic to all forms of culture (1911: 141). Boas poses the question as to whether the mental processes among 'primitive' and 'civilised' (i.e. literate) peoples are essentially the same. The question is understandable against the background and theories of much nineteenth-century thought, even (or is it especially?) among the intelligentsia. Harris draws attention to this statement by the first president of the American Anthropological Association: 'The savage stands strikingly close to sub-human species in every aspect of mentality as well as in bodily habits and bodily structure' (McGee 1901: 13).

Boas examined this question by considering four mental characteristics which where said to characterise pre-literate peoples: their inability to control impulses or emotion; their inability to concentrate or focus attention; their lack of logical thinking; and their supposed lack of originality or creativity. Boas showed that none of these assumptions is valid. The numerous cases of taboos or ritual prohibitions, the vision quest of the Plains Indians, and the perseverance exacted in the making of utensils and implements demonstrated for Boas that pre-literate people are able to control their emotional impulses. The supposed lack of concentration he suggested was hardly consonant with the effort and foresight that went into ceremonial exchanges. As for Levy-Bruhl's thesis that 'primitive' people are unable to think logically in the sense that there is a 'participation in the whole mass of subjective and objective experience which prevents a clear distinction between logically unrelated subjects' (1911: 135), Boas to some extent agrees with him. For Boas sensed that a characteristic of many pre-literate cultures was that various aspects of their cultural life were not differentiated but conjoined through 'emotional associations'. Such patterns of associated ideas – symbolic classification – were evident in all cultures but on the whole 'such associations between groups of ideas apparently unrelated are rare in civilised life'. And he continued:

–165–

In our modern society, except among the adherents of still flourishing astrology, the consideration of cosmic phenomena is constantly associated with the efforts to give adequate explanations for them, based on the principle of causality. In primitive society the consideration of the same phenomena leads to a number of typical associations different from our own, but occurring with remarkable regularity among tribes of the most remote parts of the world. (1911: 241)

Thus, for Boas, 'primitive thought' differed from European thought in the sense that the former was often characterised by a symbolic logic that served to unify disparate aspects of social life, and was evident in the supposed identification of humans and animals, the principles of magic and in religious ceremonies. But Boas contended that this did not imply that pre-literate people thought differently. Levy-Bruhl reached his conclusion – a misleading one according to Boas – 'not from a study of individual behaviour, but from the traditional beliefs and customs of primitive people'. And that if we disregarded the thinking of the individual in our own society and paid attention only to current beliefs, we would most probably conclude, Boas suggest, that the same attitudes prevail, namely that Europeans think pre-logically (1911: 135).

Thus Boas emphasised that the difference is primarily in the cultural context of thought, and the degree to which pre-literate communities systematise and integrate their culture through 'emotional associations', rather than in any qualitative difference in the processes of thinking (Berry and Dasen 1974: 6–8). We have discussed elsewhere Hallpike's study (1979) of 'primitive thought', for this writer has restated Levy-Bruhl's essential thesis using Piagetian theory (B. Morris 1987: 310–12).

The final aspect of 'primitive thought' that Boas examined, namely the supposed lack of originality among pre-literate peoples, he also challenges. He points to the complexity of esoteric doctrines formulated by priests and the existence of prophets with respect to millenial cults, both of which indicate an independence and a creativity of thought. The conclusion that Boas reached, therefore, is thus:

I think these considerations illustrate that the differences between civilised man and primitive man are in may cases more apparent than real: that the social condition, on account of their peculiar characteristics, easily convey the impression that the mind of primitive man acts in a way quite different from ours, while in reality the fundamental traits of the mind are the same. (1911: 137)

Harris has suggested that Boas was influenced throughout his life by neo-Kantian philosophy and this has been affirmed by many other writers (e.g. Hatch 1973: 42; Freeman 1983: 22–3). But Boas's stress on the autonomy of culture and on cultural determinism must be set within the historical context in which Boas was writing, and his ongoing attempts to counter the biological determinist theories of the Eugenics movement. In the early decades of the present century the biological theories of Galton and Karl Pearson crystallised in the formation of the Eugenics movement, an important social movement concerned with 'race improvement' and which, as Freeman writes, saw biology as the panacea for all the social ills of human kind (1983: 16). The cornerstone of this movement was to suggest that the human subject was largely determined by hereditary factors and its programme of selective breeding, as Boas foresaw, had dangerous and reactionary social implications. The movement did in fact culminate in the theories of the German fascists. Not all followers of Darwin were of course biological determinists – Freeman notes that Huxley, Wallace and Lankester all accepted that in the human species culture was a relatively autonomous system – but in their enthusiasm to improve the race, Pearson and the advocates of Eugenics certainly engaged a large following. In countering their racist biological doctrines and in his contribution to the nature–nurture controversy, which raged throughout the 1920s, Boas became increasingly committed to an extreme cultural deterministic theory. Drawing on the ideas of Theodor Waitz, who stressed the fundamental 'psychic unity' of humankind in his six-volume *Anthropologie Der Naturvölker* (Leipzig, 1858–71), as well as on the neo-Kantians, Boas came to postulate an unbridgeable gap between culture and biology, and to suggest that the human subject was essentially a cultural being. The whole emphasis of Boas's approach was, as George Stocking suggested: 'To distinguish the concepts of race and culture, to separate biological and cultural heredity, to focus attention on cultural process, to free the concept of culture from its heritage of evolutionary and racial assumption; so that it could subsequently become . . . completely independent of biological determinism' (1968: 264).

The essence of Boas's theoretical critiques of racism and biological theories of culture was to suggest a dichotomy between nature (biology) and culture (anthropology and history), and to overemphasise the cultural conditioning aspects of human life. With Kroeber and Lowie the total separation of biology and cultural anthropology became even more stark. Thus Freeman concludes that in opposing the unwarranted application of biological principles to cultural phenomena Boas inevitably came 'to underestimate the importance of biology in human life, and to impede the emergence of a scientifically adequate anthropological paradigm based on recognition of the pervasive interaction of biological and cultural processes' (1983: 26). Freeman's own biocultural perspective, however, ignores the psychological dimensions of human life, which Boas's was always implicitly conscious of. The similarities between the implications of Boas's cultural determinism and both Watson's psychological behaviourism and Durkheim's sociology has been noted (Freeman 1983: 46–54; Morris 1985).

In many ways Boas conceived of culture as an entity that was *sui generis*, an 'emergent' system that was independent of biological and environmental factors. Although he sensed that both environmental and psychological factors had a certain conditioning or limiting affect on human culture, his essential thesis was that culture could only be understood in terms of its own distinctive historical processes (Hatch 1973: 42–57). Thus in many ways Boas's conception of culture is similar to Durkheim's conception of the social as an entity *sui generis*. But as Service has suggested, unlike Durkheim, Kroeber and Leslie White, who tended to see culture as a level of reality *sui generis*, to be investigated and explained only in its own terms, Boas (along with Benedict and Sapir) saw culture as having its essential locus in the human mind. Boas, he writes, was a 'subjectivist' and as culture is basically mental, an appropriate science of culture would be some variant of psychology (1985: 260–2). His well-known definition of culture implies a focus on the human individual:

> Culture may be defined as the totality of the mental and physical reactions that characterise the behaviour of the individuals composing a social group collectively and individually in relation to their natural environment, to other groups, to members of the group itself, and of each individual to himself. It also includes the products of these activities and their role in the life of the groups. The mere enumeration of these various aspects of life, however, does not constitute culture. It is more, for its elements are not independent, they have a structure. (1938: 159)

Boas continually stressed that anthropology should adopt a holistic approach and study all aspects of human life, and he stressed too that culture was an integrated whole, which must be understood by developing an historical science that was distinct from the natural sciences. But because he placed a crucial emphasis on the independence of culturally patterned behaviour, on the autonomy of culture, and saw the human subject as essentially a cultural being, many other writers besides Freeman have seen Boas as an extreme cultural determinist. Just as Wundt has been wrongly interpreted as an empiricist by historians of psychology, so Boas has been seen as holding a Lockean conception of the human subject. Tim Ingold (1986), for example, has argued that Boas conceived of the human subject as simply a culture-bearing organism, as an individual who passively reflected an 'internalised cultural logic'. Boas's view of the human mind, he writes, 'ceases to be a producer and becomes a mere container of cultural ideas. The mind is no longer agent but medium: culture is correspondingly elevated from the status of an instrument to that of a director of human purposes, substituting for natural disposition rather than serving to put them into effect' (1986: 30–1). Now this Lockean approach of seeing the human subject (mind) as simply the container of a cultural logic may well be in accord with what is implied in the writings of Durkheim, Benedict, Kroeber and Leslie White, but it is misleading to interpret Boas in this light. Boas followed the same tradition as that of his compatriot Wundt, and there are undoubted affinities between the perspectives of the two scholars, for both looked upon culture as essentially a mental phenomenon that had to be understood by ethnographic and historical analysis. Thus in the Leibnizian tradition, Boas puts a focus not on culture as a reality *sui generis*, nor does he conceive of the human subject as a passive organism, but rather he sees culture as a psychological phenomenon and puts a focus on the interrelationship between the human individual and society. The relationship between culture and the self for Boas is a dialectical one:

> We have to recognise that the individual can be understood only as part of the society to which he belongs and that society can be understood only on the basis of the interrelations of the constituent individuals . . . the dynamics of social life can be understood only on the basis of the reaction of the individual to the culture in which he lives and of his influence upon society . . .
> The activities of the individual are determined to a great extent by his

social environment, but in turn his own activities influences the society in which he lives, and may bring about modifications in its form. (1940: 260–94)

Boas did not see the human subject as wholly determined by culture (as both Freeman and Ingold imply), nor did he deny that some aspects of human behaviour are not organically determined, but he saw such determining factors – both cultural and biological – as mediated by the human subject, as an active, psychological being.

Kroeber (1943: 61) described Boas as a Promethean genius of massive and acute intelligence. Looking upon anthropology as the science of humankind, Boas felt that the understanding of other cultures gave us important insights into our own cultural conditioning and thus could help us in creating a more just and humane world. Throughout his long life he expressed radical politics; he spoke out against the United States' involvement in the First World War, and condemned American anthropologists who, under the cover of anthropology, carried out secret intelligence work in Latin America. Thus Boas was a true and worthy scholar. He not only saw anthropology as an open field of inquiry rooted in empirical observations and experience, but also as a committed humanistic science with progressive aims – contributing to a better world for all people (Honigmann 1976: 195; Lesser 1981: 27).

It was Kroeber rather than Boas who looked upon the human subject in terms of a 'culture-bearing organism'. Alfred Kroeber (1876–1960) was the first of Boas's graduate students at Columbia University, and though born in New Jersey, like Boas, he came from a German background. But while Boas's early training was in the natural sciences, Kroeber had majored in the arts, and when he came under the influence of Boas he already had a masters degree in English literature, and was lecturing in that subject. To an important degree, as Harris (1969: 320) notes, Kroeber maintained a neo-Kantian perspective all his life. Unlike Boas, Kroeber argued that culture was a phenomenon *sui generis*, and in an important article (1917) he maintained that culture is 'superorganic', a 'substance' that is irreducible to the level of the individual organism. But like Durkheim the superorganic is not only irreducible to the organic level but also is inexplicable in terms of individuals. Kroeber was thus consistently anti-individualist, and saw the biological and cultural realms as radically discontinuous. 'The dawn of the social', he wrote, 'is not a link in a chain, not a step in a path, but a leap to another plane. It may be likened to the first occurence of life in the hitherto lifeless universe' (1917: 49). Thus, for Kroeber, there is a radical separation between history and biology, and cultural phenomena are to be understood in terms of historical laws, which are viewed as tendencies not as causal laws. Kroeber was therefore consistently anti-positivist, and rejected the idea that the principles of mechanistic science were applicable to social life. The historian of culture, he argued, must seek not to explain but to interpret, to seek connections, tendencies and patterns within cultural phenomena. Kroeber's monumental and important study *Configurations of Culture Growth* (1944) is aptly titled. Boas clearly distanced himself from the concept of the superorganic, noting that it 'seems hardly necessary to consider culture a mystic entity that exists outside the society of its individual carriers and that moves by its own force' (1928: 245).

Kroeber, therefore, though renouncing the nomothetic approach, is much closer to Durkheim than to Boas in his approach to the human subject, and offers a similar dualistic paradigm. Mankind, he wrote, 'compromises two aspects; he is an organic substance that can be viewed as a substance, and he is also a tablet that is written upon' (1917: 32) – and it is culture which writes the script. But unlike Comte and Durkheim, Kroeber clearly foresaw scope for a psychological science, recognising four levels of reality – inorganic (matter), organic (life), psychic (consciousness) and superorganic (culture). Collapsing the biological and physical realms, Popper, half a century later, was propounding the same schema in his 'three-world philosophy' (Popper and Eccles 1977).

It was largely in reaction to Kroeber that both Boas and Sapir stressed the need not only for an historical analysis of culture, but also of understanding the relationship of the individual to his or her culture, thus initiating the culture and personality school within anthropology. (For useful discussions of both Boas and Kroeber and the foundations of cultural anthropology in the United States, see Kardiner and Preble 1961; Harris 1969; T. Kroeber 1970; Hatch 1973; Silverman 1981; Service 1985.)

4.4 Patterns of Culture

In mapping the relationship between individual personality and culture, three very different kinds of research strategies have been noted in anthropological studies. One is that adopted by Durkheim, White and social scientists more generally (Le Vine 1973:

43–8), which suggests that personality variables have no relevance at all in the analysis of socio-cultural phenomena. Culture is an entity *sui generis*. As Durkheim put it: 'The determining cause of a social fact should be sought among the social facts preceding it and not among the states of individual consciousness' (1895: 110). Others have tempered this kind of sociologism by stressing the importance of ecological and economic variables. A second strategy accepts the autonomy of cultural analysis, and is also critical of any kind of psychological reductionism. But this approach implies the need for introducing a psychological dimension to the analysis or at least an awareness that psychological presuppositions are intrinsic to anthropological research. This strategy thus accepts, unlike the first approach, a specific psychological level of analysis, independent of both biology and social science. This is best described as a 'two system' view (Le Vine 1973: 58–9), and has been advocated by a variety of writers. Rivers, Boas and Wundt all adopt this strategy, as do more contemporary writers such as Spiro, Hallowell and Reich. Devereux has rightly suggested that what is involved here is a 'double discourse', each discipline taking cognisance of the other, but in essence independent and complementary. Any reduction of one level to the other is, he suggests, 'absolutely illusory' (1978: 3).

The orthodox Freudian approach to culture, discussed in chapter 2, seems to do precisely this, attempting to explain social phenomena by reference to psychological variables. This strategy has been described as 'psychoanalytic reductionism' (Le Vine 1973: 48), and is best exemplified by the studies of Géza Roheim. But it is worth noting that, by placing central emphasis on the Oedipal complex or on the infantile situation, this strategy or approach suggests a socio-psychological determinism, rather than an explanation in terms of the individual personality.

We turn now to another kind of research strategy, one that laid the foundations for what afterwards became known as the 'culture and personality' school in anthropology. This approach has been termed configurational (Bourguignon 1979: 82–7; Bock 1980: 63–79). It is exemplified by the writings of Ruth Benedict and Margaret Mead. Through their popular works these two scholars have had an enormous impact on the general public and have been particularly influential in educational circles, their books becoming best-sellers. Written in a clear and readable style, and in the case of Benedict also a poetic and elegant one, they have been instrumental in introducing a wide audience to anthropology. Yet surprisingly, they have all but been ignored by British anthropology and have no mention in several introductory texts.

Ruth Benedict (1887–1948) was one of the first women to 'attain major status as a social scientist' (Mead 1974: 1). She came to anthropology rather late after graduating in English literature, and after experiencing a somewhat unhappy marriage. It is interesting that she is the only woman mentioned in two collections of essays on the founders of social science (Kardiner and Preble 1961; Raison 1969). Studying under Kroeber and Boas, she conducted her first field researches among the Serrano Indians of California in 1922, when she was thirty-five. Between 1924 and 1926 she undertook further field studies among the Zuni and Pima Indians. It was while among the Pima that she was struck by the contrast between the cultures of the Plains Indians and that of the Pueblo communities of the south-west. In her doctoral thesis on the 'Concept of the Guardian Spirit' (1923), Benedict traced the nature of the beliefs in such spirits – acquired by an individual through a dream or vision quest – throughout North America. She was, however, less concerned with the distribution of cultural traits and their historical reconstruction than in indicating the social patterning of these beliefs – how the guardian spirit beliefs were integrated in a specific culture context (Bock 1980: 65–6). These seminal thoughts were developed during the next decade, and in 1934 Benedict published her classic study, *Patterns of Culture*. This was truly a 'groundbreaking work' (Barnouw 1973: 59), and a major landmark in anthropological studies. It is still recommended reading to all students in the social sciences – except those undertaking an anthropology degree.

The book focuses on the descriptive analyses of three cultures: the Pueblo Indians of New Mexico, Benedict drawing heavily on her own researches among the Zuni; the Dobuans of Melanesia, who had been the subject of a monograph by Reo Fortune (1932); and the north-west coast Indians, the studies of Boas among the Kwakuitl being a major source of reference. Each of these cultures is discussed in terms of specific and dominant cultural configurations. But before discussing these, some discussion may be devoted to the nature and sources of Benedict's theoretical perspective.

The first thing to be said is that the book hardly shows any influence of Freud; there is no psychoanalytic orientation to be discerned in its pages. Equally important, in view of White's harsh criticisms of the 'culture and personality school', is that the theoretical tenor of *Patterns of Culture* is one of cultural determinism. For as Barnouw writes, 'her emphasis was always on the culture rather than on the individual. There is no study of individuals in Benedict's book and no life histories' (1973: 72). The analysis is always focused on specific cultures. The reason for this is that Benedict, as she herself indicated (1934: 36–7), largely took her bearings from the German historical tradition and from Gestalt psychology.

As we have noted earlier, the German idealist tradition stressed that the human sciences were centrally concerned not with causal analysis but with the interpretation of meaning and thus the understanding of cultural history meant attempting to grasp intuitively the instinctive mood, or *Weltanschauung*, of a period or culture. Benedict sees Dilthey in particular as stressing the importance of integration and configuration, of the need to discern the *Zeitgeist* or spirit of the time' and of indicating the relativity of philosophical systems. In like manner, Gestalt psychology (R. Thomson 1968: 243–8), in breaking away from introspection and the experimental psychology associated with Wundt, was also acclaimed by Benedict. The Gestalt school argued that perception involved more than the simple association of sense impressions, for what was perceived was grasped, they suggested, in structured, organised wholes. Benedict felt that this notion of Gestalt or configuration had important implications for social science. (For an interesting discussion of the relation of Gestalt psychology to anthropology, see Hallowell 1976: 201–4.)

Having wide literary interests, Benedict was also influenced by two other writers, both also of German origin. The first was Oswald Spengler, who in his *Decline of the West* (1934) had indicated that two opposing philosophies were expressed in the Western tradition, the Apollonian view of life upon which the 'civilisation of the classical world was built' and the 'Faustian view' of the modern period (1934: 38). The second was the philosopher Friedrich Nietzsche, whose study of Greek drama, *The Birth of Tragedy* (1956), discussed a similar opposition, that between the Apollonian and Dionysian modes of experiences. This contrast is a central motif of Benedict's study.

The opening chapters of *Patterns of Culture* stress four essential themes.

The first is that a person's ideas, beliefs and attitudes are largely culturally determined: 'No man ever looks at the world', she writes, 'with pristine eyes. He sees it edited by a definite set of customs and institutions and ways of thinking' (1934: 2). Such cultural conditioning may not be stressed or evident in other social sciences, but it is something that is intrinsic to the anthropological enterprise.

Secondly, throughout history, Benedict suggests, mankind has expressed ethnocentric feelings, believing that there was a difference in kind between their own community and outsiders. This is but a reflection she thought of a fundamental premise, namely the 'diversity of cultures'. She notes that many tribal names – Zuni, Dene and Kiowa, for example – are names by which these communities are known, yet these are only the local terms for 'human beings'; that is, themselves. As folk classificatory terms are essentially prototypical, this did not imply that other communities were seen as non-human, as Benedict and more recently Leach (1982: 62) seem to suggest. But clearly the relativity of cultural habits is central to the human condition, and this is something that Benedict emphasises. She quotes a Digger Indian she knew, who remarked: 'In the beginning God gave to every people a cup of clay, and from this cup they drank their life', and implies that human cultures are endlessly variable. Each human society, in its cultural institutions, makes a 'selection' from a wide variety of possibilities. As she put it: 'The cultural pattern of any civilisation makes use of a certain segment of the great arc of potential human purposes and motivations' (1934: 171).

Thirdly, this stress on cultural diversity implied a radical cultural relativism. Developing ideas that are implicit in the writings of Boas, Benedict implies throughout the study that every culture has its own validity and that we should show tolerance of 'the co-existing and equally valid patterns of life which mandkind has created' (1934: 201). And she strongly argues, like Boas, that the diversity of cultures undermines any theories of racial determinism. Racial purity is a myth, she contended, and biological interpretations have no firm scientific basis. But this espousal of cultural relativism and her stress on tolerance did not mean that she was politically or morally neutral. Indeed, there are contradictions between this cultural relativism and the strong, even if implicit, democratic pluralism that pervades the work. She was essentially a reformer and a progressive, and indicates throughout her work her political standpoint. 'It is possible', she writes, 'to scrutinize different institutions and cast up their cost in terms of social capital, in terms of the less desirable behaviour traits they stimulate, and in terms of human suffering and frustration' (1934:179).

Fourthly, she suggests their cultures are integrated wholes, almost like personalities. They cannot be understood in the manner of Frazer, by cross-cultural analysis of cultural traits like totemism, or magic taken from their context. Anthropology, she writes, is the study of cultures as articulate wholes: 'A culture, like an individual is a more or less consistent pattern of thought and action. Within each culture there came into being characteristic purposes not necessarily shared by other types of societies' (1934: 33).

There is nothing mystical about this integration, she suggests; it is like an art style. Behavioural and motivated traits, she continues, develop 'in consistent patterns in accordance with unconscious canons of choice that develop within the culture' (1934: 34). She accepts, however, that cultures vary in their degree of integration and in given historical circumstances some cultures may exhibit a 'lack of integration' (1934: 161). The influences of Dilthey and the Gestalt psychologists is clearly apparent in this formulation, and as P. K. Bock (1980) rightly indicated, the writings of Sapir, who was an outstanding linguist and a close friend of Benedict, suggests a similar perspective. Culture is to be understood as like a personality, with purposes and canons of choice: It has a pattern of integration, a meaningful configuration that, on analysis, reveals a dominant concern or motif. The individual personality is, in a sense, isomorphic with culture, a kind of 'cultural microcosm' (Sapir 1949: 203).

Applying these ideas to the three ethnographic case studies, Benedict came to depict these cultures in terms of a specific configuration or value orientation. The Pueblo Indians are described as Apollonian. These matrilineal people, like the Zuni and the Hopi, have a religion that focuses on the need for rain and fertility. They have complex public ceremonials. A great emphasis is placed on co-operation and communal life, the ideal man being a person of 'dignity and affability who has never tried to lead' (1934: 71). Individuals are subordinate to the group and no value is placed on personal initiative. There is a stress on the 'middle way', and anger, aggression or assertiveness are strongly disapproved of. Ecstatic forms of religious expression are condemned.

In contrast to this, the north-west coast Indians and particularly the Indian cultures of the Plains area are described as Dionysian. Such cultures emphasise the 'path of excess', and place a central focus on individual experience and on ecstatic experiences either through hallucinogens or through the vision quest. 'They valued all violent experience, all means by which human beings may break through the usual sensory routine' (1934: 58). Supernatural power among the Pueblos comes from cult membership and through ritual, whereas in the Dionysian mode it comes through the self-induced visions, dreams or trance states.

The Kwakuitl indicate in their religious practices a Dionysian trait, but an important aspect of this community, she argues, was the strong emphasis placed on wealth, property and status. The famous potlatch ceremonies were enterprises whereby individuals, particularly the chiefs, sought to express their superior status and belittle rivals. Judged by the standards of other cultures, she writes, and the speeches at the ceremonies, the chiefs indicate little more than 'unabashed megalomania' (1934: 137).

In analysing the Dobuans, the Nietzschian dichotomy is dropped, and Benedict suggests that their cultural configuration is one best described by the term 'paranoid', though she does not label them as such. But she describes their culture as permeated by jealousy, suspicion and conflicts. Life in Dobu, she suggests, fosters extreme forms of animosity, and for the islanders every act of friendship or co-operation is thought open to possible treachery. Magical beliefs and practices are common – it is 'one of the world's strongholds' (1934: 102) – and there is much conflict and competition between spouses and between villagers. Her general conclusion, therefore, is that the Dobuan is 'dour, prudish and passionate, consumed with jealousy and suspicion and resentment' (1934: 121).

The use of psychiatric terms drawn from Western culture has often been criticised, but Benedict, like the Freudians, is easily open to misunderstanding. Although she describes the Kwakuitl as paranoid and megalomanic, she sees these as cultural traits (given her cultural relativism) that are quite normal in this culture: 'It is just those individuals among the Kwakuitl who find it congenial to give the freest expression to those attitudes who nevertheless are the leaders of Kwakuitl society and find greatest personal fulfilment in the culture' (1934: 186). She suggests that the Puritan divines of the eighteenth century were by no means considered psychotic in their community for they were part of a religious elite. Yet to a modern observer it is these divines, not the confused and tormented women they put to death as witches, who were the psychoneurotics of Puritan New England. Similarly, the 'arrogant and unbridled egoists' who are entrusted with positions of great influence in our own society 'are not described in our manuals of psychiatry because they are supported by every tenet of our civilization' (1934: 200). But a future psychiatry, she suggests, might judge them differently. Thus the Kwakuitl are not neurotic in our terms, for neurosis, like homosexuality and trance states, are differentialy evaluated in different cultures. But underlying her analysis, Benedict's own values continually erupt and it is clear that she is more positive about the Zuni cultural values of co-operation, sobriety and non-aggression – though not blind to its stifling of personal initiative.

Benedict's work has been the subject of much criticism, both on ethnographic and theoretical ground. Although there is clearly some truth in the difference between Pueblo and Plains Indian culture, a contrast suggested by other writers (e.g. Sapir 1949: 129) and Benedict's description of Dobuan social life has close affinities to the impression one gets from reading Roheim's account of the nearby Normanby Islanders, the general opinion about Benedict's work is that her configuration depictions are 'overdrawn'. By portraying a culture through the filters of a single motif she overstates the case and ignores or plays down all aspects that are contrary to her theme (Mandelbaum 1975: 47; Barnouw 1973: 59–73). For example, as Bourguignon notes (1979: 84–5), in describing both the Plains Indians and the Kwakuitl as Dionysian, as in both cultures men sought visions through ecstatic states, Benedict overlooked the crucial difference in the contexts of this ecstacy. Shamanic rites among the Kwakuitl were part of a dramatic ritual, an initiation into a secret society in a settled society divided into ranks, whereas among the Plains Indians who were egalitarian buffalo hunters, trance was an aspect of the vision quest whereby an individual sought supernatural power alone through his own initiative. Many writers have stressed that Benedict's analysis of the Pueblo culture underplayed the tension, conflict and anxieties which were all evident in these communities. In a well-known paper, John Bennett (1946) indicated that studies of Pueblo cultures tended to adopt one of two approaches: either they stressed an 'organic' view, emphasising, like Benedict, the integration of the culture and highlighting the values of co-operation, non-aggression and harmony, or they put forward a 'repressive' view, stressing the covert tension and suspicion, and the intercommunal conflicts and factions. The two views, as Bourguignon notes (1979: 86), are complementary, for both represent different aspects of Pueblo life. But the important point is that Benedict overlooked the tensions and conflicts and even the drinking of alcohol, which are evident in Pueblo culture (Harris 1969: 404–6).

The theoretical limitations of Benedict's study, however, are more serious. Her approach to social life was, as Mintz suggests (1981: 152), configurational, thematic and value-oriented , and she seems to have 'gloried' in cultural diversity. She therefore lacked any interest in class structure, and her analyses were ahistorical. Though indicating that there is variability in cultural integration, this is not directly related to ecological or technological factors, nor to cultural change or historical circumstances. The study is, as Harris writes, an 'ingenious evocation of a Dilthian feeling of understanding, achieved entirely in the absence of explanation in any scientific sense'. And he continues: 'One searches in vain through "patterns of culture" for any explanation' (1969: 402–3). The truth is, as Harris and others have discerned, that this is a work in the cultural idealist tradition; it aimed to convey meaning and interpretation in the style of the humanities, as Benedict herself admitted. This was done not so much at the emic level, but by relating the ethnographic data to abstract categories or themes. But although Benedict stressed the close links of anthropology to the humanities, like Kroeber and Evans-Pritchard, she clearly did not wish to sever the ties that link the discipline to the social sciences, as Harris implies (1969: 404). What she suggested was that anthropology stood at the boundary between science and the humanities and she writes: 'Once anthropologists include the mind of man in their subject matter, the methods of science and the methods of the humanities compliment each other. Any commitment to methods which exclude either approach is self-defeating' (1948: 585–93).

Kardiner and Preble title their biographical essay on Benedict 'Science and Poetry' – Benedict being in fact a poet as well as an anthropologist. Her plea that anthropology should drawn on the methods of both science and the humanities is, I think, salutary. But her own study *Patterns of Culture* was too poetic for most anthropologists. The difficulty is that 'understanding', as Bourguignon notes (1979: 84), does not involve a search for causes or a discovery of correlations or an unravelling of historical sequences. It is essentially ahistorical. Her insights, therefore, as Kardiner and Preble suggest, 'reflect the great virtues and minor faults of the poetic nature'. These faults can only be corrected by a more rigorous science (1961: 186).

In the configurational strategy what then is the relationship between culture and the individual personality? Le Vine (1973: 52–3) described it as the 'personality-is-culture' view, seeing the relationship as essentially isomorphic. In stressing cultural variability and relativism, and in seeing people as intrinsically 'malleable' – 'they are plastic to the moulding force of the society into which they are born' (1934: 183) – Benedict's analysis does not mention, let alone stress, cultural universals. She accepts that there are differences in temperaments among people, and that individuals are not automata, thus some individuals may be temperamentally unfitted to certain cultures or social roles. But the overriding stress is that there is mutual reinforcement between the individual and the culture. In reality there is no antagonism between society and the individual – this idea, she contends, is one of the misleading conceptions of the nineteenth-century dualism (1934: 151). Thus the conceptual distinction between culture and the individual personality breaks down, and as Bourguignon puts it, the analysis can 'shift back and forth' between these two concepts with ease (1979: 83). Honigman (1972: 126) likewise indicates the circularity of this kind of interpretation. But again there are contradictions in her writings, for Benedict, almost like Freud, writes of tradition as being neurotic and speaks of a future social order where tolerance and the encouragement of individual differences could be more evident.

This approach meant an opposition to any kind of psychological reductionism, and Benedict's views on this are akin to those of Durkheim and Rivers; indeed, as we have noted, individuals do not appear in *Patterns of Culture* at all. They are simply a 'reflection' or 'microcosm' of the cultural order. Thus Benedict's conception of the human subject is to suggest that the person is essentially a culture-bearing organism, a container, as Ingold (1986) put it, for the cultural logic. People, she suggests, are conditioned from birth by the pattern of their culture, and so she expresses, far more than her mentor Boas, a strong commitment to cultural determinism. The central focus, therefore, becomes not the dialectical interrelationship between the individual and the culture, but how cultural values and attitudes are transmitted from generation to generation. This was the central concern not only of Benedict but of her friend and mentor Margaret Mead. (For a useful biography of Benedict, though not critically examining her work, see Modell 1984.)

4.5 Margaret Mead

'A primary task of the mid-twentieth century is the increasing of understanding, understanding of our culture and of that of other countries. On our capacity to develop new forms of such understanding may well depend on the survival of our civilization' – so wrote Margaret Mead (1901–78) in the opening paragraph of her study on *Soviet Attitudes to Authority* (1951). It indicates well Mead's conception of anthropology as a mode of cross-cultural understanding, and her belief in the constructive role of education as an agency of social change. But Mead was 'brought up in a household of educators' (Metraux 1980: 263), for both her mother and grandfather had been school teachers. Born in Philadelphia, Mead's approach was similar to Benedict's: she had a 'fascination with cultural diversity' (McDowell 1980: 278), and took both a humanistic and scientific approach to the subject. She was a scrupulous and careful observer of human life, and even in her more popular studies she took pains to outline her research methodology. Many have written of her high standing and excellence as an ethnographer and even Marvin Harris, though unsympathetic to her impressionistic studies and her general disregard for statistical methods, recognised the worth of her creative and insightful writings (1969: 409–11). Her ethnographic studies were in fact remarkably extensive and in the fourteen years prior to the Second World War, she made no less than five field trips to Oceania and studied eight communities. Like Benedict, Mead was concerned with the 'understanding' of social life through interpretative studies and likened her approach to that of the physician or psychiatrist who, by careful observation and the use of 'case study' material seeks to understand human life. Her ethnographical studies therefore were 'case' materials used to illustrate or even check what she considered to be scientific questions, attempts to understand human nature. She spea! ; of societies as being 'natural laboratories' for the study of such issues (1930: 211–17). Again, like Benedict, she saw human communities as 'integrated', functional wholes. Although certainly aware of the dynamic processional aspect of social life, and never neglectful of Western contact and colonialism on the Oceanic communities (McDowell 1980) there is some substance in the suggestion that Mead tended to overstress the 'homogeneity' of the tribal communities she studied. For like many of her contemporaries, Malinowski for example, she was keen to record what was then felt to be a disappearing world. An anthropologist's first obligation, she wrote, 'is to use his training to record data on primitive society before these societies disappear' (1930: 216). Thus in her classic study on the Manus, 'culture contact' is relegated to an appendix. But unlike Benedict her early studies were not focused on a single motif; rather, they centre on a single theoretical problem. In each of the studies we shall be concerned with here, Mead expressed a cultural relativist perspective, emphasised the malleability of human nature and directly related her ethnographic findings to the understanding of Western culture, her own society. The studies, written for a lay audience, are vivid, insightful and lucid, and extremely readable, for as Barnouw put it, Margaret Mead had a 'way with words' (1973: 101).

Mead's first book, *Coming of Age in Samoa* (1928), is based on nine months' fieldwork in Samoa undertaken in 1925–6. Based on data derived from observations of a group of fifty girls from three coastal villages, the study explores the relationships between adolescence and culture. It is focused on the issue as to whether the adolescent period was a time of psychological storm and stress. In his monumental work on *Adolescence* (1904), G. Stanley Hall, following the German Romantics, had described this period of the life-cycle as not only one of emotional instability and stress, but also, because of its fluidity, a time of great potentiality. Adolescence was indeed seen by Hall as a 'new birth', and youth as the instrument for bringing about a new social order. The *Wandervögel* movement in Germany seemed to be an expression of this romantic 'revolt' of youth (Lacqueur 1962). Mead notes these general views on adolescence, indicated by Hall: 'Adolescence was characterized as the period in which idealism flowered and rebellion against authority waxed strong, a period during which difficulties and conflicts were absolutely inevitable' (1928: 10).

Was this, Mead asked, an invariable complement of our humanity or 'merely a result of civilization'? Was the idealism, the emotional conflicts and the rebellion against authority, said to characterise adolescence, universal or culturally specific? The Samoan study suggests the latter, for Mead depicts the life experiences of the adolescent girls as free of emotional stress and rebellion. There is no adolescent 'crisis'. The Samoans are described as having a rather casual attitude to sex. Pre-marital sex and clandestine encounters 'under the palm trees' are accepted as perfectly natural, but Mead suggests that such relationships, indeed relationships generally in Samoa, are diffuse and emotionally low key. Children grow up in small village communities where there are many adult figures and close kin, and until they are about fifteen are generally ignored by the community. Mead speaks of a 'lack of deep feeling', 'a diffusion of affection' as characteristic of Samoan social relationships. Moreover, the girls are not beset with confusing and conflicting alternatives, and even the influence of the missionaries, with their stress on chastity, had been, she suggests, of minimal significance. A girl's ambitions were thus focused: 'To live as a girl with many lovers as long as possible and then to marry in one's own village and to have many children' (1928: 129).

Mead therefore asks: 'Was the diffused affection and the diffused authority of the large families, the ease of moving from one family to another, the knowledge of sex and the freedom to experiment a sufficient guarantee to all Samoan girls of a perfect adjustment?' And she answers: 'In almost all cases, yes' (1928: 130).

'*Coming of Age*' in Samoa, therefore, is a simple matter, and of a casual nature, and contrasts remarkably with the situation in America and in many other cultures. Sex was considered a 'natural pleasurable thing', and the freedom to indulge in it (limited only by social status) meant a 'lack of neuroses' among the Samoans (1928: 165). Likewise, she suggests the diffuse relationships within a large family community meant that the 'crippling attitudes' of the Oedipal complex were also absent (1926: 170). But Mead was not unaware of the deviations from group norms and the Samoans' personality conflicts which occurred (1928: 135–49); these, however, are seen as exceptional to a general picture of stability and personal tranquility, or, like the issue of rape, is associated with recent culture contact.

The conclusion of the study is that the transition from infancy to adulthood is handled differently in different societies, and as Benedict later put it, in her classic paper, no specific 'cultural bridge' should be regarded as the 'natural' path to maturity: 'The adolescent period of *Storm und Drang* with which we are so familiar becomes intelligible in terms of pure discontinuous cultural institutions and demands rather than in terms of physiological necessity' (Benedict 1938: 167).

Mead's idyllic picture of Samoan life has been strongly challenged by Derek Freeman in his controversial study, *Margaret Mead and Samoa* (1983). The book was launched as a great media event with maximum publicity, and was heralded as a kind of detective story, which was to expose 'a major twentieth-century myth' – Mead's depiction of Samoa; it was brashly credited with marking the 'coming of age' of anthropology. Freeman's aim in writing the study was not to advance our understanding of Samoan cultural life, but specifically to 'refute' Margaret Mead's analysis and empirical work. It was a project on which Freeman had been working for over forty years, having first undertaken fieldwork studies in western Samoa in the early 1940s. Freeman has a positivistic conception of science and sees social reality not as something historical to be interpreted, but as something 'given', and thus his critique of Mead 's work has an aggressive and categorical quality. There is only one Samoan reality, that which Freeman knows and understands; grasping this truth Mead's study is thus depicted as 'mistaken', 'mythical' and marked by 'major errors' of interpretation.

Freeman's critique of Mead takes two forms, which he misleadingly sees as intrinsically linked. On the one hand, he makes a sustained critique of 'absolute cultural determinism' which, he contends, was espoused by both Boas and Mead, and argues that human life can be understood only in terms of an interaction between cultural and biological factors. It is doubtful if either Boas or Mead can be saddled with such an extreme cultural determinism, let alone held to be 'anti-biological' in orientation. Boas was not anti-biology; what he rejected was racial determinism, and Annette Weiner rightly suggests (1983: 912) that Freeman not only distorts Boas's tone and argument, but he neglects to indicate the significance of Boas's scholarly publications in physical anthropology. Mead, likewise, cannot be accused of such 'absolutism', for she certainly did not believe that all behaviour was determined by culture, although, like Benedict (and unlike Boas), her writings do have a strong cultural emphasis, with culture being viewed in a *sui generis* fashion. Bradd Shore poignantly asks how Freeman would account for the distinctive differences between Samoan and American adolescence. Freeman's own work, he suggests, like Mead's, provides ample evidence of such differences, but the only factors that Freeman offers to account for these differences are cultural and social factors – modes of childrearing, structures of authority. Is this, he asks, any different from Mead's own cultural determinism (1983: 944)?

On the other hand, the second form of critique is to question Mead's empirical work, and her depiction of Samoan social life. Freeman strongly questions the scientific adequacy of Mead's picture of Samoan society. Whereas she emphasised a 'relaxed dependence' on social forms, diffuse emotional ties, a lack of violent aggression and competition, casual love affairs during the adolescence years and a lack of stress or crisis during this period, Freeman presents us with almost an opposite portrait of Samoan life. He depicts Samoan society as being authoritarian and preoccupied with rank, as having competition and rivalry as its principal features, and cites ample evidence to suggest that aggression, rape, violent crime, competition and authoritarian control are ubiquitous features of Samoan social reality. He emphasises this darker side of Samoan life and seems to suggest that this is the true reality. He particularly stresses the quite savage punishments Samoan elders inflict on those who flout their authority, and the near obsession these men have for female virginity and chastity. Mead's portrait of Samoan life, he tends to think, is an affront to the Samoan people themselves. Mead's problem, he suggests, was to see Samoan society through the narrow lens of the adolescents she studied, and the fact that she was gullible young woman who accepted the statements and teasing of her informants as fact.

It is of interest how Freeman succumbs to the very mistakes that he admonishes Mead for making. Citing Einstein, he warns how a cherished idea or deep conviction can lead one unwittingly into error, but his own analysis is deeply marred by an obsession to refute Mead, and he thus misinterprets not only much of Mead's work, but also much of the empirical data on Samoa. He stresses the 'beguiling conceit' of Mead and Benedict in characterising the behaviour of an entire people in unitary terms – and then does precisely so himself. He portrays both the character and ethos of the Samoan people in a unitary fashion, and glosses over both the differences between the island communities and the differing and changing historical contexts. Freeman seems to contend that there is only one Samoan reality, and that that is unchanging.

Finally, Freeman criticises Mead for the narrowness of her field-work and her perspective. (As her focus was on adolescence, and as she was denied, because of her sex, access to the chiefly councils, she can hardly be admonished for not fully exploring the traditional political life of Samoa.) But Freeman seems to be unaware that he himself is presenting only a limited perspective of Samoan life – the viewpoint essentially of high-ranking and educated men, concerned with rank and with the control and chastity of their female kin. Evidence from other researchers on Samoa and from other Oceanic communities suggests that the 'mind-boggling contradictions' which Mead highlights, and which Freeman dismisses with such arrogance, may be much closer to the Samoan reality than Freeman's own unidimensional portrait. For the coexistence in the culture of a high stress on female virginity and control – the cult of virginity – and of pre-marital sexual adventures seems to be the norm. Bradd Shore had noted that in Samoa, while the ideal of chastity is upheld, the realisation of virginity 'is far from universal . . . pre-marital sex play is part of the growing up for many boys and girls' (1981: 197; see also Abramson (1987) on the Fijian context, where a cult of virginity upheld by a gerontocratic elite coexists with a sexual counter-culture, which conceives of the body as naturally free and predisposed to sexual pleasure).

There is validity, of course, in much of Freeman's critique of Mead's work, and earlier scholars had noted the inadequacies and limitations of Mead's account of Samoa (Barnouw 1973: 92–3). Had Freeman attempted to provide a complementary corrective to Mead's inadequate portrait, rather than simply trying to refute her, then, as Shore noted, his work would have been an important addition to Pacific studies (1983: 937; for further reading on the Mead and Freeman controversy, see Brady 1983; Strathern 1983; Patience and Smith 1986; Holmes 1987).

Mead's second study, *Growing up in New Guinea*, is, as its title suggests, also focused on socialisation. It is subtitled *A comparative study of primitive education.* The research was based on fieldwork studies among the Manus, an island community in the Admiralty Islands off the north coast of New Guinea. The community she studied lived in houses raised on stilts within a lagoon, and were engaged primarily in fishing and trading activities. Like her other study, her investigations were undertaken to solve a special problem which is 'but lightly touched upon in this book', namely the relationship between animistic thought and the thinking of neurotics and children in European culture. Although *Coming of Age in Samoa* has a clear focus on sexual matters, the book evinces no evidence of any influence of psychoanalytic theory. The problem of the second study indicates a significant change, and in fact Mead records that after she met her second husband Reo Fortune on returning from Samoa, she came into contact with the writings of Freud and Piaget: 'In Piaget I found the assumption that the "savage" and the "child" think alike; in Freud that the "child", the "savage" and the "neurotic" think alike. To each a kind of animistic thinking is attributed' (1978: 96–7).

Before responding to Mead's handling of this issue, some brief comments may be made on the study.

Mead lived in the village of Perin, together with her husband Reo Fortune, an anthropologist, for some six months. She made a remarkably intensive study of the children of the village, making ink blots tests, collecting their spontaneous drawings (around 32,000 were collected, though the children had never used pencil or paper before) and recording in detail their play activities and general behaviour within the households. The study offers, therefore, a rich descriptive account of 'growing up' in this Melanesian community. Being traders, a 'Puritan ideal' pervades the culture and there is a stress on industry, prudence and abstinence (1930: 15). Yet the children have a relatively carefree existence and live almost in a 'world of their own', relatively independent of adults. Infant mortality is high, and children are competent swimmers by the age of five, so that those who survive are healthy, independent and full of self-confidence: 'They eat when they like, play when they like, sleep when they see fit . . . the child in Manus is lord of the universe, undisciplined, unchecked by any reverence or respect for his elders' (1930: 43–4). Girls begin to perform household tasks around the age of twelve, but boys continue to live fairly carefree until they are married. The learning of adult roles is largely achieved by unconscious imitation, but a great stress is placed on taboos, and a sense of shame regarding the body and its functions is instilled in children from an early age. Affinal relationships and exchange are, as in other Melanesian countries, a 'pivotal point' of their culture and the conjugal relation tends to be difficult and rather strained.

The interesting aspect of Mead's study relates to the child's attitude to their animistic religion; Manus religion centres on the belief in ghosts, the spirits of the dead who are essentially concerned with upholding the prosperity, well-being and moral edicts of the community. 'The ghosts are an important constituent of the adult world; adults obviously act most of the time with reference to ghostly wishes; the names of ghosts are always on adults' lips' (1978 (1932): 111). Thus the Manus' religious culture is essentially animistic and adults engage in seances and divination in order to please the spirits. But Mead argues that Manus children, living largely among their age mates, have a naturalistic conception of the universe.

'Manus children', she writes, 'not only show no tendency towards spontaneous animistic thought, but they also show what may perhaps legitimately be termed a negativism towards explanations couched in animistic rather than practical cause and effect terms. The Manus child is less spontaneously animistic and less traditionally animistic than is the Manus adult' (1978 (1932): 115).

Thus Mead concludes that 'personalizing the universe is not inherent in child thought, but is a tendency bequeathed to him by his society' (1930: 103) – and that our own society tends to teach children through poetry and metaphor that the natural world and animals are personalised. In contrast, it is Manus adult world that is animistic while the children, by Western criteria, are not childlike.

Although Mead was by no mean an absolute cultural determinist as Freeman suggests (1983: 295), and certainly did not assume that the human subject was a *tabula rasa* on which culture writes its script, she undoubtedly followed Sapir and Benedict in conceiving culture as 'personality writ large', and the human subject or personality as isomorphic with culture. A strong emphasis on human plasticity nevertheless runs through her work and she follows the German idealist tradition in interpreting cultural phenomena in terms of patterns and configurations. But in spite of the drawbacks in her work, which Freeman tends to highlight, Mead was a remarkable anthropologist and, as Kroeber remarked, if you take the best ten per cent of her work, it is more in quantity and better in quality than most other anthropologists. (For useful accounts of Mead's eventful life see Mead 1972; Howard 1984; Bateson 1984.)

–5–

The Hegelian–Marxist Tradition

At the end of the eighteenth century, Germany, unlike Britain and France, was not a unified state. As a nation it existed only in a cultural sense, and although it had a growing middle class, this class had little political cohesion or status. Germany in essence consisted of a 'crazy quilt' of numerous small states, principalities, free cities and imperial domains, ruled variously by princes, bishops and knights.

Importantly, Germany had experienced no bourgeois revolution. It was said that whereas England ruled the seas and France ruled the land, Germany ruled only the clouds. The French ideals of liberty, equality and freedom were indeed in existence, but they were essentially expressed not politically, but through metaphysical and personal conceptions (Solomon 1980: 111–14). It was under these circumstances that between 1790 and 1830 there arose in Germany a remarkable and unprecedented development of metaphysical speculation. 'Magnificent spider-webs of metaphysics' (Durant 1952) were spun by academic philosophers, which possess a grandeur that can hardly be questioned, and which still arouse fascination among scholars. In the philosophical systems of Fichte, Schelling and Hegel – the triumvirate of German idealist metaphysics – a unified system of thought was offered, which purported to make full sense of the universe, and the meaning of human existence within it. These three scholars differ in many respects, but they can all be seen as engaged in developing Kant's critical philosophy into a metaphysical idealism, in which philosophical reflection is essentially seen as 'the self-awareness or self-consciousness of absolute reason in and through the human mind' (Copleston 1963: 21; Durant 1952: 292). In a sense, then, reality is conceived by these writers as a kind of rational process in which the universe becomes aware of itself in and through human consciousness. With Hegel this form of idealism reaches its highest development and elaboration. This chapter is concerned to outline the theoretical tradition that stems from Hegel, and that conceives of the human subject as essentially a social being creatively engaged in practical activities. In the first section I outline Hegel's philosophy, stressing Hegel's attempt to overcome the dualisms inherent in mechanistic science and Kantian philosophy, and focus on the theory of the subject that emerges from his early work on *Phenomenology of Spirit*. The second section is devoted to outlining the theories of Hegel's foremost disciple, Karl Marx, who as a Left-Hegelian stressed the dialectical aspects of Hegel's theory. In the third section I critically review the work of Lukács, one of the founders of Western Marxism, for its was Lukács who after the First World War attempted to reaffirm the Hegelian dimension of Marxism. In the final section I examine Sève and Vygotsky's attempt to establish a Marxist psychology. Later in the study, in chapter 8, I shall explore further the more recent developments in the Hegelian-Marxist tradition.

5.1 Hegel's Phenomenology of Spirit

Georg Wilhelm Friedrich Hegel (1770–1831) is widely regarded as one of the greatest philosophers of all time, a thinker on a par with Plato, Aristotle, Aquinas and Kant. His influence on European culture has been profound, and with the exception of Marx (who was himself influenced by Hegel), no philosopher during the last two centuries has made such an impact on the world. Marxism, phenomenology, existentialism and structuralism all bear the impress of Hegel's thought, and even currents of thought outside the Hegelian tradition have often developed in reaction to Hegel's philosophy. His fortunes however have varied over the decades. In his *Story of Philosophy*, Will Durant (1952) devotes some ninety-five pages to the philosophies of Schopenhauer and Spencer, giving Hegel only a 'note' of seven pages. Hegel's importance and influence is all the more striking given that his philosophy is expressed in a style that is extraordinarily difficult and obscure. To understand Hegel, Kaufmann (1965) writes, is like trying to comprehend the incomprehensible, and presents itself as something of a challenge. But although Hegel's prose is dense and impenetrable, making it difficult for the reader to grasp its meaning, it is also strangely fascinating, and within the forbidding prose one often finds aphoristic gems, and many subtleties of thought. His writings have been described as 'pregnant' and 'kaleidoscopic', for he attempts to write in a style that matches what he senses is the nature of the universe – a style that is shifting, transformative, dialectic.

Hegel was a great visionary , and in an important sense he tried to encompass and incorporate all previous knowledge and systems of philosophy within his own philosophy. He was a romantic, and was strongly influenced by the writings of Schiller and Goethe, as well as by his friend Schelling. He described himself as one of the sons of Goethe, and saw the writings of the poet as intrinsically woven into his own intellectual development. But Hegel refused to renounce reason, nor did he venerate the medieval age. He had a vision of a universal harmony, but he sought to convey this unity through the rational understanding of a cosmic process, which he, like Aristotle, clearly believed was moving towards perfection. He had an abhorrence of mystical intuition, and sensed that this harmony would be achieved only through the creative activity of human beings.

All the dualisms that mechanistic science and Kantian philosophy had generated, and that for Hegel were essential and necessary for the progress of human thought – spirit (mind) and nature, knowledge and passion, reason and morality, freedom and necessity, ideal and reality, human subjectivity and sociality – Hegel sought both to encompass and transcend. And he aimed to do this by reason alone. In doing so he tried to combine in one comprehensive system the following: Kant's critical philosophy and his stress on freedom and human subjectivity; the Enlightenment emphasis on empirical knowledge and reason; the view expressed by the Romantics that nature was an organic totality; the philosophical monism of Spinoza; and the holistic cosmological world-view of the Greek philosophers, for whom Hegel had a lasting admiration – particularly the writings of Heraclitus and Aristotle. In a sense, every form of knowledge and every system of philosophy has its place in Hegel's paradigm. What a vision – and what a task.

Because his writings are complex and obscure, Hegel is easily misunderstood and I cannot pretend to have fully understood the subtlety of his thoughts. I shall therefore only attempt to outline some of Hegel's basic premises, and his understanding of the human subject as conveyed in his classic study *Phenomenology of Spirit*.

The first thing to be said about Hegel is that he is, in a fundamental sense, an historical thinker. All his basic notions – *Geist* (spirit), reason, freedom and even truth itself – have meaning and significance only within an historical context, or rather within a cosmic process. If we cast a glance over the world's history, he wrote, what strikes us most is the phenomenon of change –

everything is constantly changing; we see 'a vast picture of changes and transactions; of infinitely manifold forms of peoples, states, individuals, in unresting succession' (1956: 72). Hegel praises the oriental view of the universe (the Hindu concept of karma), with its recognition of endless cycles of change. But in making a distinction between the phenomenal world of change and the infinity of spirit or the 'eternal repose' of Buddhism, as Plato and and Heraclitus did, Hegel felt that such doctrines had presented a limited viewpoint. For Hegel all reality – spirit and nature – was ever-changing. The whole universe was a kind of cosmic process, an organic unity like the development of a plant – which is how he begins his preface to the *Phenomenology*, suggesting that the diversity of philosophical systems are simply moments in the progressive unfolding of truth by the Absolute itself (1807: 2). Hegel uses the term Absolute to describe the totality, reality as a whole, the universe seen as a teleological process. The Absolute consists of two aspects, nature and spirit, which together constitute two divisions of his system, the other being logic, the way the process manifests itself both in nature and spirit.

Secondly, and significantly, Hegel conceived of the idea, or destiny, of the spirit as a potentiality that was abstract. It was a hidden, undeveloped essence. For its realisation another element, he felt, was needed, and that element was human activity in its widest sense. The 'motive power' that gives spirit or reason its actuality, that 'puts them in operation and gives them determinate existence, is the need, instinct, inclination and passion of man' (1807: 22). In a way that is difficult to comprehend, Hegel sees human activity (a blend of reason and passion) as the 'middle term' or 'medium', whereby the idea or universal essence (spirit or freedom) is translated into the domain of objectivity (nature or necessity) (1807: 27). But this is seen as a kind of historical process in which the 'world at large' through spirit (in the form of culture, or developing consciousness), becomes conscious of itself and realises, makes concrete, its own freedom in nature. It is worth stressing at this point that Hegel uses the term *Geist*, translated as either spirit or mind, in a dynamic sense. It is not for Hegel either an epistemological faculty or organ of knowledge (like mind), nor is it spiritual in a religious sense, but rather it has to be seen as a 'creative force', which is within 'objective nature' (a phrase Hegel often uses) and which manifests itself in human consciousness and human culture. This spirit is intrinsically linked to the human subject – it is subjective – and in its development through human consciousness takes different 'forms' or 'shapes', that reflect the different stages in the development of the world-spirit. The human mind for Hegel is thus not only subjective, but an aspect of a universal process.

Modern philosophers often stress Kant's claim to having wrought a Copernican revolution in philosophy by combining the rationalism of Descartes and Leibniz with the empiricism of Locke and Hume. In fact, Kant solved very little, for not only did empirical reality become an unknowable 'thing-in-itself', but his critical philosophy generated, as I have noted earlier, a plethora of antimonies. Kant never went beyond the dualistic thought of the Enlightenment and in many ways he was an important defender of mechanistic science. What is of interest about Hegel is that he attempted not only to forge conceptual categories, which went beyond both dualism and mechanism, but also to delineate a mode of thought that was radically different from that of the Enlightenment thinkers. He tried to establish a kind of philosophical anthropology that was both rationalist and empiricist. He called it objective idealism, but it could well be called dialectical materialism. Although Hegel's metaphysics has usually been described as idealism pure and simple, Hegel's writings express an unusual form of idealism, for the kind of analysis Hegel advocates always begins with empirical data, and he had nothing but praise for the empiricists. 'Whatever is true', he wrote, 'must be in the actual world, and present to sensation' (Weiss 1974: 141). But the kind of knowledge derived from sense impressions – what he calls in *Phenomenology of Spirit* (1807) 'sense certainty' – is a limited form of understanding and hardly merits the term consciousness. He demonstrates that the claim that sense certainty is the basis of knowledge is naive, and this early study is one of the earliest and most important critiques of empiricism. As Marcuse expresses it: 'To Hegel, the facts in themselves possess no authority' (1941: 27). A higher form of knowledge or reflection is therefore needed, and this Hegel describes as understanding (*Verstand*), which he seems to suggest is characteristic of ordinary mechanistic science in its explication of phenomena by reference to natural laws. But the essence of this kind of understanding is that it is static and dualistic; it sets up, Hegel suggests, a series of unnecessary oppositions; thought and life, reason and reality, mind and nature. So in order to achieve a fuller understanding and realisation of his vision, Hegel searches around for a new mode of understanding. What he required, as Copleston writes, 'for the fulfilment of this task is a new form of logic which is able to follow the movement of life and does not leave opposed concepts in irremediable opposition' (1963: 202). Hegel described this mode of thought as reason (*Vernunft*) or dialectic.

But for Hegel, the term dialectic has a wide meaning and is intrinsically associated with movement, with negation and the overcoming of static oppositions. A quotation will suffice to make Hegel's meaning clear:

> By dialectic is meant the indwelling tendency outwards by which the one-sidedness and limitation of the predicates of understanding is seen in its true light, and shown to be a negation of them . . . wherever there is movement, wherever there is life, wherever anything is carried into effect in the actual world, there dialectic is at work. It is the soul of all knowledge which is truly scientific . . . the dialectic is the same dynamic that lies at the root of every natural process. (Weiss 1974: 95–8)

Peter Singer (1983) has rightly suggested that Hegel's philosophy and his use of the term *Geist* (spirit) can properly be understood only if situated in the Western philosophical tradition. This tradition, as we have explored, was vitally concerned with the nature of the mind or consciousness, and its relation to the natural world. All earlier traditions had tended to see the human mind as essentially a subjective phenomenon and unchanging. In the Lockean tradition the human mind was conceptualised as a passive medium on which experience writes its script, while the Leibnizian tradition, adopted by Kant, viewed the mind as an active agent imposing structural forms upon the world of experience. Hegel broke completely with this tradition in viewing the mind or consciousness as a developing process, the individual mind being an aspect or 'moment' in the development of the spirit (human culture). Hegel presented his views on the human consciousness both in the *Phenomenology of Spirit* and in the third part of his *Encyclopaedia of the Philosophical Sciences*, which is entitled *Philosophy of Mind*. Hegel's views on the human subject can perhaps be delineated by outlining the substance of these two texts.

In his introduction to the *Phenomenology of Spirit*, Hegel defines the aim of philosophy as the 'actual knowledge of what truly is', the world as a totality or Absolute. And as with the earlier philosophers, he begins with the problem of knowledge itself and the standpoint of his predecessors in philosophy, who felt that as a first step in knowledge we must identify the nature of knowledge and its limits. Thus the idea is, Hegel writes, that we must first understand cognition before we can have knowledge of the world. But, Hegel argues, whether we see cognition as some kind of 'instrument' by which we can grasp reality, or as a 'medium through which the light of truth reaches us', such knowledge already presupposes a separation between knowledge and the objective world, a distinction between the knower and reality. An epistemological standpoint prior to all knowledge, Hegel felt, was an impossibility, for to scrutinise knowledge was itself an act of knowledge. As he writes in a telling phrase: 'To seek to know before we know is as absurd as the wise resolution of Scholasticus, not to venture into the water until he has learned to swim' (1892: 10).

Hegel thus rejects the whole traditional conception of epistemology assumed not only by Descartes and Kant, but by the whole tradition of British empiricism (Locke, Berkeley, Hume). He undermines their whole enterprise by not accepting an initial rigid distinction between consciousness and reality. The only possible approach to knowledge and ultimately to an understanding of reality, for Hegel, is an examination of consciousness from the inside as it appears to itself. In other words, we must conduct a phenomenology of mind; examine human consciousness as a phenomenon, as it actually appears to us in experience. Hegel's philosophy takes as its starting point ordinary consciousness, but unlike Wittgenstein he does not see the philosopher's task as merely to describe the phenomenon, but rather to explore the dialectical nature of consciousness as it develops through history. Although the *Phenomenology of Spirit* contains little historical analysis, particularly in the first part of the study, it is important to realise that for Hegel the development of human knowledge through a dialectical logic, and the changing forms of historical consciousness, embodied in cultural forms, are virtually equated. Historical change is seen by Hegel as exhibiting the same kind of dialectical movement as the development of conceptual reasoning, and both have a necessary quality, earlier forms of consciousness (knowledge) being both preserved and superseded (*aufheben*) by later forms of consciousness. The *Phenomenology of Spirit*, therefore, outlines Hegel's views on the development of human consciousness both as an historical process and as a logical development. Following his usual triadic method, the book is essentially in three parts or phases. The first is titled 'Consciousness' and outlines the development in our knowledge of the external world. The second is on 'Self-consciousnes', knowledge of consciousness itself. The third part is on 'Reason', and presents a synthesis of the first two phases, and explores in detail in the later part of the book various aspects of the human spirit – morality, culture, religion – concluding with a section on absolute mind.

Hegel begins the analysis with what he calls sense certainty, the immediate awareness or apprehension of the external world. As we have earlier noted, this is the standpoint of the earlier empiricists, who took sense data as the basis of knowledge. But Hegel argues that this immediate form of consciousness is a rather limited form of understanding, for as soon as we attempt to describe a particular object we find that we can do so only by the use of universal concepts. Sense certainty is therefore not genuine knowledge, and it is only at the level of perception that objects can be seen as things that possess distinct properties and qualities, and that can be described in language. But this too is a limited form of knowledge, and this in turn is passed beyond by human consciousness which seeks to understand an underlying order and coherence. It thus comes to postulate an 'inner essence' to explain the phenomena of sense experience. Hegel calls this form of consciousness 'understanding' and as noted earlier, sees it as particularly expressed in the laws of Newtonian physics, with the concepts of gravity and force.

Hegel sees consciousness as refusing to accept a rigid dualism between phenomena as 'appearance' and the underlying 'reality' postulated by scientific reasoning. As Richard Norman (1976: 42) has suggested, Hegel specifically rejects any forms of reductionism, rejecting both the nominalist strategy, which sees universals as simply fashioned by the mind from its experience of particulars (which are held to be the only reality), and the strategy of dogmatic metaphysics, which denied the reality of the phenomenal world of appearances. But equally, Hegel is no dualist, for he maintains that human consciousness essentially comes to understand that there is no opposition between the 'particular' and the universal, or between the empirical and the conceptual (for they are intelligible only in the light of the other), and that the reality postulated by scientific understanding to explicate phenomena is itself only a form of consciousness. Thus by a dialectical progression Hegel then comes to suggest that consciousness turns on itself, it comes to have itself, not the objective world, as its object of knowledge. It thus becomes self-consciousness.

The immediate form of self-consciousness is self-certainty; it takes the form of desire (*Begierde*) and in the immediate awareness of 'being-for-self' as an individual. But Hegel argues that self-consciousness cannot exist in isolation, that the concept of an individual self is 'pure abstraction'. He claims that the existence of other selves is essential to self-consciousness, and that one cannot be fully conscious of oneself as a self, unless one is aware of others as selves: 'Self-consciousness exists in and for itself when, and by the fact that, it so exists for another; that is, it exists only in being acknowledged' (1807: 111).

Self-consciousness becomes possible only through its awareness of other human selves, when 'it has come out of itself', as Hegel puts it. This stress on the social aspect of self-consciousness has had an important influence on both Marxist and existentialist philosophers.

Although the existence of another self is seen by Hegel as a precondition of self-consciousness (the essential social nature of the human subject is taken for granted by Hegel), historically Hegel seems to have seen consciousness (the human spirit) as developing not in terms of mutuality but in terms of conflict and assertive dominance. Self-consciousness thus expresses itself in the master–slave relationship. The master and slave, Hegel writes, 'exist as two opposed shapes of consciousness; one is the independent consciousness whose essential nature is to be for itself, the other is the dependent consciousness, whose essential nature is simply to live or to be for another' (1807: 115).

The unity of consciousness at this stage has not been achieved. The master has freedom and recognition, but is alienated from practical activity; the slave has a relationship with the world through labour, but is denied autonomy and not treated as an independent person. Marx's early writings on alienated labour were greatly influenced by this section of the *Phenomenology*. Many have suggested that Hegel's discussion on the master–slave relationship has salience only if contextualised and seen as embodied in a certain historical period, namely that of the Roman Empire. Seen in these terms, it comes as no surprise that Hegel sees the next stage in the development of self-consciousness to be that of Stoicism. As Stoic philosophy was embraced by both Marcus Aurelius, the Emperor, and by Epictetus, a slave, it represents a bridge between the master and slave, or, as Hegel sees it, a response to the universal fear and bondage of the period. Stoic consciousness, he writes, 'has a negative attitude towards the master and slave relationship' (1807: 121), but is unable to overcome the contradictions inherent in this relationship. For in steadfastly withdrawing from the 'bustle of existence', Stoicism retreats to the realm of pure thought, and to a form of freedom that is indifferent to natural existence; it is an 'abstract freedom' like that of Kant. This negative attitude towards the natural world and to social existence develops naturally into scepticism, which, as a philosophy, comes to doubt everything. But scepticism is internally contradictory, for it takes for granted common-sense understanding. 'It affirms the nullity of seeing, hearing etc., yet it is itself seeing, hearing etc. . . . . Its deeds and its words always belie one another' (1807: 125). The contradictions implicit in scepticism become explicit in what Hegel calls 'unhappy consciousness', which is a dualistic metaphysic. He seems to have in mind medieval Christianity, with its dualism between an unchanging essence, known through mystical experience, and the protean world of changing phenomena, which it devalues. But mystical union with an unchanging divine world and self-denial and asceticism are, Hegel suggests, self-defeating, for the true self is found within the individual, and in relation to an objective world, not in some remote spiritual realm. As Norman writes in his interpretation of Hegel's writings on the 'unhappy consciousness':

> In all its attempts to escape from itself and be reconciled with the unchangeable, consciousness finds only its own self. It cannot destroy its empirical self, since all the activities by which it attempts to do so are themselves the achievements of this same empirical self and therefore simply re-affirm it. (1976: 61)

The contradictions and divisions implicit in self-consciousness are overcome in the third phase of the *Phenomenology*. As reason, the finite consciousness comes to be aware that it is itself the essence or spirit of the Absolute. Reason is therefore a stage in the development of the world-spirit into self-consciousness of itself, and this represents a synthesis of consciousness of the objective world and the earlier forms of self-consciousness.

In the remainder of the study Hegel offers some important observations on a number of diverse topics – on the philosophical ideas of Fichte and Kant, on various forms of ethical theory, on the *laissez-faire* economic theory of Adam Smith, and on the philosophy of religion. Of particular interest, though little discussed by philosophers, is Hegel's devastating critique of phrenology. The relationship between the faculties of the human spirit and the physiognomy of the skull bone is about the same, he chides, as that between rainfall and a particular washday (1807: 202–3).

Two important points emerge from the *Phenomenology*. The first is that the human mind is inherently social, and as a moment in the development of the world-spirit (culture) it is also fundamentally historical. Norman has contrasted Hegel's conception of the mind with that of Kant, stressing that the latter writer regarded the human mind in terms of the individual mind, though the categories themselves might be common to all minds – a consequence, perhaps, of the existence of a common human physiology. In contrast, for Hegel, the categories of the human mind have to be seen as a social product (1976: 111–12). Robert Solomon (1983), in a lucid study also emphasises Hegel's originality in this respect, noting that all earlier philosophers – Descartes, Leibniz, Locke, Hume, Kant – hardly mentioned other people until they started doing ethics. The possibility that the self was essentially a social creation was not even considered by them, and they took consciousness to be a self-enclosed realm, and assumed as unproblematic the idea that what is 'immediately' known to us are our individual selves as knowers. Hume was in a sense correct in his insistence that he could find no immediate self in his consciousness but, as Solomon writes, 'the idea that he might be looking for it in the wrong place – namely in his own consciousness – never even occurs to him' (1983: 49). Hegel thus presented in the *Phenomenology* a radical new approach to the human subject, that the self was a social product, and that without interpersonal interaction and mutual demand for what Hegel calls 'recognition', there is no self, and no self-consciousness. This argument was later developed by such philosophers as Heidegger and George Herbert Mead, and by P. F. Strawson in his study *Individuals* (1959). Tim Ingold (1986: 95) has also recently stressed that consciousness is not a property of individual objects but is an intersubjective process, but strangely, considering the book is on 'evolution and social life' makes no mention of Hegel at all.

Secondly, as noted earlier, Hegel conceived of the dialectical overcoming of the opposition between subject and object not simply in terms of thought, but in terms of human practical activity. The human subject is not just a conscious being but also an active agent in the world, and Hegel speaks of the subject as a 'middle term' between nature and spirit. In devising a non-dualist philosophy of mind, while avoiding a reductive materialist approach, Hegel puts an important focus on rationality and on intentional agency (Elder 1980: 41–59). As Hegel expressed it in his lectures on the philosophy of art: 'Man is realised for himself by practical activity, inasmuch as he has the impulse, in the medium which is directly given to him, to produce himself, and therein at the same time to recognise himself' (Gray 1979: 58).

Thus by interacting with the natural objective world, the human subject creates its own individuality, and self-consciousness becomes self-realisation. Through human activity, reason overcomes the opposition between subject and object. But in an important sense, as Solomon insists, humanity is not a 'vehicle' for the self-realisation of spirit, but rather *Geist* is 'nothing more than human spirit writ large' (1983: 6).

Hegel sees all human history as essentially the development of consciousness or spirit. It his *Philosophy of Mind* he sees spirit as manifesting itself in a developing series, which in his typical fashion, is seen as consisting of three stages. As *subjective mind* or spirit, three phases are postulated. Anthropology studies the earliest conceptions of spirit, in which the spirit in the form of the 'soul' is seen as embedded in the body and material world. As animistic thought, spirit forms an undifferented unity with nature. Phenomenology explores the development of a separation between consciousness and the world; this forms the subject matter of the early chapters of *Phenomenology*. Finally, in psychology, the spirit emerges as reason, implying a concrete understanding of the unity between the consciousness and reality. The second stage, *objective spirit*, examines the development of consciousness as it expresses itself in objective social phenomena – in the form of legal systems, morality and political philosophy. And finally, as *Absolute spirit*, consciousness reaches its third and most developed stage; spirit aware of its own rational subjectivity. This consciousness appears in the form of art, religion and philosophy. The third part of Hegel's *Encyclopaedia of the Philosophical Sciences* outlines the final two stages of the development of human consciousness, and these ideas are developed more fully in his *Philosophy of Right*, and in his lectures on the philosophy of history, art and religion, and on the history of philosophy.

Hegel's *Phenomenology of Spirit* is not a real introduction to his system of philosophy, but it nevertheless provides us with an important guide to his vision, and to his thoughts on 'the odyssey of mind'. Spirit for Hegel is not divinity, but human consciousness and human culture, which develops as a dialectical process through history. Individual human subjects are seen not as passive observers but as active participants in this process, and thus Solomon is close to the spirit of Hegel when he describes the *Phenomenology* as 'a grand treatise on cosmic humanism' (1983: 7). Hegel was an anthropologist and an 'existentialist' of sorts, who saw human consciousness in terms of a 'series of configurations', which the human spirit takes on its 'road' or 'path' towards a full rational understanding of the world. (For important studies of Hegel's *Phenomenology*, see Lukács 1975: 466–568; Gadamer 1976; Laxer 1976; Kojève 1980; Solomon 1983).

5.2 Historical Materialism

Leszek Kolakowski (1978) begins his important study of the history of Marxism with the words 'Karl Marx was a German philosopher'. Indeed he was; but he was something more – an economist, a revolutionary scholar and something of a prophet. Recent biographical essays have compared him with religious figures like Jesus and Mahomet, as well as with intellectuals of the rank of Aristotle, Copernicus, Newton, Darwin and Einstein (Singer 1980; Callinicos 1983b: 7). He is indeed something of a colossus, but his fame largely stems from the fact that Marxism is now the official philosophy of governments like those of the Soviet Union and China, for in his own day his writings were virtually unknown. The famous *Communist Manifesto* of 1848 had a very small circulation and was hardly known outside Germany.

Karl Marx (1818–83) was born in Trier in the Rhineland of Germany, the son of a well-to-do Jewish family. He went to the universities of Bonn and Berlin to study law, but soon became interested in philosophy. He became particularly absorbed in the writings of Hegel, and he appears to have accepted Hegelian philosophy almost as if it were a religious conversion. Throughout his life Marx seems to have looked upon himself as a disciple of Hegel. After completing his doctoral thesis on the materialist philosophies of Democritus and Epicurus, he was unable to find, as he had hoped, a post as a university teacher, and became a journalist. At the end of 1843 he moved to Paris, having recently married the daughter of a local aristocrat, and there began associating with the many radicals and socialists who lived in the city – Feuerbach, Stirner, Proudhon and Bauer. All these he was to later criticise in harsh terms. In 1844 he met Friedrich Engels, the son of a German industrialist, who was to become a life-long friend and collaborator. During his stay in Paris, Marx wrote a critique of Hegel's political philosophy and began a serious study of Adam Smith, Ricardo and other political economists. These studies, together with Marx's initial reactions to Hegel and communism, constitute what has come to be known as the *Economic and Philosophic Manuscripts* (1844), which, as McLellan notes (1973: 105), were the first drafts of a major work on the capitalist system, which eventually appeared, much revised and expanded, in 1867 as *Capital*. In February 1845 Marx moved to Brussels and there, together with Engels, wrote a long critique of the Left-Hegelians, *The German Ideology* (1846), which like the Paris *Manuscripts*, remained unpublished until the present century. In 1848 with Engels he also drafted the famous *Communist Manifesto* outlining the doctrines of the newly-formed Communist League. With revolutionary movements and struggles occurring throughout Europe, Marx attempted to continue his political activities. But eventually reaction prevailed and Marx was forced into exile. He came to London in August 1849, expecting his stay to be brief. But there he remained for the rest of his life, a political emigré supported by his journalism and by financial gifts from his friend Engels. (For useful accounts of the life and work of Marx, see Berlin 1963; McLellan 1973.)

It is clearly beyond the scope of the present study to offer an account, however brief, of Marx's social and political theory, the materialist conception of history which he formulated in collaboration with Engels. The literature on this subject is now extensive and there have been many important studies published (Lichtheim 1961; Avineri 1968; Lefebvre 1968; Kolakowski 1978). I shall instead, drawing on my earlier study, focus on a number of key texts and explore Marx's conception of the human subject.

The *Economic and Philosophic Manuscripts* of 1844 represent not only, as McLellan suggests, a first draft of *Capital* but a loose, initial synthesis of the 'three sources' of Marxism. For in an important sense, as Lenin suggested (1967: 7), the genius of Marx was to continue and complete the three main ideological currents of the nineteenth century; English political economy, French socialism and German classical philosophy. Marx subjected the main representatives of these three currents of thought – Ricardo, Proudhon and Hegel – to trenchant criticisms, but he absorbed many of the essential tenets of their work. The notes of the manuscripts themselves centre on a number of key concepts – capital, labour, alienation and species-being – and reflect the combined influences of Hegel, Feuerbach and Adam Smith.

A number of themes emerge from these manuscript notes, and from Marx's other writings of the same period, that are either developed more fully in, or form an underlying premise of, his more mature writings.

First, the young Marx accepted the basic premises of Hegelian philosophy:

The outstanding thing in Hegel's phenomenology and its final outcome – that is, the dialectic of negativity as the moving and generating principle – is thus first that Hegel conceives the self-genesis of man as a process, conceives objectification as loss of the object, as alienation and as transcendence of this alienation; that he thus grasps the essence of labour and comprehends objective man – true because real man – as the outcome of man's own labour. (Marx 1959: 140)

Engels, many years later, stressed the importance of this dialectical outlook, which both he and Marx embraced. The great merit of Hegel's philosophy, he wrote, was that 'for the first time the totality of the natural, historical and spiritual aspects of the world were conceived and represented as a process of constant transformation and development and an effort was made to show the organic character of this process' (Marx and Engels 1968: 408). Callinicos (1983: 42) likewise notes that Marx took over the characteristic structure of the Hegelian dialectic.

It is worth stressing that Marx never ceased, like his mentor, to be a dialectical thinker and that he continually paid tribute to Hegel's greatness as a thinker. That Hegel was a 'monkey' hanging around Marx's neck (Harris 1980: 145), and that Marx made an epistemological leap from ideology to science in renouncing the Hegelian dialectic (Althusser 1969), are both misrepresentations of the relationship between the two men. The Hegelian dialectic, Marx wrote, in its rational form, enables us to recognise that all historical forms are transient, and is of its very nature critical and revolutionary. But Marx thought Hegel's philosophy limited and one-sided, an 'occult critique' and thus mystifying. He wrote in the preface to the second edition of *Capital* (1873):

> Although in Hegel's hand dialectic underwent a mystification, this does not obviate the fact that he was the first to expound the general forms of its movement in a comprehensive and fully conscious way. In Hegel's writings dialectic stands on its head, you must turn it right way up again if you want to discover the rational kernel that is hidden away within the wrappings of mystification. (Marx 1957)

Now it is highly unsatisfactory and misleading to interpret these words, and Hegel's philosophy in general, in terms of the old opposition between idealism and materialism, beyond which Hegel had attempted to go. When Callinicos writes of Hegel's view of nature as the 'self-estrangement of spirit' (1983: 98), and Singer says that he thought of mind as having primacy over nature in an ontological sense, and of 'the purpose or goal of history as the liberation of mind from all illusions and fetters' (1980: 41), they seriously misunderstand Hegel. They take *Geist* to be some creator-spirit in a theistic sense, whereas for Hegel spirit (culture) is immanent in the world. Hegel's notion of an 'original unity' of Being makes such an interpretation – which stems from Engels – untenable. What troubled Marx was that Hegel's conception made spirit rather than human beings the subject of history – culture was in a sense personified – therefore he puts too much emphasis on consciousness, ignoring, or at least marginalising humans' active relationships with the natural world. Thus Marx felt that for Hegel the opposition between spirit (culture) and nature was 'within thought itself' and that the 'humanness of nature' therefore appears as the product of an abstract mind. Marx challenged this kind of philosophy for its mystification and, following Feuerbach's materialistic approach, suggested both that human beings are the subject of history and offered a definition of humans as a species-being. Marx, in fact, regarded Feuerbach as the only philosopher who had taken a serious and critical look at the Hegelian dialectic. Thus in no sense can Marx be thought of as having simply 'inverted' Hegel's philosophy (the latter being seen as pure idealism) for this would attribute to Marx a crude materialism. The transition from Hegel to Marx is rather, as Marcuse and Lefebvre have suggested, a move to a different order of truth. (For other interpretations of the relationship between Hegel and Marx, see Hook 1962; Colletti 1973; Merquior 1986b.)

Second, and stemming from this, Marx offers in the Paris *Manuscripts* a definition of the human species. In doing so he took over Feuerbach's concept of species-being, but he gave it an entirely new content. Feuerbach's conception of humans essentially implied that they had a passive relationship with the world, and he gave the concept of 'man' an ethical dimension. By contrast, Marx defined human beings not in terms of their self-consciousness or their passivity or ethical attributes, but rather in terms of their essentially active relationship with the natural world. He looked upon this conception as naturalism or humanism, and significantly distinguished it from both idealism and materialism, suggesting that his approach constituted 'at the same time the unifying truth of both':

> Man is directly a natural being. As a natural being and as a living natural being he is on the one hand furnished with the natural powers of life – he is an active natural being. On the other hand, as a natural, corporeal, sensuous, objective being he is a suffering, conditioned and limited creature, like animals and plants . . . and because he feels what he suffers, a passionate being. But man is not merely a natural being; he is a human

natural being. That is to say, he is a being for himself. Therefore he is a species-being, and has to confirm and manifest himself as such both in his being and in his knowing. Therefore human objects are not natural objects as they immediately present themselves, and neither is human sense as it immediately is. . . . Neither nature objectively nor nature subjectively is directly given in a form adequate to the human being. (Marx 1959: 144–6)

Almost one hundred years before cultural anthropology, Marx was suggesting that culture could not be looked upon as something natural or given, nor is the natural world itself directly accessible to human sensibility. For Marx, as for Hegel, the mutual interdependence of man as an historical being and nature was what was essential. Marx thus combines the materialist emphasis of the Enlightenment thinkers and of Feuerbach with the spiritual (cultural) emphasis of Hegel's idealism. Humans are both natural and social beings, in essence. But Marx, like Hegel, puts a focus on the interactional aspect: thus what is called world history is 'nothing but the creation of man by human labour and the development of nature by man' (1959: 106). As Callinicos writes: 'This conception of human nature as constituted by an active, redirective, transformative relationship to nature through the labour-process is fundamental to Marx's thought' (1983: 40). It is not surprising that when the *Manuscripts* were published in 1932, they had an important impact on existentialists and socialist humanists like Erich Fromm.

Equally important is that Marx, like Hegel, completely dissolved the opposition between subjective consciousness and the objective world, which had been the essential standpoint of all classical philosophy from Descartes to Kant, and is still assumed by positivist scholars. Kolakowski has cogently interpreted Marx's basic philosophy and his divergence from classical epistemology, on the one hand, to inquire how the transition from the act of self-consciousness to the objective world is possible, is misleading, since 'the assumption of pure self-awareness as a starting point rests on the fiction of a subject capable of apprehending itself altogether independently of its being in nature and society'. (1978: 134) On the other hand, it is equally wrong to regard nature as already known and to consider humans and human subjectivity as its product, for it is not possible to contemplate nature in itself regardless of humans' practical relation to it. For Marx, therefore, 'the true starting point is man's active contact with nature, and it is only by abstraction that we divide this into self-conscious humanity on the one hand and nature on the other' (1978: 134). The importance of praxis in overcoming the subject/object dichotomy was later developed, as we shall see, by both Hegelian Marxists like Lukács and existentialist philosophers. The pragmatist philosopher Richard Rorty (1980) rather surprisingly makes no mention of Hegelian Marxists or even of Marx in his well-known critique of the epistemology derived from Cartesian dualism, although Hegel and Marx anticipate his thoughts by more than a century.

In putting an emphasis on productive relationships there is the implication that Marx is offering a Promethean ethic, the notion that humans create themselves it opposition to, and through the control and domination of, nature. There is thus the suggestion that this theory expresses the 'arrogance' of humanism and the Baconian 'man-against-nature' perspective. One writer has indeed argued that Marx never disengaged himself from the dialectic and moral philosophy of the Enlightenment (Baudrillard 1975; cf. Adorno and Horkheimer 1973: 3–42; Ehrenfeld 1978: 250). This is in a sense true, but such an approach tends to ignore entirely the fact that Marx, following Hegel, attempted to integrate into his own theory the perceptions and values articulated by Romantics, such as Schiller and Goethe. Marx's model of human activity was artistic as well as economic, and the human relationship with nature that he posited was aesthetic as well as instrumental. Callinicos again expressed Marx's orientation well when he suggested that he 'relocated this humanist, aesthetic tradition [of European romantic literature] within a materialist theory of history starting from the labour-process' (1983: 40).

There is thus a Protean as well as a Promethean dimension to Marx's thought, and the 'free conscious activity that constitutes the species–character of man' implies a potentiality for aesthetic enjoyment. Although Marx has often been criticised for the 'productivist' emphasis of his work, his conception of 'productive activity' was a wide one, and involves the total life-activity of humans. Whereas animals produce only under the dominion of immediate physical needs, 'man produces even when he is free from physical need and only truly produces in freedom therefrom' (1959: 72). Thus labour or praxis for Marx essentially entailed autonomous, conscious activity – life-activity – and in an important sense, as David Conway writes (1987: 32), Marx regarded artistic creation as the paradigm of truly human activity. His view of humankind was therefore a romantic and humanistic one, and the ideal 'all-round' personality is patterned after the Renaissance heroic model. In an oft-quoted passage in *The German Ideology*, Marx and Engels suggest that in a communist society nobody will be restricted to an exclusive sphere of activity but will be free 'to hunt in the morning, fish in afternoon, rear cattle in the evening [and] criticise after dinner' (1965: 45). For Marx labour (praxis) is essential for the self-realisation and self-creation of human beings. There is also the issue of the absence of the concept species-being in Marx's later writings. This occurred not, I think, because Marx abandoned the humanistic perspective of his early youth for a mature scientific approach evident in his analysis of *Capital*. Rather, in despiritualising Hegel's dialectic, Marx had to conceive of the human subject as an active productive being, constituted historically by his or her own interaction with nature. He did not, however, use this as an explanatory concept, and so in no sense can Marx be described as a methodological individualist, but none the less it remained an underlying premise of all his writings. For Marx, history was not 'a process without a subject' (Althusser 1972: 78); but neither did he posit a transhistorical subject. Social life is a creation of human productivity, and it is fundamentally historical. (For useful discussions of Marx's humanism, see Soper 1986: 33–9; Merquior 1986b: 51.)

Third, the Paris *Manuscripts* outline Marx's initial thoughts on, and thus criticisms of, empiricism – the theory stemming from Locke and Bacon, that knowledge is based on observation and sense experience and that scientific theories are built up by some kind of inductive inference (see Chalmers 1978: 113–15). Marx challenges the validity of this kind of theory in the social sciences. It is of interest that although Marx uses Feuerbach to criticise Hegel's idealism, he uses Hegel to criticise the empiricism of Feuerbach as well as that of the English political economists. Callinicos (1983: 155) suggests that it was Marx who initiated a process, continued by Nietzsche and Freud, that has drastically undermined the notion of reason as theoria, the disinterested contemplation of an objective reality. But in fact, it was Hegel who initiated this process in his critiques of empiricism, and Marx largely followed, and in doing so developed, Hegel's seminal thoughts.

As a close student of Hegel's *Phenomenology*, Marx was impressed, as Hook (1962) suggests, with the emphasis upon the activity of the mind in the knowing process. Knowledge is not the impress of an objective world upon a passive consciousness, but the product of the interacting development of consciousness with things existing antecedently to consciousness. Both Hegel and Marx were agreed that consciousness played an active role in knowing; they differed in that for Marx consciousness was human not absolute, and activity has a practical emphasis. As Marx put it in *The Holy Family*: 'Instead of treating self-consciousness as the self-consciousness of real men, living in a real, objective world and conditioned by it, Hegel transforms man into an attribute of self-consciousness. He turns the world upside down' (Hook 1962: 31–2).

Thus in his essay on 'estranged labour', as well as in *Capital*, Marx criticises the theories of the political economists who saw the relations of capitalist production in terms of 'natural laws', which were independent of history. Marx is equally critical of Feuerbach's materialism, and in his famous *Theses on Feuerbach* (1845) he criticises Feuerbach's naturalism as static and unhistorical, for the natural world, he suggests, is not simply given in sense-experience. In Marx's view:

> The chief defect of all hitherto existing materialism (that of Feuerbach included) is that the things, reality, sensuousness, is conceived only in the form of the object, or of contemplation, but not as sensuous human activity, practice, not subjectivity. Hence it happened that the active side, in contradistinction to materialism, was developed by idealism – but only abstractly, since of course, idealism does not know real, sensuous activity as such. (Marx and Engels 1968: 28)

Hence Marx's approach, in refusing to take the empirically given on its own terms, transcends not only the opposition between idealism and materialism, but also that between empiricism and rationalism. Again following the trend of Hegel's thought, Marx advocates neither pure empirical description (or inductive generalisations based on these – which could only be like building a house on shaky foundations) nor the imposition of preconceived concepts or schemata on existing data, whether to order or to analyse them. To read *Capital*, as do some contemporary Marxists, in order to find some theoretical template, which can then be applied universally, is a kind of scholastic and ahistorical enterprise that is quite alien to the tenor of Marx's thought.

Fourth, an underlying theme of the *Manuscripts* is the concept of alienation, which again Marx derives from Hegel, only he gives it historical substance. Feuerbach had employed the Hegelian form to criticise religion, but Marx uses the notion to describe given social conditions – that of the capitalist mode of production. He describes the antagonistic struggle between the capitalist and the worker in negative terms, suggesting that the factory system is not only injurious to the health and well-being of the worker, but reduces him or her to the status of a commodity. Thus the labour-process, which should involve the creation of wealth for human enjoyment, and involve the development of human potential, leads only to the degradation of the worker. The individual is dehumanised and alienated from his or her true species-being. The workers no longer have control over their own destiny, and even the product of their labour is alienated in the act of production. The essays present essentially a moral indictment of capitalism, but there is an embryonic analysis of the basis economic categories of capitalism – capital, labour, wages, money – that Marx was later to expand and develop in his mature works. There is also a description of the kind of society in which private property is abolished and the self-estrangement of the human subject transcended. Citing the French socialists such as Proudhon and Saint-Simon, Marx describes such a state as communism. It is the

> genuine resolution of the conflict between man and nature and between man and man – the true resolution of the strife between existence and essence, between objectification and self-confirmation, between freedom and necessity, between the individual and the species. Communism is the riddle of history solved, and it knows itself to be this solution. (1959: 95)

Although the proletariat is defined in these essays, it is not seen as the agency of social transformation, an idea that Marx was to develop in his later studies and that formed the basis of his politics. It has been suggested that Marx renounced Hegel's teleological conception of history, and consequently saw history as an open process and contradiction as a constituent of social reality. It is worth quoting, therefore, the conclusion to his notes on communism: 'Communism is the necessary form and dynamic principle of the immediate future, but communism is not as such the goal of human development, the form of human society' (1959: 106). Thus for Marx communism is not so much a social state – otherwise the dialectic would come to an end – but rather a conscious principle of movement.

Such, in brief, are some of the main themes that emerge from the *Economic and Philosophic Manuscripts*, particularly as these relate to Marx's conception of the human essence. And as Conway has indicated (1987: 28–45), both his critique of capitalism and his advocacy of communism, are based on what Marx regarded as the essential nature of the human species – the potentiality for autonomous, self-determining activity, for sociality and for aesthetic enjoyment. Marx's subsequent studies and writings were largely devoted to a detailed analysis of capitalism. But, along with Engels, he was also engaged in an important subsidiary task, namely to delineate a method of understanding and explaining social life, to construct a sociology that was both materialist and historical. And this, as Merquior notes (1986b: 48), represents a significant departure from Hegel's phenomenology, for it suggests a causal hypothesis. The fundamental ideas of historical materialism are perhaps best expressed by quoting some short extracts:

> The premises from which we begin are not arbitrary ones, not dogmas, but real premises from which abstraction can only be made in the imagination. They are the real individuals, their activity and the material conditions under which they live, both those which they find already existing and those produced by their activity. These premises can thus be verified in a purely empirical way.
>
> The fact is, therefore, that definite individuals who are productively active in a definite way enter into these definite social and political relations. Empirical observation must in each separate instance bring out empirically, and without any mystification and speculation, the connection of the social and political structure with production.
>
> We set out from real, active men, and on the basis of their real life process we demonstrate the development of ideological reflexes and echoes of this life-process . . . Morality, religion, metaphysics, all the rest of ideology and their corresponding forms of consciousness, thus no longer retain the semblance of independence. They have no history, no development; but men developing their material production and their material intercourse alter, along with their real existence, their thinking and the products of their thinking. Life is not determined by consciousness, but consciousness by life. (Marx and Engels 1965: 31–8)

A decade or so later Marx published his famous Preface to his *Critique of Political Economy* (1859) and again it is worth quoting from this seminal and much quoted work. The guiding thread of his studies, Marx suggests, can be briefly formulated as follows:

> In the social production of their life, men enter into definite relations that are indispensable and independent of their will, relations of production which correspond to a definite stage of development of their material

productive forces. The sum total of these relations of production constitute the economic structure of society, the real foundation on which rises a legal and political superstructure and to which correspond definite forms of social consciousness. The mode of production of material life conditions the social, political and intellectual life process in general.

Contradictions between the forces and relations of production engender social transformations, and Marx continues:

> In considering such transformations a distinction should always be made between the material transformation of the economic conditions of production, which can be determined with the precision of natural science, and the legal, political, religious, aesthetic or philosophic – in short, ideological forms in which men become conscious of this conflict and fight it out . . . this consciousness must be explained from the contradictions of material life. (Marx and Engels 1968: 181–2)

Marx thus makes a clear distinction between the 'real basis' of social life (the material conditions of existence) and the ideological or idealistic superstructure (politics, law and religion) which he implies have no evolutionary development.

Now although Marx speaks of the 'production of material life' as 'conditioning' or 'determining' other aspects of social life, it is clearly misleading to interpret this, as many Marxist critics have, as implying a simple causal relationship between the base and superstructure. To do so invokes a mechanistic paradigm which is quite alien to Marx's tenor of thought. As Merleau-Ponty put it, the economic base is not a 'cause' but the 'historical anchorage' or 'carrier' for law, religion and other cultural phenomena (1964: 108–12; cf. Hindess and Hirst 1975: 16). Moreover, to situate Marx's distinction between ideology and the material conditions of life in the context of the old debate between the primacy of either spirit or matter is highly misleading. For Marx, as Cole long age suggested in his introduction to *Capital* (1957), 'ideas' and 'mind' are a part of what Marx conceived of as the 'material'. The economic base for Marx was those social relations which humans had been obliged to establish among themselves in the production of their material life. In an important sense, as many writers have suggested, Marx is a sociologist concerned with 'comprehending the human condition'; not, as with Hegel, in trying to comprehend the nature of the universe. But more than this, he was concerned also, through revolutionary practice, with changing the world for the better, basing his actions on a theoretical understanding of the present.

Bloch (1983) has suggested that Marx's position was always something of a balancing act between idealism and 'vulgar' materialism; but in fact, Marx went beyond this redundant polarity. His approach was both historical and structural, and implied a dialectical form of materialism that simply dissolved the old antithesis between consciousness and nature, mind and matter. Marx had learnt his lessons well from 'good old Hegel'.

There has been a wealth of debate on Marx's historical materialism and the validity of his thesis that the material conditions of human life determine the various forms of social consciousness. (For useful recent discussions, see Cornforth 1980; Callinicos 1983; Bloch 1983.) It is beyond the scope of this study to discuss these issues here, but a little may be said about Marx's concept of ideology, a concept that has been subject to varying definitions within the Marxist tradition. Utilising the important studies by Jorge Larrain (1979, 1983), three general points may be made about this concept.

First, although Marx spoke of ideology in terms of 'illusions', 'mystification' or 'inversions', this does not imply that notions like 'God' or 'labour' are not social realities that affect human behaviour. The concept of labour is an 'abstraction', the creation of the modern capitalism; but although it has a certain objectivity, it is illusory in the sense that it reifies what are essentially social relations concealing the essential feature of capitalist relations, namely, exploitation (Marx 1973: 103; Geras 1972: 291–301).

Second, for Marx, ideology is a critical concept, and it is clearly unhelpful to equate it either with culture or with 'consciousness'. When Ricoeur (1970: 33) suggests that the 'whole of consciousness' is to Marx a false consciousness, he seriously misjudges Marx's intent. As Bloch (1983) suggests, Marx conceived of ideology as part of the superstucture, and recognised that there were forms of consciousness that were non-ideological. He never, as Larrain (1983: 112) suggests, equated ideology and consciousness. Equally, to define ideology simply in terms of symbolic practices, or cultural ideas or collective representation serves only to neutralise its critical import.

Third, the distinction between ideology and science cannot be equated with the distinction between falsehood and truth. For as Kolakowski (1973: 119) suggests, they are distinguished by their social function not by their veracity. Marx was a dialectical thinker and such an opposition is abstract and speculative. There is no sharp distinction between truth and falsity, knowledge and illusion, for the 'emergent truth is always mixed up with illusions and error' (Lefebvre 1968: 85). Nor is there a simple or direct relationship between truth and a particular social class. When Marx suggests that the 'ideas of the ruling class are in every epoch the ruling ideas', this did not imply that such ideas were simply ideological or total. The theories of the political economists involved illusory concepts but they also had their truth, which Marx attempted to extract. Science itself could have ideological functions. Marx in fact never spoke of 'false consciousness' – the expression is Engels'. (For further studies of the concept of ideology, see Seliger 1977; Centre for Contemporary Studies 1978; McCarney 1980.)

To conclude this section on the historical materialism of Marx and Engels, we can perhaps summarise some of their essential thoughts on the human subject. Early bourgeois social theorists like Hobbes tended to see the human subject as essentially an asocial being, and like Feuerbach later, postulated various attributes as being the 'essence' of humankind. Although such theorists can hardly be labelled 'idealist', as Coward and Ellis (1977) are prone to do (for idealism situates the human essence not in natural attributes or biology, but in spirit), such an approach was basically asociological. It implied a dichotomy of the individual and society which Durkheim later bequeathed. Marx criticised early bourgeois philosophy not for its idealism – in fact, he applauded the materialism of Hobbes, Bacon and Feuerbach – but for universalising what were specific historical circumstances and beliefs, and for ignoring the fact that what was fundamental about humans was neither God nor biology, but their cultural attributes. As he put it in the 6th *Thesis on Feuerbach*, humans are not 'abstract, isolated individuals', but essentially social beings. In *The German Ideology* – which is fundamentally a critique of Feuerbach's static and contemplative materialism, and Stirner's egoism – Marx and Engels state their positions even more clearly; speaking of the productive forces as 'a historically created relation of individuals to nature and to one another, which is handed down to each generation'. Marx and Engels go on to suggest that 'This sum of productive forces, capital funds and social forms of intercourse which every individual and generation finds in existence as something given, is the real basis of what the philosophers have conceived as "substance" and "essence of man"' (1965: 50–1).

They also suggest that whereas Feuerbach's conception of the sensuous world is one of ahistorical contemplation by an abstract man, in point of fact, for the 'real historical man', the normal world

– even the objects of the simplest 'sensuous certainty' – is never given, but is mediated through culture and human praxis. Marx and Engels are clearly suggesting in opposition to the contemplative materialists that the 'essence' of humans is that they are social beings. Marx's main criticism of Feuerbach, apart from challenging his naive empiricism, was to suggest that although he had indeed shown that religion was an illusion of the earthly world, he had left a vital question unanswered, namely, how it was that people got these illusions into their heads. In spite of his materialism, Marx writes, Feuerbach failed to examine the actual conditions of human existence, stopping short at the abstraction man. Marx summed up Feuerbach's approach cogently when he suggested: 'as far as Feuerbach is a materialist he does not deal with history, and as far as he considers history he is not a materialist' (Marx and Engels 1965: 59). For Marx human life could be understood only if situated in both a historical and a natural context.

Although some contemporary Marxists feel the need to stress that these insights need to be incorporated into academic psychology, with its individualistic and behaviouristic bias (e.g. Heather 1976), in point of fact these suggestions are not specifically Marxist. The whole social scientific tradition, in fact, has, over the last hundred or more years, been articulating in various ways, this essential viewpoint, namely that what characterises humankind as a species-being is their culture. The latter both mediated their perception of nature and is an adaptive mechanism. But what was specific to Marx and Engels was their stress not only on culture but on their refusal to see nature and history as separate and antithetical. For these writers humans always have an 'historical nature' (culture) and a 'natural history' (a relationship with nature) (1965: 58). The latter is too often ignored by anthropologists within the Durkheimian tradition. Hence for Marx and Engels, as was again expressed succinctly in the oft-quoted *Theses on Feuerbach*, what characterised human beings was their 'practical-critical activity'. The terms practice and practical are present in almost every one of the eleven theses (1968: 28–30). Thus as Bookchin put it: 'Marx tried to root humanity's identity and self-discovery in its productive interaction with nature' (1982: 32). This implies that for Marx, humanity is both a thinking and an active being, and that through labour they creatively produce their own 'condition of life'. In turn the mode of production of material life is seen to condition 'the social, political and intellectual life processes in general'. Praxis is therefore a key concept in Marxist theory, for 'it is just in his work upon the objective world that man really proves himself as a species-being. This production is his active species-life' (1959: 144–6).

Marx therefore counterposed Feuerbach's radical materialism and humanism with the notion of the human subject that conjoined theoretical and practical reason. To speak, therefore, of mind or ego as an abstract entity, unconnected with humanity, was for Marx pure nonsense (cf. Lefebvre 1968: 3–58; Worsley 1982: 31). This is why I think Piaget, and even Freud, are closer to Marx than Lévi-Strauss and most cultural anthropologists, and even some self-proclaimed Marxists.

For Marx, then, the individual personality is a psychosomatic unity, essentially social and rooted in nature. The 'essence' of mankind implied, therefore, a kind of complex equation involving the biological individual, nature and an ever-changing social process. Marx too was an 'essentialist' (universalist), like Feuerbach, in that he based his work on an articulated theory of 'human nature', but he simply refused to see humanity, the human subject, divorced from the social and natural worlds.

Throughout his life, as Miller suggests, Marx affirmed the aim of individual emancipation: 'Beyond the primarily political and formal emancipation envisaged by liberalism, beyond the purely technical reform of society proposed by utopian socialists like Saint-Simon, beyond the abstractly inward moral metamorphosis espoused by various strains of romanticism, Marx anticipated social conditions that might enable men to become whole' (J. Miller 1979: 40). Marx envisaged a society where institutions were under the control of the individuals who compromised them, and where humans could freely express their species-being and which would facilitate 'the full and free development of every individual'. It was a vision, however, that sat uneasily with his authoritarian politics. (For further discussions of Marx's humanism, see Fromm 1965; Schaff 1970; J. Miller 1979: 13–100.)

5.3 Lukács

Within the Marxist tradition there has been an ongoing debate, and at times harsh polemical exchanges, between two distinct interpretations of Marx. On the one hand, there is what is usually described as the critical or Hegelian Marxists, who stress the continuity of Marx with Hegel, and view Marxism as a critique rather than as a science. Thus they take a more historicist and humanistic interpretation of Marx's writings, and situate themselves in the more literary and philosophical tradition of European culture. As with Marcuse, they are often highly critical of modern science and technology. Scholars such as Lukács, Gramsci, Sartre, Marcuse, Fromm and Goldmann are placed within this critical tendency of Marxism. There are clearly important differences in the perspectives of these writers, and as we shall see, writers like Lukács were much influenced by the hermeneutic tradition of Dilthey and Weber, as well as by Hegel.

On the other hand, there are the scientific Marxists who stress that Marxism is a science of history and suggest that Marx made a clean break with Hegelian philosophy. Among the early writers, Engels, Kautsky and Plekhanov are in this tradition, and they present a more deterministic and positivistic interpretation of Marx's writings. Such writers were more mechanistic than Marx, and were often strongly influenced by social Darwinism. Modern writers who eschew critical theory include Godelier, Poulantzas and Althusser, and they stress a structural Marxism, which rejects a humanistic interpretation of Marx. This tendency is oriented towards modern technology and science, and accepts the great value placed upon them. With Althusser a radical break is stressed between the young Marx, still allegedly enrapt in Hegelian ideology, and the mature Marx, the text of *Capital* being seen as an exemplification of true science.

At extremes, the first tendency degenerates into naive romanticism and hermeneutics, whereas the second slides into positivism and mechanistic materialism. There is undoubtedly, as Wright Mills suggested (1963: 98), an 'unresolved tension' in Marx's work, and in history itself; the tension of humanism and determinism, of human freedom and historical necessity. And Marx clearly expressed an ambiguous attitude towards science, for as his criticism of abstract materialism in *Capital* suggests (1957: 393), he was trying to go beyond the mechanistic paradigm bequeathed from the Enlightenment (and adopted by the political economists), without in the process renouncing either reason or the empirical method of science. But the essence of Marx's contribution to philosophy, as Novack and Timpanaro have argued, is that he consistently tried to unify these two tendencies, advocating an approach that was both materialist and dialectical. In essence, Marx was a scientific humanist (Timpanaro 1975; Novack 1978: 230. For useful discussions of the 'two Marxisms' see Gouldner 1973, 1980; and Sahlins' (1976) critique of historical materialism.)

Although these two tendencies are in fact discernible, to see a binary contrast between the Hegelian and anti-Hegelian schools of

Marxism is problematic, for as Perry Anderson writes, it tends to obscure the interrelations between them, and the diverse influences on contemporary Marxists (1976: 73). Anderson draws instead an historical contrast between the classical tradition of Marxism that flourished until the 1920s and the 'entirely new intellectual configuration' which developed within historical materialism, and which was described by Merleau-Ponty as 'Western Marxism'. The classical tradition was represented by the writings of Labriola, Kautsky and Plekhanov, as well as Engels, who attempted to provide a philosophical foundation for historical materialism. Later, the writings of Lenin, Luxemburg, Trotsky and the Austrian Marxists led to important developments in Marxist theory. Such writings were focused on concrete analyses of capitalism, on economic issues and on political theory. The writers within the classical tradition were all closely integrated into the political and ideological life of European socialism, and the locus of the tradition was Eastern Europe. From the 1920s onwards the locus of Marxism shifted into Western Europe, and became increasingly focused on Germany, France and Italy. Anderson discusses a number of important shifts in the nature of Marxism as it developed during the next three or four decades. To begin with, Marxist theory 'migrated virtually completely into the universities – precincts at once refuge and exile from the political struggles in the world outside' (1976: 50). Thus many of the leading theorists of Western Marxism – Lukács, Lefebvre, Marcuse, Korsch, Goldmann, Adorno, Colletti and Althusser – were university professors and were essentially philosophers, not political activists. Thus the focus of Marxist studies shifted away from politics and economics and towards epistemological problems, aesthetics and cultural theory and to discourses on Marx's own writings. Inevitably, their style of writing became academic and esoteric – Anderson describes Sartre's style as 'a hermetic and unrelenting maze of neologisms', and that of Althusser's as 'a sybilline rhetoric of elusion' (1976: 54). Moreover, in their developments of Marxist theory, the Western Marxists drew increasingly on the writings of pre-Marxist philosophers like Kant and Spinoza. Although there has been another tradition operating off stage, represented by Mandel, Novack and Timpanaro, and although Western Marxists by no means represent a unified school, the tradition of Western Marxism has had an important influence on contemporary thought. Later in the study I shall discuss the work of Marcuse, Merleau-Ponty and Althusser; here I wish to discuss only one representative of the Marxist tradition. Georg Lukács, who is regarded, along with Gramsci and

Korsch, as one of the main founders of Western Marxism. (For general reviews of Western Marxism, see *New Left Review* 1978; Merquior 1986b.) Lukács has been described as one of the most original and important Marxist philosophers of the twentieth century, as well as a significant culture theorist. Even his critics pay homage to his originality and erudition. Stephen Spender described him as a 'millionaire of learning'. Lukács was born in Budapest in 1885, then the cultural centre of the Austro-Hungarian Empire. His father was a wealthy Jewish banker and a member of the nobility. The aristocratic family into which Lukács was born spoke German, and in his early years he thus became thoroughly acquainted with German literature and philosophy. He studied jurisprudence at the University of Budapest between 1902 and 1906, and after completing his doctoral studies wrote two books on aesthetics, both published in Hungarian – *A History of the Development of Modern Drama* and *The Soul and its Forms*. In the years before the First World War he moved to Germany to continue his studies at the universities of Berlin and Heidelberg. He attended the lectures of Simmel and Rickert, and met Max Weber and Emil Lask, with whom he established close friendships. At that point German sociology and philosophy were dominated by the neo-Kantian school, and Lukács was deeply influenced by its theory and perspective, particularly the theories of Rickert and the life-philosophy (*Lebensphilosophie*) of Wilhelm Dilthey. Their critiques of positivism and the distinction they stressed between the natural and the cultural sciences made a deep impression on Lukács. While at Heidelberg he wrote his famous *Theory of the Novel*, published in book form in 1920. It indicates the influence of both Dilthey and Hegel, Lukács having become interested in the latter through Dilthey's book on Hegel published in 1906. Lukács' study of the novel is in the *Geisteswissenschaft* tradition for it describes literary forms as essentially the expression of changing historical totalities. Lukács suggested that in this work 'he was searching for an historically based universal dialectic of the genres . . . that would tend towards a more intimate interrelation of the [aesthetic] categories and history than he had encountered in Hegel; he was trying to conceive something stable within the flux' (1962: Preface). But besides studying Hegel and the neo-Kantians during these pre-war years, Lukács also immersed himself in the writings of Dostoevsky and Kierkegaard, and, under the influence of the anarcho-syndicalist Ervin Szabó, the works of Marx, Luxemburg and Sorel.

The fall of the Habsburg regime at the end of the First World

War, the Russian October Revolution of 1917 and the short-lived Hungarian Soviet Republic of 1919 all had a profound effect on Lukács' thinking, culminating in his complete conversion to Marxism, both politically and philosophically. Lukács joined the newly founded Communist Party of Hungary in 1918 and the following year became Minister for Education in the Soviet Republic. With the collapse of this socialist government, Lukács sought refuge in Vienna and there he stayed until 1929. He then moved to Moscow and, apart from a short period in Germany, he remained in Moscow for the next fourteen years working at the Marx-Engels Institute. Although his writings often brought him into conflict with Stalinist orthodoxy, Lukács did his best to conform with this orthodoxy by publishing self-criticisms of his work. He remained nevertheless faithful to Lenin's conception of Marxist politics and his stress on the Vanguard party throughout the last years of his life. While in Moscow he wrote *The Young Hegel* and several books on aesthetics, all of which were published after the Second World War. In 1945 Lukács returned to Hungary and supported the short-lived revolution of 1956. After a period of exile in Romania, he again returned to Budapest and died there in 1971 aged eighty-six. He was writing books to the very end. (For useful biographical accounts of Lukács, see Mészáros 1972; Parkinson 1977: 1–18; Kolakowski 1978: 3/255–64.)

Lukács' writings are voluminous but they are mostly devoted to aesthetics and literary criticism, topics that fall outside the scope of the present study. I shall concentrate instead on the work that is regarded by many as his *magnum opus*, his *History and Class Consciousness* (1923). The book, considered as a classic in Hegelian-Marxism, consists of some eight essays that Lukács had written between 1919 and 1922. Although one of the fundamental texts of Western Marxism, *History and Class Consciousness* is a dense and scholarly work, loaded with abstractions in the style of Hegel. Its aim was to counter the evolutionist and positivist interpretations of Marx that dominated the Second International, and to provide a philosophical basis for Lenin's theory of socialism and the party. At the time it was written, Lukács, like many other socialists of the period, believed that a world revolution was imminent, involving the total transformation of European society. The study aimed to counter the scientific interpretations of Marxism outlined by Engels, Kautsky and Plekhanov, and, as Lukács put it in the Preface to the work (1967), 'to restore the revolutionary nature of Marx's theories by renovating and extending Hegel's dialectics and method'. Thus Lukács felt he was engaged in an exercise to re-establish what he regarded as orthodox Marxism as a revolutionary doctrine. The essence of orthodox Marxism for Lukács did not imply the uncritical acceptance of the result of Marx's investigation. It was not the belief in this or that thesis, still less the exegesis of a 'sacred' book. Rather, it was the conviction that the dialectical method is the road to truth. Thus even if modern research showed that many of Marx's statements were empirically invalid, this would not involve renouncing dialectical materialism as a form of knowledge. This leads Lukács to make some important criticisms of Engels' study, *Anti-Dühring* – both its conception of the dialectics of nature and its reflection theory of knowledge – which was also espoused by Lenin. Engels' understanding of dialectics as a system of natural laws that are ascertained by humans, Lukács suggests, is one-sided and involves a rigid causality. To see the 'laws of dialectic' as the property of nature which can be discovered and exploited by human technology has nothing to do, he felt, with dialectics as understood by Marx and Hegel, for it makes knowledge purely contemplative and involves a dichotomy between the subject and object. In his discussion of dialectics, Lukács writes, Engels 'does not even mention the most vital interaction, namely the dialectical relation between subject and object in the historical process, let alone give it the prominence it deserves. Yet without this factor dialectics ceases to be revolutionary despite attempts (illusory in the last analysis) to retain "fluid" concepts' (1971: 3). Lukács goes on to offer a critique of empiricism, stressing the historical character of facts and that facts always imply an interpretation; thus suggesting that knowledge is not mere contemplation but always involves practical activity. Engels' suggestion that industry and scientific experiment are forms of praxis is repudiated by Lukács, for these activities do not necessarily transform humans into the conscious creators of reality. They simply increase human mastery of the environment, and do not make a break with the bourgeois system of thought. The human person only becomes a subject when he or she assimilates and identifies with the external world, abolishing the state of affairs in which the world is mere datum, and knowledge is no more than perception or contemplation. For the same reason knowledge cannot be regarded as the mere reflection of a pre-existing reality. From the point of view of the dialectic as Lukács understands it, to treat cognition as the reflection of the external world in mental experience 'is to perpetuate the dualism of thought and being, and to assume that they are fundamentally alien to each other' (Kolakowski 1978: 3/274).

For Lukács, Engels' conception of the dialectic ignored the

creative role of human consciousness and human activity. But while Lukács is critical of the positivistic tendencies he sees as evident in Engels' study, he is also critical of Hegel, suggesting that he was unable to overcome the duality of thought and being in regarding only people and their consciousness as the true bearers of historical evolution (1971: 17). Richard Kearney cogently expresses Lukács' position when he writes:

> If the Hegelian dialectic must be superseded because of its idealist emphasis on the autonomous powers of consciousness, the 'scientific' dialectic of Engels must also be superseded in so far as it suspends the role of the subject altogether and sponsors a rigid causality which ignores the interaction of subject and object as dialectical counterparts of the historical process. In other words, while metaphysical idealism failed to 'change reality' by confining the transformative power of theory to a purely subjective consciousness, positivistic Marxism fails to provide the key to changing reality by assuming that it unfolds according to its own determinist laws independently of human initiative and intervention. (1986: 140)

Lukács links the contemplative theory of nature assumed by the empiricists to what he describes as the characteristic feature of bourgeois society, namely the tendency to reify human relationships and the human subject. Drawing on Marx's discussion of 'commodity fetishism' in the first volume of *Capital*. Lukács outlines the phenomenon of 'reification', the process whereby humans are reduced to things. As the labour process is progressively rationalised and mechanised under capitalism – and here Lukács' discussion is akin to that of Weber on rationalisation and the discussion on alienation by the early Marx – so human activity becomes less and less active and more and more contemplative. The rationalisation of the work process leads to the fragmentation of human life, as the social relations between persons are transformed into commodity relationships. The human subject becomes a mere cog in the labour process, and commodity production thus leads to the 'atomisation of the individual'. Even the worker's own labour power is treated as a commodity and his or her fate 'is typical of society as a whole in that this self-objectification, this transformation of a human function into a commodity, reveals in all its starkness the dehumanised and dehumanising function of the commodity relation' (1971: 92).

Under capitalism everything is specialised and activities become partial and fragmented. This means that the bourgeois conception of the human subject is that of an isolated, egoistic individual, whose consciousness, the source of his or her activity and knowledge, is an individual isolated consciousness *à la* Robinson Crusoe (1971: 135). Moreover, Lukács sees modern rationalist philosophy, with its antimonies of thought, as springing from the reified structure of consciousness. The essence of reification was 'the destruction of every image of the whole', a result of commodity production and exemplified in all bourgeois modes of consciousness with its dualism and mechanism and its extolling of mathematics as the ideal form of knowledge.

In the overcoming of this fragmentation of experience and the subject/object division, Lukács puts a focal emphasis on the concept of 'totality', also derived from Hegel. He argues that the development of capitalism has reached a stage where the proletariat, and the subject of the historical process, can overcome this reification. The modes of thought created by capitalism are limited and inadequate as forms of knowledge. Only through dialectical materialism, 'which sees the isolated facts of social life as aspects of the historical process and integrates them in a totality, can knowledge of the facts hope to become knowledge of reality' (1971: 8). Lukács therefore argues that what distinguishes Marxism from bourgeois thought is not the 'primacy of the economic motives in historical explanation', but the conception of totality (1971: 27). The category of concrete totality seems to be akin to Hegel's suggestion that 'truth is the whole', and his concept of reason. (For a useful discussion of Lukács' concept of totality, see Jay 1977.)

The consciousness of the human subject as a social being, that 'society becomes the reality for man' (1971: 19), became possible, Lukács suggests, only with the rise of capitalism. This implies the realisation that the human subject is both the product and the creator of social life. Unlike Kautsky and the more positivistic Marxists, Lukács stresses that 'active, working, thinking, struggling human beings were not only the products but the producers of the historical process of social development' (Novack 1978: 119). But he argues that the subject that can overcome the radical separation between subject and object, prefigured by Hegel, is a class subject, the proletariat, which, he writes, is 'the conscious subject of total social reality' (21). Thus dialectical materialism is inseparable from the 'practical and critical' activity of the proletariat, for both are aspects of the same process of social evolution. 'Socialism is not a state of affairs waiting for humanity and guaranteed by the impersonal laws of history, nor is it a moral imperative;

it is the self-knowledge of the proletariat, an aspect of its struggle' (Kolakowski 1978: 3/270).

The proletariat is thus seen by Lukács as a world-historical subject and as Novack remarks, is indeed a substitute for the logical Idea of Hegel. Humanity is alienated from its true existence, subject and object are opposed, until the proletariat arrives at class consciousness provided by Marxism (Novack 1978: 123).

There have been many critiques of Lukács' Hegelian interpretation of Marx, not least by Lukács himself. In his Preface to the work (1967), he does indeed suggest that in his study the logico-metaphysical construction of Hegel's phenomenology of mind had found its authentic realisation in the existence and the consciousness of the proletariat. But he goes on to suggest that this idea is somewhat metaphysical, and even Hegel, with his 'healthy sense of reality', had dismissed the notion of an identity between subject and object. He was rather prone, he wrote, to 'Messianic utopianism' and tended to ignore the basic category of Marxism, that of human labour, as the mediator between society and nature. Thus the ontological objectivity of nature is bypassed, and nature seen only as a societal category. Both Stedman Jones (1978) and Novack (1978) have offered important critiques of Lukács' *History and Class Consciousness*, his minimising of the materialist elements in both the background and structure of Marxism; the romantic anti-scientific thematic that prevades the study; the abstract and ethereal role assigned to the proletariat; and its general idealistic tenor. But the study has much of permanent value, and his disciple Lucian Goldman was correct in suggesting that it was a 'major event in the evolution of Marxist thought' (1977: 5). For Lukács, following Hegel and Marx, initiated a fundamental break in traditional philosophical thought, in seeing the human subject not as a being 'opposite to the world which he tries to understand and upon which he acts', but as a subject in this world (1971: 6). Lukács thus developed Hegel's and Marx's insight that history was a mediating dialectic that united human consciousness and the concrete world of praxis. He therefore clearly articulated the demand to overcome the opposition between the subject and the object of action that had been the basis of Western philosophy since the time of Descartes (1971: 11). He was thus a crucial figure in the development of both existentialism and critical theory. (For further important critiques and studies of Lukács' work, see Lichtheim 1970; Parkinson 1977; Lowy 1979; Arato and Breines 1979; Feenberg 1981.)

5.4 Marxist Psychology

Many writers in recent years have remarked on the fact that there is an 'historic gap' in Marxist theory, namely the absence of any developed theory of the human subject. In a recent interdisciplinary study of Marxist theory, discussed from the viewpoint of various disciplines, it is noteworthy that there is no mention at all of psychology (McLellan 1983). Although there are many 'indications' or 'pointers' with respect to a theory of the concrete human personality within the writings of Marx and Engels (discussed above) many Marxist scholars are agreed on the need to develop a Marxist psychology, or a 'materialist approach' to personality (P. Brown 1974; Leonard 1984). The limitations of Marxist theory in lacking a developed psychological theory was perceived by earlier scholars, and Wilhelm Reich and writers within the Frankfurt school like Fromm and Marcuse made attempts to supplement Marxist theory with concepts drawn from psychoanalysis. But many have been sceptical of the possibilities that Freudian theory could form the basis for a Marxist psychology (Brooks 1973; P. Brown 1974: 71–9; Leonard 1984: 42–7).

Although offering important critiques of academic psychology in helpful summaries of the views of Marx and Engels on the human personality, studies in Marxist psychology have been programmatic rather than substantive, leading Leonard to conclude that there does not yet exist any satisfactory materialist theory of the individual (1984: 102), though Marx and Engels are seen as having laid the foundations for such a theory. But two writers are worth discussing in the present context, for both, working consciously within the tradition of historical materialism, have attempted to formulate new theories – they are Lucien Sève and Lev Vygotsky. Lucien Sève is a French Marxist philosopher whose work is difficult to assess as he is concerned purely with outlining a coherent theory of personality based on the work of Marx and Engels. His writings are thus scholastic and abstruse, with little empirical evidence or material. Apart from nodding references to Piaget, Linton, Freud and Sheldon, there is no real engagement with academic psychology, and even important writers within Marxism – Lukács, Reich, Marcuse, Fromm, Vygotsky – are bypassed. The study in fact is firmly situated in the polemical debates, mainly of a philosophical nature, that focused on the 'theoretical anti-humanist' interpretation of Marx presented by Louis Althusser during the 1960s. While tending to agree with many of Althusser's criticisms of existentialist and Hegelian Marxists, Sève, following the lead of an earlier French Marxist, G. Politzer, whose *Critique of the Foundations of Psychology* was published in 1928, is struggling to avoid the implications of Althusser's theory, namely the collapsing of psychology into political economy. Sève is concerned with delineating the possibilities of a new psychological science, 'the science of the concrete human personality', based on Marx and Engels' conception of historical materialism. Sève in his writings (1975, 1978) is thus engaged in three tasks: a philosophical critique of academic psychology; the delineation of a Marxist conception of the human subject; and the presentation of what he descibed as 'indicative hypotheses', the basic concepts of a materialist psychology.

Sève recognises the difficulties and the problematic surrounding the notion of psychology and the fact that the abstraction 'general individual' is 'the skeleton in the cupboard of the psychology of the personality' (1975: 12). How does one avoid the Comtean reduction of psychology either to physiology or to sociology? On the one hand, if one wishes to base a materialist psychology on biology, then 'one must reduce the whole of psychological life to a merely natural process. This would bring one into continual conflict with psychological science itself which has demonstrated very clearly and convincingly that man is only psychologically man on the basis of an ensemble of social processes whereby man becomes man' (1975: 12). On the other hand, to look for the foundations of general individuality in sociology would involve psychologising the ensemble of social processes and thus enter into continual conflict with the social sciences which have shown very clearly and convincingly that society is not the sum of individuals. Differential psychology and the basic personality typologies of the culture and personality theorists are unable to understand, Sève suggests, what is fundamental about humans, namely their concrete individuality. Pavlov's theories (which many early Marxists thought of as providing a rigorous materialist psychology to supplement historical materialism), and behaviourism, Sève finds quite inadequate, for the totality of human activity 'goes beyond the limits of the individual organism and affects the individual through a vast mediation of social relations' (1975: 17). Thus for Sève sociality and individuality are intrinsically and dialectically linked; he presents the insoluble dilemma of separating them thus:

> Either one separates the personality from the social conditions in which it forms, but in doing so deprives oneself of any way of giving an account of its fundamental sociality; or else, conversely, one admits that

it is essentially resolved into social facts, but then one fails to account for each individual's concrete singularity. (1978: 231)

And he goes on to suggest that humans assume an individuality in the historical process, that 'the individual is an individual in so far as he is a general social being and a social being in so far as he is a singular individual' (1978: 239).

Both cultural anthropology and biological explanations, he concludes, run away from this contradiction. Stressing the limitations of contemporary psychology, particularly when attempting to understand the concrete personality, and convinced that a scientific psychology should be an integral part of Marxism, Sève argues that such a psychology is implied, if not elaborated, in Marx's writings, even in *Capital*. Sève follows Althusser in seeing the period 1845/6 as constituting an important break, or at least change, in Marx's philosophy. In *The German Ideology*, he suggests, Marx and Engels present a new standpoint, an irrevocable rupture with the philosophical humanism that Marx presented in the 1844 *Manuscripts*. They categorically reject the concept of 'abstract man', whose history is merely self-development, the speculative conception of the human subject as a species-being, and replace it with the idea that the 'essence' of humankind is not something abstract but an ensemble of real-life processes. Marx, Sève writes, entirely displaced the terrain of his analysis from the human essence to social relations, and this interpretation implied that the 'very concept of man . . . no longer finds a place in mature Marxism'. Marx's new approach to the human subject is seen as particularly embodied in the famous *6th Thesis on Feuerbach* which reads: 'The human essence is no abstraction, inherent in each single individual. In its reality it is the ensemble of the social relations.'

This statement is seen by Sève as introducing a radically new meaning to the concept of man, and he presents a long and detailed discussion elaborating upon the theme that the human individual is essentially a social being. Although not mentioning Sève, Norman Geras (1983) – also focusing on the *6th Thesis on Feuerbach* – has argued that within his writings Marx clearly articulated a conception of 'human nature', a conception that suggested that certain potentialities, capacities and needs are universal aspects of the human subject, however these may be mediated in specific social and historical circumstances. This thesis would appear to be contrary to the one that Sève is suggesting, for Sève puts a focal emphasis on the sociality and individuality of the human subject, not upon human 'nature'. In fact, he appears to repudiate the idea of an abstract general individual, a 'fetish of the individual' which is shared by both humanist Marxists and psychologists. Existentialism he views as the 'mirror image' of this abstract essentialism. Neither academic psychology nor existentialism 'can view the human essence as anything other than a general individual' (1975: 26).

In stressing that the human subject is fundamentally a social being, and in adopting the orthodox Marxist premise that the institutions and objective conditions of a given epoch determine the life process and the consciousness of individuals. Sève puts a focal emphasis on the social relations of production. His hypotheses for a concrete psychology therefore tend to be narrowly economistic and to be essentially derived from the nature of commodity production under capitalism. Sève therefore argues that the primary concept of a concrete psychology should not be behaviour, but the concept of act, which is social activity that has consequences not only for the individual subject but for a determinable social world. After introducing the concept of capacity, Sève makes a distinction between those activities that produce or develop specific capacities (sector one) and those acts that only make use of already existing capacities. He also makes a distinction between abstract labour – socially productive labour under capitalism which produces a surplus – and concrete labour or activity. Concrete activity he defines as all personal activity 'which directly relates to the individual himself, for example acts directly satisfying personal needs, learning of new capacities unconnected with the carrying out and requirements of social labour (i.e. commodity production)' (1978: 338). Using these two distinctions, Sève constructs a topology of personalities and activities 'produced within capitalist forms of individuality' which consist of four quadrants (ibid.: 347). The schema is abstract and formalistic and hardly adequate as a substantive materialist theory of personality which Sève envisages. Moreover, as Leonard suggests (1984: 99–101), the traditional Marxist emphasis on commodity production profoundly affects the work, for Sève gives little attention to domestic labour and to the role of the family and childhood in personality development.

Lev Vygotsky (1896–1934) is a very different kind of scholar, an original thinker and a psychologist who made important empirical studies in the fields of cognition, semiotics and educational psychology. Vygotsky was born in the provincial town of Orsha in western Russia and graduated from the University of Moscow in 1917, specialising in literature. Between 1917 and 1923 he taught literature and psychology in a local school, as well as lecturing and directing the theatre section of an adult education centre. His early interests focused on art, literary criticism and aesthetics, and in 1925 he published his first book, *The Philosophy of Art*. The previous year he had addressed a conference on psychoneurology in Leningrad, and his presentation so impressed the participants that the director of the Institute of Psychology in Moscow, K. N. Kornilov, invited Vygotsky to join its staff. For the next decade Vygotsky worked in Moscow and, surrounded by a devoted group of colleagues and students, established himself as a brilliant thinker who was driven by a seemingly boundless energy. One of his colleagues, A. R. Luria, has recalled the enormous enthusiasm that surrounded the work of Vygotsky's group as they spent most of their working hours on a 'grand plan for the reconstruction of psychology' (1979: 52). With Luria, Vygotsky worked on a cross-cultural research project and conducted important studies on semiotics, mental abnormality and educational psychology. He is credited with playing an important role in the development of Soviet psychology. He died of tuberculosis in 1934 at the early age of thirty-seven (Wertsch 1985a: 3).

Vygotsky began his career immediately after the 1917 revolution. He was thus a student during the heyday of Wundt and James, and was a contemporary of such psychologists as Kohler, Watson and Pavlov, whose work he critically studied and assimilated into his own psychology. He was also active during a crucial period in the history of Soviet psychology when there was heated debate regarding the most appropriate paradigm on the development of a Marxist theory of human intellectual functioning. Whereas G. I. Chelpanor, in his study *The Mind of Man* (1917), had, as a follower of Wundt's introspective psychology, rejected materialist theories of consciousness, his rival, Kornilov, promoted a behaviourist, Marxist theory of psychology that did not envisage a role for consciousness in human activity. It was as a critique of the latter theory that Vygotsky's talk to the 1924 congress was largely addressed. The talk was appropriately entitled 'Consciousness as an Object of the Psychology of Behaviour'.

Vygotsky's psychology is an ambitious attempt to integrate three fields of knowledge: Marxist philosophy, semiotic theory and psychology. He was acutely conscious that in his day psychology was not a unified science and was confronted with a 'crisis'. Three schools of psychology were then prominent: behaviourism, associated with Pavlov, Watson and Kornilov; the Gestalt theory associated with Kohler and Koffka; and the introspective psychology of Wundt. Vygotsky shared the Gestalt psychologists' dissatisfaction with psychological analysis that reduced phenomena to 'elements', but felt that the Gestalt psychologists had not gone beyond the description of complex phenomena towards an adequate explanation of them. He was equally dissatisfied with behaviourist psychology and its analysis in terms of stimulus/response, a psychology that ignored the problem of consciousness. Vygotsky thus attempted a synthesis of all three approaches, to construct a psychology that avoided the extremes of vulgar behaviourism on the one hand, and an exclusive focus on consciousness on the other; a psychology that would make possible both description and explanation of higher psychological processes in terms acceptable to natural science.

James Wertsch (1985) has suggested that Vygotsky followed the fundamental tenets of Marxist philosophy in three areas of his psychology, and it will be useful to discuss each of these in turn. It is worth noting that Vygotsky consciously repudiated the 'quotation method' of relating Marxism to psychology, namely the excessive citation of phrases drawn from the Marxist classics. As he wrote: 'I don't want to discover the nature of mind by patching together a lot of quotations. I want to find out how science has to be built, to approach the study of the mind having learned the whole of Marx's method' (1978: 8).

Like Lukács, what was of crucial importance for Vygotsky was the dialectical method that Marx derived from Hegel. This is the first aspect of Vygotsky's work indicating his Marxist orientation.

In adopting a dialectical approach, Vygotsky puts a focal emphasis on the genesis and development of psychological processes. A central tenet of his method, therefore, was that all phenomena must be studied as processes of change and development. The task of psychology was to reconstruct the origin and development of behaviour and consciousness. This development he felt was not simply gradual and quantitative, but involved qualitative changes:

> Our concept of development implies a rejection of the frequently held view that cognitive development results from the gradual accumulation of separate changes. We believe that child development is a complex dialectical process characterized in periodicity, unevenness in the development of different functions, metamorphosis or qualitative transformation of one form into another, intertwining of external and internal factors, and adaptive processes which overcome impediments that the child encounters. (1978: 73)

Evolutionary and revolutionary changes for Vygotsky were not incompatible, but were forms of development that presupposed one another. Thus in his important study *Thought and Language* (1962), Vygotsky argued that not only were thought and language derived from different ontogenetic roots, but in their development and interrelationships, the nature of this development itself changed from biological to sociohistorical. Verbal thought, he wrote, 'is not an innate, natural form of behaviour, but is determined by an historical–cultural process that has specific properties and laws that cannot be found in the natural forms of thought and speech' (1978: 51). The process of concept formation therefore passed through three basic phases; the first step of the young child involves the formation of unorganised congeries or 'heaps'; development then proceeds to 'thinking in complexes' on which concrete associations between objects are made, and finally there is thinking in terms of concepts. By stressing the importance of dialectical development, Vygotsky felt that the schism between experimental studies of elementary psychological processes and the speculative reflection on cultural forms of behaviour might be bridged (Cole and Scribner, Introduction to Vygotsky 1978: 7).

The second important point about Vygotsky's Marxist psychology is that he followed Marx in putting a focal emphasis on human activity. In criticising both the behaviourist perspective that reduced all behaviour to a combination of reflexes and saw consciousness as an unnecessary concept, and the subjective idealist notion of consciousness as some form of mental substance – and hence separate from behaviour – Vygotsky came to argue that consciousness was essentially the organisation of practical activity (B. Lee 1985: 68). Arguing also against the notion that consciousness was directly determined by a material substratum, such as the brain, Vygotsky stressed that human practical activity was a key explanatory principle and formed an 'intermediate link' between objective reality (the external world) and consciousness (Davydov and Radzikhoveskii 1985: 47).

The third important aspect of Vygotsky's psychology is that he followed Hegel and Marx in emphasising the social foundations of human consciousness. Stressing that culture is the product of social life and human social activity, Vygotsky argued that tools and signs – visual symbols with a definite meaning – are both social products that have historically developed and are separate from the individual. They are in essence, he wrote, social organs or social means.

ᵥests that higher mental functions are not developed in
.ᵗ are rather direct reflections of social processes in which
✓idual participated at an earlier stage of ontogenesis. 'All
. mental functions', he wrote, 'are internalized social relation-
ᵥs. Their composition, genetic structure and means of action –
ᵼ a word, their whole nature – is social' (1981: 164). Through a
process of 'internalisation' social relations and meanings become
psychological functions of the individual. Cultural development,
therefore, is not a process towards socialisation, but essentially the
conversion of social relations into mental functions, and it appears
on the social plane, and then on the psychological plane. First it
appears between people as an interpsychological category and then
within the child as an intrapsychological category. 'This is equally
true with regard to voluntary attention, logical memory, the formation of concepts and the development of volition' (1981: 163).

Vygotsky's conception of the human subject was similar to that
of Marx. He saw the human person as essentially a social being and
put a focal emphasis on human practical activity. He saw the
relationship between the individual and the society as a dialectical
process and, unlike earlier psychologists, focused on the historically shaped and culturally transmitted psychology of human beings.
Though he shared Piaget's emphasis on the active organism, he felt
that no universal schema could adequately represent the dynamic
relationship between the individual and the changing historical
conditions that determine the development of the human subject.
Moreover, Vygotsky stressed that one of the major weaknesses of
traditional psychology was that it treated cognition as an autonomous process 'segregrated from the fullness of life, from the
personal needs and interests, the inclinations and the impulses' of
the human subject (1962: 8). Vygotsky's legacy was, therefore, like
Wundt's, to suggest a cultural psychology that would bridge the
divide between the natural and the social sciences.

–6–

The Sociological Tradition

This chapter deals with the sociological tradition that stemmed from the positive philosophy of Auguste Comte which emerged in the early decades of the nineteenth century. Although close to the empiricist tradition of Hume and J. S. Mill, Comte in fact advocated, not a utilitarian individualism, but a collectivism, stressing the priority of the social over the individual. Emphasising that social life was a reality *sui generis*, Comte gave little scope for psychology, suggesting an inherent dualistic conception of the human subject. The first section of the chapter outlines Comte's positivism, while in the following two sections the sociological theory of Durkheim is explored in the light of these observations, for Durkheim had a similar dualistic conception of the subject, seeing the person as a social organism. In the final two sections I discuss three scholars who have developed Durkheim's sociology – Radcliffe-Brown, Leslie White and Louis Dumont – focusing on their theory of the human subject.

6.1 Positive Philosophy

The French revolution of 1785 has been described as an 'epochal event', which created an intellectual crisis in Europe and had a massive impact on Western thought. Along with the industrial revolution of the same period, it gave rise, directly or indirectly, to profound transformations in the fabric of European society. The revolution was regarded as the fruit of the Enlightenment, and Rousseau was held to be its clearest philosophical expression. Rousseau's social theory was based on such doctrines as equality, freedom and popular sovereignty, and on a theory of individualism based on the concept of natural law. The revolution gave credence to the idea that human beings, utilising the faculty of reason, and freed from the dogmas of religion, could effect a complete radical

human society and human nature. But the after-
olution was not merely the undermining of the old
on; it led also to an acute social and political crisis,
as much of Europe from 1789 to 1814 was embroiled in
dictably, the crisis gave rise to a conservative reaction and
early decades of the nineteenth century a number of import-
scholars emerged whose writings reflect a defence of the old
aditional order and the values of the *ancien régime*. Edmund
Burke, de Maistre and Bonald are important in this respect; they
were, Nisbet suggests, 'apostles of a stable, rooted, and hierarchical
society, enemies of any form of individualism that tended to
separate man from his primary social contexts – starting with
family, village and parish, but including social class and other close
forms of association' (1979: 88). The writings of Louis Bonald
(1754–1840), one of the most profound of the 'prophets of the past',
are of particular relevance as they had an important influence on
Auguste Comte. Bonald's philosophy represents a complete antithesis to that of the Enlightenment thinkers, for Bonald takes
society, not the individual, as his point of departure, and sees
authority, not individual liberty, as the crucial aspect of social life.
Only under the authority of the family, local community and the
Church is it possible, he felt, for the human subject to thrive, and
hierarchy was deemed to be the essence of the social bond, not
equality or contract. He stressed that society has primacy over the
individual. Thus, whereas the Enlightenment philosophers and
Rousseau had tended to derive society from human impulses,
passions and reason, Bonald takes society (created by God) as an
eternal and original force, and the vital context of the individual's
formation and development. As he wrote: 'Not only is it not true
that the individual constitutes society; it is society that constitutes
the individual, by socialization. Man does not create society; it is
society that creates man' (Nisbet 1979: 91).

This stress on the priority of the social over that of the individual
is seen by Nisbet to be intrinsically linked to other conservative
themes expressed by writers of the reaction; the conviction that
religion plays an indispensable role in social order; a functional,
organismic conception of society; and a concern for hierarchy and
historical tradition as a counter to the disintegrating effects of
modern technology. Disavowing the theory of natural rights and
profoundly sceptical with regard to the capacities of human reason
to reconstruct society, the conservative thinkers like Bonald, expressed their admiration of the medieval period, and stressed the
social nature of the human subject (Nisbet 1979: 89–105).

What is sigificant about Auguste Comte (1798–1857) is that can be firmly situated in the 'retrograde school' (as he called it) ˅ de Maistre and Bonald, yet he attempted to unite a concern fo order with some of the essential tenets of the Enlightenment tradition. Disturbed and distressed by the political disorder of his period, and by the cultural and material poverty of the people, his most fundamental preoccupation was with order and stability. But he was also concerned with the total reconstruction of society, although what he envisaged was very different from that suggested by the socialist writers (Fletcher 1966: 7).

Like Herbert Spencer, Comte was a great synthesiser of scientific knowledge, and has been rightly accredited as the founding father of both positivism and sociology. Born in Montpellier in southern France, he was brought up as a Catholic and a Royalist. Always at odds with his father, he soon renounced both doctrines and, obtaining a scholarship to the prestigious Ecole Polytechnique in Paris, attended there from 1814 until 1816. At the time this Polytechnique was the foremost centre of research in science and mathematics in Europe. On leaving the institute Comte became secretary to Saint-Simon, who was an influential precursor of socialism. Comte was associated with Saint-Simon for some seven years, until a quarrel ended their relationship in 1824. There is no doubt that Comte owed a great deal intellectually to Saint-Simon, and admitted as much, although the extent of Comte's debt to the socialist has always been a matter of debate. In 1826 he began giving lectures in a private capacity on positive philosophy, and seems for most of his life to have supported himself by tutoring. Like Spencer he never held a university post, and lived a strange, eccentric life beset with poverty, sickness and marital difficulties. Something of a megalomaniac, he quarrelled with almost everyone he met. Given his personal background, it is somewhat surprising that he achieved so much, but like Spencer he produced a vast compendium of scientific knowledge, presenting ideas that he had developed during his lecturing. Two studies are of lasting import-ance: *Cours de Philosophie Positive*, published in six volumes (1830–42), and *Système de Politique Positive* in four volumes (1851–4). The first study, 'a stylistically repellent monstrosity of nearly a million words' (as Evans-Pritchard 1981: 43, describes it), contains Comte's basic ideas on sociology. His later study is a 'polemical and rather turgid repitition' of many of the ideas ex-pressed in the *Cours*, although it has much more prophetic quality, outlining Comte's views on the future society, and his 'religion of humanity'. Comte's image as a 'tormented, dogmatic genius'

emerges clearly in these later writings. Many
...d gone a bit mad.

...and the work of Auguste Comte, Evans-Pritchard
...ests, one needs to take into account three factors – his
...ersonality which bordered on the paranoic; the social
...ons of France during Comte's formative years (characterised
...a ethos of uncertainty and despair); and Comte's position
...hin the general history of ideas. Although Comte was clearly
...nfluenced by the writings of Hume, Adam Smith, Ferguson and
Saint-Simon, his positive philosophy essentially represents a synthesis of two contrasting currents of thought. On the one hand, he
was deeply influenced by Montesquieu, d'Holbach, Turgot,
Diderot and the French Encyclopedists in general. Of particular
importance was Condorcet, whom Comte described as his 'spiritual father'. From Condorcet and the Enlightenment thinkers
Comte took the idea of the 'laws of progress' through which
human culture had passed. As he wrote, it was Condorcet who first
clearly saw that 'civilisation is subject to a progressive advance, the
stages of which are rigorously linked to one another by natural laws
which philosophical observation of the past can reveal' (Copleston
1974: 90).

On the other hand, as earlier indicated, he was also deeply
influenced by the 'traditionalists' such as Bonald and de Maistre,
who stressed the importance of order and authority, and who,
unlike the Encyclopedists, had a more sympathetic and positive
approach towards past traditions. Unlike Condorcet, they did not
have a 'blind aversion to middle ages'. Thus:

> In this respect the philosophical reaction, organised at the beginning of
> the century by the great de Maistre, was of material assistance in
> preparing the true theory of progress. His school was of brief duration,
> and it was no doubt animated by a retrograde spirit, but it will always be
> ranked among the necessary antecedent of the positive system. (so wrote
> Comte, in K. Thompson 1976: 11)

Comte's positive philosophy therefore combines two impulses
– the scientific and revolutionary impulse that stemmed from
Condorcet and the Enlightenment, and the philosophical and reactionary impulse associated with de Maistre and Bonald. Comte
himself explicitly saw his own project in these terms. His positivism thus 'preserves the theme of progress but undercuts the radicalism with which this was associated in Enlightenment

philosophy. "Progress" and "order" are more than reconciled; the one becomes dependent on the other' (Giddens 1979: 239). In counteracting the negative tendencies of rationalism, Comte, Marcuse suggests, laid the foundations for a sociology that became an ideological defence of bourgeois society and contained the seeds of a philosophical justification of authoritarianism (1941: 342).

Comte's sociology is focused on two important ideas; the 'law of three stages' and the concept of the hierarchy of sciences. Developing the ideas of the eighteenth-century philosophers of progress (Condorcet and Turgot), Comte postulated that the general intellectual development of humankind had passed through three essential stages. In the first stage, the theological, the human mind is seen as seeking the ultimate causes of events in animistic or supernatural terms. The world is held to be animate and events explained in terms of spirits, witches and deities. The theological stage had important subdivisions, constituting three successive phases; fetishism, polytheism and monotheism. The theological stage had its corresponding social order, dominated by priests and warriors. The second phase of intellectual progress, the metaphysical, is characterised by explanations in terms of abstract concepts such as nature, essence, logos, reason or vital principle. It is a period dominated by scholastics and lawyers. And finally, there is the third or positive stage, when the human mind gives up its search for absolute notions, the origin and destination of the universe, and applies itself instead to the study of the laws of phenomena, 'that is, their invariable relations of succession and resemblance. Reasoning and observation, duly combined, are the means of this knowledge' (Thompson 1976: 40). Positive knowledge, therefore, concerns itself with phenomena and the world of observed facts, which it subsumes under general descriptive laws. Comte, therefore, follows the British empiricists in adopting an empiricist theory of knowledge seeing it as little more than the systemisation of common-sense understanding. But Comte makes an important break with the classical empiricists in that the knowing subject is not the solitary individual but the human spirit as a collectivity (Benton 1977: 30). Moreover, Comte divorces positive knowledge from value judgements, seeing the scientific observer as essentially a neutral spectator. He describes the function of social science thus:

Without extolling or condemning political facts, science regards them as subjects of observational; it contemplates each phenomenon in its harmony with co-existing phenomena and in its connection with the foregoing and the following state of human development: it endeavours to discover, from both points of view, the general relations which connect all social phenomena. (Thompson 1976: 20–1)

Positive science was, therefore, concerned with 'the coordination of observed facts', of subsuming phenomena or observed facts under general descriptive laws, of linking phenomena 'to one another by relations of succession and similarity' (Copleston 1974: 77). Positive philosophy served a purpose in the scrutiny of scientific methods, and in effecting a synthesis of the various specific sciences. It was seen by Comte as having an instrumental value, as providing a 'solid basis' for the 'social reorganization which must succeed the critical condition in which the most civilized nations are now living'. What Comte envisaged was a capitalist system which would unify humankind and provide peace and stability under the guidance, if not the rule, of a scientific elite – composed of positive philosophers. He even advocated a 'religion of humanity', with appropriate cult organisation and rituals to facilitate the needed social regeneration.

It is of interest to note that Comte saw the 'law of three stages' as being recapitulated in the ontogeny of the individual, and as co-existing often within a science, or within the mind of the individual scholar.

In his *Course of Positive Philosophy* Comte outlined the development of the sciences, seeing them as forming a hierarchical system consisting of six basic sciences: mathematics, astronomy, physics, chemistry, physiology (biology) and social physics or sociology. Scientific knowledge he felt had developed in a systematic manner from the most abstract, and removed from the human condition, towards the science – sociology – which is the most complex. He argued that each successive science logically presupposed its predecessor, yet at the same time it deals with an emergent order of properties that cannot be reduced to those of the lower-order sciences. Comte, therefore, was consistently anti-reductionist, and opposed all knowledge that sought to reduce sociology to biology. Those who attempt to explain all sociological facts by the influence of climate or race show, he wrote, 'their ignorance of the fundamental laws of sociology, which can only be discovered by a series of direct inductions from history' (Thompson 1976: 78). Social physics or sociology, unlike the earlier natural sciences, tended to be holistic rather than atomistic, for a social fact could only be scientifically explained 'when it has been suitably connected with either the totality of the corresponding situation or the totality of the preceding situation'. Comte, therefore, initiated functionalist analysis and the image of society as an organism, which was to have a profound effect on later sociologists and anthropologists like Radcliffe-Brown. Indeed Evans-Pritchard (1981: 57) suggests that there is nothing in the latter's theoretical formulations that was not cogently and clearly enunciated by Comte a century earlier. Specific to sociology was the 'fourth method' of research – supplementing those of observation, experiment and comparison – which Comte described as the 'historical method'. This method seeks from history 'its own general direction' – the laws of social existence or 'human progression', which Comte clearly distinguished from the concrete histories of human societies. The 'law of three stages' encapsulated this universal history. Comte also made a distinction between social statics, concerned with the laws of coexistence, and social dynamics which studies the laws of succession. The latter is said to have a more philosophical character. But Comte insists that the two forms of sociology are intrinsically connected, for order without development leads to stasis, while change without order would lead to anarchy. Positive philosophy seeks to combine both, and thus to provide a scientific foundation for the 'systematic reformation of humanity' (Thompson 1976: 96).

Comte's writings provide the first classic statement of positivism, a philosophical doctrine which, as we have explored in chapter 3, was later developed by the logical positivists of the Vienna Circle. The basic premises of this current of thought can be summarised as follows.

First, it expressed a fundamental aversion to metaphysical thinking, the latter being repudiated as either sophistry or illusion. Comte argued that positivism superseded both the 'revolutionary metaphysics' of the Enlightenment philosophers and the reactionary connotations of the defenders, like Bonald, of Christianity and the feudal hierarchy.

Second, science is considered to deal with empirical facts, which are independent of the human subject, and scientific knowledge to consist of analytical-inductive generalisations based on sense impression. It was this approach that Hegel had criticised in his *Phenomenology*. There is some truth in the suggestion that Comte was the 'first behaviourist'.

Third, arising from this, positivism stresses a fundamental distinction between fact and value statements. Judgements of value or morality are held to have no empirical content of the sort that renders them accessible to tests of validity. Sociology is thus conceived as a value-free activity, and scientific knowledge is seen to have instrumental value.

–237–

Fourth, positivism suggests that the natural and social sciences have an essential unity and share a common logical and methodological foundation. The procedures of the natural sciences are therefore applicable to all spheres of life and culture, and positivism holds that science is the only true form of knowledge. Although there is a suggestion that this involves adopting a mechanistic paradigm, Comte's own theory, as we have noted, was functional and organismic, with respect to social statics. Such a positivistic approach tends to have a behaviouristic slant and to exclude meaning and human subjectivity from the analysis. (For useful accounts of positivism from which these points have been extracted, see Giddens 1974, 1979; Bleicher 1982: 37–51.)

What is of interest about Comte's account of the basic sciences is that he makes no mention at all of psychology – to the annoyance, Evans-Pritchard suggests, of Spencer and Mill. Indeed, he seems to express nothing but contempt for the idea of a science of the psyche regarding any attempt to study the human mind as a special field of inquiry as pure mythology. For Comte, therefore, there are only two basic sciences of human behaviour – physiology and biology. The reasons why Comte ignored psychology has been usually put down to his rejection of the introspective psychology of his day, and the fact that no empirical psychology had yet developed. But Evans-Pritchard argues that Comte, on logical grounds, believed that there could be no autonomous science of psychology. 'Man is born into the world an animal. His moral and intellectual functions are what are implanted on the organism by society, the products of culture. Consequently one must not define "humanity" by "man", but "man" by "humanity"' (1981: 44). Evans-Pritchard goes on to suggest that Durkheim took up the same position, finding no place for an intermediate science between the organic and the social sciences. We shall discuss this issue in the next section.

In his writings on social statics Comte clearly spelt out his ideas on the *tableau cérébral*, his theory of human nature. Comte postulated that human beings were essentially active beings, that human nature had a threefold character, consisting of sentiments (emotions), action (will) and intelligence, and that emotional impulses take primacy over the intellect. Each of these three elements of human nature he saw as having 'cerebral locations', and thus the mode of psychology that Comte followed was the then fashionable phrenology (Aron 1965/1: 91–3). Thus, as Leahey writes, Comte divided psychology in two, destroying it as a coherent field: 'The study of the individual he assigned to physiology and biology, as in phrenological psychology. The study of the human being as a social animal belonged to sociology' (1987: 145).

Moreover, as both Marcuse and Evans-Pritchard insist, the individual subject plays almost no part in Comte's sociology; the human subject is entirely absorbed by society and thus ceases to exist. The individual for Comte is an abstraction; only society, in the widest sense of humanity, has reality. Whereas for the mystic the human subject or self is an aspect of Brahman or the godhead, for Comte human individuality is lost in humanity, as the collective subject of history (Marcuse 1941: 359–60; Evans-Pritchard 1981: 59–60). In viewing humanity as a universal subject which develops through history, and in putting a focus on culture or intellectual progress, there are close affinities between Comte and both Hegel and Tylor, whatever their other differences.

Comte came to have an important influence on the orientation of the social sciences, and like Spencer, became almost a cult figure during the nineteenth century. Positivist groups and churches sprang up in several countries, almost justifying Comte's elevation of humanity into an object of religious devotion. Both J. S. Mill and Spencer derived key ideas from Comte's writings and these three scholars can rightly be regarded as the chief architects of sociology, a discipline which, in its modern form, is intrinsically connected with the name of Emile Durkheim. It is to Durkheim that we may now turn.

6.2 Durkheim – His Life and Work

Emile Durkheim (1858–1917) can truly be acclaimed, along with Weber, as one of the founders of modern sociology. Developing the ideas of Saint-Simon, Comte and Spencer, his seminal writings firmly established sociology as an academic discipline, and he ranks alongside Hegel, Marx, Freud and Nietzsche as one of the most important figures in the development of modern social theory. He has been variously interpreted. Evans-Pritchard described him as a militant atheist, and troubled by the fact that Durkheim's sociology completely undermined traditional religion, argued that Durkheim's theory of religion was a 'sociological metaphysics' and largely consisted of 'speculative nonsense'. Durkheim, he concluded, was a metaphysician not a scientist (1981: 157–68). It is rather ironic that Evans-Pritchard's own classic study *Nuer Religion* (1956) is an exemplary account of the kind of approach to religion that Durkheim himself advocated. Others have seen Durkheim as essentially the founder of an ahistoric, conservative theory of

society and as standing firmly in the tradition of the French theocratic reactionaries like Bonald. Even more commonly Durkheim
has been seen as 'the spiritual heir of Comte' (Parsons 1937: 307),
and thus as basically a positivist in his orientation. Giddens (1979:
245) indeed suggests that Durkheim's writings have been more
influential than those of any other author in the spread of 'positivistic sociology'. As Durkheim's writings and ideas have been
mediated largely through the functionalist perspectives of
Radcliffe-Brown and Talcott Parsons, this may well be the case,
but Durkheim had, as we shall see, a strong rationalist bent.
Edward Tiryakian (1979: 211) stresses that Kant's moral philosophy, rationalistic to the core, must be seen as the guiding philosophical orientation for much of Durkheim's concerns as a
sociologist and as an educator. Durkheim never described himself
as a positivist, only as a rationalist. As he wrote:

> The only designation we can accept is that of 'rationalist'. As a matter of
> fact, our principal objective is to extend scientific rationalism to human
> behaviour. It can be shown that behaviour of the past, when analysed,
> can be reduced to relationships of cause and effect. These relationships
> can then be transformed, by an equally logical operation, into rules of
> action for the future. What critics have called our 'positivism' is only one
> certain aspect of this rationalism. (1895: xxxix)

Durkheim thus distanced himself from the positivism of Comte
and Spencer.

Durkheim was born in the French-speaking town of Epinal
(Vosges), not far from Strasbourg. He was of Jewish background
and came from a long line of rabbis. It was intended that he should
become a rabbi and he studied Hebrew in his youth. But, under the
influence of a Catholic governess, he experienced a religious crisis,
and later came to abandon his Jewish faith. When he was twelve
years old the Germans occupied the town of Epinal during the
Franco-Prussian war, an event that was to have a decisive effect on
his life-work. For Durkheim came to develop a strong attachment
to French culture and society, particularly to the Third French
Republic, as it embodied the ideals of rationalism, democracy and
science. In 1879 Durkheim entered the famous Ecole Normale
Supérieure in Paris, and among his fellow students were Pierre
Janet and Henri Jourès. Jourès was to remain a life-long friend. The
combined influence of Jourès and Bergson is said to have led to
Durkheim's final break with Judaism. Durkheim's primary focus at

the Ecole was on philosophy but he became increasingly interested in political and social issues. During these formative years Durkheim was particularly influenced by the writings of Comte and Charles Renouvier (1815–1903), the neo-Kantian philosopher. The latter's stress on the autonomy of the individual, his concern for a scientific understanding of morality and his rigorous, uncompromising rationalism, were particularly important to Durkheim (Lukes 1973: 55). After graduating from the Ecole in 1882, Durkheim spent five years teaching philosophy in various lycées. In 1885 he obtained a scholarship to study in Germany. He visited Wundt at Leipzig and was greatly impressed by his experimental work in psychology. It has been suggested that Durkheim not only greatly admired Wundt, but adopted many of Wundt's sociological ideas – the principle that the mind is a process not a substance; the principle of 'creative synthesis' (the idea that new syntheses can emerge from component elements); and the notion that the social is an independent reality inexplicable in terms of individual psychology while also holding that collective phenomena do not exist outside individual minds. But there is no strong evidence that Durkheim's principal ideas came directly from Wundt (Gisbert 1959; Lukes 1973a: 90–1).

After his marriage in 1887, Durkheim obtained a post as a lecturer in education and social science at Bordeaux University, a post especially created for him. He remained at Bordeaux some fifteen productive years until 1902, when he was offered a professorship in sociology and education at the Sorbonne in Paris. This was the supreme accolade for a French academic. He thus became, as Robert Bellah (1973) suggests, a 'semi-official ideologist' of the Third French Republic. During his Bordeaux period he published three important studies: *The Division of Labour in Society* (1893), *The Rules of Sociological Method* (1895) and *Suicide: A study in sociology* (1897), as well as establishing an important journal, *L'Année sociologique* (1897). Around this journal Durkheim gathered a group of talented scholars, and collectively they made significant contributions to the sociological and anthropological literature. Among the more important of these scholars were Durkheim's nephew Marcel Mauss, François Simiand, Henri Hubert, Marcel Granet and Maurice Halbwachs. Many of these scholars were committed socialists, but Durkheim always remained aloof from politics. Throughout his life he remained a serious, somewhat austere, academic. Sincere and dedicated though he was, an 'atmosphere of gravity' seems to have surrounded Durkheim even from his school days.

During his period at the Sorbonne, Durkheim was mainly lecturing on the history and theory of education, but he also found time to write what is perhaps his *magnum opus*, his classic study *The Elementary Forms of the Religious Life*, first published in 1912. At the outbreak of the First World War Durkheim immersed himself in the war effort. But his health deteriorated and he died aged fifty-nine of a heart attack in 1917, no doubt exacerbated by the strains caused by the death of his only son André in the Serbian retreat of 1916 (Peyre 1960).

Talcott Parsons (1968) has interpreted Durkheim's social theory, and that of modern sociology more generally, as occupying a 'mediating' position between the two wings of the main European trends of thought, British empiricism and utilitarianism and German idealism. As we have discussed in the earlier chapters, British empiricists conceived of the human subject as not only having 'sensations or ideas in the epistemological sense of Locke, but also as having basic needs or drives that motivate action. In this tradition the point of reference throughout is 'the conception of an individual acting in pursuit of his own "interests"' (Parsons 1968: 313). On the other hand, German idealism, best exemplified by Hegel, tended to put a focal emphasis on spirit (*Geist*), a conception that was primarily cultural and thus transindividual. Durkheim tried to avoid these two extremes. He was critical of the classical economists whose theories seem to suggest that 'there is nothing real in society except the individual; it is from him that everything emanates and it is to him that everything returns. The individual is the sole tangible reality'. Economic laws are thus not derived from the observation of societies but rather deduced from the definition of the individual. This approach, Durkheim holds, distorts the social reality by abstracting 'from all circumstances of time, place and country in order to conceive of the abstract type of man in general; but, in that ideal type itself, they neglected all that did not relate to strictly individual life'. All that remained was 'the sad, portrait of the pure egoist'. The conception of the 'abstract man' is unacceptable to Durkheim, for the real man is 'of a time and place, he has a family, a city, a nation, a religious and a political faith' (Lukes 1973: 81).

But while Durkheim questions the *laissez-faire* view of the individual shared by the classical empiricists and political economists, he is equally unhappy with idealist conceptions of society as something beyond the purview of science. Collective social life cannot be reduced to individual psychology; neither does it have any reality separate from individual human subjects. We shall discuss

Durkheim's own views on the relationship between the individual and society later. Parsons suggests that Durkheim was influenced in this mediation by Rousseau – the primary philosopher of 'democratic individualism', whose 'general will' provided a conception of social solidarity that was neither economic in the sense of the classical economists, nor political in the sense of Hobbes or Hegel.

Like Comte, Durkheim was essentially concerned with two projects; the establishment of an empirical sociology, thus completing an endeavour initiated by Condorcet and Saint-Simon; and the formulation of a social ethic that would be appropriate to the new economic order, an ethic that would be based on the individualism and rationalism of the Enlightenment, and of Kant, not on its renunciation. Thus Durkheim always distanced himself from Comte's conception of social order, with its positive valuation of hierarchy and ideological conformity, and its negative valuation of human freedom and autonomy, as well as being critical of those like Bergson whose mysticism led to a critical devaluation of scientific rationalism (Lukes 1973: 75–7).

It is not my main purpose here to outline Durkheim's approach to sociological theory, but to conclude this section a few general remarks may be made on his sociology.

First, Durkheim had an evolutionary approach to social life, but it was expressed at a highly abstract level involving an ideal-type dichotomy between what he termed 'mechanical' and 'organic' forms of social solidarity. It was an etiolated version of Spencer's theory, profoundly non-historical, with a focus on the nature of social cohesion, although Wallwork (1984) has suggested that underlying this schema is a six-stage theory of sociocultural change. The questions he asked and discussed in his study *The Division of Labour in Society* were: 'What are the bonds which unite men with one another?', and 'What is the relationship of the individual to social solidarity' as the division of labour becomes more complex?

Durkheim suggests that in traditional societies with a low division of labour, the social structure consists of a 'system of homogeneous segments' and integration was achieved by a common value-system, the collective conscience, individuals in the society sharing identical beliefs and sentiments. In societies with a high division of labour, social groups and institutions are heterogeneous, and solidarity is the outcome not of shared beliefs but of mutual interdependence. In this situation sanctions are restitutive rather than repressive. Two points are worth making. The first is that the collective representations characteristic of mechanical solidarity are seen by Durkheim as essentially religious. As he wrote: 'Originally it [religion] pervades everything; everything social or religious; the two words are synonyms' (1893: 169). Secondly, Durkheim has been severely criticised for suggesting that societies based on mechanical solidarity have repressive sanctions, for anthropological studies of tribal communities have indicated the contrary, that the aim of their legal systems is to restore social relationships rather than to administer repressive justice. But interestingly, Durkheim's focus is not on tribal communities *per se*, but on early theocratic states – the repressive legislation expressed in the laws of Manu and other sacerdotal writings.

But the emergence of organic solidarity does not imply that the collective conscience will pass out of existence or be 'threatened with total disappearance'. Rather, with the loosening of social bonds, and with the possibility of people living a more autonomous existence, what has emerged is a 'cult of personality', which stresses individual dignity and individual autonomy. Far from being trammelled by the progress of specialisation, Durkheim writes, 'individual personality develops with the division of labour'. Earlier in the study he notes with respect to the 'progress of organic solidarity': 'As all the other beliefs and all the other practices take in a character less and less religious, the individual becomes the object of a sort of religion. We erect a cult on behalf of personal dignity, which, as every strong cult, has its superstitions' (1893: 172).

The collective conscience of modern society is, therefore, for Durkheim, a 'cult of the individual'. But this development is not of recent origin; it has a long history: 'Individualism, free thought, dates neither from our time, nor from 1789, nor from the Reformation, nor from scholasticism, nor from the decline of Graeco-Latin polytheism or oriental theocracies. It is a phenomenon which begins in no certain part, but which develops without cessation all through history' (1893: 171).

A second important aspect of Durkheim's sociology relates to his materialism. Although Durkheim puts a primary emphasis on social facts as phenomena *sui generis* and, like Weber, is hostile to crude economic determinism, his mode of analysis is essentially materialist. Josep Llobera (1981) has drawn attention to the way in which Durkheim came to deny Marxism's claim to scientificity by focusing on the vulgar interpretations of Marx by certain of his followers. Nevertheless Durkheim's own mode of analysis implies a social structuralist method that was causal and materialist as well as functional. For Durkheim, social reality consisted of several levels. In his review of Antonio Labriola's *Essays on the Materialist Conception of History* (1897), Durkheim wrote:

> We regard as fruitful this idea that social life must be explained, not by the conception of it held by those who participate in it, but by profound causes which escape consciousness; and we also think that these causes must be sought chiefly in the way in which the associated individuals are grouped. For in order that collective representations should be intelligible, they must come from something and, since they cannot form a circle closed upon itself, the source whence they derive must be found outside them. Either the conscience collective floats in the void or it is connected with the rest of the world through the intermediary of a substratum on which, in consequence, it depends. (quoted in Lukes 1973: 231)

Significantly, this substratum does not, for Durkheim, consist of productive relations, but the manner in which people are 'disposed upon the earth'. It has demographic rather than economic connotations. The 'multi-layered' model of social reality implied by Durkheim – substratum, institutions and collective representations – is discussed by Thompson (1982: 59–69). Also important in this context is the distinction Durkheim makes between collective representations that have been 'crystallised' and 'social currents' expressed by ecstatic movements (Durkheim 1895: 4).

Third, in arguing against the utilitarian and *lassez-faire* liberals who suggested a methodological individualism, and also against the conservative and idealist tradition of social philosophy, Durkheim came to suggest as a fundamental methodological postulate that one should 'consider social facts as things' (1895: 14). He advocated a scientific approach that is both empirical and comparative. *The Rules of Sociological Method*, in fact, is something of a manifesto suggesting two basic forms of explanation – causal analysis and functionalist interpretation. When the explanation of a social phenomenon, Durkheim wrote, 'is undertaken, we must seek separately the efficient cause which produces it and the function it fulfils' (1895: 95). While Hughes has stressed the 'unhistorical character' of Durkheim's thought and its positivistic tenor (which the above text implies) Thompson has suggested that Durkheim and his colleagues always set this kind of analysis in a comparative-historical framework (1982: 106–7). Moreover, it is important to stress that Durkheim was not a contemplative materialist or an empiricist, for as the quotation above suggests, he postulated the necessity of going beyond people's ideological pre-conceptions, as these were reflected in their collective representation. But above all, Durkheim argued for the necessity of engaging in empirical study: 'Social reality cannot be grasped by anyone who refuses to plunge into the detailed empirical investigation of social life' (Giddens 1978: 35). Durkheim's study *Suicide* (1897) was intended to be a demonstration of his method. Significantly, it was not published in English until 1951.

Finally, it is worth noting Durkheim's relationship to socialism. Durkheim's sociology has long been characterised as being concerned with 'order' and 'stability' and essentially conservative, a part of the 'counter-reaction' against the implications of the French Revolution. Emile Benoit-Smullyan remarked that it 'is a sociology of a static and monistic type, with no adequate explanation for social change' (1948: 224). The general tenor of his work implies such an assessment, although it is worth noting that his concept of 'anomie' has a critical aspect in implying that contemporary capitalism is, in a sense, pathological. The causes of this Durkheim put down to regimented and meaningless work, class conflict and an unregulated market economy. Even though his answer to this seems to be the state control of economy and an appeal to justice, Durkheim was by no means an apologist for capitalism. At the end of the nineteenth century, when the force of reaction were urging a return to Catholicism, royalism and traditionalism, Durkheim sided with the progressive forces in his advocacy of science, secularism and democracy. He was, as Hughes suggests, 'a true child of the Enlightenment'. But he was no Marxist socialist or believer in revolution. 'Socialism', in fact, he saw as a social movement, as a symptom of the malaise, rather than its cure. Essentially, Durkheim was a reformist liberal or guild socialist, believing in evolutionary change. He argued that a beneficent state regulating the economy on behalf of the people, and occupational corporations on the lines of the medieval guilds, would be the best safeguards of democracy and for the ideals of the French Revolution – equality, freedom, fraternity. It was the very antithesis of Spencer's advocacy of a free market economy with a minimal state. In noting the affinity of his political views with those of the British socialist R. H. Tawney, Lukes suggests that Durkheim was in 'many ways a moralistic conservative and a radical social reformer who would qualify, on most definitions, as a socialist of sorts' (1973: 546; cf. Gouldner 1973: 369–91).

6.3   The Dualism of Human Nature

We turn now to Durkheim's views on the human subject and on the relationship between the individual and society.

A crucial aspect of Durkheim's sociology is his antipathy towards all theories that attempt to explain social facts by reference to individual or psychological factors. Hence his hostility to Spencer's 'methodological individualism' – the theory that suggests that 'all social phenomena should always be understood as resulting from the decisions, actions, attitudes, etc., of human individuals', to use Karl Popper's phrase (1963: 98). This leads Durkheim to stress that social facts are external to the individual, and constraining towards him or her: 'We speak a language we did not make; we use instruments we did not invent; we invoke rights that we did not found; a treasury of knowledge is transmitted to each generation that it did not gather itself' (1915: 212).

Durkheim thus viewed the individual and society as a rigid dichotomy, and maintained that social facts could only be understood in terms of other social facts. In attempting to establish the 'autonomy of sociology' as a discipline, Durkheim, as Steven Lukes in his admirable study of Durkheim remarks, badly overstated his case, as well as virtually severing social life from its natural and economic moorings (1973: 20). This dichotomy between the individual and society is, as Lukes puts it, 'the keystone of Durkheim's entire system of thought' (1973: 22). Moreover, like social behaviourists and contemporary structural Marxists, the individual is conceptualised as an organism. Durkheim's famous definition of the nature of the human subject runs as follows: 'Man is double. There are two beings in him; an individual being which has its foundation in the organism. . . and a social being which represents the highest reality in the intellectual and moral order that we can know by observation – I mean society' (1915: 16). Like Comte, Durkheim seems to give little scope for a science of psychology.

But inspite of Evans-Pritchard's (1981: 45), suggestion that Durkheim followed Comte in finding no place for an intermediate science between the biological and the social sciences, this assessment is too sweeping. Durkheim's position is somewhat equivocal. For in a sense, a Bellah (1973: xx) remarks, Durkheim was radically psychological in that his most fundamental concepts, 'collective conscience' and 'representations', refer to mental or psychic realities.

In fact, Durkheim consistently referred to social facts as 'mental', 'moral' or 'spiritual' entities. Like Wundt, he was constantly pre-occupied with consciousness or conscience – the French word 'conscience' embracing both meanings. Moreover, this concept was not purely cognitive, but was also characterised by an affective element, referring also to feelings and sentiments (Tiryakian 1979: 218). Durkheim even went so far as to suggest that sociology is a 'collective psychology' that can be distinguished from individual psychology – a position similar to Wundt's. Nor, unlike Comte, did Durkheim express any antipathy towards psychology, and his writings indicate that he was not only familiar with the work of Wundt but also of William James and the British psychologists. From the work of Janet he adopted the notion of the unconscious, extending it to the collective psyche as well as to the individual. What Durkheim objected to was not psychology as a discipline but the attempt to explain social facts – collective representations such as law, morality and religion – in terms of individual psychology. Durkheim's 'collective representations' essentially has the same meaning as Hegel's and Dilthey's 'objective spirit'.

Durkheim's views on the relationship between individual and collective psychology (sociology) were clearly expressed in his essay on 'Individual and Collective Representations', first published in 1898. Essentially, Durkheim suggests that the relationship between sociology and psychology was analogous to that between psychology and physiology. Durkheim, as Bellah cogently explores, saw the human mind not as some ultimate ontological reality or some trans-empirical substance, but as an emergent property of biological organisms. It had an autonomous existence which could not be reduced to physiology, and so Durkheim argues against the efforts of Huxley and Maudsley to view the mind simply as a reflection of underlying cerebral processes. He was critical of their attempt to 'reduce the mind to nothing more than an epiphenomenon of physical life' (1974: 2). Like Nietzsche, he poses the question: Why, if mental processes are simply the 'echo' or 'shadow' of physical processes, do we need to be conscious at all? Why do we need the intervention of this 'phantom-like mind'? The defenders of epiphenomenalist theory, he concludes, deny the need for a real field of psychology. But because consciousness cannot be reduced to physiological processes, this did not imply that mental life, whether conscious or unconscious, had a life of its own, independent of the organic world. It was only relatively autonomous, for consciousness depended on organised matter for its substratum. As Durkheim wrote:

Certainly their autonomy can only be a relative one; there is no realm of nature that is not bound to others. Nothing could be more absurd than to elevate psychic life into a sort of absolute derived from nothing and unattached to the rest of the universe. It is obvious that the condition of the brain affects all the intellectual phenomena and is the immediate cause of some of them (pure sensation). But on the other hand . . . representational life is not inherent in the intrinsic nature of nervous matter, since in part it exists by its own force and has its own particular manner of being. (1974: 23–4)

The relationship of social facts (collective representations) to individual consciousness is similar to that between individual psychic life and the physiological substratum. Social facts are in a sense independent and exterior to the individuals, but nevertheless society has for its substratum the mass of associated individuals. Collective representations which form the network of social life arise from the 'relations between the individuals'; they are 'produced by the action and reaction between individual minds that form the society' (1974: 25). Social facts thus have a relative externality and independence in relation to individuals. Because he refused to reduce social life to the individual mind, this did not imply, Durkheim insists, that he left 'social life in the air', for it had its substratum in the minds of human subjects. Durkheim was thus trying to steer between two approaches. One was that of the reductive materialists, who reduced social and mental life to their underlying realities either to individual psychology (with respect to sociologists like Spencer) or to a psycho–physiological realm (with respect to the materialist 'psychologist'). Durkheim was opposed to such biological naturalism, but he was equally opposed to the approach that considered mental life to have a life of its own, 'that lifted the mental out of the world and above the ordinary methods of science' (1974: 33). The old introspectionists were thus content to describe mental phenomena without trying to explain them. Durkheim suggests a third approach, sociological naturalism, which would see 'in social phenomena specific facts, and which would undertake to explain them while preserving a religious respect for their specificity' (1974: 34). Thus Durkheim suggested an ontological distinction between three levels of reality: physiological, psychological and social, and conceived of the social as a distinctive realm. 'Society is not a mere sum of individuals, rather the system formed by their association represents a specific reality which has its own characteristics' (1895: 103). It was this reality that was the subject matter of sociology.

But although Durkheim insists on the need for a psychological naturalism, the pervasive dualism that runs through his work tends to undervalue the mediating role of the psyche, and to suggest that the human subject had essentially a 'dual nature', as the quotation above indicates. In another important essay (1914), he speaks of the 'dualism of human nature' and sees such dualism as 'constitutional' with respect to the human subject. He notes that the dualism of body and soul seems to have a universal significance, and must therefore be based on something substantial in human existence. It cannot be 'purely illusory' (Wolff 1960: 326). It is based, Durkheim argues, on the distinction between, on the one hand, our sensory appetites, which pertain to the individual organism and are egoistic, personal, individual, and, on the other, our conceptual thought and moral activity, which are impersonal, social, disinterested and derive from a 'plurality of man'. Thus our inner life and our consciousness have a 'double centre of gravity'; there are two aspects to our psychic life which are, he suggests, opposed and antagonistic. We have two beings in us, two antithetical faculties, which represent the personal/individual and the impersonal/social. We are *homo duplex*. This duality of our nature is just a particular instance, Durkheim wrote, of the division of things into the sacred and the profane that is the foundation of all religions. And as Durkheim showed in his classic study of religion, sacred things are simply collective ideals that have fixed themselves on material objects; and God is 'only a figurative expression of society' (1915: 226; for a full discussion of Durkheim's theory of religion, see my study 1987: 111–22). Thus Durkheim concludes that we are made up of two parts, that we have a double existence, 'the one purely individual and rooted in our organisms, the other social and nothing but an extension of society' (Wolff 1960: 337). We have an individuality and a personality, and the latter is eminently social.

In Durkheim's writings we find, therefore, a consistent homology between several important dichotomies:

Sociology	:	Psychology
Social	:	Individual
Concepts	:	Sensations
Sacred	:	Profane

But although Durkheim suggests a dualistic paradigm, it is clear that in stressing the sociality of the human subject he is attempting to overcome two dualisms, between reductive materialism and idealism, and between the individual and society. This synthetic approach is particularly evident in his writings on the sociology of knowledge and on individualism.

In the introduction to *The Elementary Forms of the Religious Life*, Durkheim discusses the origin of what Aristotle had termed the 'categories of understanding', the fundamental concepts that form the basis of all thought – the ideas of space, time, class and causality. Durkheim argues that currently there are two basic doctrines with regard to the problem of knowledge. On the one hand, there are those, like Kant, who view the categories of thought as prior to experience; they are immanent in the human mind itself and part of what it means to be human. On the other hand, there are those like Locke who see the categories as having been derived from experience, made up of 'bits and pieces' with the individual being the 'artisan of this construction'. Durkheim is dissatisfied with both approaches. The first he considered no explanation at all, whereas the second he felt was essentially individualist and subjective with a tendency to collapse into irrationalism. His own sociological theory, he thought, united these two conceptions; it was a form of rationalism that was midway between classical empiricism and apriorism. And with respect to the categories of understanding, it suggested that they were neither innate nor derived from individual experiences, but were socially derived, the product of human social activity, and the intellectual capital accumulated through the centuries. With Mauss he published a seminal essay on 'Primitive Classification' (1903), which exemplified this approach, suggesting that the cognitive mapping of the world is not a function of the human mind, but is essentially a product of social factors. His interpretations of religion and morality follow the same strategy, seeing them as rooted in a social substratum, and the product of social life. Edward Tiryakian argues that Durkheim's sociological approach was a major theoretical innovation, anticipating later phenomenological sociology:

> Durkheim's 'sociologism'. . . amounts to no less than an epistemological revolution from the traditional philosophical perspective that knowledge is a function of the individual knower, since Durkheim posits that knowledge is a function of aprior structures which are societal in origin. (1979: 212)

Durkheim thus grounds Kant's rationalism in a sociological theory of knowledge. His discussion of individualism adopts a similar approach, for Durkheim argues for the need to retain and develop the individualist tradition of the Enlightenment. There are, Durkheim suggests in an important essay on 'Individualism and the Intellectuals' (1895), two forms of individualism. The first is associated with the 'crass commercialism' which reduces society to nothing more than market exchanges and which is reflected in the utilitarian egoism of Spencer and the political economists. This kind of individualism is concerned with private interests, and the 'egoistic cult of the self'. The other kind of individualism associated with the moral philosophy of Kant and the political doctrines of Rousseau became embodied in the Declaration of the Rights of Man. The ethic of this individualism disregards our empirical individuality 'in order to seek out only that which our humanity requires and which we share with all our fellowmen' (Bellah 1973: 45). This ethic considers the human person almost an object of religious veneration. It has become a cult. This kind of individualism springs not from egoism but from its opposite, from a sympathy for all that is human. 'This cult of man has as its primary dogma the autonomy of reason and as its primary rite the doctrine of free inquiry' (1973: 49).

Durkheim argues that this 'religion of humanity', of which the individualistic ethic is the rational expression, is the only one possible for the modern world. This religion, like all religions, is 'socially instituted', but such individualism, articulated fully by the eighteenth-century rationalists, needs to be enlarged and made complete. Sociology is important in this task, for it emphasises what is crucial about the human subject, namely its inherently social nature. Our society Durkheim wrote, 'must regain the consciousness of its organic unity; the individual must feel the presence and influence of that social mass which envelops and penetrates him, and this feeling must continually govern his behaviour' (Lukes 1973: 102). The truth of the human subject is therefore less a point of departure than a point of arrival. We should not begin with a certain conception of human nature so as to deduce from it a sociology, he wrote, 'it is rather from sociology that we seek an increasing understanding of humanity' (Lukes 1973: 499).

Two final points need to be made. The first relates to the suggestion that Durkheim presents an 'over-socialised' conception of the human subject (cf. Wrong 1961), and that he presents the 'social' in terms of some metaphysical 'group mind', which transcends human subjectivity. Malinowski compared Durkheim with Hegel, noting that the idea that society is the origin of the divine 'reminds one somewhat of Hegel's absolute "thinking itself"'

(1963: 287). Durkheim repeatedly denied reifying or hypostasising society, noting that society has nothing metaphysical to it; it is not a substance more or less transcendent: 'There is nothing in social life that is not in individual consciences' (Lukes 1973: 11; Bellah 1973: xx). Moreover, Durkheim did not see the human subject simply as a passive being. He wrote, in one of his earlier review articles (1885):

> Since there are in society only individuals, it is they and they alone that are the factors of social life. But, it is said, the individual is an effect not a cause; he is a drop in the ocean, he does not act but is acted upon, and it is the social environment which controls him. But of what is this environment composed if not individuals? Thus we are at once active and passive, and each of us contributes in the formation of this irresistable current on which he is borne. (Lukes 1973: 93)

The second point is that Durkheim continually criticised the notion of 'man in general', the idea of an abstract individual or subject divorced from any specific social context. He criticised both Comte and the political economists on this account. Comte's sociology equated society with abstract humanity, and thus was more a philosophical meditation on human sociability in general than a study of humans as social beings. Human beings could only be understood if situated in specific social contexts (Tiryakian 1962: 22–4; Lukes 1973: 80–3). There are thus close affinities between the theories of Marx and Durkheim on the human subject, although, unlike Marx, the latter writer tends to see social relationships as divorced from the natural world, and to view specific societies as essentially homogeneous entities. Like Marx, he was trying to steer a course between idealism and reductive empiricism, and thought that in sociology he had found a way. Earlier thinkers, he suggested, faced a double alternative; either explaining human faculties and sociality by connecting them to 'inferior forms of being' – mind to matter, reason to the senses – which is equivalent to denying their uniqueness; or else attaching them to some supernatural reality, making them untenable in terms of science. Thus it is not surprising that Evans-Pritchard in his critique of Durkheim's theory of religion should accuse Durkheim of being an empiricist of the worst kind, a biological reductionist, as well as being an idealist. Perhaps in *The Elementary Forms of the Religious Life* Durkheim was trying to be what he always said he was – a scientific rationalist. (For other useful discussions of Durkheim's sociology, besides Lukes; see La Capra 1972; Nisbet 1974; Hirst 1975; and Thompson 1982.)

6.4 Durkheimian Perspectives

In earlier chapters I have discussed the contrasting rationalist and empiricist (positivist) tendencies to be found in both academic psychology and in Marxism. Similar contrasting tendencies are to be discerned in both sociology and anthropology. Both P. Cohen (1968) and Dawe (1979) have discussed sociological theories in terms of two contrasting approaches. The first is a holistic or social systems approach, the second an atomistic or social action one. Dawe, in fact, sees contemporary sociology in Durkheim fashion as being perennially concerned with the relationship between the individual and society, and as being obsessionally engaged with the 'leitmotif of reconciliation'. The 'persistent tension' between the individual and society and between the two contrasting approaches to sociology Dawe sees as an immediate expression of the 'dualism of social experience' that is central to our very existence in the modern world. On the one hand, there is the dehumanising experience under industrial capitalist production and the effects of bureaucracy and a centralised political system; on the other, there is increasing concern for personal identity, for human agency and for control over our own lives. He sums it up with the phrase: 'The machine, the bureaucracy, the system versus human agency, human creativity, human control; this is the contradictory human experience running through all our lives' (1979: 365). Thus we have two kinds of sociology. The sociology of social system sees the human subject as essentially a *tabula rasa* upon which are imprinted the values and behavioural patterns necessary for the fulfilment of social functions. Social action is a derivative of the social system. In opposition to this approach, he suggests, is the sociology of social action. This approach conceptualises the social system as the derivative of social interaction, 'a social world produced by its members who are thus pictured as active, purposeful, self- and socially-creative beings. The language of social action is thus the language of subjective meaning' (1979: 367). The tension between the two kinds of sociology, one using a natural-scientific model, the other an interpretative approach, parallels the opposition and tension between the two kinds of experience. Durkheim, Dawe suggests, expressed in his writings this dualism; a reification of society and a manifest concern with the creation of a truly moral individualism, but never, he felt, resolved the opposition (1979: 391). Robert Murphy goes so far as to suggest that there are two Emile Durkheims. The positivist sociologist from whom we have derived so much of our social scientific heritage, and a dialectical theorist who, like Marx, attempted to chart the relationship between the collectivity and the individual. The second Durkheim was more controversial and much more important (1972: 170). Dawe also notes that the sociology of both Max Weber and Talcott Parsons essentially articulated a dualistic conception of the human subject. Although the Herculean labours of Parsons were specifically motivated by a desire to overcome 'the positivistic-idealistic dualism of modern social thought' (1937: 719), and he described his own sociology as a 'voluntaristic theory of action', his normative theory remained entrenched in the social system approach, He recognised three analytical domains – the cultural, social and personality systems – but given his functionalist postulates and the 'strains to consistency' inherent in the integration of the total action system, he tends to see a homology between cultural norms and human action. Adopting the utilitarian concept of the egoistic individual, Parsons essentially argues that through the process of introjection, the common value-system becomes constitutive rather than merely regulative of the human personality. As with the culture and personality theorists, the human personality is seen as a 'mere reflex' of the cultural system. Both Murphy and Dawe have suggested that the Parsonian view allows very little scope for the concept of social action and that the personality system has as little autonomy as the social. Human agency and the subjective dimension of social life has simply disappeared in Parson's theory of action (Murphy 1972: 53–7; Dawes 1979: 400–5, see also Menzies 1977).

To turn now to the anthropological tradition. It has often been said that Durkheim's sociological legacy was handed down to later anthropologists through two divergent tendencies. On the one hand, there was the empiricist tradition of Radcliffe-Brown, which emphasised the concept of social structure, seen as a system of social relationships (see Lévi-Strauss 1963: 302–4). Influenced by Spencer's sociology and Malinowski's pragmatism, this tradition had a decidedly functionalist and symbolist bias. The writings of Talcott Parsons (1937, 1951) represent an important development of this functionalist tendency. On the other hand, there was the tradition associated with Marcel Mauss, who had co-authored with Durkheim the classic essay on symbolic classifications. This tradition focused on cosmological ideas, on the totality of 'collective representation' and it had a rationalist and structuralist bias. It is best exemplified by the writings of Lévi-Strauss. We can explore these two contrasting tendencies by discussing the writings of the two key figures Radcliffe-Brown and Mauss, particularly as these relate to the human subject. However, in this section I shall discuss the work of Radcliffe-Brown, together with that of Leslie White, who expressed even more stridently than either Durkheim or Radcliffe-Brown a dualistic conception of the human subject.

Durkheim had an immense influence on the orientation of academic sociology and British anthropology, which, in the decades following the Second World War, shared a similar structural-functionalist perspective. That Durkheimian sociology became a dominant intellectual trend can, I think, largely be attributed to the influential writings of Radcliffe-Brown, who, with Malinowski, is considered one of the founding fathers of British anthropology (Kuper 1973: 51–88).

A. R. Radcliffe-Brown (1881–1955) was born in Birmingham, of modest circumstances, his father having died when he was five, leaving his mother penniless. Supported by his brother, he won a scholarship to Cambridge University, where he read the moral sciences tripos. His tutors included Myers, Rivers and Haddon, who encouraged his interest in anthropology, and he also attended the philosophy lectures of A. N. Whitehead. These lectures were important for they gave Radcliffe-Brown's style of anthropology a decidedly organismic rather than a mechanistic quality. He always viewed social life as a process, and in functional terms. Influenced by his tutors, Radcliffe-Brown undertook ethnographic research among the Andaman Islanders (1906–8), but although he was one of the first academics to undertake fieldwork, his ethnographic studies lack the vividness and originality of those of Boas and Malinowski, and even his Andamanese text (1922) is largely an analysis of the Islanders' religious beliefs and ceremonies. Apart from this study, Radcliffe-Brown published few substantive studies and was not an original thinker; but he was a brilliant teacher and produced a number of lectures and articles, some of the more important of which were published (Radcliffe-Brown 1952; Kuper 1977). Primarily a theoretician, he wrote with great clarity – writings which Kuper suggests have a 'glacial' quality (1973: 56). But his influence is due mainly to his personal contacts and his power of inspiring enthusiasm among his students. He travelled widely, and during his academic career held chairs at Cape Town, Sydney, Chicago, Oxford, São Paolo, Yengching and Alexandria. He thus spread his teaching very wide (Evans-Pritchard 1981: 200).

Although influenced by Spencer, Radcliffe-Brown took his

main theoretical bearings from Durkheim in advocating a 'natural science of society', even though his own outlook was a good deal more empiricist. The focus of his interest, too, was more restrictive in that he took as his key concept the notion of 'social structure', viewed as a network of social relationships: 'I conceive of social anthropology as the theoretical natural science of human society, that is, the investigation of social science by methods essentially similar to those used in the physical and biological sciences' (1952: 189).

Social phenomena he felt constitute a distinct class of natural phenomena as real as living organisms, and natural science he defined as the systematic investigation of the structure of the universe as it is revealed to us through the senses. By postulating hypotheses and by the comparative method – comparing social systems of different kinds – we could establish, Radcliffe-Brown argued, the existence of 'natural laws'. Following Heraclitus's and Whitehead's contention that reality consists solely of events and relations between events, such laws were seen not as descriptive generalisations, as with empiricists such as Mach, but as being 'immanent' in the universe (1948: 13–14). Making a distinction between culture and society, Radcliffe-Brown stressed that as social structure consists of the social behaviour of actual individual human beings, it is essentially 'a priori to the existence of culture' (1952: 108). Radcliffe-Brown made two other important distinctions.

The first is that, like Comte, he made a distinction between two kinds of processes; the functional equilibrium of a specific social structure, and social evolution, the high-level processes of structural change.

Secondly, he made a clear distinction between anthropology – defined as comparative sociology – and history, suggesting that the former is a nomothetic or theoretical study, while history (like biography) is an idiographic science, concerned with the particular and the unique. Ethnograpy is also a mode of idiographic enquiry, although Radcliffe-Brown accepts that some historical studies incorporate theoretical interpretations and thus constitute a kind of historical sociology. It is important to note that Radcliffe-Brown deliberately eschews causal analysis as a scientific mode of explanation (he sees this as a limited conception applicable only to applied science and practical life), and that he is highly critical of the reification of culture. There is no 'science of culture', he argued, and the idea that culture produces effects upon people he felt to be extremely misleading. No one talks of language determining how we speak, so why treat culture as something separate from social life (1948: 96–7)? If we treat the social, he wrote, as being 'not an entity, but a process, then culture and cultural transition are names for certain recognisable aspects of that process' (1952: 5). Equally, Radcliffe-Brown denied that there could be a separate science of economics, for all economic relations are social relations.

It is therefore somewhat misleading to view Radcliffe-Brown as being anti-history and as reifying society, for as Stanner has suggested, his Heraclitean view of social life as a process is of a fundamentally historical character (Stanner 1968: 287; Ingold 1986: 153). In this there are undoubtedly similarities between the perspectives of Radcliffe-Brown and Durkheim. But Radcliffe-Brown also had affinities with Durkheim in his dualistic conception of the human personality. This is clearly expressed in his distinction between individuality and personality. In words reminiscent of Durkheim, Radcliffe-Brown wrote:

Every human being living in society is two things; he is an individual and also a person. As an individual he is a biological organism. Human beings as individuals are objects of study for physiologists and psychologists. The human being as a person is a complex of social relationships. An a person, the human being is the object of study for the social anthropologist. We cannot study persons except in terms of social structure, nor can we study social structure except in terms of the persons who are the units of which it is composed. (1952: 193–4)

As Radcliffe-Brown defines social structure as an arrangement of persons in an institutionally defined relationship, there is a certain homology between person and social structure. There are thus close affinities between Radcliffe-Brown's perspective and that of the culture and personality school. Tim Ingold has drawn attention to the similarity between Radcliffe-Brown's definition of the person and Marx's *6th Thesis on Feuerbach*, where the human essence is defined as an 'ensemble of social relations'. But given their radically different perspectives on history and social life, their conceptions of human subjectivity are quite different. The human subject in Radcliffe-Brown's sociology, like that of Parsons, is essentially a social role specified by the social structure, whereas for Marx the human subject is an agent, a practical being, enmeshed in a fabric of intersubjective relations. Ingold noted the similarity of Radcliffe-Brown's conception of the subject with that of Althusser (1986: 114–15).

Although Radcliffe-Brown's primary interest, as reflected in his later essays, is on social organisation – totemism, joking relationships, kinship – it is important to note that his first book, *The Andaman Islanders* (1922), had a significant psychological focus. For in his interpretation of Andamanese ceremonial custom, he suggests five working hypotheses, which all focus on the concept of sentiments, which Radcliffe-Brown derived from the writings of A. F. Shand (1914). These are:

1. A society depends for its existence on the presence in the minds of its members of a certain system of sentiments by which the conduct of the individual is regulated in conformity with the needs of society.
2. Any object or event that affects the well-being or cohesion of society becomes an object of this system of sentiments.
3. Such sentiments are not innate, but are developed in the individual by the action of the society upon him or her.
4. Ritual ceremonials are the means by which such sentiments are given collective expression.
5. Such rituals therefore serve to maintain and transmit the sentiments from one generation to another.

The system of sentiments will clearly be different in different societies (Radcliffe-Brown 1922: 233–4; 1952: 157).

Irving Hallowell (1976) has stressed that the broad assumptions implied in Radcliffe-Brown's hypotheses are essentially the same as those that have appeared in personality and culture studies. The difference is that Radcliffe-Brown was specifically interested in the social function of rituals, while the culture and personality theorists were concerned with delineating the actual psychological organisation and dynamics of the human personality as it functions in specific social contexts (1976: 183–4).

Although Ingold stresses Radcliffe-Brown's dualism, and his tendency to see social structure as something *sui generis*, regulative rather than interactional, nevertheless Radcliffe-Brown, like Durkheim, tended to be ambivalent about psychology. Social facts could not be explained in terms of individual psychology, but some scope for psychology as the study of the individual as a 'psycho-physical' entity was nevertheless envisaged. This could hardly be said of Leslie White, who strongly and consistently advocated a dualistic conception of the human subject and thus, like Comte, allowed little room for a science of the psyche.

Leslie White (1900–75) was born in Colorado, and studied at Louisiana State University and Columbia College, his first degree being in psychology. J. B. Watson was one of his tutors. After fieldwork studies among the Pueblo Indians in the American south-west (1926–7) he began teaching at the University of Michigan in 1930. There he taught for some forty years, although because of his atheism and radical views his promotion to full professorship was long delayed. He was a man of deep personal and professional integrity and was an important figure in contemporary anthropology, for it was largely through his writings that materialist explanations and the theory of cultural evolution were reintroduced into anthropology. Although early in his career he followed the Boasian tradition, having been a student of Goldenweiser and Sapir, he became increasingly critical of historical particularism and the anti-evolutionary stance of the Boasians. As Julian Steward wrote: 'For many years Leslie White stood virtually alone in his uncompromising support of the 19th century cultural evolutionists and in opposition to the followers of Franz Boas' (1960: 144). White had an important influence on such scholars as Sahlins, Carneiro and Service, and the three leitmotifs of Marvin Harris's *The Rise of Anthropological Theory* (1969) – evolutionism, cultural materialism and the importance of energy – were all essentially derived from White's writings, though not fully acknowledged by Harris himself (Carneiro 1981: 246).

All the basic postulates of White's anthropology – the idea of a science of culture, cultural determinism and the functional approach in general – are derived from the writings of nineteenth-century scholars, as White readily accepted. He explicitly saw himself as following in the path of Comte, Morgan, Tylor, Gumplowicz, Spencer, Durkheim and Kroeber, and argued that anthropology had actually regressed in recent years from the levels attained by Tylor and Durkheim in the nineteenth century (1949: 103). Evans-Pritchard has suggested that, apart from terminology, White accepts a rather rigid and positivistic interpretation of Durkheim, White's conception of culture being almost identical to Durkheim's concept of the social. He was always critical of the psychological tendencies evident in the writings of Rivers, Sapir and Goldenweiser. From Tylor, White derived the concept of culture and the idea of a science of culture; from Comte, he largely took his ideas on the classification of the sciences (and Comte's law of three stages permeates his work), and from Morgan's evolutionism, White absorbed a materialist outlook. White has often been described as a Marxist or an historical materialist, but he rarely mentions Marx in his writings and, as Stanley Diamond has remarked (1974: 337–41), his materialism is mechanical rather than dialectical, and more reminiscent of the eighteenth-century materialists. Ingold (1986: 82) describes his evolutionism as essentially pre-Darwinian like that of Tylor's.

Culture, L. A. White wrote, 'may be regarded as a thing *sui generis*, with a life of its own and its own laws' (1949: 123). It was a symbolic, continuous, cumulative, and progressive process that was inexplicable in terms of human psychology or human nature. It was a thermodynamic system in a mechanical sense, an elaborate mechanism whose function it is to make life secure and continuous for groups of human beings. Culture was a process of dynamic growth, dependent on the amount of energy harnessed per capita (1949: 166). Culture provides the person with the form and content of his or her behaviour as a human being, but was not explicable either biologically or psychologically. Culture, and social phenomena generally, can be explained only in terms of culture. The culture of any people, he wrote, 'at any given time is the product of antecedent cultural forces, and consequently is to be explained only in cultural terms' (1949: 79). As with Durkheim, this leads White to stress an extreme cultural determinism and a dualistic conception of the human subject. A few relevant extracts will cogently express White's position, as he writes in a vivid and forceful style.

> Human behaviour is . . . a compound of two separate and distinct kinds of elements; psychosomatic and cultural. On the one hand, we have a certain type of primate organism, man; on the other, a traditional organization of tools, ideas, beliefs, customs, attitudes etc., that we call culture. The behaviour of man as a human being . . . is an expression of the interaction of the human organism and the extra-somatic cultural tradition. (1949: 146)

> The individual is merely an organization of cultural forces and elements that have impinged upon him from the outside and which find their overt expression through him. So conceived, the individual is but the expression of a supra-biological cultural tradition in somatic form. (1949: 167)

> Culture must be explained in terms of culture. Thus, paradoxical though it may seem, 'the proper study of mankind' turns out to be not man, after all, but culture. The most realistic and scientifically adequate interpretations of culture is one that proceeds as if human beings did not exist. (1949: 141)

Although White recognises that culture is made possible only by human beings, once in existence, he felt, it comes to have a life of its own, and is explicable only in its own terms. To see culture as a simple or direct expression of the 'human mind' or of biological factors, White held to be an illusion. Human behaviour is therefore largely a function of culture and on this point there is little difference between White and the culture and personality theorists like Benedict. White recognised that it is the individual subject who acts and thinks and feels, but 'what he thinks and feels is determined not by himself but by the sociocultural system into which the accident of birth has placed him' (1949: 183). Human consciousness, therefore, is merely the individual biological aspect of a sociocultural process and both the form and content of the mind is determined by culture. As to the relationship between body and mind, this, White argues, is a 'non-problem', for had we used the word 'mind' as a verb instead of a noun, then we would have realised that mind is a function of the body. He cites an old Chinese philosopher who suggested that the spirit is to the body as sharpness is to the knife. But White is hostile also to explaining cultural phenomena in terms of human social interaction, for the latter is itself culturally determined (1949: 80). He thus maintains a rigid dichotomy between culture as an autonomous realm and the human organism, and the human subject is merely seen as a passive vehicle for culture. Diamond, quoting from Marx, criticises White's cultural determinism, stressing the importance of human agency: 'History does nothing, it possesses no colossal riches. It fights no fight. It is rather man – real, living man, who acts, possesses and fights in everything. History is nothing but the activity of man's pursuit of his ends' (1974: 339). White's 'culturology' expresses a more culturally deterministic approach than does Durkheim's, and appears to see only an interaction between culture and the human organism, a viewpoint similar to that of the sociobiologist E. O. Wilson. There is little room for a psychology of the human subject, and human social activity is largely ignored or marginalised.

6.5 Holism and Individualism

Louis Dumont explicitly situates himself in the sociological tradition of Durkheim and Mauss. Describing the teaching of Mauss as the source of his own efforts in social anthropology, he follows Mauss's theoretical style, combining philosophy with a concern for the concrete, as well as adapting his legacy – 'one of widened reason and deepened optimism' (Dumont 1986: 201). Dumont's work, extending over three decades – and still in progress (his latest work he describes as simply a 'half way report') – has been concerned essentially with two issues – an understanding of the Indian caste system and an analysis of modern ideology. With regard to the first issue he has published a seminal study *Homo Hierarchicus* (1970), as well as several important ethnographic monographs and papers on South Indian culture, his writings on kinship and marriage patterns being particularly noteworthy. His studies of modern ideology have focused on three of its aspects; the genesis of economic thought from the seventeenth century through the physiocrats to Adam Smith and Marx (1977); the comparative study of the national cultures in Europe, particularly as this throws light on the emergence of totalitarian politics (1986: 113–78); and the rise of the modern conception of the individual. The latter study is directly inspired by Mauss's classic essay, and it is with this aspect of Dumont's thought that I shall be especially concerned with here.

Although Dumont is fundamentally concerned to overcome the dualistic thought of the Enlightenment, which he sees as permeating modern ideology, he essentially expresses his own thought in terms of very general dichotomies. There are, he argues, two kinds of sociology and two kinds of society, and with respect to the latter there are concomitantly two conceptions of the human subject. Dumont suggests, in his Introduction to *Homo Hierarchicus*, that a study of the caste system has something to teach us about ourselves, and that anthropological understanding of this system has been severely hampered by our own ideological concepts. This is because sociology has been unable fully to free itself from an individualistic way of thinking, and because we are unable to conceive of hierarchy except in terms of inequalities of power. Thus there are two kinds of sociology. One is derived directly from modern ideology, the tradition of the Enlightenment. It is an approach that seems to be natural for many scholars who are unable to understand that the perception of ourselves as individuals is not innate but learned. This approach begins by positing individual human beings who are then seen as living in society; sometimes attempts are made to show that society itself arises from the interaction of individuals. This approach is often described as methodological individualism. The other kind of sociology starts from the fact that humans are essentially social beings. Thus one takes society as a global fact that is irreducible to its parts, and, moreover, this 'society' is not an abstraction 'but always of a particular, concrete society with all its specific institutions and representations' (1986: 2). This approach Dumont described as 'holism'; it is the approach advocated by Durkheim and Mauss, and it is one usually adopted by an anthropologist in studying an alien culture. Dumont felt that the more positive aspects of Radcliffe-Brown's theory indicated his adherence to holism – his stress on 'relational analysis' and his downgrading of causal analysis. The problem was that Radcliffe-Brown's holism remained too narrowly functional. But although Durkheimian sociology and anthropology adopt a holistic approach, the inclination towards individualism and nominalism, which anthropologists derive from their own culture, means that the anthropologist's task is characterised by a deep-rooted tension. Dumont warns against resolving this tension, by collapsing one of the poles of the dilemma, either by romanticising the holism of pre-literate community (which shares the same values as the anthropologists), or by taking up an objectivist position towards other cultures (1986: 218).

Corresponding to the two kinds of sociology Dumont argues there are two kinds of society – modern capitalist society with its modern ideology, and pre-capitalist society, which Dumont describes as 'traditional'. Each of these two types of society is characterised by a specific conception of the human subject. Let me first describe Dumont's assessment of modern ideology, which essentially identifies the Enlightenment tradition and certain aspects of positivism to which we have earlier alluded. Besides the individualist conception of the subject, modern ideology has the following characteristics:

1. It has a mechanistic conception of the natural world and humans are separated from nature. An absolute distinction between the subject and object is therefore seen as fundamental.
2. It views facts and values as completely separated and consistently articulates rigid dichotomies that exclude any notion of hierarchy, or a higher realm of value. Dumont notes that the literature on dual symbolic classifications neglects to explore the fact that dualisms are meaningful 'only in relation to a whole' (1986: 228).
3. Paramount importance is place on scientific knowledge, but this knowledge is distributed into a number of separate components and scientific reason is interpreted in a very instrumental fashion. Dumont notes that the theory of relativity, though by no means recent, has not yet placed mechanistic philosophy in the common representations.
4. Based on an individualistic conception of the subject, liberty and

equality become primary values in modern ideology, and the nation-state is the type of global society which corresponds to the paramountcy of the individual as a value, for it is 'composed of people who think of themselves as individuals' (1986: 10).

Dumont uses the term ideology in a non-Marxist sense to mean 'a system of ideas and values current in a given social milieu', and stresses that it is not the whole of social reality. The final task of anthropological study, he notes, is that of 'placing the ideological aspects in position relative to what may be called the non-ideological aspects' (1970: 264). But like other Durkheimian sociologists, Dumont's central focus tends to be on the collective representations themselves.

The crucial distinction between modern ideology and that of other cultures – all pre-capitalist societies it would seem – Dumont suggests centres on the conception of human subjectivity, and on this issue it is worth quoting some relevant extracts from his writings. Dumont distinguishes between two conceptions of the individual:

> (1) The empirical agent, present in every society, in virtue of which he is the main raw material for any sociology.
> (2) The rational being and normative subject of institutions; this is peculiar to us as is shown by the values of equality and liberty; it is an idea that we have, the idea of an ideal. (1970: 9)

> The individual, by which I mean the human individual as a value, appears only in the ideology of modern societies. (1986: 215)

> There are two mutually opposed configurations of this kind; one is characteristic of traditional societies and the other of modern society. In the first, as in Plato's *Republic*, the stress is placed on the society as a whole, as collective Man; the ideal derives from the organization of society with respect to its ends (and not with respect to individual happiness); it is above all a matter of order, of hierarchy. . . . In modern society, on the contrary, the human being is regarded as the indivisible, 'elementary' man, both a biological being and a thinking subject. Each particular man in a sense incarnates the whole of mankind.

> As opposed to modern society, traditional societies, which know nothing of equality and liberty as values, which know nothing, in short, of the individual, have basically a collective idea of man, and our (residual) apperception of man as a social being is the sole link which

unites us to them, and is the only angle from which we can come to understand them. This apperception is therefore the starting point of any comparative sociology. (1970: 8–9)

By making this distinction Dumont suggests 'we can avoid inadvertently attributing the presence of the individual to societies in which he is not recognised' (1970: 8–9). It is important to note that Dumont's analysis refers specifically to Indian society, but that he generalises this conception of holism to all pre-capitalist communities. It is also important to note that for Dumont, hierarchy specifically refers to the opposition between a set or whole and an element of this set: 'Essentially hierarchy is the encompassing of the contrary' (1986: 227). It is thus distinct from power relations, and his whole analysis of Indian culture is based on this distinction, which means of course that he downplays the ideological function (in a Marxist sense) of the caste hierarchy. Let me consider a criticism of this approach.

It is difficult to imagine any society where the individual is merely an 'empirical agent'. So we must presume that Dumont is suggesting that in 'traditional' Indian society a norm of 'individualism' is not articulated. That is, not only is there no articulation of the 'abstract individual' (see as the specific creation of Western capitalism – Dumont's modern society), but that the individual in India is viewed primarily as a member of a caste community. Such a formulation, it seems, is completely at variance with the ethnographic descriptions of several Indian tribal communities, with my own account (1982) of the Hill Pandaram included. In fact, Gardner (1966: 409) considers the Paliyans of Tamilnadu as exemplifying a specific cultural type, embracing several other hunter-gatherer communities, which is characterised by 'very extreme individualism'. He does indeed hint that they are more 'individualistic' than contemporary Western societies.

Let me briefly spell out the salient social patterns of some of these communities. To begin with, the Paliyans. Gardner's description of this community stresses a number of features in their social life which, in summary, are: first, a normative stress on symmetric relations and egalitarianism, both between the parents and children, and between the sexes; second, a normative stress on self-sufficiency, so that the division of labour is not marked, and co-operation between the sexes is minimal. He speaks of cohabiting couples leading almost parallel lives and many people living alone for extended periods; third, a general looseness of social ties so that camps are 'shapeless, unstructured aggregations' of related kin, there being no corporate groups of any kind; and, finally, a general lack of emphasis on formalised knowledge and ritual procedures. A second example from the Indian sub-continent are the Yanadis, as described by Raghaviah (1962). His account is at times rather colourful, but the gist of his study is consonant with Gardner's ethnograpy, and with my own description of the Hill Pandaram, all three societies being south Indian forest communities. Raghaviah writes of the extreme and uncompromising individualism that is characteristic of the Yanadi culture: 'There is very little', he suggests, 'for a Yanadi which can be called social life' (1962: 211). (Rousseau, where art thou?)

Ethnographic accounts of other hunter-gatherer communities all point to a similar cultural perspective – an explicit emphasis in these societies on the individual as an autonomous, self-sufficient being. The sex roles are important and ritualised, but an 'extreme individualism' is an underlying feature of the cultural patterns of these tribal peoples. Appellations such as 'individualistic', 'egalitarian' and 'atomistic' are frequently mentioned – terms that Dumont sees as characterising modern societies in opposition to those of the traditional type. Perhaps Lévi-Strauss has best described, in overstatement though, the situation found among some marginal communities when he wrote that the society of the Nambicuara 'had been reduced to a point at which I found nothing but human beings' (1961: 310; cf. Honigmann 1949; Henry 1964; Holmberg 1969; Ridington 1988).

But the crucial point is that these human beings are normative subjects, social individuals, not merely empirical agents. Hunter-gatherers do not wander around in a state of anomie, even though they may have little social structure. Dumont would probably agree with this. So what is he trying to convey when he suggests that so-called 'traditional' societies have a collective idea of man, and know nothing of the individual other than as an empirical agent? Have hunter-gatherers this collective idea of man? Do they conceive of themselves as merely a part of the 'social whole', when by all accounts they have so little social structure let alone hierarchy?

Even granting that they have a conception of the individual as essentially a social being, does this necessarily imply a dharma-like order? As I have attempted to answer these questions elsewhere, particularly in relation to the Indian context, little needs to be added here (Morris 1978).

We can turn now to Dumont's perceptive study of the genesis of the modern conception of the individual (1986: 23–103). This is a well-trodden trail, but Dumont's analysis is succinct and of interest, particularly as he rightly sees a marked similarity between the caste system and European society during that historical period described as the middle ages.

The prevailing ideology of this period is said to be embodied in the medieval concept of *Universitas*. This is the notion of the social body as a whole, of which living people are merely parts. Ultimate values are linked to a universal hierarchical order of several statuses – an order that is 'divinely' ordained. Dumont argues that this doctrine was the dominant ideology of the early medieval period. Several features of this ideology, not fully explored by Dumont, are worth noting.

There is an important distinction to be made between *Humanitas*, a person's natural status which is associated with flesh and carnality, and the status bestowed by the sacramental act of baptism. This rebirth made the individual a member of the Church corporation. Next, this incorporation implied that the person had become a subject of the Church, which was always defined as *Universitas Fidelium*, with the emphasis on the *fidelis* (on faith and subjection). This meant, as Ullman (1967) has cogently described, that in this ideology the individual had no autonomy. He or she was merely a part of a hierarchical ordering, divinely instituted and was expected to obey his or her superiors. To disobey was to act contrary to the divine ordering. As one fifth-century theologian put it: 'It is divine wisdom . . . that some should order and others should obey' (Ullman 1967: 11). For the medieval church took the notion of hierarchy (a concept first used in the fifth century) from a reading of Pauline tracts, significantly ignoring the egalitarian emphasis of the Gospels. This viewpoint stressed that each individual had a specific function which he should pursue for the common good, that each estate had differential rights in law, and that the authority of the king was also divinely bestowed through anointment. He was God's vicar. This gave him dominion over his subjects and thus the right to dispose of the individual's property. Such a conception was also associated with extremely repressive sanctions, because the heretic or political rebel was seen as undermining a universal moral order. Such repression evidently was not seen as violating his dignity as a Christian; by attacking the established faith (the hierarchy) he had forfeited his rights as a Christian. He was now to be treated merely as a human being. The term human still carries a certain pejorative meaning, suggesting weakness and inadequacy. Finally it is worth noting that the notion of *Universitas* or corporate unity was partly shaped by concepts derived from Roman law, but what was fundamental to the medieval notion of corporation was that it was essentially a religious conception. It was a theocratic system.

In the present context what is significant about the medieval concept of *Universitas* is that the individual did not exist for his own sake; he was, as Ullman puts it, 'submerged in society'. Individuality was absent, at least in ideology. Everything moved according to a divine plan.

Although he does not elaborate upon the above features of early medieval society, Dumont does assume that *Universitas* reflects the underlying reality of that period. In his discussion of the emergence of the abstract individual, this ideological framework is thus taken as his starting point. In doing so, Dumont takes up what, to me, are three fundamentally misleading perspectives.

First, although aware of the ideological and religious nature of this concept (*Universitas*), he does not explore or even hint that there may be other (equally social) ideas about the individual. This does not necessarily imply any notion of the abstract individual, which is a late conception in human history, but it is to suggest that human relationships are complex and are not entirely encompassed by theocratic doctrines. What comes out of Ullman's discussion is precisely this – that the Christian theocratic doctrine was largely confined to the thin upper crust of medieval society. Ullman stresses, in fact, how dangerous it is to conclude that what is official religious doctrine necessarily corresponds to the assumptions of all sections of the society. In particular he discusses four aspects of medieval society, which did not fit easily into the *Universitas* paradigm. These are, respectively, the guilds and unions which provided security for the villagers; the system of customary law which regulated to a great extent the husbandry of the village community; the concepts of *humanitas* and *civitas* which, derived from classical tradition, ran counter to the idea of the individual as merely a part of a divine order; and finally the feudal ties themselves which, though essentially unequal, are seen as involving earthly contractual relationships. Ullman indeed argues that feudal ties were an important element in the changing conception of the individual. He also stresses a theme that is prominent in Dumont's writings, namely that the king was an 'amphibious creature' having both theocratic and feudal functions.

A second misleading emphasis of Dumont is that he saw feudal society, with its emphasis on the 'social whole', or *Universitas*, as implying a notion of the individual as a 'socially-determined' person. Tribal religion, caste ideology and Durkheimian sociology are thus equated, each having the apperception of man as a social being. Now the only thing these three systems of thought have in common, it appears to me, is that they lack a conception of the abstract individual. But it is quite misleading to conclude from this that the medieval conception saw society and the individual as 'socially-determined'. This idea can only emerge when society (or the state) is itself abstracted from the *Universitas* conception. Ideologically, the medieval person was not socially determined but divinely created. As with Hegel's system, which Marx criticised precisely for its disguised theocracy, it is God or spirit which is primary and the natural world and society, as well as the individual, are derivatives. When Dumont discusses the aftermath of the French Revolution as '*Universitas* reborn', he ignores the crucial fact that although the sociality of man was reaffirmed by such writers as Marx and Durkheim, the world had by then been despiritualised by the bourgeoisie. The individual and society were now to be linked sociologically and not in terms of a spiritual entity, or a dharma-like order that was eternal and embraced the whole universe. Dumont senses this, for he saw the Christian commonwealth 'atomised' at two levels, namely into states and into abstract individuals. The two conceptions are interrelated: society for the early social theorists was equally abstract or, to put it in a more meaningful way, ahistorical. It is difficult to conceive of abstract individuals without also delineating structures equally abstract to put them in.

A final misleading perspective already broached is that Dumont suggests that all societies that do not have the Western conception of the non-social individual have instead a 'conception of the social whole'. The implication is that this implies an acceptance of hierarchical principles, or at least of an all-embracing and unifying cosmological system. I have elsewhere thrown doubt on a widespread assumption among Durkheimian sociologists, Lévi-Strauss included, that all pre-capitalist societies are characterised by symbolic classificatory systems, suggesting instead that such complex symbolism finds it apotheosis in theocratic states.

Let me now briefly discuss the factors that Dumont sees as relevant in understanding the emergence of the abstract individual, and by implication, to an understanding of the caste system itself.

Like many historians, two medieval scholars are seen by Dumont as key figures in the genesis of man as an individual. The first is the nominalist William of Ockham, who is seen as the virtual founding father of positivism. The second is Thomas Aquinas who, by combining Christian revelation with Aristotelian concepts, restructured the *Universitas* doctrine. Two things emerged. One was the notion of a 'double ordering' of reality, allowing the possibility of naturalistic interpretations. This implied a conceptual division between spiritual and temporal powers. The second point was that Aquinas stressed that each person was a private individual in relation to God, and need not obey the order of a superior if his conscience forbade it. Thus two cracks appeared in the *Universitas* ideology. The rest of Dumont's analysis follows the development and expansion of these two important themes.

On the one hand, Christian religion, with the alternative doctrine that men were equal in the sight of God, is seen as a crucial factor in the rise of individualism. Luther is the key figure here. Dumont thus suggests that modern individualism has 'religious roots'. On the other hand, the division between Church and state into independent powers gave rise to political theory, and to the eventual emergence of social contact theories. Hobbes, Locke and Rousseau are the key figures in this respect. Society, or the state, was conceived of as an association of individuals based on contract and according to the dictates of natural law.

This analysis is valid; it is what it fails to take into account that is of interest. First, Dumont completely ignores the fact that the rise of abstract individualism may have been the consequence of socio-economic changes. His analysis moves only in the realms of thought. Second, he completely conflates three quite distinct conceptions, namely: concrete socialities or groups; the idea of a sacred cosmos or norm, an all-embracing cosmology that unites into a totality all aspects of the universe (in such a conception society as well as the individual (and even spiritual beings) are but part of a total scheme); and finally, the idea of society abstractly conceived – an association of abstract individuals.

Of course, Dumont's essential thesis is that the second conception (*Universitas*) has given rise during the course of European history to the third conception (*Societas*) with its notion of the abstract individual, and that to have a true understanding of the second type of society (of which caste is a more contemporary example) we need to be aware of this fact. Our own individualism, he suggests, is a hindrance to us in this respect. He is absolutely right. But it is precisely because Dumont fails to go beyond this individualism that certain problems are created and left unresolved. He fails, for example, to emphasise that in caste ideology the individual is not a part of society in a sociological sense, but of a cosmic order that extends beyond the world we experience. As in the medieval *Universitas*, to be a member of a specific caste is to be a member of a universal order. It is precisely this point that is stressed by Khare (1975); for he rightly accuses Dumont of ignoring the implications of certain key religious concepts that imply a spiritual totality.

Third, Dumont suggests that to be an individual in India is to be a world-renouncer. Individual identity is achieved by repudiating all ties which bind a person to the caste system, and the world. According to Dumont paradoxically a person only realises his individuality by renouncing it. The only way to be an individual in such a theocratic system is, so to speak, to jump off the cosmic merry-go-round altogether – to achieve *moksha*, or liberation. It is difficult to square up these conceptions. On the one hand, he is suggesting that the individual is merely a part of social hierarchy – a member of a specific caste – and has no sense of individuality. The underlying assumption here is that only in societies like our own is there any conception of the individual. The latter term is thus equated with the notion of the abstract individual, beloved by economists and social theorists alike. On the other hand, individuality is religiously conceived as union with the universal spirit, or as a release or deliverance from the law of samsara. Thus in Dumont's terms there are three basic conceptions of the individual: the abstract individual, the 'incarnation of abstract humanity' found only in capitalist societies; the religious individual – here the person is an individual only in relation to God, or to some mystical idea of salvation; and the individual of traditional societies. This last conception, as I have said, implies a 'collective ideal' on the part of the concrete individual, an acceptance of a religious hierarchy, there thus being no conception of the person independent of the roles or structural positions he assumes.

It is beyond the scope of this study to explore the relation of the individual to social structure in tribal cosmologies, but clearly in pre-class societies the relation of the individual to the social context is variable. Variable too is the degree to which cosmological systems are a structured totality. Some, like the Dogon and Navaho, have highly structured symbolic systems; others, like the Paliyans, have hardly any, but even when present such symbolism is neither necessarily hierarchical nor does it imply (outside the ritual context) that the individual or self is 'undifferentiated' from the social. But tribal cultures, like theocratic states, invariably have a sacramental view of the world. However, one must never lose sight of the fact that life is always lived by real individuals in a real world!

It is because Dumont is unwilling to differentiate clearly between theocracy (whether tribal or hierarchical) and sociology that the problems I have tried to unravel here arise. His use of the term holism indicates this only too explicitly. This term is employed to cover the views of Saint-Simon and Durkheim, as well as those of the medieval theologians, the caste ideology and tribal cultures more generally. This obscures a crucial distinction which Dumont must be aware of, even though he significantly chooses to ignore it.

Socialism is thus seen as merely a combination of individualism and holism, and Marx denoted as even more of an individualist than either Hobbes or Rousseau! This is perversely misleading. Socialism (including Marxism) stresses the social nature of humans but abandons the notion of a spiritual cosmos, a notion that was abstractly retained by Hegel. But it is not only opposed to *Universitas* and the idea of hierarchy, it is equally critical of the abstract individual. No one criticised this idea more cogently or lampooned it with such relish than did Marx. A reading of *The German Ideology*, unabridged, is instructive in this context, for in this work Marx and Engels virtually dismember Stirnerian individualism piece by piece. And Stirner, a precursor of atheistic existentialism, is the prototypical individualist.

Socialism was not a combination of holism (or *Universitas*) and individualism; it was a conception that stressed the need to go beyond individualism. Durkheim, for all his conservatism, is closer to this tradition than many Marxists have been willing to admit. In this sense bourgeois individualism (and materialism) was applauded and seen as essentially progressive and liberating. One early socialist, Louis Blanc, put it nicely, even while displaying a limited anthropology, when he said that three great principles divided the world and history, namely, authority, individualism and fraternity. They stood respectively for theocratic states, capitalism and the socialism he – and many others, – believed was historically emerging (cf. Lukes 1973b: 12). Dumont is highly critical of Western individualism, but in his discursive thoughts about this concept he tends only too easily to become an apologist for the theocratic systems. He thus finds it natural to accept that the caste system was 'oriented to the need of all' and to play down the repressive sanctions that upheld and bolstered the ritual hierarchy. Like many trendy ecologists, he yearns for a sacramental past. Caste and sociology, Black Elk and ecology – all four express the holistic viewpoint in opposition to the individualism and the 'man against nature' attitudes of bourgeois positivism. But they part company on a crucial issue, for sociology (like ecology), or at least a sociology worthy of the name, attempts to recreate the unity without recourse to theology, or denying the oppositions. Dumont's advocacy of sociology as reaffirming the social nature of man is salutary; it is a pity his thoughts are not with the future.

Such a conclusion may seem a little harsh, for Dumont, like Durkheim, is clearly attempting a thoroughgoing critique of the Enlightenment positivist tradition, while at the same time attempting to retain its more positive aspects – the paramount values of individualism, equality and reason. Individualism is to be maintained, he writes, as the ultimate value, but not as a naive mode of describing society. We must recover the idea of hierarchy as an encompassing notion and accept the fact that humans are essentially social beings. Anthropology is thus a science in the process of becoming, and must modify and combine the two terms of the encounter between holism and individualism (1986: 207).

Pragmatism and Symbolic Interaction

This chapter outlines the philosophical tradition, of diverse origins, that came to be known as pragmatism. All the writers in this tradition were crucially concerned with the social dimensions of the human self, but unlike Durkheim, they emphasised the psychological and pragmatic aspects of human life. After some introductory remarks on the origins and ethos of pragmatism, the first two sections outline the life-work and philosophy of William James, the second section focusing on the theory of the human subject that is to be found in his classic study *The Principles of Psychology*. The following two sections deal respectively with the psychosocial aspects of the philosophies of the two most important scholars of the Chicago School, namely Dewey and George Herbert Mead. In the final section, after sketching the history of the Chicago School of Sociology, which developed the social aspects of the pragmatists, I examine the work of Erving Goffman, focusing on his seminal study *Asylums*.

7.1 Pragmatism and William James

Pragmatism has been described as America's national philosophy and as the theoretical expression of the spirit of modern industrial capitalism, with its alleged emphasis on the practical and on the utility of thinking. It is suggested that pragmatism supplied the philosophy for the liberal bourgeoisie during the progressive era in America, at a period when American capitalism was emerging as a dominant force in world affairs (Novack 1975: 41). This interpretation has been challenged by H. S. Thayer (1981) in his important study of pragmatism, for it tends, he suggests, to forget history. For the conception of human knowledge as subject to the norm of practical results, where utility is a test of significance in matters rational is a doctrine as old as the human race. It is an ancient and venerated doctrine that has its origins in pre-literate culture, and has been given, he suggests, theoretical expression throughout history. Thayer traces the development of pragmatism in Western philosophy from Descartes, seeing Fichte as a particularly key figure in this development (1981: 13–65).

Pragmatism has been described by Joad (1924) as less of a philosophical theory than a philosophical attitude, for its main proponents – Peirce, James, Dewey, Mead and F. C. S. Schiller – differed widely in their views on the nature of the universe and the place of humans within it (Joad 1924: 67). Nevertheless these writers share a common perspective that is rooted in a distinctive intellectual and historical context and all in their various ways attempted to overcome the dualistic tendencies inherent in the Western philosophical tradition, which stemmed from Descartes and Kant. Both Morton White (1955) and Scheffler (1974) describe pragmatism as a mediating philosophy. White writes that pragmatism was an attempt to mediate or steer between two extremes: the speculative philosophy of Whitehead, Bergson and absolute idealists such as Royce and Bradley on the one hand, and the narrowly conceived analytic philosophy of Moore and Wittgenstein on the other. Scheffler likewise stresses the mediating tendencies of the pragmatists, as they attempted to unify science and religion, theory and practice, positivism and romanticism, speculative thought and analysis. In particular, pragmatism tried to relate philosophy to modern scientific development, while avoiding the positivistic tendency to reduce or subordinate philosophical and other human interests to a simplified model of positive science (1974: 2).

Thomas Leahey has described pragmatism as America's only homegrown philosophy, 'a hybrid of Bain, Darwin and Kant' (1987: 248). Although rather crude, this phrase sums up some of the key influences on pragmatism, particularly as expressed by William James: British empiricist philosophy, Darwinian evolutionary theory and the Kantian focus on epistemological issues.

The originator of modern pragmatism, as William James acknowledged, was Charles S. Peirce (1839–1914), who in 1878, in a popular science magazine, set out the basic principles of the pragmatic theory of meaning and truth. Abandoning the Platonic aim of a fundamental philosophy and drawing on the Darwinian idea that viable beliefs are those that work in adopting us to our changing environment, Peirce expresses the pragmatic principle or maxim as follows:

In order to ascertain the meaning of an intellectual conception one should consider what practical consequences might conceivably result by necessity from the truth of that conception; and the sum of these consequences will constitute the entire meaning of that conception. (quoted in Copleston 1966: 311)

Peirce was concerned with establishing a theory of meaning not of truth, but although he wrote a great deal, little was published during his own lifetime. He never held a permanent university post and appears to have had an abrasive personality. He lived most of his life as a near-penniless recluse, and it was not until the 1930s when his collected papers were published that Peirce came to be recognised for what he was: one of the great philosophers of the nineteenth century. Both James and Dewey acknowledge this influence and the profound quality of his thought. Thus it was through the writings of William James that pragmatism became established as an influential current of thought in the first decades of the present century.

William James (1842–1910) was born in New York and came from a wealthy background. His grandfather was an immigrant from Ireland who had amassed a large fortune – a millionaire three times over. His father, Henry James Sr was a follower of the religious mystic Swedenborg and was, as Margaret Knight described him, 'a crank in the best sense of the word' (1950: 14). He provided a home atmosphere of 'almost stifling affection, intense intellectuality and lofty ethical idealism' (Allen 1971: vii). It was almost too much for the family, and while his younger brother Henry became a famous novelist, William James' other siblings – Alice, Wilkinson and Robertson – all suffered in later life from psychosomatic disorders. The family travelled a good deal and thus James developed a strong cosmopolitan outlook.

He had hopes of becoming an artist, but after a while gave this up and in 1863 enrolled at the Harvard Medical School. Not happy with the choice, he interrupted his medical studies to join the geologist Louis Agassiz on a collecting expedition to Brazil. It soon became clear that James was not made out to be a naturalist either: I am not cut out, he wrote home, for 'an active life'. He contracted smallpox and returned home after a year and recommenced his studies. But plagued by a variety of ailments he abandoned his medical studies again and spent some two years travelling in Europe, mainly in Germany. They were two miserable years, but James devoted most of his time to studying the physiology of the nervous system and had hopes of working under Wundt. He completed his medical studies in 1869 but never in fact practised medicine. The following year he had a nervous breakdown, which amounted to a spiritual crisis. He later recorded his near-hallucinatory experiences in his classic study on the psychology of religion, *The Varieties of the Religious Experience* (1902). He attributed his recovery to reading Renouvier's *Treatise of Psychology* (1859). Two years later came the event that was to prove a turning point in his life; he was offered a post as an instructor in physiology at Harvard University. It was 'a perfect godsend' he wrote to his brother Henry. He had at last found his vocation. For a while he taught anatomy and physiology and then in 1876 he began offering a new course in physiological psychology, as well as establishing a psychology laboratory, the first of its kind in the United States. During the next decade he began to write reviews and articles on psychology and in 1885 he became Professor of Philosophy. He thus came to join what Morton White has called 'a three-ringed philosophical circus' at Harvard University, the others being Josiah Royce and George Santayana. These three philosophers commanded world-wide respect and admiration in the decades between 1880 and 1910. It has been described as the Golden Age of American philosophy (White 1972: 170). Although intellectually they were poles apart, for Royce was a Hegelian idealist and James an empiricist to the core, the two men developed a close and intimate friendship.

After some twelve years of working on the study, in 1890 James published his monumental *The Principles of Psychology* in two volumes. (James later made an abridgment of the work entitled *Psychology: A briefer course* (1892).) The book became a classic and had a revolutionary impact on psychology. Written in a fine literary style, the tone and outlook of the book are surprisingly modern and *Principles of Psychology* is still being published and read. Can one say the same of any other nineteenth-century textbook?

Apart from *Varieties of Religious Experience*, James produced no other major psychological work, and in the latter part of his life he turned increasingly to philosophy. He published a number of important studies; all essentially consisting of lectures he had earlier delivered: these include *The Will to Believe and Other Essays* (1897), *Pragmatism* (1907), *The Meaning of Truth* (1909) and *A Pluralistic Universe* (1909). His *Essays on Radical Empiricism* were published posthumously (1912). (For useful studies of James' life and work, see Perry 1935; Allen 1967; Feinstein 1984.)

Apart from his medical studies James seems to have been largely self-taught and given his dislike of mathematics and formal logic, he has been described as a philosopher who was 'little more than a brilliant and slightly irresponsible amateur' (Knight 1950: 50). A subjectivist and anti-intellectualist tendency is seen as running through his work, and as he expressed his philosophical ideas in semi-popular lectures, they have a piecemeal and unsystematic quality. But Ellen Suckiel (1982) has suggested that a careful and thorough examination of James' philosophical writings reveals a 'coherent vision', a consistent pragmatic philosophy that hinges on two main pillars, a teleological conception of human nature and a methodological commitment to the principle of experience.

Although in philosophical temper very different from Kant – though he shared his antipathy towards the military spirit – James was motivated by an identical aim, namely to reconcile the scientific outlook with the moral and religious consciousness that he felt was intrinsic to the human condition. James was thus the most religiously-minded of the pragmatists and much of his writing can be interpreted as a defence of the religious outlook. James' own religious feelings, Russell notes, 'were very Protestant, very democratic and very full of the warmth of human kindness' – and he came to see all religion likewise; as being for the general good of humankind (1946: 839; Morris 1987: 143–4). His general philosophy has often been discussed under three headings: James' pragmatic method, his pragmatic theory of truth and his radical empiricism. We can discuss each of these in turn, leaving aside the psychological aspects of his work until the next section.

In the second lecture of his book on *Pragmatism*, James makes a distinction between pragmatism as a method and as a theory of truth. Noting that as a method pragmatism is 'nothing new' (Socrates, Locke and Hume were all forerunners of the pragmatic method), he defines it as 'primarily a method of settling metaphysical disputes that otherwise might be interminable' (1907: 28). Thus in many respects pragmatism is the spiritual ancestor of logical positivism (Knight 1950: 50) in being radically anti-metaphysical. James is quite explicit about this; the pragmatic method harmonises with many philosophical tendencies: 'It agrees with nominalism . . . in always appealing to particulars; with utilitarianism in emphasizing practical aspects; with positivism in its disdain for verbal solutions, useless questions and metaphysical abstractions.' It thus implies an attitude against dogma, and the pretence of finality in truth. The pragmatic method, he writes, turns away from abstractions, from fixed principles, from *a priori* reasons and closed systems. It is 'the attitude of looking away from first things, principles, "categories", supposed necessities, and of looking towards last things, fruits, consequences, facts' (1907: 31–2).

James explicitly acknowledges that this attitude is anti–intellectualist, and against what he felt to be the pretensions of rationalism. He makes a well-known distinction between two kinds of philosophy, which he terms 'tender-minded' and 'tough-minded'. The tender-minded or rationalist temperament (going by 'principles') he sees as idealist, intellectualist, religious, monistic and dogmatic, while the tough-minded empiricist (going by 'facts') he describes as materialist, sensationalist, irreligious, pluralistic and sceptical. Although it seems to be his intention to reconcile the two philosophical tendencies, his own writings make it clear that he was himself a tough-minded empiricist, and was highly critical of the rationalist tendency (1907: 13).

Thus James came to suggest that theories are 'instruments not answers to enigmas', and that ideas 'become true just in so far as they help us to get into satisfactory relationships with other parts of our experience' (1907: 34). Extending Peirce's pragmatic theory of meaning to truth generally, and focusing it upon particulars, James therefore came to describe pragmatism not only as a method but also as a theory of truth. It is not for determining the meanings of concepts. Pragmatism is a theory of truth which James defines as follows:

> True ideas are those that we can assimilate, validate, corroborate and verify. False ideas are those that we cannot. That is the practical difference it makes to us to have true ideas. . .the truth of an idea is not a stagnant property inherent in it. Truth happens to an idea, it becomes true, is made true by events. . . . Its verity is in fact. . .a process. . .its verification. (1907: 97)

James was thus opposed to the idea that there were *a priori* truths independent of verification, or that one could ascertain the meaning of an idea independently of its function or application. Theories and ideas, for James, were simply 'tools', whose function could only be understood in concrete life-situations. There is a certain ambiguity in James's formulation, for it could imply that even a falsehood could be 'true' if it were useful or expedient to believe it. He certainly felt that a belief in God had consequences useful to life. But it is clear that James was little concerned with formal definition of truth; he was only concerned with the empirical question of how we go about making truth ascriptions. He thus came to repudiate the two traditional theories of truth; the correspondence and coherence theories. According to the correspondence theory of truth, the truth of an idea relates to its 'agreement with reality', truth consists of a 'correspondence', 'copying' or 'mirroring' of a statement, with reality or with the facts as they are given. The coherence theory, which James associated with the objective idealism of Royce, saw truth in terms of the progression of knowledge towards a single coherent system of thought, epitomised in the notion of the absolute. James rejected both conceptions of truth; the former on the grounds that it saw knowledge as essentially a passive mirroring, and that many of our beliefs and theoretical postulates were not amenable to such one-to-one verification; the latter on account of the abstract vacuity of its metaphysical abstraction. Thus James rejected both positivism and objective idealism as modes of philosophical understanding. The human subject neither stood in opposition to the objective world, nor could it be collapsed into the absolute. In his critique of Spencer's psychology he made his own position clear:

> The knower is not simply a mirror floating with no foot-hold anywhere and passively reflecting an order that he comes upon and finds simply existing. The knower is an actor and co-efficient of the truth on one side, while on the other he registers the truth which he helps to create. Mental interests, hypotheses, postulates so far as they are based for human action. . .help to make the truth which they declare. (Allen 1971: 15)

Although, as said, James might be construed as suggesting that what is true are beliefs and theories that are useful or expedient, his intention is fundamentally to question the notion of objective or infallible truths, and to suggest that truth and meaning are integrally connected to concrete and practical concerns. For James it is pointless to inquire as to the meaning of truth or any phenomenon outside the context of its use in the fulfilment of human ends. There are thus undoubted similarities between the perspectives of James and Nietzsche. It is important to note, however, that like Nietzsche, James's interests were not exclusively epistemological and to interpret his pragmatism as essentially epistemological or cognitive in character is to distort the whole tenor of his philosophy. (For useful discussions of James's pragmatic theory of truth, see Ayer 1968: 196–208; Thayer 1981: 147–59; Suckiel 1982: 91–121; Bird 1986: 35–48.)

The third aspect of James's philosophy is his radical empiricism, which many have seen as radically distinct from his pragmatism.

James followed closely the empiricist tradition in deriving all knowledge from experience. As he wrote in the Preface to *The Meaning of Truth*, one of the first postulates of radical empiricism is 'that the only things that shall be debatable among philosophers shall be things definable in terms drawn from experience' (1909: 6). But, as we shall see, James rejected the analytic and atomistic perspective of the traditional empiricists like J. S. Mill and Spencer, who suggested that the basic content of experience consisted of discrete sensory particulars. James denied such atomism, drawing on the evidence of empirical psychology rather than by suggesting philosophical arguments. For James, experienced reality was a continuous flux; 'buzzing, blooming, confusion', as he described it, and it is human cognition based on practical interests and aims that structures and interprets this flux of sensations. Such 'common-sense' categories as reality, mind, causality, body, embedded as these are in languages, are ultimately derived from practical concerns and interests. Many have noted the similarity between James's and Bergson's views on the instrumental function of cognition. The nature of reality then, for James, had two essential referents; on the one hand, the ordinary reality of common-sense understanding, the world of physical objects. On the other hand, it referred to 'experience', which in an important sense James raised to the status of being the ultimate and only reality. As such, experience was neither mental nor physical. Bertrand Russell expressed this viewpoint well when he wrote: 'The stuff of which the world of pure experience is composed is. . .neither mind nor matter, but something more primitive than either. Both mind and matter seem to be composite, and the stuff of which they are compounded lies in a sense between the two' (1921: 10).

Both George Novack and A. J. Ayer (1982: 75) interpret James's empiricism in these terms. As Novack writes:

> James wiped out the existential priority of the external world over the mind and the essential difference between the objective and subjective parts of experience. By making nature depend upon experience and not experience upon nature, James dissolved the independent objective existence of the real world in the subjective reactions of humankind. (1975: 69)

James does indeed speak of pure experience as the 'one primal stuff or material in the world, a stuff of which everything is composed' (1912: 94), and thus his philosophy has been described as one of 'neutral monism'. But this thesis has epistemological rather than ontological import. There was, James felt, no 'aboriginal stuff' distinct from material objects, and the contrast between the subject and object was a practical distinction, 'of a functional order and in no way ontological, as classical dualism represents it' (1912: 233). It is clear that James is motivated by a desire to transcend two pervasive dualisms; that between the subjective knower and the objective world on the one hand, and between the world of values and the world of physical objects on the other (Suckiel 1982: 123–4). Whether James was a phenomenalist or a subjective idealist has been a long-debated issue, but James himself often claimed that he was, like Dewey, an epistemological realist, in postulating a reality existing independently of the human subject (1909: 104–6). Bird (1986) concludes that James avoided the reductive tendencies of traditional empiricism (as well as its atomism), and saw the relationship between the mental and physical as functional and contextual. He rejected a 'foundationalist' epistemology, advocating instead a holistic view of experience and meaning (1986: 120).

7.2   The Principles of Psychology

James's masterpiece, *The Principles of Psychology*, is a vast compendium on the state of psychology at the end of the nineteenth century. It contains much empirical data interspersed with James's philosophical reflections on a wide range of topics – the methods and subject-matter of psychology, the nature of consciousness, the mind–body problem, free will and determinism, and the concept of the self. The book had a tremendous impact on the orientation of psychology and unlike Wundt, who was essentially an academic psychologist, James appealed to a much wider audience. Murphy and Kovach write of the book bursting 'upon the world like a volcanic eruption' (1972: 195). The functionalist school of psychology, associated with J. R. Angell and Dewey, was essentially derived from the pragmatic philosophy of James. Owen Flanagan alludes to three reasons why *The Principles of Psychology* was such a crucial text in the history of psychology.

First, it came at a critical junction, at the end of the first generation when a generally recognised experimental psychology existed, when the studies of Bain, Romanes, Fechner, Wundt and Helmholtz had laid the foundations for a scientific psychology. Significantly, James himself, though instrumental in founding a psychology laboratory, had little experience or even interest in experimental work.

Secondly, the two main hypotheses on the relationship between the body and mind which derived from Descartes and mechanistic philosophy had both been found inadequate. One was the reductive materialist hypothesis derived from Hobbes, and adopted by Huxley as well as by Santayana. The other was a Cartesian dualism that denied any science of the mind. An impasse was evident, and James writes in response to the failure of both theories.

Thirdly, James's text was written in the aftermath of the Darwinian revolution in biology, which had had a profound effect on all the human sciences. Indeed, Ellen Suckiel (1982) writes that James's basic conceptions, particularly his biological model of human nature, was directly influenced by nineteenth-century Darwinism. A teleological conception of the mind is, she suggests, a guiding principle of James's philosophy, for 'he pictures the human being as a striving, goal-positing, interest-fulfilling organism, whose most important characteristic is his evolutional appropriation and projection of ends' (1982: 2). Following Darwin's theory, James postulated that human consciousness was a product of natural selection and thus situated the origin and function of mental life in the natural world. Flanagan (1984) credits James with offering the first formulation of the naturalistic position in the philosophy of mind. We can perhaps best approach James's psychology and his conception of the human subject by examining some of the key chapters and topics covered in his classic work.

Psychological Methods

James defined psychology as 'the description and explanation of states of consciousness as such' – sensations, desires, emotions, cognitions, reasonings and the like. He thought of psychology as a natural science and was critical of the earlier rational psychology in which the mind (or soul) was viewed as a spiritual entity with certain faculties that were explicated with almost no reference to the world with which such faculties deal. Accepting a Darwinian perspective, James suggests that the mind and the world have evolved together and are something of a 'mutual fit'. This leads him to postulate that 'mental life is primarily teleological; that is to say, that our various ways of feeling and thinking have grown to be what they are because of their utility in shaping our reaction on the outer world' (1892: 4).

He recognised three essential psychological methods – introspective, experimental and comparative. He seems to be critical of all three, and makes little mention of comparative studies into animal behaviour. As he defines psychology as the study of conscious mental life, and seems to equate 'mind' with the higher forms of consciousness, he tends to emphasise the methodological primacy of introspection. 'Introspective observation', he writes, 'is what we have to rely on first and foremost and always' (1890: 185), although he is critical of the 'elementism' of both Wundt and the British empiricists. Paradoxically, although James presents in the work a painstaking survey of the major experimental findings of German physiologists and psychologists, he was himself, as Boring expressed it, 'but a half-hearted experimentalist' (1950: 510). Stressing that mental life has its own distinctive existence, both behavioural and physiological experimental approaches tend to be minimised (Bird 1986: 133–4).

Habit

The notion of 'habit' had been extensively explored by earlier psychologists, particularly by Bain, whom James cites. And his chapter on 'habit' is one of the best known in the study and has been described as a 'literary classic'. The basic function of habit, for James, is to economise and simplify human action. Assuming the plasticity of organic life, and that the behaviour of humans is not rigidly determined by instincts, habit, James suggests, simplifies our movements and diminishes fatigue. If we did not economise through habit our nervous and muscular energies, we should 'be in a sorry plight'. Moreover, habit 'diminishes the conscious attention with which our acts are performed' and thus aids the functioning of the human organism. Thus habit, he suggests, is 'the enormous fly-wheel of society, its most precious conservative agent'. It therefore becomes the aim of education 'to make our nervous system our ally instead of our enemy. It is to find and capitalise our acquisitions and to live at ease upon the interest of the fund' (1982: 138–44). Habit has been seen as a key notion in James's psychology (Scheffler 1974: 122).

The Stream of Consciousness

Another famous chapter from *The Principles of Psychology* is entitled 'The Stream of Consciousness'. This chapter is essentially a critique of the British empiricist tradition and Wundt's experimental psychology. Most studies, James writes, adopt the so-called synthetic methods, and, starting with 'simple ideas' of sensation, as if they come from atoms, build up higher states of mind out of their 'association' or 'synthesis'. This is a very questionable theory, James argues, and it is more viable to adopt an analytic method and begin with the most concrete facts of human consciousness itself. James seems to reverse the normal meanings of the terms, for he was profoundly anti-analytical, and critical of the structuralist approach to consciousness, which stemmed from Locke's theory of 'simple ideas'. James felt that we cannot break up a given mental content into sensory 'elements', although it is worth noting that Bain, James Mill and Spencer had all stressed the constant flux of consciousness (Murphy and Kovach 1972: 196).

It is a fundamental fact of life and inner experience that consciousness of some sort exists, and this consciousness, James writes, has four essential characteristics.

First, consciousness is personal and subjective. A basic psychic fact is not the existence of 'thought', or this or that thought, but 'my thought, every thought being owned. . . . The universal conscious fact is not "feelings and thought exists" but "I think" and "I feel". No psychology can question the existence of personal selves' (1892: 153).

Secondly, consciousness is always changing and in flux. James stresses that 'no state once gone can recur and be identical with what it was before' (1892: 154). Thus no two ideas are ever exactly the same and, because consciousness is ever-changing, human personality is never fixed, permanent or static. James cites the Greek philosopher Heraclitus, who asserted that one never enters twice into exactly the same stream.

Thirdly, within each personal consciousness, thought is sensibly continuous and flows like a stream. In his well-known passage:

> Consciousness does not appear to itself chopped up in bits. Such words as 'chain' or 'train' do not describe it fitly as it presents itself in the first instance. It is nothing jointed; it flows. A 'river' or a 'stream' are the metaphors by which it is most naturally described. In talking of it hereafter, let us call it the stream of thought, of consciousness or of subjective life. (1892: 159)

James thus explicitly argues that personal identity is not something self-evident and given as with rationalists like Descartes; but neither is it a 'mere bundle of perceptions and ideas' as with sensationalists like Hume. Both are wrong. As Flanagan puts it:

Against the rationalist we bring the phenomenological data that we do not in fact experience ourself as exactly the same person over time. . . . Against the empiricist scepticism we bring the phenomenological data of continuity, and we locate the naturalistic ground of this continuity in our biological integrity. (1984: 33)

Fourthly, consciousness is characterised by selective attention and deliberate will; it 'chooses' all the while it thinks: 'The pursuance of future ends and the choice of means for their attainment are thus the mark and criterion of the presence of mentality in a phenomenon' (1890: 21).

Given his teleological theory of mind, James stresses that consciousness is purposeful and intentional, and he explicitly draws on the ideas of his contemporary Franz Brentano. James suggests that 'the choosing of different men is to a great extent the same', hinting that the objects and aspects selected and accentuated are fundamentally the same for all human subjects. But unlike Dewey and Mead, James seems oblivious to cultural and social factors in this selection (Scheffler 1974: 145).

The Self

James makes a distinction between two aspects of human subjectivity, the self as known, the 'empirical ego' or 'me', and the self as knower, or the 'I', the 'pure ego' of certain authors. The empirical ego or 'me' is an empirical aggregate of things objectively known, and consists of bodily, social and spiritual constituents. The 'I' which knows, then, is not itself an aggregate, 'neither for psychological purposes need it be an unchanging metaphysical entity like the soul, or a principle like the transcendental ego, viewed as "out of time"' (1892: 215). Thus, as noted earlier, James was trying to steer between the empiricist doctrine of the self (which he associates with Hume and Herbart) which, though stressing the empirical nature of personal identity, denies the unity of consciousness and the rationalist conception of the self as a transcendental ego, which he links with Kant's 'transcendental unity of apperception'. He suggests that Kant's philosophy is a 'mere curio' and that we need to 'outflank' Kant rather than go through him (Allen 1971: 154). Always with an open mind, James discusses such phenomena as insane delusions, spirit possession and mediumship, and hysteria and 'alternating personality', which were being studied by his contemporary M. Pierre Janet.

Theory of Emotions

One of the most celebrated theories formulated by James – a theory first outlined in 1884 – was his theory of emotion. The essence of James's theory is to counter the common assumption that an emotion preceded a physical movement or expression. Defining an emotion as a tendency to feel when in the presence of a certain object in the environment, James stresses that emotions also have a bodily expression and that this intervenes between the stimulus and the emotion. His theory is perhaps best expressed in his own words:

> Our natural way of thinking about these coarser emotions is that the mental perception of some fact excites the mental affection called the emotion, and that this latter state of mind gives rise to bodily expression. My theory, on the contrary, is that the bodily changes follow directly the perception of the exciting fact, and that our feeling of the same changes as they occur is the emotion. Common sense says, we lose our fortune are sorry and weep, we meet a bear, are frightened and run. . . .The hypothesis here to be defended says that this order of sequence is incorrect. . .that the more rational statement is that we feel sorry because we cry, angry because we strike, afraid because we tremble. . . (1892: 375–6)

Because in 1885 the Danish physiologist Carl Lange (1834–1900) had proposed a similar theory of the emotions, it has usually been referred to as the James–Lange theory of the emotions. The theory has generated a good deal of debate during the past century, and the general consensus is that the theory provides a limited and inadequate account of the emotions. The physiological researches of W. B. Cannon and Charles Sherrington stressed the importance of the hypothalamus and the sympathetic nervous system on emotional responses, and from another angle, Solomon has questioned the thesis that emotions can be understood in purely biological terms (see Cannon 1927; Solomon 1976; Lyons 1980). But the important point, as Allen indicates, is that James did not reduce emotional experience to automatic physiological reactions, allowing that emotions could be controlled to some extent by will power and ideas. His main point, however, was that mind and body are inseparable and functionally integrated (1971: xii).

Naturalism and Free Will

There are two tendencies in the philosophy of William James, which appear to be contradictory and to clash around the old debate between free will and determinism. On the one hand, his work is pervaded by an evolutionary tendency, which leads him to stress the dynamic and creative aspects of human life, embodied in his teleological conception of human nature. On the other hand, he advocated a conception of psychology as a natural science, as a mechanistic causal theory. Hence he faced a real dilemma; how was a scientific conception of the human subject compatible with our ordinary conception of a human being as a willing agent? In his chapter on 'will', James stressed the various types of decisions that are made in human life, and left it to the epilogue of the study to address the question of the relation of free will to a deterministic psychology. His main point is that psychology itself can never resolve the issue, and that its very methodology implied a deterministic causality. The psychologist, he wrote, 'has a great motive in favour of determinism. He wants to build a science and a science is a system of fixed relations. Wherever there are independent variables, there science stops' (1892: 457). Psychology as a science could only progress, he felt, by assuming determinism. But scientific claims were only relative. 'Science . . . must constantly be reminded that her purposes are not the only purposes and that the order of uniform causation which she has use for, and is therefore right in postulating, may be enveloped in a wider order, on which she has no claims at all' (1890: 2/576).

Like Kant, James held fast to a mechanistic conception of science; unlike Kant he advocated its application to human consciousness. But when he came to explore the nature of the human mind he abandons this mechanistic discourse and adopts a functionalist approach.

The Mind–Body Problem

James discussion of the mind–body problem has been described as remarkably modern. Although his writings are unsystematic he offers a critique of a wide variety of theories on the relationship between body and mind. He considers and rejects the epiphenomenalism of Huxley and Santayana, in which consciousness is seen as simply a by-product, like the steam whistle of a locomotive, of the physical processes of the brain; the classical psychophysical parallelism of Leibniz, which was advocated by his contemporary

W. K. Clifford; the 'mind-stuff' theory of Hume, which saw consciousness as a mere 'bundle' of impressions and ideas. His discussion of these and other positions is complex, but his own theory emerges clearly within the pages: Flanagan describes it as 'naturalistic functionalism'. James is fundamentally against the idea of treating the mind as if it were an entity. What did this imply? James writes: 'I mean only to deny that the word [consciousness] stands for an entity, but to insist most emphatically that it stands for a function.'

In other words, James is suggesting that consciousness is analogous to walking or breathing, for these activities are not things or entities in the ordinary sense of these terms, but are functions of our bodies. Thus James is suggesting, Flanagan contends, that consciousness is a functional outcome of brain–world interaction – it is not simply identical with the brain – 'it is itself' (1984: 46).

James's teleological conception of the human subject suggested that individuals were motivated towards the fulfilment of specific aims and interests. Human cognition, therefore, is not disinterested activity, but functional, dynamic and practical – and intrinsically related to human interests. Human interest, in fact, is involved in every aspect of human life – in perception, in cognition and in activity. Human consciousness, for James, is deeply rooted in the conative, personal and experiential dimensions of human life-activity. But there are two crucial aspects of human life that are significantly ignored by James. One is the social and cultural aspect of the human condition. Throughout his writings James takes a very subjectivist standpoint and seems unaware of the cultural specificity of much of human behaviour. The other is his failure to mention the sexual impulse in any of his studies. Judging from his *Principles of Psychology* he appears to see humans as asexual beings.

William James, by all accounts, was a warm-hearted person with a delightful sense of humour. Not only a fine writer, he had immense erudition and was almost universally admired. A restless spirit, his writings had an enormous impact on psychology. J. B. Watson remarked that every budding psychologist has read and loved James's chapter on 'the stream of consciousness', but that it was out of touch with modern psychology, 'as the stage coach would be in New York's Fifth Avenue' (1924: 137). But James's ideas seem much better to have stood the test of time. He directly inspired the functionalist school in psychology, which was prominent in the early years of the century, and he had an important influence on Dewey and G. H. Mead. It is to these scholars that we now turn.

7.3   Dewey's Empirical Naturalism

Although the founding triumvirate of pragmatism – Peirce, James and Dewey – are closely linked, both in their personal lives and philosophical outlook, it would be difficult to find three men with such contrasting personalities. Peirce was eccentric, creative, often obscure, and developed a pragmatism that was almost entirely technical and theoretical, a logical pragmatism that was devoted to analysing the nature of science. James was urbane, eloquent, humanistic, a member of the American genteel tradition, whose pragmatism was closely tied to his philosophy of religion. Dewey has been described as 'systematic, discursive, democratic, but often dull', and he was essentially a social philosopher. Three short quotations will perhaps give the tenor of the relationship between these three important scholars:

'If Peirce invented pragmatism and James popularised it, John Dewey applied it – that is, he applied pragmatism to social problems in general and to education in particular' (G. Miller 1964: 79).

Although Dewey 'was the youngest of the three pragmatists, one thinks of him as the father of pragmatism – not so clever as Peirce in matters of logic and science, not as witty or as brilliant as James, but in many ways a more rugged and compelling figure than either of the others' (White 1955: 175).

'The history of pragmatism begins with Peirce, who wrote as a logician, and James who wrote as a humanist and educator. Its Hegelian synthesis was achieved in the disenchanted Hegelian Dewey, who was both a logician and humanist' (Thayer 1981: 169).

John Dewey (1859–1952) was born in Burlington, Vermont, his father a merchant and his mother came from a farming family. After studying at the University of Vermont, he became a high school teacher. Studying philosophy in his spare time, he wrote an essay on the metaphysical assumptions of materialism and sent it in May 1881 to the editor of the *Journal of Speculative Philosophy*, tentively enquiring as to its worth. Given encouragement, he became a student of Johns Hopkins University the following year. He attended lectures on logic by Peirce and came under the influence of G. S. Morris, who introduced him to Hegelian philosophy. Dewey was later to recall the appeal of Hegel's thought:

It supplied a demand for unification that was doubtless an intense emotional craving. . . . Hegel's synthesis of subject and object, matter and spirit, the divine and the human, was however, no mere intellectual formula; it operated as an immense release, a liberation. Hegel's treatment of human culture, of institutions and the arts . . . had a special attraction for me.

Although Dewey gradually drifted away from Hegel, his philosophy, he noted, 'left a permanent deposit in my thinking' (Bernstein 1960: 10).

Soon after the University of Chicago opened in 1893, Dewey joined its staff, and there occupied himself mainly in logical, psychological and ethical questions. For a decade he was head of the department of philosophy there, and during this period started what was later called the 'laboratory school' (in 1896), and was associated with George Herbert Mead and James R. Angell in the promotion of the functionalist school of psychology. His first book, *Psychology*, was published in 1887. He resigned from Chicago in 1904 to become professor of philosophy at Columbia University, the centre for the rest of his career. During his long years at Columbia he produced a stream of important articles and books that established him as perhaps the foremost philosopher in the United States. Among his best-known works are *The Influence of Darwin on Philosophy* (1910), *Democracy and Education* (1916), *Reconstruction in Philosophy* (1920), *Experience and Nature* (1925), *The Quest for Certainty* (1929) and *Freedom and Culture* (1939). At the age of eighty-seven he published *Problems of Men* (1946) and was still actively engaged in writing when he reached his nineties. He died in 1952, aged ninety-three.

Throughout his long life Dewey was recognised as a liberal and progressive scholar who was deeply interested and involved in political and social issues. He travelled widely, visiting the Soviet Union in 1928 to study their experiments in education, and even as an old man he was active in the fight for freedom throughout the world. He defended the anarchists Sacco and Vanzetti, and chaired the commission of enquiry into the charges brought against Leon Trotsky, who was seeking a place of refuge from political persecution. He was reviled by both conservatives and communists, but as Morton White writes, he was, in many respects, 'the conscience of American philosophy' (1955: 174–5). In spite of world-wide acclaim, he always remained a shy and modest man, of 'almost rustic simplicity'. He was free of every variety of snobbishness and had an ingrained democratic bias. He exerted an enormous influence on his contemporaries, but as Richard Bernstein suggests, this influence did not stem from an overwhelming personality or a glittering rhetorical ability, but from the power of his ideas and the searching quality of his mind (1966: 28–9). In fact Dewey's style of writing is dense, tortuous and prosaic. It is jargon-free, but the prose lacks any sparkle and lucidity; however, it is enlivened by ideas and thought-patterns that are impressive and original. There remains something rugged and compelling about Dewey's thought. (For useful biographies of Dewey, see Hook 1939; Bernstein 1966.)

Dewey had great intellectual curiosity and an enormous capacity for work. He wrote more than forty important studies, spanning over sixty years and dealing with every branch of philosophy. His main preoccupation was with the social problems of modern urban society, particularly in the fields of education and social philosophy, though he rarely engaged himself in political or sociological analysis. We can hardly deal with this wide-ranging corpus here; instead, I shall focus on two important studies, *Democracy and Education* and *Experience and Nature*, and attempt to describe the basic tenets of his philosophy and his conception of the human subject.

Dewey described his philosophy as 'empirical naturalism' or 'instrumentalism' and many have remarked that what distinguished Dewey was his wholehearted acceptance of evolutionary theory. His starting point in every field, wrote Will Durant, was Darwinian (1952: 522). During the 1890s Dewey seems to have undergone a kind of conversion, and under the influence of Darwinism and the biological emphasis of James's *Principles of Psychology* came to stress a naturalistic, biological approach to human behaviour. As Thayer writes: 'The idealism with its categories of the organic whole, and development viewed as a passage from "contradictions" to "syntheses" gave way to the evolutionary and biologically conceived notions of growth as a process of "conflicts" and "resolutions"' (1981: 167).

Thus Dewey in the 1890s came to reinterpret Hegel's logic in terms of Darwinian notions of continuity and growth. But Dewey retained certain Hegelian emphases on wholeness and development, and it was from Hegel that he derived his abiding antipathy to the idea that there is a gulf between the mind and its object. However, Dewey transforms the Hegelian emphasis on reason and spirit into an emphasis on science and its works, and stresses more than Hegel the fundamental continuity between humans and the rest of nature. Describing continuity as the 'primary postulate of a naturalistic theory of logic', Dewey writes:

The term 'naturalistic' has many meanings. As it is here employed it means, on the one side, that there is no breach of continuity between the operations of inquiry and biological and physical operations. 'Continuity', on the other side, means that rational operations grow out of organic activities without being identical with that from which they emerge. (1938: 19)

Dewey therefore came to look upon human thought in functional terms as an instrument that is to be understood in terms of 'life processes', as a highly developed form of the active relationship between the organism and its environment. Dewey advocates a form of dialectical materialism, recognising that human consciousness is a level of reality with its own distinctive properties. But the important point about Dewey, as Copleston and others have stressed – and this is a strategy later adopted by existentialist thinkers – is that he refuses to start his analysis from the distinction between the subject and object as an absolute point of departure. For he 'sees man's intellectual life as presupposing and developing out of antecedent relations, and thus as falling wholly within the sphere of nature. Thought is one among other natural processes or activities' (Copleston 1966: 354). But equally important, as we shall see, Dewey considers human thought to be essentially social in origin; it occurs only in specific cultural contexts.

Dewey's account of the human mind is thoroughly naturalistic in that thought is seen as a product of the evolutionary process and as developing out of the relationship between an organism and its environment.

Besides 'continuity' the other key concept of Dewey's philosophy is that of 'experience'. Although Dewey is an empiricist in the sense that he sees human knowledge as derived from experience, he differs from the classical empiricists in rejecting the notion that experience consists of sense-impressions. For Dewey experience consists of situation, happenings, things going on, like eating a meal or talking to one's friends. Experience is unreflective. Knowledge, on the other hand, is the reflective or intellectual grasp of a situation. Knowledge controls thinking and makes it fruitful. It is 'reflective experience'. He writes: 'Knowledge as an act is bringing some of our dispositions to consciousness with the view to straightening out a perplexity, by conceiving the connection between ourselves and the world in which we live' (1916: 400).

Dewey sees knowledge as an activity of inquiry, beginning with perplexity and confusion, and then, through conjectures, surveys, exploration and the elaboration of hypotheses, leading to the transformation of the problematic situation. Of interest is that Dewey does not make a stark distinction between ordinary common-sense knowledge and scientific inquiry. Both are practical and concern human adaptation to the world of experience. For Dewey, therefore, the distinction between subject and object is not an attribute of human experience but only arises through reflective knowledge. Contrary to the suggestions of Marxist scholars, Dewey's stress on experience did not imply an idealist metaphysic; for Dewey never doubted that the objective world existed independently and antecedently to being experienced or thought about.

Dewey's earliest writings on psychology are embodied in his text *Psychology* and in his classic paper on 'The Reflex Arc Concept in Psychology' (1897). Later he expounded his views in the important and pioneering work *Human Nature and Conduct* (1922). The reflex arc concept had been introduced into psychology from physiology as a way of accounting for the connection between a stimulated nerve structure and motor responses. It was seen as an improvement of the atomistic psychology of the structuralists and it later became the crucial concept of behaviourist psychology. Dewey argued that such stimulus/response theory was a hangover from a redundant dualism. The older dualism of body and soul, he wrote, finds 'a distant echo in the current dualism of stimulus and response' (Thayer 1982: 263). The tendency to treat sensory stimulus and motor activity as separate and distinct – a 'patchwork of disjointed parts' – was unwarranted and Dewey suggests that sensation, ideas, and action form an organic unity, a whole and continuous process of activity. These distinctions are simply phases in a continuous process that serve specific functions. But Dewey in his later writings is equally critical of instinct theory. Having for so long ignored instincts and impulses in favour of sensations, psychology, he felt, was tending more and more to construct inventories of human instincts. But such postulates are too general and abstract to explain the complexities of personal and social life. As he wrote:

It is like saying the flea and the elephant, the lichen and the redwood, are alike products of natural selection. There may be a sense in which the statement is true, but till we know the specific environing conditions under which selection took place we really know nothing. And so we need to know about the social conditions which have educated original activities into definite and significant dispositions before we can discuss the psychological element in society. This is the true meaning of social psychology. (1922: 91; Scheffler 1974: 211–12)

The dispute of earlier psychologists as to whether humans have innate ideas or an empty, passive, wax-like mind, Dewey regarded as redundant and 'incredible', for the truth lay in neither doctrine (93). Human behaviour and capacities can only be explained in terms of specific interactions between impulses and environments. The meaning of impulses and emotions, he writes, 'depends upon interaction with a matured social medium'. Emotional responses may spring from original innate reactions to stimuli, yet they depend also on the responsive behaviour of others. They are not 'pure impulses' but habits formed under the influence of human association. Like James, Dewey stressed the importance of habits in guiding human behaviour. Consonant with his anti-dualistic tendencies, Dewey saw no opposition between reason and emotion. 'Rationality', he wrote, 'is not a force to evoke against impulse and habit. It is the attainment of a working harmony among diverse desires' (1922: 196).

Morton White (1972) describes John Dewey as a 'rebel against dualism', for a consistent opposition to the various dualisms that sprang from the Enlightenment and were advocated by positivism, permeate all his writings. White remarks that the views expressed in *Democracy and Education* were virtually theorems in Dewey's systematic attack on dualism. In the index to the book, under the heading dualism, Dewey lists a plethora of 'versuses'; activity *vs* mind, emotions *vs* intellect, capital *vs* labour, matter *vs* mind, body *vs* soul, objective *vs* subjective knowledge, experience *vs* knowledge, rationalism *vs* empiricism, nature *vs* nurture, and many more. An attempt to go beyond these dualisms is the essence not only of his educational theory but of his entire philosophy. Of particular concern to Dewey is the mind–body dualism that was so pervasive in Western thought:

> I do not know of anything so disastrously affected by the tradition of separation and isolation as is this particular theme of body-mind. In its discussion are reflected the splitting off from each other, religion, morals and science; the divorce of philosophy from science and of both from the arts of conduct. (1931: 301)

This dualism was so deeply embedded in European language and culture that we have no word for the 'mind/body in a unified wholeness of operation' and, as Dewey suggests, it goes back to antiquity.

Drawing on the writings of anthropologists like Boas and Goldenweiser, Dewey suggests that pre-literate cultures have predominantly a collectivist conception of the human subject, and the subjectivity and the 'individuality' of mind have an anomalous status. The modern conception of using the self, 'I', mind and spirit interchangeably is unconceivable in these cultures, where the family and community are solid realities. Although in earlier pre-literate communities humans were not wholly subdued to the demands of custom, such communities had a socio-centric conception of the human subject. Since then, Dewey writes, an 'extraordinary revolution' has occurred in our conception of the individual; the mind has been 'individualised'. Thus 'an individual is no longer just a particular, a part without meaning, it is a subject, self, a distinctive centre of desire, thinking and aspiration' (1925: 216). Thus, as Dumont was to suggest half a century later, the identification of the mind with the individual self and of the latter with a private psychic consciousness is a comparatively modern conception.

But Dewey sees the body-mind dualism as having developed and changed throughout the Western tradition. The dualism is seen as beginning with the Greek philosophers. Greek scholars like Plato and Aristotle, Dewey suggests, tended to identify experience with purely practical concerns and hence with material interests as to its purpose and with the body as to its organ. In contrast knowledge existed for its own sake, apart from practical interests and found its source and organ in the purely immaterial mind. It was concerned with spiritual and ideal interests. Thus practical life was in a state of perpetual flux, while intellectual knowledge, essentially contemplative, was concerned with eternal truths. Dewey sees this dichotomy in Greek thought as a direct reflection of the class structure of Greek society; the disparagement of the practical and the empirical world in terms of some higher realm of ideas or essences being directly associated with a ruling non-working aristocracy. In medieval Christianity a similar dualism continues; the body is seen as earthly, fleshy, lustful and passionate, while the spirit is godlike and incorruptible. 'Add to moral fear of the flesh, interests in resurrection into the next world for external bliss or woe, and there is present a fullfledged antithesis of spirit and matter.' Aquinas repeats the Aristotelian formulae concerning life and the body almost word for word. During the medieval period a religious individualism developed, for the deepest concern of life was the salvation of the individual soul. In the latter middle ages, this latent individualism found conscious formulation in the nominalistic philosophies which treated the structure of knowledge as something built up within the individual through his or her own acts and mental states (1916: 341; 1925: 249–50).

With the Enlightenment, Dewey writes, the scene shifts again. Nature is conceived as wholly mechanical, and an 'extraordinary revolution' in the human conception of individuality occured. Mind becomes individualised, and with the rise of economic and political individualism, the human person is seen as non-social by nature. The medieval conception of the individual soul is seen by Dewey as the precursor and source of the 'isolation of the ego', the thinking self, in all philosophies of the period. Descartes as well as Berkeley uses the notion of self as an equivalent of 'mind', and does so spontaneously. The legitimate reaction against authority in all spheres of life, and the struggle for freedom of action and enquiry led to such an emphasis upon personal observation – to an 'exaggeration of the ego' – as in effect to isolate the mind and set it apart from the world to be known. Thus Dewey concludes: 'The identification of mind with the self, and the setting up of the self as something independent and self-sufficient created such a gulf between the knowing mind and the world that it became a question how knowledge was possible at all' (1916: 342).

It became a problem to explain how a connection could be made between the mind and the world to make valid knowledge possible. Thus emerged the branch of philosophy known as epistemology. Dewey acclaims the practical individualism and the Enlightenment struggle for greater freedom of thought and action, but bewails the philosophical subjectivism which also emerged. It was a 'perversion', he contends, of Enlightenment philosophy. 'Men were not actually engaged in the absurdity of striving to be free from connection with nature and one another. They were striving for greater freedom in nature and society' (1916: 343).

Dewey notes that subjectivism is not confined to the rationalist tradition; both the empiricists and the romantics followed this dualistic perspective. The stress on the 'inner life' as an escape from the world is no modern discovery, Dewey writes: it was advocated by mystics and oppressed people long before it was formulated by philosophical romanticism. But romanticism added a new dimension to this subjectivism; new forms of art and new theories of aesthetics. Often this concern with 'inner consciousness' is a form of compensation for the technical modes of industrial life and the specialisms within science.

The problem with the Enlightenment theorists was that they were not content to conceive of the mind in the individual as the pivot upon which the reconstruction of beliefs turned, thus maintaining the continuity of the individual with the world of nature and human society. Instead, Dewey argues, they regarded the individual mind as a separate entity, complete in each person, and isolated from nature and hence from their minds. Thus a legitimate individualism, the attribute of critical revision of former beliefs, which is indispensable to progress, was explicitly formulated as a narrow social individualism.

Dewey counters this social individualism by stressing that the mind and the human subject are situated in this world, particularly in a social world. Every individual, he writes:

> Has grown up, and always must grow up, in a social medium. His responses grow intelligent, or gain meaning, simply because he lives and acts in a medium of accepting meanings and values. Through social intercourse, through sharing in the activities embodying beliefs, he gradually acquires a mind of his own. The conception of mind as a purely isolated possession of the self is at the very antipodes of the truth. The self achieves mind in the degree in which knowledge of things is incarnate in the life about him; the self is not a separate mind building up knowledge anew on its own account. (1916: 344)

And elsewhere:

> But the whole history of science, art and morals proves that the mind that appears in individuals is not as such individual mind. The former is in itself a system of belief, recognitions and ignorances . . . of expectancies and appraisal of meanings which have been instituted under the influence of custom and tradition. (1925: 219)

It says something of the insularity of British anthropology that Joanna Overing (1985) can offer a critique of dualistic thinking and Ingold (1986) can stress the social nature of human consciousness without even mentioning Dewey (or Mead) – let alone the scholar from whom he derived his essential premises, Hegel.

Dewey essentially saw the mind–body dualism as stemming from class-divisions within society. His essential purpose was to develop a pragmatic philosophy that would not so much transcend the dualism as to take a step back and to realise that the distinction between subject and object only arises through reflective experience. It is only an interpretation of the world – a 'local and provincial' one at that (1916: 239), though the dualism may be

pervasive in Western culture. And it is based on a wrong conception of knowledge which is not to be seen as a 'quest for certainty'
or divorced from the practical activities of life or from primary
experience. Thus the 'solution' to the mind–body problem, he
writes, is to be found in a revision of the preliminary assumptions
about existence that generated the problem in the first place (1916:
263). This stems not only from the intellectualism of much Western
thought (though Dewey never renounced reason), but from a
misleading conception of knowledge that is associated with the
dualistic epistemology. Dewey called this the 'spectator theory of
knowledge' – a conception he considered had been completely
undermined by the discovery of evolution which stressed that the
human subject is a part of the world: 'If the living, experiencing
being is an ultimate participant in the activities of the world to
which it belongs, then knowledge is a mode of participation,
valuable in the degree in which it is effective. It cannot be the idle
view of an unconcerned spectator' (1916: 393).

As Dewey sees knowledge as an instrument, truth also comes to
be defined in terms of utility and the useful. But Dewey did not see
this utility in terms of private gain or profit, but rather, as Copleston suggests, in terms of transforming a problematic situation. And
a problematic situation is something public and objective (1966:
366).

Dewey was concerned to advance a philosophy that undermined
all dualisms – theory and practice, intellect and emotions, empirical
and rational knowledge, mind and body, science and values – and
he did so by a philosophical method he called empirical or pragmatic. 'Its essential feature', he wrote, 'is to maintain the continuity
of knowing with an activity which purposely modifies the environment' (1916: 400).

Throughout his long life Dewey was a firm advocate of democracy, and highly distrustful of the state. His ideal was clearly a
Jeffersonian rural democracy, a pluralistic society based on diverse,
voluntary organisations. Democracy was a life-long preoccupation
with him, and at a conference celebrating his eightieth birthday he
gave a talk entitled 'Creative Democracy – The Task Before Us',
clearly demonstrating that he felt democracy was yet to be accom-
plished. By democracy he meant 'the participation of every mature
human being in formation of the values that regulate the living of
men together; which is necessary from the standpoint of both the
general social welfare and the full development of human beings as
individuals' (Scheffler 1974: 242).

Dewey always remained true to the Enlightenment tradition.

Although the legacy of Dewey has been creatively developed in the writings of Rorty (1980, 1982) and Bernstein (1983, 1986), both of whom advocate a return to the spirit of Dewey, he has not been without his critics. Santayana described him as a 'devoted spokesman of the spirit of enterprise' and as having a quasi-Hegelian tendency to dissolve the individual into his or her social functions (1951: 247). The Marxist scholar George Novack (1975) has devoted an entire text to a critical appraisal of Dewey's philosophy and influence. Although some of his criticisms have substance, this in no way detracts from Dewey's outstanding contribution as a social philosopher. In an age of disenchantment, nihilism and relativism, perhaps we need a return, Bernstein suggests, to Dewey's humanism, his sanity and courage and his refusal to submit to despair (1986: 272). (For other important discussions of Dewey's philosophy, see Schilpp 1951; Cahn 1977; Thayer 1981: 165–204; Sleeper 1986.)

7.4 Mind, Self and Society

A life-long friend of Dewey, George Herbert Mead (1863–1931) was one of the most creative and important of American philosophers. Both Dewey and Whitehead praised him highly. Whitehead described him as a 'seminal mind of the very first order', while Dewey suggested he had 'the most original mind in philosophy in America of the last generation', and he confessed 'I dislike to think what my own thinking might have been were it not for the seminal ideas which I derived from him' (Reck 1964: 1vii). Yet, aside from the students of pragmatism, Mead has all but been ignored by philosophers. Many texts have been produced on the philosophy of mind, and on Wittgenstein and the 'social construction of mind' which make no mention of Mead, though Mead was suggesting an alternative to Cartesian epistemology while the former writer was still in his positivist phase (but cf. Coulter 1979). The anthropological literature too makes little reference to Mead, or to Dewey for that matter, although, Irving Hallowell was later to suggest a theory of the development of the self that was very similar to that of Mead's. Thus though essentially a philosopher, Mead's major influence has been on social psychology and in the development of a school of sociology known as symbolic interactionism (Blumer 1969).

Mead was born in South Hadley, Massachusetts, where his father was a minister in a Congregational church. His father died when Mead was a teenager. Mead's mother was a well-educated woman who for ten years was president of Mt Holyoke College in Ohio to where the family had moved. A shy and quiet boy, Mead spent his undergraduate years at Oberlin College and there formed a close friendship with Henry Castle, who came from a wealthy family with extensive landholdings and political influence in Hawaii. Mead was later to marry Henry's sister, Helen. Encouraged by his friend, Mead went to Harvard to study philosophy and psychology and, although he met William James and for a while tutored his children, was much more influenced by the lectures of the Hegelian idealist Josiah Royce. Later, with Henry Castle, Mead spent three years in Germany, and became familiar with the writings of Wundt, and had hopes of completing a doctoral thesis in physiological psychology. In 1891, aged twenty-eight and recently married, Mead returned to America, having been offered a teaching post in the philosophy department at the University of Michigan. Dewey was head of the department. They became firm friends and seemed to discuss philosophy with each other almost every day. They had much in common. Both had experienced Hegelian idealism as a liberating force in their early youth and 'both were now searching for a more scientific foundation for philosophy. They saw the need for both a more biologically-oriented and a more socially-oriented base, and both men saw in the work of William James (whose *Principles of Philosophy* had just been published) some important new leads for a science of mind' (Schellenberg 1978: 40).

Soon after the foundation of the University of Chicago Dewey was offered a position there as head of the philosophy department, and in 1894 Mead accompanied him as an assistant professor of philosophy. After some ten years Dewey left to go to Columbia but Mead stayed at Chicago and was still a professor there when he died in 1931 aged sixty-eight. He had taught there for almost forty years, teaching a variety of courses in philosophy and social psychology. During the early days at Chicago he was instrumental, along with Dewey, Edward Ames and Addison Moore, in establishing the famous 'Chicago school of pragmatism', to which William James refers. It was the philosophical counterpart of the functionalist school of psychology associated with Dewey and James R. Angell, and the Chicago school of sociology associated with Albion Small and W. I. Thomas. All these scholars shared a common perspective at Chicago – pragmatist in philosophical orientation, imbued with the evolutionary spirit and with a concern for process, function and activity. Unlike the pragmatism of James and of the British scholar F. C. S. Schiller, whose pragmatism was individualist and subjectivist in tenor and emphasis (Thayer 1981: 232), the Chicago pragmatists stressed the social dimension of human action and were deeply involved in social and political issues. Mead especially was active in social reform circles in Chicago and was a close friend of Jane Addams, the social worker and leading figure in the settlement house movement. Schellenberg has summed up the mood of the Chicago school of pragmatism to which Mead belonged: 'Pioneering in spirit, scientific in method, and reformist in application' (1978: 44; for further discussions of the Chicago school, see Morris 1970; Rucker 1969).

Mead has been described as the 'cosmologist' of the Chicago pragmatists (Morris 1970: 89), for in his later years he seems to have been unconsciously working towards an integrated philosophical system. Between 1910 and 1920 he became especially interested in the implications of Einstein's theory of relativity for a theory of the human subject and came to develop a process philosophy similar to that of A. N. Whitehead. Unfortunately, though recognised among his contemporaries and students as an important scholar via his lectures at Chicago, Mead never published any systematic study during his lifetime and he only published about two dozen major articles (Mead 1964). All of his books were published after his death, mainly consisting of lecture notes put together by his students; four important texts have thus been published; *The Philosophy of the Present* (1932), *Mind Self and Society* (1934), *Movements of Thought in the Nineteenth Century* (1936) and *The Philosophy of the Act* (1938). These notes indicate that a major unfinished system of thought was developing and it is one that still engages the interest of contemporary scholars. (For important studies of Mead's life and work, see Blumer 1969: 61–77; D. L. Miller 1973; Goff 1980; Baldwin 1986.)

We can perhaps present Mead's thought under three headings, focusing our discussion on his seminal study *Mind, Self and Society*.

Social Behaviourism

Both Miller and Baldwin describe Mead as a naturalist and process philosopher, for a scrutiny of his writings reveals that his key method of approach was to organise all topics in terms of process, evolutionary, developmental, interactional and other types of processes. For Mead the temporal dimension cannot be excluded from our conception of reality and like Dewey he was critical of traditional philosophical systems because of their focus on static values that transcend experience. Like Dewey too, he was critical of all dualistic theories, particularly those that implied a bifurcation of the world into mental and physical domains, or into subjective and objective dimensions. As a process philosopher he was critical of the limitations of mechanistic science, but rather than totally rejecting the concept of mechanism he advocated integrating it into a larger theoretical framework that took into account the teleological dimension that was evident in the life-processes and human behaviour. He was unwilling to postulate a life-force or, with Bergson, to deny the possibility of a scientific understanding of organic life or social processes. But a mechanistic approach by itself could not account for the emergence of novelty or the essential characteristics of living organisms. What was needed was a science that combined both mechanism and teleology. Mead stressed that each were postulates and not dogmas, and that each carried distinctive methods and strategies for scientific research. And both could illuminate important aspects of the empirical world. A denial of mechanism leads to an inadequate theory, Mead argued (1936: 268–325; Baldwin 1986: 37–45).

Understandably, like Dewey, Mead felt Darwin's theory of evolution had completely undermined the static world views of the earlier philosophers and mechanistic scientists. Science, therefore, according to the pragmatic doctrine, can only produce provisional truths. Modern science ruled out the idea that any knowledge or truth could be static or absolute. The point of view which comes in with the scientific method 'implies that, so far as our experience is concerned, the world is always different. Each morning we open our eyes upon a different universe. . . . We are advancing constantly into a new universe' (1936: 291). Any scientific theory must, therefore, find a place for an emergent future with its implicated past (1964: 344). This necessarily implied a synthesis of mechanism and process; the two approaches necessary for an adequate understanding of human behaviour.

In rejecting dualistic approaches to the study of the human subject, and the introspective psychology favoured by the advocates of dualism – Mead often had Wundt in mind – Mead adopts a behaviourist standpoint. Behaviourism, he writes, 'is simply an approach to the study of the experience of the individual from the point of view of his conduct, particularly but not exclusively the conduct as it is observable by others' (1934: 2). But Mead differentiates his own point of view from that of J. B. Watson, and Charles Morris (1970), picking up a phrase that Mead had used rather incidentally in his writings, labels Mead's approach 'social behaviourism'. As Mead writes:

Social psychology is behaviouristic in the sense of starting off with an observable activity – the dynamic, on-going social process and the social acts which are its component elements – to be studied and analysed scientifically. But it is not behaviouristic in the sense of ignoring the inner experience of the individual – the inner phase of that process or activity. On the contrary it is particularly concerned with the rise of such experience within the process as a whole. (1934: 7–8)

Watson's behaviourism, it will be recalled, had completely excluded from the analysis 'mind' and all reference to mentalistic concepts in the study of human behaviour. He wished, as Mead writes, to deny the existence of human consciousness altogether (1934: 10). Such a denial, Mead suggests, is misguided, and leads inevitably to obvious absurdity. What Mead wished to do was not to deny the existence of consciousness but rather to explain it, and to explain it in naturalistic, behavioural terms. He writes: 'But though it is impossible to reduce mind or consciousness to purely behaviouristic terms – in the sense of thus explaining it away and denying its existence as such entirely – yet it is not impossible to explain it in these terms and to do so without explaining it away, or without denying its existence as such.' And he continues: 'We may deny its existence as psychical entity without denying its existence in some other sense at all; and if we then conceive it functionally and as a natural rather than a transcendental phenomenon, it becomes possible to deal with it in behaviouristic terms' (1934: 10). How he does this we shall explore in the next section.

Mead thus situated himself in the functionalist tradition of psychology, seeing the human mind not as an entity but as a function. It could be understood, he felt, only in the context of behavioural events – human social activity. Two important points stem from this. One is that, in a way similar to Durkheim, Mead assumes the priority of the social:

The behaviour of an individual can be understood only in terms of the whole social group of which he is a member since his individual acts are involved in larger, social acts which go beyond himself and which implicate the other members of that group. . . . We are not, in social psychology, building up the behaviour of the social group in terms of the behaviour of the separate individuals composing it; rather, we are starting out with a given social whole of complex group activity, into which we analyse [as elements] the behaviour of each of the separate individuals composing it. . . . For social psychology, the whole [society] is prior to the part [the individual], not the part to the whole; and the part is explained in terms of the whole, not the whole in terms of the part or parts. (1934: 6–7)

One could hardly find a better expression of the holistic tradition in sociology.

The second point is that Mead agrees with Dewey in criticising the limitations of stimulus–response theory, seeing this as but a hangover of the old atomistic psychology. Mead thus takes as his basic unit of analysis the concept of social act, which he considers to be a 'dynamic whole' and to consist of four phases, namely, impulse, perception, manipulation (involving physical contact with the world) and consummation. The act he sees as inherently social: 'The objective of the acts is then found in the life-process of the group, not in those of the separate individuals alone' (1934: 7). Unlike the Kantian unity, apperception, the act is neither simply cognitive nor simply individual (Reck 1964: xix, Baldwin 1986: 55–60).

The two points are, of course, intrinsically linked, for the behaviour of an individual can only be understood, Mead argued, as an activity within the social process.

Mind

Mind or consciousness, like the notion of self, was seen by Mead as essentially a social product derived from the social side of human experience. But he considers that there are varying levels of consciousness and awareness, ranging from simple feelings of the lower forms of animal life to the reflective intelligence of humans. A fundamental concept for Mead, denoting the basic unit of social behaviour as well as the historical origin of mind, is the concept of gesture. In his analysis of this concept, Mead drew especial inspiration from the writings of Darwin and Wundt. Darwin's early study, *Expression of the Emotions in Man and Animals*, was important for Mead in that it applied the theory of evolution to 'conscious experience'. Darwin indicated that there was a whole series of acts which called out certain responses – gestures – that do express emotions. But Darwin, Mead suggests, assumed that the emotions were psychological states, states of consciousness that found their expression in gestures, and he did not go beyond this to explore the role of gestures in the 'emergence' of consciousness. This was the important step made by Wundt, who indicated that gestures did not so much function as expressions of inner emotions, but 'were parts of complex acts in which different forms were involved. They became the tools through which other forms responded' (1934: 44). Gestures were thus parts of a social interaction, an 'interplay' functioning to generate responses from other participants. Thus we have the beginnings of a social process where a gesture functions not simply to express emotions, but to 'become the expression of a meaning, an idea'. And, Mead argues, 'when . . . that gesture means this idea behind it and it arouses that idea in the other individual, then we have a significant symbol' (1934: 345). Shaking one's fist in the face of another is an example of such a symbolic gesture. But as an advocate of psychophysical parallelism, Wundt, Mead contends, was unable to grasp that communication is fundamental to the nature of what we call 'mind'. Wundt tends, he felt, to presuppose the existence of minds which are able to communicate. For Mead, then, consciousness of meaning, rooted in gesture, is the essence of mind. But the gesture that was crucial in the development of the human mind was the vocal gesture, which is 'of peculiar importance because it reacts upon the individual who makes it in the same fashion that it reacts upon another' (1964: 243). A vocal gesture, Mead continues, has an importance which no other gesture has; it becomes a significant symbol (gestures which possess meaning), and thus functions as a form of communication, facilitating the adjustment of human individuals to one another within the social process (1934: 75).

Mead therefore concludes that mentality comes in 'when the organism is able to point out meanings to others and to himself. This is the point at which mind appears, or if you like, emerges. What we need to recognise is that we are dealing with the relationship of the organism to the environment, selected by its own sensitivity' (1934: 132). The mechanism that is important in controlling this relationship is that of language communication, and 'out of language emerges the field of mind'. Thus Mead suggests that the human mind must be regarded as arising and developing within the social process, within the empirical matrix of social interactions. 'It is absurd to look at the mind simply from the standpoint of the individual human organism; for although it has its focus there, it is essentially a social phenomenon' (1934: 133). But mind arises in the social process only when that process enters into the experience of anyone of the given individuals involved in that process. Reflexiveness – the turning back of the experience of the individual upon him/herself – is then, Mead suggests, the essential condition within the social process for the development of mind.

Self

The self Mead distinguished clearly from the human organism, although the organism is essential to it, and like the mind it arises in the process of social experience and activity. It is not there at birth; it is something which has a development. Much of human experience does not involve the self, for Mead sees individual selfhood as depending upon reflexiveness – the ability of the subject to be an object to itself. The question arises as to how self-consciousness and the notion of the self arises, and Mead's account largely focuses on this issue. Mead discusses three important facets in the emergence and development of self-reflection. The first is what is involved in children's play activities, for this entails an element of deliberate role-playing on the part of the child. The child plays at being mother or a police officer. The second involves the playing of organised games which, in contrast to normal play, enable the child who plays the game to take on the attitudes and roles of everyone else involved in the game. It involves learning a structure of rules, and, Mead writes, 'children take a great interest in rules. They make rules on the spot in order to help themselves out of difficulties. Part of the enjoyment of the game is to get these rules' (1934: 152). This leads on to a third aspect in the development of the self, the notion of a 'generalised other'. 'The organised community or social group which give to the individual his unity of self may be called "the generalised other". The attitude of the generalised other is the attitude of the whole community' (1934: 154).

Mead makes a distinction between the self that arises in social experience and other forms of subjective experience, such as memory images and the play of imagination, but he thinks it misleading to see this self as a 'more or less isolated and independent entity'. On the contrary, he sees self and self-consciousness as definitely organised about the social individual: 'The process out of which the self arises is a social process which implies interaction of individuals in the group, implies the pre-existent of the group. It implies also certain co-operative activities in which different members of the group are involved' (1934: 164).

Mead was clearly influenced by the writings of Charles Cooley, and his conception of the 'looking glass self', and William James. And in developing their ideas Mead came to make a distinction between two aspects of the self, between the 'me' and the 'I'. It will again be most useful to quote from Mead: 'The "I" is the response of the organism to the attitudes of others; the "me" is the organised set of attitudes of others which one himself assumes. The attitudes of the others constitute the organized "me" and then one reacts toward that as an "I"' (1934: 175).

Mead is eager to stress that there is a dynamic relationship between the two aspects of the self, and to counter the suggestion that during the social process the individual is simply a medium 'taking something that is objective and making it subjective' (1934: 188). The 'I' is thus the innovative and creative aspect of the self, allowing for new patterns of behaviour and to emerge in social action.

Mead saw a dialectical interrelationship existing between society and the human subject. Human society, he wrote, 'could not exist without minds and selves, since all its most characteristic features presuppose the possession of minds and selves by its individual members, but its individual members would not possess minds and selves if these had not arisen within or emerged out of the human social process in its lower stages of development' (1934: 227).

Mead's conception of the human subject was similar in many respects to that of Durkheim's, and thus a complete antithesis to the views of Hobbes, who took a mechanical, nominalistic and thoroughly individualistic view of the human subject and social organisation (Thayer 1981: 232–3). In consequence Mead's social behaviourism has been seen as essentially positivist. Some writers have tended to suggest that he represented an 'over-socialised conception of man' reducing the human subject and human thought to the status of derivations of an aprior existential social reality. Others have considered his conception of 'I' as a residual category, introduced to account for human creative and freedom, but as having no basis in the socialisation process itself (Kolb 1972: 253–61). In an important discussion of these issues Tom Goff (1980) suggests that these criticisms of Mead are not substantiated if a consideration of the broader context of Mead's writing is taken into account. A number of points may be made.

First, Mead places a persistent emphasis on the social as a process rather than as a set of absolute determinants. Like Marx he saw society as a 'form of co-operative activity', not as an entity *sui generis*, and his division of the self into conservative 'me' and creative 'I' aspects indicates an attempt to deny any total sociologism (Goff 1980: 70).

Second, Mead did not imply that the human reflexive capacity that emerges is unlimited or totally free of constraint. Consistent with his desire to avoid idealism, Mead accepted the reality of the objective world, and the need for human subjects to adapt themselves to this world. But Mead felt that humans were not simply creatures of necessity, and that human knowledge, though contingent and functional, gave us some degree of control over our destiny. Moreover, his stress on the fundamental social nature of the self and mind in no way implied a rigid social determination. To the contrary. As David Miller succinctly puts it: 'Mead does not have the problem of explaining why it is that individuals are creative despite the fact that every self has a social component and thinking involves the other. Rather, he shows that it is only because the individual is social that he can be creative' (1973: 148).

In an important sense then, like Marx, Mead is attempting to avoid two extremes; an idealistic stress on human subjectivity and existential freedom on the one hand, and the rigid social determinism of positivists on the other. Goff indeed stresses the affinities between the perspectives of Marx and Mead – their stress on the fundamental sociality of the human subject; their dialectical conception of humans and the social context, which incorporates the experience of both conformity and creativity; their tendency to conceptualise human thought as essentially functional and dynamic; and finally, their conception of truth and knowledge as being neither absolute nor totally relativistic. On this last issue Goff writes: 'Essentially, both theorists argue that thought is essentially a functional process involved in the maintenance of human life and its development. Thus they imply that ideas are to be judged in respect to their adequacy to and within human praxis' (1980: 91).

But Goff also makes some important criticisms of Mead's sociology, particularly his global functionalism and his rather naive appreciation of social structure and of human history, particularly in respect to human conflict. (For further interesting discussions of Mead's philosophy, see Joas 1985.)

7.5 Erving Goffman

The pragmatic tradition, particularly as mediated through Mead, has had an important influence on sociology, particularly in America. Symbolic interactionism, a label used to delineate a relatively distinctive sociological approach, stemming from the Chicago school of sociology – seen as 'an outpost of G. H. Mead' (Rucker 1969: 22) – has been viewed as an important tradition in American sociology. And Mead is seen as having laid the philosophical foundations for this tradition, although the writings of Dewey, Robert Park, Charles Cooley and W. I. Thomas are also considered significant. Never a clearly defined school, and overlapping the theoretical tendencies derived from the writings of Marx and Durkheim, symbolic interactionism has generated several lines of social psychological investigations. Among these areas are role theory; reference group theory, the studies of occupations which were particularly associated with the writing of Everett Hughes, Howard Becker and their associates; labelling theory in social deviance; ethnomethodology and the dramaturgical approach to social interaction. The writings of Erving Goffman exemplify this last approach. Mead's influence was also felt in the development of empirical studies of the self (cf. Mischel 1977; Marsella et al. 1985). Both the Chicago school of sociology and the symbolic interaction approach which developed from it, expressed a central interest in psychological issues and the relationship between personality and social life and culture, in ways that anticipated the culture and personality school in anthropology. W. I. Thomas's classic study *The Polish Peasant in Europe and America* (1927), written with Florian Znaniecki, was centrally concerned with tracing the influence of society and culture on the individual, although Thomas saw the human subject as essentially a product of social interaction (as did Mead) rather than being simply a recipient of cultural traits. In a later generation, at a more general level, Hans Gerth and C. Wright Mills, in their study *Character and Social Structure* (1953), made an ambitious attempt in the pragmatist tradition to integrate psychic phenomena with an analysis of institutions, the concept of role being utilised as a key variable. Their study represents a creative synthesis of the perspectives of Freud, Mead, Dewey, Weber and Marx (Martindale 1961: 369–74; Eldridge 1983: 53–63).

It is beyond the scope of this study to discuss fully the pragmatist tradition in sociology, although many important and key writers have offered thoughtful accounts of the human subject, seen not as a medium but as a social actor within a symbolic interactionist context. There have been several useful accounts of the Chicago school and symbolic interactionism, and to these the reader is referred (C. W. Mills 1966; Blumer 1969; Rock 1979; Lewis and Smith 1980; Bulmer 1984; D. Smith 1988). But there is one scholar whom we can usefully discuss here, taking him as representative of the symbolic interactionist tradition, and that is Erving Goffman.

Although Goffman has had an enormous influence on sociology, and his classic study on *Asylums* (1961) is well known, he has never become a cult figure like the other anti-psychiatrists Foucault and Laing. Nevertheless, in his oblique criticisms of the 'medical model' approach to psychiatric disorders and in his pervasive cultural relativism, he is rightly associated with these writers, as a founder member of the anti-psychiatry school. Surprisingly, he is also little known among anthropologists (Bourguignon (1979), for example, does not mention him), although both his style and his theoretical perspective stand close to the anthropological tradition. In fact, he was a postgraduate student in anthropology and his doctoral thesis was a study of a Shetland Island community. Over the past thirty years he has written a series of books on a variety of topics, all full of stimulating ideas, even though their focus is on micro-sociology (1959, 1967, 1974). It is not my intention to survey here this important corpus; I shall instead focus on his general ideas and his attempt to 'develop a sociological version of the structure of the self' via his seminal study of a mental hospital.

Goffman's approach to cultural life stands firmly within the sociological tradition of symbolic interactionism or what we have referred to as the Chicago school of sociology. This tradition, noted for its social reformist perspective and its empirical studies, some of which have become classics in sociology (e.g. Thomas and Znaniecki 1927; Whyte 1943), largely stemmed from the writings of Thomas and Park who, together with Mead, made a creative synthesis of the perspectives of Simmel, Durkheim and Marx. What emerged was a kind of social behaviourism, focused squarely on the interrelationship between the individual self and the social group or institutional setting. The concept of role was a key variable, and there was a strong assumption that personality was largely determined by social placing. Thus the tradition shared the same assumptions as Durkheim and White, discussed in the last chapter. Important to his tradition was not only its cultural determinism – 'the behaviour of an individual can be understood only in terms of the behaviour of the whole social group' – but the stress that the self was a social product. To quote again from Mead's writings: 'The self is essentially a social structure, and it arises in social experience. . . . The process out of which the self arises is a social process which implies interaction of individuals in the group, implies the pre-existence of the group' (Mead 1934: 135–64).

The self therefore is a kind of process; of social origin, not an isolated and independent entity, and the social group is adjudged to be prior to the individual – as distinct from the organism. But apart from the writings of Cooley and Mead, the Chicago school were not over-concerned with theory; its emphasis was on empirical study, particularly of urban conditions and social deviancy. The writings of Everett Hughes and Howard Becker continued this tradition, developing what came to be described as 'underdog' sociology.

Goffman's study *Asylums* combines an interactionist perspective with the kind of fieldwork approach associated with anthropology. A study of a large Washington mental hospital, made in the late 1950s, Goffman aimed to 'learn about the social world of the hospital inmate, as this world is subjectively experienced by him, believing that every social group develops a world view, a life of their own that becomes meaningful, reasonable and normal once you get close to it'. Goffman therefore attempted a phenomenological study, which largely ignored the view point of the psychiatrist. He suggested that two different kinds of framework were possible in studying the individual within the hospital setting; the psycho-physiological one, centred on stress, and the symbolic interactionist framework which concerned the 'fate of the self'. Goffman took the latter approach, but the study, consisting of four separate essays, moves well beyond any simple description of the inmates' subjective world-view. Goffman in fact is simultaneously engaged in three different theoretical strategies.

1. To suggest that the behaviour of individuals within the hospital is not an expression of their psychotic personalities but to a large degree the outcome of the way they are treated in that institutional setting (Le Vine 1973: 47).
2. To indicate that mental hospitals, as an organisational structure, share much in common with other forms of social organisations. It is a kind of total institution.
3. To explore the way in which individuals manipulate or come to terms with the institutions – the latter, in essence, being taken as a given, ahistorical structure. Goffman thus indicates a behaviourist standpoint that has much in common not only with Szasz and his 'games theory' strategy, but with such anthropologists as Leach and Barth.

The first essay is on the 'Characteristics of Total Institutions', an essay of seminal importance. Drawing on literature from a wide variety of sources, Goffman suggests that there is a common structure underlying many kinds of formal organisations, especially prisons, concentration and prison camps, monasteries and mental hospitals. All these institutions are 'forcing houses for changing persons' and are characterised by the following:

Whereas in ordinary social life, sleep, work and play tend to be distinct, and the individual has some autonomy in moving between these various spheres, in a total institution these aspects of life 'are conducted in the same place and under the same single authority'

(1961: 17). Moreover, daily activities are tightly scheduled, and the institution has an 'encompassing tendency'. Individuals are thus controlled and their activities brought within the scope of a plan and a routine designed and implemented by those in authority.

Secondly, total institutions are characterised by a dualistic social system, there being a 'basic split' between the 'staff', who have freedom of movement outside of the institution, and the 'inmates', who are the 'managed group'. The social distance between the two groups is typically great, and there is little informal contact between them. Each grouping tends to conceive of the other in terms of hostile stereotypes. Goffman notes that there are 'institutional ceremonies', which seems to function, in Durkheimian fashion, as a means of bringing together the two groups in certain periodic rituals. But as the institution is not a community, these collective ceremonies are usually 'pious and flat'. He described, however, the existence of some role differentiations within each category – lower members of staff acting as a buffer or as a channel of communication between the higher staff and the inmates, while certain of the latter group adopt the 'straw boss' role and are not too different in functional and prerogative from the lowest staff level. Often they adopt the manner of the guards or attendants.

Thirdly, in explicitly adopting a theatrical or dramatical perspective – an approach initially explored in his earlier study *The Presentation of Self in Everyday Life* (1959), which utilised the notion of 'role-playing' (cf. my article on this concept (1971)) – Goffman suggests that total institutions undermine and restrict the development and articulations of an independent self-image. Two processes are involved in the weakening of an individual's autonomy. One he describes as the 'process of mortification'. The individual is humiliated, made to express demeaning postures and verbally abused. He or she is stripped of usual clothing, and personal possessions are taken away. The clothing and possessions that are given have a uniform character and the person is thereby defaced, 'stripped of one's identity kit' (1961: 30). A person's self is systematically 'mortified' and within the mental hospital individuals are not even guaranteed their physical integrity, for they may be subjected, against their will, to beatings, shock treatment or even psychosurgery. As the individuals' personal failure is continually stressed and they are subjected to a regimented routine, life in the institution is, Goffman suggests, one of mortification. It contrasts with that of the outside world, where in normal life a person has some command over her or his world–self determination, autonomy and freedom of action (1961: 47). To ensure compliance with institutional rules, a second process is brought into play – the 'privilege system' – in which certain clearly defined rewards and privileges are given in exchange for obediance to the staff in action and spirit. Work locations and sleeping places – specifically the 'ward system' in the mental hospital – are allocated by staff in terms of rewards or punishments. Such allocation is an 'administrative device' for ensuring inmates' co-operation and compliance.

In the second essay, 'The Moral Career of the Mental Patient', described as an 'exercise in the institutional approach to the study of self' (1961: 119), Goffman, applies this perspective specifically to the mental hospital. Thus after experiencing a feeling of betrayal and of being misled by his or her next kin, who tended to stress the positive aspects of hospitalisation (Goffman describes the initial experiences as one of 'abandonment, disloyalty and embitterment'), the patient is stripped of his 'accustomed affirmation, satisfactions and defences' and, subjected to mortifying experiences, 'begins to learn about the limited extent to which a conception of oneself can be sustained' (1961: 137). In these two papers Goffman described the mental hospital in highly negative terms, as a total institution which 'mortifies' and 'degrades' the individual; it is a 'treacherous' setting, which 'assaults' the self. Goffman thus presents a picture of structural determinism where the 'primary' adaptation is the one by the individual to that of the institution. Having experienced a similar 'mortification' myself, I can but concur with Goffman's seminal insights.

But although Goffman seems to suggest that the self is not a property of the person, but rather something that 'dwells' in the pattern of social relationships or social control, he also speaks of the self as being torn away or assaulted by the total institution. He also writes of the mental hospital as a setting where a conception of the self can be sustained only to a limited extent and with difficulty (1961: 137). Thus while stressing cultural constraints and evincing an awareness that the human personality only experiences wellbeing within specific kinds of social interaction, Goffman neither collapses the individual's personality into the collectivity (the individual is not simply a 'microcosm') nor, like other behaviourists, does he expunge the self (or personality or ego) from the analysis. Indeed, self and social identity are key concepts for Goffman. Not surprisingly, his third essay 'The Underlife of a Public Institution' is not concerned with the formal organisation of the mental hospital and with its social constraints, but with how the individual 'makes out', as the subtitle suggests. Goffman is here concerned to delineate the ways in which the inmates of the hospital avoid being completely controlled and coerced by the institution.

Thus having earlier depicted the conditions of the total institution to which the inmate must adapt, Goffman in this essay explores the 'secondary adjustments', the strategies, activities and plays whereby the individual patient gets 'around the organizations assumptions as to what should he do and get and hence what he should be'. Such activities constitute the underlife of the institution.

Although *Asylums* is a study in which Goffman deliberately eschews a psychiatric viewpoint, one reads the text without any clear awareness that the inmates are in fact mental patients. To the contrary, for not only does Goffman have little to say on the psychiatric treatment the patients daily have to confront, but whenever he broaches the issue of mental illness he implies that the patients are not mentally ill. As Goffman writes:

> The student of mental hospital can discover that the craziness or 'sick behaviour' claimed for the mental patient is by and large a product of the claimant's social distance from the situation that the patient is in, and is not primarily a product of mental illness. The researcher can find that he is participating in a community not significantly different from any other he has studied. (1961: 121)

In other words, Goffman is suggesting that psychiatric disorders are simply a function of a lack of understanding on the part of those who do labelling. As in the interpretation of some allegedly 'exotic' culture, a person's behaviour seems strange or bizarre only to the degree that it is not seen as meaningful. In his final essay Goffman goes even further and questions the applicability of the medical model to functional psychoses. He seems to regard mental illness largely as a matter of labelling – a theoretical strategy later developed by other sociologists (Scheff 1966). Moreover, he strongly expresses his misgivings about institutional psychiatry, particularly mental hospitals which, rather than helping, tend to damage the life-chances of the individual. Following Szasz he therefore argues that psychiatric diagnosis is usually ethnocentric and political in nature, and that involuntary hospitalisation 'grotesque'. It involves 'a condition of life that is impoverished and desolate indeed' (1961: 321).

Goffman's study was a hallmark of sociological analysis and its social impact was possibly significant and both radical and beneficial. Criticisms of this study and of his general theory focus on four issues.

First, as Hirst and Woolley (1982: 183–8) stress in their perceptive discussion of the sociologist, Goffman's approach tends to obliterate the fact that many patients in mental hospitals *are* deranged or disturbed or suffering from mental impairment. The latter are not simply the product of labelling or social interaction within the hospital. Yet rather innocently, Goffman, in noting that anthropological understanding will tend to indicate that the inmates are in fact quite normal (as implied in the extract quoted above), actually notes that every ward contains some patients who are quite unable 'to follow the rules of social organization' (1961: 121). Again, he writes that almost all normal people have committed some social act that could get them consigned to an asylum, but the self-destructive acts that he mentions and the person who regarded his legs as not a part of himself can hardly be regarded as 'normal' as the term is generally understood.

Secondly, Goffman has been criticised for taking the institutional structures as given, for ignoring their solid historical context. As with Gouldner's critique (1973) of another symbolic interactionist, Howard Becker, Goffman is accused of an 'empty headed partisanship' which avoids macro-sociological issues. Goffman clearly sides with the mental patient and the stigmatised, but never comes to suggest that there could be an alternative. As Sedgwick (1982: 53) suggests, Goffman assumes in his compassionate work *Stigma* (1963) that stigma is almost a natural fact, that society has to accept some kind of ideal standard for the body and denigrate those who do not measure up to it. In *Asylums* Goffman presents a severe and harsh critique, as we have seen, of the mental hospital as an institution, yet in his conclusions he admits that he could not conceive of a better way of handling patients and, even if such institutions were closed down, the police and the judges, he suggests, would only clamour for new ones (1961: 334). There is a note of despair here, and acceptance of the status quo. S. Cohen and Taylor (1972: 142) also stress Goffman's tendency to emphasise adaptation to the institution rather than resistance.

Thirdly, as with Szasz, criticism can be made of Goffman's dualistic approach, and his rigid separation of two classes of illness; 'medical' and 'mental', the latter being seen not as the product of disease but of social labelling.

Finally, some critics have argued that Goffman fails to differentiate between those total institutions which may be entered voluntarily, like religious institutions and even the military, and those like mental hospitals and prisons in which membership is involuntary (Mouzelis 1971; Hirst and Woolley 1982: 188–9).

Herbert Blumer (1969: 2) has suggested that symbolic interactionism rests on three basic premises: namely that humans act towards the world on the basis of subjective meanings; that such meanings arise out of social interaction; and that these meanings are modified and acted upon by the human subject as a social being. Goffman clearly stands in this tradition, viewing the self and self-interaction as mediating between initiating factors, whether these be biological or social, and human action. Like Mead, Goffman stresses that the human subject is not merely a medium for the operation of determining forces, but an organism with a self. (For further studies of Goffman, see Drew and Wootton 1988.)

-8-

Critical Theory
and Psychoanalysis

This chapter explores the developments within the Hegelian-Marxist tradition, particularly those associated with the Frankfurt school, which attempted to integrate a cultural and a psychological dimension into Marxist theory. The first section outlines the historical background to the school, and the development of the 'critical theory' approach by Adorno and Horkheimer. The following two sections are devoted to the theories of Herbert Marcuse, particularly to his study *Eros and Civilisation*, a seminal synthesis of the theoretical perspectives of Freud and Marx. The final section outlines the more recent work of Jürgen Habermas, whose social thought, though somewhat eclectic, stands in the tradition of critical theory.

8.1 The Frankfurt School

The Frankfurt school is a term that has been used since the 1950s to describe a group of German intellectuals who founded in the early days of the Weimar Republic an Institute of Social Research in Frankfurt specifically devoted to the reaffirmation of Marxist theory. The impetus came in the summer of 1922 when Felix Weil, the socialist son of a wealthy grain merchant, organised a 'Marxist work week', attended by such left-wing scholars as Lukács, Pollock and Wittfogel. Much of the time was devoted to a discussion of Korsch's yet unpublished manuscript *Marxism and Philosophy*. The following year the Institute was established, funded by an endowment from Weil's father, and affiliated to the University of Frankfurt. The first director of the Institute was the Austro-Marxist Carl Grünberg, an economic historian of international repute, and in the early years of the Institute its work had a strong empirical bias. Several important studies were published on political economy. These include Henryk Grossman's *The Law of Accumulation and Collapse in the Capitalist System* (1929), Friedrich Pollock's *Experiments in Economic Planning in the Soviet Union 1917–1927* (1929), and Karl Wittfogel's *Economy and Society in China* (1931). All were written from a Marxist perspective. In its early years under Grünberg the Institute's work had a strong anti-philosophical flavour and little interest in psychological issues. It interpreted historical materialism as a broad interdisciplinary approach which was concerned with explicating the social world. As Grünberg put it: 'The materialist conception of history neither is, nor aims to be, a philosophical system. Its object is not abstraction but the given concrete world in its process of development and change' (Tar 1977: 16–17; Bottomore 1984: 12).

Thus Marxism was both the inspiration and the theoretical basis of the Institute's early programme. But the Institute remained officially independent of party affiliations, although its members were often active in left-wing politics. Pollock, Borkenau, Grossman and Wittfogel were all members of the German Communist Party (KPD). Most had a Jewish middle- or upper-middle-class background.

The founding of the Institute of Social Research had to be set within a specific historical context. After the unexpected success of the Bolshevik revolution in Russia, the subsequent defeat of the revolutions in Germany, Hungary and Italy had created a serious dilemma for left-wing intellectuals in Western Europe. The Marxists of the Second International had tended to see socialism as an inevitable outcome of the development of capitalism, but increasingly the German Democratic Party (SPD) adopted reformist tendencies and thus became a 'sorry spectacle to those who still maintained the purity of Marxist theory' (Jay 1973: 4). On the other hand, the 'betrayal' of the revolution and the expansion of centralised control and censorship under Stalin created uncertainty and disillusion among Marxist intellectuals and there emerged an increasingly critical view of the development of society and the state in the Soviet Union. The tendency of the KPD to follow a rigidly Bolshevik line only attenuated the dilemma of the left-wing intellectuals. Thus during the 1920s a revival of Marxism took place which entailed a searching re-examination of the central tenets of Marxist theory. Three scholars are of particular importance in the formation of a movement that came to be known as 'Western Marxism' (which we have discussed earlier) – Gramsci, Lukács and Korsch. Both Lukács and Korsch are claimed to have rediscovered the philosophical (Hegelian) and the humanist dimensions of Marx's thought, and both had an important influence on the Frankfurt school. Indeed the Frankfurt school theorists formed a significant part of the Western Marxist tradition.

After Grünberg's retirement and an interim period when Pollock was director, Max Horkheimer (1895–1973) took over as director of the Institute in January 1931. This led to a noticeable shift of emphasis in the work of the Institute; more towards philosophy and psychology and away from the focus on history and economics. But in response to the impression given by Anderson (1976: 32), this was more a shift of emphasis than a radical reorientation from historical materialism to social philosophy. As David Held writes of the Frankfurt school: 'It is wrong to characterise their work as simply replacing Marxist political economy with general concerns about social philosophy, culture, and social psychology. Neumann, Pollock and more recently Habermas, have all written extensively on the economy, the polity and their relations' (1980: 25).

Max Horkheimer came from a Jewish bourgeois family and was estranged at an early age from his authoritarian father. Appalled at the working conditions in his father's factory, he became a socialist, and during his student days in Munich with his friend Pollock, witnessed the short-lived Bavarian revolution. His earliest political sympathies were with Rosa Luxemburg, agreeing with her criticism of Bolshevik centralism, but he never joined the KPD. But as Tar writes, a protest against human suffering and social injustice, coupled with a metaphysical yearning for a more perfect world, were permanent themes in Horkheimer's thinking throughout his life (1977: 18–19). He studied at Frankfurt University under the neo-Kantian philosopher Hans Cornelius, and later at Freiburg with Husserl and Heidegger. His main interests were in psychology and philosophy, and he had a life-long preoccupation with Schopenhauer, whose writings he greatly esteemed. After serving in the army in 1916, Horkheimer became a pacifist. When he became director of the Institute he was only thirty-five years old, but quickly gathered around him a diverse group of scholars, many of whom were later to establish themselves as prominent intellectuals. Fromm, Marcuse and Franz Neumann joined the Institute, while Pollock and Leo Lowenthal, both of whom had been members since the 1920s, took on more prominent positions. Adorno, a close friend of Horkheimer's, a talented musician and philosopher, and who taught at Frankfurt University, was informally attached to the Institute. Although drawing together a diversity of different talents whose political and philosophical outlooks were often divergent, the Frankfurt school's thought, as Jay suggests, had an 'essential coherence' and it basically reflected the combined perspectives of Horkheimer and Adorno. Between them, Kolakowski writes, they may be regarded as the 'embodiment' of the Frankfurt school (1978: 344). Likewise, Tar intimates that the Frankfurt school of philosophy and sociology is 'identical' with the work of Horkheimer and Adorno by virtue of their publication record and their institutional affiliation, which lasted over three decades (1977: 8).

With the coming to power of the Nazis in 1933, the future of an avowedly Marxist institution staffed by largely Jewish intellectuals was hardly promising. After an initial move to Geneva, inevitable in the circumstances, the Institute was transferred to Columbia University in New York (1935). It was there, in exile, that leading members of the Frankfurt school under Horkheimer's direction, began to elaborate and develop their theoretical ideas and to formulate a distinctive school of Marxism known as 'critical theory'. Its principal architects were Horkheimer, Adorno and Marcuse. The heyday of the Institute was from 1933 to 1944, coinciding with the prominence of fascism, and during this period important empirical studies into the psychology of authority and on the social origins of fascism were published. In spite of this the Institute remained relatively isolated from American academic life and had relatively little influence on American sociology. By the time the Institute returned to Frankfurt in 1950, the principal ideas of critical theory had been clearly set out in a number of important texts; these include Marcuse's *Reason and Revolution* (1941), Horkheimer's *Eclipse of Reason* (1947) and the joint work of Horkheimer and Adorno, *Dialectic of Enlightenment* (1944). But it was not until the 1960s, with the growth of the radical student movement, that the Frankfurt school and critical theory came fully into the limelight and began to have an intellectual and political influence, especially due to the work of Marcuse. English translations of the studies of Adorno and Horkheimer began to appear. As Paul Connerton suggests: 'If critical theory was a creation of the early thirties, it was also a discovery of the late sixties' (1976). It reached the peak of its influence around 1970, but this influence soon declined and, with the death of Adorno in 1969 and Horkheimer four years later, the Frankfurt school as such ceased to exist. But its influence is still evident in the work of such recent scholars as Schmidt, Habermas and Wellmer, who are often referred to as the second generation of critical theorists.

The work of the Frankfurt school covered so many diverse fields that even an outline of these is quite beyond the scope of the present study. I shall therefore restrict myself to surveying some of the central themes that emerge in Horkheimer's account of critical theory, and in subsequent sections explore in more detail the work of two scholars associated with the Institute who have been particularly concerned with psychological issues, namely, Marcuse and Habermas.

Horkheimer's critical theory was formulated in a series of essays written in German, and published in the *Zeitschrift für Sozialforschung* (Journal for Social Research) between 1933 and 1940. One of these, entitled 'Traditional and Critical Theory' (1937), had a programmatic quality, and is often referred to as the 'manifesto' of critical theory. 'Traditional' theory in the social sciences, Horkheimer suggests, begins with Descartes' outline of the scientific method, which modelled itself on mathematical and deductive reasoning, and saw theory as the discovery of general laws whether the approach taken is an empirical one, focused on the investigation of facts and theories based on inductive rules, or whether, as with Husserl and the phenomenologists, theory is defined as a closed system and 'essential laws' discovered independently of empirical results, makes little difference, for the standpoint of both approaches is essentially the same. The traditional conception of theory models itself on that of the natural sciences, seen as an activity divorced from other aspects of human life, and is 'much enamoured of the methods of exact formulation and, in particular, of mathematical procedures'. This approach, whether rationalist or empiricist in style, is essentially asocial and ahistorical and involves a separation of the human subject and knowledge from the world under observation. But, Horkheimer suggests:

> The world which is given to the individual and which he must accept and take into account is in its present and continuing form a product of the activity of society as a whole. It is not only in clothing and appearance, in outward form and emotional make-up that men are the product of history. Even the way they see and hear is inseparable from the social life processes as it has evolved over the millenia. The facts which our senses present to us are socially preformed in two ways; through the historical character of the object perceived, and through the historical character of the perceiving organ. Both are not simply natural; they are shaped by human activity. (1976 (1937): 213)

In traditional theory, Horkheimer argues, the genesis of particular objective facts and the practical application of the conceptual systems by which it grasps the facts are both taken to be external to the theoretical thinking itself. This alienation finds its expression in the separation of value and research, knowledge and action and other polarities. Horkheimer accepts the Marxist premise that there will always be something extrinsic to humans' intellectual and material activity; namely nature as a totality, but the social scientific tendency to regard social reality and its product as extrinsic to the scientist is 'a sign of contemptible weakness'. Critical thinking is an effort to transcend the tensions and abolish these oppositions – but not by resort to some supra-historical external category with regard to the opposition between the individual and society. Horkheimer suggests that two tendencies are predominant. One is the bourgeois tendency, expressed by Descartes and Kant, to see the ego as an autonomous entity. This kind of thinking is essentially abstract and 'its principle is an individuality which inflatedly believes itself to be the ground of the world'. The other is to suggest that the individual is simply 'the unproblematic expression of an already constituted society'. Critical thinking, Horkheimer writes, is opposed to both tendencies:

> Critical thinking is the function neither of the isolated individual nor of a sum-total of individuals. Its subject is rather a definite individual in his real relation to other individuals and groups, in his conflict with a particular class and, finally, in the resultant web of relationships with the social totality and with nature. The subject is no mathematical point like the ego of bourgeois philosophy; his activity is the construction of the social present. (1976: 221)

Critical theory, therefore, had for its object humans as producers of their own historical way of life in its totality. Horkheimer does not deny the importance of the empirical sciences but the aim of theory should not be simply to increase knowledge but rather 'its goal is man's emancipation from slavery' (1976: 224).

Horkheimer explicitly saw critical theory as the heir to German idealism, and Kant and Hegel form an important background to his thought. The very concept of critique stems from the Enlightenment and has two essential meanings, as Connerton writes, both of which have their origin in German idealist philosophy. The first meaning, central to Kant, is epistemological and denotes reflection on the *conditions* of possible knowledge. Marx's theory of ideology and Freud's psychoanalytic theory are expressions of this form of critique. The second meaning is more political and denotes reflection on a system of *constraints* which are humanly produced; 'distorting pressures to which individuals or a group of individuals, or the human race as a whole, succumb in their process of self formation' (1976: 18). Critique in this sense has its roots in Hegel. Horkheimer and the Frankfurt school utilised both these senses of critique, offering a series of critiques on other thinkers and philosophical traditions – particularly positivism and existentialism – as well as of contemporary capitalism and its restrictions on the development of human freedom and human happiness. It was a 'gadfly of other systems'. Critical theory offered a dialectical critique of ideology, suggesting that all thought must be located in its historical context and specifically linked with human interests, while at the same time, attempting to avoid, like Hegel, a collapse into relativism or scepticism.

In an important sense, as Jay (1973) suggests, Horkheimer and the Frankfurt school in their basic premises on critical theory were returning to the concerns of the Left-Hegelians of the 1840s, and Marx, it must be remembered, was one of the Left-Hegelians. They were thus concerned with the dialectical method devised by Hegel, and like Marx sought to turn it in a materialist direction. They were interested also in integrating philosophy and social analysis, and exploring the possibilities of transforming the social order through human praxis (1973: 42).

Following the tradition of Hegel, Horkheimer (like Marx, Dewey and Lukács) is concerned above all to formulate an approach that is dialectical and materialist, and which is neither caught up in dualisms, nor reductionist in any sense. This approach can perhaps best be expressed by briefly outlining Horkheimer's criticisms of other theoretical positions: empiricism, positivism, scientism, vulgar materialism, idealism, phenomenology and existentialism.

As indicated earlier, Horkheimer was critical of the empiricist theory of knowledge. The influence of Kant not only made him sensitive to the active elements in cognition, but he also stressed that the objects of perception were themselves products of human social interaction. Echoing Marx's critique of Feuerbach he emphasises that nature itself has an historical element, in that it is both actively worked upon by humans, and conceived of differently at different times. The copy theory of perception (truth) advocated by many orthodox Marxists is a limited perspective for it ignores the subjective and historical character of perception and knowledge. In a sense there are no such things as 'facts'; perception cannot be isolated from its social genesis, both it and its object are a social and historical product (Jay 1973: 53; Kolakowski 1978: 352; see Collier (1985) for a defence of the orthodox Marxist 'objectivist' theory of truth, although Collier offers a non-empiricist version). This leads Horkheimer to criticise both positivism and vulgar materialism. Although early empiricists like Locke and Hume and those of the Enlightenment, in stressing perceptual experience as a source of knowledge, had a critical import in undermining the prevailing social order, modern logical positivism, Horkheimer contended, was quite different. It made a 'fetish of facts', ignored the active element in cognition and thus represented a reification of the existing social world. In its extreme form the subject disappears altogether. Positivism in its separation of 'facts' and 'values' essentially serves, Horkheimer argued, the status quo, offering a 'mystique of the prevailing reality' (Jay 1973: 63). In elevating science to the only valid form of knowledge, the positivists engage in unacceptable 'scientism', he suggests. He later came to identify positivism with a new form of domination, 'technocratic domination' which, although it had its roots in an earlier period, essentially emerged with the rise of capitalism, and was intrinsically linked with the Enlightenment. In the classic study *Dialectic of Enlightenment* (1973), co-authored with Adorno, Horkheimer suggests that the radical distinction between thought and reality, the disenchantment of the world, the attempt to reduce knowledge to numbers, the equation of knowledge with power – all expressed in the mechanistic philosophy of Bacon and Descartes, and still evident in modern positivistic science – implied an ethic of domination towards the natural world. Myth, they write, 'turns into Enlightenment, and nature into mere objectivity. Men pay for the increase of their power with alienation from that over which they exercise their power. Enlightenment behaves towards things as a dictator towards men. He knows them in so far as he can manipulate them' (1973: 9). And elsewhere he writes: 'The history of man's efforts to subjugate nature is also the history of man's subjugation by man. The development of the concept of the ego reflects this twofold history' (1974: 105).

Thus Horkheimer and Adorno argued that the Enlightenment dialectic, the movement of mechanistic philosophy which aimed to conquer and to emancipate reason from the shackles of religion and mythology, had by its own logic, turned into its opposite: 'It has created a positivist, pragmatic, utilitarian ideology and, by reducing the world to its purely quantitative aspects, had annihilated meaning, barbarized the arts and sciences and increasingly subjected mankind to commodity fetishism' (Kolakowski 1978: 373). The Enlightenment, instrumental reason, thus came to serve capital, to invoke a 'mastery of nature' that was totalitarian in its effects, culminating in anti-Semitism and fascism. Unlike liberal writers such as Hayek, Horkheimer saw fascism as the inevitable outcome of a developmental crisis within the capitalist system itself, and as a logical development of liberal ideology. Horkheimer agreed with the views expressed in the classic study *Behemoth* (Neumann 1944), that fascism represented the political form of monopoly capitalism. Horkheimer could therefore write: 'He who does not wish to speak of capitalism should be silent about fascism' (Held 1980: 52).

There have been many critical discussions of Horkheimer's critique of the Enlightenment and of positivism. Kolakowski suggests that Adorno and Horkheimer's concept of Enlightenment is a fanciful, unhistorical hybrid composed of everything they dislike, thus missing the gist of their critique and the problems of mechanistic science and positivism, which we have discussed in chapter 1. But some of the problems of Horkheimer's critique are nevertheless worth mentioning briefly. First, it implies a renunciation of modern science and technology and thus has affinities to the anti-science sentiments of early German idealist philosophers. Secondly, although Horkheimer stresses the importance of situating theory in a materialist and historical context, Enlightenment philosophy, as he outlines it, is treated in idealist fashion and is not related to socioeconomic factors. Thirdly, domination ceases to be regarded as domination by a particular class in any specific sense, but is focused on human domination over nature. Thus class struggle tends to have a marginal importance for Horkheimer. (For further discussions of Horkheimer's critique of positivism, see Tar 1977: 87–102; Bottomore 1984: 28–38.)

In advocating a dialectical materialist approach, Horkheimer, like Adorno, strongly argued that there could be no immutable or absolute truths. The search for 'identity' that is some kind of primordial being or substance, to which all others are ultimately reducible, is a forlorn search, even though undertaken by diverse philosophical schools – positivism, idealism, phenomenology, existentialism. As Horkheimer argued:

> There is no complete picture of reality, neither according to essence or appearance. Even the very idea of a subject who can grasp all is a

delusion. Moreover neither does the overcoming of the onesidedness of abstract concepts lead in the art of dialectical constructs, as Hegel believes, to absolute truth. It always occurs in the thought of particular historical men. (quoted in Held 1980: 179)

This led Horkheimer to reject both idealism and philosophical or monistic materialism. True materialism, he argued, did not give absolute or ontological primacy to matter, as Haeckel and many orthodox Marxists had tended to do. The tendency of vulgar Marxists to elevate materialism to a theory of knowledge and to assume the eternal primacy of the economic base was undialectical and, Horkheimer implied, encouraged the urge to dominate the natural world (Jay 1973: 53). But Horkheimer was equally critical of idealism, for though accepting Hegel's dialectical method, he rejected, like Marx, the fundamental tenet of Hegel's philosophy, namely the assumption that all knowledge is the self-knowledge of the absolute of eternal subject; in other words, 'that an identity exists between subject and object, mind and matter, based on the ultimate primacy of the absolute subject' (Jay 1973: 47). Horkheimer thus accepted Hegel's emphasis on historical process and his critical awareness that all thought is empirical and historically situated, but argued that a materialist dialectic is an 'unconducted' dialectic, that there is an irreducible tension between concept and object, between knowledge and the world as experienced.

But Horkheimer is alive to the more positive aspects of idealist philosophy, particularly its stress on the active element in cognition, and its concern for human subjectivity. The reaction against rationalism and the critiques of mechanistic materialism expressed at the end of the nineteenth century by the advocates of *Lebensphilosophie* (philosophy of life) such as Dilthey, Nietzsche and Bergson, were not simply anti-rationalist protests; they also expressed a 'protest against the fettering of individual life under the increasing concentration of capital' (Slater 1977: 49).

Horkheimer, unlike other Marxists, saw the value of these critiques of positivism and he gave qualified praise to Dilthey and Nietzsche in stressing human subjectivity and the importance of individual psychology for an understanding of history. Bottomore had drawn attention to the fact that a preoccupation with the fate of the individual in present-day capitalist society was a central theme in the thought of the Frankfurt school and this they shared with the life philosophers and with Max Weber. Horkheimer was committed to the value of individuality and he saw modern capitalism with its emphasis on planning and its centralising mechanisms as inhibiting the autonomy of the individual, particularly human spontaneity (1974: 143). But as Jay outlines, Horkheimer made three major criticisms of the kind of existentialist philosophy espoused by Dilthey, Bergson and Nietzsche.

First, although these writers were essentially correct in attempting to rescue the individual from the threats of modern society, they had gone too far in emphasising subjectivity and inwardness. They had thus undervalued the social dimension and the importance of activity in the historical world. As Horkheimer wrote:

> The absolutely isolated individual has always been an illusion. The most esteemed personal qualities such as independence, will to freedom, sympathy and the sense of justice, are social as well as individual virtues. The fully developed individual is the consummation of a fully developed society. (1974: 135)

Secondly, the life-philosophers tended to neglect the material dimensions of reality. And finally, and most importantly, 'in criticising the degeneration of bourgeois rationalism into its abstract and formal aspects, they sometimes overstated their case and seemed to be rejecting reason itself' (1973: 51).

Horkheimer was particularly critical of Bergson's advocacy of intuition, which he felt failed to come to terms with the inherent contradictions in human life.

Although the Frankfurt school's philosophical outlook has been described as one suffused with a 'defence of subjectivity', it is important to note that this subjectivity for Horkheimer could only be expressed in a communal context. As noted earlier, he constantly challenged the reification of the individual and society as polar opposites. But Horkheimer was critical of the 'subjectivism' expressed by existentialists and phenomenologists (which we shall discuss in the next chapter), and these criticisms were later developed by Adorno and Marcuse in important critiques. Adorno's study *The Jargon of Authenticity* (1973) is devoted to a critical examination of German existentialism, particularly the work of Jaspers and Heidegger. Adorno essentially argues that existentialist philosophy lacks any real analysis of the social and historical context of reification and by alluding to freedom and authenticity in an abstract way, actually sanctions the status quo by distracting people from the real causes of their slavery.

As earlier indicated, Horkheimer's understanding of the human subject and human knowledge indicated an opposition to rigid dualisms and to reductive analyses, whether of a materialist or an idealist kind. Neither matter nor spirit nor subjectivity has ontological primacy. Kolakowski sums up Horkheimer's essential thought as follows:

> The subjectivity of the individual cannot be fully described in social categories, and resolved into social causes, nor can society be described in psychological terms; the subject is not absolutely prior, nor is it a mere derivative of the object; neither the base nor the superstructure is manifestly primary; phenomenon and essence are not presented independently of each other; praxis cannot absorb theory, nor vice versa; in all these cases we have to do with mutual interaction. (1978: 346)

All this essentially expresses the philosophical viewpoints of Hegel and Marx. Truth for Horkheimer, therefore, is neither something absolute (objectivism) nor relative (subjective or purely cultural). The dichotomy between absolutism and relativism is in fact a false one, for each historical period has its own truth. If all knowledge is located in a social and historical context, and cognitive practices are to be understood by their relation to praxis, the question inevitably arises as to how we are to demarcate valid and true knowledge. Horkheimer seems to suggest that what is true is whatever fosters change in the direction of a rational society. As he writes: 'The value of a theory is not decided alone by the formal criteria of truth . . . the value of a theory is decided by its connection with the tasks which in the particular historical moment are taken up by progressive special forces' (Held 1980: 192).

The ambiguous nature of this criterion has been stressed by both Held and Kolakowski (1978: 356), but the important point is that it deviates markedly from the classical Marxist position in not seeing the proletariat as the agent of progressive change. Believing that the proletariat had been politically integrated into the modern capitalist system, Horkheimer and the critical theorists rejected the historical role of the proletariat as the primary agent of revolutionary change. There is thus some truth in Kolakowski's contention that the basic principles of critical theory are those of Lukács's Marxism but without the proletariat (1978: 355).

Although reason and praxis are the key concepts of critical theory, the Frankfurt school, particularly as reflected in the work of Adorno and Horkheimer, became increasingly divorced from economic issues and political practice. The crucial nexus between theory and praxis, as Phil Slater outlines, became progressively lost

(1977: 87). And towards the end of his life Horkheimer ceased to be a critical theorist and he adopted a religious outlook and more conservative politics.

Orthodox Marxism generally felt that Marx and Engels' outline of historical materialism was basically self-sufficient theoretically and did not need to be supplemented by a psychology derived from bourgeois science – although in the Soviet Union Pavlovian behaviourism was for a while considered a respectable supplement in Marxist theory. Marxism was generally antipathetic to Freudian theory, given its psychological and individualistic basis, and its pessimistic credo. Reich's early attempts to integrate psychoanalytic theory into Marxism met with ridicule and he was eventually, ousted from the Communist Party. The attempt made by Horkheimer and the critical theorists to introduce psychoanalysis into Marxism, therefore, was at the time 'a bold and unconventional step' (Jay 1973: 87). Horkheimer, in an early article in *History and Psychology* (1932), had argued for the need of a psychological supplement to Marxist theory, but it was in the work of Fromm and Marcuse that this integration was most cogently explored, and it is to Marcuse that we may now turn. (Besides the excellent studies by Jay (1973), Slater (1977) and Held (1980) cited earlier, other useful discussions of Horkheimer, Adorno and the Frankfurt school are Schroyer 1973; Therborn 1978; Rose 1978; and Buck-Morss 1977.)

8.2 Hegelian Marxism

By the 1940s it appeared that psychoanalysis had lost, as Robinson (1970: 114) writes, its 'shocking novelty', and had become incorporated, in various ways, into the European and American intellectual community. There was a general consensus that Freudian theory was essentially conservative in nature, with affinities to the Hobbesian tradition (cf. Rieff 1959). Herbert Marcuse's study *Eros and Civilisation*, published in 1955, was an original and important attempt to reassert the 'radical core' of Freudian theory, to insist that there was a 'hidden trend' in psychoanalysis that was liberating and critical.

Herbert Marcuse (1898–1979), like many critical theorists, was born in secure and comfortable circumstances, his father being a successful Jewish businessman. After studies at Berlin and Freiburg universities, where he came under the influence of two important phenomenologists, Husserl and Heidegger, Marcuse came in the early 1930s to join the Frankfurt school as its 'resident expert in philosophy and political theory' (Robinson 1970: 117). From his earliest years Marcuse was essentially interested in philosophical issues, and prior to joining the Frankfurt Institute made a deep study of the writings of Marx, Schiller and Hegel, his first major published work being on Hegel's ontology (1932). Although at the end of the First World War, at the age of twenty, Marcuse was politically active in the revolutionary movement, and in his sixties suddenly found himself hailed as the intellectual 'guru' of the New Left, in essence he was, like Fromm, temperamentally unsuited to the role of political activist. He was first and foremost a critical philosopher and theoretician, and although his writings are dense, allusive and academic, they are not as elitist and dogmatic as some of his critics hold (MacIntyre 1970: 17).

It is beyond the scope of the present study to discuss the social and political theory of this very important scholar, who has already been subject to a number of critical reviews (Lipshires 1974; Geoghegan 1981; Katz 1982; S. Kellner 1984; Pippin et al. 1988). I shall instead focus my discussion on his classic 'philosophical inquiry into Freud' – *Eros and Civilisation*. But before doing so, some remarks may be made on Marcuse's general theory.

Like Fromm and other members of the Frankfurt school, Marcuse advocated a humanistic interpretation of Marx, an Hegelian Marxism; a variant of the radical humanist tradition which Fromm (1962) outlines. Such an approach accepted some of the essential premises, noted above, motifs that essentially stem from Hegel. First, there was an attempt to overcome the traditional dichotomies of consciousness and nature, body and mind, fact and value, that were intrinsic to the dualistic philosophies of Descartes, Kant and Hume.

This implied, secondly, the need for an approach that would avoid the pitfalls of an uncritical empiricism or a narrowly defined instrumental rationality on the one hand, and a religious or idealist metaphysic on the other.

Thirdly, accepting an interpretation of Hegel that the unity of reason and reality was a human and historical project reflecting human potentialities (rather than the depiction of an already existing social order as rational), Marcuse came to stress the critical or negative aspect of Hegel's philosophy. For Marcuse, the essential function of philosophy was the criticism of existing culture in the light of reason, which, following Hegel, is given an almost transcendental quality.

Fourthly, this implied the acceptance of a distinction between things as they appear to be and the true nature of things – reality as a potentiality. Thus Marcuse was to pen some incisive critiques of empiricism, phenomenology, linguistic philosophy, positivism and cultural relativism (1941: 16–28, 340–59; 1968: 43–87). As Robinson puts it: 'If experience and custom were taken to be the sole guides to truth, then, according to Marcuse, man was robbed of the one faculty – reason – which enabled him to act in accordance with ideas and principles that transcended the established order' (1970: 137). Marcuse himself put it more concisely: 'To Hegel the facts in themselves possess no authority. Everything that is given has to be justified before reason' (1941: 27).

These critiques have substance, and are more than mere assertion. MacIntyre (1970: 35) ridicules this concept of negation; quoting Marcuse: 'Every fact is more than a mere fact; it is a negation and restriction of real possibilities. Wage labour is a fact, but at the same time it is a restraint on free work that might satisfy humans' needs.'

Marcuse is indicating here the exploitative nature of wage labour inherent in the capitalist system, and the 'fact' that this does not involve a fee and equal exchange, nor allow for free human creativity. MacIntyre trivialises the concept with the suggestion that when it is raining it is a negation of when it is not! The reason for the negation is not simply negation but related to Marx's concept of 'surplus value', which he (and Marcuse) inherited from the classical economists.

Fifthly, and stemming from this, Marcuse argued, following Hegel, that the realisation of reason in the world was not a fact, but rather a task. History, Hegel felt, had reached a stage at which the possibilities for realising human freedom and universal well-being were at hand, and such freedom 'presupposes the reality of reason'. People could be free to develop their potentialities only in a society based on reason, and such a society would dissolve the oppositions between the individual and society, and humans and nature. Whether or not this is considered utopian is a matter of opinion; Hegel, Marx and Marcuse clearly felt it was not; although there is certainly some truth in MacIntyre's and Kolakowski's assertion that Marcuse is something of a Left-Hegelian.

Finally, Marcuse came to stress the salience of Hegel's dialectical approach to reality. MacIntyre's (1970: 76–7) criticisms of Marcuse in this context, rather than demonstrating the absurdity of dialectics, and Marcuse's misunderstanding of traditional logic, only tend to indicate MacIntyre's own failure to understand both Marcuse and Hegel. Not only does ordinary language presuppose the laws of logic, but so does dialectical thinking. (See Cornforth 1968: 35; Novack 1971; and Stace 1955: 95 on this issue.)

Such in brief were the main philosophical premises which Marcuse adopted from his reading of Hegel, and which in a sense he shared with Reich and Fromm. They embodied an approach to society quite different from the empirical tradition of anthropology and the social sciences generally.

It was natural, however, that Marcuse should come to defend the critical integrity of Hegel, who had, with some justification, been heralded as an apologist for the Prussian state, and in essence a reactionary thinker. Hegel had even been accused of being a precursor of fascism. Marcuse in *Reason and Revolution* (1941), sought to re-establish Hegel's progressive credentials, arguing that although his political credo and personal life were conservative (like Freud), his philosophical concepts were critical and progressive. Hegel's rational theory of the state virtually precluded any political system that did not embody the freedom of the individual, and was a far cry from the 'oganicist' and irrational theory of the state espoused by the Fascists. Moreover, Hegel's conception of the rationalisation of the social reality implied the notion of transformation, the transcending of the existing (contradictory) social order. The key concepts which Marcuse felt were central to both Hegel and Marx, and crucial to the understanding and critique of capitalism, were those of labour and alienation. Indeed, he suggested that the originality and importance of Marx was that he translated or transformed Hegel's philosophical categories into sociological concepts. As with Marx, Marcuse held that labour (*Arbeit*) was humankind's means of realising its essence. Labour was humans' essence or nature, and far from being simply economic activity, labour was 'existential activity', 'free conscious activity', that not only sustained life but allowed for the development of his or her 'universal nature'. When Marx wrote that 'the outstanding achievement of Hegel's phenomenology is that Hegel grasps the self creation of man as a process, that he therefore grasps the nature of labour, and conceives of objective man, as the result of his own labour' (Bottomore 1979: 119), he anticipates the kind of interpretation that Marcuse adopted. Such a concept of human essence is a norm throughout Marx's writings, and Marcuse, accepting a humanistic interpretation of Marx, stressed that there was a basic continuity between the early and late Marx (Lefebvre 1968: 25–58, for a similar perspective). Thus Marcuse came to argue, following Marx, that labour in capitalist society is alienated, for individuals are not able to express or realise their essence through labour. Both these concepts are empirical and normative, and as Geoghegan rightly states, the concept of human essence is not only clearly evident in the writings of both Marx and Marcuse, but is a 'desideratum of any radical social theory' (1981: 16). In making human labour a fundamental concept in his social theory Marcuse, I think, is much closer to the heritage of Marx than either Reich or Fromm.

8.3 Eros and Civilisation

Let us now turn to *Eros and Civilisation*, a work, as Jay described it, 'of great complexity and richness' (1973: 107). Unlike the academic traditions of both anthropology and sociology, which tended to ignore or were hostile to psychoanalytic writings, the Frankfurt school, under Horkheimer's direction, was receptive to Freudian thought. The reasons for this, as Katz indicated, were practical, namely the need to supplement Marxist theory 'by providing it with an access to the depth dimension of the individual psyche. The pressing task had been to interpret the events of the 1930's. Why had the "revolutionary class" been largely reduced to acquiescence or even complicity? How could the potency of mass propaganda and crude ideologies be explained?' (1982: 146). The critical theorists turned to Freud, then a bold and unconventional move, for Freud was looked upon by most Marxists and radicals as an arch-conservative. As a practising psychoanalyst, Erich Fromm was the prime instigator of this 'unnatural marriage' of Freud and Marx. In these pre-war years Marcuse was not especially interested in psychoanalysis. During the 1940s, however, when he was employed by the United States government and published few academic papers, he became more involved in Freudian theory and began to read Freud extensively. The culmination was the study *Eros and Civilisation*. The pattern of interpretation exactly parallels his study of Hegel, published fourteen years earlier, for like Hegel Marcuse sought to vindicate Freud's social theory. His aim, as indicated, was to suggest that beneath Freud's pessimism and apparently conservative thesis, there was an underlying critical tendency. As MacIntyre suggests, it is something of a paradox that Marcuse should turn to a highly conservative thinker like Freud in order to explore the reasons why the working class had failed to develop a radical political consciousness. This, orthodox Marxism suggested, would emerge historically with the development of capitalism (1970: 42–3). But Marcuse also, at that period, shared another concern, namely the degeneration of the Soviet Union into a repressive form of state socialism (an issue that was the subject of another important study (1958)), and what he felt were the growing repressive tendencies in the Western democracies themselves.

As he wrote in the epilogue to *Reason and Revolution* (1941): 'The defeat of fascism has not arrested the trend towards totalitarianism. Freedom is on the retreat in the realm of thought as well as in that of society. Neither the Hegelian nor the Marxian idea of reason have come closer to realization.'

Thus it was that he turned to Freud more than a decade after Reich and Fromm. He too felt that the collapse of revolutionary hopes could not be totally explained by recourse to the writings of Marx and Engels, which, though fundamentally sound, lacked a psychological dimension (Geoghegan 1981: 43; King 1972: 116–56).

But interestingly, Marcuse felt no urge to follow in the footsteps of Fromm, although he applauded and approved of his earlier essays on psychoanalysis (1970). Indeed, he argued that Fromm, along with the other neo-Freudians, had failed to grasp the critical nature of Freud's basic concepts. Marcuse, in a well-known critique (later published as an epilogue to *Eros and Civilisation*, but, in essence, as Robinson notes, a 'prologue' to the study), expressed his misgivings with cogency and incisiveness. He acknowledges Reich's attempt to develop the critical social theory implicit in Freud and his emphasis on the degree of sexual repression which is enforced in the interests of domination and exploitation. But Marcuse felt that Reich's notion of sexual liberation as a panacea for all individual and social ills was romantic and misguided; such 'sweeping primitivism' (1969a: 191) simply obscuring his sociological insights. Jung, on the other hand, on the right wing of psychoanalysis, Marcuse curtly dismisses, calling his psychology an 'obscurantist pseudo-mythology'. The bulk of the critique, however, is devoted to the centre, to the neo-Freudians of whom Fromm is the principal target. He expresses agreement with Fromm's critique of patriarchal culture, but felt that the neo-Freudians had made a number of revisions to psychoanalytic theory, which, though motivated by a radical concern, none the less were conducive to a 'watering down' of Freud's critical insights. Three points of criticism are worth mentioning.

First, Marcuse argues that the neo-Freudians had placed a lot of emphasis on 'happiness-oriented therapy', on the development of a person's potentialities. These are laudable motives, Marcuse suggests, but essentially unattainable, not because of the limitations of therapeutic technique, but because established society itself, in its very structure, denied it. But more than this: 'In a repressive society, individual happiness is in contradiction to society, if they are defined as values to be realised within this society, they become themselves repressive' (1969a: 194).

Secondly, Marcuse strongly objected to the claim of the neo-Freudians that they had added a 'sociological dimension' to Freudian theory; the latter Marcuse insisted, 'is in its very substance "sociological"' (1969a: 24), needing no new cultural orientation to reveal this substance.

Thirdly, Marcuse was most critical of 'the playing down of biological factors [and] the mutilation of the instict theory' (ibid.) by the neo-Freudians. By abandoning the libido theory, the function of the unconscious, the importance of childhood and the Oedipal complex, and by jettisoning the death instinct, the neo-Freudians, Marcuse argued, had deprived psychoanalysis of its critical edge. The shift of emphasis from the organism to the personality, from biology to culture and ideal values, had 'flattened out' Freud's depth psychology and the conflict between the individual and his society. Thus Fromm, in particular, lapses into idealist ethics without foundation in materialist theory, and suggests an approach akin to the 'power of positive thinking' and religious reformers throughout the ages. Marcuse put it concisely in suggesting that 'the most concrete insights into the historical structure of civilization are contained precisely in the concepts that the revisionists reject' (1969a: 25); and the key concept for Marcuse is that of sexuality (Eros).

Marcuse's critique contains a good deal of truth, but as Bocock (1976: 152–3) suggests, Fromm shared with Marcuse many of the latter's misgivings about the neo-Freudian school and ego psychology – their stress on adjustment and conformity to society, and the overemphasis on the conscious ego (cf. Fromm 1970: 37). But there remained fundamental disagreements between these two scholars, once former friends and colleagues, which the ensuing controversy highlighted; both essentially deviated from Freud, but in rather different ways.

Freud's social theory (as Fromm argued) was intrinsically conservative, and implied two fundamental oppositions; between sexuality and civilisation, and between freedom and happiness. In *Civilisation and its Discontents* Freud had argued that civilisation (culture) was founded on the renunciation and the repression of instinctual pleasures (libido). In *Totems and Taboo* the emergence of culture was verily seen as an historical event. Thus culture, historically, had involved sexual renunciation. Moreover, at the level of the individual this implied the focus of sexuality on the genitals, the channeling of sex into procreation and into monogamic institutions. Sexual and psychic maturity, therefore, depended on the ego coming to terms with the reality principle, and thus controlling the instinctual impulses, the id, as well as involving the 'desexualisation' of the organism. Human freedom therefore demanded, according to Freud, the suppression or the control of the pleasure principle. 'Where the id was, there ego shall be.' Happiness and freedom were thus antithetical. As we have discussed in chapter 2, Freud was indeed troubled by this state of affairs and seriously questioned whether this unhappiness and the evident neurosis was not too high a price to pay for civilisation. As a conservative, however, he found it difficult to visualise a culture that did not involve coercive restraints and sexual repression. As Marcuse accepted: 'The notion that a non-repressive civilisation is impossible is a cornerstone of Freudian theory' (1969a: 33). But Marcuse felt that this theory contained elements that contravened western thought and even suggested its reversal. For Freud questions civilisation not from a romanticist or utopian viewpoint, but on the ground of the suffering and misery that repression involved: 'Cultural freedom thus appears in the light of unfreedom, and cultural progress in the light of constraints. Culture is not thereby refuted; unfreedom and constraint are the price that must be paid' (1969a: 33). Marcuse agrees with Freud's essential standpoint; civilisation does entail an antagonism between freedom and happiness, and between culture and sexuality. This situation, however, is the product not of the human situation as such, but of a particular historical form of civilisation – industrial capitalism. Like Reich, he essentially transforms Freud's ahistorical perceptions into historical ones, thereby enabling him to 'correlate psychoanalytic theory with presuppositions of Marxism' (Robinson 1970: 152). Interestingly, though *Eros and Civilisation* is written from a Marxist standpoint, Marx is never cited; but essentially what the study entails is the incorporation of psychoanalytic concepts into a Marxist framework. As with Fromm, Marcuse felt that analytic psychology had a legitimate place within the framework of Marxism (1970: 180), but he differed from Fromm in holding firmly to the belief that it was in Freud's instinct theory that a genuine materialist and critical perspective could be found. In this task Marcuse elaborated two important concepts – the 'performance principle' and 'surplus repression'. The terms seem a little unwieldly, but the meaning is clear enough.

Marcuse agreed with Freud that a certain amount of constraint on instinctual expression was probably necessary – basic repression

– in all human communities, but the prevailing historical form of the reality principle, which he termed the performance principle, involved surplus repression. The latter was exacted in contemporary civilisation for the purposes of domination and exploitation:

> The modifications and deflections of instinctual energy necessitated by the perpetuation of the monogamic patriarchal family, or by a hierarchical division of labour, or by public control over the individual's private existence are instances of surplus repression pertaining to the institutions of a particular reality principle. (1969: 46)

This repression implied the 'containment' of the sexual impulses and their focus on 'procreative sexuality', the desexualisation of the organism, and the subduing of the 'proximity senses' (smell and taste) – all with respect to the effectiveness of organised domination. The libido thus becomes concentrated in one part of the body. Sexuality, Marcuse suggests, following Freud, is 'polymorphous-perverse', but under capitalism 'genital primacy' is a prerequisite. But the energy thus released in the work process is unsatisfying for the individual, and drawing on Marx's concept of alienation, Marcuse writes:

> For the vast majority of the population, the scope and mode of satisfaction are determined by their own labour; but their labour is work for an apparatus they do not control, which operates as an independent power to which individuals must submit if they want to live. Men do not live their own lives, but perform pre-established functions. While they work, they do not fulfil their own needs and faculties but work in alienation . . . libido is diverted for socially useful performances in which the individual works for himself only in so far as he works for the apparatus, engaged in activities that mostly do not coincide with his own faculties and desires. (1969: 51)

Humankind, under capitalism, he writes, exists 'only part-time'; it is only during leisure hours narrowly circumscribed that a person is free for pleasurable activities, and even then leisure had become regimented and necessarily a period of passive relaxation, in order that the individual may recreate the energy for work (1952).

Anyone who has worked, like myself, for nine hours a day in an iron foundry, will sense the salience of these reflections. For Marcuse then, the dominant interests of the performance principle –

capitalism – require instinctual repression for their mode of production over and above (surplus) that which is necessary. In this way, as Robinson and Geoghegan (1981: 46) suggest, Marcuse sought to introduce a Marxist or historical perspective to Freudian theory. In doing so he developed a number of interesting themes which, for the purposes of exposition, I shall briefly enumerate.

1. With his concept of polymorphous-perverse sexuality, the idea that the whole body is potentially erotic, Marcuse came to imply that homosexuals have a revolutionary potential in the sexual sphere. Sexual perversions 'express rebellion against the subjugation of sexuality under the order of procreation, and against the institutions which guarantee this order'. And he went on to argue that in upholding sexuality as an end in itself, 'they place themselves outside the dominion of the performance and challenge its very foundation' (1969: 54).

In this respect he differed fundamentally not only from Freud but also from both Reich and Fromm, who all stressed heterosexual genitality. Fromm in particular was most critical of this apparent stress on 'pre-genital' sexuality and its implied sadistic and coprophilic tendencies (1970: 30–3). Norman Brown's well-known study *Life against Death* (1959) expresses a similar viewpoint to that of Marcuse, suggesting that not only would sexuality be completely undifferentiated in a non-repressive society, but that the self itself would be androgynous (Robinson 1970: 167–74). Marcuse looked to the Greek myths for images of a culture beyond the performance principle, and saw in Orpheus and Narcissus expressions of perversions with revolutionary potential. Narcissus was the culture hero who fell in love with his own image; while Orpheus, who is reputed to have shunned all love of womankind, is 'the poet of redemption, who brings peace and salvation by pacifying man and nature, not through force but through song' (1969: 138). Both, Marcuse suggests, protest against the repressive order of procreative sexuality. Although Marcuse, as Geoghegan points out, expressed views similar to those of the early English socialist Edward Carpenter, he did not favour exclusive homosexuality, but rather the need to 'libidinise the organism' (1981: 55–7).

Critics have invariably found this aspect of Marcuse's theory unpalatable, a 'cosmic cop-out' into a 'haze of fanciful images' is how Poster (1978: 61) describes his reference to Narcissus and Orpheus, while MacIntyre (1970: 47) refers to his discussions of sex as 'comic pomposity'. It is worth noting, however, Marcuse's discussion of desublimation, for in contemporary society, he argued, the stress on sexual liberation and on more open attitudes to sex, in advertising and in the general culture, had a 'truly conformist function' (1964: 76). Rather than leading to liberation of the individual in any real sense, the newfound sexual freedom not only inhibited the individual from the full enjoyment of his or her own sexuality, but served to bolster a repressive economic order. Marcuse was therefore in a unique position in being critical of both the puritan Christian ethic, which restricted sexuality to monogamy, and of wanton sexual abandon, which appeared to have emerged in the last decade. Criticisms of the blatant sexism in advertising and the *Playboy* philosophy and the repressive aspects of the 'new sexuality' have since been explored in further depth by writers sympathetic to Marcuse (cf. Kemnitzer 1977; Ober 1982 for interesting discussions of these issues).

2. Holding firm to Freud's instinct theory, Marcuse accepted, rather uncritically, his later version and the dualism of Thanatos and Eros, the death and life instincts. He notes that for Freud these two instincts constitute a primary dynamic, but true to his Hegelian heritage, Marcuse senses an underlying monism. He notes that there is a 'state of suspense' in Freud's writings, and that both instincts have a 'conservative nature'. Sexual impulse strives for the release of pent-up energy, while Thanatos is not destructive but the striving of all organic life for integral quiescence, the nirvana principle. Death then is 'an expression of the eternal struggle against suffering and repression' (1969: 41), an unconscious flight from pain and want. In such an underlying unity of the instincts, Marcuse suggested that the defeat of Thanatos could only be assured through the liberation of Eros. As Robinson cogently put it: 'If destructiveness was to be eliminated or curtailed, it was necessary that libido should not be attenuated nor siphoned off into the various sublimations such as work' (1970: 160).

Marcuse expressed in terms of an hydraulic conception of instincts what Fromm was suggesting in terms of moral paradigms. Like all instinct theories, the concepts of libido and Thanatos lead to theoretical difficulties. MacIntyre reflects on this problem, noting the tautological nature of the procedure. How are we to identify the presence of the death instinct independently of its manifestations – in war and destructive tendencies? And how could such an instinct serve as a causal factor in the explanation of a highly specific and variable phenomenon as modern warfare (MacIntyre 1970: 50)? Both Fromm and Reich, of course, rejected the notion of a death instinct. But two things must be said. One is that Marcuse used the term instinct in accordance with Freud's notion of *Trieb*, a primary drive of the human organism which is subject to historical modification. A second point is that Marcuse never attempted to explain war in terms of such a simplistic single factor theory.

3. With respect to the Oedipus complex Marcuse again accepts Freud's basic premises, but with an important proviso; he suggests that Freud's hypothesis only has a 'symbolic value', telescoping the 'historical dialectic of domination' and thus helping understanding. He accepts that the archaic events that the hypothesis stipulates are beyond the realm of anthropological verification. 'The difficulties', he writes, 'in scientific verification and even in logic consistency are obvious and perhaps insurmountable' (1969: 61). MacIntyre's re-iteration of the empirical and logical problems contained in Freud's theory (1970: 51–2) are therefore misplaced, and its metaphorical value only has a meaning if one senses the repressive and patriarchal tendencies in current civilisation, and MacIntyre clearly does not. But although Marcuse hinted that the father, as paterfamilias, still performed the basic regimentation of the instincts, he argued, in contrast to Reich, that the development of capitalism had effectively eliminated the family as the main agency of socialisation and as a vehicle of repression. He speaks of a decline in the social function of the family (1969: 86). Social control and sexual repression were now undertaken, he thought, by a system of extra-familial agencies such as schools, bureaucracy and the mass media. Repression was now collective, anonymous and ideological rather than familial and personal. Whether this abolition of privacy and personal autonomy, which he abhorred and criticised – the 'technological abolition of the individual' – implied that he retained an uncritical and rosy picture of the patriarchal family, as Poster (1978: 62) implies, is seriously open to question. It is clear that Marcuse was equally critical of the period of bourgeois liberalism, when the family had been a critical agent of socialisation. What he felt, however, was that in the period of monopoly capitalism, the notion of the autonomous individual itself was being seriously eroded; 'his consciousness coordinated, his privacy abolished, his emotions integrated into conformity, the individual has no longer enough "mental space" for developing himself against his sense of guilt, for living with a conscience of his own' (1969a: 88). (As we shall see, contemporary structuralism and scientific Marxism seem to agree, at the level of theory, with this portrayal.) The classical Oedipus complex, Marcuse suggested, is losing its significance for the understanding of culture. Although it may be the primary source and model of neurotic conflicts, it is, he wrote, 'certainly not the central cause of the discontents in civilization, and not the

central obstacle for their removal' (1969a: 165). Such thoughts point to the lack of any critical theory of the family in Marcuse's writings, a characteristic, Poster suggests, which is also typical of latter theorists of sexual politics (see Reiche 1970).

4. Marcuse indicated that the scientific rationality of Western civilisation, as it embodied the Promethean ethic, was essentially an approach that implied a 'subject against an object'. Nature was therefore given to the ego as something that had to be controlled, conquered, even violated. Classical logic also implied this idea of an ordering, classifying, mastering reason. Such practical reason was a 'logic of domination'. This logic equally involved the devaluation of the 'lower' faculties of the individual – the emotions, sensual experience, fantasy, imagination. Indeed for writers like Plato (and Freud), reason, and thus human freedom, demanded the subjugation of human instincts, appetites and intuitions. Yet again, within the Freudian corpus. Marcuse detected a radical element, a way beyond the present impasse. For Freud had suggested the importance of fantasy as a way of coping with reality, independent and in a sense prior to the reality principle, it was one of the two principles of mental functioning. Thus Marcuse suggested that fantasy and imagination had a truth value of their own, and a radical function in contemporary culture, a culture characterised by destructiveness, violence and poverty. Imagination, he wrote, envisages the reconciliation of humans with nature, of desire with realisation, of happiness with reason, and the possibility of a non-repressive culture. Marcuse therefore turns to a number of writers for conceptual support. To Nietzsche and his critique of Western rationalism and his affirmation of enjoyment; to the utopian socialism of Fourier and his notion of work as a pleasurable activity (*travail attrayant*); to Schiller and his concept of the aesthetic function and the idea that sensuousness (*Sinnlichkeit*) must be cultivated in order to counteract the 'order or reason'. Marcuse even turned to Kant, stressing that his aesthetic theory, outlined in *Critique of Judgement*, suggested a dimension where the 'senses and intellect meet', a third faculty linking nature (science) and freedom (morality), which his dualism held to be antagonistic. This faculty was sensuous reason. True to his Hegelian standpoint, Marcuse saw the need and the possibility of overcoming the oppositions inherent in Western culture. In the Orphic image was the possible 'erotic reconciliation (union) of man and nature in the aesthetic attitude, where order is beauty and work is play' (1969a: 145)? The antagonism that Schiller describes – sensuousness and reason, nature and freedom – reflected in the empiricist distinction between science and the arts (and

morality) – Marcuse views as embodied in the performance principle and in need of transcending. The established culture makes the intellect and the senses antagonistic, and gives the intellect, reason priority, thus giving it its controlling, destructive tendency. What is needed is the reconciling of both impulses 'by making sensuousness rational and reason sensuous' (1969a: 152). Given the primacy of repressive reason, art, fantasy, the aesthetic dimensions have revolutionary potential. In like manner, only by the strengthening of Eros will the destructive tendencies of mankind be curtained.

5. Within *Eros and Civilisation* one finds one of the most severe indictments of Western civilisation ever outlined. Yet it is interlaced with the feeling that this culture has, at the same time, opened up the possibility of a non-repressive and truly human civilisation. With intellectual courage and committed scholarship only too rare in academia, Marcuse never hesitates to indict the repressive violence and totalitarian aspects of contemporary institutions, the widespread poverty that exists in the world (which even conservative economists admit could be eliminated by a more rational organisation of production and resources) and the social systems that are organised around 'the work of destruction and waste and pollution' (18). (These issues were discussed in more detail in his other writings: 1958, 1964, 1972.) But as these negative aspects of civilisation increase with the progress of civilisation, so also did the real possibility of the elimination of oppression and poverty. For scientific knowledge and the level of productivity had reached a level when it was possible, Marcuse argued, to reduce working hours and to eliminate human suffering, allowing the individual, freed from repression, to enjoy to the full his or her human potentialities. In the diverse forms of radical protest evident in contemporary society Marcuse glimpsed the feelings of a 'great refusal' to accept the premises and the inequalities of advanced capitalism. Although he suggested that such forms of protest as the hippies and radical students may act as a catalyst for revolutionary social change, there is some substance in the criticism that Marcuse lacked any clear tactical programme for radical change. (See Swingewood 1977: 10–18, for some incisive criticisms of Marcuse and the Frankfurt school, and their theory of culture.)

Like both Reich and Fromm, Marcuse never seriously attempted a synthesis of Marxism and psychoanalysis. What he suggested and demonstrated in *Eros and Civilisation* was a need to supplement Marxist theory with a psychological dimension. This was considered lacking by all the critical theorists. In doing this he systematically translated (as Robinson notes (1970: 152)), the unhistorical, psychological categories of Freud's thought into the eminently historical and political categories of Marxism. It was fundamentally an attempt to salvage and reaffirm the critical and revolutionary potential of Marxist thought. The conception of the human subject that emerges from Marcuse's writings is akin to that of Hegel and Marx, with their central focus on reason and praxis. But drawing on Freud's depth psychology, particularly on the libido theory (Eros), Marcuse emphasises, like Nietzsche, the life-affirming, creative aspects of human nature. Many earlier philosophers, as Kellner suggests, from Plato and Augustine to Kant, have tended to stress the destructive and asocial features of the libinal instincts and thus to defend the ascetic tradition. Against this tradition Marcuse upholds the erotic energies as the very principle of life and creativity and linked with the 'aesthetic dimension' as important in explicating features of both the emancipated individual and a non-repressive society (D. Kellner 1984: 196).

Although Marcuse was a self-confessed romantic, his life-trajectory was quite different from that of Reich. Adorno and Horkheimer, for in his later life he not only remained involved in radical politics, but became more and more radicalised. A utopian socialist and a phenomenological Marxist, Marcuse left an intellectual legacy that affirms his standing as one of the most important philosophers of the present century, though he is singularly ignored by several academic texts (e.g. Passmore 1957; for a different assessment, see Kolakowski's hostile critique of Marcuse, whom he describes as an 'ideologist of obscuranticism'. Kolakowski woefully misunderstands and misinterprets both the intent and substance of Marcuse's politics (1978: 396–420.)

8.4 Knowledge and Human Interests

Jürgen Habermas has been described as the 'heir' to the Frankfurt school and there is no doubt that he sees himself as situated within this tradition. As he has noted: 'I felt a special affinity with the existentialist, ie the Marcusean variant of critical theory' (Dews 1986: 152). During the 1960s he became a friend of Marcuse, some thirty years his senior, as well as an assistant of Adorno. Born in Frankfurt in 1929, Habermas grew up during the Nazi period in a provincial German context. He studied at Göttingen and Bonn between 1949 and 1954 and was steeped in the German philosophical tradition, writing a dissertation on Schelling, which, he recalled, was strongly influenced by his reading of Heidegger. After finishing his dissertation he worked for two years as a freelance journalist, but then returned to academic life becoming Adorno's assistant between 1956 and 1959. After teaching at Heidelberg he returned to Frankfurt in 1964 to take up Horkheimer's chair in philosophy and sociology. He was then thirty-five years of age, the same age as Horkheimer when he had taken the chair more than thirty years before. With a remarkable capacity for assimilating knowledge, Habermas read widely and extensively, and his important study, *Knowledge and Human Interests*, written between 1964 and 1968, is extraordinarily detailed and scholarly. George Lichtheim wrote of Habermas, long before the latter writer had established himself as a philosopher of rank, that he indicated in his writings an unusual competence for assimilating and refashioning the ideas of other scholars 'There is no corner-cutting', he wrote,

> no facile evasion of difficulties or spurious enunciation of conclusions unsupported by research; whether he is refuting Popper, dissecting the pragmatism of Charles Peirce, delving into the medieval antecedents of Schelling's metaphysics, or bringing Marxist sociology up to date, there is always the same uncanny mastery of sources, joined to an enviable talent for clarifying intricate logical puzzles. (1971: 175)

Habermas's philosophy is undoubtedly based on the 'four pillars' of the Frankfurt school – Hegel, Marx, Weber and Freud – but as his various interviews reveal, he has in his writings drawn on a wide and eclectic range of intellectual traditions – besides that of the Frankfurt School. Of paramount influence has been the German philosophical tradition, Kant, Fichte, Hegel, Schelling, through to Lukács, whose *History and Class Consciousness* made a great impression on Habermas. His great friend Richard Bernstein has written: 'It is as if the trauma of the Nazi period required a reimmersion in the German classics of the nineteenth and early twentieth centuries in order to re-establish a thread of continuity – in order to secure a grounding and orientation' (1985: 2).

Other influences on Habermas include: writers in the hermeneutic tradition such as Dilthey and Gadamer; analytic philosophers like Wittgenstein and Austin; the sociologist Talcott Parsons and the pragmatists. Of the latter he wrote:

> I also studied Peirce as well as Mead and Dewey. From the outset I viewed American pragmatism as the third productive reply to Hegel,

after Marx and Kierkegaard, as the radical-democratic branch of Young Hegelianism, so to speak. Ever since, I have relied on this American version of the philosophy of praxis when the problem arises of compensating for the weaknesses of Marxism with respect to democratic theory. (Dews 1986: 151)

In his later writings Habermas also draws extensively on the work of Chomsky, and the theories of psychological and moral development suggested by Erikson, Piaget and Kohlberg. Although Habermas in his writings eclectically appropriates theories and ideas from a wide range of often incompatible traditions, his own work is by no means an eclectic mishmash but, as Lichtheim remarked, he has a rare faculty of digesting the material and then refashioning it into orderly wholes. Bernstein has also suggested that what is impressive in Habermas's approach is the way in which he weaves whatever he analyses into a coherent whole. 'There is a unity of vision that informs his work', he writes, 'a systematic impulse that is evident even in his earliest writings' (1985: 3). Habermas is therefore unusual in the present anti-rationalist, anti-systematic philosophical climate. He is also unusual in retaining the vision of the Frankfurt school and its project, namely 'to develop a theory of society with a practical intention; the self-emancipation of people from dominion' (Held 1980: 250). Although deviating substantially, as we shall note, from the Marxist position, Habermas always claimed to be true to the spirit of Marx. The critical theory of society, he wrote, has no need to prove its credentials; it simply needs 'a substantive foundation which will lead out of the bottleneck produced by the conceptual framework of the philosophy of consciousness, and overcome the paradigm of production, without abandoning the intentions of western Marxism in the process' (Dews 1986: 152).

During the past three decades Habermas has produced an impressive body of sociological and philosophical literature, and established himself as one of the foremost social theorists of the present day. As he has tended to follow the early critical theorists in explicating the links between social institutions and individual identity formation all his work is suffused with insights on the human subject. But given the scope of his work it is clearly impossible to cover this corpus here and I shall instead focus my discussion on his theory of cognitive interests.

The study Knowledge and Human Interests is primarily epistemological and represents Habermas's engagement with, and attempt to synthesise, five philosophical traditions: Hegelian-Marxism, the early positivism of Comte and Mach; pragmatism, as reflected in the work of Charles Peirce; the hermeneutic theory of Dilthey; and psychoanalysis. Towards the end, and in the appendix to the book, Nietzsche and Husserl come to the fore of his discussion. The aim of the work, he writes, is 'a historically-oriented attempt to reconstruct the prehistory of modern positivism with the systematic intention of analysing the connections between knowledge and human interests' (1972: vii). This entails the dissolution of epistemology, for a radical critique of knowledge is only possible as social theory; Habermas following Horkheimer's critical theory in seeing all knowledge as situated in a specific social and historical context, and as being linked with human interests. The notion of theory as knowledge that had freed itself of human interests – shared by both speculative Greek philosophy and positivist science – and thus 'value-free', Habermas considers misleading. The 'image of a reality-in-itself consisting of facts structured in a lawlike manner', which can then be grasped by theory, Habermas suggests is an 'objectivist illusion', for it prevents 'consciousness of the interlocking of knowledge with interests from the life world' (1972: 305–6). For Habermas, all knowledge is motivated by life interests, and he goes on to specify three specific human interests. But Habermas begins with Hegel's critique of Kant, and the idea that you can establish, prior to knowledge, the criteria for reliable judgements. He agrees with Hegel that such an epistemological approach inevitably 'ensnares itself'. His style of presentation is also akin to that of Hegel, in that Habermas limits himself to following immanently the movement of thought, which he felt has its own logic, rather than examining its objective context.

Yet although Habermas is sympathetic to Hegel's critique of Kant, particularly the latter's ahistorical conception of the human subject as 'a complete, fixed, knowing subject? (1972: 15), he was critical of the speculative aspect of Hegel's philosophy. As he was later to put it, he had doubts 'about whether concepts of totality, of truth and of theory derived from Hegel did not represent too heavy a mortgage for a theory of society which should also satisfy empirical claims' (Dews 1986: 152). But Habermas expressed little antipathy towards the German idealist tradition and in marked contrast to the 'structuralist' opposition towards the humanist notion of a reflective human subject. Habermas considers the history of philosophy from Kant to Marx to be a series of progressive attempts to radicalise this conception. As Richard Kearney writes:

This history of radicalization reaches modern fruition in the successive discoveries of the Kantian transcendental subject, the Fichtean ego and the Hegelian *Geist*, culminating in the Marxist synthesis of critical reflection with productive praxis – a dialectical synthesis which aims to resolve the traditional opposition between idealism and materialism. (1986: 224)

Marx's critique of Hegel's idealism – particularly the notion of an Absolute mind – and of Feuerbach's contemplative materialism, Habermas readily accepts, and he applauds Marx's conviction that the self-reflection of consciousness discloses the fundamental structures of social labour, 'discovering therein the synthesis of the objectively active natural being man and the nature that is his objective environment' (1972: 30). And Habermas goes on to suggest that although this unity can only be brought about by a human subject, Marx does not comprehend it as an absolute unity: 'The subject is originally a natural being instead of nature being originally an aspect of the subject, as in idealism. Therefore unity, which can only come about through the activity of a subject, remains in some measure imposed on nature by the subject' (1972: 32).

The implication of this premise, namely that the human subject's relationship with nature is inherently an instrumental one, we shall discuss further below, Marx's conception of the self-constitution of the human species though labour was an important insight, Habermas suggests, which Marx appropriated from Hegel and which at the same time 'demythologised' Hegel's phenomenology.

But Habermas goes on to offer a criticism of Marx's own theory, suggesting that Marx's epistemology is ambiguous and has positivist overtones. Marx, he argues, tended to reduce practical activity to labour, praxis to technique and thereby to play down the importance of language and communication in human sociality and subjectivity. By taking the natural sciences as the paradigm of knowledge, Marx, he felt, had tended to see the human subject as achieving its identity only through its comprehension of 'self-positing struggles' and through technical control:

Marx reduces the process of reflection to the level of instrumental action. By reducing the self-positing of the absolute ego to the more tangible productive activity of the species, he eliminates reflection as such as a motive force of history, even though he retains the framework of the philosophy of reflection. (1972: 44)

One may question whether Marx's concept of labour can be equated with instrumental control, for as we have earlier discussed, labour for Marx had a creative, aesthetic dimension and implied communicative action and a 'unity' between nature and the human subject. Habermas clearly finds such unity, expressed by the early Marx and by Adorno and Marcuse, as being at odds with a materialist outlook and akin to 'mysticism' (1972: 33).

From Kant to Marx the subject of cognition was comprehended as consciousness, ego, mind or the species-being. But with the critique of epistemology and 'the self-abolition of the critique of knowledge by Hegel and Marx', Habermas writes, philosophy of science came upon the scene in the form of Comte's positivism. Paradoxically, it first appeared, Habermas suggests, under the guise of a new philosophy of history. Habermas goes on to discuss in detail the positivist philosophy of Comte and Mach, highlighting its 'objectivist' orientation and its intrinsic connection with utility and technical control. Habermas is not hostile to the instrumental aspects of positivist science, but rather to its objectivism and its tendency to set itself up as the only valid knowledge. Objectivism, he writes, 'deludes the sciences with the image of a self-subsistent world of facts structured in a lawlike manner; it thus conceals the a priori constitution of these facts' (1972: 69). Positivism propagates an 'illusion of objectivism', but, as noted earlier, Habermas feels that all knowledge is motivated by interests. 'Scientism', the other limitation of positivism, means, he writes, 'science's belief in itself; that is, the conviction that we can no longer understand science as one form of possible knowledge, but rather must identify knowledge with science' (1972: 4). Although positivism had earlier a progressive function in criticising religious dogma and speculative metaphysics, it had increasingly taken on, Habermas contends, an ideological function in that instrumental knowledge had become equated with reason itself. In this Habermas is in accord with the earlier critical theorists' critique of instrumental reason. But within the philosophy of science tradition, particularly as expressed in the writings of the pragmatist Charles Peirce, self-reflection on the sciences began to indicate the limitations of positivism. For pragmatism not only showed the instrumental nature of knowledge, but stressed that the concept of the individual ego was not exclusively linked to instrumental action but rather to intersubjectivity and to symbolic interaction. Thus 'the concept of the individual ego includes a dialectical relation of the universal and the particular, which cannot be conceived on the behavioural system of instrumental action' (1972: 139). Human communication, he suggests, develops through 'the reciprocal recognition of subjects who identify one another under the category of selfhood' (1972: 138).

Habermas next considers Dilthey's writings on the hermeneutic approach to the cultural sciences, suggesting that along with Peirce he brought the self-reflection of science to a point from which their knowledge-constituting interests were visible. Habermas thus comes to outline, following the neo-Kantian tradition of Dilthey and Rickert, 'two forms of science' – the hermeneutic and the empirical-analytic sciences. Both, he argues, are governed by cognitive interests which are rooted in the life-world. The characteristics of the two sciences he describes as follows:

> Empirical-analytic inquiry is the systematic continuation of a cumulative learning process that proceeds on the pre-scientific level within the behavioural system of instrumental action. Hermeneutic inquiry lends methodical form to a process of arriving at mutual understanding (and self-understanding) which takes place on the pre-scientific level in the scientific-bound structure of symbolic interaction. The first aims at the production of technically exploitable knowledge; the second at the clarification of practically effective knowledge. Empirical analysis discloses reality from the viewpoint of possible technical control over objectified processes of nature, while hermeneutics maintains the intersubjectivity of possible action-orienting mutual understanding. (1972: 191)

Thus the natural sciences are concerned with technical control, and hermeneutics with maintaining the intersubjectivity of mutual understanding in ordinary language communication, and in action according to common norms. But in making the distinction between instrumental (*Techne*) and practical (*praxis*) reason, it is clear that Habermas conceives of praxis solely in terms of communication – specifically through language – rather than as social interaction between human subjects and nature. Habermas's sense of practice follows Kant rather than Marx. The logic of the two sciences Habermas sees as having a quasi-transcendental function, and as 'arising from actual structures of human life: from structure of a species that reproduces its life both through learning processes of socially organised labour and processes of mutual understanding in interactions mediated in ordinary language' (1973: 194).

However, Habermas did not see these two knowledge-constitutive interests as being in a sense 'biological', simply having reference to the reproduction and preservation of the human species,

but rather they are a function of the 'objectively constituted problems of the preservation of life that have been solved by the cultural
form of existence as such' (1973: 196).

Restricting empirical-analytic knowledge to our understanding
of the natural world, Habermas is equally critical of the limitations
of hermeneutics, invaluable though it is in the interpretation of
social phenomena. These limitations are made particularly explicit
in his discussion of the writings of Hans-Georg Gadamer, and of
the more recent studies by such interpretative sociologists as Schutz
and Garfinkel, Habermas makes two important points of criticism.
The first is that hermeneutics tends to lapse into pure description
and relativism, and thus is unable to assess the nature of the
ideological distortions and the truth content of various cultural
traditions. Secondly, hermeneutic understanding has an inadequate
conception of history and tends not to explore the way in which
cultural complexes are created, or the structural features of a society
that operate as unconscious determinants of social phenomena.
Hermeneutics thus tends to have a non-critical attitude towards the
dominant forms of consciousness and does not explore the way in
which these often serve to mask social inequalities and power
structures (Held 1980: 311; Keat 1981: 4).

Critical of the romantic hermeneutics expressed by Dilthey and
Gadamer, and unwilling to entertain the application of instrumental reason to social life and human subjectivity. Habermas sought
another 'path', one suggested by Hegel in the *Phenomenology*. This
he described as 'the experience of the emancipatory power of
reflection, which the subject experiences in itself to the extent that it
becomes transparent to itself in the history of its genesis' (1972:
197). Kearney expresses it well when he suggests that Habermas
'endeavours to steer a medial course between the Scylla of romantic
hermeneutics, which celebrated a mythic past of empathic fellow-
ship, and the Charybdis of positivist rationalism devoted to an
abstract system of technological administration' (1986: 223).

The path Habermas selected was that of critical theory, which is
an expression of what Habermas describes as the 'emancipatory
cognitive interests of rational reflection' (1972: 198). It seems to be
equivalent to Kant's speculative reason, which combines theoretical
and practical reason in 'one cognition', and Hegel's reason (*Vernunft*). Habermas suggests that it is only through this reason, the
'self-reflection of the sciences', and through critique that the connection of knowledge with interest emerges coherently. Habermas
describes psychoanalytic knowledge as exemplifying this form of
self-reflective knowledge. Freudian theory is a 'depth hermen-

eutics', which through self-reflection 'releases the subject from dependence on hypostatised powers. Self-reflection is determined by an emancipatory cognitive interest. Critically oriented sciences share this interest with philosophy' (1972: 310). Habermas appears to think that this interest is built into the human condition. As he suggests, emancipatory interest is not some contingent value-postulate:

> No, it is something so profoundly ingrained in the structure of human societies – the calling into question and deep-seated wish to throw off relations which repress you without necessity – so intimately built into the reproduction of human life that I don't think it can be regarded as just a subjective attitude . . . it is more. (Dews 1986: 198)

Habermas's general perspective can be summarised as follows:

Cognitive interest	Type of science	Knowledge	Social medium
Technical control	Empirical-analytic	Instrumental	Work
Mutual understanding	Hermeneutic	Practical	Interaction language
Emancipatory	Critical	Emancipatory	Power authority

One can see the influence of both Kant and Hegel in this triadic schema. As with Horkheimer, it was an attempt to lay the foundations of critical theory and bridge the gap between philosophy and the empirical sciences.

Habermas's study, *Knowledge and Human Interests*, received, as Giddens suggests, 'a barrage of critical attacks' (1985: 96), and to these Habermas has responded over the years in developing his theory of communicative action (1984). His studies are described as having taken a 'linguistic turn', but it is evident that his later sociological studies represent a development and not a break with his early ideas on cognitive interests, although he would appear now to regard the attempt to found critical theory on epistemology as misleading. But he has recently reaffirmed that his theory of cognitive interests is 'basically sound' and that he still holds to the fundamental idea that there are constitutive relationships between scientific inquiries and everyday orientations (Dews 1986: 197). As Habermas's work has now become the subject of much debate, we can hardly cover all this material here, but a number of key criticisms may be mentioned to the extent that they are central to the themes of the present study.

First, Habermas is seen as essentially presenting a dualistic neo-Kantian perspective which rigidly separates nature from the human context, seeing the human relationship with nature as purely instrumental and one of utility. As with Dilthey and the neo-Kantians, he appears to define empirical science in a positivist fashion, which, as Michael Pusey suggests (1987: 20), he defends as fervently as Kant did 200 years ago. He defends it against both metaphysics and the romantic philosophies of nature. Thus Habermas, as Thomas McCarthy writes, appears to limit our knowledge of nature to information that is technically utilisable, and our intercourse with nature to instrumental mastery of objectified processes. He allows no 'hermeneutics of nature', and unlike Horkheimer and Marcuse, is unable to conceive of a science and technology that does not imply an attitude of domination towards nature. For Habermas the real problem is not technical reason and the instrumental attitude towards nature (this is legitimate science), but rather the expansion of such science to the social life-world (1970: 90). But, as McCarthy cogently writes, is this enough? 'Are we not left in the end with only one legitimate attitude toward nature; technical mastery? And is this not seriously inadequate as an account of the multifaceted relationships with nature, both "outer nature" and the "inner nature" of our own bodies, which are in fact not only possible but necessary for a full realization of our humanity?' (1978: 67). Habermas does not exclude the possibility of other attitudes to nature – poetic, mystical, fraternal – but these are not viewed as forms of knowledge.

Secondly, in his criticisms of Marx, Habermas suggests that Marx seemed to regard the development of the human species as focused entirely on the dimension of social labour, and thus to eliminate in theory, if not in practice, the structure of symbolic interaction and the role of cultural tradition (McCarthy 1978: 68). But in linking subjectivity to communicative action Habermas seems to go to the other extreme, and to deny the creative interaction between humans and nature. Perry Anderson (1983: 61) has suggested that the trend of Habermas's thought has been increasingly to give outright primacy of communicative over productive functions in the definition of humanity and the development of history alike. It is of interest to note that Habermas specifically denies this, suggesting that the transition he has theoretically made from a production to a communication paradigm 'does not mean . . . that I am willing or bound to abandon the material reproduction of the life-world as the privileged point of reference for analysis' (Dews 1986: 177).

Thirdly, in an interesting discussion, Joel Whitebook (1985) has emphasised Habermas's dualistic framework and his opposition to the very idea of a reconciliation with external nature. External nature is unalterably constituted as an object of instrumental rationality. So how does Habermas deal with the 'inner nature', the instinctual drives of Freudian theory? Whitebook suggests that whereas Freud never doubted that instinctual drives had a somatically-based existence whose status was equal to, if not determinative of, consciousness, Habermas, in his various writings, tries to assimilate as much of inner nature as possible to the category of the linguistic by construing it as proto-linguistic. Thus while he appropriates Freud to discuss methodological problems, he ignores the significance of the libido theory, and 'leaves the dynamic unconscious behind completely when he moves to Piaget and Kohlberg'. Whitebook therefore concludes that, in essence, Habermas abandons the naturalistic tradition which ran from Feuerbach through the young Marx and Freud to the early Frankfurt school (1985: 159–160). In a response to this, Habermas defends his reading of psychoanalysis in terms of communication theory, and it is worth quoting him at length. He writes:

As I see it, nothing of significance is lost in this reading. The hydraulic model and its reliance on the mechanics of instinctual energy had only a metaphorical character. In any case, one cannot have both the analytic instrument of a depth hermeneutics and a theory of drives formulated in quasi-physicalist concepts. The Freudo-Marxism of the earlier Frankfurt School could conceptually integrate psychology and sociology only through the mechanism of internalization; but, as Whitebook shows, this results in a false antagonism which is described in biological terms and the domain of the social apparatus which invades the individual from the outside. It certainly makes more sense to attempt to integrate both disciplines from the beginning within the same conceptual framework. Such a framework would permit us to understand the development of personality as socialization, and to understand sociation as individualization. (1985: 213)

But as Bottomore notes, Habermas has never given any indication as to how (or whether) the two forms of knowledge – empirical-analytic and hermeneutic – could come together in social science theories (1984: 58). But in his later writings on the 'theory of communicative action', Habermas adopts a research strategy which he calls 'genetic structuralism', an approach clearly influenced by the writings of Piaget. Habermas sees this strategy as an alternative to the three established research orientations in sociology; the socio-historical approach of Weber and Marxist historiography, the functionalist theories of Talcott Parsons and Luhmann, and the various forms of interpretative sociology and action theory – hermeneutics, ethnomethodology and symbolic interactionism. But what eventually emerges is a grand synthesis integrating interpretative understanding and a critique of ideology with an historically-oriented analysis of social systems. An essential aspect of this synthesis is Habermas's attempt at constructing various ontogenetic models. Drawing on the studies of ego psychologists (H. S. Sullivan, Erikson), cognitive psychology (Piaget, Kohlberg) and the symbolic interactionist theory of action (Mead, Goffman), Habermas has outlined various schemas relating to the development of ego identity, and has suggested homologies between these and the evolution of world-views and collective identities (1979: 69–129).

In putting an important focus on ego identity and on the development of the human subject through social communication, Habermas indicates his distance from contemporary structuralist and post-structuralist perspectives. Although Habermas is critical of the philosophy of consciousness and the self-sufficient subject, as detailed in *Knowledge and Human Interests*, he retains the fundamental concerns of the early critical theorists – a concern for the autonomy of the human subject and for the need to develop an emancipatory reason. In an important recent text, *The Philosophical Discourse of Modernity* (1987), Habermas attempts to recapture and develop the rational and progressive aspects of the Enlightenment tradition which are embodied in the universalistic notion of morality, in democratic politics, in the subjectivity expressed in certain aesthetic forms and in the self-reflection of the sciences. He again reiterates the limitations of Marx's philosophy of praxis, suggesting that 'it remains a variant of the philosophy of the subject that locates reason in the purposive rationality of the acting subject instead of in the reflection of the knowing subject' (1987: 65). But while Habermas is critical of praxis philosophy and what he terms 'subject-centred reason', he is equally aware of the limitations and dangers of going to the other extreme and in a supposedly radical 'totalising critique' to renounce reason and human subjectivity entirely. He makes some important criticisms of Adorno's 'negative dialectics', Foucault's genealogical approach and Derrida's 'deconstruction', suggesting three limitations of their 'post-modernist' theories. First, that they give no philosophical account of their own positions, raise validity claims only to renounce them, and avoid the obligation to provide theoretical grounds by 'fleeing into the esoteric'. Their critique of reason, that 'is located everywhere and nowhere, so to speak, in discourses without a place, renders it almost immune to competing interpretations' (1987: 337). Derrida and Adorno, he suggests, make a drama out of something that is now considered rather trivial – a fallibilist conception of truth and knowledge (Dews 1986: 204). Second, in repudiating reason, they have tended to obliterate the distinction suggested by Hegel, Marx and critical theorists between the emancipatory-reconciling aspects of social rationalisation and its repressive-alienating aspects. And finally, the totalising critiques of reason tend to ignore everyday social practices, and unlike pragmaticism, hermeneutics, phenomenology and Marxism, to give it no epistemological status. Developing his earlier ideas, Habermas therefore suggests that one reformulates the concept of praxis in the sense of communicative action, and to see that language is a medium 'that draws each participant in interaction into a community of communication, as one of its members and at the same time subjects him to an unrelenting compulsion toward individuation'. Thus the process of socialisation is one of individuation and the subject has to be seen, as G. H. Mead suggested, as enmeshed in a language context, for language is the key characteristic of human life. Attempting to go beyond praxis philosophy with its 'productivist conceptual strategy' and its philosophy on the subject (espoused by the existentialist Marxists, Sartre and Merleau-Ponty, as well as by phenomenologists such as Schultz), Habermas situates the subject within a theory of communicative action. He acknowledges that reason by its very nature is incarnated in the context of communicative action and in the structures of the life-world, and stresses that the latter are not separate from the material life-processes. And this reason, he concludes, makes itself felt in the binding force of intersubjective understanding and reciprocal recognition.

Many writers have complained that Habermas reduces Marxism to a critique of ideology and that his goal of social emancipation in terms of communicative action as 'communication free of domination' is idealist and extremely vague. Kolakowski (1978: 394) likens his emancipatory reason to the pious aspiration of German metaphysics, while Göran Therborn (1978: 137) contrasts his ideas to those of Horkheimer and Marcuse, for whom emancipation was viewed in more substantial economico-political and erotic terms. Perhaps Habermas was correct to describe himself as a 'radical liberal', but he nevertheless remains an important critic of the reactionary political and philosophical tendencies of the present era. (For further discussions of Habermas, see McCarthy 1978; Keat 1981; Thompson and Held 1982; Bernstein 1985.)

–9–

Phenomenology
and Existentialism

Although the existentialist-phenomenological tradition has had an important influence on both sociology and humanistic psychology, particularly through the work of Schutz, Maslow, Binswanger and R. D. Laing, this chapter essentially concentrates on the philosophical background to that tradition. In the first section I examine the background to existentialism, its style of philosophy and its intellectual source in the ethical voluntarism of Kierkegaard, having, in chapter 2, explained the philosophy of the other precursor of existentialism, Nietzsche. In the second section I outline the basic tenets of Husserl's phenomenology, which had an important influence on Heidegger, whom many have regarded as the first true existentialist, as well as being a pivotal figure in the history of twentieth-century philosophy. I critically examine Heidegger's existentialist phenomenology in the following section. In the final two sections I discuss the work of two important French existential Marxists, Sartre and Merleau-Ponty, focusing on their conceptions of human subjectivity.

9.1 The Background to Existentialism

Existentialism is very much a twentieth-century current of thought. Although it has its precursors in the writings of Stirner, Nietzsche and Kierkegaard, it only came to prominence at the end of the Second World War. It was an expression and an awareness of the intellectual malaise and of the inexplicable horrors that had occurred in the thirty or so years that had passed. As Novack wrote: 'two world wars, the rise of fascism and totalitarian states, the slaughter of coloured peoples, the concentration camps and the extermination of six million Jews, Hiroshima and Nagasaki, all of which composed the fabric of contemporary history, had, in some quarters, given rise to a mood of extreme pessimism' (1966: 7). Existentialism thus registers a mood, an atmosphere, a 'style of philosophising', rather than any specific philosophical school, although there has been a close and intimate relationship between existentialism and phenomenology. Mary Warnock (1970) suggests that the defining characteristic of the existentialist philosopher is that he or she combines the ethical voluntarism of Kierkegaard and Nietzsche with the phenomenology of Husserl. But in many respects existentialism and phenomenology represent distinct and contrasting tendencies, as we shall observe in discussing Husserl's philosophy.

As existentialism is a style of philosophising rather than a coherent body of philosophical doctrine, it is not surprising that there is a great diversity of thought among existentialists. Two writers who are seen as central figures in the tradition, Heidegger and Jaspers, in fact deny that they are existentialists. This diversity is seen by Novack as springing not from its philosophical method but from the heterogeneous orientations and interests of dislocated middle-class intellectuals, uneasily wedged between the ruling powers and the broad mass of working people. They seek, he writes, positions between idealism and capitalist reaction on the one hand, the materialism and socialism on the other (1966: 11). Scholars such as Kierkegaard, Jaspers and Marcel were theists, while Nietzsche, Sartre, de Beauvoir and Merleau-Ponty were atheists. The political affiliations of the existentialists were equally diverse; Sartre and Merleau-Ponty were Marxists; Heidegger was a fascist and not only praised but participated in the destruction of academic freedom. But as John MacQuarrie (1973) suggests, in spite of this diversity, existentialism can be characterised by certain common themes that are shared by all the existentialists. Before going on to discuss specific scholars, it may therefore be useful, initially, drawing on the work of MacQuarrie, to outline some of these essential tenets.

The first defining characteristic of existentialism is that it is a humanistic philosophy and is centrally concerned with human and personal values, and with the realisation of an authentic existence. Unlike traditional philosophy it is not concerned with epistemology or logic, or with knowledge of the *natural* world, but with the human condition: it begins with the human subject not with nature. Although idealism and rationalist philosophy also has this focus on human subjectivity, for the existentialist the human subject is an existent, not simply a cognising, subject. The human person is seen not only as 'a thinking subject but an initiator of action and a centre of feeling. It is this whole spectrum of existence, known directly and concretely in the very act of existing that existentionalism tries to express' (MacQuarrie 1973: 2). Fundamentally, existentialism is a philosophy of existence and of the human subject; it begins with the affirmation of the subject as the central concern of philosophy.

Coupled with this focus is the tendency of existentialists to reject the main rationalist philosophical tradition that stems from Plato, and that sets up a dichotomy between the subject and the objective world. This tradition assumes a universal static reality as existing outside and independent of the individual subject, a reality that may be grasped and expressed by the rational intellect. As Tiryakian puts it: 'a fundamental presupposition of classical philosophy is that reality can be an *object* of knowledge, that this knowledge does not depend upon the peculiarities of the knower, and that rational thought is the proper instrument by which to grasp reality' (1962: 73). Existentialism breaks completely with this tradition, which had been the dominant perspective in classical philosophy from Descartes to Hegel, and which was shared by both the empiricists and rationalists. Existentialism renounces what Jaspers called 'the subject–object cleavage' – a fundamental trait of rational thought – and along with it the very foundation of traditional epistemology, the 'thinking subject' (*res cogitans*). The existentialist therefore tends to reverse Descartes' formulation, 'I think, therefore I am', and to stress that existence is prior to rational thought. Existence is primordial for the existentialist, thinking a derived mode of being. This means that existentialism tends to see the self as an agent, and such themes as freedom, choice and responsibility are prominent in all existentialist writings, and to stress that the human subject is a psychosomatic unity not simply a knower. It also means that existentialism tends to put more emphasis on the emotions – a topic that tended to be neglected by traditional philosophy, who regarded the emotions as falling within the domain of psychology.

A further important characteristic of existentialism is that its psychological tenor conveys an overwhelming sense of tragedy, which arises from the fragmentation and the meaninglessness inherent in human existence. Recurrent existentialist themes include such topics as guilt, anxiety, alienation, despair, boredom, death and loneliness. The forms of alienation that are so poignantly articulated in the existentialist 'tragic sense of life', which arise essentially from existing social realities, are depicted by the existentialists as inherent in the very nature of human life (Novack 1966: 6).

The distinction between existence and essence, stemming from Plato, relates existence to the realm of appearance, the contingent and the changeable. Reason goes beyond this realm and seeks for unchanging and universal essences, for a realm of forms and ideas. Existentialism rejects this dualism, and puts a focal emphasis on existence – concrete human experience, the basic postulate of existentialism is that existence, defined as the immediate living experience of the human subject, has priority over essence; that is, rational abstractions reflecting the laws, properties and relations of the objective reality. For the existentialist, the human subject is an ex-sistent, from the Latin term *ex-sistere* meaning to 'stand out', and thus has no predetermined nature or essence. This leads the existentialist to put prime emphasis on the uniqueness of the individual existent.

Although the general tenor of existentialist thought is subjectivist and anti-rationalist, MacQuarrie argues that it would be misleading to categorise existentialism as a form of subjective idealism, even less as a form of nihilism. Nevertheless he notes that many of the leading existentialists often pay lip-service to the truth that the human subject exists as a person only within a community, some writers like Buber and Marcel did in fact stress the importance of interpersonal relations. But on the whole, their focal concern was an individual whose quest for authentic selfhood centres on the meaning of *personal* being. But this did imply either solipsism or a subjectivist approach for the reality of the social and external world was not denied. Contrasting existentialism with idealism, Mac-Quarrie writes:

> It is true that both existentialism and idealism are philosophies of the subject rather than of the object, but whereas the idealist begins from man as thinking subject, the existentialist begins from man's total world. The idealist . . . begins from ideas, whereas the existentialist claims that we already begin with the things themselves . . . thus despite its stress on subjectivity, existentialism does not follow the same path as idealism. To exist is to be in encounter with a real world. (1973: 15)

Thus for the existentialist there is a fundamental paradox in human existence, in that the human subject can exist only in relation to a world, yet the same world that enables the person to exist also threatens his or her existence, and will eventually extinguish it entirely (1973: 59).

Likewise MacQuarrie stresses that although existentialism is at variance with the whole rationalist tradition, this does not imply the complete abandonment of rational thought, which, after all, is a basic constituent of the human existent. Socrates, the 'patron saint of reason', is seen as an early precursor of existentialism, and MacQuarrie cites Jaspers as an existentialist philosopher who reacted strongly against the irrationalism inherent in Kierkegaard's writings. As Grimsley wrote:

> To reject the perversion of overweening intellectualism does not mean that we are to be precipitated into subjectivism and irrationalism. It would be foolish to condemn reason as such. Rather we must insist on the power and efficacy of a reason which is permeated by existence as the sources of its truth. (1955: 169)

Extentialism was a reactionary move against abstract intellectualism and positivism rather than a renunciation of reason. MacQuarrie notes that in this existentialism had much in common with pragmatism, although the temper of the two outlooks were very dissimilar (1973: 15).

Although existentialism is essentially a twentieth-century phenomenon, its roots have been traced back far into history. MacQuarrie suggests that Buddhism and various mythological perspectives express an existential outlook, and the writings of Socrates, St Augustine, Luther, Pascal, Johann Hammann and Maine de Biran have all been accepted as being part of the existentialist tradition. But in its modern form the 'father' of existentialism is Kierkegaard, who along with Nietzsche, is considered one of the recognised forerunners of the movement. Also important is the neglected anarchist writer Max Stirner, a contemporary of Kierkegaard. As we have discussed Nietzsche's philosophy at some length in chapter 2, we shall confine ourselves in this section to that lonely figure Kierkegaard.

Søren Kierkegaard (1813–55) was born in Copenhagen, then the capital of a prosperous agricultural country, which was hardly involved in the tumultuous events of the early nineteenth century. He came from a well-to-do background and never had to work for a living, but had an austere religious upbringing. His father suffered from melancholia and had a morbid sense of guilt. Kierkegaard studied theology at the University of Copenhagen, but his main interests were in literature, philosophy and history, and he later gave up his training to be a Lutheran minister. After contemplating suicide in the spring of 1836, two years later he experienced a religious conversion. In 1840 he became engaged to Regina Olsen, but the next year broke off the engagement although he loved her deeply, it seems, for the remainder of his life. His reasons for ending the engagement are complex; partly due to his deep feeling of melancholy, partly to his deeply rooted religious attitude, and partly to his sense that marriage would interfere with his divinely inspired mission – to discover and express how one could be a true Christian. In an important sense, as Copleston suggests, Kierkegaard was 'first and foremost a religious thinker' (1963: 350). As Kierkegaard himself put it in speaking of his broken engagement, 'essentially I live in a spirit world' (Lowrie 1942: 140). Perhaps he was right, and was unsuited for the married life. In any event, Kierkegaard continued to live a lonely, eccentric life, alienated from many of his friends and issuing polemics against the established Church of Denmark. Crippled by a sense of guilt and physically deformed (for he had been born a hunchback), he was, he said, like a solitary fir tree, casting no shadow, and 'only the wood dove builds its nest in my branches'. He wrote voluminously, sometimes under his own name, sometimes under a pseudonym: among his more well-known works are *Either-Or* (1843), *The Concept of Dread* (1844), *Philosophical Fragments* (1845) and the *Concluding Unscientific Postscript* (1846). Politically a conservative, Kierkegaard welcomed the repression of the 1848 revolutions. He died in 1855, aged forty-two.

Kierkegaard expressed two deep and lasting antipathies: towards the established church and towards Hegelian metaphysics. As a student, Kierkegaard had been deeply impressed by Hegel's philosophy and regarded Hegel as the greatest of the speculative philosophers. But while on a short visit to Berlin in 1841 – one of the few occasions he left his native Copenhagen – he went to hear the lectures of Schelling, who expressed harsh criticisms of Hegel's philosophy. Thus influenced by Schelling and by the writings of the German dramatist Gotthold Lessing, Kierkegaard became increasingly disillusioned with Hegelian philosophy. Hegel, he felt, by focusing on the Absolute, had presented a speculative system of thought in which there was little scope or place for the existing individual. Hegel's thought was abstract, impersonal and objective, and in spinning categories that mediate between the individual and the world-process, Hegel had forgotten that he himself was an existent human subject, like everyone else. Kierkegaard writes:

> Being an individual man is a thing that has been abolished, and every
> speculative philosopher confuses himself with humanity at large,

whereby he becomes something infinitely great – and at the same time nothing at all. He confounds himself with humanity in sheer distraction of mind. (Bretall 1946: 206)

In addition, Hegel's pantheistic vision tended to collapse the distinction between God and the human subject. In the Hegelian system, he noted, 'the qualitative distinction between God and man is pantheistically abolished'. But Kierkegaard felt that for Christianity there could be no unity of the divine and the human (Bretall 1946: 230; Copleston 1963: 345) Hegel, Kierkegaard quipped – and his writings are full of ironic remarks about Hegel and his 'system' – that if a person became sufficiently steeped in Hegel's philosophy he or she would become so anonymous that they would not even have a letter addressed to them (Solomon 1988: 89).

In contrast to Hegel's speculative system, Kierkegaard stresses existence, the living human being, that is, an existing individual. The term 'existence' for Kierkegaard is a specifically human category and is not applied to the natural world. And the human subject is seen not as a knower or spectator but as a moral agent, concerned with making choices. Kierkegaard continually insists that his concern is ethical, something that he felt Hegelian philosophy ignored completely. In contrast, then, to Hegel's objectivity, Kierkegaard stresses subjectivity, focusing on 'the passionate movement of decision' when the individual makes acts of choice and specific commitments. Thus as Copleston writes:

the man who contents himself with the role of spectator of the world and of life and translates everything into a dialectic of abstract concepts exists indeed in one sense but not in another. For he wishes to understand everything and commits himself to nothing. The 'existing individual', however, is the actor rather than the spectator. He commits himself and so gives form and direction to his life. (Copleston 1963: 347)

Kierkegaard thus uses the term 'existence' in the same sense that 'authentic existence' is used by many later existentialists. Kierkegaard sees himself in this regard as essentially following the Socratic tradition:

In the principle that subjectivity, inwardness, is the truth, there is comprehended the Socratic wisdom whose everlasting merit it was to have become aware of the essential significance of existence, of the fact that the knower is an existing individual. (Bretall 1946: 215)

Whereas for Hegel truth is the whole, the totality, for Kierkegaard it is subjective. 'Subjectivity is truth, subjectivity is reality' (Bretall 1946: 231). Not since St Augustine has a philosopher stressed more the importance of the 'inner' individual human being, and equated truth with subjectivity. MacIntyre has noted the problems of holding that truth is subjective, for how is one to treat the denial of this proposition? Such a dilemma is never faced by Kierkegaard (1964: 512).

But Kierkegaard saw 'existence' not simply as a state of being, but rather as a process, as 'stages on life's way' as one of his studies is titled. He suggests three 'spheres of existence', or stages, even hinting that it is an existential 'dialectic'. The first stage or sphere is described as the *aesthetic*, when the individual chooses to be motivated by the senses and the emotions, seeking pleasurable and aesthetic experience. To break with this form of existence, and to move to the *ethical* stage, involves an either/or decision, one that is not governed by any criteria, but involves an integral commitment. A person who chooses to live an ethical existence, follows universal ethical rules, which give consistence and form to his or her life. Socrates typifies the ethical stage. Finally, there is the third choice of lifestyle, *religious* existence, one that is based fundamentally on an act of faith. This involves the radical affirmation of one's uniqueness, a leap of faith in the acceptance of God as a personal saviour. As Tiryakian in summary puts it, the human subject 'reaches genuine self-realization, selfhood, in a transcendent relation in the presence of God' (1962: 89). As with the later Jung, human subjectivity is intrinsically related to the religious life, to affirm one's relations to God, as a personal and transcendent being, an affirmation that requires faith not reason, is the essence of the religious sphere, and true subjectivity. Copleston notes that Kierkegaard's definition of truth as subjectivity and his definition of faith are the same (1963: 340). Importantly, Kierkegaard's stance does not suggest a mystical union between God and the human subject, but rather remains that of a traditional Protestant and theist.

Many writers have stressed that Kierkegaard's ethics are wholly asocial, and that he drew a stark division between the individual and the collectivity, which he castigated as the 'public', seeing the social as the realm of the anonymous and the untrue. As Blackham suggests, he lacked the historical interest and understanding for an adequate analysis of social situations. Thus his individualism 'is wholly religious and philosophic, a concentration on the individual as the sole source of the universally human' (1952: 21). There is no dialectic in Kierkegaard between society and the human subject, and he is unable to envisage any truly human community. An unhappy lonely recluse in his own life, his vision of humanity is similar and is relieved only by faith in a personal saviour. But as with Nietzsche, Kierkegaard's writings are full of interesting psychological insights, particularly his concept of dread. Distinguished from fear which always has a recognisable object, dread or anxiety is a psychological inner state that has no object, and is defined as 'sympathetic antipathy', combining attraction and repulsion. It is an emotion that implies tension, and is thus seen by Kierkegaard as essentially involving the possibility of freedom. Much of human affairs is seen by Kierkegaard as a desperate attempt by people to escape or conceal their feelings of dread. It is an intrinsic aspect of the human condition, and it can be overcome, it seems, only by an act of faith, by commitment to a transcendent God. Kierkegaard's whole viewpoint rests on the foundation of 'the individual before God' and 'individuality' can be fully attained only in the Christian religious experience. Kierkegaard's conception of the human subject, as said, is essentially that of a spiritual rather than a social being, and MacIntyre significantly suggests that Kierkegaard's depiction of the human person has affinities with what Hegel described as 'the unhappy consciousness', which, as we noted, Hegel identified with traditional Christianity (MacIntyre 1964: 513). Kierkegaard's critique of the 'public' and the 'herd mentality' led him to deny the crucial importance of human community and social interaction in the formation of the person. (For important studies on the life and philosophy of Kierkegaard, see Collins 1953; Grimsley 1973; Hannay 1983.)

9.2 Husserl and Phenomenology

We have discussed in the first section one of the intellectual sources of existentialism, the ethical voluntarism of Kierkegaard who, along with Nietzsche and Stirner, provided many of the essential doctrines and concepts of the movement – the focus on concrete existence, on freedom, choice and anxiety, and on human subjectivity. We turn now to the second element in the intellectual ancestry of existentialism, phenomenology, a philosophy that originated in Germany during the early part of the present century. Although 'phenomenology' was a term used by Hegel in his classic study (1807) of human consciousness – seen as progressing through various stages in the self-knowledge of the world-spirit or Absolute

– the meaning it came to assume in the writings of Edmund Husserl (1859–1938), the founder of phenomenology was very different. For Husserl used the concept to refer to a specific method of philosophical analysis, one quite distinct from Hegel's dialectical approach. Indeed, compared with other important scholars writing around the turn of the century – Dewey, Dilthey and Royce, for example – Husserl was little influenced by Hegel.

Husserl is one of the most important and influential philosophers of the present century, and although he has indirectly had a crucial impact on the orientation of philosophy and the social sciences, he has very much remained a marginal figure with respect to the Anglo-Saxon scene. Leszek Kolakowski (1975) remarks that when he gave a series of lectures on Husserl at Oxford in the early 1970s, it was the first time Husserl's name had been mentioned in the city since the early 1930s, and only three or four students attended the lectures. Likewise for several decades now philosophers and anthropologists have been engaged in convoluted debates relating to relativism and rationality – the 'rationality debate' as they have been described – and yet no mention is made of a rationalist philosopher who offered important critiques of cultural relativism more than sixty years ago – Husserl (B. R. Wilson 1970; Hollis and Lukes 1982; Overing 1985). Even more curious is Husserl's omission from John Cottingham's study of rationalism (1984), although it includes lengthy discussions of British analytic philosophers and empiricists!

Edmund Husserl was a German philosopher of Jewish origin. He began his career as a student of mathematics, and took his doctorate in that subject at the University of Vienna in 1883, having earlier studied at Leipzig and Berlin. But having attended Brentano's lectures from 1884 to 1886 he turned to philosophy and, on Brentano's recommendation, became Stumpfs' assistant at the University of Halle. He later taught at Gottingen and Freiburg, but something of a late developer, he was not offered a full professorship until 1916, when he was fifty-seven years old.

Although a perfectionist and expressing a 'self-disparaging humility' that bordered on masochism, his lack of academic advancement in his early years was no doubt the outcome of the anti-Semitism of that period (McCall 1983: 55).

Husserl's first important study, *Philosophy of Arithmetic*, was published in 1891. Influenced by Brentano and concerned to clarify the basic presuppositions of arithmetic, which he closely associated with logic, Husserl suggested that the basic concepts of arithmetic were based on psychological principles – a thesis similar to that of

J. S. Mill. In a harsh critique of the book, the mathematician Gottlob Frege, whose own *Foundations of Arithmetic* had appeared some seven years earlier, argued that Husserl had essentially confused logic and psychology, and that his reasoning was psychologistic and naive. The logical presuppositions of mathematical knowledge, Frege felt, were *a priori* and could not be reduced to empirical knowledge. Husserl completely accepted Frege's criticisms and did a 'complete turn-around', for in his *Logical Investigations* (1900), Husserl developed a thoroughgoing critique of what he described as 'psychologism', the attempt to subordinate logic and mathematics to psychology. We shall say more of Husserl's rejection of psychologism in a moment. But Husserl, though accepting Frege's arguments regarding the genesis of logical concepts, was critical of Frege's own theory regarding the 'objectivity' of truth. For Frege's method of logical analysis implied an 'objectivist' approach in that it failed to take into account the subjective aspect of knowledge. (Pivčevič 1970: 42). But though accepting Brentano's stress on the 'intentionality' of consciousness, Husserl is equally critical of the psychologistic premises inherent in Brentano's empirical psychology. What is needed, Husserl felt, was an approach to logic, and more generally to all forms of knowledge that took into account the 'subjective' aspect of knowledge, without collapsing into psychologism. Pivčevič expresses Husserl's position rather well when he suggests that he 'tried to unite Frege's logical objectivism with Brentano's intentionality on a Kantian basis' (1970: 70).

Husserl's philosophy contrasts in a radical fashion from those scholars who have been described as the originators of existentialism – Kierkegaard and Nietzsche – for his philosophical interests are narrowly epistemological and he is first and foremost a rationalist concerned with establishing the foundations of universal truth. The 'search for certitude' was the leitmotif of his work, from his first study on the philosophy of arithmetic to the classic essay he wrote towards the end of his life on 'philosophy and the crisis of European Man'.

Husserl's ambition is to establish philosophy as a rigorous science, to reaffirm philosophy as theoria, as a form of rational understanding that is distinct from both *doxa* (opinion) and *episteme* (knowledge). He continually makes a plea for a return to the rationalism of Plato and Socrates, 'rationality in that noble and genuine sense . . . that became the ideal in the classical period of Greek philosophy' (1965: 179). He stresses the need for a philosophy that genuinely expresses the 'imperishable demand for pure and absolute knowledge' that he sees as intrinsic to the human condition. Husserl's concern, then, is to establish a philosophy whose impulse it is to generate universal truths. He longed for the days, as Robert Solomon writes, when philosophy could call itself a science, and could declare itself a search for certainty and absolute truth without embarrassment. He sums up Husserl's credo in the following:

> Husserl perceived the loss of absolutes as a genuine 'crisis', not only in the philosophical sciences but in civilization as well. Scepticism was like a disease, an admission of failure, and Nietzsche's relativism and Dilthey's historicism were tantamount to scepticism. The simple rejection of philosophy and its foundations among scientists and empiricists was no better, for their taking the 'natural standpoint' for granted, without any attempt to show its validity, was also a virtual admission of failure. Phenomenology had as its aim nothing less than the return of philosophy to scientific status, and of European thought to the road of rationality. (1988: 130)

This passage succinctly summarises the gist of Husserl's thought as expressed in his essay 'Philosophy as Rigorous Science', published in 1911. Seeing European philosophy since Plato as retreating more and more from the ideals of philosophy as an objective science, Husserl offers a critique of three philosophical orientations which he argued have hampered philosophy in its efforts to be a universal science – naturalism, historicism and what he described as *Weltanschauung* philosophy. We may briefly consider each in turn.

Naturalistic philosophy, for Husserl, is the tendency to recognise as real only physical nature, considered as a unity of spatio-temporal being subject to exact causal laws of nature. While such a philosophy acknowledges the need for a scientific philosophy, it tends to be narrowly positivistic in either denying the reality of human consciousness, or reducing it to empirical facts of a physical nature. For Husserl all natural science is in a sense 'natural' for it takes the natural world as simply given, a 'self-evident pre-datum' (1965–85). As an empirical science psychology is a form of naturalism, for even when not taking a narrow psychophysical approach it tends to connect in an unquestioning manner consciousness with the human organism. 'To eliminate the relation to nature would deprive the psychical of its character as an objectivity and temporally determinable fact of nature, in short, of its character as a psychological fact' (1965: 86). Husserl does not deny the legitimacy of this approach, but suggests its limitations on three counts: it tends to deny consciousness the status of living intentional experience; it tends to ignore the fact that natural science itself is a cultural phenomenon, a product of 'spirit'; and finally that it tends to relativism and not to exact science. The 'intuitive environing world, purely subjective as it is, is forgotten in the scientific thematic,' Husserl writes (1965: 186). Modern psychology is therefore a form of 'objectivism' and 'simply fails to get at the proper essence of "spirit"'. By isolating human consciousness as an object of study, and by interpreting it in terms of the natural science paradigm, psychology, he contended, was inadequate and misleading.

There is a suggestion here that Husserl is following the neo-Kantian paradigm in making a clear distinction between the natural and the human sciences, but Husserl is equally critical of the efforts of Dilthey and Rickert. He suggests that both are still committed to objectivism. Husserl writes:

> There can . . . never be any improvement so long as an objectivism based on a naturalistic focusing on the environing world is not seen in all its naiveté, until men recognize thoroughly the absurdity of the dualistic interpretations of the world, according to which nature and spirit are to be looked upon as realities in the same sense. In all seriousness my opinion is this; there never has nor ever will be an objective science of the spirit. (1965: 188)

What Husserl is essentially getting at is that writers like Dilthey tend to see culture as if it were an objective reality, but to talk of the 'spirit' of a culture or notion or the 'will of a people', Husserl suggests, is pure romanticism, for these concepts only have proper sense in relation to an individual person. To speak of 'spirit' as a reality is an absurdity. But Husserl is equally concerned that Dilthey's philosophy with its historicism – the tendency to interpret reality and truth as relative to historical development – and its stress on world-views (Weltanschauung) leads inevitably to a relativistic attitude towards meaning and truth. Thus he saw Dilthey's philosophy as essentially involving the transformation of Hegel's philosophy of history into a 'sceptical historicism'.

How, then, does one obtain objective knowledge of the world and of the human subject? Husserl suggests by the phenomenological method, and, in a fashion similar to Descartes, proposes that to put philosophy on a firm basis, so as to produce universally valid knowledge, one must put into suspension all empirical and metaphysical presuppositions about the world. The world must be 'put in brackets' (*epoche*), and the 'natural standpoint' – taking the world for granted – must be suspended. This does not imply denying the existence of the natural world, simply refraining from making judgements about it, so that in this 'reduction' we are able to concentrate on pure phenomena, on what is immanently given in our own 'stream of experiences'. Consciousness in a sense must be 'disconnected' from the 'fact-world' that is there before us. Phenomenology, then, is essentially the study of consciousness, but a study quite distinct from empirical psychology for it seeks to grasp the meaning or the essense of a phenomenon as it is given to conscious experience. Husserl's phenomenology is thus the exact antithesis of Skinner's behaviouristic psychology.

Husserl argues that eidetic knowledge, which forms the foundation of all knowledge, entails a form of intellectual analysis or introspection that concentrates on psychological phenomena as they are given in immediate conscious experience, without any attempt to relate them to a non-psychological reality. Husserl's approach thus represents a development of the descriptive psychology of Wundt, Brentano and Stumpf, with whose work Husserl was well acquainted. Husserl even attended Wundt's lectures at Leipzig, but apparently was not impressed by them. And given his stress on consciousness, Husserl, as Solomon emphasises, was very much a part of the mainstream tradition of philosophy extending from Descartes to Fichte, which entailed a turn to subjectivity in order to arrive at fundamental, universal truths. The grand presumption, he writes, 'never sufficiently questioned by Husserl, is that the truth is to be found in consciousness, in the ego, and nowhere else' (1988: 130). Phenomenology is thus an examination and description of the essential structures of consciousness, with a view to ascertaining necessary and universal truths.

But for all his stress on subjectivity and consciousness Husserl's essential focus is on the human person as a cognitive being, and in this he contrasts significantly with many earlier philosophers who also each in their own way 'sought a secure harbour for the stranded ship of knowledge in the individual's existence' (Bauman 1978: 119). He lacked the cosmic vision of Kant, Schelling and Hegel, the moral self-engagement of Fichte (whom he otherwise closely resembles), and the focus on human striving and will that characterises the writings of Schopenhauer and Nietzsche (Solomon 1988: 132). The human subject of Husserl was a knowing self. But importantly, he takes a step beyond Descartes and the empiricist philosophers in that his advocacy of phenomenological reduction also puts the 'empirical ego' in 'brackets'. Thus not only is ɔnsciousness 'disconnected' from the world, but also from the ‌ubstantial ego. As Bauman puts it: 'The man, as an entity which ɔelongs to nature and as a person related to other persons, to a "society", is swept away by the broom of *epoche* together with other impurities' (1978: 120). Thus what is left after the operation of *epoche* is 'pure consciousness', consciousness that belongs to nobody, consciousness free of all earthly attachments – the transcendental ego. Bauman hints that this distinction between individual and transcendental subjectivity has affinities with the beliefs of many mystics (1978: 122), and there is no doubt that the notion of a transcendental ego is a form of subjective idealism (Ayer 1982: 215). Bauman also notes that the notion of 'pure consciousness', unadulterated by the contingencies of empirical experience, on which Husserl pinned his hopes for absolute knowledge, is in the last analysis based on an act of faith (1978: 123). It also expresses Husserl's disinterest in the mundane aspects of life.

Many have questioned whether it is possible to suspend all considerations of empirical existence, and to 'disconnect' experiences from the world of the 'natural standpoint' as required by the transcendental reduction or *epoche*. But aware that this form of analysis may lead to solipsistic conclusions, Husserl in his later writings stresses the importance of intersubjective experiences, maintaining that the experiences of 'other egos' represent an essential aspect of a person's own experience:

> to live as a person is to live in a social framework; In our continually streaming perception of the world we are not isolated but rather stand within it in contact with other men. . . . In living with one another each can participate in the life of the other. Thus, in general, the world does not exist for isolated individuals but for the community of men. (quoted in Kearney 1986: 23)

In his last study, *The Crisis of European Philosophy* (1936), Husserl argues that the transcendental ego is a 'correlative' to the world, and thus shifts the emphasis away from an individualistic viewpoint towards one that focuses on the intersubjective community. Husserl introduces the concept of *Lebenswelt*, the world of lived experience, which brings him closer to the existentialist tradition, a concept that was later developed by a close student of Husserl's philosophy, Merleau-Ponty. But as Pivčević insists, it is difficult to bridge the gap between a phenomenological method that insulates and separates the human subject from the empirical world (including the empirical self), and the reality of the historic *Lebenswelt* which suggests an intersubjective experience (1970: 90, (For further studies of Husserl, see Kockelmans 1967; Ricoeur 1967; Edie 1987.)

Husserl's phenomenology has had a tremendous impact on both philosophy and the social sciences, and his writings and method have been the starting point of many important theoretical developments. Indeed, existential phenomenology has been described by Richard H. Brown (1977) as one of the three important philosophical schools which offered a critique of positivism, and which led to the formation of a humanistic social theory. (The other two are pragmatism and the analytic philosophy associated with Wittgenstein.) There are, perhaps, four areas of enquiry that have stemmed from Husserl's phenomenology, and although it is beyond the scope of the present study to discuss all of these interpretations of Husserl fully, they may be briefly mentioned.

The first is phenomenological sociology as developed in the writings of Alfred Schutz (1899–1959) who essentially combined Husserl's 'ontology of the life-world', with its focus on consciousness and intentionality, with Max Weber's subjective theory of social action. In his *Phenomenology of the Social World* (1967), Schutz reinterpreted Weber's analysis of *Verstehen*, to suggest an interpretative sociology that has affinities with that of Dilthey, and with that of the symbolic interactionist tradition, whose approach has indeed been described as 'phenomenological in spirit' (Psathas 1973: 7; for further discussions of Schultz and phenomenological sociology, see Natanson 1970; Filmer et al. 1972; Douglas and Johnson 1977).

The second is the development of philosophical hermeneutics, which drew inspiration from twin sources – Dilthey's philosophy of historical understanding and Husserl's later writings on the centrality of the 'life world' in the interpretation of human experience. The two key scholars in this hermeneutic tradition are Hans-Georg Gadamer and Paul Ricoeur, who in recent decades have become the subject of much critical debate. (For important studies of hermeneutics, see Palmer 1969; Gadamer 1975; Ricoeur 1981; Bernstein 1983: 109–69; Kearney 1986: 90–112; Warnke 1987.)

A third area of study, which derives fundamentally from Husserl's phenomenology, is the deconstructionist theory of Jacques Derrida, whom we shall discuss more fully in the next chapter. For although Derrida studied phenomenology and wrote an important early study of Husserl, in his critique of subjectivity, Derrida has affinities with the structuralist theorists and such scholars as Foucault.

And finally, as we have suggested earlier, Husserl was one of the key figures in the development of existentialism as a philosophical tradition, and it is with this tradition that we shall be mainly concerned in the remainder of this chapter. Although many scholars have been classed as existentialists – Buber, Marcel, Jaspers, de Beauvoir, Ortega y Gasset, Berdyaev and Camus, for example – we shall confine ourselves here to three writers. For Heidegger, Sartre and Merleau-Ponty all assumed a non-religious perspective and put a central focus on human subjectivity.

9.3 Heidegger's Existentialist Phenomenology

Martin Heidegger (1889–1976) has been described as the first true existentialist and is considered by many as a pivotal figure in the history of philosophy, given his important influence on the hermeneutic theory of Gadamer and Ricoeur, on the existentialism of Sartre and Merleau-Ponty, and on the deconstructive theory of Derrida. But like Wittgenstein, Heidegger has been subject to an excess of eulogy, in that his critique of Cartesian epistemology and the subject/object dualism was a good deal less original than both he and his followers suggest. For such a critique had been initiated by Hegel and developed by both the Marxists and the pragmatists; that the human subject was a 'being-in-the world' was largely taken as self-evident by social scientists such as Boas, Durkheim and Mead. But like many academics Heidegger saw himself as a sage and a prophet who had stepped beyond the philosophical tradition he had inherited, proclaiming an entirely new way of looking at the world. This is something of an illusion, or, as Solomon puts it, a 'transcendental pretence' (1988: 153), which Heidegger shared with Kant, Hegel, Marx and Kierkegaard. Heidegger was a good deal less original than is supposed by philosophy texts.

Heidegger was born in Messkirch in the Black Forest region of Baden and his early life was steeped in the Catholic religion, for he was educated at a Jesuit seminary. He studied at Freiburg University under Husserl and the neo-Kantian philosopher Rickert, and his Catholic upbringing is reflected in his doctoral thesis on the medieval philosopher Duns Scotus (1916). From 1920 to 1923 he was Husserl's assistant at Freiburg, and after a spell of lecturing at the University of Marburg, he succeeded Husserl in the chair of philosophy at Freiburg in 1928, becoming Rector of the University five years later when Hitler assumed power. Having become a member of the Nazi Party, in his inaugural address Heidegger welcomed the new regime. He taught at Freiburg until 1944, disowning his tutor Husserl, who was Jewish. He was suspended by the Allied administration for a period after the war, and he was to spend the remainder of his life in seclusion in the Bavarian mountains, associating only with a close circle of devotees. Heidegger died in his native village aged eighty-seven. Like Kant his whole life seemed to have been rooted in one place, and devoted entirely to philosophy, 'a human existence invested wholly in abstract thought' (Steiner 1978: 23). Unlike Kant he had little interest in science and wordly affairs, and none of his progressive tendencies; Heidegger was an arch-reactionary, and even after 1945 refused to say anything candid or even intelligible about either his personal record as a Fascist, or about the general holocaust (1978: 19).

In his short but important introduction to Heidegger's thought, George Steiner outlines four difficulties in attempting to outline Heidegger's philosophy. The first is that only perhaps a third of Heidegger's philosophical output is available in anything like a definitive form. However his principal study, the monumental *Being and Time* (1927), first translated into English in the 1960s, is the one most concerned with the phenomenology of human existence, for in his later years Heidegger wrote primarily on the philosophy of language and on the metaphysics of being. And it is with *Being and Time* that we shall primarily be concerned here.

Secondly, there are very diverse and contrasting opinions relating to the status of Heidegger's philosophy. Some have regarded Heidegger as the most important philosopher since Kant, and put him in the same league as the all-time 'greats', Plato, Aristotle, Descartes and Hegel. Others have considered him as something of a charlatan or as 'meta-theologian'; it is significant that he was omitted entirely from Russell's *History of Western Philosophy*, a vulgar book, according to Steiner. But Copleston's study, which is anything but vulgar, covers Heidegger's writings in just three paragraphs (1963: 437–8). My own feeling is that neither panegyrics nor contempt does justice to Heidegger's thought. Although, as said, he has been somewhat overrated, for his essential thoughts on the human subject simply express in obscure philosophical language what many sociologists, anthropologists and Marxists (and, one might add, ordinary people of all cultures) had long taken for granted, namely that humans are essentially social beings situated in the world, Heidegger nevertheless had important things to say on this issue. Moreover, his influence on hermeneutics, existentialist phenomenology and so-called 'post-structuralist' thought three important strands in contemporary thought – make Heidegger a pivotal figure that cannot be ignored, whatever one may think of his mystical and fascist tendencies.

A third limitation to the understanding of Heidegger lies in his style of writing 'a thicket of impenetrable verbiage', an abomination that is 'nothing more than bombastic, indecipherable jargon', as Steiner expresses the thoughts of Heidegger's detractors. Carnap in fact cited an extract from Heidegger's writings to illustrate the meaningless of metaphysics, and Adorno's study *The Jargon of Authencity* (1973) is largely devoted to a critique of Heidegger's abstruse language. But it is important to realise that Heidegger is perhaps not deliberately obscure, but rather aimed to invent a new philosophical language, one that was consonant with an attempt to go beyond traditional philosophical discourse which is seen as obscuring our understanding of Being. But the creation of new terminology and concepts and the metaphorical use of language has a fascination all of its own, and many contemporary writers have seemingly followed Heidegger's example in the opaque use of language; the writings of Lacan, Derrida and others are well known for their difficult even obscurantist style. In commenting upon the 'unreadable' nature and the 'thick obscurity' of Heideggers prose, Mary Warnock (1970: 50) questions whether there can be any grounds for inventing a new language. The issue, however, is not the construction of new concepts or terminology, still less the use of poetic language or a rich metaphorical style to express meaning, but rather the importance of making one's thoughts accessible to others. The generation of new conceptual frameworks and a poetic style in the writings of Marx, Nietzsche, Schopenhauer and Freud – so different in other respects – did not affect the lucidity of their prose style. Steiner indicates that Heidegger did not want to be 'understood' in the ordinary sense of that word, but one should be careful not to equate obscurity with profundity of thought.

The final problem in coming to terms with Heidegger is his fascist affiliations, for many have tended to associate his metaphoric and obscure abstractions with his personal engagement with Nazism. Yet the relationship between his philosophy and his politics are by no means clear and straightforward, and although Heidegger became increasingly mystical in his later writings, offering an 'obscure picture of indeterminacy', his existentialist tendencies had a profound effect on Sartre and Merleau-Ponty, two Marxist scholars, as well as suggesting to Husserl the need to situate the subject in the life-world. As with Hegel one can see a rational core within what is essentially a reactionary metaphysic.

Heidegger's 'way of thought' expressed in *Being and Tin*
essentially combines two schools of philosophy, Dilthey's *Leben*
philosophie (philosophy of life) and Husserl's phenomenology. Bot.
these schools, as J. L. Mehta writes, 'were attempts to extract a
meaning out of life and consciousness and build this up conceptually by investigating them from within, immanently, without any
presuppositions and without taking any help from the discoveries
and constructions of Science and metaphysics respectively' (1971:
15).

From Dilthey, Heidegger took the lessons of hermeneutics,
Dilthey's vision of the historicity of things (for as Dilthey suggested, 'only his history tells man what he is') and his conception of
understanding as the immanent self-interpretation of the life-world
were two central ideas that were both adsorbed by Heidegger. Of
central importance to him was Dilthey's conception that 'Life is the
basic fact and it must be the starting point of philosophy.'

From Husserl, Heidegger took his phenomenological method,
and explicitly acknowledges the importance of Husserl's pioneering study *Logic Investigations* to his own thinking (1962: 62). But the
trend of Heidegger's own 'hermeneutic phenomenology' moves in
a direction that is virtually the antithesis to that of Husserl's
transcendental reduction. For whereas Husserl's method involves
putting the empirical world within brackets, thus 'disconnecting'
consciousness from it, and thereby securing through the intuiting
of essences objective understanding, Heidegger advocates the opposite, of situating the subject *within* the world. He rejects the
centrality of consciousness and the ego altogether, although he does
uphold the general method of Husserl's phenomenology in its
insistence on the first person standpoint. Thus although in *Being
and Time* (1962) Heidegger defines his philosophy as a universal
'phenomenological ontology' which takes its departure from the
hermeneutic of *Dasein* (i.e. human existence), as an 'analytic of
existence' (1962: 62), he never accepted Husserl's programmatic
conceptions of what a phenomenological analysis entailed. In an
important sense Heidegger was not a phenomenologist and Husserl
was not an existentialist, even though their respective concepts of
Dasein and *Lebenswelt* have close affinities to each other. Although
Being and Time is often interpreted as taking in the whole sweep of
traditional philosophy the other influences on Heidegger, besides
Husserl and Dilthey, are rather few in number – Parmenides,
Aristotle, Plato, Descartes, Kant, Hegel, Scheler and Bergson. The
subjective philosophy of Kierkegaard always remains in the background (Mehta 1971: 15–27; Solomon 1988: 157).

Heidegger's fundamental concern is not with epistemology or with the human subject, but with ontology, the 'meaning of being'. This is not an empirical question, and Heidegger bewails the fact that scholars since the time of pre-Socratics have been relatively uninterested in the question of being (*Sein*), with the question that Schelling raised, 'why is there anything rather than nothing?', but rather instead have been concerned with beings or entities in the world. In the past other scholars have tended to see Being as either something self-evident like 'the sky *is* blue' or as undefinable, or they have failed to make the distinction between Being and existents. Both idealists and materialists, Heidegger felt, overlooked this distinction, focusing attention on the 'Being of entities', not on Being as such. And the latter, as the foundation or ground of what *is*, is itself no-thing, nothing phenomenal. Thus Heidegger makes a clear distinction between an ontic approach, which is concerned with beings as phenomena – whether it be a person, a living organism or a social institution – and an ontological approach, which relates to the nature of Being. In *Being and Time*, however, Heidegger never gets round to an analysis of Being; the study is rather a preliminary enquiry into *Dasein*, Being-in-the-world, which Heidegger sees as having priority, over all other entities, and, as human existence, 'already comports itself' towards the meaning of Being (1962: 35). His later writings have a quasi-religious quality. Being is described as an almost metaphysical agent which 'discloses itself' in time and which can 'speak' and 'reveal' itself to us. As Heidegger writes of the poet-thinker as the 'guardian of being' these later writings have an elitist and mystical tone reminiscent of the 'oracular obscurity of the pre-Socratics' whom Heidegger admired (Blackham 1952: 109; Pivčević 1970: 113; M. Warnock 1970: 67).

We shall concern ourselves then with Heidegger's most 'existentialist' text, *Being and Time*.

The central concept of this study, indeed, the fundamental one for it is invoked on almost every page of the text, is that of *Dasein*, which literally means 'being there' (*da* = there, *sein* = being). Its essential meaning refers to human existence, which is captured in the phrase 'Being-in-the-world'. It is the mode of existence of the human subject, which is not to be conceived of as an entity or a substance with properties. This Being-in-the-world is the Being of the self in its inseparable relations with the non-self, the world of things and other persons in which the human subject always and necessarily finds itself. To stress this holistic perspective, and the centrality of our Being-in-the-world (which Heidegger takes as a fundamental starting point rather than as a result, as with Hegel (Solomon 1988; 156)). Heidegger seems deliberately to avoid using such concepts as I, subject, self, person, life, spirit, man, consciousness. *Dasein* is always the prior term. The decision to avoid these terms was not an arbitrary one, he writes, for these concepts carry with them a certain reification that Heidegger wishes to circumvent (1962: 72). When Ayer writes that Heidegger 'calls the Ego' *Dasein*, 'being-there' *probably* to underline the point that it is *supposed* to be situated in the world and not a 'detached spectator' (1982: 227, my italics), he seems not to have grasped the thrust of Heidegger's argument for there is no 'supposed' about it. For Heidegger the essence of the human subject, or rather the human condition, lies in existence, and this always necessarily implies that the person is situated in a world, of things and of people. As Blackham puts it: 'the world as I find it is constitutive of my existence, not merely the place in which I have my existence. There is no separation possible' (1952: 88). To equate Descartes' 'ego' with *Dasein*, as Ayer seems to do, is completely to misunderstand Heidegger's philosophy, which represent a fundamental break with Cartesian rationalism. As Heidegger put it:

> It is not the case that man 'is' and then has, by way of an extra, a relationship-of-Being towards the 'World' – a world with which he provides himself occasionally. *Dasein* is never 'proximally' an entity which, is, so to speak, free from Being-in . . . the world. Taking up relationships towards the world is possible only *because Dasein*, as Being-in-the-World, is as it is. (1962: 84)

Many writers have stressed the fact that Heidegger's existentialist phenomenology constitutes a fundamental rejection of Cartesian dualism. Husserl had already transformed the subjectivity of Descartes and of Hume by refusing to accept the dichotomy of the thinking subject and the world outside the mind, but Heidegger takes this critique a step further. The problem with Descartes, Heidegger writes, is that while he investigated the 'cognition' of the human subject, he ignored entirely the 'I am', the existence of the subject which is no less 'primordial' than the cognito (1962: 71). But Heidegger not only rejects the Cartesian dualism between the subject and world, and between body and mind, but an entire metaphysical tradition that stems from Plato. Steiner sums up the implications of Heidegger's emphasis on *Dasein* as follows:

All Western metaphysics, whether deliberately or not, has been Platonist in that it has sought to transpose the essence of man out of daily life. It has posited a pure perceiver, a fictive agent of cognition detached from common experience. It has disincarnated being through an artifice of introspective reductionism of the sort dramatized in Cartesian doubt and Husserlian phenomenology . . . Heidegger utterly rejects this process of abstraction and what he regards as the resultant artifice of compartmentalization in man's consideration of man. (1978: 81)

Being and Time is entirely given over to a phenomenological analysis of *Dasein*, and one can do no more here than present in summary fashion its modal characteristics. We can outline these under five headings.

Existence

The essence of *Dasein* is existence which, from a phenomenological standpoint, is in a sense prior both to the self and cognition. Existence signifies a standing-out (*ex-sistere*), and this suggests that the human condition is not something given, but implies self-reflection and that *Dasein* has 'its own possibility'. The human subject is therefore capable of 'transcendence', for existence entails an understanding in terms of possibilities and projects. The human subject is therefore, constitutionally, always pressing towards horizons that are beyond the present given condition. As Heidegger express it: 'the character of understanding as projection is constitutive of Being-in-the-World . . . *Dasein* is constantly "more" than it factually is' (1985).

Concern

The basic relationship between human beings and the world is not one of control but of concern (*Sorge*). The immediate world of the human subject is not a world of material objects but a world of preoccupations and concerns. We are in a continuous relationship with the things around us, and they are not so much inert things as entities we observe, study and use. Heidegger describes this type of existent as 'being-ready-to-hand', tools for our use. For Heidegger, therefore, the human subject is not a being separate from the surrounding world, but intrinsically connected to it, and this relationship he describes as one of concern.

Temporality

Another characteristic of *Dasein* is that of temporality, which suggests that the human subject only exists under the aspect of time and it is in this that all human activities have ultimately their roots. The Being of the human person is therefore always temporal: 'What he is *now* is determined by his possibilities and he projects them into the *future*, and by the possibilities he has realised in the *past*' (Tiryakian 1962: 109). For Heidegger time is neither an infinite series of instants or 'now points', nor a kind of spatialised container in which things are placed, but rather the setting of all understandings and interpretation of Being. Like Heraclitus and Hegel, Heidegger has a profound sense of the historicity of the world and of the human subject. As he writes, 'If *Dasein*'s being is in principle historical, then every factical science is always manifestly in the grip of this historicising' (1962: 444). The implication of this tenet has still largely to penetrate the social sciences.

Anxiety

Developing Kierkegaard's analysis of 'concept of dread', Heidegger suggests that anxiety (*Angst*) plays a vital role in the self-understanding of the human subject. Anxiety is distinct from fear, and is not focused on any particular object; it is rather the experience that arises from an awareness of our finitude. The realisation that death is a fundamental possibility for the human subject, and that 'nothing' lies within the very structure of our existence gives rise to anxiety. But this anxiety engenders an indeterminacy, and thus puts the human subject on the threshold of aunthentic self-discovery. For the experience of anxiety tends to isolate the person, who withdraws from his or her preoccupations and from the immediate context of everyday life. Separated through anxiety from the world, a person can either choose to live inauthentically, losing onself in everyday routines, or authentically, resolutely accepting death, and thereby acknowledging the experience of nothingness.

Authenticity

Concern, temporality and anxiety are all intrinsically linked by Heidegger to authenticity. But he also relates authentic living to a person's awareness and separatedness from the mode of being which he calls *Das Man*, the values and attitudes of other people.

Authenticity thus not only involves authentic concern and the fulfilment of our real potential in the world; not only an awareness of the temporal nature of being, in that the present, for the authentic human being, is a creative synthesis of the past and the future; authenticity also implies a certain kind of relationship with the social world and with other people. Although Heidegger insists that *Dasein* is not yet a self, and stresses the unity of self and the world, he nevertheless, as Solomon (1988: 161) writes, gives the notion of self, a central role in *Being and Time*. For being 'authentic' clearly involves making autonomous choices, and separating one's own individual potentialities from the impersonal world of the collectivity. Heidegger, following Marx and Durkheim (though these scholars are never cited), essentially argues that human beings are intrinsically social, and that 'Being-in is Being-with-others' (*ISS*). He uses the term *Mitsein* to emphasise the reciprocal nature of the relations between people, and the general state of 'human togetherness' (McCall 1983: 72). But Heidegger also stresses the negative aspects of human sociality, in that by nature the human subject is 'thrown' (*Geworfen*) into a world whose character he does not determine, but which to a large extent has a determining influence on the subject. Heidegger uses the term *Das Man* to describe these social influences, which is variously translated as 'one', 'they', 'people', according to the context. This concept signifies an alienation, an estrangement, a distance from the authentic being of *Dasein*. It has been linked to the Marxist conception of alienation and Durkheim's analysis of anomie (Steiner 1978: 90). Heidegger puts it this way: 'The self of everday *Dasein* is the they-self, which we distinguish from the authentic self – that is, from the self which has been taken hold of in its own way' (1962: 167). To live authentically then, *Dasein*, the human subject, must recognise and face the realities of freedom, responsibility and death, and not seek refuge in the security of the anonymous 'they' (*Das Man*), which instructs a person what to think and what to do. For the 'they' defines the person as a fixed actuality rather than as a free possibility (Kearney 1986: 37).

Authenticity does not imply a rejection of the world, nor a mystical union with spirit, but it does suggest self-reflection and an ontology that is very similar to that of Kierkegaard, though Being and not God is the Fundamental concept. And Being for Heidegger seems to be essentially finite and temporal, thus contrasting with the earlier religious traditions.

The above summary can hardly do justice to the rich analysis that Heidegger presents, even though his thoughts are enmeshed in almost impenetrable jargon. But in spite of the suggestive quality of his writings, many have drawn attention to the fact that the concept of *Dasein* is rather empty of any social content. We search his writings in vain, Bauman writes (1978: 169), for any account, or at least an acknowledgement of the myriad forms of social inter-action, while MacIntyre stresses the solitariness of Heidegger's human being. The existence of other people is certainly admitted, but it is not allowed to touch the concept of *Dasein*, and what kind of human relationship is conducive to authentic existence is never clearly specified. (MacIntyre 1964: 518).

Heidegger's conception of the human subject views the self not as inherent in the individual human being, but as a 'potentiality for Being', an aspect of *Dasein*, or 'Being-in-the-world'. The self is therefore not the subject of cognition standing outside the world, but is fundamentally a practical function of living in the world. But though the self is at the core of Heidegger's philosophy, particu-larly when he is concerned with the issue of authenticity – and here his thoughts reflect those of Kierkegaard, at other times, it is clear that *Dasein* has a transcendental quality. Thus there is a fundamen-tal ambiguity in Heidegger's exposition. At one level the subject or self is virtually equated with *Dasein*, for as a mode of being authenticity must always use a personal pronoun. At another level Heidegger paradoxically throws doubt on this equation. He writes:

> *Dasein* is an entity which is in each case I myself: its Being is in each case mine. The question of the 'who' [of *Dasein*] answers itself in terms of the 'I' itself, the 'subject', the 'self' . . . the assertion that it is I who in each case *Dasein* is, ontically obvious . . . [Yet] it remains questionable whether . . . the above assertion does proper justice to the stock of phenomena belonging to everyday *Dasein*. It could be that the 'who' of everyday *Dasein* just is *not* the 'I myself'. (1962: 150)

Heidegger seems to be suggesting what Mead and other twentieth-century social scientists have long stressed, that human subjectivity is unintelligible outside a social context, and that a socio-cultural reality – Dilthey's and Husserl's *Lebenswelt* – mediates between the cogito and the natural world. But a contemporary existentialist takes a more critical view of Heidegger's philosophy suggesting that his focus on modes of being implies that the human subject is simply an 'aggregate' of such modes, without any 'unifying centre'. He concludes:

Thus there is a gaping hole at the centre of our human being – at least as Heidegger describes this being. Consequently, we have in the end to acknowledge a certain desolate and empty quality about his thought, however we may admire the originality and novelty of its construction. (Barrett 1986: 140)

My feeling is that Heidegger does not herald the dissolution of the subject, but only the cognising, asocial subject of the philosophical tradition that stemmed from Descartes. Thus Heidegger's concept of *Dasein* is an attempt to situate the subject in the world, which for humans is primarily a social world. Husserl's comment that Heidegger had turned philosophy into anthropology is close to the truth, although Heidegger lacked any anthropological knowledge. Thus in suggesting a perspective that is essentially similar to that of many pragmatists and Marxists, Heidegger's work is less original than philosophers like Barrett contend. As Habermas suggests, Heidegger's insights are by no means unique, for they are similar to the methodology of the social sciences and for many influential philosophical trends – pragmatism, the linguistic philosophy of Wittgenstein and the hermeneutics of Gadamer. 'The philosophy of the subject is by no means an absolutely reifying power that imprisons all discursive thought and leaves open nothing but a flight into the immediacy of mystical ecstacy. There are other paths leading out of the philosophy of the subject' (1987: 137). Some of these paths we have explored in earlier chapters, including Habermas's own. We must turn now to two scholars who developed Heidegger's thoughts in an existentialist direction, with a renewed emphasis on the self and human consciousness – Sartre and Merleau-Ponty. (For further studies of Heidegger's philosophy, see Kockelmans 1965; Mehta 1971; Murray 1978; Elliston 1978.)

9.4   The Phenomenology of Consciousness

The shadow of Descartes, (Copleston 1974: 343) lies across French philosophy, and Descartes' writings certainly influenced the work of Jean-Paul Sartre (1905–80), a writer who has come to be identified with the existentialist tradition. Sartre is widely recognised as *the* existentialist, for it was his famous novel *Nausea* (1938) and his various philosophical writings, including his monumental study *Being and Nothingness* (1943), that firmly put existentialism on the

intellectual agenda at the end of the Second World War. The ot
key existentialists – Heidegger, Jaspers and Marcel – all esssentia
religious thinkers, tended to repudiate the label 'existentialism',
term that had been coined by Sartre. But though Sartre can b
firmly situated in the Cartesian rationalist tradition, it is of interes
that all the major influences on his philosophy are German scholars
– Kant, Hegel, Marx, Nietzsche, Husserl, Heidegger. Many of the
central concepts and tenets of Sartre's phenomenology stem from
these writers, and the dense prose and the systematic quality of his
major treatises have more affinity with these scholars than with the
writings of Descartes and the French Enlightenment thinkers. But
Sartre's philosophy is undeniably Cartesian in that he takes as his
fundamental standing point human consciousness and subjectivity.
As he writes, 'The epistemological point of departure must always
be *consciousness* as apodictic certainty of itself' (1976: 51).

Sartre was born in Paris. His father, a Catholic, died of a fever
while working in Indo-China as a marine engineer. Sartre was only
two at the time, and he often commented on his fatherlessness as
being a formative influence on his life. He grew up with his
Protestant mother in the house of his maternal grandfather, who
was a professor of German. At the age of nineteen he entered the
Ecole Normale Supérieure, where he studied philosophy until
1928. While at this elite institution he met a fellow student Simone
de Beauvoir, who was to become a life-long friend and companion,
although they mutually forswore marriage and parenthood. De
Beauvoir was herself to become an important existentialist writer,
and her classic and pioneering work *The Second Sex* (1949) has been
an inspiration for many feminists (cf. Okely 1986). At that period
Sartre also established friendships with two other fellow students,
Merleau-Ponty and Lévi-Strauss, both of whom were later to
establish themselves as important scholars. From 1928 to 1939 he
taught philosophy at lycées in Le Havre, Laon and Paris. Thanks to
his grandfather he knew German well and spent two years (1933–5)
in Germany studying modern German philosophy, coming particularly under the influence of Husserl and Heidegger, although he
never met them personally. Sartre was also caught up in the 'Hegel
renaissance', which took place in France during the pre-war period
(1930–9). Led by Alexandre Kojève, a Russian emigré, and Jean
Hyppolite, who both lectured in Paris, there was a rebirth of
interest in Hegel, who prior to the 1930s was for the most part
ignored by French intellectuals. The lectures of Kojève and
Hyppolite were attended by such students as Merleau-Ponty,
Aron, Lacan, Bataille and Descanti – all of whom became promi-

nent figures in French post-war intellectual life. In a later decade Hyppolite also taught Hegel to many of the thinkers associated with structuralist and post-structuralist theory – Foucault, De-Leuze, Althusser and Derrida (Poster 1975: 3–19; Hirsh 1981: 13–15).

While a provincial schoolteacher Sartre was subject to hallucinations, and de Beauvoir, in her autobiography, records that when he was in Venice Sartre believed that he was being followed by a crayfish. In 1939 Sartre joined the French Army, but was taken prisoner the following year. He managed to persuade the Germans to release him on health grounds, and returned to teaching philosophy in Paris in 1941. He was actively involved in the resistance movement, and in 1946, along with Merleau-Ponty and de Beauvoir, founded the radical periodical *Les Temps Modernes*. The success of his literary works enabled Sartre to give up teaching in 1944, and he devoted the rest of his life to writing. He never became a university professor and, on political grounds, refused to accept the Nobel Prize for literature in 1964. Sartre was a short, stocky man, rather unattractive by all accounts, but he seemed to burn with an intellectual and mental intensity. Although he never voted for or joined the French Communist Party, 'as a bohemian intellectual, he had an instinctive dislike for capitalist society, which he coupled with an honest sympathy for the poor and downtrodden – the working class' (Hirsh 1981: 23). He always supported radical causes, and in the 1960s was almost assassinated when his apartment was bombed twice during the struggle for Algerian independence. Searching, radical, encyclopaedic, Sartre, as Aronson writes, has been a major intellectual force of our generation (1978: 201; for important biographical material on Sartre, see de Beauvoir 1962).

Sartre's philosophical writings and his views on the human subject fall chronologically into three divisions:

1. His early writings on the ego, imagination and the emotions as outlined in three important early studies, *The Transcendence of the Ego* (1936), *Sketch for a Meaning of the Emotions* (1939) and *The Psychology of the Imagination* (1940).
2. His classic study of existentialist phenomenology *Being and Nothingness* (1943).
3. His ambitious attempt to combine existentialism and Marxism in *The Critique of Dialectical Reason* (1960).
We may discuss each of these divisions in turn.

In his early essay on the ego Sartre offers a phenomenological analysis of consciousness, an essay that reflects the combined influences of Husserl and Heidegger. But whereas Heidegger had focused his analysis on *Dasein* (Being-in-the-World) as a preliminary to explaining the meaning of being, Sartre devotes his whole attention to consciousness. He takes human consciousness as his point of departure. But he rejects Husserl's phenomenological reduction or *epoche*, and insists that the study of consciousness must at the same time involve an examination of the empirical world. He follows Husserl, however, in accepting that the act of consciouness is intentional, the consciousness *of* something. All this would seem to imply a thoroughly Cartesian approach, but for Sartre the basic datum is not cogito, the thinking subject, but what he describes as 'pre-reflective cogito', a pre-reflective consciousness. This form of consciousness does not imply an ego, for the ego or self-identity only arises, Sartre suggests, at the level of reflection, and is the creation of human social interaction. The 'transcendence of the ego' means that the self is never *given* in human consciousness, as Descartes, Locke and Husserl all implied. Consciousness is basically selfless, for there is no 'I' in the pre-reflective consciousness. As Solomon puts it, 'Consciousness is one thing, self and personal identity another' (1988: 175). Thus for Sartre the 'ego' is not a substance or entity, but a process, and existence comes before 'objectifying knowledge'. Thus the ego and the world arise together in correlation through reflective consciousness. In making these distinctions Sartre attempted to avoid the subjective idealism of Descartes and Husserl.

In his essay on the theory of the emotions, Sartre follows a similar strategy, suggesting that the emotions are an intentional form of pre-reflective consciousness. Sartre makes some important criticisms of the classical theories of the emotions suggested by James and Janet, as well as of psychoanalysis, and goes on to offer a phenomenological theory. These earlier theories, he suggests, tend to focus on reflective consciousness, on the consciousness *of* emotion, but although it is always possible to be aware of an emotion, the latter essentially is non-reflective, 'a certain way of apprehending the world'. It is less a bodily response than an act of consciousness, an intentional way of transforming the world that is akin to magic. Emotion, he writes, may 'be called a sudden fall of consciousness into magic', it is not an accident, 'but one of the ways in which consciousness understands its Being-in-the-World' (1962; 90–1). Sartre's study of the imagination assumes a similar perspective, for the imagination is described as an intentional mode of onsciousness, which, in contrast to perception, posits an object in its absence.

Sartre's psychological essays provide preliminary groundwork to his main philosophical treatise *Being and Nothingness*, subtitled *An essay on phenomenological ontology*. Again, Sartre's starting point is consciousness, the 'interiority of the cogito' (1943: 244), but his focus is on existence, being, not on knowledge. One of the problems of Hegel, he felt, was that for all his insights, Hegel tended to equate being with knowledge. Like Heidegger Sartre is concerned with ontology and not epistemology, and his introductory chapter is appropriately entitled 'The Pursuit of Being'. He rejects the classical dualism between appearance and essence, suggesting that a focus must be put on the phenomenon of Being. The influence of Heidegger is evident here, but Sartre contrasts Being with conscious existence – and defines the self as a 'lack of Being' – and does not stress a contrast between Being and existents, as does Heidegger. There is a trend in Sartre's thought towards 'psychologism' and as an atheist he is consistently opposed to metaphysics. Heidegger is fundamentally a metaphysician with mystical learnings, while Sartre is an existentialist who is primarily concerned with human freedom (Pivčevič 1970: 123). He thus comes to make a clear distinction between two modes of Being, Being-in-itself (*en-soi*) and Being-for-itself (*pour-soi*). To write of 'consciousness-in-itself' (as does Kearney (1986: 62)) does not seem to make much sense, for Sartre, posits a fundamental distinction between these two modes, and consciousness relates specifically to Being-for-itself. Concerned with the human condition Sartre's whole study focuses on this later category. Being-in-itself is the world as it *is*, in its opacity, the undifferentiated world prior to consciousness, for Sartre recognises that the objective world, the in-itself, has ' ontological primacy' over the for-itself, consciousness (1943: 619). The for-itself comes into Being through an act of negation of its identity with the in-itself. By its very nature Sartre argues, consciousness, for-itself, involves a distance or separation from Being, and this essential 'gap' between thought and the given world, involves a sense of lack or nothingness. As with Hegel and Heidegger, negation, for Sartre, has a crucial ontological significance, and it is unhelpful to dismiss this idea as pure obscurantism, as empiricist philosophers are prone to do. For Sartre is suggesting that the very nature of consciousness implies that the human subject is disengaged from the world, and that this disengagement is a human process. As he puts it: 'Man is the Being through whom nothingness comes to the world' (1943: 24). What a person lacks, therefore, is a self or ego as an object, and in so far as the subject is not a in-itself, nothingness forms an essential part of a person's being Equally, this disengagement implies that the human subject – the for-itself – is essentially a free being. Sartre argues that as consciousness transcends the world of objects, the human 'essence' is one of human freedom. He writes that with humans,

> the relation of existence to essence is not comparable to what it is for the things of the world. Human freedom precedes essence in man and makes it possible; the essence of the human being is suspended in his freedom. What we call freedom is impossible to distinguish from the being of 'human reality'. Man does not exist *first* in order to be free subsequently; there is no difference between the being of man and his *being-free*. (1943: 25)

Important, then, for Sartre is the view that the ego does not belong to the domain of the for-itself, but is of in-itself, and that consequently the Being-for-itself is essentially free and temporal. It has no essence; it is a nothingness, and is related to possibilities and projects.

In his well known essay 'Existentialism is a Humanism' (1945), Sartre gave a clear definition of his conception of the human subject. He stressed that existence precedes essence, and by this is meant:

> first of all, man exists, turns up, appears on the scene, and, only afterwards, defines himself. If man, as the Existentialist conceives him, is indefinable, it is because at first he is nothing. Only afterward will he be something, and he himself will have made what he will be. Thus, there is no human nature, since there is no God to conceive it. Not only is man what he conceives himself to be, but he is also only what he wills himself to be after his thrust towards existence. Man is nothing else but what he makes of himself. (Novack 1966; 74)

Existentialism, therefore was a philosophy that 'declares that every truth and every action implies a human setting and a human subjectivity' (1943: 71), and that it was one that did not lead, as its critics suggest, to an overemphasis on the dark side of human life or to an attitude of 'desperate quietness'. But Sartre did stress that this conception of the human subject necessarily implied a heightened sense of moral responsibility, and a feeling of anguish. Such anguish arises from the knowledge that our own future is absolutely open, and that 'nothing can insure me against myself'. We have total freedom and total responsibility. Anguish is the 'reflective apprehension of freedom by itself. . . . In anguish I apprehend myself at once as totally free and as not being able to derive the meaning of the world except as coming from myself' (1943: 40). The influence of Kierkegaard and Heidegger is apparent in such reflections. Sartre goes on to discuss what he describes as 'bad faith', the way in which people attempt to evade their freedom and responsibility, either by pretending to be a thing, a Being-in-itself, or by negatively accepting social roles. He provides some illuminating discussions of the way in which people engage in acts of self-deception, denying their essential freedom. The human subject, he writes, in a telling phrase, 'is condemned to be free', and though we by no means determine the conditions of our lives in being 'thrown into the world', we are in every other respect free and fully responsible for our actions. We cannot escape responsibility and, echoing Kant, Sartre writes that in choosing to be we also choose for all mankind (Novack 1966: 75–8). Not surprisingly, Sartre is critical of all theories that imply any form of determinism – as does Marxism and psychoanalysis – although he is less against these theories *per se* than in the personal embracing of such theories to evade the moral responsibility for one's actions.

Sartre essentially accepts the kind of metaphysical dualism suggested by Descartes and Kant in drawing a clear distinction between the mechanical, physical world with its causality, and a world of free, conscious, dynamic beings. Throughout the study a hiatus exists between these two modalities of being, although Sartre stresses that Being-for-itself could not exist without the in-itself, except as some kind of abstraction. Equally evident is the fact that although Sartre does stress the social nature of the human subject, in his discussion of 'Being-for-others' he tends all too easily to assume a 'psychologistic' perspective and to posit a virtual antithesis between the person and other people. Aware that the existence of others has been taken for granted by realists and positivistic psychologists, Sartre, though essentially a realist, nevertheless feels it important to question the existence of others, and the relation of my being to the being of the Other. Attempting to steer clear of the 'reef of solipsism', Sartre examines the work of Husserl, Hegel and Heidegger (in that order), and acknowledges the importance of Hegel, whose *Phenomenology of Mind* first outlined the suggestion that the appearance of the other 'is indispensable not to the constitution of the world and of my empirical' ego, 'but to the very existence of my consciousness as self-consciousness. In fact as self-consciousness, the self itself apprehends itself' (1943: 235). Thus via Hegel, Sartre attempts to go beyond the solipsism he sees inherent in Husserl's phenomenology, as well as breaking with the solitariness of the Heideggerian subject. Self-consciousness, Sartre suggests, 'passes through the other', and arises when I reflectively become aware of myself as the object of another's look or gaze. Reciprocally, I experience the other person as a free conscious subject through his or her look, whereby I become the object of the other. This leads Sartre to suggest that essentially 'conflict is the original meaning of being-for-others' (1943: 364). For we tend either to take on the role of object to the other's desires, which in an extreme form leads to masochism, or we take away the other's freedom and subjectivity, which in extremes leads to sadism. Sartre tends to equate love and masochism, and to see no way beyond the cycle of masochism and sadism, or alternatively indifference. Many have noted the negative view of social relations as expressed in *Being and Nothingness* and its similarity to the Hobbesian vision. For in seeing all social relations as essentially relations of conflict, social reciprocity and mutuality are virtually denied. The slogan 'hell is other people' expressed in one of his plays, *Huis Clos*, cogently summarises Sartre's early view of social relations. As Cranston put it, 'for Sartre, love is an impossible enterprise'. MacIntyre suggests that Sartre's individual is a secularised version of Kierkegaard's individual, who is in turn, perhaps, Hegel's unhappy consciousness (Cranston 1962: 54–6; MacIntyre 1964: 521; Hirsh 1981: 29).

Sartre's early studies in existentialist phenomenology came in for a great deal of criticism, particularly from Marxist scholars such as Garaudy, Lukács and Marcuse. Sartre was accused of being a 'false prophet' and his philosophy a form of 'idealistic mystification', which expressed the irrationalism and degeneracy of a group of alienated 'café revolutionaries' (see Novack 1966; Poster 1975: 109–60; Hirsh 1981: 30–1 for outlines of these critiques). Sartre's responded to these polemics with his lecture 'Existentialism is a Humanism', and went on the offensive in the following year with a critique of Marxism (1946). He criticises specifically the dialectical materialism of Stalin and Garaudy, questioning the whole notion of a 'dialectics of nature', and suggesting that their approach is a form of mechanistic materialism, which involves the elimination of human subjectivity. Marx and Engels, he notes, had a much richer conception of objectivity. And in the prefatory essay to his *Critique of Dialectical Reason*, published as *Marxism and Existentialism*, Sartre attempted to lay the foundations for a synthesis of Marxism and existentialism. He regards Marx, in stressing the priority of social praxis over knowledge, as in essence combining the important insights of both Kierkegaard and Hegel. He writes that Marx

> asserts that the human fact is irreducible to knowing, that it must be *lived* and produced; but he is not going to confuse it with the empty subjectivity of a puritanical and mystified petite bourgeoise . . . it is the concrete man who he puts at the centre of his research. . . . Thus Marx, rather than Kierkegaard or Hegel, is right, since he asserts with Kierkegaard the specificity of human existence and, along with Hegel, takes the concrete man in his objective reality. (1963: 14)

Claiming kinship with Marx, and critical of both dogmatic Marxism and the extreme subjectivism of certain varieties of existentialism, and recognising that Marxism was the 'philosophy of our time', Sartre felt nevertheless that Marxism lacked an adequate conception of human subjectivity. Marxist concepts had become too scholastic *a priori*, he noted, and the lived experience of humans, affirmed by existentialism, had tended to be ignored. As with other Western Marxists, Sartre sought to revitalise Marxism through the rediscovery of the subject as a free active agent. Marx's contention that 'men themselves make their history but in a given environment which conditions them' needed to be accepted and explored (1963: 85). That a synthesis of Marxism and existentialism involved a certain tension was clearly recognised by Sartre. He wrote:

> We are convinced at *one and the same time* that historical materialism furnished the only valid interpretation of history and that existentialism remained the only concrete approach to reality. I do not pretend to deny the contradictions in this attitude. . . . Many intellectuals, many students, have lived and still live with the tension of this double demand. (1963: 21)

It is beyond the scope of this study to discuss Sartre's existentialist Marxism, which has affinities to that of Marcuse, but it is of interest that while Sartre became more of a Marxist in his later writings, his friend and colleague Merleau-Ponty moved in the opposite direction. And it is to Merleau-Ponty that we may now turn. (For studies of Sartre's Marxism, see Aronson 1978, 1980; Poster 1979; J. Miller 1979: 156–96.)

9.5 Merleau-Ponty

Enigmatic, searching, withdrawn, Maurice Merleau-Ponty (1908–61) has been described as a philosopher who made people wonder. Compared with Camus and Sartre, he was an academic philosopher, for he lacked their imagination and their originality, but he was a serious scholar who opened up and explored several new avenues of thought. And it was Merleau-Ponty, rather than Sartre, who first initiated a philosophical synthesis of Marxism and existentialism, although in his later life the increasingly distanced himself from Marxism. Sartre acknowledged his deep indebtedness to Merleau-Ponty but the influence was a mutual one, for it was Sartre who first introduced his life-long friend and philosophical colleague to Husserl's phenomenology. The lives of the two men were in fact closely entwined and remarkably similar: both came from petty bourgeois backgrounds, both studied at the elite Ecole Normale, both lost their fathers early in life; both attended Kojève's lectures on Hegel and both were radical existentialists (Poster 1975: 145).

Merleau-Ponty was born at Rocheford-sur-Mer and after graduating at the Ecole Normale, taught philosophy at various lycées. During the 1930s he established friendships with Lévi-Strauss and de Beauvoir, and became increasingly interested in Husserl's phenomenology, whose influence is apparent in his first published book *The Structure of Behaviour* (1942). After serving in the infantry in the early part of the war (1939–40), he joined the resistance and worked with Sartre through the group 'Socialism and Liberty'. During the war he continued his studies of Husserl, working from 1944 on Husserl's unpublished manuscripts, which had been smuggled from Louvain to Paris. In 1945 he published his monumental study *Phenomenology of Perception*, and in the same year collaborated with Sartre in founding the review *Les Temps Modernes*, serving as its political editor until 1952 when he resigned due to political differences with Sartre. His various articles were published as *Sense and Nonsense* (1948), and formed the basis for his controversial study of the Moscow trials, *Humanism and Terror* (1947). On the strength of his philosophical writings he was offered the chair of philosophy at the Collège de France in 1952, and subsequently published another important collection of essays, *Signs* (1960) and a critique of Marxism, *Adventures of the Dialectic* (1955), which includes a bitter critique of Sartre's philosophy and politics. He died in 1961 at the early age of fifty-three, much of his work unfinished.

Merleau-Ponty has been somewhat overshadowed by Sartre, and the impression is often gained that he was a disciple of the latter. But as Copleston and others have stressed, Merleau-Ponty was an independent scholar, who made a sustained attempt to outline, within essentially the Hegelian-Marxist tradition, but infused with Husserl's phenomenology, a 'new ontology'. For he was concerned to develop a philosophy that avoided the twin intellectual hazards; represented on the one hand by Cartesian dualism, which was espoused not only by idealists and the neo-Kantians but by Sartre himself in his insistence on the separation of consciousness and being; and on the other, by reductive materialism, represented by the behaviourists and orthodox Marxists. It is a project that has affinities to that of Dewey and Lukács. In working out his ideas, Merleau-Ponty drew inspiration specifically from three scholars – Hegel, Marx and Husserl.

Merleau-Ponty had a very high opinion of Hegel, regarding him, along with Kierkegaard, as the first existentialist. All the great philosophical ideas of the past-century – the philosophies of Marx and Nietzsche, phenomenology and existentialism, and psycho-analysis – all had their beginnings, he suggested, in Hegel. For it was Hegel who started the attempt to explore the irrational and to integrate it into a wider conception of reason. Even Kierkegaard's critique of Hegel was, he felt, set within the parameters of Hegel's own paradigm, for Hegel insisted on the need to situate thought within a social and historical context (1964: 63–4).

The influence of Marx is equally important to an understanding of Merleau-Ponty's philosophy; indeed he suggests that Hegel's phenomenology is a kind of Marxism. The real debate between Marx and Hegel, he suggests, has nothing to do with the relation-ship of ideas to history; it involved the conception of historical movement which for Hegel came to an end with the Prussian state. The young Hegel and Marx had much in common, he writes, for both made 'history work on its own feet' (1964: 81). The sugges-tion that Marx was a positivist, Merleau-Ponty argues, is quite misleading, for Marx was essentially fighting on two fronts, a strategy that Merleau-Ponty continued to embrace in his own studies. Marx, he notes, was opposed, on the one hand, to all forms of mechanistic thought; and on the other, he is waging a war against idealism.

But this struggle against idealism has nothing in common with the positivist objectification of man. Marx, unlike Durkheim, would not even agree to speak of a collective consciousness whose instruments are individuals. 'Above all we must avoid once again setting society up as an abstraction over against the individual.' The individual is a social being. Man is 'a being which exists for itself', thus, a generic being. (1964: 128)

What, then, Merleau-Ponty asks, is the vehicle of history and the motivating force of the dialectic for Marx, if not the 'world spirit' or a 'social nature' given outside ourselves, or the 'collective consciousness'? And he responds: 'It is man involved in a certain way of appropriating nature in which the mode of his relationship with others takes place, it is concrete human intersubjectivity' (1964: 129).

For Merleau-Ponty, then, Marx was an existentialist and an historical materialist whose theory did not imply a reductive causality which suggested that ideologies were simply a reflection of an economic context. Economic life is the 'historical anchorage' of mental life not its cause (1964: 108).

One would think that the influence of Husserl would draw Merleau-Ponty into a direction quite at odds with that of Hegel and Marx. But this is not the case. For Merleau-Ponty interprets the two key concepts of Husserl's phenomenology – 'phenomenological reduction' and 'Lebenswelt' – in a very existentialist fashion. Husserl's search for essences is not seen as some idealistic strategy, but rather is destined, as Merleau-Ponty graphically put it, 'to bring back all the living relationships of experience, as the fisherman's net draws up from the depths of the ocean quivering fish and seaweed' (1962: xv). The *epoche* leads to a 'return to that world which precedes knowledge', the 'life-world' which we come to know through practical endeavours before we reflect on it with more theoretical interests. It brings us to the 'pre-reflective cogito' which Warnock sees as equivalent to Husserl's transcendental self (1965: 22; Schmidt 1985: 37).

Hegel, Marx and Husserl are all thus interpreted by Merleau-Ponty as existentialist philosophers, and as heralding a new non-dualistic philosophy. He expressed his thoughts well in his review of Sartre's *Being and Nothingness*, in which he wrote:

The question is that of man's relationship to his natural or social surroundings. There are two classical views: one treats man as the result of the physical, physiological, and sociological influences which shape him from the outside and made him one thing among many; the other consists of recognizing an a–cosmic freedom in him, insofar as he is spirit and represents to himself the very causes which supposedly act upon him. On the one hand, man is part of the world; on the other, he is the constituting consciousness of the world. (1964: 71–2)

Merleau-Ponty finds the viewpoints of both objective thought (positivism) and speculative rationalism untenable, and suggests that one must grant the human subject a very special way of being – intentional being – which consists of being oriented towards all things but of not residing in any. We shall outline Merleau-Ponty's conception of the human subject more fully shortly, but it is worth noting that he is also critical of the Cartesian dualism, which he finds inherent in Sartre's study. As he writes, the study remains too exclusively antithetical: 'the antithesis of my view of myself and another's view of me and the antithesis of the for-itself and the in-itself often seem to be alternatives instead of being described as the living bond and communication between one term and the other' (1964: 72). Merleau-Ponty's *Phenomenology of Perception* is primarily concerned with going beyond this Cartesian dualism, while at the same time avoiding any reductive materialist tendency.

Merleau-Ponty's earlier work, *The Structure of Behaviour*, is largely concerned with an examination of modern psychological theories, particularly behaviourism and Gestalt psychology. Although he does not deny that causal explanations of human behaviour are possible, especially under laboratory conditions, Merleau-Ponty argues that physiology and stimulus – response theory is unable to account adequately for human behaviour in the real world. For humans do not simply react as passive organisms; and thus the relationship of the subject to the environment cannot be expressed simply in terms of mechanistic reciprocal causality. Equally, human behaviour cannot be understood simply in psychical terms either, for behaviour essentially refers to a mode of existence, which can only be described in terms of a social context that involves subjective meanings. Behaviour was neither a material reality nor a psychological one, but rather involves 'a structure which does not properly belong to the external world or to the internal life'. Coplestone sums up Merleau-Ponty's views concisely when he suggests that the facts demand 'neither the reduction of the subject to a thing or object nor an idealist theory of consciousness which creates the object but rather a recognition of the basic situation of an "incarnate" subject involved in the world and in constant dialogue with it' (1974: 404).

Merleau-Ponty was clearly searching for a primordial locus of subjective meaning, of lived experience that was presupposed by reflective consciousness in making a distinction between the ego and the world. In *Phenomenology of Perception* Merleau-Ponty develops these thoughts, exploring the nature of perception, as this relates both to the body and the world. In the Preface, he outlines his guiding thoughts, Husserl's phenomenology, and offers criticisms of both the analytical reflection of Descartes and Kant, with its focus on the 'inner man' and subjective consciousness 'untouched by being and time', and of empirical science. The latter, he suggests, is built upon the world as directly experienced, and takes for granted the subjectivity of the scientist and the 'basic experience of the world' of which science is but an expression. And he goes on to suggest that

> Perception is not a science of the world, it is not even an act, a deliberate taking up of a position; it is the background from which all acts stand out, and is presupposed by them. The world is not an object such that I have in my possession the law of its making; it is the natural setting of, and field for, all my thoughts and all my explicit perceptions. Truth does not 'inhabit' only 'the inner man', or more acurately, there is no inner man, man is in the world, and only in the world does he know himself. (1962: xi)

The human subject is destined to the world, and the 'world is not what I think, but what I live through'.

In the first part of the study Merleau-Ponty discusses perceptions of the human body, as an object of empirical study, and in terms of its mobility, sexuality and as a mode of expression. And he concludes – and again I quote him in full – that the existence of the body has an ambiguous quality in having the attributes of both a thing and consciousness:

> the body is not an object. For the same reason, my awareness of it is not a thought, that is to say, I cannot take it to pieces and reform it to make any clear idea. Its unity is always implicit and vague. It is always something other than what it is, always sexuality and at the same time freedom, rooted in nature at the very moment when it is transformed by cultural influences, never hermetically sealed and never left behind. . . . I am my body, at least wholly to the extent that I possess experience, and yet at the same time my body is as it were a 'natural' subject, a provisional sketch of my total being. Thus experience of one's own body runs counter to the reflective procedure which detaches subject and object from each other. (1962: 198)

Whereas Sartre pointed to a 'pre-reflective cogito' as being prior to reflective consciousness, Merleau-Ponty suggests that perception precedes knowledge and that this is centred on the body/subject as one single reality which is inseparable from the world. The human subject for Merleau-Ponty, as for Heidegger, is a Being-in-the-world, and such a world is essentially one of subjective meanings. Merleau-Ponty sees no antithesis between the subject and the social world, and in the final chapter of the study, he questions also the rigid dichotomy between determinism and freedom. The dilemma set by both objective thought and its 'stable-companion' analytical reflection, suggests that our freedom is either total or non-existent. But, Merleau-Ponty suggests, this dilemma does not apply to our relations with the world and with our past, for our freedom does not destroy our situation but gears itself to it. He describes a man under torture refusing to betray his friends; but such a refusal, he suggests, does not arise from a solitary, unmotivated decision, but expresses the man's continued involvement with his comrades and the pattern of living that he has developed through the years. 'These motives do not cancel out freedom, but at least ensure that it does not go unbuttressed in being' (1962: 454). Freedom is thus never absolute, as Sartre tended to stress, but always 'situated', and our situation is always an open one.

Merleau-Ponty noted that the 'philosophy of the subject' had been paraded beneath lots of different banners – the self of Pascal, the thinking ego of Descartes, the transcendental subject of Kant and the subjectivity of Kierkegaard. But such subjectivity, he continues, was not waiting for philosophers to discover, as an unknown America waited for its explorers in the ocean mists – although elements of the philosophy of the subject were present in Greek philosophy. Subjectivity was created, constructed by philosophers, and in more than one way. It was seen as an absolute form of being, and was given a protean status. In the essence there were only two ideas of subjectivity – 'that of empty, unfettered, and universal subjectivity and that of full subjectivity sucked down into the world' (1964: 154). But having come on to the philosophical scene and become part of our thinking, subjectivity cannot simply be annulled. We can only digest and develop better concepts. And with Heidegger in mind, he concludes;

> The same philosopher who now regrets Parmenides and would like to give us back our relationships to Being such as they were prior to self-consciousness owes his idea of the taste for primordial ontology to just

this self-consciousness. There are some ideas which make it impossible for us to return to a time prior to their existence even and especially if we have moved beyond them, and subjectivity is one of them. (1964: 154)

Merleau-Ponty was critical of the 'philosophy of the subject', and like Marx and others before him, felt the need to go beyond its excessive subjectivism and its exclusive focus on the cogito. He was alive to developments within the social sciences, particularly within Durkheimian sociology and of those scholars who followed the path of Saussure's structural linguistics – Lévi-Strauss and Lacan. Like Sartre he hoped for a rapprochement between phenomenology and the human sciences. He felt that the proper task of anthropology was the joining together of objective structural analysis with an account of lived experience. Yet he was aware of the scientism and objectivism inherent in the structuralist approach and in one of his essays on philosophy and sociology warned that 'It is essential never to cut sociological inquiry off from our experience of social subjects' (1964b: 101). Thus, as Schmidt has outlined, Merleau-Ponty attempted to steer a path between phenomenology and structuralism. He never concluded that the human sciences could neglect completely the problem of agency: 'What was needed, and what philosophy could conceivably contribute, was an understanding of the peculiar sort of subject which these disciplines seemed to presume – a subject which both shapes and is shaped by the structures it employs' (1985: 163).

In many ways Merleau-Ponty has been a neglected figure. Although he invented the term 'Western Marxism' and made important critiques of the orthodox tradition, he has been completely ignored in many Marxist texts (e.g. Novack 1966; *New Left Review* 1978; Bottomore 1983). Modern pragmatists such as Rorty and Bernstein, although engaged in a similar project to that of Merleau-Ponty – a critique of Cartesian epistemology and the need to go beyond the alternatives of objectivism and subjectivism – also seem to bypass Merleau-Ponty (Rorty 1980; Bernstein 1983). And apart from Parkin (1985) one searches in vain among the histories of psychology or in the anthropological literature for any mention of Merleau-Ponty. But his legacy is an important one, and his philosophy, as Copleston concludes, 'can be seen as demanding reciprocal recognition among human beings, a respect for human freedom and a self-commitment to the cause of social liberation without the claim to absolute knowledge and to the right to coerce human beings in the name of this alleged knowledge' (1974: 412). It is a pity that in his last years he abandoned his existentialist Marxism and became increasingly concerned, like Heidegger, with the metaphysics of Being. (For important studies of Merleau-Ponty's philosophy, see Kwant 1963; Rabil 1967; Kruks 1981; Madison 1981; Schmidt 1985).

-10-

Structuralism and Beyond

In the previous chapter I have outlined some of the basic themes associated with the existentialist-phenomenological tradition, a tradition undoubtedly associated with the writings of Husserl, Heidegger and Sartre. This tradition, as I noted, came into prominence at the end of the Second World War, especially in France, and was to have an enormous influence on the orientation of Marxism, psychoanalysis, sociology and psychology. Conversely, existentialism hardly came within the purview of anthropological scholarship, aside from the critiques of it by Lévi-Strauss. But by the 1960s, however, this tradition had begun to decline, as radical French intellectuals became increasingly disenchanted with existentialism and its humanistic ethos. And there arose in its stead a new theoretical paradigm known as structuralism, which represented a reaction and a critique of all the central tenets of existential phenomenology, particularly as represented by Sartre. It virtually amounted, as Perry Anderson suggested (1983: 33), to an 'epistemic' shift of the type that Foucault sought to theorise, challenging the historicism, the humanism and the philosophy of the subject, which was intrinsic to the phenomenological approach. This structuralist paradigm came to exert a dominant influence on many fields, such that the two decades between 1960 and 1980 have been described as the 'age of structuralism' (Kurzweil 1980). But at the very moment structuralist thought is being introduced and advocated to a larger audience, so its commentators are declaring that the structuralist era is drawing to a close, and that we are entering a period of post-structuralism or post-modernist thought. Both the latter categories are rather empty of content, but they essentially reflect a reaffirmation of some of the themes that are evident in Nietzsche's philosophy, for Nietzsche has an underlying presence in the work of Foucault, Deleuze and Derrida.

This present chapter is concerned with outlining structuralist thought and is focused on the work of three important scholars –

Lévi-Strauss, Piaget and Althusser – who along with Lacan and Barthes represent the main proponents of this form of understanding. After some introductory discussion, the first section outlines Lévi-Strauss's structuralist theory, and in it I try to elucidate the meaning of his plea to 'dissolve' the human subject. In the following two sections I consider in turn the contrasting perspectives of Piaget and Althusser. The final two sections are devoted to two scholars who are widely recognised as important post-structuralist figures – Foucault and Derrida – and I focus my discussion on their critical thoughts relating to the human subject.

10.1 Structuralism and Lévi-Strauss

In essence structuralism represents a development of the Comtean philosophical tradition, although it would be somewhat misleading to describe it as a positivist trend, as does Hirsh (1981: 149), for its proponents consistently assume an anti-empiricist stance, structuralism, in stressing the absolute priority of the social over human subjectivity, and in its advocacy of a natural science paradigm is a development, via Durkheim, of Comtean sociology. The oft-mentioned influence of Durkheim on Saussure, who is seen as the founding father of structuralism, and the Comtean themes evident in the work of the structural Marxist Louis Althusser (cf. Elliott 1987: 53), are indications of the links between structuralism and the French philosopher. Because of this inherently scientific orientation of structuralist thought, it is all too easy for writers to define structuralism in terms that refer essentially to method, and to describe almost every social scientist from Vico to Talcott Parsons as a structuralist. In an early review of structuralism, W. G. Runciman (1969) stressed that Lévi-Strauss's outline of the structuralist method was phrased in such a way that it was in no way distinct from scientific explanations in general. Indeed, Lévi-Strauss in one of his lectures described structuralism as nothing new, but as 'a very pale and faint imitation of what the "hard sciences" have been doing all the time', namely the quest for order or invariant structures underlying diverse phenomena (1978: 9). Piaget (1971) likewise described structuralism in very general terms. He defined the notion of structure in terms of three key ideas – wholeness, transformation and self-regulation – and thus came to describe every mathematician and social scientist who came to use the concept of structure in this sense – scholars as diverse as Godel, Kohler and Talcott Parsons – as structuralists. Terence Hawkes has gone to an even further extreme and given the universal capacity of humans to formulate structures, has suggested that 'To be human . . . is to be a structuralist' (1977: 15).

Although structuralism, like existentialism in an earlier decade, became something of an intellectual fashion, it never became quite the same kind of cult phenomenon as existentionalism; there were never any structuralist night club on the Left Bank, Sturrock remarks (1979: 2). Structuralism was more a style or mode of thought born in reaction to the subjectivism of existentialism and through a disillusionment with Marxism, although it was embraced dramatically by some scholars as if it were a new form of revelation. Structuralism also expresses the growth of importance of mass communications in modern culture and is we should note intrinsically linked with the development of linguistics and semiology.

As Barthes (1968) indicated, the demand for semiology stems not from the fads of a few scholars, but from the very history of the modern world. Along with these disciplines, and with linguistic philosophy (which is situated in a very different philosophical tradition, that of Anglo-Saxon empiricism), structuralism expressed a growing awareness of the fundamental importance of language in the understanding of the human condition and human culture. In reacting against the subjectivism and historicism of the phenomenological tradition, structuralism also came to reaffirm the orthodox scientific stance of objectivity. This is particularly evident with the three key scholars with whom we shall be concerned in this chapter – Piaget, Lévi-Strauss and Althusser. Although coming from very different scientific traditions and expressing very different theoretical interests, all three scholars share a concern with uncovering and delineating universal scientific truths. Thus, for all their critiques of the philosophy of the subject and Descartes' cogito, all are firmly situated in the rationalist tradition that stems from Descartes. The other two scholars with whom we shall be concerned – Foucault and Derrida – are, as Richard Harland puts it, a 'very different kettle of fish' (1987: 2). For although they are often grouped alongside these other scholars as 'structuralists' (e.g. Sturrock 1979), and share with them an antipathy for the 'subject', their mode of intellectual analysis is quite dissimilar. Their philosophical position, as Harland writes, is 'not only incompatible with the concept of structure but also quite radically anti-scientific (1987: 3). And although both Foucault and Derrida are proclaimed as radical thinkers, their extreme relativism has disturbing, even reactionary implications.

In his introduction to modern French philosophy, Vincent Descombes described its evolution as a passage from the generation known after 1945 as that of the 'three H's' (Hegel, Husserl and Heidegger, the triumvirate of the phenomenological tradition) to the generation known since 1960 as that of the three 'masters of suspicion' (Marx, Nietzsche and Freud) (1980: 3). But though both Marx and Freud have an essential presence in the writings of the structuralists, Nietzsche's influence is only really in evidence among the *post*-structuralist writers, Foucault and Derrida. One searches in vain among the writings of the four central structuralist figures – Lacan, Piaget, Lévi-Strauss and Althusser – for any mention of Nietzsche. The two figures that are of crucial importance for the understanding of structuralism are not the 'masters of suspicion' but Durkheim and the Swiss scholar Ferdinand de Saussure (1857–1913), who is widely recognised as the father of modern linguistics. In an earlier chapter we have discussed Durkheim's sociological approach, noting that although he stressed the priority of the social, and the relative autonomy of collective representations, his approach by no means implied 'dissolution' of the subject. Saussure's approach is similar to that of Durkheim, although his focus is specifically on human language.

The structuralist writer Roland Barthes described the human subject as *homo significans*, emphasising the point that the subject was essentially a language-using animal. Lévi-Strauss likewise sees our essential humanity expressed in Cassirer's similar designation of human as an *animal symbolicism*. 'Man,' Lévi-Strauss explains,

> has been described as *homo faber*, the maker of tools, and this characteristic has been accepted as the essential mark of culture. I confess that I do not agree and that one of my essential aims has always been to establish the line of demarcation between culture and nature, not in tool making, but in articulate speech. It is with language that the leap forward occurs. (Charbonnier 1961)

As I have already discussed Lévi-Strauss's structuralist approach to anthropology at some length (1987: 264–91), I shall confine myself here to outlining briefly some of the main tenets of his thought, and his important critique of Sartre's phenomenology.

Two basic postulates underpin Lévi-Strauss's structuralist theory. The first is that social phenomena can be understood if viewed as systems of communication. He recognised that there were problems in such a semiological approach. As he said, 'In advocating the symbolic nature of its object, social anthropology does not thereby intend to cut itself off from *relia'* (1973: 11). But this is precisely what his programmatic writings entail, and there have been many criticisms of Lévi-Strauss's unwillingness to explicate social phenomena in sociological or historical terms. Some have suggested that his structuralist analyses tend to eliminate in a radical way all interest in history and human praxis, as well as in the problem of meaning (Goldman 1969: 12; I. M. Lewis 1971: 14; Diamond 1974: 300). But it is important to realise that Lévi-Strauss defines anthropology in rather narrow terms, as the study of collective representations – the 'thought-of' orders of myth, totemism and religion. The 'real situation' or the 'lived-in' orders (1963: 313), the economic infrastructures of Marxist theory, are best left to history and the empirical sciences. Thus Lévi-Strauss does not doubt the primary of the social infrastructures (1966: 130), but, like Kardiner (1939, 1945), he places the operations of the unconscious mind as a mediator between praxis (primary institutions) and cultural beliefs and practices (Kardiner's projective systems). But whereas Kardiner's basic personality structure was culturally specific, Lévi-Strauss's 'mind' is pan-human. For Lévi-Strauss, then, anthropology is fundamentally the study of 'thought' (Geertz 1975: 352).

In an important sense, therefore, Lévi-Strauss did not apply the theoretical paradigm of structural linguistics to culture as a totality, but only to those aspect of social life that constitute ideological forms: myth, religion, totemism and, as he implied, modern political ideology. As he clearly denoted, he looked upon his work in *The Savage Mind* as contributing to the Marxist 'theory of superstructure' (1966: 130). This focus on the 'superstructure' level is held to be a defining characteristic of the structuralist movement, although it seems to me to be quite misleading to interpret Lévi-Strauss as an idealist who gave explanatory priority to the superstructure (Harland 1987: 9).

The second postulate underlying Lévi-Strauss's theoretical work is that cultural facts are the manifestation at the conscious level, of fundamental structures inherent in the human mind. He writes:

If the unconscious activity of the mind consists in imposing forms upon content, and if these forms are fundamentally the same for all minds – ancient and modern, primitive and civilized – it is necessary and sufficient to grasp the unconscious structure underlying each institution and each custom, in order to obtain a principle of interpretation valid for other institutions. (1963: 21)

Thus, taking a cue from Saussure, Lévi-Strauss suggested a mode of analysis that would attempt to disclose universal structures of meaning which lay beneath the 'surface' phenomena. In his fascinating and memorable travelogue *Tristes Tropiques* (1955) (The Sad Tropics) he describes the three important influences on his work – geology, psychoanalysis and Marxism. All these three demonstrate, he wrote, 'that understanding consists in reducing one type of reality to another; that the true reality is never the most obvious; and that the nature of truth is already indicated by the care it takes to remain elusive' (1955: 70).

Throughout his studies, therefore, Lévi-Strauss was consistently critical of all empiricist theories (such as those of Malinowski and Radcliffe-Brown), as well as those theories that attempted to explain cultural phenomena by reference to emotional factors. As affectivity is the most obscure side of man, he wrote, 'there has been the constant temptation to resort to it, forgetting that what is refractory to explanation is *ipso facto* unsuitable for use in explanation' (1962: 140). He had Freud in mind. There has been a great deal of debate on Lévi-Strauss's structuralist approach, and on the epistemological status of the 'unconscious structures of the mind' as explanatory postulates (see, for example, Jenkins 1979; Harris 1980: 166–9; Augé 1982: 50–60). Jenkins accuses Lévi-Strauss of following an empiricist epistemology, while Harris chides him for his humanism and his general disdain for empirical validation. But it seems clear that Lévi-Strauss has neither a disdain for empirical data nor did he give them theoretical priority or take them as given, for his essential standpoint was to deny any simple 'continuity between experience and reality' (1955: 71). He described himself as a 'transcendental materialist' (1966: 246), and consistently stressed his scientific aspirations, to the extent that Diamond was to accuse him of making a fetish of the scientific mode of cognition (1974: 302). Inevitably, such a structuralist standpoint led him to be extremely critical of his friend Sartre's phenomenology. In *Tristes Tropiques* he writes that his 'three sources of inspiration' led him to see a fundamental discontinuity between experience and reality, and he thus questioned the legitimacy of phenomenology and existentialism as forms of reflection. Because of its overindulgent attitude towards the 'illusions of subjectivity', and its tendency to raise personal preoccupations to the dignity of philosophy, existentialism, Lévi-Strauss wrote, was likely to lead to a 'sort of shop-girl metaphysics' (1955: 71). In the final chapter of *The Savage Mind*, entitled 'History and Dialectic', Lévi-Strauss reiterated his critique of Sartre's subjectivism, suggesting that the ultimate goal of the human sciences to be 'not to constitute, but to dissolve man' (1966: 247). He also disputed the privileged position which he felt Sartre had accorded historical explanations in the human sciences. Sartre had made an absolute distinction between analytical thought, on the one hand, which describes and classifies, and dialectical thought, a mode of consciousness that attempts to account for changes in the preconceptions, and he intimated that pre-literate people were incapable of dialectical reasoning, because they had no conception of history. Although not disputing the distinction between these two modes of reasoning, Lévi-Strauss feels that they are not absolute opposites but that dialectical reasoning is complementary and 'something additional to analytical reason' (246). In giving historical understanding priority Sartre, Lévi-Strauss argued, was being ethnocentric; 'Descartes, who wanted to found a physics, separated man from society. Sartre, who claims to found an anthropology, separates his own society from others. A cogito . . . retreats into individualism and empiricism and is lost in the blind allies of social psychology' (1966: 250).

Although Lévi-Strauss challenges the priority that Sartre gives to experience, to dialectics and historical understanding, and to the human subject and consciousness, in the understanding of social life, this by no means implied a dismissive attitude towards these. Certainly Lévi-Strauss has been criticised for his anti-humanist stance and accused of 'demolishing the human person'. He has indeed, as we have noted, been a severe critic of phenomenology and existentialism. His shafts of criticism, however, are not aimed specifically at human agency *per se* but at the Cartesian notion that human consciousness has priority in cultural understanding. Like Hegel, Freud and Marx, he is anti-empiricist rather than anti-humanist. Thus his response to this kind of criticism is to say, 'The Social Sciences, following the example of the physical sciences, must grasp the fact that the reality of the object they are studying is not wholly limited to the level of the subject apprehending it' (1981: 638). But to recognise that 'consciousness is not everything' is no reason, he writes, for abandoning it, anymore than Freud or Marx suggested abandoning reason. All three were rationalists. It is noteworthy that while Sartre's Cartesian rationalism led him to put a focal emphasis on consciousness, Lévi-Strauss's rationalism was highly objectivist, bordering on scientism. The mission, he wrote, 'is to understand being in relation to itself, and not in relation to myself' (1955: 71). And it is important to note too that Lévi-Strauss's critique of Sartre was levelled at his *Critique of Dialectical Reason*, not his earlier existentialist writings.

For all his polemics against phenomenology Lévi-Strauss did not expunge the human subject or the human 'esence' from the theoretical discourse – quite the contrary. He offers only a critique of 'subjectivism' and of the transcendental subject outside of nature and society, Ricoeur, in a well-known comment, indeed described Lévi-Strauss's structuralism as 'Kantianism without a transcendental subject' (1963: 599). But unlike Marx, Lévi-Strauss conceptualises the human 'subject' in terms of thought – the human mind, *l'esprit humain* (Leach 1970b: 112; Shalvey 1979: 36), rather than in terms of human praxis, and hence as not only trans-empirical but ahistorical. The human subject for Lévi-Strauss, as for Descartes, is a cognising being, and though no longer at the centre of the knowledge process as the individual subject – as the 'human mind' it is the 'uninvited guest' in all of Lévi-Strauss's work. For this reason, he could happily write that ethnology 'is the first of all psychology' (1966: 131). Though he acknowledged that human praxis constituted the fundamental totality for the human sciences.

Lévi-Strauss described himself as an 'inconstant disciple' of Durkheim and fully acknowledged his debt to Saussure, and thus merits the title bestowed on him by Edith Kurzweil, the 'father of structuralism' (1980: 13–34). His influence on anthropological studies has been enormous, and he is now widely recognised as one of the most seminal thinkers of the present decade (see Leach 1979; Shalvey 1979; Sperber 1979). But Lévi-Strauss was only one of a number of scholars who attempted to apply the linguistic methodology of Saussure to other social domains. To these other scholars we may now turn (for useful outlines of structuralist thought, see Gardner 1972; Sturrock 1979; Kurzweil 1980; Kearney 1986: 240–331; Merquior 1986; Harland 1987).

10.2 Piaget's Genetic Structuralism

Although Lévi-Strauss is invariably credited with having instigated the 'structuralist' movement, Jean Piaget (1896–1980), it is worth noting, was writing about cognitive structures before the anthropologist had written his first anthropological paper. Like Lévi-Strauss, Piaget is one of the seminal scholars of the middle decades of the twentieth century. Born in Neuchâtel, Switzerland, he was trained as a biologist, having a boyhood interest in natural history studies. His doctoral thesis at the age of twenty-two was on molluscs. But even at an early age Piaget had pronounced philosophical interests, and both his life-work and his theoretical standpoint reflect an effort to integrate biological and an epistemological perspective. This means that although Piaget is popularly known as a child psychologist, and his theories of cognitive development have had an enormous influence on both psychology and educational practices, he is not a psychologist in the ordinary sense of the term. As Elkind and others have noted, Piaget is not interested in such issues as motivation, learning and individual differences but rather with the unfolding of universal cognitive structures. He describes his own theoretical approach as genetic epistemology, and like Freud has created his own field of study. Although, through an early confrontation with the writings of the philosopher Henri Bergson, Piaget was from the first interested in bridging the gap between biology and the problems of knowledge, it was an event that occurred in 1920 that gave Piaget the stimulus he needed. Working for a psychological laboratory in Paris he was asked to standardise intelligence tests, which had been devised by the famous psychologist Alfred Binet. It was a task that he did not initially find appealing. But Piaget soon became fascinated not by the children's correct answers, but by the nature of their incorrect responses, and this led him to explore the nature of children's thinking – how it differed from that of an adult, and how it developed over time. Such studies might be important, he felt, for the light they would throw on the nature and development of human knowledge in general. Over the next fifty or so years Piaget (and his wife and colleagues) conducted intensive researches into the nature of children's thought, and his writings on the subject are voluminous. In fact, he has published more than thirty books, mainly on the cognitive development of children and their conceptions of time, space, number and causality. His two early studies, *The Language and Thought of the Child* (1923) and *The Child's Conception of the World* (1926) have attained the status of classics. These studies were based on ingenious experiments and verbal interviews with children, including Piaget's detailed observations of his own children. His empirical work, therefore, has affinities to that of Freud, involving clinical methods, verbal questioning and close and detailed observation.

Like other dialectical thinkers such as Marx and Freud, Piaget's whole approach to the development of thought is an attempt to avoid, or transcend, the familiar dualisms of Western thought. Thus for Piaget, the separation of thought and emotion, reason and motivation as well as mind and reality is unhelpful, if not illusory, as all these aspects of human life are indissociable. In trying, then, to understand the nature of thought, and the genesis or development of cognitive structures Piaget argues against any collapse into either idealism (and its variant innatism) or empiricism (with the suggestion that thought emerges through contingent circumstances). He thus goes beyond the old nature/nurture controversy in arguing both against behaviourism and the idea that the human subject, through experience, passively records sense impressions (the copy theory) and against those theorists who, in the tradition of platonic philosophy, view cognitive structures as innate. He is particularly critical of the kind of 'static structuralism' espoused by Lévi-Strauss, which tends to see structures as 'unpolluted by history or psychology' (1971: 61). In other words, Piaget argues against the limitations of two kinds of theoretical approaches when attempting to understand human knowledge: the one is 'genesis without structures' (behaviourism); the other is 'structuralism without genesis' (Gestalt theory, and Lévi-Straussian structuralism) (Piaget 1968: 145). His approach, therefore, is akin, at the level of psychology, to the kind of sociological theory advocated by Lucien Goldmann – a genetic structuralism (Goldmann 1969; Kolakowski 1978/3: 324–40).

Human knowledge, therefore, is seen by Piaget to be neither 'ready made' nor simply 'learned', but rather it is *constructed* by the human subject (1971: 61). He termed this theory 'dialectic constructionism' implying that the individual actively builds up schemata or structures through the process of equilibration – the organisms active and self-regulated adaption to the environment. Not the human mind, but the human subject, the epistemic subject, or 'the centre of functional activity' (1971: 69) has the role of 'mediation' in this process, progressively generating structures. Only if cognitive structures were static, Piaget contended, responding to structuralists who disliked 'the subject' would the subject be 'a superfluous entity' (1971: 70). This process of equilibration he suggested involved two aspects; *assimilation* – the incorporation and modification of an external stimuli into already existing structures – and *accommodation* – the active modification of the structure itself. For Piaget then structures are wholistic, dynamic and self-regulating (1971: 3–16) and they are manifest not only in cognition, but at all levels of reality.

Given this approach, and drawing on his substantive empirical work, Piaget came to suggest that human knowledge – logical thought – developed progressively and epigenetically through four clearly defined stages.

Sensori-Motor Stage 0 to 2 Years

This is a pre-verbal stage, when the child through determined sensory and motor activities and co-ordinations develops a 'practical intelligence' in order to negotiate the environment. By the age of 18 months, in effecting a kind of 'miniature Copernican revolution' – as Piaget puts it (1968: 9) – the child through his/her movements and perceptions has cognitively organised an 'action schemata' (Piaget adopting the concept 'schemata' from Bartlett's classic writings on memory). Thus Piaget stressed that the basic organising principle of logic and science – space, time, causality, objects – start developing well before language. For a young child 'the world is essentially a thing to be sucked' (1968: 10) and by her sucking actions the child essentially, and through deliberation, constructs the categories of the object and class. But these, Piaget stresses, are practical categories, not ideas as such. Piaget also suggested that at the outset of mental awareness the child makes no clear differentiation between the self and the objective world. Thus initially the 'self is at the centre of reality' (1968: 13). It is important to realise, then, that thought and language are independent processes in Piagetian theory, and that thought can neither be reduced to language nor explained by it. As Elkind (1968) cogently puts it, in his introduction to a collection of essays by Piaget, which incidentally provide a useful introduction to his work:

> Thought and language seem to have different origins. Thought derives from the abstraction of one's own actions upon things . . . [whereas] Language . . . is derived from experiences which are not a product of the child's own activity but are rather imitations of patterns provided by adults. It is this difference in origin which accounts for the fundamental duality between thought and language. (1988: xvi)

(Vygotsky (1962: 33–51) also argued that speech and thought had different genetic roots and functionally developed along separate lines. But cf. the work of Noam Chomsky, whose rationalist theory of language suggests that grammar has its roots in an 'innate' reason, and who has suggested that Piaget's own theory is ultimately empiricist (Chomsky 1957, 1979: 84–5; Piaget 1971: 81–92).)

Intuitive or Pre-operational Stage 2 to 7 Years

Characteristic of this stage is the appearance of the semiotic functions (speech, symbolic play, imagery and the like), and this profoundly influences the child's behaviour, both cognitively and affectively. The internalisation of action, which up to then had been purely perceptual and motor, can now represent itself intuitively by means of pictures and imaginery. The child is able to evoke what is not actually perceived. Through symbolic play and intuitive thought – the simple internalisation of percepts and movements in the form of representational images – the child moves from practical intelligence to thought itself. However a child's level of understanding is limited by egocentrism, reflected in his social relationships and in a child's familiar habit of using language in the form of a spontaneous monologue, as an adjunct to immediate action. Besides the intuitive thought, which Piaget suggests (1968: 32) stands midway between actual experience and 'mental experience', this stage is also characterised by animistic thought. The child has a tendency, Piaget notes, 'to conceive things as living and endowed with intentions' (26). Physical reality is perceived by the child as essentially animate and endowed with purpose. But Piaget notes that the child does not so much impute human consciousness to inanimate objects, but rather, in expressing dissatisfaction of mechanistic explanations, seeks to know both the cause and the *purpose* of things. He thus notes the similarity between this kind of thought and that of the early Greek philosophers, like Aristotle, who (like functional anthropologists) offered teleological explanations of phenomena. (Many students have questioned whether animistic thought adequately characterises the thinking of young children. As we noted earlier, Mead suggested that among the Manus of Melanesia, this mode of thinking was a cultural belief, more evident among adults than children. For a recent survey of animistic cognition, see Ciborowski and Price-Williams 1982.)

But Piaget notes that the logic evident at this stage is limited in certain important respects: namely, that the child's thought is still tied to perception so that in ordering or classifying things no concept of 'reversibility' is involved. Lacking 'operational' thought the child is unable to 'conserve' quantities of volume, mass and number. The simple experiments which clay and water which Piaget devised, in order to ascertain whether a child has grasped the notion of *conservation*, are perhaps well known (Cole and Scribner 1974: 146–7).

Concrete Operations Stage 7 to 12 Years

The age of seven, or thereabout, marks a decisive turning point, Piaget argued, in a child's cognitive development. Egocentric language largely disappears and the child moves beyond the pre-logical stage of intuition. S/he begins to use operational thought, albeit still tied to 'concrete' things. As Piaget writes: 'In addition to causality and concepts of conservation there is the mastery of time and space, concepts which are now general schemata of thought, rather than schemata of action or intuition' (1968: 46). Thought now takes the form of a concrete logic. The conservation of substance, weight and volume are progressively attained during this period. The final stage is:

Formal Operations

A child reaches this stage around the age of 11 to 12 years. A transition is then made from concrete to 'formal' thinking, the latter essentially referring to 'hypothetical deductive' reasoning. Referring to this stage Piaget writes:

> Formal operations do not differ from concrete operations except that they are applied to hypotheses and propositions. Formal operations engender a 'logic of propositions' in contrast to the logic of relations, classes, and numbers engendered by concrete operations.

At this stage too the formation of the personality (as distinct from the self system) is achieved (1968: 63). As Gardner remarks (1972: 63–4) three broad trends seem to characterise cognitive development, as suggested by Piaget – a decline of egocentrism, the increasing interiorisation of thought, and the increasing reliance upon the use of symbols. Piaget believes that these stages of cognitive development are universal, even though they are not specifically tied to maturation or chronological age. He noted (1966) that both social and educational factors influenced cognitive growth, questioning whether knowledge could be interpreted simply as a function of innate biological factors.

Such, in brief, is Piaget's account of the 'ontogenesis of cognition'. (The number of introductory texts and critical reviews of Piaget's work is quite staggering. For interesting and important introductions to Piaget, see Flavell 1963; Gardner 1972; Furth 1969; Ginsburg and Opper 1969; Evans 1973.)

Piaget's ideas and theories stimulated much cross-cultural research into cognition; research that largely focused on whether or not children in specific cultures had reached the concrete operational stage of thought. Such research indicated the importance of cultural and environmental factors in cognitive development, and that performance in experiments depended very much on how the task was presented (Berry and Dasen 1974; Dasen 1977a; Cole and Scribner 1974).

Although in an earlier paper Piaget had hinted that the possibility that adult thinking in many cultures may not 'proceed beyond the level of concrete operations' (1966: 13), and had noted the 'parallels' between Greek science and child animism, he was generally wary about making unsubstantiated claims. But clearly Piaget's distinction between concrete and formal operational thought brings to mind similar distinctions which scholars have made in attempting to understand human thought, with Freud (and Kardiner) we have made the distinction between the 'primary processes' (fantasy, dreams, neurotic symptoms) – and their cultural manifestations in religion, myths and symbolic thought (Fromm 1951) – and the secondary processes reflected in conscious, logical thought and science. With Ernst Cassirer (1944) we have the distinction between science and mythopoeic thought. Like Lévi-Strauss, Cassirer suggested that the thought of pre-literate people did not divide life into different spheres or domains; but for Cassirer this unity was synthetic and one of feeling, rather than analytic and cognitive. Finally with Levy-Bruhl we have the distinction between science and pre-logical thought, discussed above. All these three scholars, like the 'symbolic' anthropologists, and Boas, essentially see 'symbolic' thought as non-rational, and as associated with the emotions. For these scholars, it is therefore fundamentally acausal and non-theoretical. With Freud (as with Spinoza and Malinowski) such thought is also seen as having an adaptive function, in coping with stress, cognitive uncertainty and fear (Jahoda 1969: 127–37).

The writings of Lévi-Strauss represent an essential break and departure from this kind of interpretation. 'Analogical' or untamed thought, the 'science of the concrete', is interpreted as proceeding 'through understanding, not affectivity' (1966: 268) and as being logical, rather than non- or pre-logical.

Piaget notes the affinities between his own concept of 'concrete' operations and both Levy-Bruhl's 'pre-logical thought' and Lévi-Strauss's 'thought untamed', but true to his own developmental theory he insists that such thought is pre-logical and preparatory to explicit, or scientific logic (1971: 116). Other writers on cognitive development have tended to follow Piaget in this regard. Vygotsky, for example, sees concept formation as developing through three essential phrases – thought developing in terms of congeries, complexes and concepts. Interestingly, he suggests that children, schizophrenics and pre-literate people all think in terms of 'complexes' – a mode of thought, he suggests, which is essentially concrete and symbolic (1962: 71–2). Likewise, Bruner sees cognitive growth as progressing through three stages of representation, which he terms enactive, iconic and symbolic (1966: 1–67).

The question, therefore, inevitably arises as to whether pre-literate people think primarily in terms of a concrete logic or a pre-logic, as Freud, Levy-Bruhl and Vygotsky implied. Piaget's response to this is ambiguous, but he appears to stress two points. First, that the kinship systems of pre-literate people imply an advanced logic beyond that of concrete operations. Second, he insists that a radical distinction must be made between cultural representations and the 'reasoning' of individuals in a society (1971: 116–17). Indeed Brian Rotman has suggested that Piaget makes so radical a separation between social thought and the 'logic of action' that this seems to imply that not only does cognition virtually evolve independently of language or indeed of any kind of socio-cultural influence, but that logical structures are essentially innate (something that Piaget, of course, denies) (1977: 159, 167). On the other hand, it also suggests that Piaget has an empiricist or non-structural view of language, as Chomsky argued (Moore and Harris 1978). But Lévi-Strauss had earlier sensed that Piaget (like Freud before him) was tending to equate infantile thought with that of pre-literate people (as well as with 'schizophrenic' logic) and he therefore devoted a whole chapter of his study on kinship (1969: 84–97) to discussing this issue.

Piaget's own hesitancy to equate infantile thought with that of pre-literate people was not shared by one of his disciples. For Hallpike's study on the foundations of so-called 'primitive thought' (1979) is a sustained attempt to apply Piaget's theory of cognitive development to an understanding of pre-literate thought. And so, as Shweder puts it, he rushes in 'where even Piaget feared to thread' (1982: 354). I have elsewhere discussed the limitations of this attempt (Morris 1987: 310–12).

In Piagetian theory the development of cognition and of the person essentially involves what Piaget refers to as 'a kind of decentering of the self'. As noted earlier, Piaget makes a distinction between the self and the personality, and describes the self as being 'relatively primitive', and 'is like the centre of one's activity and is characterized by its conscious or unconscious egocentricity'. Margaret Donaldson has questioned whether pre-school children are in fact so self-centred, for they are able through communication to take another's viewpoint, and are not nearly as egocentric as Piaget maintained (1978: 30–1). But for Piaget such 'decentring' (personality formation) begins in middle and late childhood (eight to twelve years) when the individual beings to internalise rules, values and moral tendencies. Piaget sees this as essentially a social process as well as presupposing formal thought and reflexive constructions:

> Personality implies co-operation and personal autonomy . . . the person and the social relationships he engenders and maintains are interdependent. . . . One might say that personality exists as soon as 'life plan' (*Lebensplan*), which is both a source of discipline for the will and an instrument of co-operation, is formed. (1968: 65)

But though Piaget is cognisant of the importance of language and the 'social world' of adults in the cognitive development of the persons, his biological tendencies – what Rotman refers to as his 'thoroughgoing organicism' (1977: 167) – lead him generally to neglect the importance of language and culture. Indeed as we have noted he makes a rigid demarcation between institutions and social facts and what he describes as the logic of 'individual invention' – a dichotomy that is reminiscent of Durkheim. Although the stress on activity, and of overcoming the dualism between empiricism and rationalistic idealism has affinities with Marxist psychology and he does indeed describe thought as 'theoretical practice', unlike Marx, Piaget's paradigm of the individual is that of an isolated organism adapting to its environment in an active way. As Rotman puts it: 'Marx's cry that man creates his nature through social practice becomes for Piaget the maxim that men create their cognition through individual activity' (1977: 177). He notes too that in his general neglect of language, Piaget contrasts radically with Lévi-Strauss and the other structuralists, although he shares their realism. Piaget, he concludes, is a 'solid empirically rooted realist' whose conception of science, and whose focus on the interaction of the organism with the environment (to the neglect of history and subjective meanings), expresses an essential continuity with the evolutionary psychology of Baldwin and Romanes, and the theories of Spencer, Darwin and Haeckel (Rotman 1977: 179), for further important studies of Piaget, see Wilden 1972: 302–50; Boden 1979; Piatelli-Palmarini 1980).

10.3 Structural Marxism

The statement of Lévi-Strauss, earliest cited, that 'the ultimate goal of the human sciences is not to constitute man but to dissolve him' (1966: 247) has been taken as the slogan of the structuralist era. But as we have suggested, neither Lévi-Strauss nor Lacan implied by this the dissolution of the human subject as a social agent; they decried only the Cartesian tendency to make the individual subject the basis of knowledge. For they followed Hegel, Marx and Durkheim in stressing that the human subject was essentially a social not an autonomous being, and that culture was relatively autonomous of the individual and could not be explained simply in terms of human psychology. But with Louis Althusser we have a form of structuralism that not only opposes the Cartesian cogito but human agency *per se*. Kate Soper entitles her chapter on Althusser 'The Death of "Marxist Man"' (1986: 96–119). With Althusser, as with the behaviourist psychologists, the human subject seems to disappear entirely from the analysis.

Louis Althusser was born in 1918, near Algiers. He went to school there and at Marseilles, and spent most of the war years in a prisoner-of-war camp. In 1948, at the age of thirty, he completed his doctoral studies under Gaston Bachelard at the prestigious Ecole Normale Supérieure, and became a teacher there in philosophy. The same year he joined the French Communist Party. For more than two decades he was a teacher at the Ecole, and during the 1960s he published two important Marxist studies, which have since come to be regarded as classics in structural Marxism – *For Marx* (1965) and *Reading Capital* (1968) (co-authored with Etienne Balibar). These studies established Althusser as a Marxist philosopher of substance and originality, and he became the focus of much controversy and critical debate within the Marxist tradition, as well has having an important influence on anthropological and sociological studies. Together with Lacan and Lévi-Strauss, Althusser came to be regarded as one of the doyens of the structuralist movement. But his notoriety as a scholar was seemingly short-lived. With the decline of structuralism as an intellectual movement, and with the emergence of a determined anti-Marxist tenor among French intellectuals, a 'virtual collective amnesia', as Elliott describes it (1987: 27) began to settle around Althusser's work. Once the subject of both adulation and a series of sustained critiques, Althusser had, by the 1990s, become almost a forgotten figure. This amnesia was no doubt aggravated by Althusser's personal circumstances. For long a sufferer of manic-depressive illness, Althusser was admitted to St Anne's psychiatric hospital in Paris in the autumn of 1980, after confessing to killing his wife Hélène. But although Althusser's intellectual career seems to have ended in tragedy and in scholarly neglect, there are signs of a 'come-back' as Althusser's work is coming to be reassessed in more balanced appraisals – studies that are free of both adulation and acrimony (Callinicos 1982: 53–80; Benton 1984; Elliott 1987).

Althusser conceived of his work, in spite of its being abstract and theoretical in both intent and style, as essentially a form of political intervention. His essays in the 1960s were motivated by a particular political conjuncture that was dominated by two important events which had profound repercussions for the French Communist Party – Krushchev's denunciation in 1956 of Stalin at the Twentieth Congress of the Communist Party of the Soviet Union, and the developing Sino-Soviet dispute. Althusser indeed remarked that he would not have written anything had it not been for Krushchev's critique of Stalinism and the subsequent 'humanist ravings' that emerged. For Althusser felt that the outcome of these events was not only the declaration by the CPS that the dictatorship of the proletariat had been 'superseded' in the Soviet Union, but in reaction – 'a profound ideological reaction' – to dogmatic Stalinism, Western Marxists had espoused a Hegelian or humanistic form of Marxism which was theoretically empty and politically reactionary. As a purported liberation from Stalinism, Communist intellectuals had, in turning to Marx's early works, spontaneously rediscovered the old philosophical themes of 'freedom', 'man', the 'human person' and 'alienation', and had thus come to develop a socialist humanist doctrine which was pre-Marxist in its essential tenets and profoundly *ideological* in character. Althusser therefore came to suggest that his 'intervention' was conducted on 'two fronts'; on the one hand, to demarcate between Marxist theory and other theoretical tendencies – and Althusser is specifically concerned with empiricism, historicism, economism and subjectivism (humanism), and on the other to demarcate between Marx's early thought, still encapsulated in pre-Marxist idealist notions, and the later scientific 'problematic' of his study *Capital*. We may discuss each of these interventions in turn.

Althusser, in a way similar to Lacan's re-reading of Freud, saw himself as engaged in the task of combatting revisionism – although whereas Lacan appealed to the early Freud for his orthodoxy, Althusser appeals to the later Marx. 'I am the defender of orthodoxy,' Althusser declared, whose aim was to counter 'the threat of bourgeois ideology' (in Hirsh 1981: 162). But such orthodoxy did not entail a defence of economic determinism, although he allowed the determination by the economic 'in the last instance'. What Althusser was particularly critical towards was the kind of mechanical materialism that was advocated by the Second International, which he dubbed 'economism' and which tended to see a direct and simple causal relationship between the economic base and the ideological superstructure. Althusser was equally critical of the interpretations of Marx as a technological determinist (cf. 1969: 108–9). But Althusser's shafts of criticism are largely directed against three tendencies, which he sees as inherent in bourgeois ideology – empiricism, historicism and humanism.

Like Lévi-Strauss, Althusser is critical of the empiricist conception of knowledge, holding that the 'real' is not directly accessible to us through observation but is mediated by our assumptions and theories about reality. He defines empiricism in a very general sense as being any theory that represents knowledge as a confrontation between a (knowing) subject and an object, such that knowledge is conceived of as an abstraction by the subject of the essence of the object. But for Althusser, knowledge is not abstraction but production. Althusser is particularly laudatory towards Spinoza, whose rationalist and determinist theory he regarded as probably the greatest philosophical revolution of all time. He regarded Spinoza as Marx's only direct ancestor. What was important about Spinoza, for Althusser, was that he made a crucial distinction between the real object and the object of knowledge, and stressed 'the opacity of the immediate' (Althusser 1970: 34–40, 102; Elliott 1987: 97).

Althusser's positive attitude towards Spinoza – whose philosophy as we earlier discussed entailed an essentially static and mechanistic conception of the world – contrasts markedly with his generally antagonistic approach towards Hegel. Althusser denies any continuity between Hegel and Marx. The notion that Marx simply 'inverted' Hegel, or that Marxism retains the 'rational kernel' of Hegel's dialectic while discarding his speculative philosophy (Engels), Althusser considers to be inappropriate images of the relationship between the two scholars. The simple inversion of Hegel's idealist metaphysic gives us Feuerbach's materialism, Althusser contends (1969: 89). And in their conceptions of the totality, of contradiction and of history, there are fundamental differences, Althusser argues, between Hegelian philosophy and Marx's historical materialism. Hegel's totality is an expressive or spiritual totality – it has 'a "spiritual" type of unity, whereas the Marxist conception is one of a complex, structured whole, which is not reducible to any single principle or substance, as with Hegel and Haeckel (1969: 202–3; 1970: 97). But more important, Hegel's conception of the historical process is teleological. Not only is the Hegelian philosophy of history teleological, in that from its origins it is in pursuit of a goal (the realisation of Absolute Knowledge by Spirit) but, Althusser argues, the structure of the Hegelian dialectic is itself teleological. In contrast, Althusser suggests, Marx postulates that 'history is a process without a subject'. He writes: 'I think I can affirm: this category of a *process without a subject*, which must of course be taken from the grip of the Hegelian teleology, undoubtedly represents the greatest theoretical debt linking Marx to Hegel' (1972: 182–3). This is as much as Althusser was willing to concede to Hegel, whose influence on Marx he sees as minimal.

This leads us directly to Althusser's critique of humanism, the notion that human subjects create the social world in which they live by intentional acts. His well-known essay 'Marxism and Humanism' (1963) is an explicit critique of such humanism, which Althusser sees as a recurrent problem in Marxism. Marx's criticisms of Feuerbach's ethical humanism, Engels' struggle against Dühring, and Lenin's long battle with the Russian populists are all precedents, Althusser contends, of a continuing struggle against humanist ideology. The gist of Althusser's argument is that around 1845 Marx broke completely with the kind of theory that based history and politics on an 'essence of man'. Marx's new paradigm had three essential elements. The first was the formation of a social theory based on radically new concepts – Althusser's outline of this theory we shall come to shortly. Secondly, a radical critique of the *theoretical* pretensions of every philosophical humanism, and finally, the definition of humanism as an ideology. Althusser cites a quotation from Marx's 'Marginal Notes on Wagner' (1879–80) to the effect that 'my analytic method . . . does not start from man but from the economically given period of society', and he argues that Marx broke completely with the 'empiricism of the subject'. This type of humanist theory postulates that there is a universal essence of man, and that this essence is an attribute of 'each single individual' who is its real subject. Such a theory could be recognised not only in contract theories of society (from Hobbes to Rousseau), of political economy (from Petty to Ricardo), of ethics (from Descartes to Kant), but such 'subjectivism' was the very principle of both idealist and empiricist theories of knowledge (from Locke to Feuerbach, via Kant). The content of the human essence or of the empirical subjects may vary, but a philosophical humanism formed the basis of all pre-Marxist theories. And Althusser continues:

By rejecting the essence of man as his theoretical basis, Marx rejected the whole of this organic system of postulates. He drove the philosophical categories of the subject, of empiricism, of the ideal essence, etc. from all the domains in which they had been supreme. Not only from political economy (rejection of the myth of *homo economicus* . . .), not just from history (rejection of social atomism and ethico-political idealism); not just from ethics (rejection of the Kantian ethical idea); but also from philosophy itself; for Marx's materialism excludes the empiricism of the subject. (1969: 228)

This, Althusser felt, constituted a total theoretical revolution, and there are thus grounds for suggesting that Marx's theory was essentially a 'theoretical anti-humanism'. As a structuralist, therefore, Althusser goes on to claim that the social structure is prior to the human subject, and is not created by it. There are clearly echoes of Comte in Althusser's formulations, and it is of interest that in bewailing the complete lack of any radical thinker in France since the revolution, Althusser notes the hostility of French philosophy towards Comte – the 'only mind worthy of interest' that France has produced (1969: 25).

In postulating that history is a 'process without a subject', it follows the humans are not subjects of social and historical structures but merely their 'supports' or 'carriers' (the similarity between Althusser's Marxism and the theories of cultural determinists like Benedict are here apparent). As Althusser explicitly puts it in an frequently quoted passage:

The structure of the relations of production determines the *places* and *functions* occupied and adopted by the agents of production, who are never anything more than the occupants of these places, in so far as they are the 'supports' (*Träger*) of these functions. The true 'subjects' (in the sense of the constitutive subjects of the process) are therefore not these occupants or functionaries, are not despite all appearances, the 'obviousness' of the 'given' of naive anthropology, 'concrete individuals'. 'real men' – but *the definition and distribution of these places and functions. The true 'subjects' are these defines and distributors: the relations of production* (and political and ideological social relations). But since these are 'relations', they cannot be thought with the category *subject*. (1970: 180)

Whereas Marx in the 6th Thesis on Feuerbach had suggested displacing the 'abstract man' with the 'real man', that is the recognition of individuals as historical and social subjects, Althusser dispenses with the concept of the human subject entirely, and social structures and historical processes are seemingly independent of humans. The subject is a function of ideology: history and society are not the creations of a human subject either singular or collective. But the suggestion that 'the "subjects" of history are given human societies' (1969: 231) is tempered elsewhere in his writings with the postulate that it 'is the masses which make history. The class struggle is the motor of history' (1969: 215; Mepham 1985: 141).

In the second intervention, Althusser sought to demonstrate that there was a complete disjuncture – an 'epistemological break' – between Marx's early writings and the kind of social theory that is evident in his mature work, particularly in *Capital*. Drawing on the ideas of his tutor Gaston Bachelard, Althusser argues that this break occurred around 1845, when, with Engels, Marx wrote *The German Ideology*, and it involved the abandonment of an early pre-scientific humanistic standpoint, one that was heavily influenced by Hegelian idealism. The break was a fundamental one, involving a leap from ideology to science and the creation of a whole new problematic. Marx, around the middle of the nineteenth century, Althusser argues, established a new science – 'the science of the history of "social formations"'. Marx, he writes, 'opened up' for scientific knowledge 'a new continent', that of history, just as Thales opened up the 'continent' of mathematics for scientific knowledge, and Galileo opened up the 'continent' of physical nature for scientific knowledge (1969: 13–14). As mechanistic science had 'induced' the birth of Cartesian philosophy, so had Marx's science of history induced a Marxist philosophy – dialectical materialism – which was still in the process of formation.

In forging a new science of history that was fundamentally distinct from his earlier philosophical humanism, Marx created radically new concepts of social formation, productive forces, relations of production, determination in the last instance by the economy, superstructure, ideologies, etc. Such a social theory entailed a conception of 'society' as consisting of four 'instances', 'levels' or 'practices' – the 'economic', political, ideological and theoretical (science) – which form a complex, structural whole. But although Althusser sees the 'economic' as the determinant in the 'last instance', he argues that each of these levels has a relative autonomy, and that there is no simple mechanical determination of the political and ideological levels by the economic 'base'. Important in this formulation is the autonomy that Althusser gives to theoretical (scientific) practices and the sharp dichotomy he makes between science and ideology. There has been much critical debate on Althusser's conception of Marxism, with its static, functionalist overtones, and his conception of science. For in taking *Capital* as a given exemplification of social science, and in severing theory from any real referent, there is a certain circularity and ambiguity in Althusser's arguments. As Elliott sums it up:

> If science was separated from the social, it was similarly sundered from the empirical. Rationalism and conventionalism converged here to exclude the latter from scientific practice. Conflating the empirical and empiricist, Althusser furthermore equated the experiental with the ideological-realm of the imaginary and 'false conceptions', antithesis of conceptual science and objective knowledge. These collapses . . . debarred any genuine input on the part of empirical evidence into theoretical practice. (1987: 110)

Not surprisingly, Althusser has been accused of scientism, and has having a very narrow positivistic conception of science (Hirsh 1981: 166; for further discussions of Althusser's structural Marxism, see Geras 1978: 5; Clarke 1980; Elliott 1987: 91–114).

These debates fall outside the present study, but Althusser's discussion of ideology is particularly relevant, as he sees the subjectivity of the subject as being specifically constructed in ideology. Althusser defines ideology as an organic part of every social totality and as being a matter of the *lived* relation between humans and their world. Ideology is a system of representations, but it is ill-understood as a collective *consciousness*, for it is largely – profoundly – unconscious, and its images and concepts largely impose themselves on human beings through *structures* rather than through their consciousness. Humans, he writes, 'live' their ideologies, 'not at all as a form of consciousness, but as an object of the "world" – as their "world" itself' (1969: 233). Althusser seems to use the term ideology not in its critical Marxist sense as a form of consciousness that cloaks inequalities, but in a more anthropological sense, as a synonym of culture. He thus sees ideology as a part of every human society, and cannot conceive of even a future communist society as being without ideology. (1969: 231–5). Holding to a more orthodox interpretation of ideology, many Marxists have naturally found such formulations unacceptable, although it is difficult to conceive of humans living in a 'cultureless' world.

Ideology, for Althusser, thus has a practico-social function in contrast to the theoretical function of science. Bourgeois ideology has a humanistic bias and its principal function is to make the human subject 'the principle of all theory' (1969: 237). But Althusser goes on to imply that the primary function of all ideologies is to transform individuals into subjects, to 'constitute' individuals as conscious subjects of society ('free subjectivities, centres of initiatives) so as to enforce their *subjection* to the social order and its demands on them. For Althusser 'there is no ideology except by the subject and for the subject'. And he continues: 'The category of the subject is constitutive of all ideology but . . . the category of the subject is only constitutive of all ideology insofar as all ideology has the function [which defines it] of "constituting" concrete individuals as subjects' (1971: 153–65). Althusser thus deliberately explains the ambiguity of the term 'subject', meaning both freedom and agency, and constraint (Kearney 1986: 305; Elliott 1987: 299). If ideology is universal in all societies, and its main function is the creation of autonomous subjects then it follows that the culture of all societies is to some extent humanistic – a formulation that tends to obliterate the specificity of the Western bourgeois conception of the individual. But the centrepoint of Althusser's theory is to repudiate the category of human nature, and to postulate that the subject is entirely an ideological – a cultural – construct.

In reacting against the 'essentialism' of the early bourgeois theorists and in uncritically accepting Althusser's formulations, contemporary structuralists seem to suggest that the human subject is simply a creation of culture (or language). They thus join forces with both the cultural relativists (who are close to the German idealist tradition) and the Durkheimian sociologists in playing down the natural world, and the creative labour of the human subject. Although entitled *Language and Materialism* (1977), Coward and Ellis's study of semiology and the 'theory of the subject' is significant in that it hardly mentions the natural world, and makes no reference at all to the findings of Vygotsky, Whorf, Piaget and Schaff.

If, as Coward and Ellis seem to suggest, the 'social process has no centre' or subject, or 'motivating force', (1977: 74) and if the concept of the 'subject' is simply an 'ideological construct' of the bourgeoisie, it is, I think, difficult to conceive how social life ever originated. And if it is conceded that 'morality' depends on the 'category of subject' for its functioning, then it is clearly problematic to postulate culture without a subject. Whereas the early bourgeois theorists had taken the human subject as given and 'natural', and society as in some sense artificial and imposed (Mészáros 1970: 254) – methodological individualism – we now have the inversion of this: the 'social system' is given (almost a transcendental entity) and the 'subject' results from it construction in sociality (Coward and Ellis 1977; 2). But: the human subject and culture are dialectically related and coexistent. Of course, one can conceptualise the human subject abstracted from any social context – this is precisely the kind of theory that Coward and Ellis cogently criticise. Equally, one can treat culture (and language) as an abstract system without a subject: this is precisely what Durkheim does. The dangers are that either one collapses into cultural relativism, or to keep theoretically afloat, postulates an ahistoric human 'mind' like Lévi-Strauss or the kind of structuralism that Althusser espouses. (In this context it is hardly surprising that both Althusser and Durkheim – as well as Lévi-Strauss – have been accused of following a neo-Kantian dualistic paradigm (Rose 1981: 1–39).) But inevitably without a human subject, as defined by Marx, history is divorced from nature. Social structures are only prior to the subject if the latter is conceptualised – as writers in the behaviourist tradition do (Malinowski, Durkheim, White) – as an organism, or as the idiosyncratic individual at birth. A viewpoint that Coward and Ellis are surely trying to counter. It would, of course, be highly misleading to equate the 'abstract individual' of the early social contract theorists with the human 'subject' of sociological analysis – as it would be to conflate empiricism with empirical data. (For some interesting discussions by Marxists on the relationship between the 'individual' and 'society' – those two 'great abstractions' of Western culture, as Williams called them – see Williams 1961: 89–119; Mészáros 1970: 254, 288; Sève 1978; for an important critique of Coward and Ellis's text, see Rée 1985.)

There have been many critiques of Althusser's structural Marxism, particularly of its anti-humanist aspects. E. P. Thompson (1978), in a well-known but harsh polemic, stresses the ahistoric and mechanistic tenor in Althusser's formulations, noting that in repudiating historicism and empiricism Althusser went to an unjustified extreme, virtually denying the epistemological legitimacy of both empirical and historical knowledge. Thompson berates Althusser for evicting process from history, and for also excluding human agency from the analysis (1978: 281–2). Others in a more temperate manner have presented critiques of Althusser's antihumanism. Norman Geras (1983), as earlier noted, has been critical of Althusser's sociologistic perspective and has argued that Marx continued to employ the idea of a human nature as a normative concept, as well as giving it an explanatory role in historical materialism. Elliott concurs with this general assessment of Marx's position (1978: 129–30). Soper has even suggested that in his stress on collective action there is not such a wide gulf between Althusser and such humanist Marxists as Sartre, and that Althusser's 'moderate' form of anti-humanism may in reality be a thinly veiled humanism (1986: 107). But the general consensus among many Marxist scholars seems to be that Althusser's structural Marxism was too extreme in its exclusion of both historical analysis and subjective agency from the Marxist paradigm.

One writer who has presented a more balanced interpretation of Marx's materialism is Lucien Goldman. Like Marx, Goldman rejects as untenable the many radical dualisms that pervade contemporary thought – philosophy and science, theory and praxis, interpretation and explanation. And on the concept of the subject he argues persuasively against the two main approaches: one is to give the subject, specifically the cogito, analytical priority – a line of thought that stems from Descartes and is expressed by existentialists, phenomenologists, as well as by humanistic psychologists and interpretative sociologists. The other approach, characteristic of contemporary structuralism (and he specifically cites Althusser and Lévi-Strauss, whose theories Coward and Ellis closely follow), leads to the 'negation of the subject'. Although the 'subject' has the status of other scientific concepts in that it is constructed, Goldman holds that such a concept is a grounded one in having a necessary function of 'rendering the facts we propose to study intelligible and comprehensible' (1977b: 92). He therefore criticises both approaches. The first approach, which begins with the individual subject, and puts a focal emphasis on meaning, is, Goldman argues, essentially non-explanatory, and unable to account for the relationship among phenomena. The second approach – structuralism – in negating the subject is unable to account for the becoming or genesis of a structure, or its functioning: 'the first does not see structure; the second does not see the subject which creates genesis, becoming and functionality' (1977b: 106).

Goldman, therefore, rightly argues that it is necessary to integrate consciousness in behaviour and praxis, and to seek both the meaning and functionality of structures. To do this one needs a dialectic approach that situates a 'creative subject at the interior of social life'. Goldman thus concludes:

> To comprehend a phenomenon is to describe its structure and to isolate its meaning. To explicate a phenomenon is to explain its genesis on the basis of a developing functionality which begins with a subject. And there is no radical difference between comprehension and explication. (1977b: 106)

But to argue against the theoretical negation of the human subject is not in the least to deny that the 'self' or 'mind' is not socially constituted: the subject, human existence, is no more conceivable outside of culture than is culture without a subject. Althusser, of course, does not deny the social reality of the human subject, which is present in all cultures, he simply sees this as an ideological construct, and thus outside true scientific discourse – that is Marxism. (For further studies on the limitations of Althusser's structural Marxism and emphasising the need to integrate structural analysis with a focus on history and subjective meaning, see Timpanaro 1975: 192–6; Schmidt 1983; Callinicos 1987.)

Although Althusser felt he was offering a left-wing critique of Stalinism, his politics were always firmly entrenched, like Lukács', in the Marxist-Leninist tradition. He affirmed the role of the revolutionary party and never made any serious or public criticism of either the Communist Party or the Soviet Union. He rarely stepped outside his theoretical activity, and as Sheridan remarks, that activity was carried on at such an exalted level of abstraction that only the Althusserians were capable of practising it. History and the real world are almost entirely absent from his writing; they are peopled entirely with concepts drawn from Marxism and Freud (Sheridan 1980: 201–2). As with Lévi-Strauss and Lacan, Althusser seemed to be engaged in a 'flight from history'. The same could not be said of Michel Foucault, a one-time student of Althusser, who has often been labelled a structuralist, but whose relations with the structuralist movement, as we shall observe, was to say the least an ambiguous one. And it is to the writings of Foucault that we may now turn.

10.4   The Archaeology of Knowledge

Michel Foucault (1926–84) was born in Poitiers, France, of middle-class parents. He belongs to the same generation as Chomsky and Habermas and was thus a much younger scholar than Lacan and Lévi-Strauss. His father, a local surgeon, sent him to a Catholic school, and he went on to study philosophy at the Ecole Normale Supérieure. There, and at the Sorbonne, he studied under Hyppolite, Althusser and the French historian of science Georges Canguilhem. At the age of twenty-three he received his diploma of philosophy, and shortly afterwards joined the Communist Party (PCF). But he soon became disillusioned both with philosophy and with the politics of the Communist Party, and his interest shifted to psychology and psychopathology. He undertook research studies into psychiatric practice and mental illness and in 1954 published his first book, on psychopathology. This was revised and republished eight years later under the title *Mental Illness and Psychology*. But still estranged from French academic life, Foucault left Paris and obtained a post in the French department at Uppsala University in Sweden. There he stayed four years, later moving to Warsaw and Hamburg. While at Hamburg he completed his studies on the history of madness, and under the aegis of Canguilhem, was awarded a doctorate. Of interest is that the study, translated as *Madness and Civilisation*, and which was later to establish Foucault's reputation as a scholar, had initially been turned down by two leading Paris publishers, and was very scantily reviewed when it first came out. Foucault's history of medicine, *The Birth of the Clinic*, published two years after *Madness and Civilisation* (in 1963) fared even worse; it had even lower sales and virtually no reviews at all (Sheridan 1980: 47). But the tide changed in 1966 when Foucault published his *Les Mots et les choses* (*Words and Things*, translated under the title *The Order of Things* (1970)). It came out in the same year as Lacan's long awaited *Ecrits*, and became an immediate best-seller. By then the structuralist movement had become firmly established – a translation of Lévi-Strauss's *The Savage Mind* was published that same year – and Foucault's reputation as one of the most original and important scholar of the decade was firmly assured. On returning to Paris in 1960 he became head of the philosophy department of the University of Clermont Ferrand, and after a spell at the University of Vincennes, became 'Professor of the History of Systems of Thought' (his own designation) at the College de France in 1970. A great media figure and an outspoken polemicist, Foucault was also a committed scholar, and was a relentless campaigner for human rights, particularly the rights of oppressed women, homosexuals and prisoners. He died at the age of fifty-eight of a cerebral tumour.

Foucault was an elusive scholar who hated to be pigeon-holed. He came to maturity in the 1960s when there were student debates taking place between the proponents of four intellectual traditions – Marxism, phenomenology, hermeneutics and structuralism. He was clearly influenced by all these currents of thought but at the same time he distanced himself from all of them, attempting to plough his own unique theoretical furrow. Foucault always maintained a certain aloofness towards Marxism, and some have described his writings as essentially anti-Marxist. Marx is hardly mentioned in his early writings, and even in *Discipline and Punish* he gets no more than three or four references. Foucault always seemed to question the usefulness of historical materialism, regarding it as the epitome of nineteenth-century historicist thought, which was now outmoded and in the process of being superseded. Foucaults antipathy towards global theorising also distanced him from Marxism, for Foucault's work has focused on the analysis of specific institutions and he has been concerned to rediscover 'subjugated knowledge' rather than to construct systematic theory. Indeed one important characteristic of Foucault's thought is that it is consistently anti-system, Foucault rejecting the notion that his work dealt with any form of 'totality'.

Foucault was equally circumspect towards existentialism and phenomenology. At the Sorbonne Foucault had attended Merleau-Ponty's lectures on the phenomenology of experience, and steeped himself in the writings of Heidegger and the phenomenologists. He wrote a long, sympathetic introduction to a translation of Ludwig Binswanger's study in *Le Rêve et l'existence* (1954). Phenomenology, as we have seen, was essentially a philosophy of the subject, especially as initially presented by Husserl. Phenomenology placed acquired knowledge 'in brackets' and attempted to return to a pure, unprejudiced apprehension of the world. Human beings were conceptualised as meaning-giving subjects, and thus priority was given to subjectivity as the focus or origin of meaning. For Husserl, it is the transcendental ego which gives meaning to the world and to the culture and history which it 'constitutes' as conditioning its empirical self. Existentialism stressed the importance of 'authentic' free choice and situated the individual in the world, but like phenomenology remained essentially a philosophy of the subject (Dreyfus and Rabinow 1982: xvi; Smart 1985: 16). Foucault, like the structuralists, broke entirely with this tradition, rejecting not only a history based on such notions as causality, contradiction and teleology, but also the whole philosophy of the subject (Sheridan 1980: 204). As Foucault puts it:

> I don't believe the problem [of historical contextualisation] can be solved by historicising the subject as posited by the phenomenologists, fabricating a subject that evolves through the course of history. One has to dispense with the constituent subject, to get rid of the subject itself, that's to say, to arrive at an analysis which can account for the constitution of the subject within a historical framework. And this is what I would call genealogy, that is, a form of history which can account for the constitution of knowledges, discourses, domains of objects, etc.,

without having to make reference to a subject which is either transcendental in relation to the field of events or runs its empty sameness throughout the course of history. (1980: 117)

But while Foucault agrees with the structuralists in his critique of the philosophy of the subject, and his own early studies certainly have a structuralist flavour, Foucault, unlike the structuralists, has an acute sense of history. Like the scholars with whom he has most frequently been compared – Nietzsche and Weber – Foucault's project throughout has an historical import, and the description of him as a 'philosopher-historian' is a valid one (Smart 1985: 13). His political concerns also make his theoretical standpoint 'at a far remove from the textual navel-gazing' of the post-structuralists (Merquior 1985: 14). But besides his historical emphasis, Foucault differs from the structuralists in that the underlying 'structures' which his analyses reveal are not universal, but, as we shall see, specific to given historical epochs. While structuralists such as Althusser and Lévi-Strauss rejected nineteenth-century subjectivism and historicism only to fall back into a nineteenth-century scientism of truth and objectivity, Foucault relinquished the view of science as the embodiment of an objective and universal reason. Many have stressed his preoccupation, like Weber, with rationality, but Foucault's concerns are with concrete forms of reason, and this thus leads to a consistent relativism. The kind of history he envisaged was an 'internal ethnology of our culture and our rationality', and this meant that 'we must limit the sense of the word "rationalisation" to an instrumental and relative use . . . and to see how forms of rationalisation became embodied in practices or systems of practices' (Sheridan 1980: 204–5; Dreyfus and Rabinow 1982: 133). Foucault is therefore concerned with meaning, and with delineating the social forms of reason, not, as with the structuralist, of finding universal structures or objective laws which govern all human activity. However, in his early writings Foucault has affinities with the structuralists in treating discourses – on madness, medical knowledge and the human sciences – as autonomous practices, not only independent of the human subject, but also of socioeconomic conditions. However, in spite of certain structuralist tendencies evident in Foucault's early work he was always adamant that he was *not* a structuralist. In the Foreword to the English edition on *The Order of Things* (1970) he wrote, with some petulance:

In France, certain half-witted 'commentators' persist in labelling me a 'structuralist'. I have been unable to get it into their tiny minds that I have used none of the methods, concepts, or key terms that characterize structural analysis. (1970: xiv)

And in distinguishing his own historical form of analysis from structuralism he elsewhere wrote:

> One can agree that structuralism formed the most systematic effort to evacuate the concept of the event, not only from ethnology but from a whole series of other sciences and in the extreme case from history. In that sense, I don't see who could be more of an anti-structuralist than myself. But the important thing is to avoid trying to do for the event what was previously done with the concept of structure. It's not a matter of locating everything on one level, that of the event, but of realising that there are actually a whole order of levels of different types of events differing in amplitude, chronological breadth, and capacity to produce effects. (1980: 114)

Such an analysis did not imply what Foucault refers to as 'commentary', a form of descriptive hermeneutics. In their study of Foucault, Dreyfus and Rabinow suggest that two different kinds of hermeneutic inquiry stemmed from Heidegger, constrasting both with Husserl's phenomenology (in which meaning and subjectivity are intrinsic) and with structuralism (which excludes both). The first kind of hermeneutics they describe as the 'hermeneutics of the everyday', interpretative understanding, as exemplified by Garfunkel and Geertz. Their suggestion that this is simply an 'offshoot' of Heidegger's work is certainly misplaced, for as we have noted, hermeneutics has a long tradition in the social sciences going back to Dilthey, Weber and Boas at the beginning of the present century. The second form of hermeneutics they refer to as the 'hermeneutics of suspicion' and see this approach as exemplified by Freud and Marx who sought to uncover an underlying truth. They suggest that Foucault rejects both forms of hermeneutics. On the one hand, he agrees with Nietzsche, Marx and Freud, that interpretative understanding or hermeneutics in its normal sense, is limited in 'that such an interpretation is surely deluded about what is really going on' (1982: xix). On the other hand, Foucault questioned the validity of some deep underlying truth which analysis revealed, and expressed certain reservations about Marx's theory of ideology (1980: 118).

So if Foucault is not a Marxist, or a structuralist or a phenomenologist, and rejects both forms of hermeneutics, what kind of approach does he advocate? Foucault is very reluctant to situate his writings in any specific tradition – he was, he wrote, creating a 'labyrinth' into which his discourse could venture (1972: 17) – but essentially he advocates a mode of *historical* understanding purged of what he describes as 'anthropologism', that is, the assumption that there is some 'anonymous and general subject of history'. He called this approach, following Nietzsche, 'genealogical'. Dreyfus and Rabinow describe this method of history as 'interpretive analytics'. It is an historical analysis which focuses almost exclusively on three key concepts – knowledge (truth, reason), power and the human subject.

Rather than advocating the 'dissolution' of the subject, Foucault's almost entire corpus has been concerned with, as he put it, presenting a 'genealogy of the modern subject as a historical and cultural reality'. His aim was not to analyse the phenomenon of power, but rather to 'create a history of the different modes by which, in our culture, human beings are made subjects' (1982: 208; Smart 1985: 18). Like Lévi-Strauss and Lacan, Foucault's critique of phenomenology and existentialist-humanism does not imply the elimination of subjectivity and agency from social scientific discourse, but rather involves a critique of the epistemological subject, a refusal to base knowledge on the postulate of a subject that transcends history and society. But such issues we can perhaps best leave aside until we have discussed his seminal study of the human sciences, *The Order of Things*, which is specifically concerned, as an underlying thematic, with delineating how the human subject became an 'object' of knowledge in Western culture.

The Order of Things, subtitled *An archaeology of the human sciences*, provides an historical analysis of three intellectual discourses – on life (biology), wealth (economics) and language (linguistics) – in order to understand the emergence of the human sciences. He deliberately eschews the 'history of thought' approach, which tends to see academic disciplines like biology as autonomous totalities, and which puts a focal emphasis on historical continuity. Instead, following (like Althusser) the suggestions of Bachelard, Foucault puts an emphasis on discontinuity, rupture, series, thresholds and transformations, his aim being, as he put it, 'to uncover the principles and consequences of an autochthonous transformation that is taking place in the field of historical knowledge' (1972: 15). Thus Foucault rejects the notion of a linear evolution of knowledge, and comes to postulate a series of epistemes that characterise three historical epochs – The Renaissance, (to 1650), the Classical (1650–1800) and the Modern (1800–1950) epistemes. He thus sees two great discontinuities in the episteme of Western culture – the first inaugurating the classical age, the second, at the beginning of the nineteenth century, marking the beginning of the modern period. He defines episteme as

> the total set of relations that unite, at a given period, the discursive practices that give rise to epistemological figures, sciences, and possibly formalize systems. . . . The episteme is not a form of knowledge or a type of rationality which, crossing the boundaries of the most varied sciences, manifests the sovereign unity of a subject, a spirit, or a period; it is the totality of relations that can be discovered, for a given period, between the sciences when one analyses them at the level of discursive regularities. (1972: 191)

Many have noted the similarity between this conception and Thomas Kuhn's (1962) notion of a scientific paradigm.

The episteme of the Renaissance period Foucault describes as the 'prose of the world', a cosmological world-view defined by the unity of words and things. The relation of languages to the world, Foucault wrote, during the period, was one of analogy rather than signification (1970: 37). Language possessed a symbolic function, and such notions as resemblance and sympathy played a constructive role in the knowledge of the period. Quoting from obscure sources – rather than from the more familiar Renaissance texts – Foucault outlines the doctrine of signatures and the Greek symbolic classification of the four elements, but otherwise his portrait of Renaissance cosmology is shallow compared with the rich accounts of Koyré (1958) and Lovejoy (1936).

Then towards the middle of the seventeenth century, the episteme of symbolic correspondences, the cosmological world-view, collapsed with the emergence of mechanistic philosophy, although given his focus, Foucault makes little mention of the mechanistic science of Galileo and Newton. The conception of knowledge shifted, and 'the activity of the mind' no longer consisted in 'drawing things together, in setting out on a quest for everything that might reveal some sort of kinship, attraction, or secretly shared nature . . . but on the contrary, in discriminating' (1970: 55). The stress was now not on analogy but on analysis, not on resemblance but on representation. A gap emerges between words and things, and words come to function as ideas whose role is to represent, measure and classify the structure, the things of the world. The main projects of the classical episteme involves mathesis a 'general science of order' whose universal method is algebra, and taxonomia, the ordering of things through classificatory schemata. Foucault devotes a chapter to each of the empirical knowledges of the classical age – 'natural history' exemplified in the work of Buffon and Linnaeus, the 'analysis of wealth' associated with the work of Cantillon, Quesnay and the Physiocrats, and 'general grammar' as portrayed in the discourses of Condillac, and the 'Port Royal' logic (1662). Foucault stresses the shared episteme of each of these empirical sciences, and notes that what was common to them was probably unconscious to the scientists of the period (1970: xi).

At the end of the eighteenth century a similar discontinuity occurred to that which destroyed Renaissance thought, and the classical episteme was in turn dislocated and replaced. It essentially involved the 'mutation of order into history', and thus history became the 'unavoidable element in our thought' (1970: 219–20). History therefore comes to play the same role in modern thought that order and classification played in classical thought, and during the early years of the nineteenth century notions of 'development' and 'historicity' came to define the new empirical sciences – those of philology, biology and political economy. As Foucault writes: 'Within a few years (around 1800) the tradition of general grammar was replaced by an essentially historical philology; natural classifications were ordered according to the analyses of comparative anatomy; and a political economy was founded whose main themes were labour and production' (1970: xii). The key figures in this transformation were Bopp, Cuvier and Ricardo, all of whom, along with their contemporaries, sought to 'historicise' the knowledges of language, life and labour. Foucault stresses that 'Philology, biology and political economy were established, not in the places formerly occupied by general grammar, natural history, and the analysis of wealth, but in an area where those forms of knowledge did not exist, in the spaces they left blank' (1970: 207). But although Foucault puts an emphasis on the disjuncture between epistemes, it is evident that he does not see a particular period in monolithic terms as some critics have suggested (1970: x).

But the crucial characteristic of the modern episteme for Foucault is not simply its historical perspective but the fact that discourses became 'self-referential'. The human subject emerged not only as an 'object' of knowledge, but as a 'subject', as the locus and basis of knowledge . The human subject became an 'operational concept' in the sciences and the philosophy that emerged at the turn of the nineteenth century. Before this decade, Foucault contends, 'man', the human subject, did not exist. 'He is a quite recent creature, which the demiurge of knowledge fabricated with its own hands less than two hundred years ago' (1970: 308). Of course, early forms of knowledge, during the classical period, recognised the existence of human beings, but, Foucault suggests, a distinction needs to be made, for what they did not have was 'an epistemological consciousness of man as such. The classical episteme is articulated along lines that do not isolate, in any way, a specific domain proper to man' (1970: 309). And Foucault continues:

> Modern culture can conceive of man because it conceives of the finite on the basis of itself. Given these conditions, it is understandable that classical thought, and all forms of thought that preceded it, were able to speak of the mind and the body, of the human being . . . but that not one of them was ever able to know man as he is posited in modern knowledge. Renaissance 'humanism' and classical 'rationalism' were indeed able to allot human beings a privileged position in the order of the world, but they were not able to conceive of man. (1970: 318)

Foucault sees Kant as an important philosophical exponent of this 'anthropologism' – the formation of 'man' as a self-sufficient subject, a 'strange empirico-transcendental doublet' who is both the subject and the object of his or her own knowledge. Both Marxism and phenomenology are steeped in this 'anthropology', and Foucault sees the recent raprochement between them (suggested by Sartre) as anything but a tardy reconciliation, for they both needed each other (1970: 321–2). But Foucault implores us to awaken from this 'anthropological sleep', to recognise the limitations of this mode of thought. And he concludes:

> To all those who still wish to talk about man, about his reign or liberation, to all those who still ask themselves questions about what man is in his essence, to all those who wish to take him as their starting point in their attempts to reach the truth, to all those. . .who refuse to think without immediately thinking that it is man who is thinking, to all these warped and twisted forms of reflection we can answer only with a philosophical laugh – which means, to a certain extent, a silent one. (1970: 342–3)

Nietzsche's promise of the superman signifies first and foremost, Foucault writes, the 'imminence of the death of man', thus marking the threshold to a new episteme. The human subject – 'man' – an invention of recent date, is now nearing its end. For Lévi-Strauss 'man' – the 'epistemological subject' – needs to be dissolved; for Foucault it is in the process of being 'erased, like a face drawn in sand at the edge of the sea' (1970: 387).

In the final chapter of the study Foucault discusses the human sciences. The empirical sciences of biology, economics and philology have as their object of knowledge not the human subject but life, labour and language respectively. But the human sciences – psychology, sociology and the study of culture – are, Foucault suggests, quite different, for in taking the human subject *per se* as their primary object of investigation they inevitably became self-critical. Although they are in some sense parasitic on the nineteenth-century sciences in their use of analytic models drawn from these sciences, the essential function of the human sciences is a critical one, that of demystification. They are not real sciences; what gives them their 'positivity' is their critical reflection on the human condition, the unveiling of a social reality that is unconscious to the individual subject. Psychoanalysis and ethnology in particular are 'counter-sciences' for they 'ceaselessly unmake' that very man who is creating and recreating his positivity in the human sciences' (1970: 379). Foucault thus comes to align himself with the structuralist perspectives of Lacan and Lévi-Strauss seeing structuralism as essentially a 'post-modern' movement and its anti-humanist tendencies. A human science, for Foucault, exists, 'wherever there is analysis – within the dimension proper to the unconscious – of norms, rules, and signifying totalities which unveil to consciousness the conditions of its forms and contents' (1970: 364). Foucault's affinities with the structuralists has been noted by many writers and this has inevitably given rise to some misunderstanding. Alan Sheridan has discussed this issue succinctly. These all revolve, he writes,

around a single problem: the status and role of the human subject, the concept of 'man', in history and in the 'human sciences'. Now it was precisely a desire to displace the human subject, consciousness, from the centre of theoretical concern – a position it had enjoyed in French philosophy during the three hundred years separating Descartes and Sartre – rather than a concern to extend the application of the concepts and methods of structural linguistics, that Foucault shared with the so-called 'structuralists'. (1980: 90)

And Sheridan goes on to stress that in other respects Foucault is profoundly anti-structuralist. Far from wishing to 'freeze' the movement of history in unconscious structures, his whole work has been an examination of the nature of historical change. It is worth noting, however, that Foucault's anti-humanism is specifically directed against the epistemological subject for he makes a distinction, as said, between the subject as an existential reality and the subject as the locus and basis of human knowledge.

Foucault's archaeology of the human sciences – whose epistemic analysis also forms the framework for his histories of madness and medicine – has given rise to a wealth of critical commentary. Merquior (1985: 56–75) outlines some of the main criticisms with Foucault's historical account – the pluralistic nature of both Renaissance and classical culture, the historical continuity in the development of many of the natural sciences, its relativism. Marxists have bewailed the fact that in *The Order of Things* Foucault completely ignores the political, social and economic practices of the period, seeing the epistemic transformations as being unrelated to non-discursive practices. But after the events of May 1968 – an event that Foucault did not participate in (he was teaching in Tunisia at the time) – Foucault's writings indicate a marked shift in emphasis, a change of direction characterised as a move 'from archaeology to genealogy'. Becoming increasingly aware of the close and intimate relationship between knowledge and power, Foucault abandoned the 'archaeological' approach to knowledge – and the concepts of 'archaeology' and 'episteme' are hardly used after 1970. His attention instead turns to the role of power in social discourse, and he adopts the form of historical analysis which, following Nietzsche, he calls 'genealogy'.

10.5 Power and the Human Subject

In an essay on Nietzsche, Foucault defined genealogy not in opposition to history, but as a kind of historical analysis that forsakes the search for origins and the attempt to capture the exact essence of things. It does not pretend to go back in time in an attempt to restore an unbroken continuity, but rather it tries to 'identify the accidents, the minute deviations . . . the errors, the false appraisals, and the faulty calculations that gave birth to those things that continue to exist and have value for us; it is to discover that truth or being does not lie at the root of what we know and what we are, but the exteriority of accidents' (Rabinow 1984: 81). It makes no claims to scientificity but has value as a critique, and as providing expression to local or subjugated forms of knowledge. Genealogical analysis and the rediscovery of local memories, of the submerged histories that global theorising has tended to suppress and silence (1980: 81–3). But above all, genealogical analysis is concerned with the insurrection of knowledges 'that are opposed primarily not to the contents, methods or concepts of a science, but to the effects of the centralising powers which are linked to the institution and functioning of an organised scientific discourse within a society such as ours' (1980: 84).

Thus whereas Althusser saw scientific knowledge and politics as distinct practices, Foucault saw knowledge and power as intimately connected, and argues that it is 'really against the effects of the power of a discourse that is considered to be scientific that the genealogy must wage its struggle' (ibid.). For Foucault power and knowledge are not linked together solely by the play of interests or ideologies. The problem, therefore, is not that of determining how power subjugates knowledge and makes it serve its end. There is not, he writes, 'knowledge on the one side and society on the other, or science and the State, but only the fundamental forms of knowledge/power' (Sheridan 1980: 131) or as he expressed it elsewhere, 'there is no power relation without the correlative constitution of a field of knowledge, nor any knowledge that does not presuppose and constitute at the same time power relations' (1977: 27). Moreover, Foucault insists that we must eschew the model of Leviathan in the study of power. We must escape from the liberal conception of power in terms of juridical sovereignty and Marxist conception of equating power with the state, and instead base our analysis of power on the study of the techniques and tactics of domination. For it is Foucault's contention that since the end of the eighteenth century new forms of power have emerged that involve techniques of surveillance, discipline, and what he describes a 'bio-power'. His important study *Discipline and Punish* explores these new forms of 'disciplinary technology', which were not confined to prisons, but extended to workshops, schools and hospitals. This form of power, which is focused on the body, is not localised: it is never in anybody's hands or appropriated as a commodity, but rather is employed and exercised through a net-like organisation:

When I think of the mechanics of power, I think of its capillary form of existence, of the extent of which power seeps into the very grain of individuals, reaches right into their bodies, permeates their gestures, their posture, what they say, how they learn 'o live and work with other people. (Sheridan 1980: 217)

Foucault notes that the term 'subject' has a double meaning. On the one hand, it is tied to a person's identity by a conscience or self-knowledge; on the other hand, it refers to control and dependence on someone else (1982: 212). The two senses are linked by Foucault, for he suggests that power/knowledge relations are not to be analysed on the basis of a subject of knowledge, but rather the subject as well as the modalities of knowledge 'must be regarded as so many effects of these fundamental implications of power-knowledge and their historical transformations' (1977: 27–8).

As with Comte, Durkheim, and Althusser, the 'subject' for Foucault is largely conceptualised in sociological terms, as an 'effect' of social power and practices.

In one of his later essays Foucault argues that the general theme of his researches has not really been the issue of power, but the human subject. He has been primarily concerned, he writes, to create a history of the various modes by which in Western culture, humans are made into subjects, and he has dealt with three such 'modes of objectification'. The first he explored in the order of things – the way in which the human subject became an object in scientific discourses. The second mode of 'objectification' he describes as 'dividing practices', which he dealt with in his important studies of three institutions – the asylum, clinic and prison. 'The subject is either divided inside himself or divided from others. This process objectivises him. Examples are the mad and the sane, the sick and the healthy, the criminals and the 'good boys''' (1982: 208). And finally, in his latter work, particularly on sexuality and on 'techniques of the self', Foucault has sought to study the ways in which a human being turns him- or herself into a subject. His later studies would thus seem to imply that Foucault does not see the subject as simply an 'effect' of knowledge/power relations. But what is of interest about his later writing is that he describes the new technologies of power as having essentially a pastoral function, and thus being a 'kind of individualising power':

I don't think that one should consider the 'modern state' as an entity which was developed above individuals, ignoring what they are and even their very existence, but on the contrary as a very sophisticated structure, in which individuals can be integrated, under one condition:

that this individuality would be shaped in a new form, and submitted to a set of very specific patterns. (1982: 214)

This kind of power, derived from Christianity and salvation-oriented, is, Foucault suggests, both a totalising and an individualising form of political power. The emergence of social science cannot be isolated, he feels from these developments, from the rise of this new political technology (Martin et al. 1988: 162).

But although Foucault stresses the ubiquity of power and the intimate connection between knowledge and power, and appears to suggest that the 'subject' is to an important degree an 'effect' of power/knowledge structures, all his writings express a radical, libertarian impulse. Where there is power, he writes, there is always resistance, and he conceives the role of the intellectual as an engaged scholar who is concerned not with emancipating truth from every system of power, but with detaching the power of truth from the forms of hegemony, social, economic and political, within which it operates at the present time (1980: 133). Many have noted the Nietzschian perspective that pervades Foucault's work, a point that is fully acknowledged by Foucault himself. But Foucault sides with the oppressed, and lacks any elitist or aristocratic aspirations. But he also lacks Nietzsche's sense of joy and the latter's paean towards life and the instincts – indeed, in his studies of sexuality Foucault is a consistent critic of what he terms the 'repressive hypothesis', the notion that increased sexual repression is associated with the development of modern industrial societies. Foucault thus distances himself from sexual radicals such as Reich and Marcuse, who he felt had given the notion of repression an exaggerated role. Power, he writes, would be a fragile thing if its only function were to repress (1980: 59). And Foucault is quite critical of the notion that there is some basic human nature, as his debate with Noam Chomsky indicated (Elders 1974). But if knowledge is linked with the 'will to power', and Foucault appears to follow Nietzsche in also adopting a relativist position, what the latter called 'perspectivism', Foucault's becomes enmeshed in intractable problems regarding the truth-value of his own analyses (Merquior 1985: 146; Dews 1987: 185). Many have been critical of the irrationalism inherent in Foucault's work – over his historico-philosophical frescoes, writes Merquior, there hovers the shadow of Nietzschean irrationalism unstained by any major echo from Hegel, Husserl or Heidegger (1985: 143). Whether or not Foucault can be accused of irrationalism, or of denying the possibility of objective knowledge, are debatable issues, but certainly, as Habermas suggests, while offering an illuminating critique of the philosophy of the subject, Foucault provided no account of the normative foundations of his own position. 'To the objectivism of self-mastery on the part of the human sciences there corresponds a subjectivism of self-forgetfulness on Foucault's part' (1987: 294). Others have suggested that in seeing power as coextensive with the social body, and in allowing no agency of social change, Foucault also denied the possibility of social emancipation. His political theory lacked any vision of non-alienated social relations (Callinicos 1982: 108–11; Merquior 1985: 143). He has indeed been described as a neo-anarchist, although his perspective is closer to that of Stirner than to the social anarchists such as Kropotkin. And similarities between Foucault and such critical theorists as Horkheimer and Marcuse have been noted, although Foucault would certainly have repudiated the Hegelian tendencies in their work (Smart 1985: 139–40).

Foucault always revelled in the fact that he had been 'situated in most of the squares on the political checkerboard' – idealist, anarchist, crypto-Marxist, neo-conservative, nihilist, liberal, anti-Marxist. But his own characterisation of himself was a modest one: 'I am not a writer, a philosopher, a great figure of intellectual life. I am a teacher'. And he summed up his own work thus:

> Man is a thinking being, the way he thinks is related to society, politics, economics, and history and is also related to very general and universal categories and formal structures. But thought is something other than societal relations. The way people really think is not adequately analysed by the universal categories, of logic. Between social history and formal analyses of thought there is a path, a lane – maybe very narrow – which is the path of the historian of thought. (in Martin et al. 1988: 10)

In spite of his 'hyperactive pessimism', reminiscent of Schopenhauer, and his exclusive focus on Western culture, it was a path that Foucault trod with credit and originality. (For further important studies of Foucault, see Dreyfus and Rabinow 1982; Smart 1983; Hoy 1986; Dews 1987: 144–220).

10.6 Post-Structuralism

'I think it's an occupational hazard for intellectuals, regardless of their politics, to lose touch with the stuff and flow of everyday life,' so wrote Marshall Berman (1984: 123). This is a hazard to which Jacques Derrida has certainly succumbed. Although he is often linked with Foucault as one of the key 'post-structuralist' thinkers, and shares with Foucault an admiration for Nietzsche's philosophy, he lacks the historian's engagement with social and political realities. Unlike Foucault he remains, as Hayden White has said, 'imprisoned in structuralism's hypostatized labyrinth of language' (1978: 280), and thus his writings have an idealist tenor and are inherently conservative, offering little hope for overcoming present inequalities. His thoughts never seem to move outside academia and the world of the text. In this he contrasts with some of the more important figures in philosophy – Descartes, Locke, Kant, Hegel, Dewey, Sartre – whose philosophical writings all engage themselves with a world beyond philosophy itself.

Jacques Derrida was born in the suburbs of Algeria in 1930, the son of a petit-bourgeois Jewish family. He moved to France when he was nineteen, and, stimulated by a radio programme on Camus, he entered philosophy classes at the Ecole Normale. Among his tutors were Levinas (who introduced Derrida to the work of Husserl), Ricoeur and Foucault. He was recognised from the outset as a student of brilliance and originality, and his first published work was a long introduction to a translation of Husserl's *Origin of Geometry* (1962). Shortly thereafter he began publishing a series of critical essays in French intellectual periodicals, and, in 1967, many of these were published in three studies, which soon established Derrida as one of the key philosophers of the decade – Of *Grammatology*, *Writing and Difference* and *Speech and Phenomena*. Such texts defy classification, and although like Foucault, Derrida has been linked with structuralist thinking, his whole mode of thought is profoundly anti-structuralist. Since then Derrida has become something of an intellectual cult figure, particularly among American literary critics, and he has been described as 'probably the most famous living philosopher in the English-speaking world' (Rée 1984: 31), although he fails to get a mention in a recent *Dictionary of Philosophy*.

Derrida is usually described, along with Adorno, Foucault, Deleuze, Lacan and Lyotard, as a 'post-structuralist', a label that seems to me to have little real substance or meaning. Unlike existentialism and structuralism itself, it has little intellectual coherence, for these scholars have precious little in common with each other apart from a critique of the 'epistemological subject'. And as writers such as Adorno and Derrida were formulating their thoughts about the same time that 'structuralism' became in vogue, even the term *post*-structuralism is something of a misnomer. But what is clear about Derrida is that he drew on ideas from a wide range of intellectual sources. Due to his early studies he essentially emerged from a phenomenological background, and even acknowledged the early influence of Sartre, although he later expressed surprise as to how such a scholar – who he felt was wrong on so many issues – could have achieved such extraordinary intellectual prominence in his own lifetime (Norris 1987: 12). But the three influences that Derrida most fully acknowledged were Husserl, Heidegger and Hegel, all of whom had a formative influence on his philosophy. Heidegger has a constant presence in Derrida's work, particularly Heidegger's project of overcoming/deconstructing Western metaphysics – Western philosophy being seen in rather monolithic terms. From Husserl, Derrida took a concern for detailed and painstaking analysis – his 'rigorous technique' – though he never shared Husserl's pathos for, and commitment to, a 'phenomenology of presence' – Husserl's philosophy of 'essences' and subjectivity. The debate with Hegel, Derrida admits, is infinite and interminable. But Derrida's approach represents 'the radicalisation of phenomenology' (Descombes 1980: 136–52), and to do this Derrida draws on the perspectives of essentially three scholars – Saussure, Lacan and Nietzsche, Merquior interprets Derrida's work as a combination of Heideggerian metaphysics with a radicalised pan-semiotic theory derived from Saussure and Lacan, and stresses that Derrida's originality is more rhetorical than real. It is a 'philosophical antique', he suggests, with a more theological than epistemological origin (1986: 213–24). But what is important about Derrida is not his own theoretical standpoint, which apart from a kind of messianic scepticism he does not appear to have, but rather his critiques of a whole range of Western scholars from Plato, Rousseau and Hegel, through to more contemporary scholars such as Saussure, Husserl, Freud, Lacan and Lévi-Strauss. All are alleged to be representatives of the Western metaphysical tradition, and all are subjected to essentially the same critique. Derrida's critiques are all variations on the same theme, and although his ideas are expressed in a very elliptical fashion, such critiques do indicate wide erudition and a serious engagement with the work under review.

Derrida's critique of Western philosophy essentially focuses on what he sees as three basic problems. These we may outline in summary fashion.

First, Western metaphysics, Derrida contends, is logocentric. It tends to devalue written language, and thus gives priority – if only unconsciously – to spoken over written language. In a series of illuminating, but difficult, analyses on the writings of Plato, Husserl, Saussure, Rousseau and Lévi-Strauss, Derrida attempts to demonstrate that writing is invariably treated by these scholars as merely a derivative or secondary form of communication. There is a dualism inherent in their writings and a privileged status is invariably given to natural speech. Although he applauds Lévi-Strauss's search for a new status of discourse, a structuralist account that abandons 'all reference to a centre, to a subject, to a privileged reference, to an origin' (1978: 286), he nevertheless stresses that Lévi-Strauss, like his mentor Rousseau, has a romantic vision, and privileges 'living speech' – even linking writing to political violence. He cites *Tristes Tropiques* as exemplifying a metaphysics that constitutes an 'exemplary system of defence against the threat of writing' and discusses Lévi-Strauss's notion that writing seems to favour the exploitation rather than the enlightenment of humankind (1976: 101). But underlying this 'scorn' for writing that Lévi-Strauss shares with Rousseau (whom Lévi-Strauss described as the founder of anthropology), there is, Derrida suggests, a romantic image of 'a community immediately present to itself, without difference, a community of speech where all the members are within earshot' (1976: 136). Derrida's discussion of Saussure's important work on language and writing (in the essay 'Linguistics and Grammatology' (1976: 27–73) offers essentially the same critique, for he suggests that Saussure tends to relegate writing to a secondary, derivative status as compared with speaking. Derrida makes these critiques not, it seems, because he wishes to privilege writing over ordinary speech, but because he senses that such logocentrism is symptomatic of the misleading way in which language itself has generally been understood. This leads us to the second problem associated with Western metaphysics, which Derrida describes as the 'metaphysics of presence'.

But before moving on to this, it is worth noting that Derrida's characterisation of Western philosophy as being logocentric has not gone without challenge. Indeed it has been suggested by both Searle and Merquior that the thesis that Western philosophy has always privileged speech over writing is ill-conceived. For not only were many earlier philosophers – Aristotle, Hume, Kant – not particularly concerned with the speech/writing distinction, but one could argue, from the evidence, the opposite view – that philosophy has tended to emphasise the priority of written language (Merquior 1986a: 216).

A second feature of Western philosophy that Derrida criticises is what he describes, following his mentor Heidegger, as the 'determination of Being as presence'. In *Being and Time* Heidegger had described Western philosophy since the time of the Greeks as involving 'the treatment of the meaning of Being as *parousia* or *ousia* which signifies, in ontologico-temporal terms, "presence". Entities are grasped in their Being as "presence"; this means that they are understood with regard to a definite mode of time – the "Present"' (1962: 47). Derrida, though critical of Heidegger's own nostalgia for 'Being', takes up Heidegger's own critique of metaphysics (under whose rubric the whole of Western philosophy, in spite of its diverse and contrasting currents of thought, seem to be placed). Thus Derrida writes – and this often quoted passage expresses his essential thoughts – that the whole matrix of Western metaphysics

> is the determination of Being as *presence* in all senses of this word. It could be shown that all the names related to fundamentals, to principles, or to the centre have always designated an invariable presence – *eidos, arche, telos, energia, ousia* (essence, existence, substance, subject) *atethia*, transcendentality, consciousness, God, man, and so forth. (1978: 279–80)

What Derrida appears to be suggesting is that there is no immediate, intuitive access to meaning, that knowledge and truth cannot be based on the idea of an authentic, self-present awareness of the human subject. Meaning is not something given either through the Cartesian cogito or through immediate experience (or through any other 'principle' or 'centre') which is then expressed through signs or signals. As Derrida puts it in his critique of Husserl:

> speech is no longer simply the expression of what, without it, would *already* be an object, caught again in its primordial purity: speech constitutes the object and is a concrete juridical condition of truth. The paradox is that, without the apparent fall back into language and thereby into history . . . sense would remain an empirical formation imprisoned as fact in a psychological subjectivity – *in the inventor's head*. (1978b: 76)

For Derrida there is thus 'no transcendental or privileged signified' (1978: 281). The realisation that there is no 'centre' and that meaning is bound up, as it were, with language; the moment when language, as Derrida puts it, involves 'the universal problematic', then 'everything became discourse' – 'the domain or play of signification henceforth has no limit' (1978a: 280–1). All discourse is on par with what Lévi-Strauss called 'bricolage'. The architects of this decentring, Derrida suggests, are Nietzsche, Heidegger and Freud – the first two scholars presented a critique of metaphysics (Nietzsche introducing the notions of play and interpretation) while Freud provided a 'critique self-presence, that is, the critique of consciousness, of the subject, of self-identity' (1978a: 280).

Developing Saussure's thesis that 'difference' is the source of linguistic value, Derrida stresses that meaning and signification depend not only on difference – in the sense of contrast – but on the flow of events and on reference to other signifying terms in a complex system of signifiers. As he writes:

> Whether in written or spoken discourse, no element can function as a sign without relating to another element which itself is not simply present. This linkage means that each 'element' – phoneme or grapheme – is constituted with reference to the trace in it of the other elements of the sequence or system. (Culler 1979: 164)

Derrida coined the term 'difference' to suggest that meanings were at once 'differential' and 'deferred'. But Derrida goes much further than Saussure, for whom the sign was always a unitary concept consisting of a signifier (sound-image) and a signified (the concept) – whose relationship could be compared with two sides of a single sheet of paper (1959: 113). For like Lacan, Derrida gives primacy to the signifier, and suggests that every signifier serves as a metaphor for a signified, and that every signified is also in the position of the signifier. Language thus becomes an absolutely self-referential process; there being no reference outside language. Meaning is thus indeterminate, and the search for meaning involves infinite regression (Merquior 1986: 222; Dews 1987: 30). As Derrida put it in a well-known phrase, 'there is nothing outside of the text' (1976: 158). Derrida's critique – his 'deconstruction' of Western metaphysics would therefore appear to be a form of idealism, and to involve the subversion of the traditional concepts of science and truth, resting as these do on some notion of a real world independent of discourse (Callinicos 1982: 46). It is noteworthy that, like Foucault, Derrida seems to have little concern or interest in modern science.

Two points can perhaps be made about Derrida's critique of the 'metaphysics of presence'. The first is that it does not seem to be all that original in the sense that long ago Hegel had stressed the limitations of immediate perception and the philosophy of 'representation'.

As Merquior notes, 'whereas Hegel conceived of philosophy as a knowledge beyond representation, Derrida *equates* philosophy with representation' (1986: 227; Rose 1984: 160).

Secondly, there is the important issue as to whether meaning can be generated by the differential relation between linguistic elements alone. Although a condition of meaning, differentiality cannot be seen as the sole determinant of meaning since the structure of differences can itself only be semantically discriminated. Thus the reciprocal relation between meaning and structure must be seen as mediated by 'an indispensable third term' – the human subject (Dews 1987: 28).

The third aspect of Derrida's critique of Western philosophy is his stress that in a 'close reading' of the classical text it can be shown that they are infused with a series of binary oppositions – public/private, culture/nature, masculine/feminine, rational/irrational, real/imaginary, speech/writing, philosophy/literature – in which one of the terms is, as he puts it, 'privileged'. Derrida in his analyses sought to subvert the either/or logic of Western metaphysics, and its hierarchical tendency. This did not involve simply inverting the received order of priorities but of dismantling the oppositions 'resisting and disorganising it, without ever constituting a third term, without ever leaving room for a solution in the form of a speculative dialectics' (Kearney 1986: 125; Rée 1984: 31).

Where is the human subject in Derrida's programme of deconstruction? One has to admit that s/he is hardly to be seen, for as with the structuralists an anti-humanist tendency runs through Derrida's work. For Derrida appears to see nothing between the subject as the 'centre' of meaning, a core of self-certainty akin to Descartes cogito, and the acceptance of a position – which he advocates – that there is no subject at all, except as an 'effect' of the play of the text (Dews 1987: 327) 'Language' for Derrida, seems to have the same role as Lacan's 'symbolic', Durkheim's 'society', and Foucault's power/knowledge structure – and the subject is essentially bypassed. One commentator interprets Derrida's philosophy in almost lyrical fashion, personifying language in a manner that would have made even Hegel's *Geist* shudder!

By removing the signified, Derrida thus removes the last human control over language. In the absence of all signifiers, language takes on its own kind of energy and creativity, quite distinct from any subjective energy or creativity on the part of individual writers or readers. This is an energy and creativity to which individual writers and readers can only *abandon* themselves. (Harland 1987: 135–6)

Language on this reading has a life of its own to which humans simply abandon themselves. Others, however, have stressed the nihilistic tendency inherent in Derrida's writings, emphasising his affinities with Nietzsche . . . although it is worth noting that Nietzsche, as we have discussed, is also seen as a precusor of existentialism. William Barrett thus writes of Derrida's doctrine.

Language is . . . cut off from its human base and becomes a free-floating system of signs. Without a reference to this human base, the self, deconstructionism becomes merely another manifestation of the nihilism that in so many guises, subtle and otherwise, prevades our culture. (1986: 130–1)

Thus paradoxically, as Anderson (1983: 54) indicates, a wholesale attack on the category of the subject – which is always interdependent with that of structure – invariably ends up as 'unbridled subjectivity'. Solomon concludes his discussion of Derrida in a very similar fashion. 'Between the self as absolute spirit and the self as nothing at all there is, it turns out, very little difference – as Kierkegaard in particular told us some time ago' (1988: 202).

But it has been suggested that in deconstructing transcendental subjectivity into the spatio-temporal play of language, Derrida does not do away with the subject altogether. As Derrida himself noted:

The subject is not some meta-linguistic substance or identity, some pure cogito of self-presence, it is always inscribed in language and this very inscription constitutes a form of liberty . . . for it shows the subject that it is not tied to a single identity or essence, but lives in language. (Kearney 1986: 125–6)

Is such a viewpoint so very far from that of the early Sartre?

The philosophy of Derrida along with that of Nietzsche, Heidegger and Foucault, has been seen as essentially a reaction against the Enlightenment and the progressive tradition, the tradition that classical Marxism still represents, and which embodies a Cartesian faith in science, a Kantian faith in humanity and a Hegelian faith in history (Merquior 1986: 242). This tradition during the recent decades has been increasingly under scrutiny. But surely there is a path between the objectivism of certain structuralist and behaviourist discourses, and the relativism espoused by Derrida, between a 'metaphysics of presence' embodied in the Cartesian cogito and the kind of anti-humanist analysis that reduces the subject to a subordinate category constituted by impersonal structures (Althusser) or simply inscribed in language (Derrida). There is then an account of subjectivity that sees it emerging from and entwined with the natural and historical world – an account that is implicit in many of the theoretical positions we have discussed in earlier chapters of this study. (For further useful studies of Derrida, see Culler 1979; Norris, 1982, 1987; Megill 1985; Ryan 1982; Lawson 1985: 90–124.)

References

Aaron, R. I. (1937) *John Locke* (2nd edition 1965), Oxford: Clarendon Press

Aberle, D. F. (1960) 'The Influence of Linguistics on Early Personality Theory'. In G. E. Dole and R. L. Carneiro, *Essays on the Science of Culture*, New York: Crowell

Abramson, A. (1987) 'Beyond the Samoan Controversy in Anthropology'. In P. Caplan (ed.), *The Cultural Construction of Sexuality*, London: Tavistock

Adler, A. (1927) *The Practice and Theory of Individual Psychology*, New York: Harcourt

—— (1955) *Individual Psychology*, London: Routledge & Kegan Paul

Adorno, T. W. (1966) *Negative Dialectics*, trans. E. B. Ashton, New York: Seabury Press

—— (1968) 'Sociology and Psychology', *New Left Review*, 47: 86–93

—— (1973) *The Jargon of Authenticity*, London: Routledge & Kegan Paul

—— and M. Horkheimer (1973) *Dialectic of Enlightenment* (original 1944), trans. J. Cumming, London: Verso

Aiken, H. D. (1956) *The Age of Ideology: the 19th century philosophers*, New York: Mentor

Alexander, R. D. (1979) *Darwinism and Human Affairs*, Seattle: University of Washington Press

Alland, A. Jr (1985) *Human Nature: Darwin's view*, New York: Columbia University Press

Allen, G. W. (1967) *William James: A biography*, New York: Viking Press

—— (ed.) (1971) with Introduction, *A William James Reader*, Boston, Mass.: Houghton Mifflin

Allport, G. W. (1955) *Becoming*, New Haven, Conn.: Yale University Press

—— (1961) *Pattern and Growth in Personality*, New York: Holt, Rinehart & Winston

Althusser, L. (1969) 'Marxism and Humanism'. In *For Marx*, Harmondsworth: Penguin Books

—— (1969) *For Marx*, trans. B. Brewster, London: New Left Books

References

—— (1971) *Lenin and Philosophy and Other Essays*, London: New Left Books

—— (1972) *Politics and History*, London: New Left Books

—— and E. Balibar (1970) *Reading Capital*, trans. B. Brewster, London: New Left Books

Ameriks, K. (1982) *Kant's Theory of Mind*, London: Oxford University Press

Anderson, P. (1976) *Considerations on Western Marxism*, London: New Left Books

—— (1983) *In the Tracks of Historical Materialism*, London: Verso

Anscombe, G. E. M. and P. T. Geach (eds) (1954). *Descartes: Philosophical writings*, introd. A. Koyré, Wokingham, Berks: Van Nostrand

Arato, A. and P. Breines (1979) *The Young Lukács and the Origins of Western Marxism*, London: Pluto Press

—— and E. Gebhardt (1978) *The Essential Frankfurt School Reader*, Oxford: Basil Blackwell

Ardrey, R. (1966) *The Territorial Imperative*, New York: Dell

Arens, W. (1979) *The Man-Eating Myth*, London: Oxford University Press

Aron, R. (1965) *Main Currents in Sociological Thought 1*, trans. R. Howard and H. Weaver, Harmondsworth: Penguin Books

—— (1967) *Main Currents in Sociological Thought 2*, Harmondsworth: Penguin Books

—— (1969) *Marxism and Existentialists*, New York: Harper

Aronson, R. (1978) 'The Individualist Social Theory of Jean-Paul Sartre', In *New Left Review, Western Marxism*: 201–31

—— (1980) *Jean-Paul Sartre – Philosophy in the world*, London: New Left Books

Augé, M. (1982) *The Anthropological Circle*, Cambridge: Cambridge University Press

Avineri, S. (1968) *The Social and Political Thought of Karl Marx*, Cambridge: Cambridge University Press

Ayer, A. J. (1936) *Language, Truth and Logic* (1971 edition), Harmondsworth: Penguin Books

—— (ed.) (1959) *Logical Positivism*, Glencoe, Illinois: Free Press

—— (1968) *The Origins of Pragmatism*, London: Macmillan

—— (1980) *Hume*, London: Oxford University Press

—— (1982) *Philosophy in the Twentieth Century*, London: Allen & Unwin

—— (1985) *Ludwig Wittgenstein*, Harmondsworth: Penguin Books

Badcock, C. R. (1975) *Lévi-Strauss: Structuralism and sociological theory*, London: Hutchinson

—— (1980) *The Psychoanalysis of Culture*, Oxford: Basil Blackwell

Bain, A. (1855) *The Senses and the Intellect*, London: Parker

—— (1859) *The Emotions and the Will*, London: Parker

Bakunin, M. (1973) *Bakunin on Anarchy*, trans. S. Dolgoff, London: Allen & Unwin

References

Baldwin, J. D. (1986) *George Herbert Mead: A unifying theory for sociology*, Beverly Hills, Calif.: Sage

Bannan, J. F. (1967) *The Philosophy of Merleau-Ponty*, New York: Harcourt Brace

Barash, D. P. (1977) *Sociobiology and Behaviour*, London: Heinemann

—— (1981) *Sociobiology: The whispering within*, London: Fontana

Barkow, J. H. (1978) 'Culture and Sociobiology', *Amer. Anthr.*, 80: 5–20

Barnouw, V. (1973) *Culture and Personality*, rev. ed., Homewood, Ill.: Dorsey

Barral, M. (1965) *Merleau-Ponty: The role of the body-subject in interpersonal relations*, Pittsburgh: Duguesue University Press

Barrett, W. (1958) *Irrational Man: A study in existential philosophy*, New York: Doubleday

—— (1986) *Death of the Soul: From Descartes to the computer*, London: Oxford University Press

Barthes, R. (1968) *Elements of Semiology*, trans. A. Lavers and C. Smith, New York: Hill & Wang

Bartley III, W. W. (1973) *Wittgenstein*, Philadelphia: Lippincott

Bateson, M. C. (1984) *With a Daughter's Eye: A memoir of Margaret Mead and Gregory Bateson*, New York: Morrow

Baudrillard, J. (1975) *The Mirror of Production*, St Louis: Telos

Bauman, Z. (1978) *Hermeneutics and Social Science: Approaches to understanding*, London: Hutchinson

Becker, E. (1962) *The Birth and Death of Meaning* (1972 edition), Harmondsworth: Penguin Books

Bellah, R. N. (1964) 'Religious Evolution', *Amer. Sociol. Rev.*, 29: 358–74

—— (1973) *Emile Durkheim on Morality and Society*, ed. and introd., Chicago: University of Chicago Press

Beloff, J. (1973) *Psychological Sciences: A review of modern psychology*, London: Crosby Lockwood

Benedict, R. (1923) 'The Concept of the Guardian Spirit in North America', *Memoirs AAA*, 29

—— (1934) *Patterns of Culture*, London: Routledge & Kegan Paul

—— (1938) 'Continuities and Discontinuities in Cultural Conditioning', *Psychiatry*, 1: 161–7. Reprinted in M. Mead and M. Wolfenstein, *Childhood in Contemporary Cultures*, Chicago: University of Chicago Press: 21–30

—— (1943) 'Franz Boas as an Ethnologist', *Amer. Anthrop. Assoc. Memoir*, 45: 3

—— (1946) *The Chrysanthemum and the Sword*, Boston, Mass.: Houghton Mifflin

—— (1948) 'Anthropology and the Humanists', *Amer. Anthr.*, 30: 585–93

Bennet, E. A. (1961) *C. G. Jung*, London: Barne & Rockcliffe

—— (1966) *What Jung Really Said*, London: MacDonald

Bennett, J. W. (1946) 'The Interpretation of Pueblo Cultures: A question of values', *SWJA*, 2: 361–74. Reprinted in D. S. Haring (1956) *Personal*

Character and Cultural Mileu, New York: Syracuse University Press

—— and M. Nagai (1953) 'Echoes-Reactions to American Anthropology: Japanese critique of Benedict's *Chrysanthemum and the Sword*', *Amer. Anthrop.*, 55: 404–11

Benoit-Smullyan, E. (1948) 'the Sociologism of Emile Durkheim and his School'. In H. E. Barnes (ed.), *An Introduction to the History of Sociology*, Chicago: University of Chicago Press: 205–43

Benton, T. (1977) *Philosophical Foundations of Three Sociologies*, London: Routledge & Kegan Paul

—— (1984) *The Rise and Fall of Structural Marxism*, London: Macmillan

Berlin, I. (1956) *The Age of Enlightenment: The 18th century philosophers*, New York: Mentor

—— (1963) *Karl Marx: His life and environment* (3rd edition), Oxford: Oxford University Press

Berman, M. (1984) 'The Signs in the Street: a response to Perry Anderson', *New Left Review*, 144: 114–25

Bernard, J. (1945) 'Observation and Generalization in Cultural Anthropology'. *Amer. J. Sociol.*, 50: 284–91

Bernstein, R. J. (ed.) (1960) *John Dewey: On experience, nature and freedom*, New York: Liberal Arts Press

—— (1966) *John Dewey*, New York: Washington Square Press

—— (1983) *Beyond Objectivism and Relativism: Science, hermeneutics and praxis*, Oxford: Basil Blackwell

—— (ed.) (1985) *Habermas and Modernity*, Cambridge: Cambridge University Press

—— (1986) *Philosophical Profiles: Essays on a pragmatic mode*, Cambridge: Polity Press

Berry, J. W. and P. R. Dasen (eds) (1974) *Culture and Cognition: Readings in cross-cultural psychology*, London: Methuen

Bettelheim, B. (1943) 'Individual and Mass Behaviour in Extreme Situations'. *J. Abn. Soc, Psychol.*, 38: 417–52

—— (1960) *The Informed Heart: Autonomy in a mass age*, New York: Avon Books

—— (1962) *Symbolic Wounds*, New York: Collier

—— (1967) *The Empty Fortress*, New York: Free Press

—— (1969) *The Children of the Dream*, New York: Avon

—— (1976) *The Uses of Enchantment: The meaning and importance of fairy tales*, New York: Vintage/London: Thames & Hudson

—— (1983) *Freud and Man's Soul*, New York: Knopf/Fontana paperback 1985

Binswanger, L. (1957) *Sigmund Freud: Reminiscences of a friendship*, Trans. N. Guterman, New York: Grune & Stratton

—— (1963) *Being-in-the-World*. trans. and introd. J. Needleman, New York: Basic Books

Bird, G. (1986) *William James*, London: Rootledge & Kegan Paul

References

Black, M. (1959) 'Linguistic Relativity: The views of Benjamin Lee Whorf'. *Phil. Rev.*, 68: 228–38
—— (1973) 'Some Aversive Responses to a Would-be Reinforcer'. In H. Wheeler (ed.), *Beyond the Primitive Society*: 125–34
Blackham, H. J. (1952) *Six Existentialist Thinkers*, London: Routledge & Kegan Paul
Bleicher, J. (1980) *Contemporary Hermeneutics: Hermeneutics as method, philosophy and critique*, London: Routledge & Kegan Paul
—— (1982) *The Hermeneutic Imagination*, London: Routledge & Kegan Paul
Bloch, M. (1977) 'The Past and the Present in the Present'. *Man*, 12: 278–92
—— (1983) *Marxism and Anthropology*, London: Oxford University Press
Blumenthal, A. L. (1980) 'Wilhelm Wundt and Early American Psychology: A clash of cultures'. In R. W. Rieber (ed.) *Wilhelm Wundt and the Making of a Scientific Psychology*: 117–36
Blumer, H. (1969) *Symbolic Interactionism: Perspective and method*, Englewood Cliffs, NJ: Prentice Hall
Boadella, D. (1973) *Wilhelm Reich – The evolution of his work*, London: Vision Press
Boas, F. (1910) 'Psychological Problems in Anthropology'. *Amer. J. Psychol.*, 21: 371–84
—— (1911) *The Mind of Primitive Man*, (1938 edition), New York: Macmillan
—— (1928) *Anthropology and Modern Life*, New York: Norton
—— (ed.) (1938) *General Anthropology*, Boston, Mass.: D. C. Heath
—— (1940) *Race, Language and Culture*, New York: Free Press
Bock, K. E. (1980) *Human Nature and History: A response to sociobiology*, New York: Columbia University Press
Bock, P. K. (1980) *Continuities in Psychological Anthropology*, San Francisco: Freeman
Bocock, R. (1976) *Freud and Modern Society: An outline and analysis of Freud's sociology*, London: Nelson
Boden, M. (1979) *Piaget*, London: Fontana
Bonelli, M. and W. Shea (eds) (1975) *Reason, Experiment and Mysticism in the Scientific Revolution*, New York: Science History Publ
Bookchin, M. (1982) *The Ecology of Freedom*, Palo Alto, Calif: Cheshire Books
Boring, E. G. (1950) *A History of Experimental Psychology* (original 1929), New York: Appleton-Crofts
Bottomore, T. (1979) 'Marxism and Sociology'. In T. Bottomore and R. Nisbet *A History of Sociological Analysis*, London: Heinemann: 118–48
—— (1984) *The Frankfurt School*, London: Tavistock Press
—— et al. (eds) (1983) *Dictionary of Marxist Thought*, Cambridge, Mass.: Harvard University Press
—— and R. Nisbet (eds) (1979) *A History of Sociological Analysis*, London:

Heinemann

Bourguignon, E. (1979) *Psychological Anthropology*, New York: Holt Rinehart

Bowie, M. (1979) 'Jacques Lacan', In Sturrock (ed.), *Structuralism and Science*: 116–53

Boyers, R. and R. Orrill (eds) (1972) *Laing and Anti-Psychiatry*, Harmondsworth: Penguin Books

Bradley, F. H. (1893) *Appearance and Reality*, Oxford: Clarendon Press

Brady, I. (ed.) (1983) 'Speaking in the Name of the Real: Freeman and Mead on Samoa'. *Amer. Anthr.*, 85: 908–47

Brainerd, C. L. (1978) *Piaget's Theory of Intelligence*, Englewood Cliffs, NJ: Prentice Hall

Breines, P. (ed.) (1972) *Critical Interruptions: New Left perspectives on Herbert Marcuse*, New York: Herder & Herder

Brentano, F. (1973) *Psychology from an Empirical Standpoint*, trans. L. L. McAlister (original 1874), London: Routledge & Kegan Paul

Bretall, R. (ed.) (1946) *A Kierkegaard Anthology*, Princeton, NJ: Princeton University Press

Bridgman, P. W. (1927) *The Logic of Modern Physics*

Broad, C. D. (1975) *Leibniz: An introduction*, Cambridge: Cambridge University Press

Brome, V. (1969) *Freud and His Early Circle*, New York: Humanities Press
—— (1978) *Jung*, London: Paladin

Bronowski, J. and B. Mazlish (1960) *The Western Intellectual Tradition: From Leonardo to Hegel*, Harmondsworth: Penguin Books

Brooks, K. (1973) 'Freudianism is not a Basis for a Marxist Psychology'. In P. Brown (ed.), *Radical Psychology*, New York: Harper & Row: 315–74

Brown, B. (1973) *Marx, Freud and the Critique of Everyday Life: Toward a permanent cultural revolution*, New York: Monthly Review Press

Brown, J. A. C. (1961) *Freud and the Post Freudians* (1967 edition), Harmondsworth: Penguin Books

Brown, N. O. (1959) *Life Against Death: The psychological meaning of history*, New York: Vintage Books, Random House

Brown, P. (ed.) (1973) *Radical Psychology*, New York: Harper & Row
—— (1974) *Toward a Marxist Psychology*, New York: Harper & Row

Brown, R. H. (1977) 'The Emergence of Existential Thought: Philosophical perspectives on positivist and humanist forms of social theory'. In J. D. Douglas and J. M. Johnson (eds), *Existential Sociology*: 77–100

Brown, R. W. and E. H. Lenneberg (1954) 'A Study in Language and Cognition'. *J. Abn. Soc. Psychol.*, 49: 454–62

Bruner, J. S. (1966) *Studies in Cognitive Growth*, New York: Wiley

Bruner, J. (1985) 'Vygotsky: A historical and conceptual perspective'. In J. V. Wertsch (ed.): 21–34

Buck-Morss, S. (1977) *The Origin of Negative Dialectics: Adorno, Benjamin and the Frankfurt School*, Hassocks: Harvester Press

Bugenthal, J. F. T. (1967) *Challenges of Humanistic Psychology*, New York: McGraw-Hill

Bulmer, M. (1984) *The Chicago School of Sociology*, Chicago: University of Chicago Press

Cahn, S. M. (1977) *New Studies in the Philosophy of John Dewey*, Hanover: University of Vermont

Callinicos, A. (1976) *Althusser's Marxism*, London: Pluto Press

—— (1982) *Is there a Future for Marxism?* London: Macmillan

—— (1983a) *Marxism and Philosophy*, London: Oxford University Press

—— (1983b) *The Revolutionary Ideas of Marx*, London: Bookmarks

—— (1987) *Making History: Agency, structure and change in social theory*, Oxford: Polity Press

Campbell, J. (1949) *The Hero with a Thousand Faces*, New York: Pantheon Books

Cannon, W. B. (1927) 'The James–Lange Theory of Emotion'. *A. J. Psychol.*, 39: 106–24

Carneiro, R. L. (1981) 'Leslie White'. In S. Silveran (ed.), *Totems and Teachers*, New York: Columbia University Press: 209–54

Carrithers, M. (1985) 'An Alternative Social History of the Self'. In M. Carrithers et al. (eds.), *The Category of the Person*: 234–56

Carrithers, M., S. Collins and S. Lukes (eds) (1985) *The Category of the Person: Anthropology, philosophy, history*, Cambridge: Cambridge University Press

Carver, T. (1981) *Engels*, London: Oxford University Press

Cassirer, E. (1944) *An Essay on Man*, New Haven, Conn.: Yale University Press

—— (1951) *The Philosophy of the Enlightenment*, Princeton, NJ: Princeton University Press

—— (1953) *The Philosophy of Symbolic Forms*, 3 vols, New Haven, Conn.: Yale University Press

—— (1981) *Kant's Life and Thought*, trans. J. Haden, New Haven, Conn.: Yale University Press

Caton, H. (1973) *The Origin of Subjectivity: An essay on Descartes*, New Haven, Conn.: Yale University Press

Centre for Contemporary Studies (1978) *On Ideology*, London: Hutchinson Press

Chagnon, N. and W. Irons (eds) (1979) *Evolutionary Biology and Human Social Behaviour: An anthropological perspective*, N. Scituate, Mass.: Duxbury Press

Chalmers, A. F. (1978) *What is This Thing Called Science?* Milton Keynes: Open University Books

Charbonnier, G. (ed.) (1961) *Conversations with Claude Lévi-Strauss*, London: Cape

Chasseguet-Smirgel, J. and B. Grunberger (1986) *Freud or Reich? Psychoanalysis and illusion*, trans. C. Pajaczkowska, London: Free Assoc. Books

Chattopadhyaya, D. (1959) *Lokayata: A study of an ancient Indian material-ism*, New Delhi: Peoples Publishing House

Chisholm, R. M. (1986) *Brentano and Intrinsic Value*, Cambridge: Cambridge University Press

Chomsky, N. (1957) *Syntactic Structures*, The Hague: Mouton

—— (1959) 'Review of Verbal Behaviour. B. F. Skinner'. *Language*, 35: 26–58. Reprinted in J. Fodor and J. Katz (eds) (1964) *The Structure of Language*, Englewood Cliffs, NJ: Prentice Hall

—— (1966) *Cartesian Linguistics*, New York: Harper

—— (1968) *Language and Mind*, New York: Harcourt Brace

—— (1976) *Reflection of Language*, London: Fontana/Collins

—— (1979) *Language and Responsibility*, Brighton, Sussex: Harvester Press

Churchland, P. M. (1984) *Matter and Consciousness: A contemporary Introduction to the Philosophy of Mind*, Cambridge, Mass.: MIT Press

Ciborowski, T. and D. Price-Williams (1982) 'Animistic Cognition: Some cultural, conceptual and methodological questions for Piagetian research'. In D. A. Wagner and H. W. Stevenson, *Cultural Perspectives on Child Development*, San Francisco: W. H. Freeman: 166–80

Cioffi, F. (1970) 'Freud and the Idea of Pseudo-Science'. In R. Borger and F. Cioffi, *Explanations and the Behavioural Sciences*, Cambridge: Cambridge University Press

Clare, A. (1976) *Psychiatry in Dissent*, London: Tavistock

Clark, R. W. (1980) *Freud: The man and the cause*, New York: Random House

Clarke, S. (1980) 'Althusserian Marxism'. In S. Clare et al., *One-Dimensional Marxism*, London: Allison & Busby: 7–102

Cohen, D. (1979) *J. B. Watson: The founder of behaviourism*, London: Routledge & Kegan Paul

Cohen, P. S. (1968) *Modern Social Theory*, London: Heinemann

Cohen, S. and L. Taylor (1972) *Psychological Survival: The experience of long-term imprisonment*, Harmondsworth: Penguin Books

Cole, M. (1985) 'The Zone of Proximal Development: Where culture and cognitions create each other'. In J. V. Wertsch (ed.) *Culture, Communication and Cognition*: 146–61

—— and S. Scribner (1974) *Culture and Thought: A Psychological introduction*, New York: Wiley

Colegrave, S. (1979) *The Spirit of the Valley*, London: Virago

Coles, R. (1970) *Erik H. Erikson: The growth of his work*, Boston, Mass.: Little, Brown

Colletti, L. (1973) *Marxism and Hegel*, London: New Left Books

Collier, A. (1977) *R. D. Laing: The philosophy and politics of psychotherapy*, Hassocks: Harvester Press

—— (1985) 'Truth and Practice'. In R. Edgley and R. Osborne (eds), *Radical Philosophy Reader*: 193–214

Collingwood, R. G. (1945) *The Idea of Nature*, Oxford: Clarendon Press

References

—— (1946) *The Idea of History*, Oxford: Oxford University Press
Collins, J. (1952) *The Existentialists: A critical study*, Chicago: Regnery
—— (1953) *The Mind of Kierkegaard*, Princeton, NJ: Princeton University Press
Comfort, A. (1964) *Sex in Society*, Harmondsworth: Penguin Books
Comte, A. (1830–42). *Cours de philosophie positive*, 6 vols, Paris: Bachelier
Connerton, P. (ed.) (1976) *Critical Sociology: Selected readings*, Harmondsworth: Penguin Books
Conway, D. (1987) *A Farewell to Marx*, Harmondsworth: Penguin Books
Cooley, C. H. (1902) *Human Nature and the Social Order*, New York: Scribners
Cooper, B. (1981) *Michel Foucault: An introduction to his thought*, Toronto: E. Mellen
Copleston, F. (1946) *Arthur Schopenhauer: Philosopher of pessimism*, London
—— (1959) *A History of Philosophy*, volume V, *Hobbes to Hume*, London: Burns and Oates
—— (1960) *A History of Philosophy*, volume VI, *Part One. The French Enlightenment to Kant*, New York: Doubleday
—— (1963) *A History of Philosophy*, volume IV, *Descartes to Leibniz*, New York: Doubleday
—— (1963) *A History of Philosophy*, volume VII, *Fichte to Nietzsche*
—— (1966) volume VIII, *Bentham to Russell*
—— (1974) volume IX, *Main de Biran to Sartre* (1985 edition in one volume), New York: Doubleday
Cornforth, M. (1965) *Marxism and the Linguistic Philosophy*, New York
—— (1968) *The Open Philosophy and the Open Society*, London: Lawrence & Wishart
—— (1980) *Communism and Philosophy*, London: Lawrence & Wishart
Cottingham, J. (1984) *Rationalism*, London: Paladin Books
Coulter, J. (1979) *The Social Construction of Mind: Studies in ethnomethodology and linguistic philosophy*, London: Macmillan
Cousins, M. and A. Hussain (1984) *Michel Foucault*, London: Macmillan
Coward, R. (1983) *Patriarchal Precedents: Sexuality and social relations*, London: Routledge & Kegan Paul
—— and J. Ellis (1977) *Language and Materialism: Developments in semiology and the theory of the subject*, London: Routledge & Kegan Paul
Cranston, M. (1962) *Sartre*, Edinburgh: Oliver & Boyd
—— (1972) 'Thomas Hobbes'. In B. Mazlish (ed.), *Makers of Modern Thought*, New York: American Heritage Press: 112–21
—— (1972) 'John Locke 1632–1704'. In B. Mazlish (ed.), *Makers of Modern Thought*, New York: American Heritage Press
Culler, J. (1976) *Saussure*, London: Fontana
—— (1979) 'Jacques Derrida'. In J. Sturrock (ed.), *Structuralism and Science*: 154–80
—— (1983) *On Deconstruction: Theory and criticism after structuralism*,

London: Routledge & Kegan Paul

Danto, A. C. (1964) 'Nietzsche'. In D. J. O'Connor: A Critical History of Western Philosophy, New York: Free Press 384–401

—— (1965) Nietszsche as Philosopher, New York: Macmillan

Danziger, K. (1980) 'Wundt and the Two Traditions in Psychology. Wundt's theory of behaviour and volition'. In R. W. Rieber. (ed.) Wilhelm Wundt and the Making of a Scientific Psychology: 73–88, 89–116

Darwin, C. (1859) The Origin of Species, ed. J. B. Burrow (1968 edition), Harmondsworth: Penguin Books

Dasen, P. (ed.) (1977a) Piagetian Psychology: Cross-cultural contributions, New York: Gardner Press

—— (1977b) 'Are Cognitive Processes Universal?: A contribution to cross-cultural Piagetian psychology'. In N. Warren, Studies in Cross-Cultural Psychology I, London: Academic Press: 155–201

—— (1977c)'Cross-cultural Cognitive Development', Annals New York Acad. Sc., 285: 332–7

Davydov, V. V. and L. A. Radzikhovskii, (1985) 'Vygotsky's Theory of the Activity-Oriented Approach in Psychology'. In J. V. Wertsch (ed.), Culture, Communication and Cognition: 35–65

Dawe, A. (1979). 'Theories of Social Action'. In Bottomore and Nisbet (eds), A History of Sociological Analysis: 362–417

Dawkins, R. (1976) The Selfish Gene, Oxford: Oxford University Press

—— (1982) The Extended Phenotype, San Francisco: Freeman

De Beauvoir, S. (1962) The Prime of Life, Harmondsworth: Penguin Books

Derrida, J. (1972) Margins of Philosophy, trans. A. Bates, Brighton: Harvester Press

—— (1976) Of Grammatology, trans. G. C. Spivak, Baltimore, Md: Johns Hopkins University Press

—— (1978a) Writing and Difference, trans. and introd. A. Bass, London: Routledge & Kegan Paul

—— (1978b) Edmund Husserl's Origin of Geometry: An introduction, trans. J. P. Leavey, Pittsburgh: Duguesne University Press

Desan, W. (1960) The Tragic Finale: An essay on the philosophy of Jean-Paul Sartre, New York: Harper

Descartes, R. (1637) A Discourse on Method, trans. J. Veitch, London: Dent

—— (1650) The Passions of the Soul (Les Passions de l'âme), Paris: Loyson In Discourse on Method and Other Writings, trans. and introd. F. E. Sutcliffe, Harmondsworth: Penguin Books

Descombes, V. (1980) Modern French Philosophy, Cambridge: Cambridge University Press

Deutsch, H. (1945) The Psychology of Women, 2 vols, New York: Grune & Stratton

Devereux, G. (1978) Ethnopsychoanalysis. Psychoanalysis and anthropology as complementary frames of reference, Berkeley, Calif.: University of California Press

—— (1980) *Basic Problems of Ethnopsychiatry*, Chicago: University of Chicago Press

Dewey, J. (1886) *Psychology*, New York: Harper

—— (1916) *Democracy and Education*, New York: Macmillan

—— (1917) 'The Need for a Social Psychology'. *Psychol. Rev.*, 24: 266–77

—— (1922) *Human Nature and Conduct: An introduction to social psychology*, New York: Holt

—— (1925) *Experience and Nature*, New York: Dover

—— (1931) *Philosophy and Civilization*, New York: Minton, Balch & Co.

—— (1938) *Logic: The theory of inquiry*, New York: Holt & Co.

Dews, P. (ed) (1986) *Habermas: Autonomy and solidarity*, London: Verso

—— (1987) *Logics of Disintegration: Post-structuralist thought and the claims of critical theory*, London: Verso

Diamond, S. (1974) *In Search of the Primitive*, New York: Transaction Books

—— (1980) 'Wundt before Leipzig'. In R. W. Rieber (ed.) *Wilhelm Wundt and the Making of a Scientific Psychology* (ed) 3–70

Dijksterhuis, E. J. (1961) *The Mechanization of the World Picture*, trans. C. Dikshoorn, Oxford: Oxford University Press

Donaldson, M. (1978) *Children's Minds*, London: Fontana

Douglas, J. D. and J. M. Johnson (eds) (1977) *Existential Sociology*, Cambridge: Cambridge University Press

Drew, P. and A. Wootton (1988) *Erving Goffman: Exploring the interaction order*, Oxford: Polity Press

Dreyfus, H. and P. Rabinow (1982) *Michel Foucault. Beyond structuralism and hermeneutics*, Chicago: University of Chicago Press

Dumont, L. (1965) 'The Modern Conception of the Individual'. *Contrib. Ind. Sociol.*, 8: 13–61

—— (1970) *Homo Hierarchicus: The caste system and its implications*, London: Weidenfeld & Nicolson

—— (1977) *From Mandeville to Marx*, Chicago: University of Chicago Press

—— (1985) 'A Modified View of our Origins: The Christian beginnings of modern individualism'. In M. Carrithers et al. (eds), *The Category of the Person*: 93–122

—— (1986) *Essays on Individualism: Modern ideology in anthropological Perspective*, Chicago: University of Chicago Press

—— (1986b) 'Are Cultures Living Beings? German identity in interaction'. *Man*, 21: 587–604

Dunn, J. (1984) *Locke*, London: Oxford University Press

Durant, W. (1952) *The Story of Philosophy*, New York: Washington Square Press

Durham, W. H. (1979) 'Toward a Co-evolutionary Theory of Human Biology and Culture'. In N. Chagnon and W. Irons (eds), *Evolutionary – Biology and Human Social Behaviour*: 39–58

Durkheim, E. (1893) *The Division of Labour in Society*, Glencoe, Ill: Free Press

—— (1895) *The Rules of the Sociological Method* (1950 edition), Glencoe, Ill: Free Press

—— (1915) *The Elementary Forms of the Religious Life* (1964 edition), London: Allen & Unwin

—— (1974) *Sociology and Philosophy*, trans. D. F. Pocock, New York: Free Press

Eccles, J. and D. N. Robinson (1985) *The Wonder of Being Human*, Boston, Mass.: Shanbhala

Edgley, R. and R. Osborne (eds) (1985) *Radical Philosophy Reader*, London: Verso

Edie, J. M. (1987) *Edmund Husserl's Phenomenology*, Bloomington, Ind.: Indiana University Press

Edinger, D. (1968) *Bertha Poppenheim – Freud's Anna O.*, Highland Park, Ill.: Congregation Solel

Edman, I. (1928) *The Philosophy of Schopenhauer*, New York: Random House

Ehrenfeld, D. (1978) *The Arrogance of Humanism*, Oxford: Oxford University Press

Eisendrath, C. R. (1971) *The Unifying Moment: The psychological philosophy of William James and Alfred North Whitehead*, Cambridge, Mass.: Harvard University Press

Ekirch, Jr A. A. (1973) *Man and Nature in America*, Nebraska: University of Nebraska Press

Elder, C. (1980) *Appropriating Hegel*, Aberdeen: Aberdeen University Press

Elders, F. (1974) *Reflexive Water: The basic concerns of mankind*, London: Souvenir Press

Eldridge, J. (1983) *C. Wright Mills*, London: Tavistock

Eliade, M. (1975) *Patanjali and Yoga*, trans. C. L. Markmann (original 1962), New York: Schocken Books

Elkind, D. (1975) 'Giant in the Nursery – Jean Piaget', and 'Erik Erikson's Eight Ages of Man'. In J. Rubinstein, *Readings in Anthropology 75/76*, Guildford, Conn: Pushkin Publ.: 165–77, 178–91

Ellenberger, H. F. (1970) *The Discovery of the Unconscious: The history and evolution of dynamic psychiatry*, London: Allen Lane

Elliott, G. (1987) *Althusser: The detour of theory*, London: Verso

Elliston, F. (ed.) (1978) *Heidegger's Existential Analytic*, The Hague: Mouton

Engels, F. (1886) 'Ludwig Feuerbach and the End of Classical German Philosophy'. In Marx and Engels, *Selected Works*: 586–622

Erdelyi, M. H. (1985) *Psychoanalysis: Freud's cognitive psychology*, San Francisco: W. H. Freeman

Evans, R. I. (1968) *B. F. Skinner: The man and his ideas*, New York: Dutton

References

—— (1973) *Jean Piaget: The man and his ideas,* New York: Dutton

Evans-Pritchard, E. E. (1965) *Theories of Primitive Religion,* Oxford: Clarendon Press

—— (1981) *A History of Anthropological Thought,* ed. E. Gellner, London: Faber & Faber

Eysenck, H. J. (1953) *The Uses and Abuses of Psychology,* Harmondsworth: Penguin Books

—— (1985) *Decline and Fall of the Freudian Empire,* Harmondsworth: Penguin Books

Fancher, R. E. (1973) *Psychoanalytic Psychology: The development of Freud's thought,* New York: Norton

—— (1979) *Pioneers of Psychology,* New York: Norton

Farber, M. (1943) *The Foundations of Phenomenology,* Cambridge, Mass.: Harvard University Press

Farrell, B. A. (1981) *The Standing of Psychoanalysis,* London: Oxford University Press

Farrington, B. (1949) *Francis Bacon: Philosopher of industrial science,* New York: Schumann

Feenberg, A. (1981) *Lukács, Marx and the Sources of Critical Theory,* Oxford: Martin Robertson

Feinstein, H. M. (1984) *Becoming William James,* Ithaca, NY: Cornell University Press

Feuerbach, L. (1957) *The Essence of Christianity,* trans. G. Eliot (original 1841), New York: Harper

Figes, E. (1970) *Patriarchal Attitudes,* London: Faber & Faber

Filmer, P. et al. (1972) *New Directions in Sociological Theory,* London: Collier-Macmillan

Findlay, J. N. (1964) 'Hegel'. In D. J. O'Connor *A Critical History of Western Philosophy* New York: Free Press 319–40

Firth, R. (1970) *Man and Culture: An evaluation of the work of Bronislow Malinowski,* London: Routledge & Kegan Paul

—— (1972) *The Sceptical Anthropologist? Social anthropology and Marxist views on society,* British Academy, Oxford University Press

Fisher, B. M. and A. L. Strauss (1979) 'Interactionism'. In T. Bottomore and R. Nisbet, *A History of Sociological Analysis,* London: Heinemann: 457–98

Fisher, E. (1980) *Woman's Creation: Sexual evolution and the shaping of society,* London: Wildwood House

Flanagan, Jr O. J. (1984) *The Science of the Mind,* Cambridge, Mass.: MIT Press

Flavell, J. H. (1963) *The Developmental Psychology of Jean Piaget,* New York: Van Nostrand

Fleming, M. (1979) *The Anarchist Way to Socialism,* London: Croom Helm

Fletcher, R. (1966) *Auguste Comte and the Making of Sociology,* London: Athlone Press

Flew, A. (1984) *Darwinian Evolution*, London: Paladin Books

Flügel, J. C. (1921) *The Psychoanalytic Study of the Family*, London: Hogarth Press

—— (1964) *A Hundred Years of Psychology*, rev. D. J. West, London: Macmillan

Fodor, J. A. (1983) *The Modularity of Mind: An essay on faculty psychology*, Cambridge, Mass.: MIT Press Bradford Books

Fortune, R. (1932) *The Sorcerors of Dobu*, London: Routledge & Kegan Paul

Foucault, M. (1954) *Mental Illness and Psychology* (1976 edition), New York: Harper & Row

—— (1963) *The Birth of the Clinic*, trans. A. M. Sheridan, London: Tavistock

—— (1965) *Madness and Civilization: A history of insanity in the Age of Reason*, New York: Mentor/ London: Tavistock

—— (1970) *The Order of Things: An archaeology of the human species*, (original 1966), London: Tavistock

—— (1972) *The Archaeology of Knowledge*, trans. A. M. Sheridan Smith (original 1965), London: Tavistock

—— (1976) *History of Sexuality*. vol. 1. *An Introduction*, trans. R. Hurly, London: Allen Lane

—— (1977) *Discipline and Punish: The birth of the prison*, trans. A. M. Sheridan (original 1975), London: Allen Lane

—— (1980) *Power/Knowledge: Selected interviews and other writings 1972–1977*. ed. C. Gordon, New York: Pantheon

—— (1982) 'The Subject and Power'. In H. L. Dreyfus and P. Rabinow, *Michel Foucault*: 208–26

Frankfurt, H. G. (ed.) (1972) *Leibniz: A collection of critical essays*, London: University of Notre Dame Press

Frankl, V. E. (1963) *Man's Search for Meaning: An introduction to logotherapy*, New York: Beacon Press

Freedman, D. G. (1979) *Human Sociobiology: A holistic approach*, New York: Free Press

Freeman, D. (1969) 'Totem and Taboo: A reappraisal'. In W. Muenster Berger, *Man and his Culture*, London: Rapp & Whiting 53–80

—— (1983) *Margaret Mead and Samoa*, Harmondsworth: Penguin Books

Freud, A. (1936) *The Ego and the Mechanisms of Defence* (1964 edition), London: Hogarth Press

Freud, S. with J. Breuer (1895) *Studies on Hysteria*, London: Hogarth Press

—— (1900) *Interpretation of Dreams*, London: Allen & Unwin/Hogarth Press (Harmondsworth: Penguin Books, 1976 edition)

—— (1901) *Psychopathology of Everyday Life*, New York: Modern Library

—— (1905) *Three Essays on the Theory of Sexuality* (1982 edition), London: Hogarth Press

—— (1913) *Totem and Taboo*, London: Routledge & Kegan Paul, 1983 edition, Harmondsworth: Penguin Books

References

(1916–17) *Introductory Lectures on Psychoanalysis*, trans. J. Reviere (London: Allen & Unwin, 1929; New York: Doubleday, 1953)

—— (1914) *History of the Psychoanalytic Movement*, London: Hogarth Press

—— (1920) *Beyond the Pleasure Principle*, London: Hogarth Press, 1950; New York: Norton, 1961

—— (1921) *Group Psychology and the Analysis of the Ego* (1959 edition), London: Hogarth Press

—— (1923) *The Ego and the Id* (1962 edition), London: Hogarth Press

—— (1928) *The Future of an Illusion*, London: Hogarth Press (1978 edition, Int. Psy. Libr. No. 15)

—— (1930) *Civilization and its Discontents*, London: Hogarth Press/ New York: Norton

—— (1937) *General Selection from the Works of Sigmund Freud (1910–1923)*, J. Rickman, New York: Doubleday

—— (1946) *An Autobiographical Study*, London: Hogarth Press

—— (1953) *A General Introduction to Psychoanalysis* (original 1915–17)

—— *Introductory Lectures on Psychoanalysis*, University of Vienna, New York: Doubleday

—— (1954) *The Origins of Psychoanalysis. Letters to Wilhelm Fliess 1887–1902*. ed. M. Bonaparte et al., introd. E. Kris, New York: Basic Books

—— (1962) *Two Short Accounts on Psychoanalysis. (Five Lectures on Psychoanalysis, 1909. The Question of Long Analysis, 1926)*, Harmondsworth: Penguin Books

—— (1986) *Historical and Expository Works on Psychoanalysis*, Harmondsworth: Penguin Books

Friedman, M. (1967) *To Deny our Nothingness*, Chicago: University Chicago Press

Fromm, E. (1942) *The Fear of Freedom*, London: Routledge & Kegan Paul

—— (1949) *Man for Himself: An enquiry into the psychology of ethics*, London: Routledge & Kegan Paul

—— (1950) *Psychoanalysis and Religion*, New Haven, Conn.: Yale University Press

—— (1951) *The Forgotten Language*, New York: Grove Press

—— (1955) 'The Human Implications of Instinctivistic Radicalism', *Dissent*, 2: 342–9

—— (1956) *The Sane Society*, London: Routledge & Kegan Paul

—— (1957) *The Art of Loving*, London: Allen & Unwin

—— (1959) 'Value, Psychology and Human Existence'. In A. Maslow (ed.), *New Knowledge in Human Values*, South Bend, Ind.: Regnery

—— (1961) *Marx's Concept of Man*, New York: Frederick Wagner

—— (1962) *Beyond the Chains of Illusion: My encounter with Marx and Freud* (1980 edition), London: Sphere Books

—— (1965) 'The Application of Humanist Psychoanalysis to Marx's Theory'. In E. Fromm (ed.), *Socialist Humanism*, London: Allen Lane: 207–24

—— (1970) *The Crisis of Psychoanalysis: Essays on Freud, Marx and social psychology*, Harmondsworth: Penguin Books

—— (1974) *The Anatomy of Human Destructiveness* (1977 edition), London: J. Cape/Harmondsworth: Penguin Books

—— (1976) *To Have or to Be?* (1979 edition), London: Sphere Books

—— (1984) *On Disobedience and other Essays*, London: Routledge & Kegan Paul

Frosh, S. (1987) *The Politics of Psychoanalysis: An introduction to Freudian and post-Freudian theory*, London: Macmillan

Fry, J. (1978) *Marcuse: Dilemma and liberation*, Brighton: Harvester Press

Furth, H. G. (1969) *Piaget and Knowledge: Theoretical foundations*, Englewood Cliffs, NJ: Prentice Hall

Gadamer, H. (1975) *Truth and Method*, New York: Seabury Press

—— (1976) *Hegel's Dialectic: Five hermeneutic studies*, trans. P. C. Smith, New Haven, Conn.: Yale University Press

Galton, F. (1883) *Inquiries into Human Faculty and its Development*, London: J. M. Dent

Gardner, H. (1972) *The Quest of Mind: Piaget, Lévi-Strauss and the Structuralist Movement*, New York: Knopf

Gardner, P. M. (1966) 'Symmetric Respect and Memorate Knowledge'. *Southwestern J. Anthrop.*, 22: 389–415

Geertz, C. (1975) *The Interpretation of Cultures* London: Hutchinson

Gellner, E. (1959) *Words and Things*, London: Gollancz/ Harmondsworth: Penguin Books, 1968

—— (1985) *The Psychoanalytic Movement or the Coming of Unreason*, London: Paladin Books

Geoghegan, V. (1981) *Reason and Eros: The social theory of Herbert Marcuse*, London: Pluto Press

George, W. (1982) *Darwin*, London: Fontana

Geras, N. (1972) 'Marx and the Critique of Political Economy'. In R. Blackburn (ed.), *Ideology in Social Science*, London: Fontana/Collins: 284–305

—— (1978) 'Althusser's Marxism: An assessment'. In *New Left Rev.* (ed.), *Western Marxism*: 232–72

—— (1983) *Marx and Human Nature, Refutation of a legend*, London: Verso

Gerth, H. and C. W. Mills (1953) *Character and Social Structure*, London: Routledge & Kegan Paul

Giddens, A. (ed.) (1974) *Positivism and Sociology*, London: Heinemann

—— (1978) *Durkheim*, London: Fontana/Collins

—— (1979) 'Positivism and its Critics'. In T. Bottomore and R. Nisbet (eds), *A History of Sociological Analysis*: 237–86

—— (1985) 'Reason without Revolution? Habermas's *Theories des Kommunikativen Hardelns*'. In R. J. Bernstein (ed.), *Habermas and Modernity*: 95–124

Ginsburg, H. and S. Opper (1969) *Piaget's Theory of Intellectual Develop-*

ment: An introduction, Englewood Cliffs, NJ: Prentice Hall

Gisbert, P. (1959) 'Social Facts and Durkheim's System'. *Anthropos.*, 54: 353–69

Glenn, M. and R. Kunnes (1973) *Repression or Revolution: Therapy in the United States today*, New York: Harper Colophon

Glover, E. (1950) *Freud or Jung*, New York: Norton

Goble, F. (1971) *The Third Force: The psychology of Abraham Maslow*, New York: Grossman

Goff, T. W. (1980) *Marx and Mead: Contributions to a sociology of knowledge*, London: Routledge & Kegan Paul

Goffman, E. (1959) *The Presentation of Self in Everyday Life*, London: Allen Lane

—— (1961) *Asylums: Essays in the social situation of mental patients and other inmates*, Harmondsworth: Penguin Books

—— (1963) *Stigma: Notes on the management of spoiled identity*, Harmondsworth: Penguin Books

—— (1967) *Interaction Ritual: Essays on face-to-face behaviour*, New York: Doubleday

—— (1974) *Frame Analysis*, New York: Harper & Row

Goldenweiser, A. (1941) 'Recent Trends in American Anthropology'. *Amer. Anthrop.*, 43: 151–63

Goldmann, L. (1969) *The Human Sciences and Philosophy*, London: Cape.

—— (1971) *Immanuel Kant*, London: New Left Books

—— (1977a) *Lukács and Heidegger: Towards a new philosophy*, London: Routledge & Kegan Paul

—— (1977b) 'Dialectical Thought and Transindividual Subject'. In *Cultural Creation in Modern Society*, Oxford: Basil Blackwell

Gould, J. (1969) 'Auguste Comte'. In T. Raison (ed.), *The Founding Fathers of Social Science*: 35–42

Gould, S. J. (1980) *The Panda's Thumb*, Harmondsworth: Penguin Books

Gouldner, A. W. (1973) *For Sociology*, Harmondsworth: Penguin Books

—— (1980), *The Two Marxisms*, London: Macmillan

Gower, B. (1987) *Logical Positivism in Perspective*, London: Croom Helm

Gray, J. G. (1979) 'Introduction'. In J. G. Gray (ed.), *G. W. F. Hegel: On art, religion, and philosophy*, New York: Harper & Row

Greenberg, J. R. and S. A. Mitchell (1983) *Object Relation in Psychoanalytic Theory*, Cambridge, Mass.: Harvard University Press

Gregory, R. L. (1981) *Mind in Science: A history of explanations in psychology and physics*, London: Weidenfeld & Nicolson

Grimsley, R. (1955) *Existentialist Thought*, Cardiff: University of Wales Press

—— (1973) *Kierkegaard: A biographical introduction*, New York: Scribner

Grossman, R. (1984) *Phenomenology and Existentialism: An introduction*, London: Routledge & Kegan Paul

Gruber, H. E. (1974) *Darwin on Man: A psychological study of scientific* creativity, Chicago: University of Chicago Press

Gruenbaum, A. (1984) The Foundations of Psychoanalysis, Berkeley, Calif.: University of California Press

Habermas, J. (1970) Toward a Rational Society, trans. J. J. Shapiro, Boston, Mass.: Beacon Press

—— (1972) Knowledge and Human Interests, London: Heinemann

—— (1979) Communication and the Evolution of Society, London: Heinemann

—— (1984) Reason and the Rationalisation of Society, Boston, Mass.: Beacon Press

—— (1985) 'Questions and Counter-question'. In R. J. Berstein (ed.): 192–216

—— (1987) The Philosophical Discourse of Modernity, trans. F. Lawrence, Cambridge: Polity Press

Haeckel, E. (1899) The Riddle of the Universe (1929 edition), London: Watts

Hale, N. G. (1971) Freud and the Americans: The beginning of psychoanalysis in the United States, New York: Oxford University Press

Hall, C. S. and G. Lindzey (1957) Theories of Personality, New York: Wiley

Hall, G. S. (1904) Adolescence: Its psychology, 2 vols, New York: Appleton

Hallowell, A. I. (1953) 'Culture, Personality and Society'. In A. Kroeber (1962) Anthropology Today, Chicago: University Chicago Press: 597–620

—— (1955) Culture and Experience, Philadelphia: University of Pennsylvania Press

—— (1959) 'Behavioural Evolution and the Emergence of Self'. In B. J. Meggars (ed.), Evolution and Anthropology: A centennial appraisal, Anthrop. Soc. Washington

—— (1960) 'Ojibwa Ontology, Behaviour and World View'. In S. Diamond, Primitive Views of the World, New York: Columbia University Press: 49–84

—— (1960) 'Self, Culture and Society in Phylogenetic Perspective'. In S. Tax (ed.), The Evolution of Man, Mind, Culture and Society, Chicago: University of Chicago Press

—— (1961) 'The Protocultural Foundations of Human Adaptation'. In S. L. Washburn (ed.), Social Life of Early Man, New York: Werner Gren

—— (1976) Contributions to Anthropology: Selected Papers of A. I. Hallowell, introd. R. D. Fogelson, Chicago: University of Chicago Press

Hallpike, C. R. (1979) The Foundations of Primitive Thought, Oxford: Clarendon Press

Hampshire, S. (1951) Spinoza, Harmondsworth: Penguin Books

—— (1956) The Age of Reason: The 17th century philosophers, New York: Mentor

Hanfling, O. (1981) Logical Positivism, Oxford: Basil Blackwell

Hannay, A. (1983) Kierkegaard, London: Routledge & Kegan Paul

Harland, R. (1987) Superstructuralism, London: Methuen

Harris, M. (1969) The Rise of Anthropological Theory, London: Routledge & Kegan Paul

References

——— (1977) *Cannibals and Kings: The origins of cultures*, London: Fontana/ Collins

——— (1980) *Cultural Materialism*, New York: Vintage Books

Hartley, D. (1749) *Observations on Man, His Frame, His Duty and His Expectations*, London: Johnson

Hartmann, H. (1939) *Ego Psychology and the Problem of Adaptation*, New York: Intern. University Press

Hatch, E. (1973) *Theories of Man and Culture*, New York: Columbia University Press

Hawkes, T. (1977) *Structuralism and Semiotics*, London: Methuen

Hawton, H. (1956) *Philosophy for Pleasure*, Greenwich, Conn.: Fawcett

Heather, N. (1976) *Radical Perspectives in Psychology*, London: Methuen

Heelas, P. and A. Lock (eds) (1981) *Indigenous Psychologies: The anthropology of self*, New York: Academic Press

Hegel, G. W. F. (1807) *Phenomenology of Spirit*, trans. A. V. Miller (1977 edition), Oxford: Oxford University Press

——— (1892) *The Logic of Hegel*, trans. from *Encyclopaedia of the Philosophical Sciences* by W. Wallace, Oxford: Oxford University Press

——— (1942) *Philosophy of Right*, trans. and ed. T. Knox, Oxford: Oxford University Press

——— (1956) *The Philosophy of History* (original 1840), New York: Dover

Heidegger, M. (1949) *Existence and Being*, intro. W. Brock, Chicago: H. Regnery

——— (1962) *Being and Time*, trans. J. MacQuarrie and E. S. Robinson (original 1927), Oxford: Basil Blackwell

Held, D. (1980) *Introduction to Critical Theory: Horkheimer to Habermas*, London: Hutchinson

Henry, J. (1964) *The Jungle People*, New York: Random Press

Hindness, B. and P. Q. Hirst (1975) *Pre-Capitalist Modes of Production*, London: Routledge & Kegan Paul

Hirsh, A. (1981) *The French New Left: An intellectual history from Sartre to Gorz*, Boston, Mass.: South End Press

Hirst, P. Q. (1975) *Durkheim, Bernard and Epistemology*, London: Routledge & Kegan Paul

Hirst, P. and P. Woolley (1982) *Social Relations and Human Attributes*, London: Tavistock Press

Hobbes, T. (1651) *Leviathan*, ed. M. Oakeshott (1962 edition), London: Collier-Macmillan

Hodges, H. A. (1944) *Wilhelm Dilthey: An introduction*, London: Routledge & Kegan Paul

——— (1952) *The Philosophy of W. Dilthey*, London: Routledge & Kegan Paul

Hollingdale, R. J. (1965) *Nietzsche: The man and his philosophy*, London: Routledge & Kegan Paul

——— (1970) *Introduction to Schopenhauer, Essays and Aphorisms*, Harmondsworth:

References

Penguin Books

Hollis, M. and S. Lukes (eds) (1982) *Rationality and Relativism*, Oxford: Basil Blackwell

Holmberg, A. R. (1969) *Nomads of the Long Bow*, New York: American Museum of Natural History

Holmes, L. D. (1987) *The Quest for the Real Samoa*, S. Hadley: Bergin & Garvey

Homans, G. C. (1950) *The Human Group*, New York: Harcourt Brace

—— (1961) *Social Behaviour: Its elementary forms*, New York: Harcourt Brace

Home, H. J. (1966) 'The Concept of Mind'. *Int. J. Psychoanalysis*, 47: 42–9

Honigmann, J. J. (1949) *Culture and Ethos of Kaska Society*. New Haven, Conn.: Yale University Press

—— (1967) *Personality in Culture*, New York: Harper & Row

—— (1972) 'North America'. In F. L. K. Hsu, *Psychological Anthropology*, Schenkman, Cambr.: 121–66

—— (1975) 'Psychological Anthropology'. In T. R. Williams (ed.), *Psychological Anthropology*, The Hague: Mouton

—— (1976) *The Development of Anthropological Ideas*, Homewood, Ill.: Dorsey

Hook. S. (1939) *John Dewey: An intellectual portrait*, New York: J. Day

—— (1962) *From Hegel to Marx*, Ann Arbor, Mich.: University of Michigan Press

Horkheimer, M. (1974a) *Eclipse of Reason* (original 1947), New York: Seabury Press

—— (1974b) *Critique of Instrumental Reason*, trans. M. J. O'Connell (original 1967), New York: Seabury Press

—— (1976) 'Traditional and Critical Theory' (original 1937). In Connerton (ed.), *Critical Sociology*: 206–24

Howard, J. (1984) *Margaret Mead – A life*, London: Harvill Press

Hoy, D. C. (ed.) (1986) *Foucault: A critical reader*, Oxford: Basil Blackwell

Hubert, H. and M. Mauss (1964) *Sacrifice: Its nature and function*, London: Cohen & West

Hughes, H. S. (1958) *Consciousness and Society: The reorientation of European Social Thought 1890–1930*, New York: Vintage Books

—— (1966) *The Obstructed Path: French social thought in the years of desperation 1930–1966*, New York: Harper & Row

Hull, C. L. (1943) *Principles of Behaviour*, New York: Appleton-Century.

Hume, D. (1739–40) *A Treatise of Human Nature* (1975 edition), ed. L. A. Selby-Bigge, Oxford: Oxford University Press

—— (1955) *An Inquiry Concerning Human Understanding*, ed. C. W. Hendel (original 1748), Indianapolis: Bobbs-Merrill

Husserl, E. (1952) *Ideas for a Pure Phenomenology*, trans. W. R. Boyce Gibson (original 1931), New York: Collier

—— (1960) *Cartesian Meditations*, trans. D. Carins (original 1931), The

References

Hague: M. Nijhoff
—— (1964) *The Idea of Phenomenology*, trans. W. Palston and G. Nakhnikian (original 1907), The Hague: M. Nijhoff
—— (1965) *Phenomenology and the Crisis of Philosophy*, trans. and introd. Q. Laver, New York: Harper & Row
—— (1970) *The Crisis of European Sciences and Transcendental Phenomenology*, trans. D. Carr, Evanston, Ill.: Northwestern University Press
Ingold, T. (1986) *Evolution and Social Life*, Cambridge Cambridge University Press
Inkeles, A. (1961) 'National Character and Modern Political Systems'. In F. Hsu (ed.), *Psychological Anthropology*: 172–208
Jacoby, R. (1975) *Social Amnesia: A critique of conformist psychology from Adler to Laing*, Hassocks: Harvester Press
Jahoda, G. (1969) *The Psychology of Superstition*, Harmondsworth: Penguin Books
—— (1982) *Psychology and Anthropology: A psychological perspective*, New York: Academic Press
Jahoda, M. (1977) *Freud and the Dilemmas of Psychology*, London: Hogarth Press
James, W. (1890) *The Principles of Psychology*, 2 vols, New York: Dover Press
—— (1892) *Psychology: A briefer course*, London: Macmillan
—— (1897) *The Will to Believe and other Essays in Popular Philosophy*, New York: Longmans Green
—— (1902) *Varieties of Religious Experience* (1980 edition), London: Fontana/Collins
—— (1907) *Pragmatism: A new name for some old ways of thinking*, New York: Longmans Green
—— (1909) *The Meaning of Truth* (1978 edition), Cambridge, Mass.: Harvard University Press
—— (1912) *Essays in Radical Empiricism*, New York: Longmans Green
—— (1967) *Selected Papers on Philosophy*, introd. C. M. Blakewell, London: Dent Everyman's Library
—— (1971) *A William James Reader*, ed. and Introd. G. W. Allen, Boston, Mass.: Houghton Mifflin
Jay, M. (1973) *The Dialectical Imagination*. London: Tavistock
—— (1977) 'The Concept of Totality in Lukács and Adorno'. In S. Avineri (ed.), *Varieties of Marxism*, The Hague: M. Nijhoff: 147–74
—— (1984) *Marxism and Totality*, London: Oxford University Press
Jenkins, A. (1979) *The Social Theory of Claude Lévi-Strauss*, London: Macmillan
Joad, C. E. M. (1924) *Introduction to Modern Philosophy*, Oxford: Clarendon Press
—— (1936) *Guide to Philosophy* (1957 edition), New York: Dover
Joas, H. (1985) *G. H. Mead: A contemporary re-examination of his thought*,

Cambridge: Polity Press

Jones, E. (1964) *The Life and Work of Sigmund Freud* (original 1953–7), 3 vols, ed. L. Trilling (abridged.), London: Hogarth Harmondsworth: Penguin Books

Jones, H. E. (1971) *Kant's Principle of Personality*, Madison, Wisc.: University of Wisconsin Press

Kant, I. (1781) *The Critique of Pure Reason*, trans. N. Kemp Smith (1959 edition), London: Dent

—— (1783) *Prolegomena to any Future Metaphysics*, introd. L. W. Beck, New York: Bobbs-Merrill

—— (1798) *Anthropology from a Pragmatic Point of View*, trans. M. J. Gregor (1974 edition), The Hague: M. Nijhoff

Kaplan, B. (1957) 'Personality and Social Structure'. In R. A. Manners and D. Kaplan (eds), *Theory in Anthropology*, London: Routledge & Kegan Paul, 318–41

Kaplan, D. and R. A. Manners (1972) *Culture Theory*, Englewood Cliffs, NJ: Prentice Hall

Kardiner, A. (1939) *The Individual and his Society*, New York: Columbia University Press

—— et. al. (1945) *The Psychological Frontiers of Society*, New York: Columbia University Press

—— (1957) 'Freud – The Man I Knew'. In B. Nelson (ed.), *Freud and the Twentieth Century*, New York

—— and E. Preble (1961) *They Studied Man*, New York: Mentor Books

Katz, B. (1982) *Herbert Marcuse and the Art of Liberation*, London: Verso, New Left Books

Kaufmann, W. (1950) *Nietzsche: Philosopher, psychologist, anti-Christ* (4th edition), Princeton, NJ: Princeton University Press

—— (1956) *Existentialism from Dostoevsky to Sartre*, New York: Meridian

—— (1965) *Hegel – A Reinterpretation*, Notre Dame, Ind.: University Notre Dame Press

—— (1971) *The Portable Nietzsche*, London: Chatto & Windus

Kearney, R. (1986) *Modern Movements in European Philosophy*, Manchester: Manchester University Press

Kearns, E. J. (1979) *Ideas in Seventeenth Century France*, Manchester: Manchester University Press

Keat, R. (1981) *The Politics of Social Theory*, Oxford: Basil Blackwell

Kellner, D. (1984) *Herbert Marcuse and the Crisis of Marxism*, London: Macmillan

Kellner, L. (1963) *Alexander von Humboldt*, Oxford: Oxford University Press

Kemnitzer, D. S. (1977) 'Sexuality as a Social Form: Performance and anxiety in America'. In J. L. Dolgin et al., *Symbolic Anthropology. A reader*, New York: Columbia University Press: 292–309

Kempton, W. and P. Kay (1984) 'What is the Sapir–Whorf Hypothesis?' *Amer. Anthrop.*, 86: 65–79

References

Kenny, A. (1968) *Descartes: A study of his philosophy*, New York: Random House
—— (1973) *Wittgenstein*, London: Allen Lane
Khare, R. S. (1975) Hindu Social Inequality and some Ideological Entailments. In B. N. Nair (ed.) *Culture and Society*, Delhi: Thomson Press pp. 97–114
Kiefer, C. W. (1977) 'Psychological Anthropology'. *Ann. Rev. Anthrop.*, 6: 103–19
King, R. (1972) *The Party of Eros: Radical thought and the realm of freedom*, Chapel Hill, NC: University of North Carolian Press
Kitcher, P. (1984) 'Kant's Real Self'. In H. W. Wood (ed.), *Self and Nature in Kant's Philosophy*, Ithaca, NY: Cornell University Press: 113–41
—— (1985) *Vaulting Ambition: Sociobiology and the quest for human nature*, Cambridge, Mass.: MIT
Kluckhohn, C. (1944) *Navaho Witchcraft* (1967 edition), Boston, Mass.: Beacon Press
—— (1953) 'Universal Categories of Culture'. In A. L. Kroeber (ed.), *Anthropology Today*, Chicago: University Chicago Press
—— (1954) 'Culture and Behaviour'. In G. Lindzey (ed.), *Handbook of Social Psychology*, vol. 2, Cambridge, Mass.: Addison-Wesley
Knight, M. (1950) *William James: A selection from his writings on psychology*, Harmondsworth: Penguin Books
Kockelmans, J. (1965) *Martin Heidegger: A first introduction to his philosophy*, Pittsburg: Duquesne University Press
—— (1967) *Husserl's Phenomenological Psychology*, Pittsburgh: Duquesne University Press
Koestler, A. (1959) *The Sleepwalkers: A history of man's changing vision of the universe*, Harmondsworth: Penguin Books
Koffka, K. (1925) *The Growth of the Mind*, London: Routledge
—— (1935) *Principles of Gestalt Psychology*, New York: Harcourt Brace
Köhler, W. (1938) *The Place of Value in a World of Facts* (1966 edition), New York: Mentor Books
—— (1947) *Gestalt Psychology*, New York: Liveright
Kojève, A. (1980) *Introduction to the Reading of Hegel*, Ithaca, NY: Cornell University Press
Kolakowski, L. (1973) 'Ideology and Theory'. In T. Bottomore (ed.), *Karl Marx*, Englewood Cliffs, NJ: Prentice Hall: 119–22
—— (1975) *Husserl and the Search for Certitude* (1987 edition), Chicago: University of Chicago Press
—— (1978) *Main Currents of Marxism* Vol. 1: *The Founders*. Vol. 2: *The Golden Age*. Vol. 3: *The Breakdown*, Oxford: Oxford University Press
Kolb, W. L. (1972) 'A Critical Evaluation of Mead's "I" and "Me" Concepts'. In J. G. Manis and S. N. Meltzer, *Symbolic Interactionism: A reader in social psychology* (2nd edition). Boston, Mass.: Allyn & Bacon: 253–61

References

Körner, S. (1955) *Kant*, Harmondsworth: Penguin Books

Kovel, J. (1978) *A Complete Guide to Therapy*, Harmondsworth: Penguin Books

—— (1981) *The Age of Desire: Reflections of a radical psychoanalyst*, New York: Pantheon Books

Koyré, A. (1958) *From the Closed World to the Infinite Universe*, New York: Johns Hopkins University Press

Kroeber, A. L. (1917) 'The Superorganic'. *Amer. Anthrop.*, 19: 163–213

—— (1935) 'History and Science in Anthropology'. *Amer. Anthrop.*, 37: 539–9

—— (1943) 'Franz Boas: The Man'. *Memoirs Amer. Anthrop. Assoc.*, 61

—— (1944) *Configuration of Culture Growth*, Berkely, Calif.: University California Press

—— (1952) *The Nature of Culture*, Chicago: University of Chicago Press

Kroeber, T. (1970) *Alfred Kroeber: A personal configuration*, Berkeley, Calif.: University of California Press

Kropotkin, P. (1970) *Selected Writings on Anarchism and Revolution*, ed. M. A. Miller, Cambridge, Mass: MIT

Kruks, S. (1981) *The Political Philosophy of Merleau-Ponty*, Brighton: Harvester Press

Kuhn, T. S. (1962) *The Structure of Scientific Revolutions*, Chicago: University of Chicago Press

Kuper, A. (1973) *Anthropologists and Anthropology*, Harmondsworth: Penguin Books

—— (ed.) (1977) *The Social Anthropology of Radcliffe-Brown*, London: Routledge & Kegan Paul

Kurzweil, E. (1980) *The Age of Structuralism: Lévi-Strauss to Foucault*, New York: Columbia University Press

Kwant, R. C. (1963) *From Phenomenology to Metaphysics (Merleau-Ponty)*. Pittsburgh: Duquesne University Press

La Barre, W. (1945) 'Some Observations on Character Structure in the Orient: The Japanese'. *Psychiatry*, 8: 319–42

Lacan, J. (1968) *The Language of the Self: The function of language in psychoanalysis*, trans. A. Wilden, Baltimore, Md: Johns Hopkins University Press

—— (1977a) *Four Fundamental Concepts of Psychoanalysis*, London: Hogarth

—— (1977b) *Escrits: A Selection*, trans. A. Sheridan, New York: Norton

La Capra, D. (1972) *Emile Durkheim, Sociologist and Philosopher*, Ithaca, NY: Cornell University Press

Lacqueur, W. Z. (1962) *Young Germany*, London: Routledge & Kegan Paul

La Mettrie, J. O. De (1748) *Man as Machine. L'Homme Machine*. Leyden: Luzac

Lange, F. A. (1866) *History of Materialism (Geschichte des Materialismus)*

Langham, I. (1981) *The Building of British Social Anthropology*, Holland: Reidel Dordrecht

References

Laplache, J. and J. Pontalis (1973) *The Language of Psychoanalysis*, London: Hogarth Press

Larrain, J. (1979) *The Concept of Ideology*, London: Hutchinson

—— (1983) *Marxism and Ideology*, London: Macmillan

Lauer, Q. (1965) *Phenomenology: Its genesis and prospects*, New York: Harper & Row

—— (1976) *A Reading of Hegel's 'Phenomenology of Spirit'*, New York: Fordham University Press

Lavrin, J. (1971) *Nietzsche: A Biographical Introduction*, London: Studio Vista

Lawson, H. (1985) *Reflexity: The post-modern predicament*, London: Hutchinson

Lea, F. A. (1957) *The Tragic Philosopher: A study of Friedrich Nietzsche*, New York: Philosophical Library

Leach, E. (1964) 'Anthropological Aspects of Language: Animal categories and verbal abuse'. In E. H. Lenneberg (ed.), *New Directions in the Study of Language*, Cambridge, Mass.: MIT

—— (1970a) 'The Epistemological Background to Malinowski's Empiricism'. In R. Firth (ed.), *Man and Culture*: 119–38

—— (1970b) *Lévi-Strauss*, London: Fontana/Collins

—— (1981) 'Biology and Social Science: Wedding or Rape?' *Nature*, 291: 267–8

—— (1982) *Social Anthropology*, London: Fontana

Leacock, E. B. (1981) *Myths of Male Dominance*, New York: Monthly Review Press

Leaf, M. J. (1979) *Man, Mind and Science. A history of anthropology*, New York: Columbia University Press

Leahey, T. H. (1987) *A History of Psychology: Main currents in Psychological thought* (2nd edition), Englewood Cliffs, NJ: Prentice Hall

Lee, B. (1985) 'Intellectual Origins of Vygotsky's Semiotic Analysis'. In J. V. Wertsch (ed.), *Culture, Communication and Cognition*: 66–93

Lee, D. (1959) *Freedom and Culture*, Englewood Cliffs, NJ: Prentice Hall

Lefebvre, H. (1968) *The Sociology of Marx*, Harmondsworth: Penguin Books

Lemaire, A. (1977) *Jacques Lacan*, trans. D. Macey, London: Routledge & Kegan Paul

Lemert, C. C. and G. Gillan (1982) *Michel Foucault: Social theory and transgression*, New York: Columbia University Press

Lenin, V. I. (1909) *Materialism and Empirio-Criticism* (1972 edition), Peking: Foreign Language Press

—— (1967) *Karl Marx*, Peking: Foreign Language Press

Leonard, P. (1984) *Personality and Ideology: Towards a materialist understanding of the individual*, London: Macmillan

Lesser, A. (1981) 'Franz Boas', In S. Silverman (ed.), *Totems and Teachers*, Columbia: Columbia University Press: 1–34

LeVine, R. (1973) *Culture, Behaviour and Personality*, Chicago: Aldine

References

Lévi-Strauss, C. (1955) *Tristes Tropiques*, Harmondsworth: Penguin Books
—— (1962) *Totemism*, Harmondsworth: Penguin Books
—— (1963) *Structural Anthropology*, Harmondsworth: Penguin Books
—— (1966) *The Savage Mind*, London: Weidenfeld & Nicolson
—— (1969) *The Elementary Structure of Kinship*, London: Eyre & Spottiswoode
—— (1973) *Structural Anthropology II*, Harmondsworth: Penguin Books
—— (1978) *Myth and Meaning*, London: Routledge & Kegan Paul
—— (1981) *The Naked Man*. Vol. 4: *Introduction to a Science of Mythology*, London: Cape
—— (1987) *Introduction to the Work of Marcel Mauss*, London: Routledge & Kegan Paul
Lewin, K. (1935) *A Dynamic Theory of Personality*, New York: McGraw-Hill
Lewis, D. J. and R. L. Smith (1980) *American Sociology and Pragmatism: Mead, Chicago and symbolic interactionism*, Chicago: University of Chicago Press
Lewis, I. M. (1971) *Ecstatic Religion*, Harmondsworth: Penguin Books
—— (ed.) (1977) *Symbols and Sentiments*, New York: Academic Press
Lichtheim, G. (1961) *Marxism: An Historical and Critical Study*, London: Routledge & Kegan Paul
—— (1970) *Lukács*, London: Fontana/Collins
—— (1971) *From Historicism to Marxist Humanism*. In *From Marx to Hegel*, New York: Seabury Press
Lipshires, S. S. (1974) *Herbert Marcuse: From Marx to Freud and beyond*, Cambridge, Mass.: Schenkmann
Llobera, J. (1981) 'Durkheim, the Durkheimians and their Collective Misrepresentations of Marx'. In J. S. Kahn and J. R. Llobera (eds), *The Anthropology of Pre-capitalist Societies*, London: Macmillan: 214–40
Lock, A. (1981) 'Universals in Human Cognition'. In P. Heelas and A. Cock, *Indigenous Psychologies*, London: Academic Press: 19–36
Locke, J. (1690) *An Essay Concerning Human Understanding*, abridg. and introd. A. D. Woozlet (1964 edition) London: Collins
Lomas, P. (1966) 'Psychoanalysis – Freudian or existential'. In C. Rycroft, *Psychoanalysis Observed*, Harmondsworth: Penguin Books: 116–44
Lorenz, K. (1966) *On Aggression*, trans. M. Latzke, London: Methuen
Lovejoy, A. O. (1936) *The Great Chain of Being* (1982 edition), Cambridge, Mass.: Harvard University Press
Lowen, A. (1975) *Bioenergetics*, Harmondsworth: Penguin Books
Löwith, K. (1967) *From Hegel to Nietzsche: The revolution in nineteenth century thought*, trans. D. E. Green, Garden City, NY: Doubleday London: Constable
Lowrie, W. (1942) *A Short Life of Kierkegaard*, Princeton, NJ: Princeton University Press
Lowy, M. (1979) *Georg Lukács: From Romanticism to Bolshevism*, trans.

P. Camiller, London: New Left Books

Lukács, G. (1971) *History and Class Consciousness: Studies in Marxist dialectics*, trans. R. Livingstone, London: Merlin Press

—— (1975) *The Young Hegel: Studies on the relations between dialectics and economics*, trans. R. Livingstone, London: Merlin Press

Lukes, S. (1973a) *Emile Durkheim: His life and work*, Harmondsworth: Penguin Books

—— (1973b) *Individualism*, Oxford: Basil Blackwell

Lumsden, C. J. and E. O. Wilson (1981) *Genes, Mind and Culture*, Cambridge, Mass.: Harvard University Press

—— (1983) *Promethean Fire: Reflections on the origin of mind*, Cambridge, Mass.: Harvard University Press

Luria, A. R. (1979) *The Making of Mind: A personal account of Soviet pychology*, ed. M. Cole and S. Cole, Cambridge, Mass.: Harvard University Press

Lyons, W. (1980) *Emotion*, Cambridge: Cambridge University Press

McCall, R. J. (1983) *Phenomenological Psychology: An introduction*, Madison, Wisc.: University of Wisconsin Press

McCarney, J. (1980) *The Real World of Ideology*, Brighton: Harvester Press

McCarthy, T. (1978) *The Critical Theory of Jürgen Habermas*, London: Hutchinson

McCloskey, H. J. (1971) *John Stuart Mill: A critical study*, London: Macmillan

McDermott, J. J. (ed.) (1967) *The Writings of William James*, New York: Random House

McDougall, L. (1975) 'The Quest of the Argonauts'. In T. R. Williams, *Psychological Anthropology*, Monitor: 59–102

McDowell, N. (1980) 'The Oceanic Ethnography of Margaret Mead'. *Amer. Anthr.*, 82: 278–303

McGee, W. J. (1901) 'Man's Place in Nature'. *Amer. Anthr.*, 3: 1–13

McGuire, W. (1974) *The Freud/Jung Letters*, trans. R. Manheim and R. F. C. Hull. London: Routledge & Kegan Paul

MacIntyre, A. (1964) 'Existentialism'. In D. J. O'Connor (ed.): *A Critical History of Western Philosophy* New York: Free Press 509–29

—— (1970) *Marcuse*, London: Fontana/Collins

MacKenzie, B. (1977) *Behaviourism and the Limits of Scientific Method*, London: Routledge & Kegan Paul

McLellan, D. (1973) *Karl Marx: His life and thought*, London: Granada

—— (ed.) (1983) *Marx: The first hundred years*, London: Fontana

MacLeod, R. B. (1947) 'The Phenomenological Approach to Social Psychology'. *Psychol. Rev.*, 54: 193–210

MacPherson, C. B. (1962) *The Political Theory of Possessive Individualism*, Oxford: Oxford University Press

MacQuarrie, J. (1973) *Existentialism*, Harmondsworth: Penguin Books

McRae, R. (1976) *Leibniz, Perception, Apperception and Thought*, Toronto:

References

University of Toronto Press

McTaggart, J. M. E. (1896) *Studies in the Hegelian Dialectic*, Cambridge: Cambridge University Press

Mach, E. (1893) *The Science of Mechanics*, trans. T. J. McCormick (original 1883) Chicago: Open Court

—— (1914) *The Analysis of Sensations*, trans. C. M. Williams (original 1886), Chicago: Open Court

Madison, G. B. (1981) *The Phenomenology of Merleau Ponty: A search for the limits of consciousness*, Athens, Ohio: Ohio University Press

Magee, B. (1983) *The Philosophy of Schopenhauer*, Oxford: Clarendon Press

Maier, H. W. (1965) *Three Theories of Child Development*, (rev. edition 1909), New York: Harper & Row

Makkreel, R. A. (1975) *Dilthey: Philosopher of the human sciences*, Princeton, NJ: Princeton University Press

Malcolm, J. (1984) *In the Freud Archives*, New York: Knopf

Malcolm, N. (1964) 'Behaviourism as a Philosophy of Psychology'. In T. E. Wann (ed.), *Behaviour and Phenomenology*: 141–54

—— (1977) *Thought and Knowledge*, Ithaca, NY: Cornell University Press

—— (1984) *Ludwig Wittgenstein: A memoir*, with a biographical sketch by G. H. Von Wright, London: Oxford University Press

Malinowski, B. (1922) *Argonauts of the Western Pacific*, London: Routledge & Kegan Paul

—— (1972) *Sex and Repression in a Savage Society* (1979 edition), London: Routledge & Kegan Paul

—— (1929) *Sexual Life of Savages in New Melanesia* (1908 edition), London: Routledge & Kegan Paul

—— (1963) *Sex, Culture and Myth*, London: Hart Davies

Mandelbaum, D. G. (1971) *History, Man and Reason: A study in nineteenth century thought*, Baltimore, Md: Johns Hopkins University Press

—— (1973) 'The Study of Life History: Gandhi'. *Current Anthrop.*: 177–96

—— (1975) 'Variations on a Theme by Ruth Benedict'. In T. R. Williams, *Psychological Anthropology*: 45–58

Mannoni, O. (1971) *Freud – The theory of the unconscious*, London: New Left Books

Marcel, G. (1952) *Man Against Society*, Chicago: Regnery

Marcuse, H. (1941) *Reason and Revolution: Hegel and the Rise of Social Theory*, London: Routledge & Kegan Paul

—— (1958) *Soviet Marxism: A critical analysis*, Columbia: Columbia University Press (New York: Random Books, 1961 edition)

—— (1964) *One-Dimensional Man*, Boston, Mass.: Beacon Press

—— (1968) *Negation: Essays in critical theory*, London: Allen Lane

—— (1969a) *Eros and Civilization* (original 1955), London: Sphere Books

—— (1969b) *An Essay on Liberation*, Harmondsworth: Penguin Books Boston, Mass.: Beacon Press

—— (1970) *Five Lectures*, London: Allen Lane Boston, Mass.: Beacon Press

—— (1972a) *Studies in Critical Philosophy*, London: New Left Books

—— (1972b) *Counter-Revolution and Revolt*, London: Allen Lane Boston, Mass.: Beacon Press

—— (1978) *The Aesthetic Dimension*, Boston, Mass.: Beacon Press

Marsella, A. J., G. De Vos and F. L. K. Hsu (eds) (1985) *Culture and Self: Asian and western perspectives*, New York: Tavistock

Martin, L. H., H. Gutman and P. H. Hutton (1988) *Technologies of the Self: A seminar with Michel Foucault*, London: Tavistock

Martindale, D. (1961) *The Nature and Types of Sociological Theory*, London: Routledge & Kegan Paul

Marx, K. (1957) *Capital* (original 1867), trans. E. Paul and C. Paul, ed. G. D. H. Cole, vol. 1, London: Dent

—— (1959) *Economic and Philosophical Manuscripts of 1844*, Moscow: Progress Publishers

—— (1973) *Grundrisse*, trans. and ed. M. Nicolaus, Harmondsworth: Penguin Books

—— and F. Engels (1965) *The German Ideology*, London: Lawrence & Wishart

—— (1968) *Selected Works*, London: Lawrence & Wishart

Maslow, A. H. (1962) *Toward a Psychology of Being*, New York: Van Nostrand

Masson, J. M. (1984) *The Assault on Truth: Freud's suppression of the seduction theory*, Harmondsworth: Penguin Books

Masterson, P. (1973) *Atheism and Alienation*, Harmondsworth: Penguin Books

Mattick, P. (1972) *Critique of Marcuse*, London: Merlin Press

Mauss, M. (1925) *The Gift* (1970 edition), trans. I. Cunnison, London: Cohen & West

—— (1972) *A General Theory of Magic* (with H. Hubert), London: Routledge & Kegan Paul

—— (1979) *Sociology and Psychology*, trans. B. Brewster, London: Routledge & Kegan Paul

—— (1985) *A Category of the Human Mind: The notion of person, the notion of self*, trans. W. D. Halls (original 1938). Reprinted in *J. Anthr. Inst.*, 68; and M. Carrithers et al. (eds), *The Category of the Person*: 1–25

May, R. et al. (eds) (1958) *Existence: A new dimension in psychiatry and psychology*, New York: Basic Books

—— (ed.) (1961) *Existential Psychology*, New York: Random House

—— (1983) *The Discovery of Being: Writings in existential psychology*, New York: Norton

Mead, G. H. (1934) *Mind, Self and Society: from the standpoint of a social behaviourist* (1965 edition), Chicago: University of Chicago Press

—— (1936) ed. M. H. Moore, *Movements of Thought in the Nineteenth Century*, Chicago: University of Chicago Press

—— (1964) *Selected Writings*, ed. and Introd. A. J. Reck, Indianapolis:

Bobbs-Merrill
—— (1965) *The Social Psychology of George Herbert Mead*, ed. and introd. A. Strauss, Chicago: Chicago University Press (Phoenix edition)

Mead, M. (1928) *Coming of Age in Samoa* (1963 edition), Harmondsworth: Penguin Books

—— (1920) *Growing up in New Guinea* (1954 edition), Harmondsworth: Penguin Books

—— (1932) 'An Investigation of the Thought of Primitive Children with Special Reference to Animism'. *J. R. Anthr. Soc.*, 62: 173–90. Also in Spindler (1978) *The Making of Psychological Anthropology*.

—— (1935) *Sex and Temperament in Three Primitive Societies*, London: Routledge & Kegan Paul

—— (1942) *And Keep Your Powder Dry* (1975 edition), New York: Morrow

—— (1950) *Male and Female* (1967 edition), Harmondsworth: Penguin Books

—— (1951) *Soviet Attitudes to Authority*, New York: Rand Corporation

—— (1952) 'Some Relationships between Social Anthropology and Psychiatry'. In F. Alexander and H. Ross, *Dynamic Psychology*, Chicago: University of Chicago Press: 401–48

—— (1953) 'National Character'. In A. L. Kroeber (ed.), *Anthropology Today*, Chicago: University of Chicago Press: 396–421

—— (1954) 'The Swaddling Hypothesis: Its reception'. *Amer. Anthr.*, 56: 395–409

—— (1959) *An Anthropologist at Work: The writings of Ruth Benedict*, Boston, Mass.: Houghton Mifflin

—— (1964) *Continuity in Cultural Evolution*, New Haven, Conn.: Yale University Press.

—— (1972) *Blackberry Winter: My earlier years*, New York: Washington Square Press

—— (1974) *Ruth Benedict*, New York: Columbia University Press

—— (1978) 'The Evocation of Psychologically Relevant Response in Ethnological Fieldwork'. In G. D. Spindler (ed.), *The Making of Psychological Anthropology*: 89–139

—— and G. Bateson (1942) *Balinese Character: A photographic analysis*, New York: Academy of Sciences

Megill, A. (1985) *Prophets of Extremity: Nietzsche, Heidegger, Foucault, Derrida*, Berkeley, Calif.: University of California Press

Mehta, J. L. (1971) *The Philosophy of Martin Heidegger*, New York: Harper & Row

Menzies, K. (1977) *Talcott Parsons and the Social Image of Man*, London: Routledge & Kegan Paul

Mepham, J. (1985) 'Who Makes History: Althusser's anti-humanism'. In R. Edgley and R. Osborne, *Radical Philosophy* Reader: 137–57

Merchant, C. (1980) *The Death of Nature*, New York: Harper

Merleau-Ponty, M. (1962) *Phenomenology of Perception*, trans. C. Smith

References

(original 1945), London: Routledge & Kegan Paul
—— (1963) *The Structure of Behaviour* (original 1942), trans. A. Fisher, Boston, Mass.: Beacon Press
—— (1964a) *Sense and Non-Sense*, trans. H. L. and P. A. Dreyfus (original 1948), Evanston, Ill.: Northwestern University Press
—— (1964b) *Signs*, trans. and introd. R. C. McCleary (original 1960), Evanston, Ill.: Northwestern University Press
Merquior, J. G. (1985) *Foucault*, London: Fontana
—— (1986a) *From Prague to Paris: A critique of structuralist and post-structuralist thought*, London: Verso
—— (1986b) *Western Marxism*, London: Granada
Mészáros, I. (1970) *Marx's Theory of Alienation*, London: Merlin
—— (1972) *Lukács' Concept of Dialectic*, London: Merlin Press
—— (1986) *Philosophy, Ideology and Social Science: Essays in negation and affirmation*, Brighton: Wheatsheaf Books
Metraux, R. (1980) 'Margaret Mead: A biographical sketch'. *Amer. Anthrop.*, 82: 262–9
Midgley (1985) *Evolution as a Religion* London: Methuen
Milgram, S. (1963) 'Behavioural Study of Obedience'. *J. Abn. Soc. Psychol.*, 67: 371–8
—— (1974) *Obedience to Authority*, New York: Harper & Row
Mill, J. (1829) *Analysis of the Phenomenon of the Human Mind*, London: Longmans & Dyer
Mill, J. S. (1962) *Utilitarianism, (Including 'On Liberty', 'Essay on Bentham' and Writings by Bentham & Austin)*, ed. and introd. M. Warnock, London: Collins/Fontana
Miller, D. L. (1973) *George Herbert Mead: Self, language and the world*, Austin, IX: University of Texas Press
Miller, G. (1964) *Psychology: The science of mental life*, Harmondsworth: Penguin Books
Miller, J. (1979) *History and Human Existence: From Marx to Merleau-Ponty*, Berkeley, Calif.: University of California Press
Millett, K. (1971) *Sexual Politics*, London: Sphere Books
Mills, C. W. (1963) *The Marxists*, Harmondsworth: Penguin Books
—— (1966) *Sociology and Pragmatism: The higher learning in America*, ed. and introd. I. I. Horowitz, Oxford: Oxford University Press
Mintz, S. W. (1981) 'Ruth Benedict'. In S. Silverman (ed.), *Totems and Teachers*, Columbia: Columbia University Press: 141–70
Mischel, W. (1980) *Introduction to Personality*, New York: Holt Rinehart
Mitchell, J. (1974) *Psychoanalysis and Feminism*, Harmondsworth: Penguin Books
Modell, J. (1984) *Ruth Benedict: Patterns of a life*, London: Chatto & Windus
Moore, T. E. and A. E. Harris (1978) 'Language and Thought in Piagetian Theory'. In L. S. Siegel and C. J. Brainerd, *Alternatives to Piaget*, New York: Academic Press: 131–52

Moorehead, A. (1969) *Darwin and the 'Beagle'*, Harmondsworth: Penguin Books

Morris, B. (1971) 'Reflections on Role Analysis'. *Brit. J. Sociol.*, 22: 395–409

—— (1978) 'Are There Any Individuals in India? A Critique of Dumont's Theory of the Individual'. *Eastern Anthrop.*, 31: 365–77

—— (1979) 'Scientific Myths: Man the Mighty Hunter'. *New Humanist*, 94: 129–30

—— (1981) 'Changing Views of Nature'. *The Ecologist* 11: 130–7

—— (1982) *Forest Traders*, London: Athlone Press

—— (1985) 'The Rise and Fall of the Human Subject'. *Man*, 20: 722–42

—— (1987) *Anthropological Studies of Religion*, Cambridge: Cambridge University Press

Morris, C. W. (1970) *The Pragmatic Movement in American Philosophy*, New York: G. Braziller

Morris, D. (1967) *The Naked Ape*, London: Cape

Moscovici, S. (1981) Foreword to P. Heelas and A. Lock *Indigenous Psychologies* New York: Academic Press

Mossner, E. C. (1954) *The Life of David Hume*, Oxford: Clarendon Press

Mouzelis, N. (1971) 'A Critical Note on Total Institutions'. *Sociology*, 5: 1

Murdoch, I. (1971) *Sartre*, London: Fontana

Murdock, G. P. (1945) 'The Common Denominators of Cultures'. In R. Linton (ed.), *The Science of Man in the World Crisis*, New York: Columbia University Press

Murphy, G. and J. K. Kovach (1972) *Historical Introduction to Modern Psychology* (original 1949), London: Routledge & Kegan Paul

Murphy, R. F. (1972) *The Dialectics of Social Life*, London: Allen & Unwin

Murray, M. (ed.) (1978) *Heidegger and Modern Philosophy*, New Haven, Conn.: Yale University Press

Muuss, R. E. (1962) *Theories of Adolescence*, New York: Random House

Nadel, S. F. (1970) 'Malinowski on Magic and Religion'. In R. Firth (ed.), *Man and Culture*: 189–208

Nash, R. (1967) *Wilderness and the American Mind*, New Haven, Conn.: Yale University Press

Natanson, M. (ed.) (1970) *Phenomenology and Social Reality: Essays in memory of Alfred Schutz*, The Hague: M. Nijhoff

Neumann, E. (1955) *The Great Mother: An analysis of the archetype*, Princeton University Press

Neumann, F. (1944) *Bohemoth: The structure and practice of national socialism 1933–1944*, London: Gollancz

New Left Review (1978) *Western Marxism: A Critical Reader*, London: Verso

Nietzsche, F. (1956) *The Brith of Tragedy* and *The Genealogy of Morals*, trans. F. Golffing, New York: Doubleday

—— (1961) *Thus Spoke Zarathustra*, trans. and introd. R. J. Hollingdale,

References

Harmondsworth: Penguin Books
—— (1968) *Twilight of the Idols and the Anti-Christ*, trans. and introd. R. J. Hollingdale, Harmondsworth: Penguin Books
—— (1972) *Beyond Good and Evil*, trans. and introd. R. J. Hollingdale, Harmondsworth: Penguin Books
—— (1977) *A Nietzsche Reader*, trans. and introd. R. J. Hollingdale, Harmondsworth: Penguin Books
—— (1986) *Human, All Too Human*, Cambridge: Cambridge University Press
Niehardt, J. G. (1972) *Black Elk Speaks*, London: Barrie & Jenkins
Nisbet, R. A. (1974) *The Sociology of Emile Durkheim*, Oxford: Oxford University Press
—— (1979) 'Conservatism'. In Bottomore and Nisbet (eds), *A History of Sociological Analysis*: 80–117
Norman, R. (1976) *Hegel's Phenomenology: A philosophical introduction*, Hassocks: Harvester Press
Norris, C. (1982) *Deconstruction: Theory and Practice*, London: Methuen
—— (1987) *Derrida*, London: Fontana
Nova, F. (1968) *Freidrich Engels: His contribution to political theory*, London: Vision
Novack, G. (1965) *The Origins of Materialism*, New York: Pathfinder Press
—— (1966) *Existentialism Versus Marxism*, ed. and introd. New York: Dell Publishing
—— (1969) *Empiricism and its Evolution: A Marxist view*, New York: Pathfinder Press
—— (1971) *An Introduction to the Logic of Marxism*, New York: Pathfinder Press
—— (1973) *Humanism and Socialism*, New York: Pathfinder Press
—— (1975) *Pragmatism versus Marxism*, New York: Pathfinder Press
—— (1978) *Polemics in Marxist Philosophy*, New York: Monad Press
Nugent, S. L. (1985) 'Replacing the Mind: Implicit and explicit models of cognition'. *Critique of Anthrop.*, 5: 3–21
Nyiti, R. M. (1982) 'The Validity of "Cultural Differences Explanations" for Cross-Cultural Variations in the Rate of Piagetian Cognitive Development'. In D. A. Wagner and H. W. Stevenson, *Cultural Perspectives on Child Development*, San Francisco: W. H. Freeman: 146–65
Oakley, A. (1972) *Sex, Gender and Society*, London: Temple Smith
Ober, J. D. (1982) 'On Sexuality and Politics in the Work of Herbert Marcuse'. In M. Brace (ed.), *Human Sexual Relations*, Harmondsworth: Penguin Books: 82–107
O'Donnell, J. M. (1985) *The Origins of Behaviourism: American psychology 1870–1920*, New York: University Press
Okely, J. (1975) 'The Self and Scienticism'. *J. Oxford Anthr. Soc.*, 6: 171–88
—— (1986) *Simone de Beauvoir: A re-reading*, London: Virago
Ornstein, R. E. (1972) *The Psychology of Consciousness*, Harmondsworth:

Penguin Books

Osborn, R. (1965) *Marxism and Psychoanalysis*, New York: Delta

Overing, J. (ed.) (1985) *Reason and Morality*, London: Tavistock

Palmer, R. E. (1969) *Hermeneutics: Interpretation Theory in Schleiermacher, Dilthey, Heidegger and Gadamer*, Evanston, Ill.: Northwestern University Press

Parkin, D. (1985) 'Reason, Emotion and the Embodiment of Power'. In J. Overing (ed), Reason and Morality: 131–51

Parkinson, G. H. R. (1973) *Leibniz: Philosophical writings*, ed. and trans. M. Morris and G. H. R. Parkinson, London: Dent

—— (1977) *Georg Lukács*, London: Routledge & Kegan Paul

Parsons, A. (1969) 'Is the Oedipus Complex Universal?' In W. Muensterberger and S. Axeland (eds), *The Psychoanalytic Study of Society*, vol. 3, New York: Intern. University Press: 278–301, 310–26

Parsons, T. (1937) *The Structure of Social Action*, New York: McGraw-Hill.

—— (1951) *The Social System*, New York: Free Press

—— et al. (1955) *Family, Socialization and Interaction Process*, Glencoe, Ill.: Free Press

—— (1964) *Social Structure and Personality*, New York: Free Press

—— (1968) 'Emile Durkheim'. In D. L. Sills (ed.), *International Encyclopaedia of the Social Sciences*, vol. 4, New York: Macmillan: 311–20

Passmore, J. (1952) *Hume's Intentions*, Cambridge: Cambridge University Press

—— (1957) *A Hundred Years of Philosophy* (1968 edition), Harmondsworth: Penguin Books

Paterson, R. W. K. (1971) *The Nihilistic Egoist: Max Stirner*, Oxford: Oxford University Press

Patience, A. and J. W. Smith (1986) 'Derek Freeman and Samoa: The making and unmaking of a biobehavioural myth'. *Amer. Anthrop.*, 88: 157–62

Paulsen, F. (1963) *Immanuel Kant: His life and doctrine*, New York: Ungar

Pavlov, I. P. (1927) *Conditioned Reflexes*, trans. G. V. Anrep, Oxford: Oxford University Press

—— (1928) *Lectures on Conditional Reflexes*, trans. W. H. Gantt, New York: Intern Publ

Peacock, J. L. (1975) *Consciousness and Change: Symbolic anthropology in evolutionary perspective*, Oxford: Basil Blackwell

Pearce, R. H. (1953) *Savagism and Civilization*, Baltimore, Md: Johns Hopkins University Press

Pears, D. (1971) *Wittgenstein*, London: Fontana/Collins

Peel, J. D. Y. (1971) *Herbert Spencer, the Evolution of a Sociologist*, London: Heinemann

Perry, R. B. (1935) *The Thought and Character of William James*, 2 vols, Boston, Mass.: Little, Brown

Peters, R. S. (ed.) (1953) *Brett's History of Psychology*, London: Allen &

References

Unwin

Peyre, H. (1960) 'Durkheim: The man, his time and his intellectual background'. In K. H. Wolff (ed.), *Emile Durkheim 1858–1917*. Columbus, Ohio: State University Press: 32–76

Piaget, J. (1926) *The Language and Thought of the Child* (original 1923), London: Routledge & Kegan Paul

—— (1929) *The Child's Conception of the World* (original 1926), London: Kegan Paul

—— (1953) *Logic and Psychology*, Manchester: Manchester University Press

—— (1954) *The Child's Construction of Reality* (original 1936), London: Routledge & Kegan Paul

—— (1966) 'Need and Significance of Cross-Cultural Studies in Genetic Psychology'. *Int. J. Psychol.*, 1: 3–13

—— (1968) *Six Psychological Studies*, trans. A. Tenzer, ed. and introd. D. Elkind, New York: Vintage Books

—— (1970) *Genetic Epistemology*, Columbia: Columbia University Press

—— (1971) *Structuralism*, trans. C. Maschler, London: Routledge & Kegan Paul

—— (1972) *Insights and Illusions of Philosophy*, trans. W. Mays, London: Routledge & Kegan Paul

Piatelli-Palmarini, M. (1980) *Language and Learning: The debate between Jean Piaget and Noam Chomsky*, Cambridge, Mass.: Harvard University Press

Piers, G. and M. Singer (1953) *Shame and Guilt*, Springfield, Ill.: C. Thomas

Pippin, R., A. Feenberg and C. P. Webel (1988) *Marcuse: Critical theory and the promise of Utopia*, London: Macmillan

Pitcher, P. (1984) 'Kant's Real Self'. In A. W. Wood (ed.), *Self and Nature in Kant's Philosophy*: 113–47

Pivčević, E. (1970) *Husserl and Phenomenology*, London: Hutchinson

—— (ed) (1975) *Phenomenology and Philosophical Understanding*, Cambridge: Cambridge University Press

Plamenatz, J. (1966) *The Eight Utilitarians*, Oxford: Basil Blackwell

—— (1975) *Karl Marx's Philosophy of Man*, Oxford: Oxford University Press

Polhemus, T. (1978) *Social Aspects of the Human Body*, Harmondsworth: Penguin Books

Popper, K. R. (1945) *The Open Society and its Enemies*, vol. 2: *Hegel and Marx*, London: Routledge & Kegan Paul

—— (1957) *The Poverty of Historicism*, London: Routledge & Kegan Paul

—— (1963) *Conjectures and Refutations*, London: Routledge & Kegan Paul

—— and J. Eccles (1977) *The Self and its Brain*, New York: Springer

Poster, M. (1975) *Existential Marxism in Postwar France: Sartre to Althusser*, Princeton, NJ: Princeton University Press

—— (1978) *Critical Theory of the Family*, London: Pluto Press

—— (1979) *Sartre's Marxism*, London: Pluto Press

—— (1984) *Foucault, Marxism and History: Mode of production versus mode of information*, Cambridge: Polity Press

Pribram, K. H. (1973) 'Operant Behaviourism: Fad, factory and fantasy'. In H. Wheeler (ed.), *Beyond the Primitive Society*: 101–12

Prigogine, I. and I. Stengers (1984) *Order out of Chaos: Man's new dialogue with nature*, New York: Bantam

Progoff, I. (1953) *Jung's Psychology and its Social Meaning*, New York: Grove Press

Psathas, G. (ed.) (1973) *Phenomenological Sociology: Issues and applications*, New York: Wiley

Pusey, M. (1987) *Jürgen Habermas*, London: Tavistock

Quinn, S. (1987) *A Mind of Her Own: The life of Karen Horney*, London: Macmillan

Rabil, A. (1967) *Merleau-Ponty: Existentialist of the social world*, New York: Columbia University Press

Rabinow, P. (1984) *The Foucault Reader*, Harmondsworth: Penguin Books

Radcliffe-Brown, A. R. (1922) *The Andaman Islanders* (1964 edition), Glencoe, Ill.: Free Press

—— (1948) *A Natural Science of Society*, New York: Free Press

—— (1952) *Structure and Function in Primitive Society* (1968 edition), London: Cohen & West

Raghaviah, V. (1962) *The Yanadis*, New Delhi: Bharatiya Adimjati Sevk Songh

Ragland-Sullivan, E. (1985) *Lacques Jacan and the Philosophy of Psychoanalysis*, London: Croom Helm

Raison, T. (1969) *The Founding Fathers of Social Science*, Harmondsworth: Penguin Books

Rancurello, A. C. (1968) *A Study of Franz Brentano. His psychological standpoint and his significance in the history of psychology*, New York: Academic Press

Reardon, B. M. G. (1977) *Hegel's Philosophy of Religion*, London: Macmillan

Reck, A. J. (ed. and introd.) (1964) *George Herbert Mead: Selected writings*. Indianapolis: Bobbs-Merrill

Rée, J. (1974) *Descartes*, London: Allen Lane

—— (1984) 'Metaphor and Metaphysics: The end of philosophy and Derrida'. *Radical Philosophy*, 38: 29–33

—— (1985) 'Marxist Modes'. In R. Edgley and R. Osborne, *Radical Philosophy Reader*: 337–60

Reed, E. (1975) *Woman's Evolution*, New York: Pathfinder Press

Reich, I. O. (1969) *Wilhelm Reich: A personal biography*, London: Elek Books

Reich, W. (1929) *Dialectical Materialism and Psychoanalysis* (1934 edition), London: Socialist Reproduction

—— (1930) *The Sexual Revolution*, trans. T. P. Wolfe (1951 edition), London: Vision

References

—— (1932) *The Invasion of Compulsory Sex-Morality* (1972 edition), Harmondsworth: Penguin Books

—— (1933a) *Character Analysis*, New York: Farrar, Strauss

—— (1933b) *The Mass Psychology of Fascism*, trans. V. R. Carfagno, Harmondsworth: Penguin Books

—— (1942) *The Function of the Orgasm* (original 1927), London: Panther Books

—— (1949) *Character Analysis*, New York: Farrar, Strauss

—— (1972) *Sex-Pol Essays 1929–1934*, ed. L. Baxandall, New York: Vintage Books

Reiche, R. (1970) *Sexuality and Class Struggle*, trans. S. Bennett, London: New Left Books

Rescher, N. (1979) *Leibniz: An introduction to his philosophy*, Oxford: Basil Blackwell

Rickert, H. (1986) *The Limits of Concept Formation in Natural Science*, Cambridge: Cambridge University Press

Rickman, H. P. (1961) *Meaning in History: W. Dilthey's thoughts on history and society*. London: Allen & Unwin

—— (ed.) (1976) with introduction, *Wilhelm Dilthey: Selected writings*, Cambridge: Cambridge University Press

Ricoeur, P. (1963) 'Structure et Hermeneutique'. *Esprit* no. 11

—— (1967) *Husserl, An analysis of his phenomenology*. Evanston, Ill.: Northwestern University Press

—— (1970) *Freud and Philosophy: An essay in interpretation*, New Haven, Conn.: Yale University Press

—— (1974) 'The Question of the Subject'. In *The Conflict of Interpretations*, ed. D. Ihde, Evanston, Ill.: Northwestern University Press

—— (1981) *Hermeneutics and the Human Sciences*, ed. J. B. Thompson, Cambridge: Cambridge University Press

Ridington, R. (1988) 'Knowledge, Power and the Individual in Subarctic Hunting Societies'. *Amer. Anthrop.*, 90: 98–110

Rieber, R. W. (ed.) (1980) *Wilhelm Wundt and the Making of a Scientific Psychology*, New York: Plenum Press

Rieff, P. (1959) *Freud: The mind of the moralist* (3rd edition, 1979), Chicago: University of Chicago Press

—— (1966) *The Triumph of the Therapeutic: Uses of faith after Freud*, Harmondsworth: Penguin Books

Riesman, D. et al. (1950) *The Lonely Crowd*, New Haven, Conn.: Yale University Press

Ritter, P. (1958) *Wilhelm Reich*, Nottingham: Ritter Press

Rivers, W. H. R. (1920) *Instinct and the Unconscious*, Cambridge: Cambridge University Press

—— (1923) *Conflict and Dream*, London: Kegan Paul

—— (1926) *Psychology and Ethnology*, ed. G. E. Smith, London: Kegan Paul

Roazen, P. (1968) *Freud: Political and social thought*, New York: Knopf
—— (1976a) *Freud and his Followers*, London: Allen Lane
Robert, M. (1966) *The Psychoanalytic Revolution: Sigmund Freud's life and achievement*, trans. K. Morgan, London: Allen & Unwin
Robinson, P. A. (1970) *The Sexual Radicals: Reich, Roheim, Marcuse*, London: Paladin
Rock, P. (1979) *The Making of Symbolic Interactionism*. Totowa, N.J.: Rowan & Littlefield
Rogers, C. (1961) *On Becoming a Person*, New York: Houghton Mifflin
Roheim, G. (1925) *Australian Totemism*, London: Allen & Unwin
—— (1930) *Animism and the Divine King*, London: Kegan Paul
—— (1932) 'Psychoanalysis of Primitive Cultural Types'. *Intern. J. Psychoanal.*, 8: 1–224
—— (1934) *The Riddle of the Sphinx*, New York: Harper
—— (1945) *The Eternal Ones of the Dream*, New York: Intern. University Press
—— (1950) *Psychoanalysis and Anthropology*, New York: Intern, University Press
—— (1969) 'The Psychoanalytic Interpretation of Culture'. In W. Muensterberger (ed.), *Man and his Culture*, New York: Rapp & Whiting: 31–52
Rorty, R. (1980) *Philosophy and the Mirror of Nature* (1986 edition), Oxford: Basil Blackwell
—— (1982) *The Consequence of Pragmatism*, Minneapolis: University of Minnesota Press
Rosaldo, M. Z. (1974) 'Women, Culture and Society: Theoretical overview'. In M. Rosaldo and L. Lamphere, *Woman, Culture and Society*, Stanford, Calif.: University of California Press: 17–42
Rose, G. (1978) *The Melancholy Science: An introduction to the thought of T. W. Adorno*, London: Macmillan
—— (1981) *Hegel contra Sociology*, London: Athlone Press
—— (1984) *Dialectic of Nihilism: Post-structuralism and law*, Oxford: Basil Blackwell
Rose, S., L. J. Kamin and R. C. Lewontin (1984) *Not in our Genes*, Harmondsworth: Penguin Books
Rosen, S. (1974) *G. W. F. Hegel: An introduction to the science of wisdom*, New Haven, Conn.: Yale University Press
Rossi, I. (ed.) (1974) *The Unconscious in Culture*, London: E. P. Dutton
—— (1983) *From the Sociology of Symbols to the Sociology of Signs*, New York: Columbia University Press
Rossi, P. (1968) *Francis Bacon: From magic to science*, London: Routledge & Kegan Paul
Roszak, T. (1969) *The Making of a Counter-Culture*, New York: Doubleday
Rotman, B. (1977) *Jean Piaget: psychologist of the real*, Hassocks: Harvester Press

Roy, M. N. (1940) *Materialism – An outline of the history of scientific thought* (1982 edition), Delhi: Ajanta Books

Royce, J. (1885) *The Religious Aspect of Philosophy*, Boston: Houghton Mifflin

—— (1892) *The Spirit of Modern Philosophy*, Boston, Mass.: Houghton Mifflin

Rubins, J. (1978) *Karen Horney: Gentle rebel of psychoanalysis*, New York: Dial Press

Rucker, D. (1969) *The Chicago Pragmatism*, Minneapolis: University of Minnesota Press

Runciman, W. G. (1969) 'What is Structuralism?' *Brit. J. Sociol.*, 20: 253–65

Ruse, M. (1979) *Sociobiology: Sense or nonsense?* Dordrecht: Reider

Russell, B. (1921) *The Analysis of Mind*, London: Allen & Unwin

—— (1946) *History of Western Philosophy*, London: Allen & Unwin

—— (1959) *My Philosophical Development*, London: Allen & Unwin

Ryan, A. (1970) *The Philosophy of John Stuart Mill*, London: Macmillan

—— (1974) *J. S. Mill*, London: Routledge & Kegan Paul

Ryan, M. (1982) *Marxism and Deconstruction: A critical articulation*, Baltimore, Md.: Johns Hopkins University Press

Rycroft, C. (1966) 'Introduction: Causes and meanings'. In *Psychoanalysis Observed*, Harmondsworth: Penguin Books

—— (1971) *Reich*, London: Fontana

—— (1985) *Psychoanalysis and Beyond*, London: Chatto & Windus

Ryle, G. (1949) *The Concept of Mind*, Harmondsworth: Penguin Books

Sahlins, M. (1976a) *Culture and Practical Reason*, Chicago: Chicago University Press

—— (1976b) *The Use and Abuse of Biology: An anthropological critique of sociobiology*, London: Tavistock

Santayana, G. (1951) 'Dewey's Naturalistic Metaphysics'. In P. A. Schilpp (ed.), *The Philosophy of John Dewey*: 245–61

Sapir, E. (1949) *Culture, Language and Personality: Selected essays*, ed. D. G. Mandelbaum, Berkeley, Calif.: University of California Press

Sartre, J. P. (1943) *Being and Nothingness*, trans. H. E. Barnes (1969 university paperback edition), London: Methuen

—— (1945) 'Existentialism is a Humanism'. In G. Novack (ed.), *Existentialism versus Marxism* (1966), New York: Dell: 70–84

—— (1948) *The Emotions: Outlines of a theory*, trans. B. Frechtman, New York: Philosophical Library

—— (1948) *The Psychology of Imagination*, trans. B. Frechtman, New York: Citadel Press

—— (1962) *Existential Psychoanalysis*, Chicago: Regnery

—— (1963) *Existentialism and Humanism*, trans. P. Mairet (original 1948), London: Methuen

—— (1963) *Search for a Method*, trans. H. E. Barnes, New York: Knopf,

References

Random House
—— (1971) *Sketch for a Theory of the Emotions*, trans. P. Mairet (original 1939), London: Methuen
—— (1976) *Critique of a Dialectical Reason. Theory of practical ensembles*, trans. A. Sheridan-Smith (original 1960), London: New Left Books
Sarup, M. (1983) *Marxism/Structuralism/Education*, London: Falmer Press
Saussure, F. de (1959) *Course in General Linguistics*, trans. W. Baskin, London: Owen
Saxe, G. B. (1983) 'Piaget and Anthropology'. *Amer. Anthrop.*, 85: 136–43
Schaff, A. (1963) *A Philosophy of Man*, New York: Monthly Review Press
—— (1970) *Marxism and the Human Individual*, New York: McGraw-Hill
—— (1973) *Language and Cognition*, New York: McGraw-Hill
—— (1978) *Structuralism and Marxism*, Oxford: Pergamon
Scheff, T. J. (1966) *Being Mentally Ill*, Chicago: Aldine
Scheffler, I. (1974) *Four Pragmatists: A critical introduction to Peirce, James, Mead and Dewey*, London: Routledge & Kegan Paul
Schellenberg, J. A. (1978) *Masters of Social Psychology. Freud, Mead, Levin, Skinner*, New York: Oxford: University Press
Schilpp, P. A. (ed.) (1951) *The Philosophy of John Dewey* (2nd edition), La Salle, Ill.: Open Court
Schmidt, A. (1983) *History and Structure*, trans. J. Herf (original 1971), Cambridge, Mass.: MIT
Schmidt, J. (1985) *Maurice Merleau-Ponty: Between phenomenology and structuralism*, London: Macmillan
Schnädelbach, H. (1984) *Philosophy in Germany 1831–1933*, Cambridge: Cambridge University Press
Schneewind, J. B. (ed.) (1968) *Mill: A collection of critical essays*, London: Macmillan
Scholte, B. (1966) 'Epistemic Paradigms'. *Amer. Anthrop.*, 68: 1192–201. Reprinted in In E. N. and T. Hayes, *C. Lévi-Strauss. The anthropologist as hero*, Cambridge, Mass.: MIT. 108–22
Schopenhauer, A. (1819) *The World as Will and Representation*, trans. E. F. J. Payne, Colorado: Falcon's Wing Press
—— (1970) *Essays and Aphorisms*, trans. and introd. R. J. Hollingdale, Harmondsworth: Penguin Books
Schroyer, T. (1973) *The Critique of Domination: The origins and development of critical theory*. Boston, Mass.: Beacon Press
Schutz, A. (1967) *The Phenomenology of the Social World*, trans. G. Walsh and F. Lehnert, Evanston, Ill.: Northwestern University Press
Scruton, R. (1981) *A Short History of Modern Philosophy, from Descartes to Wittgenstein*, London: Routledge & Kegan Paul (Ark)
Sears, R. et al. (1957) *Patterns of Child Rearing*, Evanston, Ill.: Row Peterson
Sedgwick, P. (1972) 'R. D. Laing: Self, symptom and society'. In Boyers and Orrill, *Laing and Anti-Psychiatry*: 11–47

References

—— (1982) *Psychopolitics*, London: Pluto Press

Seliger, M. (1977) *The Marxist Conception of Ideology*, Cambridge: Cambridge University Press

Service, E. R. (1985) *A Century of Controversy. Ethnological issues from 1860 to 1960*, New York: Academic Press

Sève, L. (1975) *Marxism and the Theory of Human Personality*, London: Lawrence & Wishart

—— (1978) *Man In Marxist Theory: And the psychology of personality*, Hassocks: Harvester Press

Shalvey, T. (1979) *Claude Lévi-Strauss: Social psychotherapy and the collective unconscious*, Brighton: Harvester Press

Shand, A. F. (1914) *The Foundations of Character*, London

Sharaf, M. (1983) *Fury on Earth: A biography of Wilhelm Reich*, London: Hutchinson

Sheridan, A. (1980) *Michel Foucault. The will to truth*, London: Tavistock

Shore, B. (1981) 'Sexuality and Gender in Samoa: Conceptions and missed conceptions'. In S. B. Ortiner and H. Whitehead (eds), *Sexual Meanings: The cultural construction of gender and sexuality*, Cambridge: Cambridge University Press

—— (1983) 'Paradox Regained: Freeman's Margaret Mead and Samoa'. *Amer. Anthrop.*, 85: 935–44

Shotter, J. (1975) *Images of Man in Psychological Research*, London: Methuen

Showalter, E. (1985) *The Female Malady: Women, madness and English culture 1830–1980*, London: Virago Press

Shweder, R. A. (1982) 'On Savages and other Children' (review of C. R. Hallpike, *The Foundations of Primitive Thought*). *Amer. Anthrop.*, 83: 354–66

—— and E. Bourne (1982) 'Does the concept of the Person Vary Cross-Culturally?' In A. J. Marsella and G. White (eds), *Cultural Conceptions of Mental Health and Therapy*, Boston, Mass.: Reidel: 97–137

—— and R. A. LeVine (eds) (1984) *Culture Theory: Essays on mind, self and emotion*, Cambridge: Cambridge University Press

Silverman, S. (ed.) (1981) *Totems and Teachers*, New York: Columbia University Press

Singer, J. (1977) *Androgyny: Towards a new theory of sexuality*, London: Routledge & Kegan Paul

Singer, M. (1978) 'For a Semiotic Anthropology'. In T. A. Sebeck (ed.), *Sight, Sound and Vision*, Bloomington, Ind.: Indiana University Press

—— (1980) 'Signs of the Self: An exploration in semiotic anthropology'. *Amer. Anthrop.*, 82: 485–50

Singer, P. (1980) *Marx*, London: Oxford University Press

—— (1983) *Hegel*, London: Oxford University Press

Skinner, B. F. (1938) *The Behaviour of Organism: An experimental analysis*, New York: Appleton-Century

—— (1953) *Science and Human Behaviour*, New York: Macmillan/Free

References

Press

—— (1954) 'Critique of Psychoanalytic Concepts and Theories'. *Scient. Monthly*. Reprinted in H. Feigl and M. Scriven (eds), *The Foundations of Science and the Concepts of Psychology and Psychoanalysis*, Minneapolis: University of Minnesota Press: 77–87

—— (1957) *Verbal Behaviour*, New York: Appleton-Century

—— (1971) *Beyond Freedom and Dignity*, New York: Knopf Harmondsworth: Penguin Books

—— (1974) *About Behaviourism*, New York: Knopf

—— (1976) *Particulars of My Life*, New York: Knopf

Slater, P. (1977) *Origins and Significance of the Frankfurt School: A Marxist perspective*, London: Routledge & Kegan Paul

Sleeper, R. W. (1986) *The Necessity of Pragmatism: John Dewey's conception of philosophy*, New Haven, Conn.: Yale University Press

Smart, B. (1983) *Foucault, Marxism and Critique*, London: Routledge & Kegan Paul

—— (1985) *Michel Foucault*, London: Tavistock

Smith, D. (1988) *The Chicago School: A liberal critique of capitalism*, London: Macmillan

Smith, N. K. (1941) *The Philosophy of David Hume*, London: Macmillan

Smuts, J. C. (1926) *Holism and Evolution*, London: Macmillan

Solomon, R. C. (1976) *Passions*, New York. Doubleday

—— (1980) *History and Human Nature: A philosophical review of European philosophy and culture 1750–1850*, Brighton: Harvester Press

—— (1983) *In the Spirit of Hegel*, London: Oxford University Press

—— (1984) 'Getting Angry: The Jamesian theory of emotion in anthropology'. In Schweder and LeVine, *Culture Theory*: 238–54

—— (1988) *Continental Philosophy since 1750: The rise and fall of the self*, London: Oxford University Press

Soper, K. (1986) *Humanism and Anti-Humanism*, London: Hutchinson

Sorell, T. (1987) *Descartes*, London: Oxford University Press

Spencer, H. (1855) *The Principles of Psychology*, 2 vols (1870 edition), London: Williams & Nangate

Spengler, O. (1934) *Decline of the West*, New York: Knopf

Sperber, D. (1975) *Rethinking Symbolism*, trans. A. L. Morton, Cambridge: Cambridge University Press

—— (1979) 'Lévi-Strauss'. In Sturrock. (ed.), *Structuralism and Since*: 19–51

Spindler, G. D. (ed.) (1978) *The Making of Psychological Anthropology*, Berkeley, Calif.: University of California Press

Spinoza, B. (1977) *Ethics and on the Correction of the Understanding*, trans. A. Boyle, introd. T. S. Gregory (original 1677), London: Dent

Stace, W. T. (1955) *The Philosophy of Hegel* (original 1924), New York: Dover

Stanner, W. E. H. (1968) 'A. R. Radcliffe-Brown'. In *Intern. Encyc. Soc. Sciences*, 13, New York: Macmillan: 285–90

References

Stedman Jones, G. (1978). 'The Marxism of the Early Lukács'. In *New Left Review, Western Marxism*: 11–60

Steiner, G. (1978) *Heidegger*, London: Fontana

Stern, J. P. (1978) *Nietzsche*, London: Fontana/Collins

Stevens, R. (1983) *Freud and Psychoanalysis*, Milton Keynes: Open University Press

Steward, J. H. (1960) Review of *The Evolution of Culture* by L. A. White. *Amer. Anthrop.*, 62: 144–8

Stirner, M. (1973) *The Ego and his Own*, trans. S. T. Byington (original 1845), New York: Dover

Stocking, G. W. (1968) *Race, Culture and Evolution: Essays in the history of Anthropology*, New York: Free Press

Stoetzel, J. (1955) *Without the Chrysanthemum and the Sword*, New York: Columbia University Press

Strathern, M. (1983) 'The Punishment of Margaret Mead'. *London Rev. of Books*, May: 5–18

Strawson, P. F. (1959) *Individuals: An essay in descriptive metaphysics*, London: Methuen

——— (1966) *The Bounds of Sense*, London: Methuen

Sturrock, J. (ed.) (1979) *Structuralism and Since: From Lévi-Strauss to Derrida*, Oxford: Oxford University Press

——— (1986) *Structuralism*, Londons: Collins (Paladin)

Suckiel, E. K. (1982) *The Pragmatic Philosophy of William James*, Notre Dame, Ind.: University of Notre Dame Press

Sullivan, H. S. (1953) *The Interpersonal Theory of Psychiatry*, New York: Norton

Sulloway, F. J. (1979) *Freud, Biologist of the Mind*, London: Barrett Fontana paperbacks

Swingewood, A. (1977) *The Myth of Mass Culture*, London: Macmillan

Tar, Z. (1977) *The Frankfurt School: The critical theories of Max Horkheimer and Theodor W. Adorno*, New York: Schocken Books

Taylor, C. (1979) *Hegel and Modern Society*, Cambridge: Cambridge University Press

Taylor, R. (1964) 'Schopenhauer', In D. J. O'Connor *A Critical History of Western Philosophy*, New York: Free Press: 365–83

Thayer, H. S. (1953) *Newton's Philosophy of Nature*, New York: Harper

——— (1964) 'Pragmatism'. In D. J. O'Connor *A Critical History of Western Philosophy*, New York: Free Press: 438–62

——— (1981) *Meaning and Action: A critical history of pragmatism*, Indianapolis: Hackett

——— (1982) *Pragmatism: The classic writings*, Indianapolis: Hackett

Therborn, G. (1978) 'The Frankfurt School'. In *New Left Review, Western Marxism*: 83–139

Thomas, K. (1983) *Man and the Natural World*, London: Allen Lane

Thomas, W. (1985) *Mill*, London: Oxford University Press

Thomas, W. I. and F. Znaniecki (1927) *The Polish Peasant in Europe and America*, 2 vols (original 1918–19), New York: Knopf

Thompson, E. P. (1978) *The Poverty of Theory and Other Essays*, London: Merlin

Thompson, J. B. and D. Held (eds) (1982) *Habermas: Critical debates*, London: Macmillan

Thompson, K. (1976) *Auguste Comte: The foundation of sociology*, London: Nelson

—— (1982) *Emile Durkheim*, London: Tavistock

Thomson, R. (1968) *The Pelican History of Psychology*, Harmondsworth: Penguin Books

Thornton, E. N. (1983) *Freud and Cocaine: The Freudian fallacy*, London: Paladin

Thurnwald, R. (1936) Review of *Sex and Temperament in Three Primitive Societies* by M. Mead. *Amer. Anthrop.*, 38: 558–61

Tiger, L. and R. Fox (1970) *The Imperial Animal*, London: Secker & Warburg

Timpanaro, S. (1974) *The Freudian Slip*, London: New Left Books

—— (1975) *On Materialism*, London: New Left Books

Tiryakian, E. A. (1962) *Sociologism and Existentialism: Two perspectives on the individual and society*, Englewood Cliffs, NJ: Prentice Hall

—— (1979) *Emile Durkheim*. In T. Bottomore and R. Nisbet, *A History of Sociological Analysis*: 187–236

Titchener, E. B. (1921) 'Wilhelm Wundt'. *Amer. J. Psychol.*, 32: 161–78

Toulmin, S. and J. Goodfield (1965) *The Discovery of Time*, Harmondsworth: Penguin Books

Toynbee, A. (1973) 'Great Expectations' In H. Wheeler (ed.), *Beyond the Primitive Society*: 113–20

—— (1976) *Mankind and Mother Earth*, Oxford: Oxford University Press

Turkel, S. (1978) *Psychoanalytic Politics: Jacques Lacan and Freud's French revolution*, London: Burnett Books

Turner, V. (1975) *Dramas, Fields and Metaphors*, Ithaca, NY: Cornell University Press

Ullman, W. (1967) *The Individual and Society in the Middle Ages*, London: Methuen

Voget, F. W. (1975) *A History of Ethnology*, New York: Holt Rinehart

Volosinov, V. N. (1973) *Marxism and the Philosophy of Language*, Cambridge, Mass.: Harvard University Press

Vygotsky, L. S. (1962) *Thought and Language*, Cambridge, Mass.: MIT

—— et al. (1978) *Mind in Society: The development of higher psychological processes*, ed. M. Cole., Cambridge, Mass.: Harvard University Press

—— (1981) 'The Genesis of Higher Mental Functions'. In J. V. Wertsch (ed.), *The Concept of Activity in Soviet Psychology*, Armork, N.J.: Sharpe: 144–88

Wallwork, E. (1984) 'Religion and Social Structure in "The Division of

Labour"' *Amer. Anthrop.*, 86: 43–64

Wann, T. E. (ed.) (1964) *Behaviour and Phenomenology*, Chicago: University of Chicago Press

Warnke, G. (1987) *Gadamer: Hermeneutics, tradition and reason*, Oxford: Polity Press

Warnock, G. J. (1964) 'Kant'. In D. J. O'Connor (ed.) *A Critical History of Western Philosophy*, New York: Free Press: 296–318

Warnock, M. (1965) *The Philosophy of Sartre*, London: Hutchinson

—— (1970) *Existentialism*, Oxford: Oxford University Press

Warrender, H. (1957) The *Political Philosophy of Hobbes*, Oxford: Oxford University Press

Watson, J. B. (1913) 'Psychology as a Behaviourist Views it'. *Psychol. Review*, 20: 158–77

—— (1914) *Behaviour: An introduction to comparative psychology*, New York: Holt Rinehart

—— (1919) *Psychology from the Standpoint of a Behaviourist*, New York: Lippincott

—— (1924) *Behaviourism*, New York: Norton

—— (1936) 'Autobiography'. In C. Murchison (ed.), *A History of Psychology in Autobiography*, Worcester, Mass.: Clark University Press

Watson, R. I. (1963) *The Great Psychologists: From Aristotle to Freud*, New York: Lippincott

—— (1979) *Basic Writings in the History of Psychology*, New York: Oxford University Press

Weeks, J. (1985) *Sexuality and its Discontents*, London: Routledge & Kegan Paul

Weiner, A. B. (1983) 'Ethnographic Determinism: Samoa and the Margaret Mead controversy'. *Amer. Anthrop.*, 85: 909–18

Weiss, F. G. (ed.) (1974) *Hegel: The essential writings*, New York: Harper & Row

Wells, H. K. (1956) *Ivan P. Pavlov: Toward a scientific psychology and psychiatry*, New York: Intern. Publ

Wertheimer, M. (1945) *Productive Thinking*, New York: Harper

Wertsch, J. V. (ed.) (1985a) *Culture, Communication and Cognition: Vygotskian perspectives*, Cambridge: Cambridge University Press

—— (1985b) *Vygotsky and the Social Formation of Mind*, Cambridge University Press

Wheeler, H. (ed.) (1973) *Beyond the Primitive Society: Operant conditioning; social and political aspects*, London: Wildwood House

Wheelis, A. (1959) *The Quest for Identity*, London: Gollancz

White, H. (1978) *Tropics of Discourse: Essays in cultural criticism*, Baltimore, Md: Johns Hopkins University Press

White, L. A. (1949) *The Science of Culture: A study of man and civilization*, New York: Grove Press

White, Jr L. (1967) 'The Historical Roots of our Ecological Crisis'. *Science*,

155: 1203–7. Reprinted in R. Clarke (ed.) (1975), *Notes for a Future*, London: Thames & Hudson: 99–106

White, M. (1955) *The Age of Analysis: The 20th century philosophers*, New York: Mentor

—— (1957) *Social Thought in America*, Boston, Mass.: Beacon Press

—— (1972) *Science and Sentiment in America: Philosophical thought from Edwards to Dewey*, Oxford: Oxford University Press

White, R. W. (1960) 'Competence and the Psychosexual Stages of Development'. In M. R. Jones (ed.), *Nebraska Symposium on Motivation*, Nebraska: University of Nebraska Press: 97–141

Whitebook, J. (1985) 'Reason and Happiness: Some psychoanalytic themes in critical theory'. In R. J. Bernstein, *Habermas and Modernity*: 140–60

Whitehead, A. (1926) *Science and the Modern World* (1975 edition), London: Fontana Books

—— (1929) *Process and Reality*, Cambridge: Cambridge University Press

Whitehead, A. N. (1938) *Modes of Thought*, New York: Capricorn Books

Whorf, B. L. (ed.) (1956) *Language, Thought and Reality*, introd. J. B. Carroll (original 1940), Cambridge, Mass.: MIT

Whyte, L. L. (1960) *The Unconscious before Freud*, New York: Basic Books

Whyte, W. F. (1943) *Street Corner Society*, Chicago: University of Chicago Press

Wilden, A. (1972) *System and Structure*, London: Tavistock

Wilkinson, J. (1973) 'How Good is Current Behaviour Therapy'. In H. Wheeler (ed.), *Beyond the Primitive Society*: 149–59

Williams, B. (1979) *Descartes: The project of pure enquiry*, Harmondsworth: Penguin Books

Williams, R. (1961) *The Long Revolution*, Harmondsworth: Penguin Books

Williams, T. R. (ed.) (1975) *Psychological Anthropology*, The Hague: Mouton

Wilson, B. R. (ed.) (1970) *Rationality*, Oxford: Basil Blackwell

Wilson, C. (1972) *New Pathways in Psychology; Maslow and the Post-Freudian revolution* (1979 edition), London: Gollancz

—— (1981) *The Quest for Wilhelm Reich*, London: Granada

Wilson, E. O. (1975) *Sociobiology: The new synthesis*, Cambridge, Mass.: Harvard University Press

—— (1978) *On Human Nature*, Cambridge, Mass.: Harvard University Press

Wilson, M. et al. (1969) *The Essential Descartes*, New York: Mentor

—— (1978) *Descartes*, London: Routledge & Kegan Paul

Wing, J. K. (1978) *Reasoning about Madness*, Oxford: Oxford University Press

Wittgenstein, L. (1921) *Tractatus Logico-Philosophicus*, trans. C. K. Ogden and F. P. Ramsey, London: Routledge & Kegan Paul

—— (1953) *Philosophical Investigation*, trans. G. E. M. Anscombe, Oxford: Basil Blackwell

Wolff, K. H. (ed.) (1960) *Emile Durkheim, 1858–1917*, Columbus, Ohio:

References

Ohio State University Press

Wollheim, R. (1971) *Freud*, London: Fontana/Collins

—— and J. Hopkins (eds) (1982) *Philosophical Essays on Freud*, Cambridge: Cambridge University Press

Woolhouse, R. (1971) *Locke's Philosophy of Science and Knowledge*, Oxford: Basil Blackwell

Wolman, B. (ed.) (1968) *Historical Roots of Modern Psychology*, New York: Harper & Row

Wood, A. W. (ed.) (1984) *Self and Nature in Kant's Philosophy*, Ithaca, NY: Cornell University Press

Woodworth, R. S. (1931) *Contemporary Schools of Psychology*, London: Methuen

Worsley, P. (1982) *Marx and Marxism*, London: Tavistock

Wright, E. (1984) *Psychoanalytic Criticism: Therapy in practice*, London: Methuen

Wrong, D. 1961 'The Oversocialized Conception of Man in Modern Society'. *Amer. Sociol. Rev.*, 26: 183–93

Wundt, W. (1894) *Lectures on Human and Animal Psychology*, trans. J. E. Creightom and E. B. Titchener, London: Allen & Unwin

—— (1897) *Outlines of Psychology (Grundisse der Psychologie)*, trans. C. H. Judd (1907 edition), Leipzig: Stechert Engelmann

—— (1912) *An Introduction to Psychology*, trans. R. Pinter, London: Allen

—— (1916) *The Elements of Folk Psychology (Völkerpsychologie)*, trans. E. L. Schaub (Leipzig 1900–20), London: Allen & Unwin

Yates, F. A. (1964) *Gordano Bruno and the Hermetic Tradition*, London: Routledge & Kegan Paul

Yolton, J. W. (1956) *John Locke and the Way of Ideas*, Oxford: Clarendon Press

—— (1970) *Locke and the Compass of Human Understanding*, Cambridge: Cambridge University Press

Index

Index

Index

Evans-Pritchard E. E., 233–4, 238–9
evolutionary theory, 103, 106–7, 304
existentialism, 359–63, 375–6, 396, 402
experimental psychology, 155–6, 283–5
Eysenck, H. J., 80–1, 83

faculty psychology, 13
Fancher, R. E., 116
Fechner, Gustav, 156
Feuerbach, Ludwig, 201, 203, 212–13, 349, 422
Fichte, Johann, 372
Flanagan, Owen J., 140–1
Flew, Anthony, 133
Fliess, Wilhelm, 89
Flügel, J. C., 102
Fortune, Reo, 173, 186
Foucault, Michel, 404, 428–42
  his archaeology of knowledge, 429–38
  life and background, 428–9
  on power, 439
  on the human subject, 440–2
  'Order of Things', 433–8
Frankfurt School, 319–20, 332, 345, 347
Frege, Gottlob, 369
Freeman J. D., 169, 183
Freud, Sigmund, 27, 79–101, 336–45, 410, 415, 419
  depth psychology, 92–5
  his humanism, 83–6
  life and work, 87–92
  on the libido, 64, 93–5
  on the Oedipus complex, 96
  on the unconscious, 93
Fromm, Erich, 86, 97, 225, 332, 336–8, 344
functionalism
  psychological, 283, 302
  sociological, 236–7, 245, 255

Gadamer, Hans-George, 346, 352, 374, 385
Galileo, 423, 434
Gall, Franz, 102
Galton, Francis, 117, 167
Gardner, Howard, 414
Gardner, Peter M., 266–7
Geisteswissenschaft (human sciences), 84, 146
genetic structuralism, 410–11
Geoghegan, V., 340
George, Wilma, 105
Geras, Norman, 225, 426

Gestalt psychology, 153, 174
Giddens, Anthony, 353
God, 9, 23–4, 38, 42, 53–4, 250, 280, 366
Goethe, Johann, 190
Goff, Tom, 309–10
Goffman, Erving, 310–18
  his symbolic interactionism, 312
  on asylums, 313–17
  on the self, 312, 314–15, 318
Goldmann, Lucien, 58, 141, 222, 427
Gruber, H. E., 110
Grunberg, Carl, 319–20

Habermas, Jürgen, 345–58
  defence of rationalism, 356–7
  his critical theory, 352
  knowledge and human interests, 347–53
  life and background, 345–6
  theory of communicative action, 356
habit, 285
Haeckel, Ernst, 113
Hall, C. Stanley, 91, 182
Hallowell, A. Irving, 161, 259, 301
Hallpike, C. R., 416
Hampshire, Stuart, 10, 25, 28
Harland, Richard, 404
Harris, Marvin, 141, 149, 152, 163, 167, 178–9, 181, 202, 407
Hartley, David, 41
Harvey, William, 11
Hawkes, Terence, 403
Hegel, G. W. F., 106, 143, 150, 189–99, 201–4, 208, 221, 299, 332–4, 389, 395, 420–1, 444
  his philosophy, 190–2, 364–5
  on the master-slave relationship, 196
  phenomenology of spirit, 193–9
Hegelian Marxism, 214–15, 331–4
Heidegger, Martin, 198, 375–85, 388–9, 444, 446
  Being and Time, 379–84
  his existentialism, 376–9
  life and background, 375–6
Helmholtz, Hermann, 84, 113, 155–6
Heraclitus, 189
hermeneutics, 83, 146–50, 354, 378, 432
Hill Pandaram, 266
Hirsh, Arthur, 403
historical materialism, 204–12
historical particularism, 163
Hobbes, Thomas, 14–22, 100, 119, 309

Index

Index

Index

Index